WORKING IN AMERICA

Continuity, Conflict, and Change

SECOND EDITION

Amy S. Wharton

Washington State University

McGraw Hill

Boston   Burr Ridge, IL   Dubuque, IA   Madison, WI   New York
San Francisco   St. Louis   Bangkok   Bogotá   Caracas   Kuala Lumpur
Lisbon   London   Madrid   Mexico City   Milan   Montreal   New Delhi
Santiago   Seoul   Singapore   Sydney   Taipei   Toronto

McGraw-Hill Higher Education ⚛

*A Division of The **McGraw-Hill** Companies*

1 2 3 4 5 6 7 8 9 0 MAL/MAL 0 9 8 7 6 5 4 3 2 1

Library of Congress Cataloging-in-Publication Data

Wharton, Amy S.
  Working in America : continuity, conflict, and change / Amy S. Wharton.—2nd ed.
    p. cm.
  ISBN 0-7674-2077-2
    1. Work—Sociological aspects. 2. Work—Social aspects—United States. I. Title.
  HD4904 .W485 2001
  306.3'6—dc21

                                                                        2001030426

Sponsoring editor, Serina Beauparlant; production editor, April Wells-Hayes; manuscript
editor, Sheryl Rose; design manager, Violeta Diaz; cover designer, Laurie Anderson; manufacturing manager, Randy Hurst. Cover image: © John Freeman/Stone. The text was set in
10/12 Book Antiqua by Carlisle Communications and printed on 45# Scholarly Matte by
Malloy Lithographing.

www.mhhe.com

To my father, William Wharton, and the
memory of my mother, Marilyn Wharton (1921–1964)

Preface

College students today are more anxious about their futures than in the past, particularly with respect to their places in the world of work. The social contract that promised steadily increasing wages and secure employment has unraveled, leaving many uncertain about their lives and livelihoods. In these times, a sociological perspective on work is more important than ever. Analysis and understanding of the societal conditions that shape people's work lives may be the best tools for conquering their anxiety and uncertainty. To prepare for and reshape the future demands knowledge of the social forces that influenced the past and help structure the present.

The study of work is central to the discipline of sociology. From the industrial revolution to the service economy, sociologists have contributed much to our understanding of the forces shaping workers' lives and the workplace. This anthology contains a sampling of some of the best that sociologists of work have to offer. Through a variety of methods and approaches, the readings address several pertinent questions about the American workplace: What have been the most important changes in workers' lives and work organization during the twentieth century? What factors shape employment today? What does the future hold for work and workers?

By examining how sociologists have pursued answers to these questions, I hope students will acquire tools to address their own concerns and come away better equipped to make sense of their past, present, and future work experiences.

Selecting the readings for this anthology was both a challenge and a pleasure. It was challenging because my colleagues have produced such a tremendous amount of valuable research on the workplace that I could have filled several volumes easily; deciding what to exclude was a difficult task. At the same time, compiling these readings provided me with an opportunity to explore and appreciate sociologists' contributions to our knowledge about workers and work. This process reaffirmed my belief that a sociological perspective remains the best vantage point from which to understand the social world.

In the end, the readings that appear here were selected with several considerations in mind. First, I aimed for a degree of comprehensiveness in the coverage of topics. While no anthology can address everything, the anthology remains one of the best vehicles for presenting information to students on a range of topics. Second, I wanted to present the key pieces of research in a particular area. I included some classics but primarily used examples of contemporary research that have made an impact. Third, attending to gender, racial, and ethnic differentiation in the workplace was important to me. Hence, these issues are addressed throughout the anthology. Finally, I selected readings with a student audience in mind. When all is said and done, this anthology is for them.

Intellectual work is, at its best, a collective enterprise. In editing this anthology, I benefited from the valuable comments and suggestions of many colleagues around the country.

These included William Canak, Middle Tennessee State University; Samuel Cohn, Texas A&M University; Daniel Cornfield, Vanderbilt University; Barbara Thomas Coventry, The University of Toledo; Patricia Craig, Ohio State University; William Finlay, University of Georgia; Robin Leidner, University of Pennsylvania; Garth Massey, University of Wyoming; Peter Meiksins, Cleveland State University; Stephen Petterson, University of Virginia; Patricia A. Roos, Rutgers University; and Vicki Smith, University of California–Davis. At Washington State University, my friend and colleague in the English Department, Anne Maxham, cheerfully volunteered to give critical feedback on my introductions; Nathan Lauster provided crucial research assistance.

The division of labor involved in producing this book extends beyond academe to include many others' contributions. I owe tremendous thanks to Mayfield Senior Editor Serina Beauparlant, whose gentle prodding, enthusiasm, and constant positive reinforcement helped this anthology move from idea to reality in what seems like record time. Others at Mayfield, including Sara Early and April Wells-Hayes, have been equally helpful and conscientious. In fact, from the beginning to the end of this project, I have benefited from the efforts of many people who are very good at their jobs. They have my thanks and appreciation.

Changes to the Second Edition

The second edition contains several changes, most inspired by comments and suggestions from colleagues around the country. I have added a new introductory section that includes readings on the history of work. I have also added several readings that address the global economy. Contingent, marginal, and low-wage jobs receive more attention than in the first edition, as does work in the household. Throughout the anthology, I have replaced older readings with more updated research. In making all of these changes, however, I have adhered to the themes that guided my selection of readings for the first edition.

As always, I have benefited from reviewers' comments. Reviewers for the second edition include Robert Althauser, Indiana University; Spencer Blakeslee, Framingham State College; William T. Clute, University of Nebraska at Omaha; Richard H. Hall, University at Albany; Kevin D. Henson, Loyola University of Chicago; Linda Markowitz, Southern Illinois University, Edwardsville; Carol Ray, San Jose State University; Raymond Russell, University of California, Riverside; and Denise Scott, State University of New York, Geneseo. I have also been privileged to continue my association with McGraw-Hill and its fine staff. Special thanks to my editor and friend, Serina Beauparlant. I also wish to thank Serina's assistant, Kate Schubert, for her assistance.

Contents

General Introduction

The beginning of a new century offers an opportune time to assess the past, reflect on the present, and imagine the future. As the millennium begins, a course in the sociology of work can provide a conceptual and theoretical platform from which to explore a variety of enduring sociological issues. Though this anthology focuses mainly on the contemporary workplace, it also looks at workplaces of the past and the future through a critical, sociological lens. Work is among the most important social institutions; indeed, in the late nineteenth and early twentieth centuries, sociologists Karl Marx, Max Weber, and Emile Durkheim placed work at the center of their analyses. Contemplating the development of capitalism in the West and the burgeoning industrial revolution, these "founding fathers of sociology" understood that the organization of work helps to determine the fates of individuals as well as their societies.

Three major themes guided the selection of readings for this anthology—the first reflects a methodological concern, the second stems from an empirical observation, and the third emphasizes conceptual and theoretical issues. Each theme has continuity with past efforts to understand the American workplace, yet each also directs attention to important questions about the present and future.

The first theme is that workers' lives are shaped not only by daily life on the job but also by larger trends that are transforming work in the country and across the globe. This theme has methodological implications because it suggests that any study of work must concern itself not only with workers' experiences but also with the larger histori-cal, economic, and social contexts within which these experiences occur. Multiple levels of analysis are thus necessary to address the important questions in the sociology of work.

The second major theme is that workers are demographically more diverse than ever, and this changing demography plays an important role in the organization and experience of work. This theme is drawn from an empirical observation: The American workplace—like the larger society—has always been composed of workers from diverse racial and ethnic backgrounds, genders, ages, religions, and sexual orienta-tions—to name but a few characteristics. As American society moves into the next century, this demographic diversity is increas-ing: Most new entrants to the labor force are expected to be nonwhites, females, or immigrants (Johnston and Packer 1987). Sociologists have come to believe that we cannot fully understand work without con-sidering the characteristics of the people who perform it.

The third theme of this book is perhaps the most significant to sociologists: Work is not strictly an instrumental activity, nor can it be understood only in economic terms. Instead, as Friedland and Robertson (1990, p. 25) explain, "Work provides identities as much as it provides bread for the table; par-ticipation in commodity and labor markets is as much an expression of who you are as what you want." Moreover, from this per-spective work is not an isolated institution, closed off from the rest of society, but is pro-foundly interconnected with the larger social world. Not only are its boundaries permeable, making the workplace subject to influences from other institutions, but the influence of work on other aspects of society is also great. Indeed, work shapes every aspect of life—from people's conceptions of self to the degree of inequality in a society. Through the years sociologists studying work have disagreed as to which effects of work they consider most important, but there has been no dispute with the basic premise that the study of work is a vehicle for examining some of the most fundamental aspects of social life.

Linking the Micro and the Macro in Sociological Studies of Work

Like the field of sociology as a whole, teaching and scholarship in the sociology of work reflect a range of approaches, which typically have been characterized as either *micro* or *macro*. Micro-level approaches tend to focus on individuals or small groups in a particular workplace and examine processes or outcomes that operate at these levels of analysis. Though by no means all micro-level research is ethnographic, many researchers prefer qualitative methodologies that allow for close, in-depth scrutiny of particular social phenomena. Indeed, there is a long and rich tradition of micro-level ethnographic research in the sociology of work. This research has provided useful accounts of many jobs, offering the student a way to vicariously experience life as a machine shop worker, a medical student, a flight attendant, or a McDonald's employee (Roy 1959; Becker, Geer, Hughes, and Strauss 1961; Hochschild 1983; Leidner 1993).

In contrast, macro-level studies in the sociology of work tend to be less concerned with "flesh-and-blood workers" and more attentive to larger processes, trends, and outcomes (Simpson 1989, p. 565). Studies of this type typically analyze data collected from representative samples of people, jobs, or workplaces and seek to identify patterns and relationships between key variables. Macro-level research thus is often quantitative, driven by the desire to test hypotheses or produce generalizable results. The popularity of macro-level research has grown in recent years, as sociologists have borrowed concepts and theories from economists. Sociological studies of wage determination, for example, attempt to explain what factors determine the "worth" of jobs and cause some jobs to command higher wages than others (Tomaskovic-Devey 1993).

Micro and macro research traditions are often perceived as distinct, and sometimes even conflicting, approaches. Courses in the sociology of work have thus traditionally emphasized one or the other approach, but not both. Ideally, however, micro and macro studies should inform one another, as no single approach can address everything. Moreover, in my view, important sociological questions cannot be answered by only one type of study or approach but require a "division of labor" among researchers. For example, to understand the role of race in the workplace we need both fine-grained, ethnographic studies *and* more large-scale, quantitative analyses. The former can help us understand such issues as workers' experiences of discrimination and the meaning of race to employers (Kirschenman and Neckerman 1991), and the latter may address such issues as the racial gap in earnings or the consequences of corporate restructuring for the employment chances of African Americans (Wilson 1996). This view is reflected in the selection of readings for this anthology, which incorporates studies employing diverse methodologies and approaches. By studying both the micro and the macro dimensions of work, we can begin to see how work is shaped by its social context and, conversely, how workplace dynamics may shape the larger society.

The Changing Demographics of the Workplace

Anyone who takes even a cursory look around any place of work in industrialized countries can see that workers doing the same or similar jobs tend to be of the same gender and racial and ethnic group. In a workplace in New York City—for instance, a handbag factory—a walk through the various departments might reveal that the owners and managers are white men; their secretaries and book-keepers are white and Asian women; the order takers and data processors are African-American women; the factory hands are Hispanic men cutting pieces and Hispanic women sewing them together; African-American men are packing and loading the finished product; and non-English-speaking Eastern European women are cleaning up after everyone. (Lorber 1994, p. 194)

Although the labor force is becoming increasingly diverse, jobs and workplaces continue to be highly segregated along gender, racial, and ethnic lines. The continuing association between jobs and workers of a particular gender, race, or ethnic background suggests that these social categories are as powerful in shaping life inside the workplace as they have been shown to be in shaping life in other societal institutions.

Gender, race, and ethnicity in the workplace are often studied by focusing on discrimination and inequality, and these remain important topics. Despite widespread social changes, as well as the passage of legislation and social policies designed to prevent discrimination and reduce inequality, the costs and rewards of work remain unevenly distributed across social categories. The desire to understand the sources of these work-related inequalities, the forces that perpetuate them, and the consequences of these inequalities for workers and their families has generated a tremendous amount of research in recent years. We thus know a great deal about some aspects of gender, racial, and ethnic inequality in the workplace. Changes in the organization of work brought on by a global economy and the changing demographics of workers raise new questions for analysis, however. How will these changes affect the costs and rewards of work? More important, how will the relative situations of different groups of workers be affected by the changing workplace? Will economic inequality increase or diminish in the twenty-first century? Questions such as these are important topics for research and debate.

The impacts of gender, race, and ethnicity on the workplace are not confined to their roles in producing inequality and discrimination, nor do these factors affect only the personal consequences of work. Rather, sociologists argue that, at a more fundamental level, the structure and organization of work also reflect the influences of gender, race, and ethnicity. From this perspective, gender, race, and ethnicity are not just characteristics of workers but may also be considered characteristics of work roles and jobs or seen as embedded in work arrangements and technologies (Acker 1991). Understanding how the workplace is gendered and how it is imbued with racial symbolism have become important concerns in recent years. Addressing these issues requires us to examine how work structures and practices that may appear "neutral" in design or application may nevertheless contribute to the construction and maintenance of gender and racial distinctions in the workplace. Including issues pertaining to gender, race, and ethnicity throughout this anthology, instead of confining them to a section on discrimination, allows the reader to see the many ways in which these social categories shape work experience and organization.

Work and Society

Viewing work through a sociological lens enables us to consider the varied ways in which work and society are interrelated. For example, at the individual level, work shapes identity, values, and beliefs, as well as a host of other outcomes ranging from mental and physical health to political attitudes (see, e.g., Kohn and Schooler 1983; Karasek and Theorell 1990; Brint 1985). Thus, while sociologists tend to view families as the primary agents of socialization in American society, it is also important to recognize the ways in which people are socialized by their jobs and work experiences. Indeed, some argue that work is an increasingly "greedy" institution, capable of "outcompeting" other institutions for people's time, emotional energies, and commitments.

One often-overlooked feature of work is that it typically brings people into contact with others—co-workers, subordinates, supervisors, and, increasingly for many, the public. Hence, social interaction and group dynamics are just as important in the workplace as they are in other social arenas. An early, influential sociological study first called attention to the ways that the social relations of work shaped workers' reactions to their jobs (Mayo 1933). For contemporary researchers, this insight is reflected in the claim that workers are not "atomized optimizers," unaffected by their interactions with other workplace members (Baron and Pfeffer 1994). Instead, both the content and quality of these relations are seen as important for understanding the consequences and significance of work. Along these lines, some suggest that it is not so much workers' own characteristics that shape their views and behavior; rather, it is the relation between their characteristics and the characteristics of those with whom they interact. From this perspective, workplaces are settings in which both expressive and instrumental ties between people are important—not only for understanding workers' responses to their jobs, but also for understanding the broader ways in which work shapes meanings and life experience. As Marks (1994, p. 855) explains, "With the help of co-workers, ethnic statuses may get reaffirmed and enlivened, and age and gender identities may be consolidated, celebrated, reorganized, and even transformed. The same is true, of course, of worker identities."

Though the workplace has never been truly separate from other societal institutions and trends, its interdependence with the larger environment has perhaps never been greater. This point can best be illustrated by considering the relations between work and another important social institution: family life. Societal changes, such as women's rising participation in the labor force, declining birth rates, and changing gender roles, have transformed relations between families and work. In the process, new conceptual approaches have emerged, and there has been a change in the way social institutions, including work, are understood. In particular, there has been a move away from rigid dichotomies, such as public and private or impersonal and personal, that compartmentalized work and family life, toward more complex portrayals of these social institutions and those who negotiate the work-family boundary (Marks 1994). Work, family, and the relations between them are not static but rather reflect and respond to developments in the wider society.

People's lives in advanced, capitalist societies are largely dependent on forces emanating from the workplace. The organization and availability of work determine—to a great extent—the social and economic well-being of individuals, neighborhoods, cities, and societies. Work is thus among the most important social institutions, with influential consequences for just about all arenas of social life.

REFERENCES

Acker, Joan. 1991. "Hierarchies, Jobs, Bodies: A Theory of Gendered Organizations." Pp. 162–179 in *The Social Construction of Gender,* edited by Judith Lorber and Susan A. Farrell. Newbury Park, CA: Sage Publications.

Baron, James N. and Jeffrey Pfeffer. 1994. "The Social Psychology of Organizations and Inequality." *Social Psychology Quarterly* 57: 190–209.

Becker, Howard S., Blanche Geer, Everett C. Hughes, and Anselm L. Strauss. 1961. *Boys in White: Student Culture in Medical School.* Chicago: University of Chicago Press.

Brint, Steven G. 1985. "The Political Attitudes of Professionals." *Annual Review of Sociology* 11: 389–414.

Friedland, Roger and A. F. Robertson. 1990. "Beyond the Marketplace." Pp. 3–49 in *Beyond the Marketplace,* edited by Roger Friedland and A. F. Robertson. New York: Aldine de Gruyter.

Hochschild, Arlie Russell. 1983. *The Managed Heart.* Berkeley: University of California Press.

Johnston, William B. and Arnold E. Packer. 1987. *Workforce 2000: Work and Workers for the 21st Century.* Indianapolis, IN: The Hudson Institute, Inc.

Karasek, Robert and Tores Theorell. 1990. *Healthy Work: Stress, Productivity, and the Reconstruction of Working Life.* New York: Basic Books.

Kirschenman, Joleen and Kathryn M. Neckerman. 1991. "We'd Love to Hire Them, But . . . : The Meaning of Race for Employers." Pp. 203–232 in *The Urban Underclass,* edited by C. Jencks and P. E. Peterson. Washington, DC: The Brookings Institution.

Kohn, Melvin L. and Carmi Schooler. 1983. *Work and Personality: An Inquiry into the Impact of Social Stratification.* Norwood, NJ: Ablex Publishing Company.

Leidner, Robin. 1993. *Fast Food, Fast Talk: Service Work and the Routinization of Everyday Life.* Berkeley: University of California Press.

Lorber, Judith. 1994. *Paradoxes of Gender.* New Haven, CT: Yale University Press.

Marks, Stephen R. 1994. "Intimacy in the Public Realm: The Case of Co-Workers." *Social Forces* 72: 843–858.

Mayo, Elton. 1933. *The Human Problems of an Industrial Civilization.* New York: The Macmillan Company.

Roy, Donald. 1959. " 'Banana Time': Job Satisfaction and Informal Interaction." *Human Organization* 18: 158–168.

Simpson, Ida Harper. 1989. "The Sociology of Work: Where Have the Workers Gone?" *Social Forces* 67: 563–581.

Tomaskovic-Devey, Donald. 1993. *Gender and Racial Inequality at Work.* Ithaca, NY: ILR Press.

Wilson, William Julius. 1996. *When Work Disappears: The World of the New Urban Poor.* New York: Knopf.

PART I
Historical Perspectives

A glimpse at the past can help frame our study of the present and future. For this reason, we begin with three selections focused on life and work during the early stages of industrialization.

Historical Perspectives

For most American workers, the boundaries between work and leisure are clearly drawn. For many, the weekend marks the end of the workweek and offers, if not time for play and recreation, at least time away from paid work. In Reading 1, Witold Rybczynski examines the origins of the "weekend." He traces this particular way of organizing non-work time to nineteenth-century England and the changes brought about by industrialization. Rybczynski also explores the origin and demise of "Saint Monday," another

tradition related to the changing boundaries between work and leisure.

What was work like for those laboring in factories during the early years of industrialization in the United States? In Reading 2, Sanford Jacoby describes the harsh conditions confronted by factory workers. These conditions stemmed in part from the brutality of foremen and their reliance on the "drive system" as a method of labor control.

In Reading 3, we turn our attention to the American household in the nineteenth century. Ruth Schwartz Cowan chronicles the ways that households were transformed by industrialization and the consequences of these changes for those who did the work necessary to maintain a home. Cowan shows that industrialization increased, rather than decreased, household work, and she demonstrates how this work became the primary responsibility of women.

HISTORICAL PERSPECTIVES

1

Keeping Saint Monday

Witold Rybczynski

The Oxford English Dictionary finds the earliest recorded use of the word "weekend" in an 1879 issue of *Notes and queries,* an English magazine. "In Staffordshire, if a person leaves home at the end of his week's work on the Saturday afternoon to spend the evening of Saturday and the following Sunday with friends at a distance," the entry goes, "he is said to be spending his week-end at So-and-so." The quotation is obviously a definition, which suggests that the word had only recently come into use. It is also important to note that the "week's work" is described as ending on Saturday afternoon. It was precisely this early ending to the week that produced a holiday period of a day and a half—the first weekend. This innovation—and it was a uniquely British one—occurred in roughly the third quarter of the nineteenth century. To understand how and why the weekend appeared when it did, let's examine how the nature of free time changed during the previous hundred years.

Throughout the eighteenth century, the work-week ended on Saturday evening; Sunday was the weekly day off. The Reformation and, later, Puritanism had made Sunday the weekly holy day in an attempt to displace the saints' days and religious festivals of Catholicism. Although the taboo on

work was more or less respected, the strictures of Sabbatarianism that prohibited merriment and levity on the Lord's Day were rejected by most Englishmen, who saw the holiday as a chance to drink, gamble, and generally have a good time.

Only one official weekly holiday did not necessarily mean that the life of the average British worker was one of unremitting toil. Far from it. Work was always interrupted to commemorate the annual feasts of Christmas, New Year, and Whitsuntide (the days following the seventh Sunday after Easter). These traditional holidays were universally observed, but the length of the breaks varied. Depending on local convention, work stopped for anywhere from a few days to two weeks. In addition to the religious holidays, villages and rural parishes observed their own annual festivals or "wakes." These celebratory rituals, which dated from medieval times, were mainly secular and involved sports, dancing, and other public amusements.

Towns had their own festivals, less bucolic than those of the countryside. Stamford, in Lincolnshire, celebrated a special holiday; each November 13th, thousands of men and boys gathered in the streets for bull running, an event reminiscent of the famous festival that still takes place in Pamplona. The British today deride the Spanish passion for bullfighting, but their sensibility in this regard is, at least culturally speaking, recent—the Stamford run ended with the

From Witold Rybczynski, *Waiting for the Weekend.* New York: Viking, 1991.

bull's being pushed off a bridge into the river, and then fished out and killed. The Stamford run is famous because it lasted the longest (well into the nineteenth century), but similar runs took place in many English towns. In London, bull running involved workers and apprentices in the Spitalfields weaving trades, who merrily chased and goaded the animal, provided by a local butcher; the popular event persisted until 1826 and it took several violent police actions to stop it.

Annual festivals like the bull run were not the only days off. There were also communal holidays associated with special, occasional events such as prizefights, horse races, and other sporting competitions, as well as fairs, circuses, and traveling menageries. When one of these attractions arrived in a village or town, regular work more or less stopped while people flocked to gape and marvel at the exotic animals, equestrian acrobats, and assorted human freaks and oddities.

The idea of spontaneously closing up shop or leaving the workbench for the pursuit of pleasure strikes the modern reader as irresponsible, but for the eighteenth-century worker the line between work and play was blurred; work was engaged in with a certain amount of playfulness, and play was always given serious attention. Moreover, many recreational activities were directly linked to the workplace, since trade guilds often organized their own outings, had their own singing and drinking clubs and their own preferred taverns.

Eighteenth-century workers had, as Hugh Cunningham puts it, "a high preference for leisure, and for long periods of it." This preference was hardly something new; what *was* new was the ability, in prosperous Georgian England, of so many people to indulge it. For the first time in their lives, many workers earned more than survival wages. Now they had choices: they could buy goods

or leisure. They could work more and earn more, or they could forgo the extra wages and enjoy more free time instead. Most chose the latter course. This was especially true for the highly paid skilled workers, who had the most economic freedom; but even general laborers, who were employed at day rates, had a choice in the matter. Many of these worked intensively, often for much more than the customary ten hours a day, and then quit to enjoy themselves until their money ran out.

Of course, the amount of regular free time varied according to local custom and the strength of each trade union. But many—too many—were left out. The poorest people, especially women and children, who were paid the lowest wages, did not share in the prosperity and were obliged to work continuous and unremitting days, often twelve to fourteen hours long. Sunday was their only opportunity for rest, and for some, who were obliged to work seven days a week, not even that break was available. But the occupation that offered the least chance for leisure had nothing to do with factory work—it was domestic service. Servants were at their masters' beck and call and had little time of their own. One afternoon a week was the typical maid's day off.

Whenever people had a choice in the matter, however, work was characterized by an irregular mixture of days on and days off, a pattern that the historian E. P. Thompson described as "alternate bouts of intense labor and of idleness." This irregularity was exacerbated by the way holidays were prolonged. The London bull run, for example, which traditionally took place on Easter Monday, was almost always extended to the following day; other runs began on Sunday and continued for one or two days thereafter. Village wakes followed a similar pattern. It was not unusual for sporting events, fairs, and other celebrations to last several days. Since Sunday was always the official holiday, it was usually the days following that were added on. This produced a regular custom of staying away from work on Monday, frequently also on Tuesday, and then working long hours at the end of the week to catch up. Among some trades, the Monday holiday achieved what amounted to an official status. Weavers and miners, for example, regularly took a holiday on the Monday after payday—which occurred weekly, or bi-weekly. This practice became so common that it was called "keeping Saint Monday."

The origin of the Saint Monday tradition is obscure. Like the seven-day week, it was a custom that spread rapidly, despite the fact that it lacked any official sanction, because it appealed to people. Like the week, it was an institution whose genesis was explained by legends and folktales. According to some, keeping Saint Monday originated among tailors, whose shops were generally closed on Mondays. According to another story, the custom began with cobblers, tradesmen who were not held in high esteem since they, unlike real shoemakers, had only enough skill to mend shoes.* These slow-witted fellows were supposed to have forgotten the exact date of the feast day of their patron, Saint Crispin; remembering only that it occurred on a Monday, they celebrated each "Saint" Monday instead. It is a charming tale, though unlikely to be true, for the Monday tradition also existed in France, Belgium, Prussia, and Sweden. Its widespread observance suggests that it may have been a popular reaction against the loss of the cherished medieval saints' days, which had been eliminated by Reformation clerics in Protestant countries and by demanding employers in Catholic Europe.

Cobblers had a reputation as great tipplers—"cobbler's punch" was a cure for a hangover—and in some versions of the story they were said to have needed the Monday holiday to recover from their Sunday excesses. That part of the legend rings true, for the custom of keeping Saint Monday was undoubtedly linked to heavy drinking. The eighteenth century's propensity for heavy drinking has already been mentioned; if anything, the consumption of alcohol increased during the first half of the nineteenth century, and did not begin to decline until the early 1900s. Since binges rarely lasted only one day, those workers who chose to "do a lushington" found themselves unable to get to work on the Monday morning. Here is Benjamin Disraeli writing about the fictitious industrial town of Wodgate, in his novel *Sybil, or the Two Nations:* "The men seldom exceed four days of labour in the week. On Sunday the master workmen begin to drink; for the apprentices there is dog-fighting without stint. On the Monday and Tuesday the whole population is drunk."

The habit of keeping Saint Monday was not ancient—it probably started at the end of the eighteenth century. It was directly linked to industrialization, since it was a way for workers to redress the balance between their free time and the longer and longer workdays being demanded by factory owners. This improvised temporal device also allowed the worker to thumb his nose at authority and assert his traditional freedom to come and go from the workplace as he willed. Once the practice of keeping Saint Monday took hold, it was hard to dislodge. It was still common when Disraeli published his novel, in 1845, and it lasted for decades more. Thomas Wright's well-known book on the habits and customs of the working classes, which appeared in 1867, describes Saint Monday as "the most noticeable holiday, the most thoroughly self-made and characteristic of them all . . . that greatest of small holidays." Wright described himself as a journeyman engineer, that is, a mechanic, and his views are therefore those of someone

---

*Hence something "cobbled together" is considered to be clumsily or poorly made.

who was not unsympathetic to his subject. On Monday, he wrote, "[the workers] are refreshed by the rest of the previous day; the money received on the Saturday is not all spent; and those among them who consign their best suits to the custody of the pawnbroker during the greatest part of each week are still in the possession of the suits which they have redeemed from limbo on Saturday night." Dressed in his Sunday clothes, with a few shillings in his pocket, the idle worker could go out on the town and enjoy himself. Not a small part of this enjoyment was meeting friends and fellow tradesmen who were engaged in the same recreation.

According to E. P. Thompson, Saint Monday was observed "almost universally wherever small-scale, domestic and outwork industries existed"; it was also common among factory workers. Saint Monday may have started as an individual preference for staying away from work—whether for relaxation, for recovering from drunkenness, or both—but its popularity during the 1850s and '60s was ensured by the enterprise of the leisure industry. During that period, most sporting events such as horse races and cricket matches took place on Mondays, since their organizers knew that many of their working-class customers would be prepared to take the day off. Saint Monday was not only a day for animal baiting and prizefighting, however. Since many public events were prohibited on the Sabbath, Monday became the chief occasion for secular recreations. Attendance at botanical gardens and museums soared on Monday, which was also the day that ordinary people went to the theater and the dance hall and when workingmen's social clubs held their weekly meetings.

Michael R. Marrus, a British historian, defines leisure as "a free activity which an individual engages in for his own purposes, whatever these may be." The implication is that not all free time should be considered as leisure time, and that what distinguishes leisure from other recreations is the element of *personal choice*. This exercise of individual choice became a reality for a significant number of people for the first time during the late eighteenth and early nineteenth centuries, partly as the result of prosperity, partly as work habits changed, and partly as leisure activities passed from the world of custom and tradition (which offered little real choice) to the commercial world of the marketplace.

Chesterton maintained that the truest form of leisure was the freedom to do nothing. This was precisely the choice that the worker who kept Saint Monday made. This involved not only taking a particular day off but also the idea that it was the individual who was the master of his—and, more rarely, her—leisure. Because of its association with personal liberty, Saint Monday is sometimes described as if it were a preindustrial custom, like Maypole dancing or the village wake. Although this description is chronologically inaccurate, it is true that the ability to exercise the personal freedom to do nothing reflected preindustrial mores and stood in sharp contrast to the late-Victorian attitude to work, which stressed discipline and regularity, promoted creative recreation, and was critical of inactivity and idleness.

Saint Monday was a reflection of old habits, but it was also a premonition of what was to come. The "small holiday" prepared the way for the weekend. First, because it accustomed people to the advantages of a regular weekly break that consisted of more than one day. Second, because it served to popularize a new type of recreational activity—travel for pleasure.

Until the coming of the railway in the 1830s, modes of travel had been basically unchanged since ancient times. Short distances were covered on foot; longer trips were undertaken on horseback (although only by young and fit males) or in a horse-drawn carriage. Both involved bad roads, mishaps, and, for a long time, the perils of highwaymen. By the early 1800s, the last was no longer a problem, but travel continued to be something undertaken out of necessity, rarely for amusement. In Jane Austen's *Emma,* Mr. Knightley frets about the "evils of the journey" that he and his family are about to undertake from London to Highbury, and about the "fatigues of his own horses and coachmen." The modern reader is surprised to discover that the journey is a distance of only sixteen miles. But sixteen miles, by coach, took almost four hours, and it would have been an exceedingly unpleasant and uncomfortable four hours, swaying and bumping over rutted, muddy country roads.* In the same novel Emma's father, Mr. Woodhouse, has a horror of carriages and hardly ever travels—except on foot; Emma's sister visits Highbury from London, but she does so infrequently. Most houseguests in *Emma* stay at Highbury for at least a week or two, since the slowness and discomfort of coach travel makes shorter visits impractical.

The time involved, as well as the expense, ensured that travel was a luxury, if not exactly enjoyed by, then at least restricted to, the moneyed and leisured classes. But the railway and Saint Monday changed all that. According to Douglas A. Reid, a historian at the University of Birmingham in England, cheap railway excursions in that city began in the summer of 1841. The custom established itself quickly, and in 1846, twenty-two excursions (many

_____
Emma was written in 1816. It wasn't until the 1830s that metaled roads became common, at least between major cities, and coach travel, in turn, became somewhat more comfortable and more rapid. On a good road, with frequent change of horses, a coach could attain the unprecedented speed of ten miles per hour.

organized by workers' clubs) took place; more than three quarters of them occurred on a Monday. The train furnished the workingman and his family with a rapid and cheap means of travel, and the weekday holiday provided an entire free day to indulge it. "Eight hours at the seaside for three-and-sixpence," announced a contemporary advertisement. The Sunday-to-Monday holiday also meant that people could leave on a trip one day and return the next. This was not called "spending a weekend," but it differed little from the later practice. It only remained to transpose the holiday from Monday to Saturday.

The energy of entrepreneurs, assisted by advertising, was an important influence not only on the diffusion and persistence of Saint Monday but on leisure in general. Hence a curious and apparently contradictory situation: not so much the commercialization of leisure as the discovery of leisure, thanks to commerce. Beginning in the eighteenth century with magazines, coffeehouses, and music rooms, and continuing throughout the nineteenth century, with professional sports and holiday travel, the modern idea of personal leisure emerged at the same time as the business of leisure. The first could not have happened without the second.

Saint Monday had many critics. Religious groups actively campaigned against the tradition which they saw as linked to the drinking and dissipation that, in their eyes, dishonored the Sabbath. They were joined by middle-class social reformers and by proponents of rational recreation, who also had an interest in altering Sunday behavior. . . .

Attacked on all sides, the Saint Monday tradition suffered a decline—though not all at once and not everywhere at the same rate. The idea of a Monday holiday did persist in the Bank Holidays Act of 1871, which required that three of the four new official national holidays fall on a Monday.* A few trades, such as cutlers, printers, and potters, held fast to Saint Monday until the turn of the century; E. P. Thompson tells of British coal miners' keeping Saint Monday as late as the 1960s, but that was unusual. Sometimes the old custom managed to coexist with the new. As late as 1874, the American consul in Sheffield wrote that "every Monday is so generally a holiday, that it has come to be called Saint Monday . . . And this holiday is, in thousands of instances, protracted through the next day, so that large numbers of the workmen, stopping work on Saturday noon, do not commence again until the following Wednesday." But on the whole such behavior, once so common, was becoming the exception. For more and more workers, the week was assuming its modern shape: regular workdays followed by a regular period of leisure.

It was in the 1870s that people began to speak of "week-ending" or "spending the week-end." The country houses of the wealthy were generally located in the Home Counties, in the vicinity of London, and were now easily reached by train. It became fashionable to go there on Friday afternoon and return to the city on Monday, and these house parties became an important feature of upper-class social life.† Weekend outings, often to the seashore, were also available to the lower classes, although their weekend

was shorter, extending from Saturday afternoon until Sunday evening.

According to one contemporary observer, Thomas Wright, "that the Saturday half-holiday movement is one of the most practically beneficial that has ever been inaugurated with a view to the social improvement of 'the masses,' no one who is acquainted with its workings will for a moment doubt." He approvingly described a variety of activities that working people indulged in on the Saturday half-holiday. The afternoon began with a leisurely midday meal at home, and was often followed by a weekly bath in the neighborhood bathhouse, an important institution at a time when few homes had running water, and one that was common in British and North American cities until well into the twentieth century. The rest of the daytime hours might be spent reading the paper, working around the house, attending a club, or strolling around town window-shopping. Saturday afternoon became a customary time for park concerts, soccer games, rowing, and bicycling. And, of course, drinking in the local pub, for despite the hopes of the reformers and Evangelicals, drinking was still the main leisure pastime of the working classes, whether the holiday occurred on Saturday or on Monday.

Wright emphasized that the afternoon was usually brought to a close in time for five o'clock tea, to leave plenty of time for the chief entertainment of the week—Saturday night. This was the time for an outing to the theater; most people brought their own food and drink into the cheap seats in the gallery. The music hall, an important influence on the spread of Saturday night, began as an adjunct to taverns but emerged as an independent entity in the 1840s, and proceeded to dominate British entertainment for the next eighty years. Like American vaudeville, the music hall presented its working-class audience with variety entertainment, chiefly songs.

---

*This raised the total number of bank holidays to eight. Lest this appear magnanimous, it is worth noting that before the first Bank Holidays Act of 1834, banks were closed on certain saints' days and anniversaries—thirty-three days every year.
†According to Ralph Dutton, the Victorian weekend was a backward step; whereas eighteenth-century country-house life had provided a leisurely setting for visiting poets, painters, and writers, who would stay one or two weeks, the emphasis of the abbreviated house party was on entertainment, not culture.

One of these catches the spirit of the new holiday, and of a new ritual:

Sweet Saturday night,
When your week's work is over,
That's the evening you make a throng,
Take your dear little girls along.
Sweet Saturday night:
But this hour is Monday morning—
To work you must go
Though longing, I know
For next Saturday night.

Michael R. Marrus provocatively suggested that "for the broad masses of Europeans, leisure became a reality only in the nineteenth century." This is a slight exaggeration, since many recreational habits were established a hundred years earlier, and the Saint Monday tradition was already a kind of improvised leisure. But it is true that the nineteenth century saw, for the first time, a conception of leisure that was markedly different from what had come before. This was not the elite leisure of the aristocracy and landed gentry, for whom recreations such as shooting and fox hunting had become an all-consuming way of life. Nor was it like the traditional mix of leisure and work of ordinary people. No longer were work and play interchanged at will, no longer did they occur in the same milieu; there was now a special time for leisure, as well as a special place. Neither play as work nor work as play, middle-class leisure, which eventually infiltrated and in-fluenced all of society, involved something new: a strict demarcation of a temporal and a physical boundary between leisure and work. This boundary—exemplified by the weekend—more than anything else characterizes modern leisure.

REFERENCES

Much of the historical material in this [reading] is drawn from Douglas A. Reid's essay, "The Decline of Saint Monday 1766–1876" (*Past and Present,* 71, 1976). Other sources for the Saint Monday tradition and eighteenth-century leisure are: E. P. Thompson's "Time, Work-Discipline, and Industrial Capitalism" (*Past & Present,* 38, 1967), and Michael R. Marrus's "Introduction" to *The Emergence of Leisure* (Michael R. Marrus, ed., New York, 1974). Thomas Wright's contemporary account is *Some Habits and Customs of the Working Classes by a Journeyman Engineer* (London, 1867). On the Early Closing Association, Wilfred B. Whitaker's *Victorian and Edwardian Shopworkers: The Struggle to Obtain Better Conditions and a Half-Holiday* (Newton Abbot, 1973); and on Victorian leisure, Peter Bailey's *Leisure and Class in Victorian England* (London, 1978), Ralph Dutton's *The Victorian Home* (London, 1954), and Colin MacInnes's charming *Sweet Saturday Night* (London, 1967), which is the source for the music-hall song.

2

The Way It Was: Factory Labor Before 1915

Sanford M. Jacoby

At the beginning of the nineteenth century, most commodities in the United States were produced either in the workshops of artisans or at home. Skilled tradesmen—carpenters, cobblers, potters—crafted their wares in small shops, owned by merchants or master craftsmen, that had not yet been significantly affected by machine methods. Goods made at home were usually consumed there, although in urban areas the putting-out system was common: Merchants distributed raw materials and tools to household workers, who then wove the cloth or made the shoes and returned the finished product to the merchants for distribution and sale. By the end of the century, however, everything had changed: Most commodities were now manufactured in factories, which were enormous agglomerations of machinery and men.

America's first factories were New England's textile mills, which supplanted home methods of production between 1790 and 1840. These early mills shared a number of features that distinguished the factory system from other modes of production: a reliance on power-driven machinery; the integration of different production processes at a single site; an elaborate division of labor; and finally, new methods of administration based on the overseer or foreman.

The overseer was the key figure in the early New England mills. Large mills employed a number of them, each in charge of a room full of machinery and workers. Although there was an agent who dealt with the mill's owners, the overseer did most of the work of maintaining mechanical and human order. In addition to tending machines, he selected the workers, assigned them to their tasks, and made sure that they labored diligently. Indeed, one advantage of the textile factories was that they permitted more effective labor supervision than was previously possible. Under the putting-out system, merchants could manipulate only the piece prices they paid; effort was controlled by the worker, who could take anywhere from two days to two weeks to turn in his goods. But in the factory, workers had less discretion over their work pace and methods. As one Rhode Island merchant wrote in 1809, "We have several hundred pieces now out weaving, but a hundred looms in families will not weave so much cloth as ten at least constantly employed under the immediate inspection of a workman."[1]

Until the 1840s, the factory system was limited chiefly to the textile industry. By 1880, it had become the dominant production mode in most manufacturing industries. As Carroll D. Wright observed in his introduction to the census of manufactures for 1880:

> Of the nearly three millions of people employed in mechanical industries of this country at least four-fifths are working under the factory system. Some of the other [than textiles] remarkable instances of the application of this system are to be found in the manufacture of

From Sanford M. Jacoby, *Employing Bureaucracy: Managers, Unions, and the Transformation of Work in American Industry, 1900–1945*. New York: Columbia University Press, 1985.

boots and shoes, of watches, musical instruments, clothing, agricultural implements, metallic goods generally, firearms, carriages and wagons, wooden goods, rubber goods, and even the slaughtering of hogs. Most of these industries have been brought under the factory system during the past thirty years.

Despite this dramatic growth, the factory did not immediately displace older organizational forms. In the iron and steel industry, rural forges and small foundries coexisted during the 1860s and 1870s with giant rail mills employing more than a thousand workers. Similarly, although steam-powered machinery provided the impetus to establish shoe factories in the 1850s, certain types of women's shoes and slippers were manufactured on a putting-out basis until the end of the century.[2]

Older methods persisted in yet another way. Many of the industries that shifted to the factory system after 1850 continued to depend on techniques from the earlier period. In these industries, the factory was often no more than a congeries of artisanal workshops which had been mechanized and enlarged. A steady infusion of craft skills was still required, particularly when the factory turned out small batches of an unstandardized product. As a result, proprietors in these industries were content to let their foremen and skilled workers make most of the decisions about the timing and manner of production.[3]

At one extreme, this practice took the form of internal contracting, which was less a system of production management than a ceding of managerial control to the contractor. The contractor, who was a highly skilled foreman, arranged with the proprietor to deliver the product within a specified time at a specified cost. The proprietor provided the contractor with tools, materials, and money, and then left him in charge of production. The contractor hired and supervised a group of skilled workers, who in turn might employ their own unskilled helpers. This system was most common in metalworking industries—sewing machinery, locomotives, guns—where a high degree of skill was needed to process component parts to exacting tolerances.[4]

At the other extreme were industries that left production decisions entirely to the skilled workers, with no foreman or contractor involved. For instance, at the Columbus Iron Works during the early 1870s, workers negotiated with the firm's owners on a tonnage rate for each rolling job undertaken by the firm. The gang members decided collectively how to pay themselves, how to allocate assignments, whom to hire, and how to train helpers. Unlike internal contracting, this was a highly egalitarian method for production management; no one interposed between the skilled workers and the owners.[5]

Neither the syndicalism of the rolling mill workers nor internal contracting was, however, very common. Rather, in most nineteenth-century factories, salaried foremen and skilled workers shared responsibility for administering production. Although the salaried foreman occupied a position inferior to the internal contractor's, he nevertheless had authority to make most of the decisions about how a production task was to be accomplished, including work methods, technical processes, and work organization.

The foreman exercised his authority within limits set by the skilled workers, who guarded their autonomy in production through a multitude of working rules that governed methods of shop organization and through what one historian has called the craftsman's "moral code." The code included output quotas set by the workers to protect themselves from overexertion, as well as an ethos of manly defiance to any foreman who tried to subvert traditional shop rules.[6]

Foremen had their own moral code, one which owed a great deal to the skilled worker's shop culture. They were arrogant, proud, conservative men, mindful of the position to which their skill and knowledge had elevated them. Often they wore white shirts to work and seated themselves at raised desks in the middle of the shop floor. But despite their former status as skilled workers, most foremen were strenuously antiunion. They were well aware that their authority depended on severing ties to their pasts. As one observer noted, "They spurn the rungs by which they did ascend."[7]

By the 1880s, winds of change were beginning to erode the power of foremen and skilled workers over production management. The new industries, such as electrical machinery and chemicals, were based on a technology that had little continuity with artisanal techniques. The older industries, like iron and steel, had mechanized to the point where craft skills were no longer essential to production. After the introduction of continuous flow methods in steel manufacturing, the foreman was left with little authority. Most production decisions were now made by engineers and metallurgists. Among skilled steelworkers, who had once been "strong, even arrogant in their indispensability," the "strong sense of independence disappeared." In machine-paced industries like textiles, the overseer was forced to share authority with an increasing number of specialists equal or superior in rank: the chief engineer, the chief electrician, and the supervisors of piping and the waste house. Other than making occasional repairs or inspecting goods to insure their quality, the overseer had fewer and fewer responsibilities in production. In textiles, as in steel and other industries, most of the foreman's tasks were related to employing and supervising labor. Here, however, the methods of the 1850s persisted, with little modification.[8]

I. Foremen in Control, 1880–1915

Whereas the foreman's degree of control over production varied by industry, his authority in employment matters was uniform across industries. Whether in a machine shop or on the assembly line, the foreman was given free rein in hiring, paying, and supervising workers. To the worker, the foreman was a despot—rarely benevolent—who made and interpreted employment policy as he saw fit. Any checks on the foreman's power emanated from the workers he supervised, not from the proprietor.

Recruiting and Hiring

The foreman's control over employment began literally at the factory gates. On mornings when the firm was hiring—a fact advertised by signs hung outside the plant, by newspaper ads, or by word of mouth—a crowd gathered in front of the factory, and the foreman picked out those workers who appeared suitable or had managed to get near the front. At one Philadelphia factory, the foreman tossed apples into the throng; if a man caught an apple, he got the job. Foremen could be less arbitrary. For instance, they frequently hired their friends, the relatives of those already employed, and even their own relatives: "Oftentimes he [the foreman] is connected by blood ties with those who come under his control and he will inevitably be swayed by considerations of previous friendship no matter how hard he may strive not to be." New foremen might dismiss current employees to make room for their friends and relatives, as occurred in a Lawrence textile mill during the 1880s. The overseers "made changes very freely in the departments committed to them, and the result was that for several months a feeling of great insecurity prevailed among the hands."[9]

In addition to blood ties, foremen relied on ethnic stereotypes to determine who would get a job and which job they would get. The Irish and Germans were considered good skilled workers, while Poles and "Hunkies" were thought to be suited for heavy labor. Jews were said to be dexterous, Rumanians dishonest, Slovaks stupid, and Italians "so susceptible to the opposite sex that they could not be satisfactorily employed." When an investigator in the steel mills asked for a job on a blast furnace, he was told "only Hunkies work on those jobs, they're too damn dirty and too damn hot for a white man."[10]

To get a job, workers often resorted to bribing the foreman with whiskey, cigars, or cash, a practice that one study found to be "exceedingly common" in Ohio's factories. The study included an affidavit from an immigrant worker who, to get a factory job, had paid the foreman a five-dollar bribe. Several days later the foreman told the man that he would be fired unless he paid another five dollars right away, because someone else had just paid ten dollars for a similar job.[11]

Assignment to a job was determined in large part by favoritism or ethnic prejudice. The foreman had little interest in or knowledge of an employee's previous work experience. If a newly hired employee proved unsatisfactory, he was easily replaced by someone else. Although intradepartmental promotions occurred, transfers and promotions between departments were rare, as were definite lines of promotion (except on skilled work). The foreman had a parochial view of the factory and was reluctant to give up his best workers to another foreman.

Few companies kept detailed employment records before 1900. Only the foreman knew with any accuracy how many workers were employed in his shop and how much they were paid. In a large firm, a worker could quit his job in the morning and get taken on by the foreman of another department in the afternoon. In 1915, the top man-

agers of a large hosiery factory reported that they had little idea of how many people their firm hired and dismissed each week.[12]

The one exception to this lack of information was the bureau that specialized in screening skilled labor for open-shop employers. Henry Leland, founder of the Cadillac Motor Company, started the Employers' Association of Detroit in 1897 to ensure that Detroit remained an open-shop city. The organization kept records on every individual who had worked for a member firm and blacklisted those who were "agitators" and union supporters. To get a job at a member firm, a worker had to apply through the Employers' Association. By 1911, the association's employment bureau had in its files names of more than 160,000 workers, a figure equalling nearly 90 percent of the Detroit labor force. Other employer organizations (including the National Metal Trades Association and the National Founders Association) set up similar local agencies to blacklist radicals and trade unionists and to supply member firms with the names of "good men" who needed work.[13]

Although direct recruitment was common during the nineteenth century, it was not usually done by the foreman. Instead, employers either sent their own special recruiters to the New York docks to secure immigrant workers or else relied on private agencies like the American Emigrant Company, which kept scouts in several foreign ports to recruit emigrating workers. After the 1890s, however, immigration flows had become large enough and cyclically sensitive enough to meet industrial demand. Consequently, direct recruitment was rare, except in sectors like construction and the railroads, where work was seasonal and labor requirements for certain projects could run into the thousands.[14]

During the heyday of mass immigration, employers recruited through the immigrants' own informal network: Newcomers to America headed for areas where their countrymen, often men from the same European villages, had found jobs. As more men of a given nationality arrived, benefit societies were organized, priests appeared, and wives and children were sent for. Gradually a new ethnic community developed in the area. The news that a company was seeking help was transmitted to friends and relatives in the old country; sometimes, tickets were purchased for them. Letters might also warn of a shortage of jobs.[15]

Wages and Effort

The foreman also had considerable power in determining the wages of the workers he hired, whether for piecework or daywork. As a result, different individuals doing the same job were often paid very different rates. Because top management monitored labor costs but not the wage determination process, the foreman had an incentive to hire individuals at the lowest rate possible. It was common practice for a foreman "to beat the applicant down from the wage he states he wishes to the lowest which the interviewer believes he can be induced to accept." Moreover, by being secretive about wage rates and production records, foremen could play favorites, varying the day rate or assigning workers to jobs where piece rates were loose. Since each foreman ran his shop autonomously, rate variations across departments were also common. In their report on the stove industry, Frey and Commons found that "molding [piece] prices were far from equal on similar work in the same shop or district."[16]

Despite—or perhaps because of—the latitude they gave him in determining rates, the firm's owners expected the foreman to hold down labor costs. This meant paying a wage no greater than the "going rate" for a particular job. But it also meant keeping effort levels up in order to reduce unit costs. When the going rate rose, effort became the key variable to be manipulated by the foreman.

The methods used by foremen to maintain or increase effort levels were known collectively as the "drive system": close supervision, abuse, profanity, and threats. Informal rules regulating such work behavior as rest periods were arbitrarily and harshly enforced. Workers were constantly urged to move faster and work harder. Sumner Slichter defined the drive system as "the policy of obtaining efficiency not by rewarding merit, not by seeking to interest men in their work . . . but by putting pressure on them to turn out a large output. The dominating note of the drive policy is to inspire the worker with awe and fear of the management, and having developed fear among them, to take advantage of it."[17]

Driving was more prevalent with daywork, where the effort wage was indeterminate. But it occurred with straight piecework too, when foremen sought to prevent workers from restricting output. An official of the machinists complained that "in many cases the rapidity with which the workingmen have been driven under the piecework and similar systems have been the means of driving the mechanics to the insane asylum." Under the bonus wage systems that began to appear after 1890, wages did not rise in proportion to output. Thus, unit labor costs fell with additional production, creating an incentive for the foreman to drive his men even harder and arousing the unions' anger over these new "scientific" payment plans.[18]

The drive system depended, ultimately, on fear of unemployment to ensure obedience to the foreman. Workers were more submissive when jobs were scarce, as was often the case before World War I. A discharge was usually devastating, since few workers had savings to cushion the hardships of unemployment and only meager relief was available. On the other hand, a tight labor market tended to undermine the foreman's authority, forcing him to rely more heavily on discharges to maintain discipline. Data from a metalworking plant illustrate this point. In 1914, a depressed year, the plant had 225 dismissals, many of them for "unadaptability" or "slow work"; this suggests that workers who could not keep up to standard were fired during hard times. By 1916, when the economy had improved and workers could afford to be feisty, the number of dismissals rose to 467, and a relatively large number of workers were fired for "insubordination," "troublemaking," and "positive misconduct." But whether times were tough or easy, the foreman was free to fire anyone as he saw fit, and discharges were meted out liberally. One critic of this system told the story of an assistant superintendent making his rounds through the shop: "Bill," he said to the foreman, "has anyone been fired from this shop today?" "No," the foreman meekly replied. "Well, then, fire a couple of 'em!" barked the assistant superintendent, in a voice that carried. "It'll put the fear of God in their hearts."[19]

Employment Security

Employment instability involved more than high dismissal rates. In its cyclical and seasonal forms, unemployment regularly touched a large portion of the working class. Between 1854 and 1914, recessions or depressions occurred every three or four years, with about twenty-five of these sixty years spent in contraction. In Massachusetts, unemployment was high even during relatively prosperous periods such as 1900–1906, when about one in every five of the state's manufacturing workers was unemployed for at least part of each year. Even Massachusetts' trade union members, a relatively skilled group, were not immune to job loss. An average of 29 percent of these workers had a spell of joblessness each year between 1890 and 1916. The amount of time spent in unemployment was considerable: In 1890 and again in 1900, over 40 percent of the na-

tion's unemployed were jobless for more than four months.[20]

Because of dismissals and seasonal instability, unemployment was widespread throughout the labor force even during good years. Paul H. Douglas, the noted labor economist, estimated that approximately two-thirds of the unemployment that occurred in the three decades after 1896 was due to seasonal and chronic, as opposed to cyclical, causes. During the 1900s, workers in highly seasonal industries—men's clothing, glass containers, textiles—were on average employed only about three-fourths of a full working year. Employment tended to be more stable in consumer goods industries which produced items unaffected by style changes. But in 1909 even the most stable industry—bread and bakery goods—had monthly employment levels that varied 7 percent from peak to trough. That same year, the industrial average fluctuated 14 percent over the year, rising to 45 percent in the automobile industry. The seasonal instability of employment perpetuated the drive system. Activity became frenzied during the busy season as firms rushed to fill orders. Capacity utilization rates and employment levels rose by magnitudes rarely encountered today. A Fall River textile worker said that during the industry's busy season, "The Board of Trade drives the agent, the agent drives the superintendent, he drives the overseer, and the overseer drives the operative. They drive us, and we drive each other."[21]

However, the existence of widespread unemployment is not by itself an indication of the impermanence of the employment relationship. Had there been some understanding that laid-off workers would be recalled when needed, periodic unemployment need not have severed the relationship. But few firms made systematic attempts to rehire their workers after layoffs. For example, statistics from a large Chicago metalworking plant, whose records distinguished between new hires and rehires, reveal that only 8 percent of all new hires during the 1908–1910 period were rehires of workers who had been laid off during the depression that began late in 1907. Average industrial rehire rates were probably much lower. Of course, rehiring was more common in seasonal industries, since layoffs and their durations were more predictable. Even here, however, reemployment was by no means guaranteed. A government study of seven dressmaking establishments found that from 32 percent to 75 percent of those employed during the spring busy season were rehired after the summer lull.[22]

In addition to rehiring, mechanisms to maintain the employment relationship during downturns included guaranteed employment plans and work-sharing arrangements. By 1920, only 15 companies had employment guarantee plans. Work-sharing plans, though more prevalent, were usually initiated by trade unions in cooperation with unionized employers. Employers in nonunion firms maintained that work-sharing was cumbersome and inefficient.[23]

Few workers had anything resembling equity in their jobs. When layoffs came, it was the rare employer who ordered his foremen to reduce the work force systematically. Employment security was determined by the same arbitrary criteria as hiring. Bribes were a common means of ensuring job security. Shortly after the turn of the century, a group of Lithuanian workers in a rubber factory were forced to hand over a regular portion of their wages to the foreman as a sort of unemployment insurance. In other shops, according to an article in *Engineering Magazine*, everyone had to "pay some sort of tribute to his foreman. The tribute is usually in the form of money or service, but there are cases where the tribute is of a nature which cannot be mentioned in an open paper."[24]

In short, prior to World War I employment for most manufacturing workers was unstable, unpredictable, and frequently unjust. The worker's economic success and job satisfaction depended on a highly personal relationship with his foreman, with management and "the company" playing only a minor role. A foreman interviewed in 1920 noted that "before the war, most workmen worked where they did not so much because of the company they worked for but because of the foreman. To them the foreman represented the company, and workers in the barroom and other hangouts didn't talk so much about this company or that company as they did about this foreman or that foreman they had worked for." There *was* an implicit system of employment here, but it was not bureaucratic. Foremen had many favors to offer those whom they had befriended or those who had bought their friendship. Personal ties and loyalty counted for much, although later reformers were horrified by the particularism and brutality that infused the drive system. Those changes that made employment practices more rational, stable, and equitable were not a managerial innovation; rather, they were imposed from below.[25]

II. The Union Response

Trade unionism helped to curb the foreman's arbitrary exercise of power and gave the skilled worker some control over the terms of his employment. The trade union ensured that strict rules and equitable procedures would govern allocative decisions. While only a minority of all workers belonged to unions, those unions were a persistent reminder that the employer's authority, and that of his agents, could be circumscribed through collective action.[26]

Prior to the 1880s, local trade unions unilaterally adopted working rules or "legislation" that governed wages and working conditions for union members. Enforcement depended upon members' refusing—under threat of punishment by the union—to obey any order that contravened the union's rules. But after 1880, as the unions and their national organizations grew more powerful, the status of these rules changed from unilateral group codes to contractual and bargained restrictions on the employer and his foremen. These contracts were extensive documents that strictly regulated work methods and effort norms as well as such issues as apprenticeship standards and wage scales. An 1889 Memorandum of Agreement for members of the Amalgamated Association of Iron, Steel and Tin Workers at the Homestead Works contained fifty-eight pages of "footnotes" defining work rules for union members.[27]

Hiring

Controlling access to a trade was a fundamental element of the unions' power, and regulating apprenticeship standards was an important method for effecting this control. By limiting the number of apprentices or by lengthening the time required to become a journeyman, the union ensured that there would not be an oversupply of men in the trade and thus that the living standards to which union members were accustomed would not deteriorate. Moreover, by overseeing the training process, the union made certain that persons entering the trade were exposed to the virtues of unionism and had absorbed its moral code.

By the turn of the century, however, the apprenticeship system was fading out in many occupations where an ever finer division of labor reduced the demand for versatile craftsmen who knew all the "secrets" of a trade. The ratio of apprentices to the total number employed in manufacturing

steadily declined, from 1:33 in 1860 to 1:88 in 1900. In testimony to Congress in 1901, Samuel Gompers noted that "the apprenticeship system is not so generally in vogue now as formerly. The introduction of new machinery . . . and the division and subdivision of labor have rendered a high class of skill, in which workmen have whole work, scarcely necessary (except the demand for the highest skill in a particular branch)."[28]

Nevertheless, the unions had other ways to bolster their control. One important mechanism was the closed or preferential shop, which restricted the foreman's discretion to hire whomever he chose and enhanced the demand for union labor. This protected union members against discrimination in hiring and guaranteed that vacancies would be filled by them. In some trades, the closed shop led to more restrictive union admissions policies so that a fixed number of potential vacancies could be divided among a smaller body of members. Some unions required that the foreman apply to a union hiring hall when in need of labor; this practice allowed the union to dispense jobs to the workers of its choice. Such arrangements also allowed unions to provide employment for older members and to prohibit the use of tests and other screening devices deemed objectionable. But basically they were a powerful demonstration to the worker that his well-being was best served by allegiance to the union rather than to his foreman.[29]

Wages and Effort

In their approach to wage determination, trade unions sought to protect not only absolute wage levels but also relative and effort wages. The central feature of this approach was the so-called standard rate, which all union members were supposed to receive. Reflecting the principle of equal pay for equal work, the standard rate ruled out all incentive wage systems under which earnings did not rise in proportion to output and effort, as well as all payment systems which "graded" workers: that is, classified them by some criterion such as merit or competence or sometimes even seniority. (One union said that seniority allowed the employer to get "first class service from a man getting less than a first class wage.") The unions' strong emphasis on the standard rate was based on the premise that foremen would always prefer to deal with individuals and that grading was the surest way to divide and conquer.

The unions were opposed to grading on other grounds as well. First, they argued that grading was unnecessary since apprenticeship standards insured that all journeymen were equally competent. Second, they feared that grouping workers by competence would undercut the standard rate and lead inevitably to the substitution of relatively cheap labor for higher priced men. Third, they believed that grading encouraged specialization within the trade, thereby lessening the demand for all-around craftsmen and eroding wage levels. Finally, they viewed grading and other meritocratic wage determination methods as an affront to their egalitarianism and their insistence on occupational autonomy. When the United Typothetae, an employers' association, proposed a graded wage system in 1887, the Typographical Union replied that "it would be impossible to satisfactorily grade all workmen except by an elaborate system of examination which would be appalling to undertake."[30]

In practice, however, the unions permitted the payment of different rates for the various steps within a trade and for especially skilled or dangerous work. Among machinists and molders, for example, journeymen who had recently advanced from apprenticeship could be paid wages below the standard rate. Other unions allowed grading by skill, but only if the different grades were nonsub-

stitutable. The photoengravers permitted half-tone etchers to be paid more than line-etchers, but the latter—however capable—were never permitted to do half-tone work.[31]

The standard rate represented a level of well-being for which union members had fought and to which they felt entitled. Consequently, organized workers viewed wage cuts as a threat to their living standards and stood ready to strike in defense of the standard rate. As early as 1870, textile manufacturers in Fall River, and then coal operators in Ohio's Hocking Valley, deliberately provoked strikes by cutting the wages of their unionized workers, hoping to break the unions in the ensuing disputes.[32]

Unions were equally concerned about how hard members had to work to receive their pay. To check the foreman's driving and to protect the effort wage, skilled workers made effective use of "the stint," the deliberate restriction of output. In many instances, the union specified output limits in the trade agreement and imposed fines on pieceworkers whose earnings were excessive. Typically, however, union members policed themselves. Skilled workers who restricted their output did not think of themselves as Luddites but instead as "sober and trustworthy masters of the trade" whose stinting demonstrated "unselfish brotherhood."[33]

While the stint was also used to deter foremen from playing favorites in assigning piecework jobs, the unions had other ways to limit favoritism. For example, in 1896 the molders demanded that piece rates be listed in a price-book, so as to prevent foremen from paying different rates for similar work. In one stovemaking shop, both the foreman and a union representative were given keys to the locker in which the price-book was kept. In the Chicago meatpacking industry, the cattle butchers devised a detailed system of promotion lines governed by seniority that was intended to curtail favoritism in job allocation and to create a sense of equity among the union's members. Foremen and other managers were strongly opposed to the practice. As John R. Commons observed, "These rules of promotion do not find favor with the superintendents, who contend that forced promotion takes a man away from work he does well."[34]

Elsewhere, promotion lines were devised primarily to enhance the prospects of a shop's incumbent workers. During the 1870s, unskilled helpers in the steel industry demanded that they be given preference over outsiders whenever a skilled position became vacant. By the late 1880s, the steelworkers' union had adopted rules calling for promotion lines governed by seniority. "We endeavor," said the union, "to prevent men from learning the skilled positions before they have served in the minor ones. If they are permitted to learn the skilled jobs, it would necessarily mean that those holding the minor positions would have no opportunity for improvement."[35] . . .

III. The Less Skilled

The unskilled worker dissatisfied with his job had few options. He could complain to higher officials, but they invariably supported the foreman in any dispute. Daniel McCallum, president of the Erie Railroad, justified this practice by asserting that "obedience cannot be enforced where the foreman is interfered with by a superior officer giving orders directly to his subordinates." More was involved here than the application of a military model to industry. As one economist perceptively observed, managers feared that any show of liberality would "give the workmen exaggerated notions of their rights and management desires to keep the workers' minds off their rights." In the early 1900s a group of nineteen unskilled rubber workers presented their employer with signed affidavits that described how

they had been forced to bribe a foreman to retain their jobs. All nineteen were fired within two weeks.[36]

Occasionally the unskilled were able to establish their own workplace organizations, which regulated employment in much the same way as the craft unions did. During the 1880s, the Knights of Labor included local assemblies made up of less skilled workers who banded together to press for higher wages and to protect themselves from arbitrary foremen. Some of the locals even achieved the closed shop and a seniority-based layoff system. But unskilled workers had relatively little bargaining power and were rarely able to sustain sizable, stable organizations.

The absence of organization did not, however, deter them from engaging in militant activity. In steel, for instance, pitched battles were fought at Cleveland (1899), East Chicago (1905), McKees Rocks (1909), and Bethlehem (1910), with the unskilled, immigrant work force on one side and the militia and police on the other. The particularly violent strike at McKees Rocks was touched off when the company fired a group of workers who had protested pay practices and fee-charging by the company's foremen. But these strikes, while spectacular, were sporadic and seldom successful.[37]

Limitation of output was a somewhat more effective means of checking the foreman. The Commissioner of Labor's 1904 report on *Regulation and Restriction of Output* found that stints and slowdowns were "enforced in nonunion establishments" and were widely accepted "among all wage earners." But lacking the discipline provided by a union, and sundered by ethnic conflicts and language barriers that stymied cooperation, unskilled workers—even those belonging to assemblies of the Knights of Labor—had less success with this method than did their skilled counterparts.[38]

Because his actions were so ineffectual, the unskilled worker seeking higher wages or better working conditions usually had no alternative but to quit. Data from the 1900s and 1910s show labor turnover levels that were extraordinarily high by modern standards, especially among less skilled workers. Many companies experienced monthly separation rates in excess of 10 percent. In one Milwaukee engine factory, whose experience was typical of other factories, the separation rates for unskilled and semiskilled workers in 1912 were three times as high as the rates for skilled workers in the tool and pattern department. A government official termed labor turnover "the individualistic strike": Just as the number of strikes by skilled trade unionists tended to increase during a recovery period, so did the number of quits by the less skilled.[39]

High turnover rates also reflected the immigrant backgrounds of the unskilled. Almost two-thirds of the immigrants arriving in the United States between 1870 and 1910 were unskilled, and they became the backbone of the manufacturing labor force. Around the turn of the century, when the foreign-born constituted nearly one-quarter of the labor force, they represented about half of all unskilled laborers in manufacturing. Foreign-born workers accounted for 58 percent of all workers in iron and steel manufacturing, 61 percent in meatpacking, 62 percent in bituminous coal mining, and 69 percent in the cotton mills.[40]

While it is well known that immigration flows were large and cyclically sensitive, it is less well known that emigration flows followed the same pattern. Between 1870 and 1914, one person left the United States for every three that arrived. While emigration decreased and immigration increased during good years, the annual proportion of emigrants to immigrants never fell below 20 percent. Emigration rose during depressed years, as recent immigrants—the first to lose their jobs—decided to return home. Ninety percent of the Bulgarians who made up most

of the unskilled labor force in an Illinois steel mill had left town by the end of the 1908 depression. That year, immigration fell, and the national proportion of emigrants to immigrants rose to 75 percent. Although more immigrants stayed than left, the large backflow contributed to the instability of the unskilled labor force and to high rates of turnover.[41]

Immigrants often came to the United States with no intention of permanently settling here. Many were single men or married men with families back home. This was true of about half of the unskilled Italian laborers living in Buffalo in 1905, and of four in five of the nation's immigrant steelworkers. These men came to make their "stake," planning to return to Europe to buy land, open shops, or pay off debts. The transience of the immigrant labor force was part of an older European pattern of peasant mobility. In Italy, landless day laborers roamed from place to place looking for work, often spending weeks or months away from home. Slovaks worked seasonally on their plots and then supplemented their incomes as roving peddlers; Polish peasants went to Germany. The fact that many immigrant workers viewed their stay in the United States as temporary made it difficult to organize them into unions. A strike just lengthened the time a man was away from home and family, while the prospect of returning home made one's privations more bearable.[42]

Finally, quitting was a form of resistance to the rigors of factory life. Here there was a continuity of experience among the early New England textile workers, their French-Canadian and Irish replacements, and the southeastern Europeans who filled the factories after 1880. Each group brought to the factories a preindustrial work ethic that was attuned to the seasons, migratory, and uncomfortable with industrial discipline. Ellen Collins quit the mill at Lowell in the 1840s complaining about her "obedience to the ding-dong of the bell—just as though we were so many living machines." During the

1870s, managers of New England textile mills complained that absenteeism and quits made it difficult to run their machines on the hottest summer days. One manufacturer said in 1878 that "our mill operatives are much like other people and take their frequent holidays for pleasure and visiting." Forty years later, the quit rate at a Connecticut silk mill quadrupled during the hot summer months of 1915. Thus, each group successively went through the process of internalizing factory discipline; this was one of the props to high turnover before 1920.[43]

Although they were relatively less mobile, skilled workers also had a tradition of itinerancy that formed at the intersection of artisanal work habits and the requisites of learning a trade. It was supported by craft institutions, especially the trade union, and by repeated waves of immigrant artisans carrying similar traditions to the United States.

A familiar figure in industrializing societies, the footloose craftsman moved from shop to shop, acquiring the secrets of his trade. Employers often approved of this type of mobility. The labor supervisor at National Cash Register wrote in 1907 that for a skilled worker, "it is of value, not a detriment, if he has had several employers—he is learning the trade." Reinforcing this mobility was a work ethic that emphasized manliness and independence. Acceptance of demeaning working conditions, or even long tenure, would compromise that ethic. One trade union representative noted that, for many skilled workers, "a job may be satisfactory in every respect, quite as good as they are likely to find anywhere, yet they will leave because they do not want to remain in one shop too long. . . . It rests upon a fear of losing their independence, of getting into a frame of mind wherein they will come to attach disproportionate importance to the retention of a certain job."[44]

The craft union facilitated the skilled worker's propensity to move. The constitutions of the early national unions required lo-

cal secretaries to furnish reports on the conditions of the trade in their area and to help traveling members find jobs. Some unions loaned their members money to finance a search for work if none was to be found near home. But this loan system was on the decline by the beginning of this century, partly "because, as in the case of the iron molders, it was made use of to secure a free holiday."[45]

IV. A Market of Movement

Because the employment relationship was one of weak attachment on both sides, the industrial labor market prior to 1915 was a market of movement, characterized by high rates of mobility. Indeed, the few available company records indicate a pattern of continuously high turnover rates before World War I. The earliest turnover data come from the New England textile industry of the 1830s and 1840s, and they show that the young Yankee women who worked in the mills were an unstable labor force. Most were unmarried and could return to their parents' farms if they were dissatisfied or if work was scarce. But the immigrants who began to replace native workers in the 1850s had high turnover rates too. A study of 151 Scottish weavers recruited by Lyman Mills in 1853 found that nearly 80 percent of the women had left the firm within three years.[46]

A similar picture emerges in other companies, especially those employing relatively more men. A Massachusetts firm that manufactured textile machinery recruited large numbers of French-Canadians between 1860 and 1890. But "so rapid was the turnover" that, of every three workers hired, only one stayed with the firm. Rates of persistence were also very low at the Boston Manufacturing Company. For quinquennial periods between 1850 and 1865, only 10–12 percent of the male workers employed at the beginning of a period were still working for the firm five years later.[47]

Nineteenth-century employers sometimes complained about what one of them called "the nomadic system of employing men." Employers often responded to high quit rates by withholding the wages of those who left without prior notice, a practice that also deterred strikes. When a Massachusetts mill owner was asked in the 1870s to explain these wage forfeitures, he replied, "If a mill did not keep back workers' wages, it would simply awake to find all its hands gone by the morning."[48]

The better records available for the first two decades of the twentieth century show continuing high levels of turnover throughout the manufacturing sector. But because the overall data are so fragmentary, especially for the nineteenth century, some other source of information is needed to gauge labor turnover levels. . . .

. . . There is no doubt that employment under the drive system was a tenuous relationship. Both parties in the relationship took full advantage of their legal rights, acquired early in the nineteenth century, to quit or to dismiss at will. In fact, this was the only worker right consistently recognized by the courts of the day, and most managers did little to discourage its exercise. During the McKees Rocks dispute of 1909, the president of the struck company was succinct in his opinion of the strikers: "If a man is dissatisfied, it is his privilege to quit."[49]

NOTES

1. Samual Batchelder, *Introduction and Early Progress of the Cotton Manufacture in the United States* (Boston, 1863), passim; Stephen Marglin, "What Do Bosses Do? The Origins and Functions of Hierarchy in Capitalist Production," *Review of Radical Political Economics* (Summer 1974), 6:33–60; Caroline F. Ware, *The Early New England Cotton Manufacture* (Boston, 1931), pp. 23, 50–51, 263–266; Howard M. Gitelman, "The Waltham System and the Coming of the Irish," *Labor History* (Fall 1967), 8:227–253; Hannah Josephson, *The Golden Threads: New England's Mill Girls* (New York, 1949), pp. 220–221; Thomas Dublin, *Women at Work: The Transformation of Work and Community in Lowell, Massachusetts, 1826–1860* (New York, 1979).

2. Carroll D. Wright, "The Factory System of the United States," U.S. Bureau of the Census, *Report of the United States at the Tenth Census* (Washington, D.C., 1883), p. 548; Victor S. Clark, *History of Manufacturers in the United States* (Washington, D.C., 1929), 3:15–16, 76–80, 473; Daniel Nelson, *Managers and Workers: Origins of the New Factory System in the United States, 1880–1920* (Madison, Wis., 1975), p. 4.

3. The authority of the foreman and the skilled worker, said Frederick W. Taylor, come from "knowledge handed down to them by word of mouth. . . . This mass of rule-of-thumb or traditional knowledge may be said to be the principal asset or possession of every tradesman." *The Principles of Scientific Management* (New York, 1912), pp. 31–32.

4. Dan Clawson, *Bureaucracy and the Labor Process: The Transformation of U.S. Industry, 1860–1920* (New York, 1980), pp. 75–83, 115; John Buttrick, "The Inside Contract System," *Journal of Economic History* (September 1952), 12:205–221; Nelson, *Managers and Workers*, pp. 31, 38.

5. David Montgomery, "Workers' Control of Machine Production in the Nineteenth Century," *Labor History* (Fall 1976), 17:488–489; Clawson, *Bureaucracy*, pp. 130–166.

6. George S. Gibb, *The Whitesmiths of Taunton: A History of Reed and Barton, 1824–1843* (Cambridge, Mass., 1943), pp. 282–286; Clawson, *Bureaucracy*, pp. 126–130; Nelson, *Managers and Workers*, p. 40; Montgomery, "Workers' Control," p. 491.

7. Alexander Hamilton Church, "The Twelve Principles of Efficiency: The Eleventh Principle—Written Standard Practice Instructions," *The Engineering Magazine* (June 1911), 41:445; Gibb, *Whitesmiths*, p. 184; Ordway Tead, "The Importance of Being a Foreman," *Industrial Management* (June 1917), 53:353.

8. David Brody, *Steelworkers in America: The Nonunion Era* (New York, 1969), p. 85; "The Characteristics of a Foreman," *The Engineering Magazine* (February 1909), 36:847; Evelyn H. Knowlton, *Pepperell's Progress: History of a*

Cotton Textile Company, 1844–1945 (Cambridge, Mass., 1948), pp. 159–161.

9. Joseph H. Willits, "Steadying Employment," *The Annals* (May 1916), vol. 65, suppl., p. 72; H. Keith Trask, "The Problem of the Minor Executive," *The Engineering Magazine* (January 1910), 38:501; "Fall River, Lowell, and Lawrence," Massachusetts Bureau of the Statistics of Labor, *Thirteenth Annual Report* (Boston, 1882), p. 381.

10. Brody, *Steelworkers*, p. 120; Virginia Yans-McLaughlin, *Family and Community: Italian Immigrants in Buffalo, 1880–1930* (1977; reprint, Urbana, Ill., 1982), p. 43; Arthur Hanko, "Reducing Foreign Labor Turnover," *Industrial Management* (May 1921), 61:351.

11. Fred H. Rindge, Jr., "From Boss to Foreman," *Industrial Management* (July 1917), 53:508–509; C. J. Morrison, "Short-Sighted Methods in Dealing with Labor," *The Engineering Magazine* (January 1914), 46:568.

12. Charles E. Fouhy, "Relations Between the Employment Manager and the Foreman," *Industrial Management* (October 1919), 58:336; Henry Eilbirt, "The Development of Personnel Management in the United States," *Business History Review* (Autumn 1959), 33:346; Willits, "Steadying," p. 72.

13. "Detroit's Great Growth Due to Its Open Shop Policy," *Iron Trade Review* (July 15, 1915), 57:143–145; Clarence E. Bonnett, *Employer's Associations in the United States* (New York, 1922), p. 80; Edwin E. Witte, *The Government in Labor Disputes* (New York, 1932), pp. 211–218.

14. Charlotte Erickson, *American Industry and the European Immigrant, 1860–1885* (Cambridge, Mass., 1957), pp. 17–28, 67–87; Brody, *Steelworkers*, p. 109; Don D. Lescohier, "Working Conditions," in J. R. Commons et al., *History of Labor in the United States* (New York, 1935), 3:188; Isaac A. Hourwich, *Immigration and Labor* (New York, 1912), pp. 93–101; Harry Jerome, *Migration and Business Cycles* (New York, 1926).

15. Yans-McLaughlin, *Italian Immigrants*, pp. 59–64, 72–73; William I. Thomas and Florian Znaniecki, *The Polish Peasant in Europe and America*, abridged by Eli Zaretsky (1918; reprint, Urbana, Ill., 1984), pp. 139–255.

16. Sumner H. Slichter, *The Turnover of Factory Labor* (1919; reprint, New York, 1921), p. 319; Dwight T. Farnham, "Adjusting the Employment Department to the Rest of the Plant," *Industrial Management* (September 1919), 58:202;

Commission of Inquiry, Interchurch World Movement, *Report on the Steel Strike of 1919* (New York, 1920), p. 139; Nelson, *Managers and Workers*, pp. 44–45; John P. Frey and John R. Commons, "Conciliation in the Stove Industry," U.S. Bureau of Labor Statistics (BLS) Bulletin No. 62 (Washington, D.C., 1906), p. 128.

17. John R. Commons, "Labor Conditions in Meat Packing and the Recent Strike," *Quarterly Journal of Economics* (November 1904), 19:8; Nelson, *Managers and Workers*, p. 43; Slichter, *Turnover*, p. 202.

18. Lloyd Ulman, *The Rise of the National Trade Union* (Cambridge, Mass., 1955), p. 549.

19. Philip Klein, *The Burden of Unemployment* (New York, 1923), pp. 13–37; Paul F. Brissenden and Emil Frankel, *Labor Turnover in Industry: A Statistical Analysis* (New York, 1922), pp. 80–81; Slichter, *Turnover*, p. 184; *Industrial Relations* (also known as *Bloomfield's Labor Digest*) (May 12, 1923), 15:1530.

20. Alexander Keyssar, "Men Out of Work: A Social History of Unemployment in Massachusetts, 1870–1916" (Ph.D. dissertation, Harvard University, 1977), pp. 43, 72, 76–77, 79, 107; Robert A. Gordon, *Business Fluctuations* (New York, 1961), p. 251.

21. Paul H. Douglas, "Can Management Prevent Unemployment?" *American Labor Legislation Review* (September 1930), 20:273; Mary Van Kleeck, "The Effect of Unemployment on the Wage Scale," *The Annals* (September 1915), 61:97–98; Irene O. Andrews, "The Relation of Irregular Employment to the Living Wage for Women," *American Labor Legislation Review* (June 1915), 5:319–374; Massachusetts Commission on Minimum Wage Boards, *Report* (Boston, 1912), passim; U.S. Bureau of the Census, *Census of Manufacturers: 1909* (Washington, D.C., 1912), pt. 1, pp. 37–54; "Fall River," p. 306.

22. Slichter, *Turnover*, pp. 126–127, 129.

23. Keyssar, "Out of Work," p. 129; "How to Meet Hard Times: A Program for the Prevention and Relief of Abnormal Unemployment," Mayor's Committee on Unemployment, City of New York (New York, 1917), p. 24; "Guaranteed Wages: Report to the President by the Advisory Board," Office of War Mobilization and Reconversion and Office of Temporary Controls (Washington, D.C., 1947), app. C, pp. 290, 293.

24. Keyssar, "Out of Work," p. 153; Morrison, "Short-Sighted," p. 568.

25. *Industrial Relations* (December 11, 1920), 5:484.

26. At its pre-Wagner Act peak in 1920, the proportion of nonagricultural employees who belonged to unions was 18.5 percent. Leo Wolman, *Ebb and Flow in Trade Unions* (New York, 1936), pp. 172–193.

27. F. W. Hilbert, "Trade-Union Agreements in the Iron Molders' Union," in Jacob H. Hollander and George E. Barnett, *Studies in American Trade Unionism* (London, 1906), pp. 221–260; Bruno Ramirez, *When Workers Fight: The Politics of Industrial Relations in the Progressive Era, 1898–1916* (Westport, Conn., 1978), pp. 17–48; Brody, *Steelworkers*, p. 52.

28. James M. Motley, *Apprenticeship in American Trade Unions* (Baltimore, 1907); Paul H. Douglas, *American Apprenticeship and Industrial Education* (New York, 1921), p. 74; "Testimony of Samuel Gompers," in U.S. Industrial Commission, *Report on the Relations and Conditions of Capital and Labor* (Washington, D.C., 1901), 7:620.

29. Sumner H. Slichter, *Union Policies and Industrial Management* (Washington, D.C., 1941), p. 63; "Gompers," p. 603; Sanford M. Jacoby and Daniel J. B. Mitchell, "Development of Contractual Features of the Union-Management Relationship," *Labor Law Journal* (August 1982), 33:515; Howard T. Lewis, "The Economic Basis of the Fight for the Closed Shop," *Journal of Political Economy* (November 1912), 20:928–952; D. P. Smelser, *Unemployment and American Trade Unions* (Baltimore, 1919), pp. 57–74.

30. Sidney and Beatrice Webb, *Industrial Democracy* (1897; reprint, London, 1920), pp. 279–323; David A. McCabe, *The Standard Rate in American Trade Unions* (Baltimore, 1912), pp. 101–111; William H. Buckler, "The Minimum Wage in the Machinists' Union," in Hollander and Barnett, *Studies*, pp. 111–151.

31. Ulman, *National Trade Union*, pp. 483–484.

32. Montgomery, "Workers' Control," p. 496.

33. "Regulation and Restriction of Output," Eleventh Special Report of the U.S. Commissioner of Labor (Washington, D.C., 1904); Slichter, *Union Policies*, pp. 166–167; Montgomery, "Workers' Control," p. 491; G. G. Groat, *An Introduction to the Study of Organized Labor in America* (1916; reprint, New York, 1926), pp. 358–365. Unions also practiced output limitation as a way to stave off unemployment. Smelser, *Unemployment*, pp. 46–50.

34. Ulman, *National Trade Union*, pp. 542–543; Frey and Commons, "Stove Industry," pp. 128, 157; Commons, "Meat Packing," p. 17.

35. Quoted in Bernard L. Elbaum, "Industrial Relations and Uneven Development: Wage Structure and Industrial Organization in the British and U.S. Iron and Steel Industries, 1870–1970" (Ph.D. dissertation, Harvard University, 1982), p. 171.

36. McCallum quoted in Richard Edwards, *Contested Terrain: The Transformation of the Workplace in the Twentieth Century* (New York, 1979), p. 31; Slichter, *Turnover*, p. 387; Keyssar, "Out of Work," p. 153.

37. Montgomery, "Workers' Control," p. 489; Perlman, *History*, pp. 98–99, 116; Brody, *Steelworkers*, pp. 138–139.

38. "Restriction of Output," pp. 22, 29; Montgomery, "Workers' Control," p. 499. Also see Stanley B. Mathewson, *Restriction of Output Among Unorganized Workers* (New York, 1931).

39. Brissenden and Frankel, *Labor Turnover*, pp. 41, 48; Slichter, *Turnover*, pp. 57–69; William B. Wilson, "Labor Program of the Department of Labor," BLS Bulletin No. 247 (1918), p. 166. At a large metalworking plant, the number of quits rose from 581 in 1914, a depressed year, to 3,035 in 1916. The plant's proportion of quits due to "dissatisfaction" rose from 27 percent in 1914 to 34 percent in 1915, the beginning of the recovery; by 1916, these accounted for 64 percent of all quits. Slichter, *Turnover*, p. 180.

40. Stanley Lebergott, *Manpower in Economic Growth: The American Record Since 1800* (New York, 1964), p. 28; Hourwich, *Immigration*, p. 503; Walter Fogel, "Immigrants and the Labor Market: Historical Perspectives and Current Issues," in D. G. Papademetriou and M. J. Miller, eds., *The Unavoidable Issue: U.S. Immigration Policy in the 1980s* (Philadelphia, 1983), p. 73.

41. Ulman, *National Trade Union*, p. 9; Jerome, *Migration*, p. 106; Federated American Engineering Societies, *Waste in Industry* (New York, 1921), p. 300; Brody, *Steelworkers*, pp. 105–106.

42. Yans-McLaughlin, *Italian Immigrants*, pp. 26–30, 49, 78; Brody, *Steelworkers*, pp. 97–98; Stephen Hickey, "The Shaping of the German Labor Movement: Miners in the Ruhr," in Richard J. Evans, ed., *Society and Politics in Wilhelmine Germany* (New York, 1978), pp. 215–240.

43. Herbert Gutman, *Work, Culture and Society in Industrializing America* (New York, 1976), p. 28; Massachusetts Bureau of Statistics of Labor, *Tenth Annual Report* (Boston, 1978), cited in Daniel T. Rodgers, *The Work Ethic in Industrializing America, 1850–1920* (Chicago, 1978), p. 162; Slichter, *Turnover*, p. 184.

44. Gutman, *Work, Culture and Society*, pp. 38–40; H. A. Worman, "How to Secure Factory Workers," in Clarence M. Wooley et al., *Employer and Employee* (New York, 1907), p. 57; A. J. Portenar, "Centralized Labor Responsibility from a Labor Union Standpoint," *The Annals* (May 1917), 71:193.

45. Ulman, *National Trade Union*, pp. 57–59; E. J. Hobsbawm, "The Tramping Artisan," in his *Labouring Men: Studies in the History of Labour* (London, 1964), p. 34; John Davidson, *The Bargain Theory of Wages* (New York, 1898), p. 178; Smelser, *Unemployment*, pp. 75–108.

46. Ware, *Cotton Manufacture*, pp. 224–226; Norman Ware, *The Industrial Worker, 1840–1860* (Boston, 1924), p. 149; Ray Ginger, "Labor in a Massachusetts Cotton Mill: 1853–1860," *Business History Review* (March 1954), 28:84, 87.

47. Thomas R. Navin, *The Whitin Machine Works Since 1831: A Textile Machinery Company in an Industrial Village* (Cambridge, Mass., 1950), pp. 160–161; Howard M. Gitelman, *Workingmen of Waltham: Mobility in American Urban Industrial Development, 1850–1890* (Baltimore, 1974), p. 71.

48. Rodgers, *Work Ethic*, p. 164. In an 1853 case involving a weaver who quit without giving prior notice, a Maine court said that, "The only valuable protection which the manufacturer can provide against such liability to loss and against what are in these days denominated 'strikes,' is to make an agreement with his laborers that if they willfully leave their machines and his employment without notice, all or a certain amount of wages that may be due to them shall be forfeited." *Harmon v. Salmon Falls Mfg. Co.*, 35 Me. 450 (1853).

49. Sanford M. Jacoby, "The Duration of Indefinite Employment Contracts in the United States and England: An Historical Analysis," *Comparative Labor Law* (Winter 1982), 5:85–128; Brody, *Steelworkers*, p. 78.

3

The Invention of Housework

Ruth Schwartz Cowan

During the nineteenth century the United States became an industrialized country—indeed, probably the most industrialized of all countries in the world. The process took a long time and, for the country as a whole, had many facets. For international merchants it meant a shift from

dealing in raw materials to dealing in manufactured goods. For landless laborers it meant a shift from the farm to the factory as the locus for their work. For politicians it meant having to cope with complex questions of finance and corporate structure for which there were few legal precedents. For bankers it meant modifications of routine practices so as to satisfy the needs of capitalists who wished to invest—not in land but in machinery. For poor young men who had big plans for themselves, it meant casting

From Ruth Schwartz Cowan, *More Work for Mother: The Ironies of Household Technology from the Open Hearth to the Microwave.* New York: Basic Books, 1983.

those plans in terms of new businesses, new inventions, and technical training rather than in terms of one of the professions or progressive farming. For local merchants, proprietors of general stores, and rural peddlers, it meant learning to insist on payments in cash rather than in kind. For farmers it also meant learning to deal in cash and to acquire cash, for the new implements that could increase yields and replace farm laborers—the harvesters and combines, the nurserymen's seeds and chemists' fertilizers—could be paid for only in cash. Industrialization brought with it new forms of transport (the canal and the railroad), new forms of communication (the telegraph, the telephone, the typewriter, the daily newspaper), and new kinds of goods that would alter social relations of all kinds: ready-made cloth, which might eliminate home spinning and weaving; ready-made clothing, which might eliminate home sewing or jobs for seamstresses; canned milk to substitute for the fresh and perishable kind; iceboxes, which required the invention of a new social role, the iceman; and so on.

The household was affected by and implicated in this process, just as much as were the law courts, the countinghouses, the workplaces, and the general stores. For it was from the households of the countryside and the cities that young people and adults went out to work in the factories, and it was to those households that their wages were returned, providing the cash that was traded for goods. Furthermore, it was the demand for those goods that continued to fuel the economy being formed by those who were organizing the manufacture of the goods. During the nineteenth century, households ceased to manufacture cloth and began to buy it; they similarly ceased to manufacture candles and, instead, purchased kerosene; they ceased to chop wood and, instead, began to purchase coal; they ceased to butcher their own meat and, instead, began to pur-

chase the products of the meat packers in Chicago. There were a variety of reasons for these changes. Some once-rural, now-urban households found that many of these activities were not possible in an urban setting. Other households ceased carrying them on out of economic considerations, since the wages of the young or of parents were able to buy more goods or a higher standard of goods than any of these individuals could have produced by themselves. Other people were forced to give up these activities, having lost whatever stake they had had in the land and its products upon voyaging from the Old World to the New. For whatever reasons, and there were many more reasons than those I have alluded to, the relationship between the household and the economy in which it was placed was profoundly—and irreversibly—altered by the process of industrialization. Whatever disadvantages some of us may now see in the alteration of this relationship, the fact remains that some of the people who made decisions about the conduct of life in their own households in the nineteenth century wanted those changes to occur and acted on that impulse: buying manufactured goods, willingly selling their labor in return for cash, bringing up their children so as to be socialized appropriately for the role of employee rather than of owner, or, alternatively, by bringing up their children to expect the perquisites of being owners. Some people were dragged unwillingly into the industrialized world; but others, for their own good reasons, greeted it with open arms. The latter group appear to have been in the majority or, at the very least, in the places of power.

It has proved difficult, however, to assess the relationship between the work that women did in their homes—"housework," as it came to be called in this century—and the process of industrialization. Many historians have concluded that the substitution of manufactured goods for homemade goods eased the burden of women's work: for example, it is surely easier to buy kerosene than to make candles; to purchase cotton cloth than to comb, card, spin, and weave it; to buy milk from a vendor than to tend to the milking and management of a cow. Furthermore, since the process of industrialization involved a growth in the size both of the urban population and of the middle classes, it is easy to argue, on structural grounds alone, that in the nineteenth century fewer women had to work their fingers to the bone in order to maintain the health and security of their families than in any previous century. Surely it must be easier to do housework under urban conditions and with the assistance of servants (the possession of which was, in that century, virtually the only sure way of defining who was a member of the middle classes). This argument becomes even more persuasive when we remember that it was during the nineteenth century that, by whatever mechanism, white American families succeeded in limiting their fertility; the total fertility rate (the average number of children borne by a woman) fell from 7.04 in 1800 to 3.56 in 1900; fewer children, almost by necessity, must have meant fewer women with broken health (and broken backs!). It seems easy to conclude that, during the nineteenth century, the many facets of industrialization conspired together to make life easier for the average American woman.[1]

Unfortunately contemporary documents tell a different tale: from the beginning of the century until its end, from one coast to the other, American women seem to have been exhausted a lot of the time. "A woman's work is never done, and happy she whose strength holds out to the end of the [sun's] rays," wrote Martha Moore Ballard in her diary in 1795, after she had spent a full day preparing wool for spinning.[2] Her sentiments were echoed almost a century later in a letter written by Mary Hallock Foote: "I am

daily dropped in little pieces and passed around and devoured and expected to be whole again next day and all days and I am never *alone* for a single minute."[3] Famous women, even when they had several servants, were not immune to pressure either. "The arranging of the whole house . . . the cleaning . . . the children's clothes and the baby have seemed to press on my mind all at once. Sometimes it seems as if anxious thought has become a disease with me from which I could not be free," wrote Harriet Beecher Stowe to her husband, Calvin, in 1844.[4] Observers of the American scene frequently commented on the ill health of American married women. In 1832, Frances Trollope attributed their waxen complexions, stooped shoulders, and careworn faces to the burdens of their domestic work.[5] Twenty years later Gro Svendsen, a young Norwegian immigrant, made a similar observation in a letter to her parents:

> We are told that the women of America have much leisure time but I haven't yet met any woman who thought so! Here the mistress of the house must do all the work that the cook, the maid and the housekeeper would do in an upper class family at home. Moreover she must do her work as well as these three together do it in Norway.[6]

Catherine Beecher, an early disciple of what later came to be called "home economics," waged many a long campaign against what she regarded as the widespread ill health of American married women, and also laid a good part of the blame on the nature of the work that they did:

> There is nothing which so demands system and regularity as the affairs of a housekeeper . . . and yet the perpetually fluctuating state of society seems forever to bar any such system and regularity. The anxieties, vexations, perplexities

and even hard labor that come upon American women . . . are endless; and many a woman has, in consequence, been disheartened, discouraged and ruined in health.[7]

Census statistics, articles in women's magazines, economic histories, genre paintings, patent records, and the extant artifacts themselves all converge to tell us that hundreds of household conveniences were invented and diffused during the nineteenth century. There were hand-driven washing machines and taps for indoor cisterns, eggbeaters and pulley-driven butter churns, tinned milk and store-bought flour, porcelainized cookware, air-tight heating stoves, and a multitude of additional small gadgets and large utilities, from apple parers to piped coal gas, that were intended to make housework easier.[8] Yet, when discussed by the people who actually did housework, or by the people who watched the people who were actually doing it, it seems not to have become one whit more convenient—or less tiring—during the whole of the century. What a strange paradox that in the face of so many labor-saving devices, little labor appears to have been saved!

One is tempted to resolve the paradox by assuming that the commentators were, in some ways, biased: that, as housewives, Mary Hallock Foote and Harriet Beecher Stowe were either a bit paranoid, or a bit spoiled, or particularly poor organizers, or perhaps that they were trying, as some housewives always have, to "do too much." Similarly, we might want to argue that, as observers, Frances Trollope, Gro Svendsen, and Catherine Beecher were either misguided, or observing the wrong housewives, or grinding some other, unstated, historical axe. The paradox can be resolved, however, without impugning either the reputations or the motives of these, and many other, participants in and observers of the patterns of daily life in nineteenth-century America. Labor-saving devices were invented and diffused throughout the country during those hundred years that witnessed the first stages of industrialization, but they reorganized the work processes of housework in ways that did not save the labor of the average housewife.

This point can best be dramatized if we analyze the work processes and the technological systems involved in preparing a beef stew in 1850. Meat was still a dominant constituent of the average American diet, and stewing was still (as it is today) a standard form of preparation. Let us imagine what it might have been like . . . to be preparing [this] dish . . . some place in Connecticut, perhaps in a farm town in the Connecticut River valley which was just beginning to feel the impact of industrialization.

The stew would require, then as it does now, roughly the same ingredients: meat, vegetables, salt and other spices, water to do the stewing, fuel to heat the water, and grain to thicken the resultant liquid so that it could be served effectively as sauce. In a farm household in rural Connecticut in 1850, these ingredients would have been obtained in much the same fashion as was common one hundred years earlier—with one exception. The meat would have come from an animal that was owned by the family and butchered at home, and the vegetables from a garden that was likely to have been tended by the wife; the fuel to have been cut by the husband and his assistant on their own woodlot; the salt and some of the spices obtained by trade (either in cash or in kind); and the water carried, by hand, from their own well or from a nearby spring. The single exception would have been the grain—the thickening agent for the stewing juices; and thereby hangs a significant point about the ways in which household labor changed in the early years of industrialization. . . .

More Chores for Women, Fewer for Men

If we imagine our Connecticut family making the transition, over several generations, from a wood-burning fireplace (with fuel supplied by the husband from his own woodlot) to a wood-burning stove (with some of the wood purchased in any given year) to a coal-burning stove (when local supplies of wood had given out, and the railroad had made it possible to bring in coal), we can understand precisely why men were more likely to enter the labor force than were women, and why, eventually, these rural Connecticut families became dependent upon the cash that wage labor supplied. The stove reduced the amount of labor that a man had to do in order to maintain the standard of comfort to which his family was accustomed; with his time thus freed, he could look for seasonal or part-time work that might bring in cash with which to purchase luxuries or necessities. When coal was substituted for wood, cash became itself such a necessity; coal could rarely be obtained by barter or by trade in kind, since the people who sold coal had to purchase it from the people who had transported it (as well as from other "middle" men); and this series of transactions required cash. As each generation of fathers ceased to cut, haul, and split wood, each generation of sons knew less and less about how it should be done—and more and more about how to find and to keep a job that paid wages. Each generation of mothers, on the other hand, would have found the burden of their domestic chores more or less the same—perhaps even heavier—and thus would have been less likely to look outside their homes for employment, unless dire necessity intervened. Each generation of young girls, consequently, continued to be trained in the pursuits of domesticity—despite the fact that their brothers had gone on to other sorts of enterprise.

And what was true of cooking was true of other household chores as well. As the nineteenth century wore on, in almost every aspect of household work, industrialization served to eliminate the work that men (and children) had once been assigned to do, while at the same time leaving the work of women either untouched or even augmented. Factories made boots and shoes (this was one of the ten leading industries in the United States in 1860), so men no longer had to work in leather at home. Factories also made pottery and tin ware, so men no longer had to whittle. Piped household water (which was introduced in several eastern cities even before the Civil War and was fairly common in middle-class homes throughout the country by the end of the century) meant that children no longer had to be burdened with perpetual bucket carrying. The growth of the meat-packing industry, coupled with the introduction of refrigerated transport in the 1870s and 1880s, meant that men no longer spent much time in butchering. Virtually all of the stereotypically male household occupations were eliminated by technological and economic innovations during the nineteenth century, and many of those that had previously been allotted to children were gone as well.

But not so with the occupations of women. If the advent of manufactured cloth eliminated the need for women to spin (as well as for men to weave and children to card), it did not in the least affect the need for them to sew—and sewing was the part of clothing preparation which had always been exclusively female. Indeed, the advent of manufactured cloth seems to have been accompanied by an increase in the amount of clothing that people expected to own—and since ready-made clothing had not yet appeared on the scene, there was a radical increase in the amount of sewing that had to be done. The diaries and letters of women who lived during the middle decades of the nineteenth century are filled with comments about the pervasiveness and tediousness of sewing. Here is a representative sample, from a letter written by Ellen Birdseye Wheaton, a middle-class housewife living in Syracuse, New York, in April of 1850:

> Since the second week, in March, I have been preparing garments, for children's summer wear, having shirts altered and made, for Charles [her husband], and having dresses made, and fixed till I am at times, almost bewildered. I began this work earlier than usual, this season, hoping much to get the main part of my sewing done, before the extreme heat of summer, but oh! it seems at times as tho' it could never be done.[9]

Like many of her contemporaries, Mrs. Wheaton hired seamstresses to come into her home to help during these sewing seasons (another occurred during the early fall, when cold-weather clothing was prepared), but the seamstresses assisted and did not replace her labor: they might work on the girls' dresses, while she worked on the boys' pants; or she might cut out fabrics, while they did the plain stitching. According to letters and diaries of women living later in the century, the advent of the sewing machine eliminated the need to hire seamstresses but not the hours spent by the housewife herself.

Manufactured cloth also served to augment women's work by increasing the amount of household laundry that had to be done, laundry—like sewing—having been one of those tasks that had long been exclusively female. Prior to industrialization, much of the clothing that people wore was virtually unwashable: the woven woolen goods, the alpacas and felts and leathers of which outer clothing was made, were cleaned by brushing; and the linen or knitted wools of which underclothing was composed, although potentially washable, were in fact rarely laundered. When cotton replaced linen and wool as the most frequently utilized fabric, laundering increased; indeed, one of cotton's attractions as a fabric was that it could be washed fairly easily. This development was no doubt viewed as an improvement by many people, but there is no question that it altered the pattern of women's household labor for the worse. In the diaries and letters of nineteenth-century women, laundering appears, for the first time, as a weekly—and a dreaded—chore. Since it was exceedingly hard work (what with the rubbing, wringing, toting, and ironing), children rarely became involved in it. Whether done by a female servant or by the housewife herself, laundry was a major component of women's work in the nineteenth century—and arduous work at that.

Like clothmaking, some female chores disappeared during the century, but almost every one was replaced by other chores, equally time and energy consuming. Candlemaking became a lost art. In its place there were the glass globes of oil and the gas lamps from which soot had to be removed almost every day—a chore that housewives were advised not to assign either to children or to servants, since the globes could not survive rough handling. Waste-water systems (commonly known as "water closets") eliminated the chore of collecting "slops" but added the chore of cleaning toilets. Furthermore, in those cities in which the cleaning of outhouses and cesspools had been a commercial enterprise undertaken by men, the water closet privatized this work—and shifted it to women. Home canning equipment made it possible to preserve more fruits and vegetables for consumption during the winter but vastly increased the amount of work that women were expected to do when the season was "on."

Small wonder, then, that so many people commented on the exhaustion and ill health of American women during the nineteenth century. Industrialization had introduced many novelties to their homes and probably had, overall, improved their standard of living—but they still had a great deal of hard work to do. With the exception of the very poorest women, or those who were dwelling on the most primitive frontiers, American women living toward the end of the century probably ate a more varied diet, suffered less from the cold, enjoyed more space and more luxuries in their homes, and kept their bodies and their clothes cleaner than their mothers and grandmothers who had lived earlier. These improvements had not, however, lifted the burden of women's domestic cares, in spite of radical changes in the patterns of daily work at home. The processes of housework had changed in such a way that adult males and small children of both sexes were no longer needed to do domestic labor: wood did not have to be chopped, nor water carried, nor grain hauled to the mill. Men and children could be spared, to the schools, to the factories, to the offices of the burgeoning industrial economy. Adult women and their grown daughters, on the other hand, could not be spared: meals still had to be cooked; sick children had to be tended; infants to be nursed; clothes to be made, mended, and laundered—and industrialization had done nothing at all to ease the burden of those particular chores.

Industrialization, at least in these its earliest phases, had in fact created the material conditions under which the doctrine of separate spheres could take root and flourish. Merchant flour, cast-iron stoves, municipal water, and manufactured boots had made it possible for men to work at wage labor without endangering (indeed, with some chance of improving) the standard of living of their families. As time wore on, the need to pay cash for flour, or for coal, or for any of the other commodities that were so swiftly appearing on the market, ensured that, once having entered

the market for wage labor, men would stay there. Once that had happened, they ceased to train their sons in the multitudinous crafts that had been the heritage of men's work at home—preparing fuel, mending ironware, working in leather, building fireplaces, making cider, butchering pigs—and then the process was complete. A new generation of men came into adulthood having learned the skills needed to work for wages, not the skills needed to work at home. For these men the doctrine of separate spheres served to make sense of the new patterns by which they were living, and it was this new pattern of living and thinking that they taught to their sons.

For women the transition to the industrial order was different. Merchant flour, cast-iron stoves, municipal water, and manufactured boots did not free them from their labors. Insofar as these commodities allowed men and boys to leave their homes, and insofar as these commodities also created new jobs that only women could perform, women were tied even more strongly than they had been before to their cast-iron hearths. Angel food cakes, strawberry preserves, clean clothes, ironed ruffles, and leavened bread may have made life easier and pleasanter for their families, but they also kept women working at home. The factories and the schoolrooms may have sung a siren call to some women, but most of these were either unmarried or in dire distress. For the rest, the material conditions of domestic life during the first phases of industrialization required women to stay at home so as to protect (and even to enhance) the standard of living of their families: when women were absent, meals were irregular, infant mortality was higher, clothes were dirtier, and houses poorly maintained. Grown daughters were needed at home as well (at least until they married) because, in the absence of servants, who was left to help? Girls learned the crafts that their mothers practiced; boys did not. In this way the obverse side of the doctrine of separate spheres, the side that identified women with home and with homely virtues, was sealed in the best social cement of all: the patterns of daily life and the relations between parents and children.

NOTES

1. The assumption that housework became easier in the nineteenth century is implicit, for example, in Carl Degler, *At Odds: Women and the Family in America from the Revolution to the Present* (New York, 1980), especially chaps. 2 and 8; and explicit in Alice Kessler-Harris, *Out to Work: A History of Wage Earning Women in the United States* (New York, 1982), pp. 110–12. It also underlies many older and more specialized treatments, such as Elizabeth Mickle Bacon, "The Growth of Household Conveniences in the United States from 1865 to 1900" (Ph.D. dissertation, Radcliffe College, 1942). The demographic data comes from Ansley J. Coale and Melvin Zelnick, *New Estimates of Fertility and Population in the United States* (Princeton, 1963), pp. 34–36.

2. Entry for 26 November 1795 in the diary of Martha Moore Ballard, 1785–1812, in Charles Elventon Nash, ed., *The History of Augusta* (Augusta, Me., 1904), p. 348, as quoted in Nancy Cott, *Bonds of Womanhood* (New Haven, 1977), p. 19.

3. Letter, 6 February 1888, from Mary Hallock Foote to Helena Gilder, Mary Hallock Foote Papers, Stanford University Library, as quoted in Degler, *At Odds* [1], p. 54.

4. Harriet Beecher Stowe to Calvin Stowe, 23 May 1844, in Stowe Papers, Schlesinger Library, Radcliffe College.

5. Frances Trollope, *Domestic Manners of the Americans* [1832] edited by Donald Smalley (New York, 1949), pp. 117–18.

6. Gro Svendsen to her parents, 20 November 1862, in *Frontier Mother: The Letters of Gro Svendsen* (Northfield, Minn., 1950), p. 28.

7. Catherine Beecher, *A Treatise on Domestic Economy* (Boston, 1841), p. 18.

8. The best sources for information on the changing technologies of housework in the nineteenth century are Bacon, "Growth of Household Conveniences" [1]; Walter Buehr, *Home, Sweet Home, in the Nineteenth Century* (New York, 1965); Siegfried Giedion, *Mechanization Takes Command* (New York, 1948), parts VI and VII; and Susan Strasser, *Never Done: A History of American Housework* (New York, 1982).

9. Letter from Ellen Birdseye Wheaton to Charlotte Amelia Birdseye, 21 April 1850, in Donald Gordon, ed., *The Diary of Ellen Birdseye Wheaton* (Boston, 1923), p. 14.

The Social Organization of Work

What factors shape the organization of work? Does work organization reflect managerial interests in control? The outcome of struggles between conflicting interests? The dictates of technology? What does it mean to live in a global economy? Part II addresses these issues. In the course of exploring different perspectives on the organization of work, the readings introduce several key concepts that have played a role in understanding work over the past century.

Classical Sociology and the Organization of Work

Sociology in the West is a product of the industrial revolution and the rise of capitalism; thus, the history of sociology and the history of the sociology of work are closely intertwined. This makes readings by Karl Marx and Max Weber an appropriate starting point for a historical survey of work organization. The selections by these sociological theorists have more than just historical value, however. As classics, they have a "privileged status" in the discipline, meaning that "contemporary [sociologists] . . . believe they can learn as much about their field through understanding this earlier work as they can from the work of their own contemporaries" (Alexander 1987). Although their views diverge in important respects, Marx and Weber each were highly critical of the industrial, capitalist society that was emerging during their lifetimes. As Watson (1987, p. 3) explains: "The founding fathers of sociology can be seen as striving to make sense of the dislocations of their age. Their attempts to make sense of their situation are invaluable

to us because these men, in an historical location more marginal than our own, were better able to look at the industrial capitalist world in light of conceptions of alternatives. This is their humanistic significance."

Marx's theory of capitalism has shaped sociologists' views of work for more than a century. Adherents and critics alike continue to discuss and debate Marx's ideas about private property, social class, and capitalist society. The selection titled "Alienated Labour" that leads off this section may be one of Marx's most well-known writings, especially among sociologists of work. Marx's analysis of alienation is important for two primary reasons. First, the concept of alienation is important in its own right as an expression of Marx's critique of capitalist society. No other concept in sociology conveys as well the dehumanizing potential of industrial work. However, in addition to developing this concept, Marx demonstrates the connections between the experience of work and the conditions under which it is performed. Although contemporary sociologists sometimes portray alienation as a purely subjective state, Marx viewed alienation as a product of the social organization of work.

Like Marx, Weber was also concerned with the transition to an industrial, capitalist economy and sought to develop a narrative that would capture the totality of this change. Thus emerged the concept of "rationalization," an orientation and a process that Weber saw as the dominant feature of the modern capitalist world. In his view, a rationalized society is dominated by concerns for efficiency, productivity, and the ability to subject life to rational calculation.

For Weber, bureaucracy represented the epitome of rational organization. His discussion of this concept in Reading 5 has served as the foundation for all subsequent sociological analyses of bureaucracy.

The remaining two readings in this section move us from the classical sociologists of Europe to the work of social scientists in the United States. Frederick Winslow Taylor (1856–1915) is best known as the "Father of Scientific Management" (Merkle 1980, p. 10), and in Reading 6 he outlines the "fundamentals" of his system. As Taylor's discussion reveals, scientific management (or "Taylorism," as it is sometimes called) was much more than a set of techniques for improving workplace efficiency. Taylor combined technical, organizational, and ideological elements into an integrated system that he offered as a solution to the problems of modern industrial society. The legacy of scientific management thus derives from its vision of work organization. As later readings reveal, this legacy has continued to shape the organization of work.

Taylor's belief that scientific methods could be used to understand workers' behavior was shared by others during the first half of the twentieth century. Studies by Elton Mayo and his colleagues conducted during the 1930s and 1940s at the Western Electric factory in Chicago represent the most well known example of such research. In his detailed description of the famous "Hawthorne experiment," Mayo lays the foundation for what would become another influential view of work organization: the human relations movement. In contrast to Taylor's conception of workers as machines or "beasts of burden," Mayo and his colleagues argued that workers were social beings and that the workplace thus must be understood as a social system. These studies and those following in the human relations tradition were scathingly labeled "cow soci-

ology" by critics, who viewed sociological interest in workers' morale as merely attempts to help managers achieve control and higher productivity (Whyte 1987). Nevertheless, studies by Mayo and his colleagues also inspired an ongoing tradition of sociological research on occupational cultures, groups, and the social relations of work (Whyte 1987; Simpson 1989).

Conceptualizing Work

In the 1960s and 1970s the sociology of work took an economic turn. Rising levels of industrial conflict, as well as social movements outside the workplace, provided a context for the emergence of more critical conceptions of work organization. The next two readings are examples of these views. Harry Braverman's 1974 study, *Labor and Monopoly Capitalism*, is among the most influential books on the workplace in the twentieth century. Paying particular attention to the relations between the division of labor, skills, and technology, Braverman echoed Marx's critique of work in a capitalist society. Braverman described the degradation, deskilling, and managerial control that he viewed as inevitable consequences of work organization under capitalism. Although later sociologists have faulted Braverman for his lack of attention to workers and their resistance to management initiatives, Braverman inspired numerous followers. Studies exploring the "labor process" and the effects of technological change on skill levels are just two examples of his legacy.

While Braverman focused on the forces that were "homogenizing" workers, sociologists of work in the late 1970s and 1980s began to examine the ways that the organization of work divided (or "segmented") groups of workers from one another. This research produced concepts such as "dual economy," "dual labor market," and "labor market segmentation." For Richard Edwards and others, these divisions derived from differences between industries, between firms, and between jobs within firms. Edwards suggests that three "labor market segments," each with a different type of control system, emerged in the latter half of the twentieth century. The jobs of Maureen, Fred, and Stanley described in the first part of Reading 9 are examples of these three forms of control.

The growth of the service economy has fueled sociological interest in jobs that require interaction with customers or clients. These "interactive service jobs" are the focus of Arlie Russell Hochschild's classic book, *The Managed Heart,* a portion of which is excerpted in Reading 10. Hochschild argues that many service jobs require "emotional labor," which she defines as "the management of feeling to create a publicly observable facial and bodily display" (p. 7). Unlike industrial jobs where workers' labor is primarily physical or professional jobs that involve mental labor, service jobs require workers to manage their emotions as part of performing work tasks. In Hochschild's view, performance of emotional labor may have negative consequences for workers. Just as Marx warned of the dangers of alienation in an industrial society, Hochschild cautions that there may be psychological and social costs associated with emotional labor as well.

The final selection critiques several earlier ways of thinking about work and workers, and it offers a new approach. Randy Hodson advocates treating workers as "active subjects"—that is, as participants involved in shaping work processes and relations—not simply as passive objects of structural forces. Hodson explores the implications of this new approach and shows how it can help us understand many types of workplace issues.

Technology, Flexibility, and the Transformation of Work

Change is an inevitable and ongoing feature of work. The occupations employing the most workers at the beginning of the twentieth century are much different from those most prominent at the century's end. Some occupations, like stenography, have virtually disappeared, while others, such as systems analyst, emerged only recently. In addition, other changes have transformed the conditions under which many occupations are performed. Some jobs have been so altered by technological change that only their name remains the same. Technology is not the only force transforming the occupational landscape, however. Corporate restructuring, aimed at creating a more flexible workplace, is also reshaping the conditions under which work is performed. The readings in this section examine these forces that are transforming the occupational world.

Reading 12, drawn from Shoshana Zuboff's 1988 book, *In the Age of the Smart Machine,* describes the experiences of pulp and paper mill workers as their jobs undergo computerization. Zuboff is particularly interested in the potential impact of computerization on workers' skills. Rather than focus simply on the gain or loss of skill, Zuboff suggests that computerization potentially alters the *types* of skills required by pulp and paper mill workers. Whether this potential is deployed to expand workers' control and responsibilities, or to restrict them, depends upon how the technology is introduced and used. Zuboff shows that computers can have powerful effects on how workers conceive and perform their jobs, but these effects depend on organizational and social factors as much as on the technological possibilities of the machines.

The next reading offers a more macro-historical view of workplace technologies. In

"Labor and Management in Uncertain Times," Ruth Milkman examines the auto industry, where technological change has coincided with increased international competition. Milkman reveals the challenges both factors pose for organized labor, and she examines how labor and management have coped with a rapidly changing auto industry. She illustrates how technological change has the potential not only to alter jobs, but also to transform relations between workers and between workers and management. Moreover, Milkman shows how technological change in the auto industry is linked to other factors, such as international competition, that are transforming the American auto industry.

Technology and industrial transformation in manufacturing are also the subjects of Reading 14 by Steven Vallas and John Beck. These authors engage the debate surrounding "post-Fordist" forms of work organization. On one side of this debate are those claiming that traditional bureaucratic forms of work organization are ill-suited to current technological and economic conditions (Piore and Sabel 1984). According to this post-Fordist view, the postindustrial workplace should exhibit much more flexibility and less hierarchy than in the past. Alternatively, others suggest that the post-Fordist view is overstated. These researchers expect much more continuity between the mechanized, mass production era of Fordism and postindustrial forms of work organization.

Vallas and Beck find only weak evidence supporting the post-Fordist position. Although the pulp and paper mills they studied were seemingly well positioned to adopt post-Fordist work practices, Vallas and Beck identified several obstacles to greater flexibility. Hence, they conclude that American manufacturing remains in the grip of what they call a "technological iron cage" (p. 34).

A somewhat different view of current changes is provided by Vicki Smith in her case study of white-collar service workers. Smith suggests that the move toward flexible, more decentralized work may have some positive consequences for lower-level workers. Involvement in employee participation programs can empower workers by teaching the types of interpersonal skills valued in higher level jobs. Smith reminds us that change produces intended and *unintended* consequences. Sociologists of work thus should not assume that conceptual frameworks and assumptions drawn from the past will be useful for understanding the workplaces of the present and future.

The Global Economy

What does it mean to say that we live in a global economy? How has this economy changed the meaning and experience of work? What are the larger social, political, and cultural implications of a global workplace? The three readings in this section attempt to answer some of these questions.

Far-reaching changes in communications and information technology have helped fuel the creation of a global economy. We begin by focusing on a group of workers at the center of these developments. Ó Riain's study of Irish software developers is an ethnographic account of one "global informational workplace." He explores the shifting meanings of space and time in the work lives of his informants and suggests that globalization has intensified, rather than diminished, the salience of time and space. Globalization, for Ó Riain, is "a contested terrain," whose social, cultural, and political consequences have barely begun to be understood.

Robert Perrucci and Earl Wysong provide a different kind of take on the global economy by examining its implications for U.S. workers. These authors argue that globalization has benefited the "privileged classes," while workers have become more divided.

The final reading in this section looks at one of the most successful, U.S.-based global corporations: McDonald's. Through a case study of McDonald's in Beijing—the largest McDonald's in the world—Yunxiang Yan identifies some of the factors that have enabled this company to market its products worldwide. Offering customers a Chinese version of American culture, McDonald's has managed to "localize" its appeal, while at the same time presenting itself as a symbol of a modern, transnational world.

REFERENCES

Alexander, Jeffrey C. 1987. "The Centrality of the Classics." Pp. 11–57 in *Social Theory Today*, edited by Anthony Giddens and Jonathon H. Turner. Stanford, CA: Stanford University Press.

Braverman, Harry. 1974. *Labor and Monopoly Capitalism.* New York: Monthly Review Press.

Edwards, Richard. 1978. *Contested Terrain: The Transformation of the Workplace in the Twentieth Century.* New York: Basic Books.

Giddens, Anthony. 1972. *Emile Durkheim: Selected Writings.* Cambridge: Cambridge University Press.

Hochschild, Arlie Russell. 1977. *The Managed Heart: The Commercialization of Human Feeling.* Berkeley: University of California Press.

Mayo, Elton. 1933. *The Human Problems of an Industrial Civilization.* New York: The Macmillan Company.

Merkle, Judith A. 1980. *Management and Ideology: The Legacy of the International Scientific Management Movement.* Berkeley: University of California Press.

Piore, Michael and Charles F. Sabel. 1984. *The Second Industrial Divide: Possibilities for Prosperity.* New York: Basic Books.

Simpson, Ida Harper. 1989. "The Sociology of Work: Where Have the Workers Gone?" *Social Forces* 67: 563–581.

Thompson, Paul. 1989. *The Nature of Work.* London: Macmillan.

Vallas, Steven P. and John P. Beck. 1996. "The Transformation of Work Revisited: The Limits of Flexibility in American Manufacturing." *Social Problems* 43:339–361.

Watson, Tony J. 1987. *Sociology, Work, and Industry.* London: Routledge and Kegan Paul.

Whyte, William Foote. 1987. "From Human Relations to Organizational Behavior: Reflections on the Changing Scene." *Industrial and Labor Relations Review* 40:487–490.

Zuboff, Shoshana. 1988. *In the Age of the Smart Machine.* New York: Basic Books.

4

Alienated Labour

Karl Marx

We started from the presuppositions of political economy. We accepted its vocabulary and its laws. We presupposed private property, the separation of labour, capital, and land, and likewise of wages, profit, and ground rent; also division of labour; competition; the concept of exchange value, etc. Using the very words of political economy we have demonstrated that the worker is degraded to the most miserable sort of commodity; that the misery of the worker is in inverse proportion to the power and size of his production; that the necessary result of competition is the accumulation of capital in a few hands, and thus a more terrible restoration of monopoly; and that finally the distinction between capitalist and landlord, and that between peasant and industrial worker disappears and the whole of society must fall apart into the two classes of the property owners and the propertyless workers.

Political economy starts with the fact of private property, it does not explain it to us. It conceives of the material process that private property goes through in reality in general abstract formulas which then have for it a value of laws. It does not understand these laws, i.e. it does not demonstrate how they arise from the nature of private property. Po-

litical economy does not afford us any explanation of the reason for the separation of labour and capital, of capital and land. When, for example, political economy defines the relationship of wages to profit from capital, the interest of the capitalist is the ultimate court of appeal, that is, it presupposes what should be its result. In the same way competition enters the argument everywhere. It is explained by exterior circumstances. But political economy tells us nothing about how far these exterior, apparently fortuitous circumstances are merely the expression of a necessary development. We have seen how it regards exchange itself as something fortuitous. The only wheels that political economy sets in motion are greed and war among the greedy, competition.

It is just because political economy has not grasped the connections in the movement that new contradictions have arisen in its doctrines, for example, between that of monopoly and that of competition, freedom of craft and corporations, division of landed property and large estates. For competition, free trade, and the division of landed property were only seen as fortuitous circumstances created by will and force, not developed and comprehended as necessary, inevitable, and natural results of monopoly, corporations, and feudal property.

So what we have to understand now is the essential connection of private property, selfishness, the separation of labour, capital, and landed property, of exchange and competition, of the value and degradation of man, of monopoly and competition, etc.— the connection of all this alienation with the money system.

Let us not be like the political economist who, when he wishes to explain something, puts himself in an imaginary original state of affairs. Such an original state of affairs explains nothing. He simply pushes the question back into a grey and nebulous distance. He presupposes as a fact and an event what he ought to be deducing, namely the necessary connection between the two things, for example, between the division of labour and exchange. Similarly, the theologian explains the origin of evil through the fall, i.e. he presupposes as an historical fact what he should be explaining.

We start with a contemporary fact of political economy:

The worker becomes poorer the richer is his production, the more it increases in power and scope. The worker becomes a commodity that is all the cheaper the more commodities he creates. The depreciation of the human world progresses in direct proportion to the increase in value of the world of things. Labour does not only produce commodities; it produces itself and the labourer as a commodity and that to the extent to which it produces commodities in general.

What this fact expresses is merely this: the object that labour produces, its product, confronts it as an alien being, as a power independent of the producer. The product of labour is labour that has solidified itself into an object, made itself into a thing, the objectification of labour. The realization of labour is its objectification. In political economy this realization of labour appears as a loss of reality for the worker, objectification as a loss of the object of slavery to it, and appropriation as alienation, as externalization.

The realization of labour appears as a loss of reality to an extent that the worker loses his reality by dying of starvation. Objectification appears as a loss of the object to such an extent that the worker is robbed not only of the objects necessary for his life but also of the objects of his work. Indeed, labour itself becomes an object he can only have in his power with the greatest of efforts and at irregular intervals. The appropriation of the object appears as alienation to such an extent that the more objects the worker produces, the less he can possess and the more he falls under the domination of his product, capital.

All these consequences follow from the fact that the worker relates to the product of his labour as to an alien object. For it is evident from this presupposition that the more the worker externalizes himself in his work, the more powerful becomes the alien, objective world that he creates opposite himself, the poorer he becomes himself in his inner life and the less he can call his own. It is just the same in religion. The more man puts into God, the less he retains in himself. The worker puts his life into the object and this means that it no longer belongs to him but to the object. So the greater this activity, the more the worker is without an object. What the product of his labour is, that he is not. So the greater this product the less he is himself. The externalization of the worker in his product implies not only that his labour becomes an object, an exterior existence but also that it exists outside him, independent and alien, and becomes a self-sufficient power opposite him, that the life that he has lent to the object affronts him, hostile and alien.

Let us now deal in more detail with objectification, the production of the worker, and the alienation, the loss of the object, his product, which is involved in it.

The worker can create nothing without nature, the sensuous exterior world. It is the matter in which his labour realizes itself, in which it is active, out of which and through which it produces.

But as nature affords the means of life for labour in the sense that labour cannot live without objects on which it exercises itself, so it affords a means of life in the narrower sense, namely the means for the physical subsistence of the worker himself.

Thus the more the worker appropriates the exterior world of sensuous nature by his labour, the more he doubly deprives himself of the means of subsistence, firstly since the exterior sensuous world increasingly ceases to be an object belonging to his work, a means of subsistence for his labour; secondly, since it increasingly ceases to be a means of subsistence in the direct sense, a means for the physical subsistence of the worker.

Thus in these two ways the worker becomes a slave to his object: firstly he receives an object of labour, that is he receives labour, and secondly, he receives the means of subsistence. Thus it is his object that permits him to exist first as a worker and secondly as a physical subject. The climax of this slavery is that only as a worker can he maintain himself as a physical subject and it is only as a physical subject that he is a worker.

(According to the laws of political economy the alienation of the worker in his object is expressed as follows: the more the worker produces the less he has to consume, the more values he creates the more valueless and worthless he becomes, the more formed the product the more deformed the worker, the more civilized the product, the more barbaric the worker, the more powerful the work the more powerless becomes the worker, the more cultured the work the more philistine the worker becomes and more of a slave to nature.)

Political economy hides the alienation in the essence of labour by not considering the immediate relationship between the worker (labour) and production. Labour produces works of wonder for the rich, but nakedness for the worker. It produces palaces, but only hovels for the worker; it produces beauty, but cripples the worker; it replaces labour by machines but throws a part of the workers back to a barbaric labour and turns the other part into machines. It produces culture, but also imbecility and cretinism for the worker.

The immediate relationship of labour to its products is the relationship of the worker to the objects of his production. The relationship of the man of means to the objects of production and to production itself is only a consequence of this first relationship. And it confirms it. We shall examine this other aspect later.

So when we ask the question: what relationship is essential to labour, we are asking about the relationship of the worker to production.

Up to now we have considered only one aspect of the alienation or externalization of the worker, his relationship to the products of his labour. But alienation shows itself not only in the result, but also in the act of production, inside productive activity itself. How would the worker be able to affront the product of his work as an alien being if he did not alienate himself in the act of production itself? For the product is merely the summary of the activity of production. So if the product of labour is externalization, production itself must be active externalization, the externalization of activity, the activity of externalization. The alienation of the object of labour is only the résumé of the alienation, the externalization in the activity of labour itself.

What does the externalization of labour consist of then?

Firstly, that labour is exterior to the worker, that is, it does not belong to his essence. Therefore he does not confirm himself in his work, he denies himself, feels miserable instead of happy, deploys no free physical and intellectual energy, but mortifies his body and ruins his mind. Thus the worker only feels a stranger. He is at home when he is not working and when he works he is not at home. His labour is therefore not voluntary but compulsory, forced labour. It is therefore not the satisfaction of a need but only a means to satisfy needs outside itself. How alien it really is is very evident from the fact that when there is no physical or other compulsion, labour is avoided like the plague. External labour, labour in which man externalizes himself, is a labour of self-sacrifice and mortification. Finally, the external character of labour for the worker shows itself in the fact that it is not his own but someone else's, that it does not belong to him, that he does not belong to himself in his labour but to someone else. As in religion the human imagination's own activity, the activity of man's head and his heart, reacts independently on the individual as an alien activity of gods or devils, so the activity of the worker is not his own spontaneous activity. It belongs to another and it is the loss of himself.

The result we arrive at then is that man (the worker) only feels himself freely active in his animal functions of eating, drinking, and procreating, at most also in his dwelling and dress, and feels himself an animal in his human functions.

Eating, drinking, procreating, etc. are indeed truly human functions. But in the abstraction that separates them from the other round of human activity and makes them into final and exclusive ends they become animal.

We have treated the act of alienation of practical human activity, labour, from two aspects. (1) The relationship of the worker to the product of his labour as an alien object that has power over him. This relationship is at the same time the relationship to the sensuous exterior world and to natural objects as to an alien and hostile world opposed to him. (2) The relationship of labour to the act of production inside labour. This relationship is the relationship of the worker to his own activity as something that is alien and does not belong to him; it is activity that is

passivity, power that is weakness, procreation that is castration, the worker's own physical and intellectual energy, his personal life (for what is life except activity?) as an activity directed against himself, independent of him and not belonging to him. It is self-alienation, as above it was the alienation of the object.

We now have to draw a third characteristic of alienated labour from the two previous ones.

Man is a species-being not only in that practically and theoretically he makes both his own and other species into his objects, but also, and this is only another way of putting the same thing, he relates to himself as to the present, living species, in that he relates to himself as to a universal and therefore free being.

Both with man and with animals the species-life consists physically in the fact that man (like animals) lives from inorganic nature, and the more universal man is than animals the more universal is the area of inorganic nature from which he lives. From the theoretical point of view, plants, animals, stones, air, light, etc. form part of human consciousness, partly as objects of natural science, partly as objects of art; they are his intellectual inorganic nature, his intellectual means of subsistence, which he must first prepare before he can enjoy and assimilate them. From the practical point of view, too, they form a part of human life and activity. Physically man lives solely from these products of nature, whether they appear as food, heating, clothing, habitation, etc. The universality of man appears in practice precisely in the universality that makes the whole of nature into his inorganic body in that it is both (i) his immediate means of subsistence and also (ii) the material object and tool of his vital activity. Nature is the inorganic body of a man, that is, in so far as it is not itself a human body. That man lives from nature means that nature is his body with which he must maintain a constant interchange so as not to die. That man's physical and intellectual life depends on nature merely means that nature depends on itself, for man is part of nature.

While alienated labour alienates (1) nature from man, and (2) man from himself, his own active function, his vital activity, it also alienates the species from man; it turns his species-life into a means towards his individual life. Firstly it alienates species-life and individual life, and secondly in its abstraction it makes the latter into the aim of the former which is also conceived of in its abstract and alien form. For firstly, work, vital activity, and productive life itself appear to man only as a means to the satisfaction of a need, the need to preserve his physical existence. But productive life is species-life. It is life producing life. The whole character of a species, its generic character, is contained in its manner of vital activity, and free conscious activity is the species-characteristic of man. Life itself appears merely as a means to life.

The animal is immediately one with its vital activity. It is not distinct from it. They are identical. Man makes his vital activity itself into an object of his will and consciousness. He has a conscious vital activity. He is not immediately identical to any of his characterizations. Conscious vital activity differentiates man immediately from animal vital activity. It is this and this alone that makes man a species-being. He is only a conscious being, that is, his own life is an object to him, precisely because he is a species-being. This is the only reason for his activity being free activity. Alienated labour reverses the relationship so that, just because he is a conscious being, man makes his vital activity and essence a mere means to his existence.

The practical creation of an objective world, the working-over of inorganic nature, is the confirmation of man as a conscious species-being, that is, as a being that relates to the species as to himself and to himself as to the species. It is true that the animal, too, produces. It builds itself a nest, a dwelling, like the bee, the beaver, the ant, etc. But it only produces what it needs immediately for itself or its offspring; it produces one-sidedly whereas man produces universally; it produces only under the pressure of immediate physical need, whereas man produces freely from physical need and only truly produces when he is thus free; it produces only itself whereas man reproduces the whole of nature. Its product belongs immediately to its physical body whereas man can freely separate himself from his product. The animal only fashions things according to the standards and needs of the species it belongs to, whereas man knows how to produce according to the measure of every species and knows everywhere how to apply its inherent standard to the object; thus man also fashions things according to the laws of beauty.

Thus it is in the working over of the objective world that man first really affirms himself as a species-being. This production is his active species-life. Through it nature appears as his work and his reality. The object of work is therefore the objectification of the species-life of man; for he duplicates himself not only intellectually, in his mind, but also actively in reality and thus can look at his image in a world he has created. Therefore when alienated labour tears from man the object of his production, it also tears from him his species-life, the real objectivity of his species and turns the advantage he has over animals into a disadvantage in that his inorganic body, nature, is torn from him.

Similarly, in that alienated labour degrades man's own free activity to a means, it turns the species-life of man into a means for his physical existence.

Thus consciousness, which man derives from his species, changes itself through alienation so that species-life becomes a means for him.

Therefore alienated labor:

(3) makes the species-being of man, both nature and the intellectual faculties of his species, into a being that is alien to him, into a means for his individual existence. It alienates from man his own body, nature exterior to him, and his intellectual being, his human essence.

(4) An immediate consequence of man's alienation from the product of his work, his vital activity and his species-being, is the alienation of man from man. When man is opposed to himself, it is another man that is opposed to him. What is valid for the relationship of a man to his work, of the product of his work and himself, is also valid for the relationship of man to other men and of their labour and the objects of their labour.

In general, the statement that man is alienated from his species-being, means that one man is alienated from another as each of them is alienated from the human essence.

The alienation of man and in general of every relationship in which man stands to himself is first realized and expressed in the relationship with which man stands to other men.

Thus in the situation of alienated labour each man measures his relationship to other men by the relationship in which he finds himself placed as a worker.

We began with a fact of political economy, the alienation of the worker and his production. We have expressed this fact in conceptual terms: alienated, externalized labour. We have analysed this concept and thus analysed a purely economic fact.

Let us now see further how the concept of alienated, externalized labour must express and represent itself in reality.

If the product of work is alien to me, opposes me as an alien power, whom does it belong to then?

If my own activity does not belong to me and is an alien, forced activity to whom does it belong then?

To another being than myself.

Who is this being?

The gods? Of course in the beginning of history the chief production, as for example, the building of temples etc. in Egypt, India, and Mexico was both in the service of the gods and also belonged to them. But the gods alone were never the masters of the work. And nature just as little. And what a paradox it would be if, the more man mastered nature through his work and the more the miracles of the gods were rendered superfluous by the miracles of industry, the more man had to give up his pleasure in producing and the enjoyment in his product for the sake of these powers.

The alien being to whom the labour and the product of the labour belongs, whom the labour serves and who enjoys its product, can only be man himself. If the product of labour does not belong to the worker but stands over against him as an alien power, this is only possible in that it belongs to another man apart from the worker.

If his activity torments him it must be a joy and a pleasure to someone else. This alien power above man can be neither the gods nor nature, only man himself.

Consider further the above sentence that the relationship of man to himself first becomes objective and real to him through his relationship to other men. So if he relates to the product of his labour, his objectified labour, as to an object that is alien, hostile, powerful, and independent of him, this relationship implies that another man is the alien, hostile, powerful, and independent master of this object. If he relates to his own activity as to something unfree, it is a relationship to an activity that is under the domination, oppression, and yoke of another man.

Every self-alienation of man from himself and nature appears in the relationship in which he places himself and nature to other men distinct from himself. Therefore religious self-alienation necessarily appears in the relationship of layman to priest, or, because here we are dealing with a spiritual world, to a mediator, etc. In the practical, real world, the self-alienation can only appear through the practical, real relationship to other men. The means through which alienation makes progress are themselves practical. Through alienated labour, then, man creates not only his relationship to the object and act of production as to alien and hostile men; he creates too the relationship in which other men stand to his production and his product and the relationship in which he stands to these other men. Just as he turns his production into his own loss of reality and punishment and his own product into a loss, a product that does not belong to him, so he creates the domination of the man who does not produce over the production and the product. As he alienates his activity from himself, so he hands over to an alien person an activity that does not belong to him.

Up till now we have considered the relationship only from the side of the worker and we will later consider it from the side of the non-worker.

Thus through alienated, externalized labour the worker creates the relationship to this labour of a man who is alien to it and remains exterior to it. The relationship of the worker to his labour creates the relationship to it of the capitalist, or whatever else one wishes to call the master of the labour. Private property is thus the product, result, and necessary consequence of externalized labour, of the exterior relationship of the worker to nature and to himself.

Thus private property is the result of the analysis of the concept of externalized labour, i.e. externalized man, alienated work, alienated life, alienated man.

We have, of course, obtained the concept of externalized labour (externalized life) from political economy as the result of the movement of private property. But it is evident from the analysis of this concept that, although private property appears to be the ground and reason for externalized labour, it is rather a consequence of it, just as the gods are originally not the cause but the effect of the aberration of the human mind, although later this relationship reverses itself.

It is only in the final culmination of the development of private property that these hidden characteristics come once more to the fore, in that firstly it is the product of externalized labour and secondly it is the means through which labour externalizes itself, the realization of this externalization.

5

Bureaucracy

Max Weber

I: Characteristics of Bureaucracy

Modern officialdom functions in the following specific manner:

I. There is the principle of fixed and official jurisdictional areas, which are generally ordered by rules, that is, by laws or administrative regulations.

1. The regular activities required for the purposes of the bureaucratically governed structure are distributed in a fixed way as official duties.

2. The authority to give the commands required for the discharge of these duties is distributed in a stable way and is strictly delimited by rules concerning the coercive means, physical, sacerdotal, or otherwise, which may be placed at the disposal of officials.

3. Methodical provision is made for the regular and continuous fulfillment of these duties and for the execution of the corresponding rights; only persons who have the generally regulated qualifications to serve are employed.

In public and lawful government these three elements constitute "bureaucratic authority." In private economic domination, they constitute bureaucratic "management." Bureaucracy, thus understood, is fully developed in political and ecclesiastical communities only in the modern state, and, in the private economy, only in the most advanced institutions of capitalism. Permanent and public office authority, with fixed jurisdiction, is not the historical rule but rather the exception. This is so even in large political structures such as those of the ancient Orient, the Germanic and Mongolian empires of conquest, or of many feudal structures of state. In all these cases, the ruler executes the most important measures through personal trustees, table-companions, or court-servants. Their commissions and authority are not precisely delimited and are temporarily called into being for each case.

II. The principles of office hierarchy and of levels of graded authority mean a firmly ordered system of super- and subordination in which there is a supervision of the lower offices by the higher ones. Such a system offers the governed the possibility of appealing the decision of a lower office to its higher authority, in a definitely regulated manner. With the full development of the bureaucratic type, the office hierarchy is monocratically organized. The principle of hierarchical office authority is found in all bureaucratic structures: in state and ecclesiastical structures as well as in large party organizations and private enterprises. It does not matter for the character of bureaucracy whether its authority is called "private" or "public."

When the principle of jurisdictional "competency" is fully carried through, hierarchical subordination—at least in public office—does not mean that the "higher" authority is simply authorized to take over the business of the "lower." Indeed, the opposite is the rule. Once established and having fulfilled its task, an office tends to continue in existence and be held by another incumbent.

III. The management of the modern office is based upon written documents ("the files"), which are preserved in their original or draught form. There is, therefore, a staff of subaltern officials and scribes of all sorts. The body of officials actively engaged in a "public" office, along with the respective apparatus of material implements and the files, make up a "bureau." In private enterprise, "the bureau" is often called "the office."

In principle, the modern organization of the civil service separates the bureau from the private domicile of the official, and, in general, bureaucracy segregates official activity as something distinct from the sphere of private life. Public monies and equipment are divorced from the private property of the official. This condition is everywhere the product of a long development. Nowadays, it is found in public as well as in private enterprises; in the latter, the principle extends even to the leading entrepreneur. In principle, the executive office is separated from the household, business from private correspondence, and business assets from private fortune. The more consistently the modern type of business management had been carried through the more are these separations the case. The beginnings of this process are to be found as early as the Middle Ages.

It is the peculiarity of the modern entrepreneur that he conducts himself as the "first official" of his enterprise, in the very same way in which the ruler of a specifically modern bureaucratic state spoke of himself as "the first servant" of the state. The idea that the bureau activities of the state are intrinsically different in character from the management of private economic offices is a continental European notion and, by way of contrast, is totally foreign to the American way.

IV. Office management, at least all specialized office management—and such man-

agement is distinctly modern—usually presupposes thorough and expert training. This increasingly holds for the modern executive and employee of private enterprises, in the same manner as it holds for the state official.

V. When the office is fully developed, official activity demands the full working capacity of the official, irrespective of the fact that his obligatory time in the bureau may be firmly delimited. In the normal case, this is only the product of a long development, in the public as well as in the private office. Formerly, in all cases, the normal state of affairs was reversed: official business was discharged as a secondary activity.

VI. The management of the office follows general rules, which are more or less stable, more or less exhaustive, and which can be learned. Knowledge of these rules represents a special technical learning which the officials possess. It involves jurisprudence, or administrative or business management.

The reduction of modern office management to rules is deeply embedded in its very nature. The theory of modern public administration, for instance, assumes that the authority to order certain matters by decree—which has been legally granted to public authorities—does not entitle the bureau to regulate the matter by commands given for each case, but only to regulate the matter abstractly. This stands in extreme contrast to the regulation of all relationships through individual privileges and bestowals of favor, which is absolutely dominant in patrimonialism, at least in so far as such relationships are not fixed by sacred tradition.

2: The Position of the Official

All this results in the following for the internal and external position of the official:

I. Office holding is a "vocation." This is shown, first, in the requirement of a firmly prescribed course of training, which demands the entire capacity for work for a long period of time, and in the generally prescribed and special examinations which are prerequisites of employment. Furthermore, the position of the official is in the nature of a duty. This determines the internal structure of his relations, in the following manner: Legally and actually, office holding is not considered a source to be exploited for rents or emoluments, as was normally the case during the Middle Ages and frequently up to the threshold of recent times. Nor is office holding considered a usual exchange of services for equivalents, as is the case with free labor contracts. Entrance into an office, including one in the private economy, is considered an acceptance of a specific obligation of faithful management in return for a secure existence. It is decisive for the specific nature of modern loyalty to an office that, in the pure type, it does not establish a relationship to a *person*, like the vassal's or disciple's faith in feudal or in patrimonial relations of authority. Modern loyalty is devoted to impersonal and functional purposes. Behind the functional purposes, of course, "ideas of culture-values" usually stand. These are *ersatz* for the earthly or supra-mundane personal master: ideas such as "state," "church," "community," "party," or "enterprise" are thought of as being realized in a community; they provide an ideological halo for the master.

The political official—at least in the fully developed modern state—is not considered the personal servant of a ruler. Today, the bishop, the priest, and the preacher are in fact no longer, as in early Christian times, holders of purely personal charisma. The supra-mundane and sacred values which they offer are given to everybody who seems to be worthy of them and who asks for them. In former times, such leaders acted upon the personal command of their master; in principle, they were responsible only to him. Nowadays, in spite of the partial survival of the old theory, such religious

leaders are officials in the service of a functional purpose, which in the present-day "church" has become routinized and, in turn, ideologically hallowed.

II. The personal position of the official is patterned in the following way:

1. Whether he is in a private office or a public bureau, the modern official always strives and usually enjoys a distinct *social esteem* as compared with the governed. His social position is guaranteed by the prescriptive rules of rank order and, for the political official, by special definitions of the criminal code against "insults of officials" and "contempt" of state and church authorities.

The actual social position of the official is normally highest where, as in old civilized countries, the following conditions prevail: a strong demand for administration by trained experts; a strong and stable social differentiation, where the official predominantly derives from socially and economically privileged strata because of the social distribution of power; or where the costliness of the required training and status conventions are binding upon him. The possession of educational certificates—to be discussed elsewhere—are usually linked with qualification for office. Naturally, such certificates or patents enhance the "status element" in the social position of the official. For the rest this status factor in individual cases is explicitly and impassively acknowledged; for example, in the prescription that the acceptance or rejection of an aspirant to an official career depends upon the consent ("election") of the members of the official body. This is the case in the German army with the officer corps. Similar phenomena, which promote this guild-like closure of officialdom, are typically found in patrimonial and, particularly, in prebendal officialdoms of the past. The desire to resurrect such phenomena in changed forms is by no means infrequent among modern bureaucrats. For instance, they have played a role among the demands of the quite proletarian and expert officials (the *tretyj* element) during the Russian revolution.

Usually the social esteem of the officials as such is especially low where the demand for expert administration and the dominance of status conventions are weak. This is especially the case in the United States; it is often the case in new settlements by virtue of their wide fields for profit-making and the great instability of their social stratification.

2. The pure type of bureaucratic official is *appointed* by a superior authority. An official elected by the governed is not a purely bureaucratic figure. Of course, the formal existence of an election does not by itself mean that no appointment hides behind the election—in the state, especially, appointment by party chiefs. Whether or not this is the case does not depend upon legal statutes but upon the way in which the party mechanism functions. Once firmly organized, the parties can turn a formally free election into the mere acclamation of a candidate designated by the party chief. As a rule, however, a formally free election is turned into a fight, conducted according to definite rules, for votes in favor of one of two designed candidates.

In all circumstances, the designation of officials by means of an election among the governed modifies the strictness of hierarchical subordination. In principle, an official who is so elected has an autonomous position opposite the superordinate official. The elected official does not derive his position "from above" but "from below," or at least not from a superior authority of the official hierarchy but from powerful party men ("bosses"), who also determine his further career. The career of the elected official is not, or at least not primarily, dependent upon his chief in the administration.

The official who is not elected but appointed by a chief normally functions more exactly, from a technical point of view, because, all other circumstances being equal, it is more likely that purely functional points of consideration and qualities will determine his selection and career. As laymen, the governed can become acquainted with the extent to which a candidate is expertly qualified for office only in terms of experience, and hence only after his service. Moreover, in every sort of selection of officials by election, parties quite naturally give decisive weight not to expert considerations but to the services a follower renders to the party boss. This holds for all kinds of procurement of officials by elections, for the designation of formally free, elected officials by party bosses when they determine the slate of candidates, or the free appointment by a chief who has himself been elected. The contrast, however, is relative: substantially similar conditions hold where legitimate monarchs and their subordinates appoint officials, except that the influence of the followings are then less controllable.

Where the demand for administration by trained experts is considerable, and the party followings have to recognize an intellectually developed, educated, and freely moving "public opinion," the use of unqualified officials falls back upon the party in power at the next election. Naturally, this is more likely to happen when the officials are appointed by the chief. The demand for a trained administration now exists in the United States, but in the large cities, where immigrant votes are "corralled," there is, of course, no educated public opinion. Therefore, popular elections of the administrative chief and also of his subordinate officials usually endanger the expert qualification of the official as well as the precise functioning of the bureaucratic mechanism. It also weakens the dependence of the officials upon the hierarchy. This holds at least for the large administrative bodies that are difficult to supervise. The superior qualification and integrity of federal judges, appointed by the President, as over against elected judges in the United States is well known, although both types of officials have been selected primarily in terms of party considerations. The great changes in American metropolitan administrations demanded by reformers have proceeded essentially from elected mayors working with an apparatus of officials who were appointed by them. These reforms have thus come about in a "Caesarist" fashion. Viewed technically, as an organized form of authority, the efficiency of "Caesarism," which often grows out of democracy, rests in general upon the position of the "Caesar" as a free trustee of the masses (of the army or of the citizenry), who is unfettered by tradition. The "Caesar" is thus the unrestrained master of a body of highly qualified military officers and officials whom he selects freely and personally without regard to tradition or to any other considerations. This "rule of the personal genius," however, stands in contradiction to the formally "democratic" principle of a universally elected officialdom.

3. Normally, the position of the official is held for life, at least in public bureaucracies; and this is increasingly the case for all similar structures. As a factual rule, *tenure for life* is presupposed, even where the giving of notice or periodic reappointment occurs. In contrast to the worker in a private enterprise, the official normally holds tenure. Legal or actual life-tenure, however, is not recognized as the official's right to the possession of office, as was the case with many structures of authority in the past. Where legal guarantees against arbitrary dismissal or transfer are developed, they merely serve to guarantee a strictly objective discharge of specific office duties free from all personal considerations. In Germany, this is the case for all juridical and, increasingly, for all administrative officials.

Within the bureaucracy, therefore, the measure of "independence," legally guaranteed by tenure is not always a source of increased status for the official whose position is thus secured. Indeed, often the reverse holds, especially in old cultures and communities that are highly differentiated. In such communities, the stricter the subordination under the arbitrary rule of the master, the more it guarantees the maintenance of the conventional seigneurial style of living for the official. Because of the very absence of these legal guarantees of tenure, the conventional esteem for the official may rise in the same way as, during the Middle Ages, the esteem of the nobility of office rose at the expense of esteem for the freemen, and as the king's judge surpassed that of the people's judge. In Germany, the military officer or the administrative official can be removed from office at any time, or at least far more readily than the "independent judge," who never pays with loss of his office for even the grossest offense against the "code of honor" or against social conventions of the salon. For this very reason, if other things are equal, in the eyes of the master stratum the judge is considered less qualified for the social intercourse than are officers and administrative officials, whose greater dependence on the master is a greater guarantee of their conformity with status conventions. Of course, the average official strives for a civil-service law, which would materially secure his old age and provide increased guarantees against his arbitrary removal from office. This striving, however, has its limits. A very strong development of the "right to the office" naturally makes it more difficult to staff them with regard to technical efficiency, for such a development decreases the career-opportunities of ambitious candidates for office.

This makes for the fact that officials, on the whole, do not feel their dependency upon those at the top. This lack of a feeling of dependency, however, rests primarily upon the inclination to depend upon one's equals rather than upon the socially inferior and governed strata. The present conservative movement among the Badenia clergy, occasioned by the anxiety of a presumably threatening separation of church and state, has been expressly determined by the desire not to be turned "from a master into a servant of the parish."

4. The official receives the regular *pecuniary* compensation of a normally fixed *salary* and the old age security provided by a pension. The salary is not measured like a wage in terms of work done, but according to "status," that is, according to the kind of function (the "rank") and, in addition, possibly, according to the length of service. The relatively great security of the official's income, as well as the rewards of social esteem, make the office a sought-after position, especially in countries which no longer provide opportunities for colonial profits. In such countries, this situation permits relatively low salaries for officials.

5. The official is set for a *"career"* within the hierarchical order of the public service. He moves from the lower, less important, and lower paid to the higher positions. The average official naturally desires a mechanical fixing of the conditions of promotion: if not the offices, at least of the salary levels. He wants these conditions fixed in terms of "seniority," or possibly according to grades achieved in a developed system of expert examinations. Here and there, such examinations actually form a character *indelebilis* of the official and have lifelong effects on his career. To this is joined the desire to qualify the right to office and the increasing tendency toward status group closure and economic security. All of this makes for a tendency to consider the offices as "prebends" of those who are qualified by educational certificates. The necessity of taking general personal and intellectual qualifications into consideration, irrespective of the often subaltern character of the educational certificate, has led to a condition in which the highest political offices, especially the positions of "ministers," are principally filled without reference to such certificates.

6

Fundamentals of Scientific Management

Frederick Winslow Taylor

The principal object of management should be to secure the maximum prosperity for the employer, coupled with the maximum prosperity for each employé.

The words "maximum prosperity" are used, in their broad sense, to mean not only large dividends for the company or owner, but the development of every branch of the business to its highest state of excellence, so that the prosperity may be permanent.

In the same way maximum prosperity for each employé means not only higher wages than are usually received by men of his class, but, of more importance still, it also means the development of each man to his state of maximum efficiency, so that he may be able to do, generally speaking, the highest grade of work for which his natural abilities fit him, and it further means giving him, when possible, this class of work to do.

It would seem to be so self-evident that maximum prosperity for the employer, coupled with maximum prosperity for the employé, ought to be the two leading objects of management, that even to state this fact should be unnecessary. And yet there is no question that, throughout the industrial world, a large part of the organization of employers, as well as employés, is for war rather than for peace, and that perhaps the majority on either side do not believe that it is possible so to arrange their mutual relations that their interests become identical.

The majority of these men believe that the fundamental interests of employés and employers are necessarily antagonistic. Scientific management, on the contrary, has for its very foundation the firm conviction that the true interests of the two are one and the same; that prosperity for the employer cannot exist through a long term of years unless it is accompanied by prosperity for the employé, and *vice versa*; and that it is possible to give the workman what he most wants—high wages—and the employer what he wants—a low labor cost—for his manufactures.

It is hoped that some at least of those who do not sympathize with each of these objects may be led to modify their views; that some employers, whose attitude toward their workmen has been that of trying to get the largest amount of work out of them for the smallest possible wages, may be led to see that a more liberal policy toward their men will pay them better; and that some of those workmen who begrudge a fair and even a large profit to their employers, and who feel that all of the fruits of their labor should belong to them, and that those for whom they work and the capital invested in the business are entitled to little or nothing, may be led to modify these views.

No one can be found who will deny that in the case of any single individual the greatest prosperity can exist only when that individual has reached his highest state of

From Taylor, Frederick Winslow, *The Principles of Scientific Management.* New York: Harper & Brothers, 1911.

efficiency; that is, when he is turning out his largest daily output.

The truth of this fact is also perfectly clear in the case of two men working together. To illustrate: if you and your workman have become so skilful that you and he together are making two pairs of shoes in a day, while your competitor and his workman are making only one pair, it is clear that after selling your two pairs of shoes you can pay your workman much higher wages than your competitor who produces only one pair of shoes is able to pay his man, and that there will still be enough money left over for you to have a larger profit than your competitor.

In the case of a more complicated manufacturing establishment, it should also be perfectly clear that the greatest permanent prosperity for the workman, coupled with the greatest prosperity for the employer, can be brought about only when the work of the establishment is done with the smallest combined expenditure of human effort, plus nature's resources, plus the cost for the use of capital in the shape of machines, buildings, etc. Or, to state the same thing in a different way: that the greatest prosperity can exist only as the result of the greatest possible productivity of the men and machines of the establishment—that is, when each man and each machine are turning out the largest possible output; because unless your men and your machines are daily turning out more work than others around you, it is clear that competition will prevent your paying higher wages to your workmen than are paid to those of your competitor. And what is true as to the possibility of paying high wages in the case of two companies competing close beside one another is also true as to whole districts of the country and even as to nations which are in competition. In a word, that maximum prosperity can exist only as the result of maximum productivity. Later in this paper illustrations will be given of several companies which are earn-

ing large dividends and at the same time paying from 30 per cent. to 100 per cent. higher wages to their men than are paid to similar men immediately around them, and with whose employers they are in competition. These illustrations will cover different types of work, from the most elementary to the most complicated.

If the above reasoning is correct, it follows that the most important object of both the workmen and the management should be the training and development of each individual in the establishment, so that he can do (at his fastest pace and with the maximum of efficiency) the highest class of work for which his natural abilities fit him.

These principles appear to be so self-evident that many men may think it almost childish to state them. Let us, however, turn to the facts, as they actually exist in this country and in England. The English and American peoples are the greatest sportsmen in the world. Whenever an American workman plays baseball, or an English workman plays cricket, it is safe to say that he strains every nerve to secure victory for his side. He does his very best to make the largest possible number of runs. The universal sentiment is so strong that any man who fails to give out all there is in him in sport is branded as a "quitter," and treated with contempt by those who are around him.

When the same workman returns to work on the following day, instead of using every effort to turn out the largest possible amount of work, in a majority of the cases this man deliberately plans to do as little as he safely can—to turn out far less work than he is well able to do—in many instances to do not more than one-third to one-half of a proper day's work. And in fact if he were to do his best to turn out his largest possible day's work, he would be abused by his fellow-workers for so doing, even more than if he had proved himself a "quitter" in sport. Underworking, that is, deliberately working slowly so as to avoid doing a full day's work, "soldiering," as it is called in this country, "hanging it out," as it is called in England, "ca canae," as it is called in Scotland, is almost universal in industrial establishments, and prevails also to a large extent in the building trades; and the writer asserts without fear of contradiction that this constitutes the greatest evil with which the working-people of both England and America are now afflicted.

It will be shown later in this paper that doing away with slow working and "soldiering" in all its forms and so arranging the relations between employer and employé that each workman will work to his very best advantage and at his best speed, accompanied by the intimate cooperation with the management and the help (which the workman should receive) from the management, would result on the average in nearly doubling the output of each man and each machine. What other reforms, among those which are being discussed by these two nations, could do as much toward promoting prosperity, toward the diminution of poverty, and the alleviation of suffering? America and England have been recently agitated over such subjects as the tariff, the control of the large corporations on the one hand, and of hereditary power on the other hand, and over various more or less socialistic proposals for taxation, etc. On these subjects both peoples have been profoundly stirred, and yet hardly a voice has been raised to call attention to this vastly greater and more important subject of "soldiering," which directly and powerfully affects the wages, the prosperity, and the life of almost every working-man, and also quite as much the prosperity of every industrial establishment in the nation.

The elimination of "soldiering" and of the several causes of slow working would so lower the cost of production that both our home and foreign markets would be greatly enlarged, and we could compete on more than even terms with our rivals. It would remove one of the fundamental causes for dull times, for lack of employment, and for poverty, and therefore would have a more permanent and far-reaching effect upon these misfortunes than any of the curative remedies that are now being used to soften their consequences. It would insure higher wages and make shorter working hours and better working and home conditions possible.

Why is it, then, in the face of the self-evident fact that maximum prosperity can exist only as the result of the determined effort of each workman to turn out each day his largest possible day's work, that the great majority of our men are deliberately doing just the opposite, and that even when the men have the best of intentions their work is in most cases far from efficient?

There are three causes for this condition, which may be briefly summarized as:

First. The fallacy, which has from time immemorial been almost universal among workmen, that a material increase in the output of each man or each machine in the trade would result in the end in throwing a large number of men out of work.

Second. The defective systems of management which are in common use, and which make it necessary for each workman to soldier, or work slowly, in order that he may protect his own best interests.

Third. The inefficient rule-of-thumb methods, which are still almost universal in all trades, and in practising which our workmen waste a large part of their effort.

This paper will attempt to show the enormous gains which would result from the substitution by our workmen of scientific for rule-of-thumb methods.

To explain a little more fully these three causes:

First. The great majority of workmen still believe that if they were to work at their best speed they would be doing a great injustice to the whole trade by throwing a lot of men out of work, and yet the history of the development of each trade shows that each improvement, whether it be the invention of a new machine or the introduction of a better method, which results in increasing the productive capacity of the men in the trade and cheapening the costs, instead of throwing men out of work makes in the end work for more men.

The cheapening of any article in common use almost immediately results in a largely increased demand for that article. Take the case of shoes, for instance. The introduction of machinery for doing every element of the work which was formerly done by hand has resulted in making shoes at a fraction of their former labor cost, and in selling them so cheap that now almost every man, woman, and child in the working-classes buys one or two pairs of shoes per year, and wears shoes all the time, whereas formerly each workman bought perhaps one pair of shoes every five years, and went barefoot most of the time, wearing shoes only as a luxury or as a matter of the sternest necessity. In spite of the enormously increased output of shoes per workman, which has come with shoe machinery, the demand for shoes has so increased that there are relatively more men working in the shoe industry now than ever before.

The workmen in almost every trade have before them an object lesson of this kind, and yet, because they are ignorant of the history of their own trade even, they still firmly believe, as their fathers did before them, that it is against their best interests for each man to turn out each day as much work as possible.

Under this fallacious idea a large proportion of the workmen of both countries each day deliberately work slowly so as to curtail the output. Almost every labor union has made, or is contemplating making, rules which have for their object curtailing the output of their members, and those men who have the greatest influence with the working-people, the labor leaders as well as many people with philanthropic feelings who are helping them, are daily spreading this fallacy and at the same time telling them that they are overworked.

A great deal has been and is being constantly said about "sweat-shop" work and conditions. The writer has great sympathy with those who are overworked, but on the whole a greater sympathy for those who are *under paid.* For every individual, however, who is overworked, there are a hundred who intentionally underwork—greatly underwork—every day of their lives, and who for this reason deliberately aid in establishing those conditions which in the end inevitably result in low wages. And yet hardly a single voice is being raised in an endeavor to correct this evil.

As engineers and managers, we are more intimately acquainted with these facts than any other class in the community, and are therefore best fitted to lead in a movement to combat this fallacious idea by educating not only the workmen but the whole of the country as to the true facts. And yet we are practically doing nothing in this direction, and are leaving this field entirely in the hands of the labor agitators (many of whom are misinformed and misguided), and of sentimentalists who are ignorant as to actual working conditions.

Second. As to the second cause for soldiering—the relations which exist between employers and employés under almost all of the systems of management which are in common use—it is impossible in a few words to make it clear to one not familiar with this problem why it is that the *ignorance of employers* as to the proper time in which work of various kinds should be done makes it for the interest of the workman to "soldier."

The writer therefore quotes herewith from a paper read before The American Society of Mechanical Engineers, in June, 1903, entitled "Shop Management," which it is hoped will explain fully this cause for soldiering:

"This loafing or soldiering proceeds from two causes. First, from the natural instinct and tendency of men to take it easy, which may be called natural soldiering. Second, from more intricate second thought and reasoning caused by their relations with other men, which may be called systematic soldiering.

"There is no question that the tendency of the average man (in all walks of life) is toward working at a slow, easy gait, and that it is only after a good deal of thought and observation on his part or as a result of example, conscience, or external pressure that he takes a more rapid pace.

"There are, of course, men of unusual energy, vitality, and ambition who naturally choose the fastest gait, who set up their own standards, and who work hard, even though it may be against their best interests. But these few uncommon men only serve by forming a contrast to emphasize the tendency of the average.

"This common tendency to 'take it easy' is greatly increased by bringing a number of men together on similar work and at a uniform standard rate of pay by the day.

"Under this plan the better men gradually but surely slow down their gait to that of the poorest and least efficient. When a naturally energetic man works for a few days beside a lazy one, the logic of the situation is unanswerable. 'Why should I work hard when that lazy fellow gets the same pay that I do and does only half as much work?'

"A careful time study of men working under these conditions will disclose facts which are ludicrous as well as pitiable.

"To illustrate: The writer has timed a naturally energetic workman who, while going and coming from work, would walk at a speed of from three to four miles per hour, and not infrequently trot home after a day's work. On arriving at his work he would immediately slow down to a speed of about one mile an hour. When, for example, wheeling a loaded wheelbarrow, he would go at a good fast pace even up hill in order to be as short a time as possible under load, and immediately on the return walk slow down to a mile an hour, improving every opportunity for delay short of actually sitting down. In order to be sure not to do more than his lazy neighbor, he would actually tire himself in his effort to go slow.

"These men were working under a foreman of good reputation and highly thought of by his employer, who, when his attention was called to this state of things, answered: 'Well, I can keep them from sitting down, but the devil can't make them get a move on while they are at work.'

"The natural laziness of men is serious, but by far the greatest evil from which both workmen and employers are suffering is the *systematic soldiering* which is almost universal under all of the ordinary schemes of management and which results from a careful study on the part of the workmen of what will promote their best interests.

"The writer was much interested recently in hearing one small but experienced golf caddy boy of twelve explaining to a green caddy, who had shown special energy and interest, the necessity of going slow and lagging behind his man when he came up to the ball, showing him that since they were paid by the hour, the faster they went the less money they got, and finally telling him that if he went too fast the other boys would give him a licking.

"This represents a type of *systematic soldiering* which is not, however, very serious, since it is done with the knowledge of the employer, who can quite easily break it up if he wishes.

"The greater part of the *systematic soldiering,* however, is done by the men with the deliberate object of keeping their employers ignorant of how fast work can be done.

"So universal is soldiering for this purpose that hardly a competent workman can be found in a large establishment, whether he works by the day or on piece work, contract work, or under any of the ordinary systems, who does not devote a considerable part of his time to studying just how slow he can work and still convince his employer that he is going at a good pace.

"The causes for this are, briefly, that practically all employers determine upon a maximum sum which they feel it is right for each of their classes of employees to earn per day, whether their men work by the day or piece.

"Each workman soon finds out about what this figure is for his particular case, and he also realizes that when his employer is convinced that a man is capable of doing more work than he has done, he will find sooner or later some way of compelling him to do it with little or no increase of pay.

"Employers derive their knowledge of how much of a given class of work can be done in a day from either their own experience, which has frequently grown hazy with age, from casual and unsystematic observation of their men, or at best from records which are kept, showing the quickest time in which each job has been done. In many cases the employer will feel almost certain that a given job can be done faster than it has been, but he rarely cares to take the drastic measures necessary to force men to do it in the quickest time, unless he has an actual record proving conclusively how fast the work can be done.

"It evidently becomes for each man's interest, then, to see that no job is done faster than it has been in the past. The younger and less experienced men are taught this by their elders, and all possible persuasion and social pressure is brought to bear upon the greedy and selfish men to keep them from making new records which result in temporarily increasing their wages,

while all those who come after them are made to work harder for the same old pay.

"Under the best day work of the ordinary type, when accurate records are kept of the amount of work done by each man and of his efficiency, and when each man's wages are raised as he improves, and those who fail to rise to a certain standard are discharged and a fresh supply of carefully selected men are given work in their places, both the natural loafing and systematic soldiering can be largely broken up. This can only be done, however, when the men are thoroughly convinced that there is no intention of establishing piece work even in the remote future, and it is next to impossible to make men believe this when the work is of such a nature that they believe piece work to be practicable. In most cases their fear of making a record which will be used as a basis for piece work will cause them to soldier as much as they dare.

"It is, however, under piece work that the art of systematic soldiering is thoroughly developed; after a workman has had the price per piece of the work he is doing lowered two or three times as a result of his having worked harder and increased his output, he is likely entirely to lose sight of his employer's side of the case and become imbued with a grim determination to have no more cuts if soldiering can prevent it. Unfortunately for the character of the workman, soldiering involves a deliberate attempt to mislead and deceive his employer, and thus upright and straightforward workmen are compelled to become more or less hypocritical. The employer is soon looked upon as an antagonist, if not an enemy, and the mutual confidence which should exist between a leader and his men, the enthusiasm, the feeling that they are all working for the same end and will share in the results is entirely lacking.

"The feeling of antagonism under the ordinary piece-work system becomes in many cases so marked on the part of the men that any proposition made by their employers, however reasonable, is looked upon with suspicion, and soldiering becomes such a fixed habit that men will frequently take pains to restrict the product of machines which they are running when even a large increase in output would involve no more work on their part."

Third. As to the third cause for slow work, considerable space will later in this paper be devoted to illustrating the great gain, both to employers and employés, which results from the substitution of scientific for rule-of-thumb methods in even the smallest details of the work of every trade. The enormous saving of time and therefore increase in the output which it is possible to effect through eliminating unnecessary motions and substituting fast for slow and inefficient motions for the men working in any of our trades can be fully realized only after one has personally seen the improvement which results from a thorough motion and time study, made by a competent man.

To explain briefly: owing to the fact that the workmen in all of our trades have been taught the details of their work by observation of those immediately around them, there are many different ways in common use for doing the same thing, perhaps forty, fifty, or a hundred ways of doing each act in each trade, and for the same reason there is a great variety in the implements used for each class of work. Now, among the various methods and implements used in each element of each trade there is always one method and one implement which is quicker and better than any of the rest. And this one best method and best implement can only be discovered or developed through a scientific study and analysis of all of the methods and implements in use, together with accurate, minute, motion and time study. This involves the gradual substitution of science for rule of thumb throughout the mechanic arts.

This paper will show that the underlying philosophy of all of the old systems of management in common use makes it imperative that each workman shall be left with the final responsibility for doing his job practically as he thinks best, with comparatively little help and advice from the management. And it will also show that because of this isolation of workmen, it is in most cases impossible for the men working under these systems to do their work in accordance with the rules and laws of a science or art, even where one exists.

The writer asserts as a general principle (and he proposes to give illustrations tending to prove the fact later in this paper) that in almost all of the mechanic arts the science which underlies each act of each workman is so great and amounts to so much that the workman who is best suited to actually doing the work is incapable of fully understanding this science, without the guidance and help of those who are working with him or over him, either through lack of education or through insufficient mental capacity. In order that the work may be done in accordance with scientific laws, it is necessary that there shall be a far more equal division of the responsibility between the management and the workmen than exists under any of the ordinary types of management. Those in the management whose duty it is to develop this science should also guide and help the workman in working under it, and should assume a much larger share of the responsibility for results than under usual conditions is assumed by the management.

The body of this paper will make it clear that, to work according to scientific laws, the management must take over and perform much of the work which is now left to the men; almost every act of the workman should be preceded by one or more preparatory acts of the management which enable him to do his work better and quicker than he otherwise could. And each man should daily be taught by and receive the most friendly help from those who are over him, instead of being, at the one extreme, driven or coerced by his bosses, and at the other left to his own unaided devices.

This close, intimate, personal cooperation between the management and the men is of the essence of modern scientific or task management.

It will be shown by a series of practical illustrations that, through this friendly cooperation, namely, through sharing equally in every day's burden, all of the great obstacles (above described) to obtaining the maximum output for each man and each machine in the establishment are swept away. The 30 per cent. to 100 per cent. increase in wages which the workmen are able to earn beyond what they receive under the old type of management, coupled with the daily intimate shoulder to shoulder contact with the management, entirely removes all cause for soldiering. And in a few years, under this system, the workmen have before them the object lesson of seeing that a great increase in the output per man results in giving employment to more men, instead of throwing men out of work, thus completely eradicating the fallacy that a larger output for each man will throw other men out of work.

It is the writer's judgment, then, that while much can be done and should be done by writing and talking toward educating not only workmen, but all classes in the community, as to the importance of obtaining the maximum output of each man and each machine, it is only through the adoption of modern scientific management that this great problem can be finally solved. Probably most of the readers of this paper will say that all of this is mere theory. On the contrary, the theory, or philosophy, of scientific management is just beginning to be understood, whereas the management itself has been a gradual evolution, extending over a period of nearly thirty years. And during this time the employés of one company after another, including a large

range and diversity of industries, have gradually changed from the ordinary to the scientific type of management. At least 50,000 workmen in the United States are now employed under this system; and they are receiving from 30 per cent. to 100 per cent. higher wages daily than are paid to men of similar caliber with whom they are surrounded, while the companies employing them are more prosperous than ever before. In these companies the output, per man and per machine, has on an average been doubled. During all these years there has never been a single strike among the men working under this system. In place of the suspicious watchfulness and the more or less open warfare which characterizes the ordinary types of management, there is universally friendly cooperation between the management and the men.

Several papers have been written, describing the expedients which have been adopted and the details which have been developed under scientific management and the steps to be taken in changing from the ordinary to the scientific type. But unfortunately most of the readers of these papers have mistaken the mechanism for the true essence. Scientific management fundamentally consists of certain broad general principles, a certain philosophy, which can be applied in many ways, and a description of what any one man or men may believe to be the best mechanism for applying these general principles should in no way be confused with the principles themselves.

It is not here claimed that any single panacea exists for all of the troubles of the working-people or of employers. As long as some people are born lazy or inefficient, and others are born greedy and brutal, as long as vice and crime are with us, just so long will a certain amount of poverty, misery, and unhappiness be with us also. No system of management, no single expedient within the control of any man or any set of men can insure continuous prosperity to either workmen or employers. Prosperity depends upon so many factors entirely beyond the control of any one set of men, any state, or even any one country, that certain periods will inevitably come when both sides must suffer, more or less. It is claimed, however, that under scientific management the intermediate periods will be far more prosperous, far happier, and more free from discord and dissension. And also, that the periods will be fewer, shorter and the suffering less. And this will be particularly true in any one town, any one section of the country, or any one state which first substitutes the principles of scientific management for the rule of thumb.

That these principles are certain to come into general use practically throughout the civilized world, sooner or later, the writer is profoundly convinced, and the sooner they come the better for all the people.

7

The Hawthorne Experiment
Western Electric Company

Elton Mayo

. . Acting in collaboration with the National Research Council, the Western Electric Company had for three years been engaged upon an attempt to assess the effect of illumination upon the worker and his work. No official report of these experiments has yet been published, and it is consequently impossible to quote chapter and verse as to the methods employed and the results obtained. I can, however, state with confidence that the inquiry involved in one phase the segregation of two groups of workers, engaged upon the same task, in two rooms equally illuminated. The experimental diminution of the lighting, in ordered quantities, in one room only, gave no sufficiently significant difference, expressed in terms of measured out-

put, as compared with the other still fully illuminated room. Somehow or other that complex of mutually dependent factors, the human organism, shifted its equilibrium and unintentionally defeated the purpose of the experiment. . . .

In the institution of a second inquiry full heed was paid to the lesson of the first experiment. A group of workers was segregated for observation of the effect of various changes in the conditions of work. No attempt was made to "test for the effect of single variables." Where human beings are concerned one cannot change one condition without inadvertently changing others—so much the illumination experiment had shown. The group was kept small—six operatives—because the Company officers had become alert to the possible significance for the inquiry of changes of mental attitude; it was believed that such changes

Excerpts from *The Human Problems of an Industrial Civilization,* by Elton Mayo. Reprinted by permission of Baker Library, Harvard Business School.

were more likely to be noticed by the official observers if the group were small. Arrangements were made to measure accurately all changes in output; this also meant that the group must be small. An accurate record of output was desired for two reasons: first, changes in production differ from many other human changes in that they lend themselves to exact and continuous determination; second, variations in output do effectively show "the combined effect" of all the conditions affecting a group. The work of Vernon and Wyatt supports the view that an output curve does indicate the relative equilibrium or disequilibrium of the individual and the group.

The operation selected was that of assembling telephone relays. . . . The operation ranks as repetitive; it is performed by women. A standard assembly bench with places for five workers and the appropriate equipment were put into one of the experimental rooms. This room was separated from the main assembly department by a ten-foot wooden partition. The bench was well illuminated; arrangements were made for observation of temperature and humidity changes. An attempt was made to provide for the observation of other changes and especially of unanticipated changes as well as those experimentally introduced. This again reflected the experience gained in the illumination experiments. Thus constituted, presumably for a relatively short period of observation, the experimental room actually ran on from April, 1927, to the middle of 1932, a period of over five years. And the increasing interest of the experiment justified its continuance until the economic depression made further development impossible.

Six female operatives were chosen, five to work at the bench, one to procure and distribute parts for those engaged in assembly. I shall not discuss the method of choosing these operatives, except to say that all were experienced workers. This was arranged by those in charge because they wished to avoid the complications which learning would introduce. Within the first year the two operatives first chosen—numbers one and two at the outset—dropped out, and their places were taken by two other workers of equal or superior skill who remained as numbers one and two until the end. The original number five left the Hawthorne Works for a time in the middle period but subsequently returned to her place in the group. In effect, then, there exist continuous records of the output of five workers for approximately five years. These records were obtained by means of a specially devised apparatus which, as each relay was completed, punched a hole in a moving tape. The tape moved at a constant speed, approximately one-quarter of an inch per minute; it punched five rows of holes, one row for each worker. At the right of each worker's place at the bench was a chute within which was an electric gate. When the worker finished a relay she placed it in the chute; as it passed through, it operated the electric gate and the punching apparatus duly recorded the relay. By measuring the distance on the tape between one hole and the next it is possible to calculate the time elapsing between the completion of one relay and another. The Company thus has a record of every relay assembled by every operative in the experimental room for five years and in almost every instance has also a record of the time taken to assemble it. . . .

The transfer of the five workers into the experimental room was carefully arranged. It was clear that changes in output, as measured by the recording device, would constitute the most important series of observations. The continuity and accuracy of this record would obviously make it the chief point of reference for other observations. Consequently, for two weeks before the five operatives were moved into the special room, a record was kept of the production of each one without her knowledge. This is stated as the base output from which she starts. After this, the girls were moved into the experimental room and again for five weeks their output was recorded without the introduction of any change of working conditions or procedures. This, it was assumed, would sufficiently account for any changes incidental to the transfer. In the third period, which lasted for eight weeks, the experimental change introduced was a variation in the method of payment. In the department the girls had been paid a group piece rate as members of a group of approximately one hundred workers. The change in the third period was to constitute the five a unitary group for piece-rate payment. . . . It . . . meant that each girl was given a strong, though indirect, interest in the achievement of the group. After watching the effect of this change of grouping for eight weeks, the Company officers felt that the more significant experimentation might begin.

In the fourth experimental period the group was given two rest-pauses of five minutes each, beginning at 10:00 in the mid-morning and at 2:00 in the afternoon respectively. The question had been discussed beforehand with the operatives—as all subsequent changes were—and the decision had been in favor of a five minute rather than a ten or fifteen minute pause partly because there was some feeling that, if the break were longer, the lost time would perhaps not be made up. This was continued for five weeks, at which time it was clear that just as total output had increased perceptibly after the constitution of the workers as a group for payment, so also had it definitely risen again in response to the rests. The alternative of the original proposals, two ten-minute rest-pauses, was therefore adopted as the experimental change in period five. This change was retained for four weeks, in which time

both the daily and weekly output of the group showed a greater rise than for any former change. In the sixth period the group was given six five-minute rests for four weeks. The girl operatives expressed some dislike of the constant interruption and the output curve showed a small recession.

The seventh experimental period was destined to become standard for the remaining years of the experiment. The subsequent changes are, for the most part, some variation of it. It may be regarded as concluding the first phase of the inquiry which was devoted, first, to the transfer of the operative and the establishment of routines of observation and, second, to experiment with rest-pauses of varying incidence and length. Period seven was originally intended to discover the effect of giving some refreshment—coffee or soup and a sandwich—to the workers in the mid-morning period. The observers in charge had, in process of talking with the girls, found out that they frequently came to work in the morning after little or no breakfast. They became hungry long before lunch and it was thought that there was an indication of this in a downward trend of the output record before the midday break. It was therefore decided that the Company should supply each member of the group with adequate refection in the middle of the working morning and perhaps some slighter refreshment in the mid-afternoon. This, however, meant an abandonment of the six five-minute rests and a return to the two ten-minute rest-pauses. Such a return was in any event justified both by the expressed preference of the workers and by the fact that the output records seemed to indicate it as the better arrangement. The refreshment provided, however, made necessary some extension of the morning break. Period seven accordingly is characterized by a mid-morning break of fifteen minutes (9:30 A.M.) with lunch and a mid-afternoon break of ten minutes (2:30 P.M.). This arrangement persisted in uncomplicated form for eleven weeks and in that time production returned to its former high level and remained there.

In the second phase of experimentation, periods eight to eleven inclusive, the conditions of period seven are held constant and other changes are introduced. In period eight the group stopped work half an hour earlier every day—at 4:30 P.M. This was attended with a remarkable rise in both daily and weekly output. This continued for seven weeks until the tenth of March, 1928. Early in this period the original numbers one and two dropped out and their places were taken by those who rank as one and two for the greater part of the inquiry. In the ninth period the working day was shortened still further and the group stopped at 4:00 P.M. daily. This lasted for four weeks and in that time there was a slight fall both in daily and weekly output—although the average hourly output rose. In the tenth period the group returned to the conditions of work of period seven—fifteen-minute morning rest-pause with refreshment, ten-minute rest-pause in the mid-afternoon and a full working day to five o'clock. This period lasted for twelve weeks and in that time the group in respect of its recorded daily and weekly output achieved and held a production very much higher than at any previous time. It was, perhaps, this "high" of production which brought to expression certain grave doubts which had been growing in the minds of the Company officers responsible for the experiment. Many changes other than those in production had been observed to be occurring; up to this time it had been possible to assume for practical purposes that such changes were of the nature of adaptation to special circumstance and not necessarily otherwise significant. Equally it had been possible to assume that the changes recorded in output were, at

least for the most part, related to the experimental changes in working conditions—rest-pauses or whatnot—singly and successively imposed. At this stage these assumptions had become untenable—especially in the light of the previously expressed determination "not to test for single variables" but to study the situation.

Period eleven was a concession to the workers, at least in part. I do not mean that the Company had not intended to extend their second experimental phase—observation of the effect of shorter working time—to include a record of the effect of a five-day week. I am convinced that this was intended; but the introduction of a shorter working week—no work on Saturday—at this time refers itself to two facts, first, that the twelve weeks of this period run between the second of July and the first of September in the summer of 1928 and, second, it refers itself also by anticipation to the next experimental change. For it had already been agreed between the workers and the officers in charge that the next experiment, twelve, should be the restoration of the original conditions of work—no rest-pauses, no lunch, no shortened day or week. In period eleven—the shortened week in summer—the daily output continued to increase; it did not, however, increase sufficiently to compensate for the loss of Saturday morning's work, consequently the weekly output shows a small recession. It is important to note that although the weekly output shows this recession, it nevertheless remains above the weekly output of all other periods except periods eight and ten.

September, 1928, was an important month in the development of the inquiry. In September, the twelfth experimental change began and, by arrangement with the workers, continued for twelve weeks. In this period, as I have said, the group returned to the conditions of work which obtained in period three at the beginning of the inquiry;

rest-periods, special refreshments, and other concessions were all abolished for approximately three months. In September, 1928, also began that extension of the inquiry known as "The Interview Programme." . . . Both of these events must be regarded as having strongly influenced the course of the inquiry.

The history of the twelve-week return to the so-called original conditions of work is soon told. The daily and weekly output rose to a point higher than at any other time and in the whole period "there was no downward trend." At the end of twelve weeks, in period thirteen, the group returned, as had been arranged, to the conditions of period seven with the sole difference that whereas the Company continued to supply coffee or other beverage for the mid-morning lunch, the girls now provided their own food. This arrangement lasted for thirty-one weeks— much longer than any previous change. Whereas in period twelve the group's output had exceeded that of all the other performances, in period thirteen, with rest-pauses and refreshment restored, their output rose once again to even greater heights. It had become clear that the itemized changes experimentally imposed, although they could perhaps be used to account for minor differences between one period and another, yet could not be used to explain the major change—the continually increasing production. This steady increase as represented by all the contemporary records seemed to ignore the experimental changes in its upward development.

The fourteenth experimental period was a repetition of period eleven; it permitted the group to give up work on Saturday between the first of July and the thirty-first of August, 1929. The fifteenth period returned again to the conditions of the thirteenth, and at this point we may regard the conditions of period seven as the established standard for the group.

It had been the habit of the officers in charge to issue reports of the progress of the experiment from time to time. These reports were published privately to the Western Electric Company and certain of its officers. From these documents one can gain some idea of the contemporary attitude to the inquiry of those who were directing it. The third of these reports was issued on August 15, 1928, and consequently did not carry its comment or description beyond period ten. The fourth was issued on May 11, 1929, and in it one finds interesting discussion of the events I have just described. . . .

. . . From the "conclusions" I select the following passages:

"(b) There has been a continual upward trend in output which has been independent of the changes in rest-pauses. This upward trend has continued too long to be ascribed to an initial stimulus from the novelty of starting a special study."

"(c) The reduction of muscular fatigue has not been the primary factor in increasing output. Cumulative fatigue is not present."

"(f) There has been an important increase in contentment among the girls working under test-room conditions."

"(g) There has been a decrease in absences of about 80 per cent among the girls since entering the test-room group. Test-room operators have had approximately one-third as many sick absences as the regular department during the last six months" (p. 126).

"(v) Output is more directly related to the type of working day than to the number of (working) days in the week . . ." (p. 127).

"(y) Observations of operators in the relay assembly test room indicate that their health is being maintained or improved and that they are working within their capacity. . ." (p. 129).

The following conclusions in former reports are reaffirmed:

"(n) The changed working conditions have resulted in creating an eagerness on the part of operators to come to work in the morning" (p. 130).

"(s) Important factors in the production of a better mental attitude and greater enjoyment of work have been the greater freedom, less strict supervision and the opportunity to vary from a fixed pace without reprimand from a gang boss."

"The operators have no clear idea as to why they are able to produce more in the test room; but as shown in the replies to questionnaires . . . there is the feeling that better output is in some way related to the distinctly pleasanter, freer, and happier working conditions" (p. 131).

The report proceeds to remark that "much can be gained industrially by carrying greater personal consideration to the lowest levels of employment."

Mr. G. A. Pennock in a paper read before a conference of the Personnel Research Federation on September 15, 1929, in New York says: ". . . this unexpected and continual upward trend in productivity throughout the periods, even in period twelve when the girls were put on a full forty-eight hour week with no rest period or lunch, led us to seek some explanation or analysis." He goes on to mention three possibilities: first, fatigue which he finds it easy to exclude on the medical evidence, on the basis of certain physiological findings and on the obvious ground that the "gradually rising production over a period of two years" precludes such a possibility. He considers that the payment incentive of the higher group earnings may play some small part, but proceeds to state his conviction that the results are mainly due to changes in mental attitude. . . .

. . . Undoubtedly, there had been a remarkable change of mental attitude in the group. This showed in their recurrent conferences with high executive authorities. At first shy and uneasy, silent and perhaps somewhat suspicious of the Company's intention, later their attitude is marked by confidence and candor. Before every change of programme, the group is consulted. Their comments are listened to and discussed; sometimes their objections are allowed to negative a suggestion. The group unquestionably develops a sense of participation in the critical determinations and becomes something of a social unit. This developing social unity is illustrated by the entertainment of each other in their respective homes, especially operatives one, two, three, and four. . . .

The most significant change that the Western Electric Company introduced into its "test room" bore only a casual relation to the experimental changes. What the Company actually did for the group was to reconstruct entirely its whole industrial situation. Miss May Smith has wisely observed that the repetition work is "a thread of the total pattern," but "is not the total pattern." The Company, in the interest of developing a new form of scientific control—namely, measurement and accurate observation—incidentally altered the total pattern, in Miss Smith's analogy, and then experimented with that thread which, in this instance, was the work of assembling relays. The consequence was that there was a period during which the individual workers and the group had to re-adapt themselves to a new industrial milieu, a milieu in which their own self-determination and their social well-being ranked first and the work was incidental.

CONCEPTUALIZING WORK

8

The Division of Labor

Harry Braverman

The earliest innovative principle of the capitalist mode of production was the manufacturing division of labor, and in one form or another the division of labor has remained the fundamental principle of industrial organization. The division of labor in capitalist industry is not at all identical with the phenomenon of the distribution of tasks, crafts, or specialties of production throughout society, for while all known societies have divided their work into productive specialties, no society before capitalism systematically subdivided the work of each productive specialty into limited operations. This form of the division of labor becomes generalized only with capitalism. . . .

Our concern at this point, therefore, is not with the division of labor in society at large, but within the enterprise; not with the distribution of labor among various industries and occupations, but with the breakdown of occupations and industrial processes; not with the division of labor in "production in general," but within the capitalist mode of production in particular. It is not "pure technique" that concerns us, but rather the marriage of technique with the special needs of capital.

The division of labor in production begins with the *analysis of the labor process—*

that is to say, the separation of the work of production into its constituent elements. But this, in itself, is not what brings into being the detail worker. Such an analysis or separation, in fact, is characteristic in every labor process organized by workers to suit their own needs.

For example, a tinsmith makes a funnel: he draws the elevation view on sheetmetal, and from this develops the outline of an unrolled funnel and its bottom spout. He then cuts out each piece with snips and shears, rolls it to its proper shape, and crimps or rivets the seams. He then rolls the top edge, solders the seams, solders on a hanging ring, washes away the acid used in soldering, and rounds the funnel to its final shape. But when he applies the same process to a quantity of identical funnels, his mode of operation changes. Instead of laying out the work directly on the material, he makes a pattern and uses it to mark off the total quantity of funnels needed; then he cuts them all out, one after the other, rolls them, etc. In this case, instead of making a single funnel in the course of an hour or two, he spends hours or even days on each step of the process, creating in each case fixtures, clamps, devices, etc. which would not be worth making for a single funnel but which, where a sufficiently large quantity of funnels is to be made, speed each step sufficiently so that the saving justifies the extra outlay of time. Quantities, he has discovered, will be produced with less trouble and greater economy of time in this way than by finishing each funnel individually before starting the next.

In the same way a bookkeeper whose job it is to make out bills and maintain office records against their future collection will, if he or she works for a lawyer who has only a few clients at a time, prepare a bill and post it at once to the proper accounts and the customer statement. But if there are hundreds of bills each month, the bookkeeper will accumulate them and spend a full day or two, from time to time, posting them to the proper accounts. Some of these postings will now be made by daily, weekly, or monthly totals instead of bill by bill, a practice which saves a great deal of labor when large quantities are involved; at the same time, the bookkeeper will now make use of other shortcuts or aids, which become practicable when operations are analyzed or broken up in this way, such as specially prepared ledger cards, or carbon forms which combine into a single operation the posting to the customer's account and the preparation of a monthly statement.

Such methods of analysis of the labor process and its division into constituent elements have always been and are to this day common in all trades and crafts, and represent the first form of the subdivision of labor in detail. It is clear that they satisfy, essentially if not fully, the three advantages of the division of labor given by Adam Smith in his famous discussion in the first chapter of *The Wealth of Nations:*

This great increase in the quantity of work, which, in consequence of the division of labour, the same number of people are capable of performing, is owing to three different circumstances; first, to the increase of dexterity in every particular workman; secondly, to the saving of the time which is commonly lost in passing from one species of work to another; and lastly, to the invention of a great number of machines which facilitate and abridge labour, and enable one man to do the work of many.

The example which Smith gives is the making of pins, and his description is as follows:

One man draws out the wire, another straightens it, a third cuts it, a fourth points it, a fifth grinds it at the top for receiving the head; to make the head requires two or three distinct operations; to put it on, is a peculiar business, to whiten the pins is another; it is even a trade by itself to put them into the paper; and the important business of making a pin is, in this manner, divided into about eighteen distinct operations, which, in some manufactories, are all performed by distinct hands, though in others the same man will sometimes perform two or three of them.

In this example, the division of labor is carried one step further than in the examples of the tinsmith and the bookkeeper. Not only are the operations separated from each other, but *they are assigned to different workers.* Here we have not just the analysis of the labor process but the creation of the detail worker. Both steps depend upon the scale of production: without sufficient quantities they are impracticable. Each step represents a saving in labor time. The greatest saving is embodied in the analysis of the process, and a further saving, the extent varying with the nature of the process, is to be found in the separation of operations among different workers.

The worker may break the process down, but he never voluntarily converts himself into a lifelong detail worker. This is the contribution of the capitalist, who sees no reason why, if so much is to be gained from the first step—analysis—and something more gained from the second—breakdown among workers—he should not take the second step as well as the first. That the first step breaks up only the process, while the second dismembers the worker as well, means nothing to the capitalist, and all the less since, in destroying the craft as a process under the control of the worker, he reconstitutes it as a process under his own control. He can now count his gains in a double sense, not only in productivity but in management control, since that which mortally injures the worker is in this case advantageous to him.

The effect of these advantages is heightened by still another which, while it is given surprisingly little mention in economic literature, is certainly the most compelling reason of all for the immense popularity of the division of tasks among workers in the capitalist mode of production, and for its rapid spread. It was not formulated clearly nor emphasized strongly until a half-century after Smith, by Charles Babbage.

In "On the Division of Labour," Chapter XIX of his *On the Economy of Machinery and Manufactures,* the first edition of which was published in 1832, Babbage noted that "the most important and influential cause [of savings from the division of labor] has been altogether unnoticed." He recapitulates the classic arguments of William Petty, Adam Smith, and the other political economists, quotes from Smith the passage reproduced above about the "three different circumstances" of the division of labor which add to the productivity of labor, and continues:

> Now, although all these are important causes, and each has its influence on the result; yet it appears to me, that any explanation of the cheapness of manufactured articles, as consequent upon the division of labour, would be incomplete if the following principle were omitted to be stated.

> *That the master manufacturer, by dividing the work to be executed into different processes, each requiring different degrees of skill or of force, can purchase exactly that precise quantity of both which is necessary for each process; whereas, if the whole work were executed by one workman, that person must possess sufficient skill to perform the most difficult, and sufficient strength to execute the most laborious, of the operations into which the art is divided.*

To put this all-important principle another way, in a society based upon the purchase and sale of labor power, dividing the craft cheapens its individual parts. To clarify this point, Babbage gives us an example drawn, like Smith's, from pin manufacture. He presents a table for the labor employed, by type (that is, by age and sex) and by pay, in the English manufacture of those pins known in his day as "Elevens."

Drawing wire	Man	3s. 3d. per day
Straightening wire	Woman	1s. 0d.
	Girl	0s. 6d.
Pointing	Man	5s. 3d.
Twisting and cutting heads	Boy	0s. 4½d.
	Man	5s. 4½d.
Heading	Woman	1s. 3d.
Tinning or whitening	Man	6s. 0d.
	Woman	3s. 0d.
Papering	Woman	1s. 6d.

It is clear from this tabulation, as Babbage points out, that if the minimum pay for a craftsman capable of performing all operations is no more than the highest pay in the above listing, and if such craftsmen are employed exclusively, then the labor costs of manufacture would be more than doubled, *even if the very same division of labor were employed and even if the craftsmen produced pins at the very same speed as the detail workers.*

Let us add another and later example, taken from the first assembly line in American industry, the meatpacking conveyor (actually a *disassembly* line). J. R. Commons has realistically included in this description, along with the usual details, the rates of pay of the workers:

> It would be difficult to find another industry where division of labor has been so ingeniously and microscopically worked out. The animal has been surveyed and laid off like a map; and the men have been classified in over thirty specialties and twenty rates of pay, from 16 cents to 50 cents an hour. The 50-cent man is restricted to using the knife on the most delicate parts of the hide (floorman) or to using the ax in splitting the backbone (splitter); and wherever a less-skilled man can be slipped in at 18 cents, 18½ cents, 20 cents, 21 cents, 22½ cents, 24 cents, 25 cents, and so on, a place is made for him, and an occupation mapped out. In working on the hide alone there are nine positions, at eight different rates of pay. A 20-cent man pulls off the tail, a 22½-cent man pounds off another part where good leather is not found, and the knife of the 40-cent man cuts a different texture and has a different "feel" from that of the 50-cent man.

Babbage's principle is fundamental to the evolution of the division of labor in capitalist society. It gives expression not to a technical aspect of the division of labor, but to its social aspect. Insofar as the labor process may be dissociated, it may be separated into elements some of which are simpler than others and each of which is simpler than the whole. Translated into market terms, this means that the labor power capable of performing the process may be purchased more cheaply as dissociated elements than as a capacity integrated in a single worker. Applied first to the handicrafts and then to the mechanical crafts, Babbage's principle eventually becomes the underlying force governing all forms of work in capitalist society, no matter in what setting or at what hierarchical level.

In the mythology of capitalism, the Babbage principle is presented as an effort to "preserve scarce skills" by putting qualified workers to tasks which "only they can perform," and not wasting "social resources." It is presented as a response to "shortages" of skilled workers or technically trained people, whose time is best used "efficiently" for the advantage of "society." But however much this principle may manifest itself at times in the form of a response to the scarcity of skilled labor—for example, during wars or other periods of rapid expansion of production—this apology is on the whole false. The capitalist mode of production systematically destroys all-around skills where they exist, and brings into being skills and occupations that correspond to its needs. Technical capacities are henceforth distributed on a strict "need to know" basis. The generalized distribution of knowledge of the productive process among all its participants becomes, from this point on, not merely "unnecessary," but a positive barrier to the functioning of the capitalist mode of production.

Labor power has become a commodity. Its uses are no longer organized according to the needs and desires of those who sell it, but rather according to the needs of its purchasers, who are, primarily, employers seeking to expand the value of their capital. And it is the special and permanent interest of these purchasers to cheapen this commodity. The most common mode of cheapening labor power is exemplified by the Babbage principle: break it up into its simplest elements. And, as the capitalist mode of production creates a working population suitable to its needs, the Babbage principle is, by the very shape of this "labor market," enforced upon the capitalists themselves.

Every step in the labor process is divorced, so far as possible, from special knowledge and training and reduced to simple labor. Meanwhile, the relatively few persons for whom special knowledge and training are reserved are freed so far as possible from the obligations of simple labor. In this way, a structure is given to all labor processes that at its extremes polarizes those whose time is infinitely valuable and those whose time is worth almost nothing. This might even be called the general law of the capitalist division of labor. It is not the sole force acting upon the organization of work, but it is certainly the most powerful and general. Its results, more or less advanced in every industry and occupation, give massive testimony to its validity. It shapes not only work, but populations as well, because over the long run it creates that mass of simple labor which is the primary feature of populations in developed capitalist countries.

9

Contested Terrain
The Transformation of the Workplace in the Twentieth Century

Richard C. Edwards

Roughly one hundred million Americans must work for a living. About ninety-five million of them, when they can find jobs, work for someone else. Three of those workers, who reflect both the unity and the diversity of the American working class, are Maureen Agnati, Fred Doyal, and Stanley Miller. These three share a condition common to all workers, past and present: they must sell their labor time to support themselves. Yet they also lead very different work lives, and the differences contain in kernel form the evolving history of work in twentieth-century America. Indeed, the study of how their jobs came to be so different goes far toward explaining the present weakness and future potential of the American working class.

Maureen Agnati assembles coils at Digitex, Incorporated, a small Boston-area manufacturer of electronics components.[1] Digitex's founder established the firm in the 1930s and continues to manage it today. The company employs about 450 people, four-fifths of whom are production workers. The labor force is mainly female and Portuguese, with a sprinkling of other ethnic workers—Italian, Haitian, Greek, Polish, and Asian.

Maureen is a white, twenty-six-year-old mother of two girls. Her husband Tom works in a warehouse at a nearby sheet-metal company. Maureen has worked for Digitex off and on for a number of years; she started after her junior year in high school, quit at nineteen when her first child was born, returned for one month to get Christmas money, quit again, and then returned again to work the spring months until the end of her older daughter's school term. Frequent job changes do not seem to be any problem at Digitex, and indeed, in some ways the company appears to encourage high turnover.

Maureen's work involves winding coil forms with copper wire. To do this, Maureen operates a machine that counts and controls the number of wraps put on each collar. She does the same task all day.

Nearly half of Digitex's workers are on the piece-rate system, which means that their wages partly depend on how fast they work. The company pays both a guaranteed base wage and a piece-rate bonus on top of the base. But the guaranteed wage is always low—roughly equal to the legal minimum wage—so the worker's attention turns to making the bonus. To be eligible for extra pay, a worker must exceed the particular job's "rate"; that is, the assigned minimum level of output needed to trigger the incentive system. The worker then earns a bonus depending on how many units she produces above the rate. The problem is that the rates are high and are often changed. For example, when Maureen returned to work this last time, she found that the rates were so "tight" that she frequently did not make any incentive pay at all. It seems to be common that when workers begin to make large premiums, the time-study man appears to "restudy" the job, and the rates cause a great deal of resentment.

The pay system causes resentment among the hourly workers too. The company keeps most of the information about wages secret; a worker cannot learn, for example, what her job's top pay is, how the job is classified, or even what the wage schedule is. Often two workers will discov-

er that, while they are doing nearly the same work, their pay differs greatly.

As for the conditions of work, employees are watched constantly, like children in a classroom. The design of the machinery pretty much dictates what tasks have to be done at each work station, but in other ways the foreman actively directs the work. One way he does this is by assigning workers to particular stations. For example, Maureen was not hired specifically for "winding" and when she returned to work her foreman simply put her at the station. But he can change job assignments whenever he wishes, and he often moves people around. Since some jobs have easy rates and others have tight ones, the job he assigns Maureen to will determine both how much she makes and how hard she has to work.

The foreman and supervisors at Digitex have other ways of directing the work, too. They watch closely over the hours and pace of work, and they ring a bell to signal the beginning and end of work breaks. Workers must get permission to make phone calls or leave the work area. And despite the piece-rate system (which might seem to leave it up to the individual worker to determine how fast to work and hence how much pay she would receive), the bosses take a direct hand in speeding up production; workers who talk to nearby workers, who fail to make the rates, or who return late from breaks or lunch are likely to be targets for reprimands and threats. The various bosses (foremen, general foreman, and other officials) spend their days walking among the workers, noting and correcting any laggard performance.

The supervisors' immediate role in directing production gives them considerable power, of course, yet their full power springs from other sources as well. No real grievance process exists at Digitex, and supervisors can dismiss workers on the spot. Less drastically, foremen maintain a certain degree of control because they must approve any "benefits" the workers receive. They must approve in advance any requests for time off to attend a funeral, see a doctor, and so on. For hourly workers, the supervisors determine any pay raises; since the wage schedules are secret, supervisors can choose when and whom to reward, and in what amount. For piece-rate workers, who are not eligible for raises, the supervisors' decisions on rejects—what to count as faulty output and whether to penalize the workers for it—weigh heavily in bonus calculations. Foremen also choose favored workers for the opportunity to earn overtime pay. And when business falls off and the company needs to reduce its workforce, no seniority or other considerations intervene; the foremen decide which workers to lay off. Through these powers, supervisors effectively rule over all aspects of factory life. Getting on the foreman's good side means much; being on his bad side tends to make life miserable.

Maureen, like other production workers at Digitex, has few prospects for advancing beyond her current position. All people working under the piece-rate system, regardless of seniority, earn the same base pay. There are a few supervisory slots, but these jobs are necessarily limited in number and are currently filled. There simply is no place for them to grow. This fact perhaps accounts for the high turnover at Digitex: over half the employees have worked for the company for less than three years, and Maureen's pattern of frequently quitting her job does not seem to be unusual.

There has recently been a bitter struggle to build a union at Digitex. Maureen's attitude—"We could sure use one around here, I'll tell you that"—was perhaps typical, but the real issue was whether the company's powers of intimidation would prove stronger than the workers' desire for better conditions. Initially, the union won a federally monitored election to be the workers' bargaining agent.

The company's hostility toward the union persisted, however; after signing an initial contract with the union it launched a vicious campaign to decertify the union. The second time around, the union lost. No union exists at Digitex today.

Fred Doyal works as process control inspector at General Electric's Ashland (Massachusetts) assembly plant. The plant used to be run by Telechron Clock Company, a small independent firm, but GE bought it out. Today, the plant's thousand or so workers manufacture small electrical motors, the kind used in clocks, kitchen timers, and other very small appliances. The plant is highly automated, and slightly over half of its workers are women.

Fred operates sound-testing machinery to check the motors' noise levels. He monitors two hundred or so motors a day. The procedure is routine—he picks up the motors from the assembly area, returns to the "silent room," mounts them on the decibel counter, and records the result—and he performs virtually the same sequence every day. GE pays Fred about $13,000 a year.

There is little need for the supervisor to direct the work pace; the machinery does that, and when "you come on the job, you learn that routine; unless there is some change in that routine, the foreman would not be coming to you and telling you what to do; he just expects you (and you do) to know your daily routine, when you do repetitious work." In fact, the foreman generally appears only when a special situation arises, such as defective materials or machine breakdown. Other than that, workers mainly have contact with their bosses on disciplinary problems.

Evaluation and discipline do bring in the supervisors, but the union's presence tends to restrict their power. In a sense, the company evaluates Fred's work daily: "Everything I do, I record, and I turn in daily reports." The reports provide information not only about the decibel level of the motors but also coincidentally about Fred's output. Yet he is very confident that if he does a reasonable amount of work, his job will be secure. If the company tried to fire him, it would have to demonstrate to an outside arbitrator that its action is justified. In fact, any time the company takes disciplinary action, the union contract says that arbitration is automatic. In arbitration, Fred notes, the union has found that "discharge on a long-service employee, unless there's a horrendous record on this person, or if it was for something like striking a supervisor or stealing, discharge would be considered too severe by an arbitrator. Usually, you know? Don't bet on it, but that's the usual case."

There are, of course, lesser penalties. The disciplinary procedure begins with the written warning, and when the worker gets three written warnings, he or she can be suspended. Fred himself has been suspended for two days for "refusing to do a certain type of work." Suspension means the loss of pay, and it is probably the most common discipline at Ashland. Fred has known people who were suspended for up to a week because of absenteeism, and for lesser periods because of tardiness and insubordination.

Fred is in his mid-fifties, and he has worked for GE for thirty years. He started as a stock handler in the Worcester (Massachusetts) plant, moved up to be a group leader in the packing department, then transferred to shipping. At one point he had several employees under him, but he was "knocked off that job in a cutback." When they consolidated the plants he moved to Ashland to work in quality control. Presently he does not supervise anyone.

While Fred was moving up, the company had no formal procedure for filling vacancies. Switching from one job to another depended on "merit and so forth . . . some of it was ass-kissing." Now, however, in a change that Fred traces directly to the com-

ing of the union, a new system prevails. If any job opens up, it must be posted, and everyone can apply for it. Qualifications and seniority are supposed to be taken into account in determining who gets the job. The company usually wants to decide unilaterally who is qualified, but "the union fights the company on this all the way." In fact, in Fred's experience the union is usually successful: "The company, rather than get in a hassle, and if they have no particular bitch against this individual who has the most seniority, the company will give that person the job."

Men do a lot better at Ashland than women. The plant jobs seem quite rigidly stereotyped. Women fill most of the lower-paying positions on the clock-assembly conveyors, while the men tend to get the more skilled jobs elsewhere in the plant. Men's jobs are also more secure. In the event of a partial layoff, any worker in a higher-classified job can bump any other worker of equal or lesser seniority in a lower-classified job; but of course one cannot bump upwards. Women, since they tend to be in the lower classifications, have few others (mainly women) whom they can bump. Men have most of the women to bump.

Fred believes that General Electric has not overlooked the benefits of this system.

> Where that company has made all its money is on the conveyors; that's where they really build the clocks, see—a long assembly conveyor, thirty-five, forty women working on it. Those women are working every minute of the day; those women *really* make money for the company! The company didn't get rich on me, and the older I get, the less rich it's gonna get on me. But they got rich on those women. Those women are there every second, every second of their time is taken up. Now, they have on each of these conveyors what they call a group

leader, and it's a woman, right? . . . These women are *highly* qualified, *highly* skilled, these group leaders. Way underpaid. There's a man that stock-handles the conveyor—man or a boy, whichever you want—he's just a "hunky," picks up boxes and puts them on the conveyor for the girls or moves heavy stuff. That man makes ten to fifteen dollars a week more than a woman who's a group leader.

In the supervisory staff, the sexual stereotyping is even more apparent. There are quite a few bosses, counting all the foremen, general foremen, and higher managers. Yet there are only two women. "There have always been two; not always the same two, but two."

Recently, the rigid sexual division seems to have lessened somewhat, and women have applied for jobs that formerly were off limits. According to Fred, the company is wary of turning them down, because it is worried about a government anti-discrimination suit. (GE subsequently settled the suit, agreeing to pay damages.) The union has made some attempt to change the ratio of women's to men's wages, but Fred acknowledges that it has been "unsuccessful."

At the plant, men and women alike are very concerned about the possibilities of a general layoff. As Fred puts it,

I'll give it to the company; they're great with the public relations bit. GE puts out two, three bulletins a week, and they're always telling those people [the plant's workers] about the foreign competition. What they're trying to do, and they're successful, is getting the idea across that if they don't work harder, if they don't stop taking off days off, and quit taking so much time on their coffee break, and so forth, that they're gonna have to take the plant and move it to Singapore, which, by the way, they have a plant in Singapore that makes clocks. . . . They've

been very successful at this productivity thing, you know. They've scared people with it. This company, like a lot of companies, runs the thing by fear.

Fred is a strong supporter of the union (the United Electrical Workers), and he has from time to time held various official positions in the local. He is completely disillusioned about the AFL-CIO ("They sold out a long time ago"). For him, just following the Democratic Party is not enough: "Any union movement that doesn't have a political philosophy in this country is doomed."

Stanley Harris works as a research chemist at the Polaroid Corporation. "Research chemist" may sound like a high-powered position, and indeed the pay is quite good: Stanley makes about $18,000. But in terms of the actual work involved, the position is more mundane. Stanley's bachelor degree equips him to do only relatively routine laboratory procedures. He cannot choose his own research, and he does not have a special area of expertise. He supervises no one, and instead his own work is done under supervision. Stanley is, in effect, a technical worker.

On first meeting Stanley, one is not surprised to learn of his middle-level occupation. He is white, roughly fifty years old, and seems well educated. Despite the fact that it is the middle of the workday, his proffered hand is clean (and soft). He wears no special work clothes, spurning both the heavy fabrics necessary in production jobs and the suit and tie affected by the managers. In the lab, of course, he wears a white protective smock, but beneath is an unstylish, small-collar Dacron sports shirt and chino pants.

Here and there, traces of a blue-collar background appear. Stanley has a few teeth missing. His speech retains a slight working-class accent, and occasionally his grammar betrays him. He mentions that he lives in Lynn (Massachusetts), an old working-class city outside of Boston.

Stanley's career tells much about the employment system at Polaroid. He joined the company nineteen years ago as a production worker, when he "ran out of money going through college." Having already completed the science curriculum, he went to night school to fulfill his liberal arts requirements while continuing to work at Polaroid. After obtaining his BS degree, he began applying for the research openings advertised on the company's bulletin boards, and since Polaroid's hiring policies give preference to those who are already employees, the company eventually promoted Stanley into one of the lab jobs. These jobs encompass many ranks, from assistant scientist all the way up to senior scientist. Stanley started at the bottom, and his current position, research scientist, appears in the middle of the hierarchy.

In most of the research jobs, the specific work to be done combines a particular product assignment with the general skills and work behavior expected of a research chemist. Stanley's supervisor assigns him a project within the "general sweep of problems, anything having to do with a company product." Stanley then methodically applies standard tests ("the state of the art"), one after the other, until he finds the answer or his supervisor redirects his efforts. Rather than having his workday closely supervised by his boss or directed by a machine, Stanley follows professional work patterns, habits that are, in fact, common to the eight hundred or so other research workers at Polaroid's Tech Square facility.

Stanley's supervisor formally evaluates his work performance in the annual review. Although the evaluation format seems to change frequently—"Right now it is very curt, either 'good,' 'bad,' or 'indifferent'; but in previous years it was something like four pages"—the purpose and importance of the review have not changed. Stanley believes that the evaluation is crucial to his chances for promotion. "It goes to someone who has to okay it, and if he doesn't know you and he sees on a piece of paper 'poor worker,' it hurts you."

The formal evaluations are especially important because, while Stanley's boss assigns him projects and evaluates his work, he has little say in Stanley's promotions or pay raises or discipline. Those decisions are made higher up, by applying the company's rules to the individual's case. As Stanley explains it, the company contributes the formula while the individual provides the numbers, and then somebody "upstairs" just has to do the calculation. The rules for advancement seem pretty clear.

An important illustration of Stanley's point is the company's layoff policy. When demand for Polaroid's cameras fell off during the 1974–1975 recession, the company laid off sixteen hundred workers, about 15 percent of its entire workforce. Such a deep cut could be expected to create lasting insecurity among Polaroid's workers, and it undoubtedly did among the younger workers. But not for Stanley; the company's seniority-based bumping system protects him. If Polaroid eliminates Stanley's current job, he can displace any worker with less seniority in any of the jobs that he has previously held. "I'm not worried because of the fact that I started at the bottom, and so in theory I could bump my way all the way back to the bottom." In Stanley's view, such an enormous economic disaster would be required before layoffs reached him that, "I figure we'll all be out of work."

Stanley summed up his attitude toward unions in one word: "antagonistic." But the reason for his hostility is, perhaps, surprising. "Like all the movements that are idealistic at the beginning, they [unions] have degenerated to where they benefit a select group. . . . I'm not saying the idea is bad, but they have been corrupted." Stanley sees no use for a union in his own job, since, "if I put out, I'll get the rewards; at least, that's what I've found."

Maureen Agnati, Fred Doyal, Stanley Miller. Three different workers, three different ways of organizing work. Today we observe their situations as simply different arrangements in production, but they are in fact endpoints in a long process of capitalist development that has transformed (and continues to transform) the American workplace. The change does not reflect inevitable consequences of modern technology or of industrial society, but rather . . . the transformation occurred because continuing capital accumulation has propelled workers and their employers into virtually perpetual conflict. And while both technology and the requirements of modern social production play a part in the story to come, the roots of this conflict lie in the basic arrangements of capitalist production. . . .

The Dimensions of Control

How much work gets done every hour or every day emerges as a result of the struggle between workers and capitalists. . . . Each side seeks to tip the balance and influence or determine the outcome with the weapons at its disposal. On one side, the workers use hidden or open resistance to protect themselves against the constant pressure for speed-up; on the other side, capitalists employ a variety of sophisticated or brutal devices for tipping the balance their way. But this is not exactly an equal fight, for employers retain their power to hire and fire, and on this foundation they have developed various methods of control by which to organize, shape, and affect the workers' exertions.

Control in this sense differs from coordination, a term that appears more frequently in popular literature describing what managers do, and it may be useful at the outset to distinguish the two. Coordination is required, of course, in all social production, since the product of such production is by definition the result of labor by many persons. Hence, whether a pair of shoes is produced in a Moroccan cobbler's shop, a Chinese commune, or an American factory, it is an inherent technical characteristic of the production process that the persons cutting and tanning the leather must mesh their efforts with those who sew the leather, those who attach the heels, and others. Without such coordinations, production would be haphazard, wasteful, and—where products more complex than shoes are involved—probably impossible as well. Hence, coordination of social production is essential.

Coordination may be achieved in a variety of ways, however, and the differences are crucial. Coordination may be achieved by tradition—through long-established ways of doing the work and the passing on of these trade secrets from master to apprentices. Or it may be achieved directly by the producers themselves, as occurs when the members of a cooperative or commune discuss their parts in the production process to ensure that their tasks are harmonized. As the scale of production increases, workers may designate one member (or even choose someone from the outside) to act as a full-time coordinator of their interests, thus establishing a manager. As long as the managerial staff, no matter how large, remains accountable to the producers themselves, we may properly speak of their efforts as "coordination" or "administration."

A different type of coordination characterizes capitalist workplaces, however; in capitalist production, labor power is purchased, and with that purchase—as with the purchase of every commodity in a capitalist economy—goes the right to designate the use (consumption) of the object bought. Hence there is a presumption, indeed a contractual right backed by legal force, for the capitalist, as owner of the purchased labor power, to direct its use. A corollary presumption (again backed by legal force) follows: that the workers whose labor power has been purchased have no right to participate in the conception and planning of production. Coordination occurs in capitalist production as it must inevitably occur in all social production, but it necessarily takes the specific form of top-down coordination, for the exercise of which the top (capitalists) must be able to control the bottom (workers). In analyzing capitalist production, then, it is more appropriate to speak of control than of coordination, although of course, control is a means of coordination.

"Control" is here defined as the ability of capitalists and/or managers to obtain desired work behavior from workers. Such ability exists in greater or lesser degrees, depending upon the relative strength of workers and their bosses. As long as capitalist production continues, control exists to some degree, and the crucial questions are: to what degree? how is control obtained? and how does control lead to or inhibit resistance on a wider scale? At one extreme, capitalists try to avoid strikes, sit-downs, and other militant actions that stop production; but equally important to their success, they attempt to extract, day by day, greater amounts of labor for a given amount of labor power.

In what follows, the *system of control* (in other words, the social relations of production within the firm) are thought of as a way in which three elements are coordinated:

1. Direction, or a mechanism or method by which the employer directs work tasks, specifying what needs to be done, in what order, with what degree of precision or accuracy, and in what period of time.

2. Evaluation, or a procedure whereby the employer supervises and evaluates to correct mistakes or other failures in production, to assess each worker's performance, and to identify individual workers or group of workers who are not performing work tasks adequately.

3. Discipline, or an apparatus that the employer uses to discipline and reward workers, in order to elicit cooperation and enforce compliance with the capitalist's direction of the labor process.

The Types of Control

Systems of control in the firm have undergone dramatic changes in response to changes in the firm's size, operations, and environment and in the workers' success in imposing their own goals at the workplace. The new forms did not emerge as sharp, discrete discontinuities in historical evolution, but neither were they simply points in a smooth and inevitable evolution. Rather, each transformation occurred as a resolution of intensifying conflict and contradiction in the firm's operations. Pressures built up, making the old forms of control untenable. The period of increasing tension was followed by a relatively rapid process of discovery, experimentation, and implementation, in which new systems of control were substituted for the older, more primitive ones. Once instituted, these new relations tend to persist until they no longer effectively contain worker resistance or until further changes occur in the firm's operations.

In the nineteenth century, most businesses were small and were subject to the relatively tight discipline of substantial competition in product markets. The typical firm had few resources and little energy to invest in creating more sophisticated management structures. A single entrepreneur, usually flanked by a small coterie of fore-men and managers, ruled the firm. These bosses exercised power personally, interven-ing in the labor process often to exhort workers, bully and threaten them, reward good performance, hire and fire on the spot, favor loyal workers, and generally act as despots, benevolent or otherwise. They had a direct stake in translating labor power into labor, and they combined both incentives and sanctions in an idiosyncratic and unsys-tematic mix. There was little structure to the way power was exercised, and workers were often treated arbitrarily. Since work-forces were small and the boss was both close and powerful, workers had limited success when they tried to oppose his rule. This system of "simple" control survives today in the small-business sector of the American economy, where it has necessarily been amended by the passage of time and by the borrowings of management practices from the more advanced corporate sector, but it retains its essential principles and mode of operation. It is the system of simple control that governs Maureen Agnati's job at Digitex.

Near the end of the nineteenth century, the tendencies toward concentration of eco-nomic resources undermined simple control; while firms' needs for control increased, the efficacy of simple control declined. The need for coordination appeared to increase not only with the complexity of the product but also with the scale of production. By bring-ing under one corporate roof what were for-merly small independent groups linked through the market, the corporation more than proportionately raised the degree of coordination needed. Production assumed an increasingly social character, requiring greater "social" planning and implying an increased need for control. But as firms began to employ thousands of workers, the distance between capitalists and workers expanded, and the intervening space was filled by growing numbers of foremen, gen-eral foremen, supervisors, superintendents, and other minor officials. Whereas petty tyranny had been more or less successful when conducted by entrepreneurs (or fore-men close to them), the system did not work well when staffed by hired bosses. The fore-men came into increasingly severe conflict with both their bosses and their workers.

The workers themselves resisted speed-up and arbitrary rule more successfully, since they were now concentrated by the very growth of the enterprise. From the Home-stead and Pullman strikes to the great 1919–1920 steel strike, workers fought with their bosses over control of the actual process of production. The maturing labor move-ment and an emergent Socialist Party orga-nized the first serious challenge to capitalist rule. Intensifying conflict in society at large and the specific contradictions of simple con-trol in the workplace combined to produce an acute crisis of control on the shop floor.

The large corporations fashioned the most far-reaching response to this crisis. During the conflict, big employers joined small ones in supporting direct repression of their adversaries. But the large corporations also began to move in systematic ways to reorganize work. They confronted the most serious problems of control, but they also commanded the greatest resources with which to attack the problems. Their size and their substantial market power released them from the tight grip of the short-run market discipline and made possible for the first time planning in the service of long-term profits. The initial steps taken by large companies—welfare capitalism, scientific management, and company unions—consti-tuted experiments, trials with serious inher-ent errors, but useful learning experiences nonetheless. In retrospect, these efforts appear as beginnings in the corporations' larger project of establishing more secure control over the labor process.

Large firms developed methods of organization that are more formalized and more consciously contrived than simple control; they are "structural" forms of control. Two possibilities existed: more formal, consciously contrived controls could be embedded in either the physical structure of the labor process (producing "technical" control) or in its social structure (producing "bureaucratic" control). In time, employers used both, for they found that the new systems made control more institutional and hence less visible to workers, and they also provided a means for capitalists to control the "intermediate layers," those extended lines of supervision and power.

Technical control emerged from employers' experiences in attempting to control the production (or blue-collar) operations of the firm. The assembly line came to be the classic image, but the actual application of technical control was much broader. Machinery itself directed the labor process and set the pace. For a time, employers had the best of two worlds. Inside the firm, technical control turned the tide of conflict in their favor, reducing workers to attendants of prepaced machinery; externally, the system strengthened the employer's hands by expanding the number of potential substitute workers. But as factory workers in the late 1930s struck back with sit-downs, their action exposed the deep dangers to employers in thus linking all workers' labor together in one technical apparatus. The conflict at the workplace propelled labor into its "giant step," the CIO.

These forces have produced today a second type of work organization. Whereas simple control persists in the small firms of the industrial periphery, in large firms, especially those in the mass-production industries, work is subject to technical control. The system is mutually administered by management and (as a junior partner) unions. Jobs in the GE plant where Fred Doyal works fit this pattern.

There exists a third method for organizing work, and it too appeared in the large firms. This system, bureaucratic control, rests on the principle of embedding control in the social structure or the social relations of the workplace. The defining feature of bureaucratic control is the institutionalization of hierarchical power. "Rule of law"—the firm's law—replaces "rule by supervisor command" in the direction of work, the procedures for evaluating workers' performance, and the exercise of the firm's sanctions and rewards; supervisors and workers alike become subject to the dictates of "company policy." Work becomes highly stratified; each job is given its distinct title and description; and impersonal rules govern promotion. "Stick with the corporation," the worker is told, "and you can ascend up the ladder." The company promises the workers a *career*.

Bureaucratic control originated in employers' attempts to subject nonproduction workers to more strict control, but its success impelled firms to apply the system more broadly than just to the white-collar staff. Especially in the last three decades, bureaucratic control has appeared as the organizing principle in both production and nonproduction jobs in many large firms, and not the least of its attractions is that the system has proven especially effective in forestalling unionism. Stanley Miller's job at Polaroid is subject to bureaucratic control.

Continuing conflict in the workplace and employers' attempts to contain it have thus brought the modern American working class under the sway of three quite different systems for organizing and controlling their work: simple control, technical control (with union participation), and bureaucratic control. Of course, the specific labor processes vary greatly: Maureen Agnati's coil wrapper might have been a typewriter or a cash register, Fred Doyal's job might have been in a tire plant or a tractor factory, and Stanley Miller's work might have involved being a supervisor or skilled craftsman. Yet within this variety of concrete labors, the three patterns for organizing work prevail.

The typology of control embodies both the pattern of historical evolution and the array of contemporary methods of organizing work. On the one hand, each form of control corresponds to a definite stage in the development of the representative or most important firms; in this sense structural control succeeded simple control and bureaucratic control succeeded technical control, and the systems of control correspond to or characterize stages of capitalism. On the other hand, capitalist production has developed unevenly, with some sectors pushing far in advance of other sectors, and so each type of control represents an alternate method of organizing work; so long as uneven development produces disparate circumstances, alternate methods will coexist.

10

The Managed Heart

Arlie Russell Hochschild

The one area of her occupational life in which she might be "free to act," the area of her own personality, must now also be managed, must become the alert yet obsequious instrument by which goods are distributed.

—C. WRIGHT MILLS

In a section in *Das Kapital* entitled "The Working Day," Karl Marx examines depositions submitted in 1863 to the Children's Employment Commission in England. One deposition was given by the mother of a child laborer in a wallpaper factory: "When he was seven years old I used to carry him [to work] on my back to and fro through the snow, and he used to work 16 hours a day.... I have often knelt down to feed him, as he stood by the machine, for he could not leave it or stop." Fed meals as he worked, as a steam engine is fed coal and water, this child was "an instrument of labor."[1] Marx questioned how many hours a day it was fair to use a human being as an instrument, and how much pay for being an instrument was fair, considering the profits that factory owners made. But he was also concerned with something he thought more fundamental: the human cost of becoming an "instrument of labor" at all.

On another continent 117 years later, a twenty-year-old flight attendant trainee sat with 122 others listening to a pilot speak in the auditorium of the Delta Airlines Stewardess Training Center. Even by modern

Excerpts from *The Managed Heart* by Arlie Russell Hochschild. 1983. Berkeley, CA: University of California Press. Copyright © 1983, The Regents of the University of California. Reprinted by permission.

American standards, and certainly by standards for women's work, she had landed an excellent job. The 1980 pay scale began at $850 a month for the first six months and would increase within seven years to about $20,000 a year. Health and accident insurance is provided, and the hours are good.*

The young trainee sitting next to me wrote on her notepad, "Important to smile. Don't forget smile." The admonition came from the speaker in the front of the room, a crewcut pilot in his early fifties, speaking in a Southern drawl: "Now girls, I want you to go out there and really *smile*. Your smile is your biggest *asset*. I want you to go out there and use it. Smile. *Really* smile. Really *lay it on*."

The pilot spoke of the smile as the *flight attendant's* asset. But as novices like the one next to me move through training, the value of a personal smile is groomed to reflect the company's disposition—its confidence that its planes will not crash, its reassurance that departures and arrivals will be on time, its welcome and its invitation to return. Trainers take it as their job to attach to the trainee's smile an attitude, a viewpoint, a rhythm of feeling that is, as they often say, "professional." This deeper extension of the professional smile is not always easy to retract at the end of the workday, as one worker in her first year at World Airways noted: "Sometimes I come off a long trip in a state of utter exhaustion, but I find I can't relax. I giggle a lot, I chatter, I call friends. It's as if I can't release myself from an artificially created elation that kept me 'up' on the trip. I hope to be able to come down from it better as I get better at the job."

---

*For stylistic convenience, I shall use the pronoun "she" when referring to a flight attendant, except when a specific male flight attendant is being discussed. Otherwise I shall try to avoid verbally excluding either gender.

As the PSA jingle says, "Our smiles are not just painted on." Our flight attendants' smiles, the company emphasizes, will be more human than the phony smiles you're resigned to seeing on people who are paid to smile. There is a smile-like strip of paint on the nose of each PSA plane. Indeed, the plane and the flight attendant advertise each other. The radio advertisement goes on to promise not just smiles and service but a travel experience of real happiness and calm. Seen in one way, this is no more than delivering a service. Seen in another, it estranges workers from their own smiles and convinces customers that on-the-job behavior is calculated. Now that advertisements, training, notions of professionalism, and dollar bills have intervened between the smiler and the smiled upon, it takes an extra effort to imagine that spontaneous warmth can exist in uniform—because companies now advertise spontaneous warmth, too.

At first glance, it might seem that the circumstances of the nineteenth-century factory child and the twentieth-century flight attendant could not be more different. To the boy's mother, to Marx, to the members of the Children's Employment Commission, perhaps to the manager of the wallpaper factory, and almost certainly to the contemporary reader, the boy was a victim, even a symbol, of the brutalizing conditions of his time. We might imagine that he had an emotional half-life, conscious of little more than fatigue, hunger, and boredom. On the other hand, the flight attendant enjoys the upper-class freedom to travel, and she participates in the glamour she creates for others. She is the envy of clerks in duller, less well-paid jobs.

But a close examination of the differences between the two can lead us to some unexpected common ground. On the surface there is a difference in how we know what labor actually produces. How could the worker in the wallpaper factory tell when his job was done? Count the rolls of wallpaper; a good has been produced. How can the flight attendant tell when her job is done? A service has been produced; the customer seems content. In the case of the flight attendant, the *emotional style of offering the service is part of the service itself,* in a way that loving or hating wallpaper is not a part of producing wallpaper. Seeming to "love the job" becomes part of the job; and actually trying to love it, and to enjoy the customers, helps the worker in this effort.

In processing people, the product is a state of mind. Like firms in other industries, airline companies are ranked according to the quality of service their personnel offer. Egon Ronay's yearly *Lucas Guide* offers such a ranking; besides being sold in airports and drugstores and reported in newspapers, it is cited in management memoranda and passed down to those who train and supervise flight attendants. Because it influences consumers, airline companies use it in setting their criteria for successful job performance by a flight attendant. In 1980 the *Lucas Guide* ranked Delta Airlines first in service out of fourteen airlines that fly regularly between the United States and both Canada and the British Isles. Its report on Delta included passages like this:

> [Drinks were served] not only with a smile but with concerned enquiry such as, "Anything else I can get you, madam?" The atmosphere was that of a civilized party—with the passengers, in response, behaving like civilized guests. . . . Once or twice our inspectors tested stewardesses by being deliberately exacting, but they were never roused, and at the end of the flight they lined up to say farewell with undiminished brightness. . . .
>
> [Passengers are] quick to detect strained or forced smiles, and they come

aboard wanting to *enjoy* the flight. One of us looked forward to his next trip on Delta "because it's fun." Surely that is how passengers ought to feel."[2]

The work done by the boy in the wallpaper factory called for a coordination of mind and arm, mind and finger, and mind and shoulder. We refer to it simply as physical labor. The flight attendant does physical labor when she pushes heavy meal carts through the aisles, and she does mental work when she prepares for and actually organizes emergency landings and evacuations. But in the course of doing this physical and mental labor, she is also doing something more, something I define as *emotional labor.** This labor requires one to induce or suppress feeling in order to sustain the outward countenance that produces the proper state of mind in others—in this case, the sense of being cared for in a convivial and safe place. This kind of labor calls for a coordination of mind and feeling, and it sometimes draws on a source of self that we honor as deep and integral to our individuality.

Beneath the difference between physical and emotional labor there lies a similarity in the possible cost of doing the work: the worker can become estranged or alienated from an aspect of self—either the body or the margins of the soul—that is *used* to do the work. The factory boy's arm functioned like a piece of machinery used to produce wallpaper. His employer, regarding that arm as an instrument, claimed control over its speed and motions. In this situation, what

---

*I use the term *emotional labor* to mean the management of feeling to create a publicly observable facial and bodily display; emotional labor is sold for a wage and therefore has *exchange value.* I use the synonymous terms *emotion work* or *emotion management* to refer to these same acts done in a private context where they have *use value.*

was the relation between the boy's arm and his mind? Was his arm in any meaningful sense his *own?*

This is an old issue, but as the comparison with airline attendants suggests, it is still very much alive. If we can become alienated from goods in a goods-producing society, we can become alienated from service in a service-producing society. This is what C. Wright Mills, one of our keenest social observers, meant when he wrote in 1956, "We need to characterize American society of the mid-twentieth century in more psychological terms, for now the problems that concern us most border on the psychiatric."[3]

When she came off the job, what relation had the flight attendant to the "artificial elation" she had induced on the job? In what sense was it her *own* elation on the job? The company lays claim not simply to her physical motions—how she handles food trays—but to her emotional actions and the way they show in the ease of a smile. The workers I talked to often spoke of their smiles as being *on* them but not *of* them. They were seen as an extension of the make-up, the uniform, the recorded music, the soothing pastel colors of the airplane decor, and the daytime drinks, which taken together orchestrate the mood of the passengers. The final commodity is not a certain number of smiles to be counted like rolls of wallpaper. For the flight attendant, the smiles are a *part of her work,* a part that requires her to coordinate self and feeling so that the work seems to be effortless. To show that the enjoyment takes effort is to do the job poorly. Similarly, part of the job is to disguise fatigue and irritation, for otherwise the labor would show in an unseemly way, and the product—passenger contentment—would be damaged.* Because it is easier to disguise fatigue and irritation if they can be banished altogether,

at least for brief periods, this feat calls for emotional labor.

The reason for comparing these dissimilar jobs is that the modern assembly-line worker has for some time been an outmoded symbol of modern industrial labor; fewer than 6 percent of workers now work on assembly lines. Another kind of labor has now come into symbolic prominence—the voice-to-voice or face-to-face delivery of service—and the flight attendant is an appropriate model for it. There have always been public-service jobs, of course; what is new is that they are now socially engineered and thoroughly organized from the top. Though the flight attendant's job is no worse and in many ways better than other service jobs, it makes the worker more vulnerable to the social engineering of her emotional labor and reduces her control over that labor. Her problems, therefore, may be a sign of what is to come in other such jobs.

Emotional labor is potentially good. No customer wants to deal with a surly waitress, a crabby bank clerk, or a flight attendant who avoids eye contact in order to avoid getting a request. Lapses in courtesy by those paid to be courteous are very real and fairly common. What they show us is how fragile public civility really is. We are brought back to the question of what the social carpet actu-

---

*Like a commodity, service that calls for emotional labor is subject to the laws of supply and demand. Recently the demand for this labor has increased and the supply of it drastically decreased. The airline industry speed-up since the 1970s has been followed by a worker slowdown. The slowdown reveals how much emotional labor the job required all along. It suggests what costs even happy workers under normal conditions pay for this labor without a name. The speed-up has sharpened the ambivalence many workers feel about how much of oneself to give over to the role and how much of oneself to protect from it.

ally consists of and what it requires of those who are supposed to keep it beautiful. The laggards and sluff-offs of emotional labor return us to the basic questions. What is emotional labor? What do we do when we manage emotion? What, in fact, is emotion? What are the costs and benefits of managing emotion, in private life and at work?

The Private and Public Faces of an Emotional System

Our search for answers to these questions leads to three separate but equally relevant discourses: one concerning labor, one concerning display, and one concerning emotion.

Those who discuss labor often comment that nowadays most jobs call for a capacity to deal with people rather than with things, for more interpersonal skills and fewer mechanical skills. In *The Coming of Post-Industrial Society* (1973), Daniel Bell argues that the growth of the service sector means that "communication" and "encounter"—"the response of ego to alter and back"—is the central work relationship today.* As he puts it, "The fact that individuals now talk to other individuals, rather than interact with a machine, is the fundamental fact about work in the post-industrial society." Critics of labor studies, such as Harry Braverman in *Labor and Monopoly Capital* (1974), point out a continual subdivision of work in many branches of the economy. Complex tasks in

which a craftsman used to take pride are divided into simpler, more repetitive segments, each more boring and less well paid than the original job. Work is deskilled and the worker belittled. But celebrants and critics alike have not inspected at close hand or with a social-psychological eye what it is that "people jobs" *actually require* of workers. They have not inquired into the actual nature of this labor. Some do not know exactly what, in the case of emotional labor, becomes deskilled.

A second discourse, closer to the person and more remote from the overall organization of work, concerns the display of feeling. The works of Erving Goffman introduce us to the many minor traffic rules of face-to-face interaction, as they emerge at a card game, in an elevator, on the street, or at the dining table of an insane asylum. He prevents us from dismissing the small as trivial by showing how small rules, transgressions, and punishments add up to form the longer strips of experience we call "work." At the same time, it is hard to use Goffman's focus to explain why companies train flight attendants in smiling, or how emotional tone is supervised, or what profit is ultimately tied to emotional labor. It is hard, in other words, to draw on this discourse alone and see how "display work" fits into the larger scheme of things.

The third discourse takes place in a quiet side street of American social science; it deals with the timeless issues of what an emotion is and how we can manage it. . . .

To uncover the heart of emotional labor, to understand what it takes to do it and what it does to people, I have drawn on elements from all three discourses. Certain events in economic history cannot be fully understood unless we pay attention to the filigreed patterns of feeling and their management because the details of these patterns are an important part of what many men and women do for a living.

---

*Jobs that Bell includes in the service sector are those in transportation and utilities, distribution and trade, finance and insurance, professional and business services, jobs deriving from demands for leisure activities (recreation and travel), and jobs that deal with communal services (health, education, and government). Only some of these service-sector jobs call for much emotion management.

Because such different traditions are joined here, my inquiry will have a different relevance for different readers. Perhaps it will be most relevant for those who do the work it describes—the flight attendants. But most of us have jobs that require some handling of other people's feelings and our own, and in this sense we are all partly flight attendants. The secretary who creates a cheerful office that announces her company as "friendly and dependable" and her boss as "up-and-coming," the waitress or waiter who creates an "atmosphere of pleasant dining," the tour guide or hotel receptionist who makes us feel welcome, the social worker whose look of solicitous concern makes the client feel cared for, the salesman who creates the sense of a "hot commodity," the bill collector who inspires fear, the funeral parlor director who makes the bereaved feel understood, the minister who creates a sense of protective outreach but even-handed warmth—all of them must confront in some way or another the requirements of *emotional labor.*

Emotional labor does not observe conventional distinctions between types of jobs. By my estimate, roughly one-third of American workers today have jobs that subject them to substantial demands for emotional labor. Moreover, of all *women* working, roughly one-half have jobs that call for emotional labor. . . . Thus this inquiry has special relevance for women, and it probably also describes more of their experience. As traditionally more accomplished managers of feeling in private life, women more than men have put emotional labor on the market, and they know more about its personal costs.

This inquiry might at first seem relevant only to workers living under capitalism, but the engineering of a managed heart is not unknown to socialism; the enthusiastic "hero of labor" bears the emotional standard for the socialist state as much as the Flight Attendant of the Year does for the capitalist airline industry. Any functioning society makes effective use of its members' emotional labor. We do not think twice about the use of feeling in the theater, or in psychotherapy, or in forms of group life that we admire. It is when we come to speak of the *exploitation* of the bottom by the top in any society that we become morally concerned. In any system, exploitation depends on the actual distribution of many kinds of profits— money, authority, status, honor, well-being. It is not emotional labor itself, therefore, but the underlying system of recompense that raises the question of what the cost of it is. . . .

Private and Commercial Uses of Feeling

A nineteenth-century child working in a brutalizing English wallpaper factory and a well-paid twentieth-century American flight attendant have something in common: in order to survive in their jobs, they must mentally detach themselves—the factory worker from his own body and physical labor, and the flight attendant from her own feelings and emotional labor. Marx and many others have told us the factory worker's story. I am interested in telling the flight attendant's story in order to promote a fuller appreciation of the costs of what she does. And I want to base this appreciation on a prior demonstration of what can happen to any of us when we become estranged from our feelings and the management of them.

We feel. But what is a feeling? I would define feeling, like emotion, as a sense, like the sense of hearing or sight. In a general way, we experience it when bodily sensations are joined with what we see or imagine. Like the sense of hearing, emotion communicates information. It has, as Freud said of anxiety, a "signal function." From feeling we discover our own viewpoint on the world.

We often say that we *try* to feel. But how can we do this? Feelings, I suggest, are not stored "inside" us, and they are not independent of acts of management. Both the act of "getting in touch with" feeling and the act of "trying to" feel may become part of the process that makes the thing we get in touch with, or the thing we manage, *into* a feeling or emotion. In managing feeling, we contribute to the creation of it.

If this is so, what we think of as intrinsic to feeling or emotion may have always been shaped to social form and put to civic use. Consider what happens when young men roused to anger go willingly to war, or when followers rally enthusiastically around their king, or mullah, or football team. Private social life may always have called for the management of feeling. The party guest summons up a gaiety owed to the host, the mourner summons up a proper sadness for a funeral. Each offers up feeling as a momentary contribution to the collective good. In the absence of an English-language name for feelings-as-contribution-to-the-group (which the more group-centered Hopi culture called *arofa*), I shall offer the concept of a gift exchange.[4] Muted anger, conjured gratitude, and suppressed envy are offerings back and forth from parent to child, wife to husband, friend to friend, and lover to lover. . . .

What gives social pattern to our acts of emotion management? I believe that when we try to feel, we apply latent feeling rules. . . . We say, "I shouldn't feel so angry at what she did," or "given our agreement, I have no right to feel jealous." Acts of emotion management are not simply private acts; they are used in exchanges under the guidance of feeling rules. Feeling rules are standards used in emotional conversation to determine what is rightly owed and owing in the currency of feeling. Through them, we tell what is "due" in each relation, each role. We pay tribute to each other in the currency of the managing act. In interaction we

pay, overpay, underpay, play with paying, acknowledge our dues, pretend to pay, or acknowledge what is emotionally due another person. In these ways, . . . we make our try at sincere civility.

Because the distribution of power and authority is unequal in some of the relations of private life, the managing acts can also be unequal. The myriad momentary acts of management compose part of what we summarize in the terms *relation* and *role*. Like the tiny dots of a Seurat painting, the microacts of emotion management compose, through repetition and change over time, a movement of form. Some forms express inequality, others equality.

Now what happens when the managing of emotion comes to be sold as labor? What happens when feeling rules, like rules of behavioral display, are established not through private negotiation but by company manuals? What happens when social exchanges are not, as they are in private life, subject to change or termination but ritually sealed and almost inescapable?

What happens when the emotional display that one person owes another reflects a certain inherent inequality? The airline passenger may choose not to smile, but the flight attendant is obliged not only to smile but to try to work up some warmth behind it. What happens, in other words, when there is a *transmutation* of the private ways we use feeling?

One sometimes needs a grand word to point out a coherent pattern between occurrences that would otherwise seem totally unconnected. My word is "transmutation." When I speak of the transmutation of an emotional system, I mean to point out a link between a private act, such as attempting to enjoy a party, and a public act, such as summoning up good feeling for a customer. I mean to expose the relation between the private act of trying to dampen liking for a person—which overcommitted lovers sometimes attempt—and the public act of a bill collector who suppresses empathy for a debtor. By the grand phrase "transmutation of an emotional system" I mean to convey what it is that we do privately, often unconsciously, to feelings that nowadays often fall under the sway of large organizations, social engineering, and the profit motive.

Trying to feel what one wants, expects, or thinks one ought to feel is probably no newer than emotion itself. Conforming to or deviating from feeling rules is also hardly new. In organized society, rules have probably never been applied only to observable behavior. "Crimes of the heart" have long been recognized because proscriptions have long guarded the "preactions" of the heart; the Bible says not to covet your neighbor's wife, not simply to avoid acting on that feeling. What is new in our time is an increasingly prevalent *instrumental stance* toward our native capacity to play, wittingly and actively, upon a range of feelings for a private purpose and the way in which that stance is engineered and administered by large organizations.

This transmutation of the private use of feeling affects the two sexes and the various social classes in distinctly different ways. . . . As a matter of tradition, emotion management has been better understood and more often used by women as one of the offerings they trade for economic support. Especially among dependent women of the middle and upper classes, women have the job (or think they ought to) of creating the emotional tone of social encounters: expressing joy at the Christmas presents others open, creating the sense of surprise at birthdays, or displaying alarm at the mouse in the kitchen. Gender is not the only determinant of skill in such managed expression and in the emotion work needed to do it well. But men who do this work well have slightly less in common with other men than women who do it well have with other women. When the "wom-anly" art of living up to *private* emotional conventions goes public, it attaches itself to a different profit-and-loss statement.

Similarly, emotional labor affects the various social classes differently. If it is women, members of the less advantaged gender, who specialize in emotional labor, it is the middle and upper reaches of the class system that seem to call most for it. And parents who do emotional labor on the job will convey the importance of emotion management to their children and will prepare them to learn the skills they will probably need for the jobs they will probably get.

In general, lower-class and working-class people tend to work more with things, and middle-class and upper-class people tend to work more with people. More working women than men deal with people as a job. Thus, there are both gender patterns and class patterns to the civic and commercial use of human feeling. That is the social point.

But there is a personal point, too. There is a cost to emotion work: it affects the degree to which we listen to feeling and sometimes our very capacity to feel. Managing feeling is an art fundamental to civilized living, and I assume that in broad terms the cost is usually worth the fundamental benefit. Freud, in *Civilization and Its Discontents*, argued analogously about the sexual instinct: enjoyable as that instinct is, we are wise in the long run to give up some gratification of it. But when the transmutation of the private use of feeling is successfully accomplished—when we succeed in lending our feelings to the organizational engineers of worker-customer relations—we may pay a cost in how we hear our feelings and a cost in what, for better or worse, they tell us about ourselves. When a speed-up of the human assembly line makes "genuine" personal service harder to deliver, the worker may withdraw emotional labor and offer instead a thin crust of display. Then the cost shifts: the penalty becomes a sense of being phony or insincere.

In short, when the transmutation works, the worker risks losing the signal function of feeling. When it does not work, the risk is losing the signal function of display.

Certain social conditions have increased the cost of feeling management. One is an overall unpredictability about our social world. Ordinary people nowadays move through many social worlds and get the gist of dozens of social roles. Compare this with the life of the fourteenth-century baker's apprentice described in Peter Laslett's *The World We Have Lost* (1968): it is a life that begins and ends in one locale, in one occupation, in one household, within one world view, and according to one set of rules.[5] It has become much less common that given circumstances seem to dictate the proper interpretation of them or that they indicate in a plainly visible way what feeling is owed to whom, and when, and how. As a result, we moderns spend more mental time on the question "What, in this situation, should I be feeling?" Oddly enough, a second condition more appropriate to Laslett's baker's apprentice has survived into more modern and fluid times. We still, it seems, ask of ourselves, "Who am I?" as if the question permitted a single neat answer. We still search for a solid, predictable core of self even though the conditions for the existence of such a self have long since vanished.

In the face of these two conditions, people turn to feelings in order to locate themselves or at least to see what their own reactions are to a given event. That is, in the absence of unquestioned external guidelines, the signal function of emotion becomes more important, and the commercial distortion of the managed heart becomes all the more important as a human cost.

We may well be seeing a response to all this in the rising approval of the unmanaged heart, the greater virtue now attached to what is "natural" or spontaneous. Ironically, the person like Rousseau's Noble Savage, who only smiles "naturally," without ulterior purpose, is a poor prospect for the job of waiter, hotel manager, or flight attendant. The high regard for "natural feeling," then, may coincide with the culturally imposed need to develop the precise opposite—an instrumental stance toward feeling. We treat spontaneous feeling, for this reason, as if it were scarce and precious; we raise it up as a virtue. It may not be too much to suggest that we are witnessing a call for the conservation of "inner resources," a call to save another wilderness from corporate use and keep it "forever wild."

With the growing celebration of spontaneity have come the robot jokes. Robot humor plays with the tension between being human—that is to say, having feeling—and being a cog in a socioeconomic machine. The charm of the little robot R2-D2, in the film *Star Wars*, is that he seems so human. Films like this bring us the familiar in reverse: every day, outside the movie house, we see human beings whose show of feeling has a robot quality. The ambiguities are funny now.

Both the growing celebration of spontaneity and the jokes we tell about being robots suggest that in the realm of feeling, Orwell's 1984 came in disguise several years ago, leaving behind a laugh and perhaps the idea of a private way out.

NOTES

Epigraph: C. Wright Mills, *White Collar,* p. 184.

1. Marx, *Capital* (1977), pp. 356–357, 358.
2. *Lucas Guide 1980,* pp. 66, 76. (Fourteen aspects of air travel at the stages of departure, arrival, and the flight itself are ranked. Each aspect is given one of sixteen differently weighted marks. For example, "The friendliness or efficiency of the staff is more important than the quality of the pilot's flight announcement or the selection of newspapers and magazines offered.")
3. Mills (1956), p. xx.
4. Lee (1959) discusses the concept of *arofa.*
5. Laslett (1968); Stone (1965); Swidler (1979).

REFERENCES

Laslett, Peter. 1968. *The World We Have Lost.* London: Methuen.

Lee, Dorothy. 1959. *Freedom and Culture.* New York: Prentice-Hall.

Marx, Karl. 1977. *Capital,* Vol. 1. Intro. by Ernest Mandel. Tr. Ben Fowkes. New York: Vintage.

Mills, C. Wright. 1956. *White Collar.* New York: Oxford University Press.

Stone, Lawrence, ed. 1965. *Social Change and the Revolution in England, 1540–1640.* London: Longmans.

Swidler, Ann. 1979. *Organization Without Authority.* Cambridge, MA, and London: Harvard University Press.

11

The Worker as Active Subject
Enlivening the "New Sociology of Work"

Randy Hodson

The theory and practice of workplace relations was dominated until recently by industrial psychologists, human relations sociologists, organizational theorists, and management consultants (see Walton and Hackman 1986). The theories and goals of these researchers led them to an analysis of individual and small group phenomena in the workplace. When problems occurred at work, individuals and group processes were identified as the cause. The proposed solutions to workplace problems typically involved changes in management style, in payment systems, in the socialization and values of workers, in the socio-technical organization of work, and in small group structure (see Mayo 1945).

Recent decades have seen the emergence of a sustained critique of this individual and small group approach to the workplace.

Excerpts from "The Worker as Active Subject: Enlivening the 'New Sociology of Work'" by Randy Hodson in *The New Modern Times: Factors Reshaping the World of Work,* edited by David B. Bills. 1995. Albany, NY: State University of New York Press. Copyright © 1995, State University of New York. All rights reserved. Reprinted by permission.

Those who have participated in this critique have argued that individualistic and small group approaches miss the "big structures" that mold work and the workplace. These critiques have come from several different sources including the dual economy and dual labor market literatures (Averitt 1968; Gordon 1972; Bonacich 1976), the labor process literature (Braverman 1974), and the "new industrial sociology" centered in Great Britain (Edwards 1986; Edwards and Scullion 1982; Friedman 1977; Thompson 1983). The large scale structures these critics feel have been overlooked include those of exploitation, deskilling, and labor market segmentation.

The structuralist critique has generated new energy and insight in fields that had grown increasingly stagnant. It has not, however, been without its costs (see Simpson 1989). The earlier management-inspired view of the worker as an object to be either cajoled or encouraged into cooperation has been replaced by a view of workers as manipulated by forces even further removed from workers' immediate control. Rather than theoretically liberating the worker from control by management, such theories have replaced supervisory and management control with control emanating from system imperatives. In such accounts, the worker is allowed even less of a theoretical role as active participant in the workplace. These earlier theories explicitly recognized that workers had at least a limited role as active subjects in the workplace and recognized this role through studies of soldiering and other types of output restriction in work groups (Roy 1954).

This theoretical shortcoming in the structural critique of industrial sociology, organizational behavior research, and social stratification research has led to difficulties in explaining and interpreting current changes in the workplace. These changes include management practices entailing an increased focus on quality circles and worker participation and changing technologies based on the application of microprocessor related technologies to the workplace. The structural analysis of the workplace has generated few insights that inform us about these processes, their implications and limitations, or their probable future directions.

While the structural critique has produced many valuable concepts, including those of economic segmentation, deskilling, and core-periphery relations, we need to extend this critique by incorporating a vision of the worker as active agent in organizing the nature of work. This new sociology of work, which includes both structural elements and an image of the worker as an active agent in determining the nature of work, can be used to inform related literatures on human relations, complex organizations, working-class culture, workplace democracy, and collective action. A new sociology of work that includes both structure and agency has the potential to reestablish for industrial sociology a leading role in addressing questions at the mainstream of sociology (Hodson and Sullivan 1990).

A Typology of Worker Behaviors

In this section I develop a typology of worker behaviors that incorporates the worker as active agent. Worker behavior can be conceptualized around three central dimensions: behavior oriented toward the individual's goals, behavior oriented toward group goals, and behavior oriented toward the organization's goals. A typology based on these three goals of worker behavior is presented in Figure 1. In this typology each dimension is divided between positive and negative poles. Thus, behavior may meet or fail to meet individual, group, or organizational goals.

Eight cells depicting possible worker behaviors are created by cross-classifying individual, group, and organizational goals. The group may be defined as a small shop floor

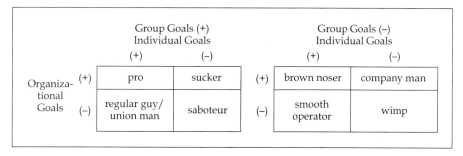

		Group Goals (+) Individual Goals			Group Goals (−) Individual Goals	
		(+)	(−)		(+)	(−)
Organizational Goals	(+)	pro	sucker	(+)	brown noser	company man
	(−)	regular guy/ union man	saboteur	(−)	smooth operator	wimp

FIGURE 1   A Typology of Worker Behaviors

group or as a broader group, such as an occupational community or a social class. Behaviors that are oriented toward small group
goals are much more common than behaviors that are oriented toward social class
goals. As the literature on social movements
informs us, revolutionary class behaviors, or
even genuinely reformist class-oriented behaviors, are relatively uncommon. Instead,
workers generally struggle to "get by," or to
"make out" (Burawoy 1979). The literature
on strikes and collective bargaining tells us
that class-oriented behaviors are unlikely
unless workers have power, based on their
position in the division of labor or in the labor market, and they possess a strong organization and a strong organizing ideology
(Cornfield 1989). Class-oriented behaviors
are, however, a possibility. The literature on
workplace democracy argues that such behaviors are capable of overcoming schisms
between various factions of workers and
that organized workers are capable of carrying out the functions of management. The
dimension depicting group goals can thus be
interpreted either in terms of shop floor
groups or in terms of larger social groups
such as classes or occupational communities.

In the left-hand table in Figure 1, four
cells depict possible behaviors that meet
group goals. Workers who meet personal, organizational, *and* group goals can be labeled
"pros." At some level, this is what we all
want to be. Those who meet personal and
group goals but resist organizational goals
are labeled "regular guys," or they might be
called a "union man" in a unionized context.
Such workers use the power based on their
position in the division of labor to attain both
individual and group goals and to resist the
imposition of organizational goals. Those
who fail to meet individual goals but who act
to meet group and organizational goals
might be labeled "suckers." We all feel like
we have acted like this at times, that we have
been taken advantage of, that we have not

looked out for ourselves. The final cell in this
table is defined by meeting group goals but
not meeting individual and organizational
goals. I hesitatingly label such behaviors
"sabotage" in recognition of their antithesis
to organizational goals, their generally collective character, and their non-constructive
nature for the individual (Taylor and Walton
1971). However, there are forms of sabotage
that do not fit in this cell. Some acts of sabotage may be purely for the release of individual frustrations (Molstad 1988; Westwood
1984). Such behaviors would fall into the
"regular guy" cell. Other acts of sabotage
may be for the purpose of pressuring management to change objectional job conditions
(Jermier 1988). Such acts are oriented toward
the attainment of individual and group goals
and would thus also fall in the "regular guy"
cell (Hodson 1991; Weinstein 1979). I label
this behavioral cell saboteur with an awareness that not all acts of sabotage are counterproductive for the individual.

The right-hand table in Figure 1 depicts behaviors that do *not* meet group
goals. Individuals engaging in these sorts
of behaviors may meet their own needs or
organizational needs but rarely meet group
needs. Thus, they will tend to be social isolates to some degree. Most of us try to avoid
being identified with these types of behaviors. Those who meet organizational and
personal goals but not group goals can be labeled "brown nosers." We have all encountered this type. The literature on human
resource management is full of suggestions
on how to set up organizational rewards so
that individuals experience an overlap between their own interests and those of the organization and so that the attraction of
alternative group goals is minimized. It is
perhaps surprising that this cell does not include even a larger share of behavior at the
workplace given the potential rewards of
such behaviors. Those who meet individual
goals but neither group nor organizational

goals can be labeled "smooth operators." Such behaviors feather the individual's own nest. These behaviors may be at the expense of organizational and group goals. Or, they may facilitate organizational and group goals. Indeed, a good smooth operator often selects behaviors that both facilitate their own goals and group and organizational goals. Such behaviors would be identical with those of the "pro." However, for the smooth operator, the leading motivation is personal gain, not group or organizational gain. When these goals come into conflict, the behaviors of smooth operators and pros become differentiated. Those who do not meet individual or group goals, but who act to meet organizational goals, are labeled "company men." Their behavior recognizes only the goals of the formal organization as valid and ignores both individual and work group goals. The final type of behavior is that which fails to meet individual, group, or organizational goals. Such behaviors are anemic and the individuals who engage in them are often labeled "wimps" or some equally pejorative term. Such behaviors are unsuccessful at meeting any goals and are counterproductive for all concerned.

It will perhaps be illuminating for the reader to review again the behavioral categories we have just discussed but in a different order. This can be done by first considering the four types of behavior that meet individual goals and the four types of behavior that do not meet individual goals. Next, review the four types of behavior that meet organizational goals and the four types of behavior that do not meet organizational goals. Finally, review the four types of behavior that meet group goals and the four types of behavior that do not meet group goals.

A Model of Worker Behaviors

At this point we turn to the task of modeling the behaviors outlined above. This model includes a central role for the worker as active participant. A schematic version of this model is presented in Figure 2. On the left side of Figure 2 are measures of objective job and workplace characteristics. These factors create motivations and provide resources that eventually become translated into behaviors. Thus, organizational structure and technology allow certain types of behaviors,

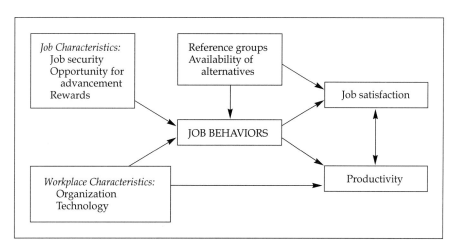

FIGURE 2 A Model of Worker Behaviors

but prohibit others, or make them more difficult. For example, the use of a new technology, the output potential of which is understood only by workers, empowers workers with greater control over their work. Similarly, the opportunities for advancement in a job create motivations in workers to engage in certain types of behavior if these are available. High pay and opportunities for advancement reduce quits, even if the work is onerous. These job and workplace characteristics, which create the motivations and opportunities for action, play a similar conceptual role to the concepts of grievances and resources for action identified by the sociological analysis of collective action. Small group processes, cultural factors, organized worker power, and ideology enter this model as mediating factors that facilitate or discourage the selection and utilization of specific behaviors.

The job behaviors positioned in the center of Figure 2 are diverse and impossible to reduce to a single dimension of positive versus negative, constructive versus destructive, or rational versus irrational. Figure 1 offers a tentative model of these behaviors based on how the behaviors reflect individual, group, and organizational goals. The behavior selected by a worker in turn gives rise to both job satisfaction and productivity. The job satisfaction and productivity of workers depend on the behavioral strategy they select and on their success in implementing those strategies. In this model, job satisfaction is influenced by working conditions but only after these conditions are mediated by workers' selection of behavioral strategies.

Job satisfaction also depends on the reference groups that workers use to evaluate their situation and on the availability of alternative employment opportunities (Hodson 1985). If a worker's friends and relatives are doing better than the worker, then he or she will be dissatisfied. However, if few opportunities for improving his or her condition exist, then expectations will be downgraded and job dissatisfaction will be repressed in the interests of reducing cognitive dissonance that might arise from being stuck in a dissatisfying job. Workers' reference groups and the availability of alternatives may also influence their selection of behaviors at work. Job satisfaction is thus a result of workers' behaviors and their expectations and options; it is a result of job and workplace conditions only as these are mediated by the behavioral options workers select.

Productivity in this model results from workers' behavioral strategies and from the organizational structure and technology used in production. Note that productivity and job satisfaction are not causally related in this model. Thus, any relationship between them results from their common roots in workers' behavioral strategies. For instance, a successful strategy of being a pro will increase both productivity and job satisfaction, giving rise to the appearance of a relationship between productivity and job satisfaction. Being a sucker, however, will increase productivity but not necessarily satisfaction.

The model of worker behaviors outlined in Figures 1 and 2 has important implications for how we approach the study of the workplace. These implications are developed in the following sections by analyzing recent development in the major subfields of industrial sociology.

Implications of Conceptualizing the Worker as an Active Subject . . .

Organizational Behavior

Much of the early organizational behavior literature was motivated by a desire to increase worker productivity and to reduce worker resistance to work through soldiering, working to rule, sabotage, striking, or forming unions. Not all early studies in industrial sociology, however, were motivated by these goals (see for example, Nosow and Form 1962). Nor should the findings of these studies be completely discounted because of their motivating question. Serendipitous findings abound in this field: recall for a moment the discovery of the Hawthorne effect (Roethlisberger and Dickson 1939). Even though increasing productivity was the common orienting goal of these studies, the existence and importance of small group processes among workers was the most important and lasting finding.

Much of this literature was organized and presented to a generation (or more) of sociologists in Miller and Form's seminal text, *Industrial Sociology* (1951, 1964, 1980). The materials covered in this text include small group processes, informal work behavior, cliques, ceremonies, rituals, and beliefs and myths. Informal processes and emergent cultures in small groups have continued as favored topics in the human relations literature and in several related literatures influenced by its traditions, including urban anthropology (Bensman and Gerver 1963; Mars 1982) and the sociology of occupations (Abbott 1988; Haas 1987; Pavalko 1988). It is important not to lose these insights about small group processes and workplace cultures as we develop theories that also take larger scale structures into account.

Contemporary theories of human relations in industry continue to be dominated by concerns for productivity. Yet such theories sometimes also include an active view of the worker. The new theories that have emerged are often referred to collectively as Theory Z (Ouchi 1981). These theories view productivity as embedded in workers, in their skills, in their attitudes, and, most centrally, in the small group structure of work, rather than as embedded in specific bureaucratic procedures or in particular management styles. Indeed, much of the new theorizing about human relations at work

has been motivated by the inefficiencies and rigidities associated with bureaucratic means of motivating workers and allocating rewards. In Europe, these theories have helped motivate and legitimate the widespread use of work groups in the labor process. Under the group organization of work, teams of workers have at least a limited degree of control over decision making about their day-to-day operations and activities (Gyllenhammar 1977; see also Dohse, Jurgens and Malsch 1985; Grenier 1988; Parker 1985).

Such theories of productivity have been implemented in Japan through the concept of "life-time employment" (Abegglen and Stalk 1985). Guaranteeing life-time employment to workers insures their job security and thus their trust in the organization and their enthusiasm for work. It also retains workers' presence in the organization as a repository of skills and knowledge (Cole 1989). These benefits are amplified by having workers rotate through a variety of jobs during their careers, thus building their reservoirs of knowledge. This accumulated knowledge is invaluable for coordinating activities between different parts of the organization and is a more efficient mechanism for coordinating and integrating production than more bureaucratic structures.

Potential tensions between the worker as active agent and the labor process as worker control are highlighted by Burawoy's analysis of "making out" on the shop floor. Burawoy (1979) argues that workers devise a variety of ways to "make out" on their jobs. Often this entails maneuvering to keep piece rates up and to keep time allocations for work high. Burawoy argues that organized and individual acts of resistance are the everyday stuff of workplace life and he observes that workers take great pride in devising creative ways to make out.

Burawoy also notes, however, that workplace struggles are often displaced from management onto relations between co-workers. Thus, in the factory Burawoy studied, struggles over making out were often translated into struggles between production workers and tool crib attendants or struggles between production workers and fork lift drivers. Such conflicts between workers are also noted by Sabel (1982, 16): "Each group's defense of its own niche in the division of labor can isolate it from its most likely allies against management, the other groups in the plant." Such conflicts are labeled "lateral displacements" by Thompson (1983).

In *The Politics of Production,* Burawoy (1985) takes an even more pessimistic view of worker struggle on the shop floor. He refers to the new shop floor relations as "hegemonic despotism." He argues that the despotism of early factory regimes is replaced by a hegemonic despotism in contemporary capitalism in which workers' patterns of making out become part of the system that reproduces exploitation. That is, capitalists have organized the production process so that the available means of making out serve to displace conflict from the management-worker relationship to relationships between different groups of workers or to make the only available solutions ones in which workers participate in their own heightened exploitation. Thus, workers' solutions (ways of making out) serve to reproduce the system of exploitation rather than to change it. This view seems overly negative and may overlook important ways in which workers' activities of resistance limit and condition the labor process and structure the nature of work life (Tucker 1993).

The analysis of small group processes and effort bargaining at the workplace need to be incorporated into the new sociology of work. These insights and observations are frequently either treated with disdain by critical theorists because of their association with the management goal of increased productivity or relegated to the theoretical dust-

bin of obscurity by considering them "displacements" that serve only to reproduce the existing system. However, the insights that workers are social animals, work best in small groups, help each other to learn, and can be controlled by peer pressure need to be taken seriously, rather than jettisoned as excess baggage or rejected as theoretically trivial. These insights provide essential building blocks toward a more active vision of the role of workers in structuring the nature of work. . . .

Collective Bargaining and Strikes

There is a vast literature on collective bargaining and strike behavior. (See Cornfield 1989 and Lewin and Feuille 1983 for recent reviews of this literature.) A central finding in this literature is that workers with power tend to strike in response to job related problems, while workers without power tend to quit their jobs (Cornfield 1985). "Power" can be derived from an effective union, location in an industry that is sheltered by a product market monopoly, or employment in a growing industry. Workers without power are forced to respond to unsatisfactory job conditions by quitting the job rather than by taking collective action to improve conditions. As Bluestone (1970) writes, "for such workers, losing a job is not much worse than keeping it." Besides power, the most important factor facilitating collective action among workers is the availability of ideologies that support such action (Snyder 1975). Without ideological support, few workers are willing to accept the individual sacrifices that may accompany strike activity (Hodson 1987).

There is also a large literature on how the individual characteristics of workers influence strike behavior (Leicht 1989). A principal finding from this literature is that a wide variety of types of workers are potentially available for collective action (Batstone, Boraston and Frankel 1978). Many fewer workers, however, are interested in the types of action that involve direct violent confrontations with management (Grant and Wallace 1991).

The analysis of workers' responses at the workplace has been conceptualized by Hirschman (1971) as a three category typology: exit, voice, and loyalty. Voice refers to a variety of individual and collective behaviors (including union activity, professional association lobbying, and individual acts of bargaining and resistance) through which workers can express their complaints at the workplace and push for redress. Exit refers primarily to quitting, but also includes more subtle and partial forms of withdrawal such as absenteeism, apathy, and carelessness. Loyalty refers to commitment to the organization and to working to achieve individual goals within the parameters laid out by the organization, its rules, and goals. The model of workplace behaviors suggested in this [reading] shares common terrain with Hirschman's three category model but it covers a more comprehensive range of behaviors. This range of behaviors is especially important for extending Hirschman's model to include collective responses. . . .

Technology: Control versus Empowerment

A final research area to be considered for developing the implications of a model of the worker as active agent is the rapidly growing literature on technology and work. Two areas are of particular interest: the effects of new technology on skills and the consequences of new technology for the organization of work.

Deskilling or Skill Upgrading? Blauner's (1964) classic study of continuous process automation in the chemical industry is among the most widely cited empirical studies on the relationship between advanced technology and skill. Blauner finds that continuous process automation requires a greater proportion of skilled maintenance workers than mass production and that operators in automated settings have greater responsibility for the care and functioning of expensive capital equipment. Riche (1982), in a review of technological change in four industries, and Adler (1984), in a study of banks and bank tellers, arrive at similar conclusions. Both emphasize the increasing level of skill required by advanced technology. These studies can be interpreted as providing support for Bell's (1973) thesis that new, knowledge-based industries are creating a "post-industrial society" typified by increased skill and autonomy.

Research on the computerized numeric control (CNC) in the machine tool industry supports Blauner's contention that automation produces increased demands for skill.

> CNC operators are likely to have to deal with a greater and more frequently changing range of jobs; part of this is related to the increased sophistication of the machine control-system through which more flexible change-overs and improvements of programmes can be achieved (Hartmann, Nicholas, Sorge and Warner 1983, 226).

Increased skills were also needed in settings such as those described above to prevent bottle-necks in production that result from system components with highly differential levels of flexibility and efficiency.

Advanced technologies may thus demand greater skills from workers, allowing them greater power. Hirschhorn (1984, 58) quotes a management consultant in a high technology power plant in this regard: "The operator can achieve better results than the engineer. This can probably be put down to his ability, derived from intimate experience of the plant, to take into account the many ill-understood factors which affect the plant's running but which he cannot communicate to the engineer." Hirschhorn

(1984, 73) argues for an historical progression in which the worker moves "from being the controlled element in the production process to operating the controls to controlling the controls."

Other researchers argue that *deskilling* is the most likely consequence of advanced technology. Bright (1966) argues that, as mechanization progresses, initial changes demanding increased skill levels yield to a progressive loss of skill, resulting in an inverted "U-shaped" skill curve. Bright's thesis has been popularized by Braverman (1974), who coined the phrase "deskilling" to typify the progressive loss of skill.

Boddy and Buchanan (1983), basing their analysis on a series of case studies, illustrate how new technologies are creating a growing proportion of deskilled occupations. One of the cases documented by Boddy and Buchanan involved the introduction of automated mixing equipment at a biscuit factory. The major effect of advanced technology on work in the biscuit factory was to transform the "doughman" into a mixer operator. Previously, the position of doughman was held by a master baker. However, once automated equipment was introduced into the mixing process, the doughman suffered a substantial loss of craft skills. In addition, as control of the operation was moved further up the organizational hierarchy, the doughman was left with less discretion over other aspects of work as well. (See also Finlay 1987, and Francis et al. 1981.)

The literature on advanced technology and skills suggests that the tasks required of workers in high technology settings may involve both skill upgrading and deskilling. Workers may experience skill upgrading through an increased role in decision-making and through an increased range of skills required on the job. Deskilling may occur as craft skills are lost to increasing automation and as previous elements of worker autonomy are captured by the organizational hier-

archy or incorporated into new computerized "management information systems." . . .

Hypotheses Emerging from the Study of the Active Worker

The model of the active worker developed in this [reading] is capable of producing a variety of new hypotheses about the nature of work in the 1990s and beyond. The generation of such hypotheses is an important first step in further developing and refining a model of the worker as an active partner in defining the nature of work. Five such hypotheses are listed below:

> Hypothesis 1: A culture of solidarity is necessary for transforming grievances into behaviors that further class goals.

> Hypothesis 2: A supportive small group structure is necessary for transforming grievances into behaviors that further group goals.

> Hypothesis 3: The absence of class solidarity and supportive group structures will result in the selection of individualistic behaviors which may or may not be supportive of organizational goals.

> Hypothesis 4: Bureaucratic organizational structures move behavioral strategies toward resistance to rules rather than individuals.

> Hypothesis 5: After controlling for behavioral strategies, productivity and job satisfaction have no net relationship.

The systematic investigation of these and other hypotheses derived from the model of the active worker developed in this [reading] has the potential to yield new insights that could enliven the study of workplace conditions, behaviors and attitudes. From such research we may be able to develop models of the conditions giving rise to various workplace behaviors analogous to those suggested by Tilly (1978) for larger scale collective action.

Conclusions

The typology of workplace behaviors and the causal model of how these behaviors emerge and operate in the workplace proposed in this [reading] are compatible with insights drawn from recent work in a variety of fields, including industrial sociology, the study of complex organizations, class culture, and workplace democracy, and the study of strikes and other forms of collective behavior. This unifying model has the potential to yield significant new insights into the relationships between workplace conditions, worker behaviors and workplace outcomes. . . .

. . . It is hoped that the model of the worker as an active agent proposed in this [reading] can serve as a starting framework for the pursuit of these and other research questions which incorporate a fuller role for the worker as active subject in the new sociology of work.

REFERENCES

Abbott, Andrew. 1988. *The System of Professions.* Chicago: University of Chicago.

Abegglen, James and George Stalk. 1985. *The Japanese Corporation.* New York: Basic.

Adler, Paul. 1984. "Tools for Resistance: Workers Can Make Automation Their Ally." *Dollars and Sense* 100 (October):7–8.

Averitt, Robert T. 1968. *The Dual Economy.* New York: W. W. Norton.

Batstone, E., I. Boraston and S. Franke. 1978. *The Social Organization of Strikes.* Oxford: Basil Blackwell.

Bell, Daniel. 1973. *The Coming of Post-Industrial Society.* New York: Basic.

Bensman, Joseph and Israel Gerver. 1963. "Crime and Punishment in the Factory." *American Sociological Review* 28 (4):588–98.

Blauner, Robert. 1964. *Alienation and Freedom.* Chicago: University of Chicago.

Bluestone, Barry. 1970. "The Tripartite Economy: Labor Markets and the Working Poor." *Poverty and Human Resources* 5:15–35.

Boddy, D. and D. Buchanan. 1983. "Advanced Technology and the Quality of Working Life: The Effects of Computerized Controls on Biscuit-Making Operators." *Journal of Occupational Psychology* 56 (2):109–19.

Bonacich, Edna. 1976. "Advanced Capitalism and Black/White Race Relations in the United States: A Split Labor Market Interpretation." *American Sociological Review* 41:34–51.

Braverman, Harry. 1974. *Labor and Monopoly Capital.* New York: Monthly Review.

Bright, James R. 1966. "The Relationship of Increasing Automation and Skill Requirements." In *The Employment Impact of Technological Change, Volume 2: Technology and the American Economy,* National Commission on Technology, Automation and Economic Progress. Washington, D.C.: U.S. Government Printing Office, 203–221.

Burawoy, Michael. 1985. *The Politics of Production.* London: New Left Books.

———. 1979. *Manufacturing Consent.* Chicago: University of Chicago.

Cole, Robert E. 1989. *Strategies for Learning: Small-Group Activities in American, Japanese, and Swedish Industry.* Berkeley: University of California Press.

Cornfield, Daniel B. 1989. *Becoming a Mighty Voice: Conflict and Change in the United Furniture Workers of America.* New York: Russell Sage Foundation.

Cornfield, Daniel B. 1985. "Economic Segmentation and the Expression of Labor Unrest." *Social Science Quarterly* 66 (2):247–65.

Dohse, Knuth, Ulrich Jurgens and Thomas Malsch. 1985. "From 'Fordism' to 'Toyotism'? The Social Organization of the Labor Process in the Japanese Automobile Factory." *Politics and Society* 14 (2):115–45.

Edwards, P. K. 1986. *Conflict at Work.* London: Basil Blackwell.

Edwards, P. K. and Hugh Scullion. 1982. *The Social Organization of Industrial Conflict.* London: Basil Blackwell.

Finlay, William. 1987. "Commitment and Control in the High-tech Workplace." Paper presented at the Annual Meetings of the American Sociological Association.

Francis, Arthus, Mandy Snell, Paul Willman, and Graham Winch. 1981. "The Impact of Information Technology at Work: The Case of CAD/CAM and MIS in Engineering Plants." In *Information Technology: Impact on the Way of Life.* Dublin, Ireland: Tycooly, 182–193.

Friedman, Andrew L. 1977. *Industry and Labor: Class Struggle at Work and Monopoly Capitalism.* London: MacMillan.

Gordon, David M. 1972. *Theories of Poverty and Underemployment.* Lexington, Massachusetts: Heath.

Grant, Don Sherman, II, and Michael Wallace. 1991. "Why Do Strikes Turn Violent?" *American Journal of Sociology* 96 (5):1117–50.

Grenier, G. J. 1988. *Inhuman Relations: Quality Circles and Anti-unionism in American Industry.* Philadelphia: Temple University Press.

Gyllenhammar, Pehr G. 1977. "How Volvo Adapts Work to People." In Richard M. Steers and Lyman W. Porter (Eds.), *Motivation and Work Behavior, Third Edition.* New York: McGraw-Hill, 564–576.

Haas, J. 1987. *Becoming Doctors: The Adoption of a Cloak of Competence.* Greenwich, Connecticut: JAI Press.

Hartmann, Gert, Ian Nicholas, Arndt Sorge and Malcolm Warner. 1983. "Computerized Machine Tools, Manpower Consequences and Skill Utilization." *British Journal of Industrial Relations* 21 (2):221–31.

Hirschhorn, Larry. 1984. *Beyond Mechanization.* Cambridge: MIT.

Hirschman, Albert O. 1971. *Exit, Voice, and Loyalty.* Cambridge, Massachusetts: Harvard University.

Hodson, Randy. 1991. "Good Soldiers, Smooth Operators, and Saboteurs: A Model of Workplace Behaviors." *Work and Occupations* 18 (3):271–90.

———.1987. "Who Crosses the Picket Line? An Analysis of the CWA Strike of 1983." *Labor Studies Journal* 12 (2):19–37.

———. 1985. "Workers' Comparisons and Job Satisfaction." *Social Science Quarterly* 66 (2): 266–80.

Hodson, Randy and Teresa A. Sullivan. 1990. *The Social Organization of Work.* Belmont, California: Wadsworth.

Jermier, John M. 1988. "Sabotage at Work." In Nancy DiTomaso (Ed.), *Research in the Sociology of Organizations,* Volume 6. Greenwich, Connecticut: JAI Press, 101–135.

Leicht, Kevin. 1989. "Unions, Plants, Jobs and Workers: An Analysis of Union Satisfaction and Participation." *Sociological Quarterly* 30 (2):331–62.

Lewin, David and Peter Feuille. 1983. "Behavioral Research in Industrial Relations." *Industrial and Labor Relations Review* 36 (3):341–60.

Mars, Gerald. 1982. *Cheats at Work.* London: Unwin.

Mayo, Elton. 1945. *The Social Problems of an Industrial Civilization.* Cambridge, Massachusetts: Harvard University.

Miller, Delbert C. and William H. Form. 1951, 1964, 1980. *Industrial Sociology,* 1st, 2nd, and 3rd editions. New York: Harper and Row.

Molstad, Clark. 1988. "Control Strategies Used by Industrial Brewery Workers: Work Avoidance, Impression Management and Solidarity." *Human Organization* 47 (4):354–60.

Nosow, Sigmund and William H. Form (Eds.). 1962. *Man, Work, and Society.* New York: Basic.

Ouchi, William G. 1981. *Theory Z.* Reading, Massachusetts: Addison-Wesley.

Parker, Mike. 1985. *Inside the Circle: A Union Guide to QWL.* Boston: South End Press.

Pavalko, Ronald M. 1988. *Sociology of Occupations and Professions, 2nd Edition.* Itasca, Illinois: Peacock.

Riche, Richard W. 1982. "Impact of New Electronic Technology." *Monthly Labor Review* 105 (3):37–9.

Roethlisberger, F. J. and William J. Dickson. 1939. *Management and the Worker.* Cambridge, Massachusetts: Harvard University.

Roy, Donald. 1954. "Efficiency and 'The Fix': Informal Intergroup Relations in a Piecework Machine Shop." *American Journal of Sociology* 60:255–66.

Sabel, Charles F. 1982. *Work and Politics.* Cambridge, England: Cambridge University.

Simpson, Ida Harper. 1989. "The Sociology of Work: Where Have All the Workers Gone?" *Social Forces* 67 (3):563–81.

Snyder, David. 1975. "Institutional Setting and Industrial Conflict: Comparative Analyses of France, Italy and the United States." *American Sociological Review* 40:259–78.

Taylor, Laurie and Paul Walton. 1971. "Industrial Sabotage: Motives and Meanings." In Stanley Cohen (Ed.), *Images of Deviance.* London: Penguin, 219–245.

Thompson, Paul. 1983. *The Nature of Work.* London: MacMillan.

Tilly, Charles. 1978. *From Mobilization to Revolution.* Reading, Massachusetts: Addison-Wesley.

Tucker, James. 1993. "Everyday Forms of Employee Resistance." *Sociological Forum* 8 (1):25–45.

Walton, Richard E. and J. Richard Hackman. 1986. "Groups under Contrasting Management Strategies." In Paul S. Goodman and Associates (Eds.), *Designing Effective Work Groups.* San Francisco: Jossey Bass, 168–201.

Weinstein, Deena. 1979. *Bureaucratic Opposition.* New York: Pergamon.

Westwood, Sallie. 1984. *All Day Every Day: Factory and Family in the Making of Women's Lives.* London: Pluto.

TECHNOLOGY, FLEXIBILITY, AND THE TRANSFORMATION OF WORK

12

In the Age of the Smart Machine

Shoshana Zuboff

Without a doubt, the part of mankind which has advanced intellectually is quite under the spell of technology. Its charms are twofold. On the one hand, there is the enticement of increasingly comfortable living standards; on the other, there is a reduction in the amount of work which is necessary to do. . . . The irresistible pull toward technological development . . . is caused, we should remember, by the unconscious and deep-rooted desire to free ourselves from the material oppression of the material world.
—FOLKERT WILKEN, *THE LIBERATION OF CAPITAL*

The Body's Virtuosity at Work

In the older pulp and paper mills of Piney Wood and Tiger Creek, where a highly experienced work force was making the transition to a new computer-based technology, operators had many ways of using their bodies to achieve precise knowledge. One man judged the condition of paper coming off a dry roller by the sensitivity of his hair to electricity in the atmosphere around the machine. Another could judge the moisture content of a roll of pulp by a quick slap of his hand. Immediacy was the mode in which things were

known; it provided a feeling of certainty, of knowing "what's going on." One worker in Piney Wood described how it felt to be removed from the physical presence of the process equipment and asked to perform his tasks from a computerized control room:

> It is very different now. . . . It is hard to get used to not being out there with the process. I miss it a lot. I miss being able to see it. You can see when the pulp runs over a vat. You know what's happening.

The worker's capacity "to know" has been lodged in sentience and displayed in action. The physical presence of the process equipment has been the setting that corresponded to this knowledge, which could, in turn, be displayed only in that context. As long as the action context remained intact, it was possible for knowledge to remain implicit. In this sense, the worker knew a great deal, but very little of that knowledge was ever articulated, written down, or made explicit in any fashion. Instead, operators went about their business, displaying their know-how and rarely attempting to translate that knowledge into terms that were publicly accessible. This is what managers mean when they speak of the "art" involved in operating these plants. As one manager at Piney Wood described it:

> There are a lot of operators working here who cannot verbally give a description of some piece of the process. I

can ask them what is going on at the far end of the plant, and they can't tell me, but they can draw it for me. By taking away this physical contact that he understands, it's like we have taken away his blueprint. He can't verbalize his way around the process.

In this regard, the pulp and paper mills embody a historical sweep that is unavailable in many other forms of work. Unlike other continuous-process industries, such as oil refining or chemical production, the pulp-and-paper-making process has not yet yielded a full scientific explication. This has retarded the spread of automation and also has worked to preserve the integrity of a certain amount of craft know-how among those operators with lengthy experience in the industry. Like other continuous-process operations, the technological environment in these mills has created work that was more mediated by equipment and dependent upon indirect data than, say, work on an assembly line. However, discrete instrumentation typically was located on or close to the actual operating equipment, allowing the operator to combine data from an instrument reading with data from his or her own senses. Most workers believed that they "knew" what was going on at any particular moment because of what they saw and felt, and they used past experience to relate these perceptions to a set of likely consequences. The required sequences and routines necessary to control certain parts of the process and to make proper adjustments for achieving the best results represented a form of knowledge that the worker displayed in action as a continual reflection of this sentient involvement. Acquired experience made it possible to relate current conditions to past events; thus, an operator's competence increased as the passing of time enabled him or her to experience the action possibilities of a wide variety of operating conditions.

In Piney Wood and Tiger Creek, the technology change did not mean simply trading one form of instrumentation for another. Because the traditional basis of competence, like skilled work in most industries, was still heavily dependent upon sentient involvement, information technology was experienced as a radical departure from the taken-for-granted approach to daily work. In this sense, workers' experiences in these mills bridge two manufacturing domains. They not only illustrate the next phase of technological change within the continuous-process industries but also foreshadow the dilemmas that will emerge in other industrial organizations (for example, batch and assembly-line production) with the transition from machine to computer mediation.

When a process engineer attempts to construct a set of algorithms that will be the basis for automating some portion of the production process, he or she first interviews those individuals who currently perform the tasks that will be automated. The process engineer must learn the detail of their actions in order to translate their practice into the terms of a mathematical model. The algorithms in such a model explicate, rationalize, and institutionalize know-how. In the course of these interviews, the process engineer is likely to run up against the limits of implicit knowledge. A worker may perform competently yet be unable to communicate the structure of his or her actions. As one engineer discovered:

> There are operators who can run the paper machine with tremendous efficiency, but they cannot describe to you how they do it. They have built-in actions and senses that they are not aware of. One operation required pulling two levers simultaneously, and they were not conscious of the fact that they were pulling two levers. They said they were pulling one. The operators run the mill,

but they don't understand how. There are operators who know exactly what to do, but they cannot tell you how they do it.

Though every operator with similar responsibilities performs the same functions, each will perform them in a unique way, fashioned according to a personal interpretation of what works best. A process engineer contrasted the personal rendering of skill with the impersonal but consistently optimal performance of the computer:

> There is no question that the computer takes the human factor out of running the machine. Each new person who comes on shift will make their own distinct changes, according to their sense of what is the best setting. In contrast, the computer runs exactly the same way all the time. Each operator thinks he does a better job, each one thinks he has a better intimate understanding of the equipment than another operator. But none of them can compete with the computer.

These comments describe a particular quality of skill that I refer to as *action-centered*. Four components of action-centered skill are highlighted in the experiences of these workers:

1. *Sentience.* Action-centered skill is based upon sentient information derived from physical cues.
2. *Action-dependence.* Action-centered skill is developed in physical performance. Although in principle it may be made explicit in language, it typically remains unexplicated—implicit in action.
3. *Context-dependence.* Action-centered skill only has meaning within the context in which its associated physical activities can occur.
4. *Personalism.* It is the individual body that takes in the situation and an individual's

actions that display the required competence. There is a felt linkage between the knower and the known. The implicit quality of knowledge provides it with a sense of interiority, much like physical experience.

The Dissociation of Sentience and Knowledge

Computerization brings about an essential change in the way the worker can know the world and, with it, a crisis of confidence in the possibility of certain knowledge. For the workers of Piney Wood and Tiger Creek, achieving a sense of knowing the world was rarely problematical in their conventional environments. Certain knowledge was conveyed through the immediacy of their sensory experience. Instead of Descartes's "I think, therefore I am," these workers might say, "I see, I touch, I smell, I hear; therefore, I know." Their capacity to trust their knowledge was reflected in the assumption of its validity. In the precomputerized environment, belief was a seamless extension of sensory experience.

As the medium of knowing was transformed by computerization, the placid unity of experience and knowledge was disturbed. Accomplishing work depended upon the ability to manipulate symbolic, electronically presented data. Instead of using their bodies as instruments of *acting-on* equipment and materials, the task relationship became mediated by the information system. Operators had to work through the medium of what I will call the "data interface," represented most visibly by the computer terminals they monitored from central control rooms. The workers in this transition were at first overwhelmed with the feeling that they could no longer see or touch their work, as if it has been made both invisible and intangible by computer mediation.

It's just different getting this information in the control room. The man in here can't see. Out there you can look around until you find something.

The chlorine has overflowed, and it's all over the third floor. You see, this is what I mean . . . it's all over the floor, but you can't see it. You have to remember how to get into the system to do something about it. Before you could see it and you knew what was happening—you just knew.

The hardest thing for us operators is not to have the physical part. I can chew pulp and tell you its physical properties. We knew things from experience. Now we have to try and figure out what is happening. The hardest part is to give up that physical control.

In a world in which skills were honed over long years of physical experience, work was associated with concrete objects and the cues they provided. A worker's sense of occupational identity was deeply marked by his or her understanding of and attachment to discrete tangible entities, such as a piece of operating equipment. Years of service meant continued opportunities to master new objects. It was the immediate knowledge one could gain of these tangible objects that engendered feelings of competence and control. For workers, the new computer-mediated relationship to work often felt like being yanked away from a world that could be known because it could be sensed.

Our operators did their job by feeling a pipe—"Is it hot?" We can't just tell them it's 150 degrees. They have to believe it.

With computerization I am further away from my job than I have ever been before. I used to listen to the sounds the boiler makes and know just how it was running. I could look at the fire in the furnace and tell by its color how it was burning. I knew what kinds of adjustments were needed by the shades of color I saw. A lot of the men also said that there were smells that told you different things about how it was running. I feel uncomfortable being away from these sights and smells. Now I only have numbers to go by. I am scared of that boiler, and I feel that I should be closer to it in order to control it.

It is as if one's job had vanished into a two-dimensional space of abstractions, where digital symbols replace a concrete reality. Workers reiterated a spontaneous emotional response countless times—defined by feelings of loss of control, of vulnerability, and of frustration. It was sharpened with a sense of crisis and a need for steeling oneself with courage and not a little adrenaline in order to meet the challenge. It was shot through with the bewilderment of a man suddenly blind, groping with his hands outstretched in a vast, unfamiliar space. "We are in uncharted water now," they said. "We have to control our operations blind." This oft-repeated metaphor spoke of being robbed of one's senses and plunged into darkness. The tangible world had always been thick with landmarks; it was difficult to cast off from these familiar moorings with only abstractions as guides.

One operator described learning to work with the new computer system in Tiger Creek's pulping area. "The difficulty," he said, "is not being able to touch things." As he spoke, his hands shot out before him and he wiggled all his fingers, as if to emphasize the sense of incompleteness and loss. He continued:

When I go out and touch something, I know what will happen. There is a fear of not being out on the floor watching things. It is like turning your back in a dark alley. You don't know what is behind you; you don't know what might be happening. It all becomes remote from you, and it makes you feel vulnerable. It was like being a new operator all over again. Today I push buttons instead of opening valves on the digester. If I push the wrong button, will I screw up? Will anything happen?

Many other descriptions conveyed a similar feeling:

> With the change to the computer it's like driving down the highway with your lights out and someone else pushing the accelerator.

> It's like flying an airplane and taking all the instruments out so you can't see. It's like if you had an airplane and you put pieces over each instrument to hide it. Then, if something went wrong, you have to uncover the right one in a split second.

> Doing my job through the computer, it feels different. It is like you are riding a big, powerful horse, but someone is sitting behind you on the saddle holding the reins, and you just have to be on that ride and hold on. You see what is coming, but you can't do anything to control it. You can't steer yourself left and right; you can't control that horse that you are on. You have got to do whatever the guy behind you holding the reins wants you to do. Well, I would rather be holding the reins than have someone behind me holding the reins.

The feeling of being in control and the willingness to be held accountable require a reservoir of critical judgment with which to initiate informed action. In the past, operators like those at Piney Wood derived their critical judgment from their "gut feel" of the production process. Becoming a "good" operator—the kind that workers and managers alike refer to as an "artist" and invest with the authority of expertise—required the years of experience to develop a finely nuanced, felt sense of the equipment, the product, and the overall process. With computerization, many managers acknowledged that operators had lost their ability "to feel the machine." Without considering the new skill implications of this loss, many managers feared it would eliminate the kind of critical judgment that would have allowed operators to take action based upon an understanding that reached beyond the computer system.

Piney Wood's plant manager, as he presided over the massive technology conversion, asked himself what the loss of such art might mean:

> In the digester area, we used to have guys doing it who had an art. After we put the computer in, when they went down we could go to manual backup. People remembered how to run the digesters. Now if we try to go back, they can't remember what to do. They have lost the feel for it. We are really stuck now without the computer; we can't successfully operate that unit without it. If you are watching a screen, do you see the same things you would if you were there, face-to-face with the process and the equipment? I am concerned we are losing the art and skills that are not replenishable.

There were many operators who agreed. In one area of Piney Wood, the crew leader explained it this way:

> The new people are not going to understand, see, or feel as well as the old guys. Something is wrong with this fan, for example. You may not know what; you just feel it in your feet. The sound, the tone, the volume, the vibrations . . . the computer will control it, but you will have lost something, too. It's a trade-off. The computer can't feel what is going on out there. The new operators will need to have more written down, because

they will not know it in their guts. I can't understand how new people coming in are ever going to learn how to run a pulp mill. They are not going to know what is going on. They will only learn what these computers tell them.

Sam Gimbel was a young production co-ordinator in Piney Wood. Though trained as a chemical engineer, he had been particularly close to the operators whom he managed. He had shepherded them through the technology conversion and construction of the new control room, and worked closely with them as they grappled with new ways of operating:

> We are losing the context where hands-on experience makes sense. If you don't have actual experience, you have to believe everything the computer says, and you can't beat it at its own game. You can't stand up to it. And yet who will have the experience to make these kinds of judgments? It will surely be a different world. You lose the checkpoints in reality to know if you are doing it right; therefore, how will anyone be able to confront the computer information?

Piney Wood's management had approached the technology conversion with the following message: "We are simply providing you with new tools to do your job. Your job is to operate the equipment, and this is a new tool to operate the equipment with." Managers repeatedly made statements such as, "We told them this was a tool just like a hammer or a wrench." One manager even went so far as to say, "We hoped they wouldn't figure out that the terminal we were giving them was really a computer."

As experience with the new operating conditions began to accumulate, many managers began to see that treating the computer system like a physical object, "just another tool," could lead to chronic suboptimiza-

tion of the technology's potential. A powerhouse worker with over twenty-five years of experience had developed a special way of kicking the boiler in order to make it function smoothly. He used the same approach with the terminal; if he hit a certain button on the keyboard, a particular reading would change in the desired direction, but he did not know why or how. Piney Wood's powerhouse manager put it this way:

> The guy who kicks the boiler is the same guy who mashes the button a certain way just to make the line go down. This person will never optimize the process. He will use too much chemical and too high pressure. He will never make you money because he doesn't understand the problem.

Just as the digester operators had lost their ability to cook manually, other workers throughout the mill felt equally powerless:

> In the old way, you had control over the job. The computer now tells you what to do. There is more responsibility but less control. We lost a boiler that was on computer control. We just had to sit there and stare. We were all shook up.

> Sometimes I am amazed when I realize that we stare at the screen even when it has gone down. You get in the habit and you just keep staring even if there is nothing there.

Ironically, as managers and operators across the mill watched the level of artistry decline, the senior technical designers continued to assume that manual skills would provide the necessary backup to their systems.

The problem was even more acute in Cedar Bluff, where most of the work force lacked the experience base from which felt sense and critical judgment are developed. Managers at Cedar Bluff engaged in a quiet debate as to how much of a problem this lack of experience would ultimately be. On one side of the argument were the "old-timers"—managers with years of experience in the industry:

> I like to smell and feel the pulp some-times. It can be slick, it can be slimy, it can be all different consistencies. These are the artistic aspects of making pulp that the computer doesn't know about. Some of the operators have been picking up these aspects, but there are so many numbers so readily accessible, we have to shortcut it at times and solve more problems from the office. The informa-tion is so good and rapid we have to use it. . . . You have got to be able to recog-nize when you can run things from the office and when you have to go and look. Yet, I recognize that I am not as good a pulp maker as the people who trained me, and the new operators are not as good as I am. They are better man-agers and planners. I am very happy with the new managers, but not with the new pulp makers.

The younger engineers, schooled in computer-based analytic techniques, had lit-tle patience with anxious laments over the loss of the art of pulp making. They were re-lentlessly confident that a good computer model could reproduce anything that opera-tors knew from experience—only better. Here is how the process engineers articu-lated the argument:

> Computer analysis lets us see the effects of many variables and their interactions. This is a picture of truth that we could not have achieved before. It is superior to the experience-based knowledge of an operator. You might say that truth re-places knowledge.

> People who have this analytic power do not need to have been around to know what is going on. All you need is to be able to formulate a model and perform

the necessary confirmation checks. With the right model you can manage the sys-tem just fine.

Most Cedar Bluff managers agreed that the computer system made it possible to do a better job running the plant with an inex-perienced work force than otherwise would have been possible, though some wondered whether the levels of expertise would ever be as high as among workers with hands-on exposure to the pulping process. Yet even as managers argued over the essentiality of action-centered skill, technology was irreversibly altering the context in which the operators performed. The opportunities to develop such skills were becoming increasingly rare as the ac-tion context was paved over by the data highway.

Many of Cedar Bluff's managers be-lieved that the traditional knowledge of the pulp mill worker would actually inhibit the development of creativity and flexibility. Under the new technological conditions, the young operators would develop their capac-ity to "know better" than the systems with which they worked as they struggled with the complexities of the new technology and the data it provided. The data interface would replace the physical equipment as the primary arena for learning.

Yet as months passed, other managers observed a disturbing pattern of interactions between the operators and the computer system. Some believed that the highly com-puterized task environment resulted in a greater than usual bifurcation of skills. One group of operators would use the informa-tion systems to learn an extraordinary amount about the process, while another group would make itself an appendage to the system, mechanically carrying out the computer's directives. These managers com-plained that the computer system was be-coming a crutch that prevented many operators from developing a superior knowledge of the process. One "old-timer" provided an example:

> When there is a shift change and new operators come on, the good operator will take the process from the computer, put it on manual, make certain changes that the operator thinks are necessary, and then gives it back to the computer. The average operator will come in, see this thing on automatic control, and leave it with the computer. Sometimes that operator won't even realize that things are getting bad or getting worse. They should have known better, but they didn't.

Most Cedar Bluff operators spoke enthusiastically about the convenience of the computer interface, and some freely admitted what they perceived to be a dependence on the computer system:

> The computer provides your hands. I don't think I could work in a conventional mill. This is so much more convenient. You have so much control without having to go out to the equipment and adjust things.

> We can't run this mill manually. There are too many controls, and it is too complex. The average person can only run four or five variables at once in a manual mode, and the automatic system runs it all. If the computer goes down, we have to sit back and wait. We sit and we stare at the screens and we hope something pipes in.

Many managers observed with growing alarm the things that occurred when operators neither enjoyed the traditional sources of critical judgment nor had developed enough new knowledge for informed action.

> In a conventional mill, you have to go and look at the equipment because you cannot get enough data in the control room. Here, you get all the data you need. The computer becomes a substi-

tute tool. It replaces all the sensual data instead of being an addition. We had another experience with the feedwater pumps, which supply water to the boiler to make steam. There was a power outage. Something in the computer canceled the alarm. The operator had a lot of trouble and did not look at the readout of the water level and never got an alarm. The tank ran empty, the pumps tripped. The pump finally tore up because there was no water feeding it.

> We have so much data from the computer, I find that hard drives out soft. Operators are tempted not to tour the plant. They just sit at the computer and watch for alarms. One weekend I found a tank overflowing in digesting. I went to the operator and told him, and he said, "It can't be; the computer says my level is fine." I am afraid of what happens if we trust the computer too much.

At least since the introduction of the moving assembly line in Ford's Highland Park plant, it has been second nature for managers to use technology to delimit worker discretion and, in this process, to concentrate knowledge within the managerial domain. The special dilemmas raised by information technology require managers to reconsider these assumptions. When information and control technology is used to turn the worker into "just another mechanical variable," one immediate result is the withdrawal of the worker's commitment to and accountability for the work. This lack of care requires additional managerial vigilance and leads to a need for increased automatic control. As this dynamic unfolds, it no longer seems shocking to contemplate an image of work laced with stupefaction and passivity, in which the human being is a hapless bystander at the margins of productive activity. One young operator in Cedar Bluff discussed his prior job as a bank clerk. I asked him if his two employment experiences had anything in common. "Yes," he said, "in both cases you punch the buttons and watch it happen."

As automation intensifies, information technology becomes the receptacle for larger and larger portions of the organization's operating intelligence. Algorithms become the functional equivalent of a once diffuse know-how, and the action context in which know-how can be developed and sustained vanishes. Because many managers assume that more technology means a diminished need for human operating skill, they may recognize the waning of worker know-how without becoming concerned enough to chart a different course. Left unchallenged, these systems become more potent, as they are invested with an escalating degree of authority. Technical experts temporarily serve as resources, but once their knowledge has been depleted, and converted into systematic rules for decision making, their usefulness is attenuated. The analysts and engineers, who construct programs and models, have the capacity to manipulate data and, presumably, to make discoveries. Ultimately, they will become the most important human presence to offer any counterpoint to the growing density and opacity of the automated systems.

There is an alternative, one that involves understanding this technological change as an occasion for developing a new set of skills—skills that are able to exploit the information capacity of the technology and to become a new source of critical judgment. In order to assess the likelihood of this alternative—the forces that will drive organizations in this direction and those that will impede them—we first have to understand the nature of these new skills. What can the experiences of workers in these three mills teach us about the emerging requirements for competence at the data interface?

From Action-Centered to Intellective Skill

The pulp and paper mills reveal the shift in the grounds of knowledge associated with a technology that informates. Men and women accustomed to an intimate physical association with the production process found themselves removed from the action. Now they had to know and to do based upon their ability to understand and manipulate electronic data. In Piney Wood, a $200 million investment in technology was radically altering every phase of mill life. Managers believed they were merely "upgrading" in order to modernize production and to improve productivity. Tiger Creek was undergoing a similar modernization process. In both cases, informating dynamics tended to unfold as an unintended and undermanaged consequence of these efforts. Cedar Bluff had been designed with a technological infrastructure based on integrated information and control systems. In that organization, managers were somewhat more self-conscious about using the informating capacity of the technology as the basis for developing new operating skills.

The experiences of the skilled workers in these mills provide a frame of reference for a general appraisal of the forms of knowledge that are required in an informated environment. My contention is that the skill demands that can be deciphered from their experiences have relevance for a wider range of organizational settings in both manufacturing and service sectors. Later chapters will compare the experiences of clerks and managers to those of the mill operators. This joint appraisal will help to unravel the intrinsic and the contingent aspects of change and to gauge the generalizations that follow from the dilemmas of transformation described here.

A fundamental quality of this technological transformation, as it is experienced by workers and observed by their managers, involves a reorientation of the means by which one can have a palpable effect upon the world. Immediate physical responses must be replaced by an abstract thought process in which options are considered, and choices are made and then translated into the terms of the information system. For many, physical action is restricted to the play of fingers on the terminal keyboard. As one operator put it, "Your past physical mobility must be translated into a mental thought process." A Cedar Bluff manager with prior experience in pulping contemplates the distinct capacities that had become necessary in a highly computerized environment:

> In 1953 we put operation and control as close together as possible. We did a lot of localizing so that when you made a change you could watch the change, actually see the motor start up. With the evolution of computer technology, you centralize controls and move away from the actual physical process. If you don't have an understanding of what is happening and how all the pieces interact, it is more difficult. You need a new learning capability, because when you operate with the computer, you can't see what is happening. There is a difference in the mental and conceptual capabilities you need—you have to do things in your mind.

When operators in Piney Wood and Tiger Creek discuss their traditional skills, they speak of knowing things by habit and association. They talk about "cause-and-effect" knowledge and being able to see the things to which they must respond. They refer to "folk medicine" and knowledge that you don't even know you have until it is suddenly displayed in the ability to take a decisive action and make something work.

In plants like Piney Wood and Tiger Creek, where operators have relied upon action-centered skill, management must convince the operator to leave behind a world in which things were immediately

known, comprehensively sensed, and able to be acted upon directly, in order to embrace a world that is dominated by objective data, is removed from the action context, and requires a qualitatively different kind of response. In this new world, personal interpretations of how to make things happen count for little. The worker who has relied upon an intimate knowledge of a piece of equipment—the operators talk about having "pet knobs" or knowing just where to kick a machine to make it hum—feels adrift. To be effective, he or she must now trade immediate knowledge for a more explicit understanding of the science that undergirds the operation. One Piney Wood manager described it this way:

> The workers have an intuitive feel of what the process needs to be. Someone in the process will listen to things, and that is their information. All of their senses are supplying data. But once they are in the control room, all they have to do is look at the screen. Things are concentrated right in front of you. You don't have sensory feedback. You have to draw inferences by watching the data, so you must understand the theory behind it. In the long run, you would like people who can take data and draw broad conclusions from it. They must be more scientific.

Many managers are not optimistic about the ability of experienced workers to trade their embodied knowledge for a more explicit, "scientific" inference.

> The operators today know if I do "x," then "y" will happen. But they don't understand the real logic of the system. Their cause-and-effect reasoning comes from their experience. Once we put things under automatic control and ask them to relate to the process using the computer, their personal judgments about how to relate to equipment go by the wayside. We

are saying your intuition is no longer valuable. Now you must understand the whole process and the theory behind it.

Now a new kind of learning must begin. It is slow and scary, and many workers are timid, not wanting to appear foolish and incompetent. Hammers and wrenches have been replaced by numbers and buttons. An operator with thirty years of service in the Piney Wood Mill described his experience in the computer-mediated environment:

> Anytime you mash a button you should have in mind exactly what is going to happen. You need to have in your mind where it is at, what it is doing, and why it is doing it. Out there in the plant, you can know things just by habit. You can know them without knowing that you know them. In here you have to watch the numbers, whereas out there you have to watch the actual process.

"You need to have in your mind where it is at"—it is a simple phrase, but deceptive. What it takes to have things "in your mind" is far different from the knowledge associated with action-centered skill.

This does not imply that action-centered skills exist independent of cognitive activity. Rather, it means that the process of learning, remembering, and displaying action-centered skills do not necessarily require that the knowledge they contain be made explicit. Physical cues do not require inference; learning in an action-centered context is more likely to be analogical than analytical. In contrast, the abstract cues available through the data interface do require explicit inferential reasoning, particularly in the early phases of the learning process. It is necessary to reason out the meaning of those cues—what is their relation to each other and to the world "out there"?

It is also necessary to understand the procedures according to which these abstract cues can be manipulated to result in the desired effects. Procedural reasoning means having an understanding of the internal structure of the information system and its functional capacities. This makes it possible both to operate skillfully through the system and to use the system as a source of learning and feedback. For example, one operation might require sixteen control actions spread across four groups of variables. The operator must first think about what has to be done. Second, he or she must know how data elements (abstract cues) correspond to actual processes and their systemic relations. Third, the operator must have a conception of the information system itself, in order to know how actions taken at the information interface can result in appropriate outcomes. Fourth, having decided what to do and executed that command, he or she must scan new data and check for results. Each of these processes folds back upon a kind of thinking that can stand independent from the physical context. An operator summed it up this way:

> Before computers, we didn't have to think as much, just react. You just knew what to do because it was physically there. Now, the most important thing to learn is to think before you do something, to think about what you are planning to do. You have to know which variables are the most critical and therefore what to be the most cautious about, what to spend time thinking about before you take action.

The vital element here is that these workers feel a stark difference in the forms of knowledge they must now use. Their experience of competence has been radically altered. "We never got paid to have ideas," said one Tiger Creek worker. "We got paid to work." Work was the exertion that could be known by its material results. The fact that a material world must be created required physical exertion. Most of the operators believed that some people in society are paid to "think," but they were not among them.

They knew themselves to be the ones who gave their bodies in effort and skill, and through their bodies, they made things. Accustomed to gauging their integrity in intimate measures of strain and sweat, these workers find that information technology has challenged their assumptions and thrown them into turmoil. There was a gradual dawning that the rules of the game had changed. For some, this created panic; they did not believe in their ability to think in this new way and were afraid of being revealed as incompetent.

Such feelings are no mere accident of personality, but the sedimentation of long years of conditioned learning about who does the "thinking"—a boundary that is not meant to be crossed. As a Tiger Creek manager observed:

> Currently, managers make all the decisions. . . . Operators don't want to hear about alternatives. They have been trained to *do,* not to *think.* There is a fear of being punished if you think. This translates into a fear of the new technology.

In each control room, a tale is told about one or two old-timers who, though they knew more about the process than anyone else, "just up and quit" when they heard the new technology was coming. From one plant to another, reports of these cases were remarkably similar:

> He felt that because he had never graduated high school, he would never be able to keep up with this new stuff. We tried to tell him different, but he just wouldn't listen.

Despite the anxiety of change, those who left were not the majority. Most men and women need their jobs and will do whatever it takes to keep them. Beyond this, there were many who were honestly intrigued with the opportunity this change offered. They seemed to get pulled in gradually, observing their own experiences and savoring with secret surprise each new bit of evidence of their unexpected abilities. They discussed the newness and strangeness of having to act upon the world by exerting a more strictly intellectual effort. Under the gentle stimulus of a researcher's questions, they thought about this new kind of thinking. What does it feel like? Here are the observations of an operator who spent twenty years in one of the most manually intensive parts of the Tiger Creek Mill, which has recently been computerized:

> If something is happening, if something is going wrong, you don't go down and fix it. Instead, you stay up here and think about the sequence, and you think about how you want to affect the sequence. You get it done through your thinking. But dealing with information instead of things is very . . . well, very intriguing. I am very aware of the need for my mental involvement now. I am always wondering: Where am I at? What is happening? It all occurs in your mind now.

Another operator discussed the same experience but added an additional dimension. After describing the demand for thinking and mental involvement, he observed:

> Things occur to me now that never would have occurred to me before. With all of this information in front of me, I begin to think about how to do the job better. And, being freed from all that manual activity, you really have time to look at things, to think about them, and to anticipate.

As information technology restructures the work situation, it abstracts thought from action. Absorption, immediacy, and organic responsiveness are superseded by distance, coolness, and remoteness. Such distance brings an opportunity for reflection. There was little doubt in these workers' minds that the logic of their jobs had been fundamentally altered. As another worker from Tiger Creek summed it up, "Sitting in this room and just thinking has become part of my job. It's the technology that lets me do these things."

The thinking this operator refers to is of a different quality from the thinking that attended the display of action-centered skills. It combines abstraction, explicit inference, and procedural reasoning. Taken together, these elements make possible a new set of competencies that I call *intellective skills.* As long as the new technology signals only deskilling—the diminished importance of action-centered skills—there will be little probability of developing critical judgment at the data interface. To rekindle such judgment, though on a new, more abstract footing, a reskilling process is required. Mastery in a computer-mediated environment depends upon developing intellective skills. . . .

13

Labor and Management in Uncertain Times
Renegotiating the Social Contract

Ruth Milkman

The U.A.W. . . . is the largest labor union on earth. Its membership of 1,300,000 embraces most of the production workers in three major American industries. . . . The U.A.W. itself is diverse and discordant, both in its leaders and its members, among whom are represented every race and shape of political opinion. . . . The union's sharp insistence on democratic expression permits bloc to battle bloc and both to rebel at higher-ups' orders. They often do. But U.A.W. is a smart, aggressive, ambitious outfit with young, skillful leaders. . . . It has improved the working conditions in the sometimes frantically paced production lines. And it has firmly established the union shop in an industry which was once firmly open shop. . . . It is not a rich union. Its dues are one dollar a month, which is low. . . . U.A.W. makes its money go a long way. It sets up social, medical, and educational benefits. . . . In its high ranks are men like Reuther, who believes labor must more and more be given a voice in long-range economic planning of the country.[1]

Curious as it may seem to late-twentieth-century sensibility, this homage to the United Auto Workers is not from a union publication or some obscure left-wing tract. It appeared in *Life* magazine in 1945, a month after V-J Day and not long before the century's largest wave of industrial strikes, led by the auto workers, rocked the nation. The cover photo featured a 1940s Everyman: an unnamed auto worker in his work clothes, with factory smokestacks in the background. Blue-collar men in heavy industry, with powerful democratic unions and, at least implicitly, a strong class consciousness—only forty-five years ago this was standard iconography in the mass media and in the popular thinking that it both reflected and helped shape. Organized labor, then embracing over a third of the nation's nonfarm workers and 67 percent of those in manufacturing, was a central force in the Democratic party and a vital influence in public debate on a wide range of social questions. The industrial unions founded in the New Deal era were leaders in opposing race discrimination (and to some extent even sex discrimination) in this period, and their political agenda went far beyond the narrow, sectional interests of their members. Indeed, as historian Nelson Lichtenstein has written, in the 1940s "the union movement defined the left wing of what was possible in the political affairs of the day."[2]

Today, the history is all but forgotten. Blue-collar workers and labor unions are conspicuous by their absence from the mainstream of public discourse. Across the political spectrum, the conventional wisdom is that both industrial work and the forms of unionism it generated are fading relics of a bygone age, obsolete and irrelevant in today's postindustrial society. As everybody knows, while the unionized male factory worker was prototypical in 1945, today the labor force includes nearly as many women as men, and workers of both genders are more likely to sit behind a desk or perform a service than to toil on an assembly line. Union density has fallen dramatically, and organized labor is so isolated from the larger society that the right-wing characterization of it as a "special interest" prevails unchallenged. Public approval ratings of unions are at a postwar low, and such new social movements as environmentalism and feminism are as likely to define themselves in opposi-

tion to as in alliance with organized labor (if they take any notice of it at all).

What has happened in the postwar decades to produce this change? Part of the story involves structural economic shifts. Most obviously, the manufacturing sector has decreased drastically in importance, accounting for only 20 percent of civilian wage and salary employment in the United States in 1987, compared to 34 percent in 1948.[3] And for complex political as well as economic reasons, unionization has declined even more sharply, especially in manufacturing, its historical stronghold. Although numbers fail to capture the qualitative aspects of this decline, they do indicate its massive scale: in 1989, only 16 percent of all U.S. workers, and 22 percent of those in manufacturing, were union members—half and one-third, respectively, of the 1945 density levels.[4] Alongside these massive processes of deindustrialization and deunionization, the widespread introduction of new technologies and the growing diffusion of the "new" industrial relations, with its emphasis on worker participation, have in recent years dramatically transformed both work and unionism in the manufacturing sector itself.

Few workplaces have been affected by these changes as dramatically as those in the automobile industry, the historical prototype of mass production manufacturing and the core of the U.S. economy for most of this century. Since the mid-1970s, hundreds of thousands of auto workers have been thrown out of work as some factories have closed and others have been modernized. And although the U.A.W. still represents the vast bulk of workers employed by the "Big Three" auto firms (General Motors, Ford, and Chrysler), in recent years the non-union sector of the industry has grown dramatically. Union coverage in the auto parts industry has fallen sharply since the mid-1970s, and the establishment of new Japanese-owned "transplants" in the 1980s has created a non-union beachhead in the otherwise solidly organized assembly sector. Profoundly weakened by these developments, the U.A.W. has gingerly entered a new era of "cooperation" with management, jettisoning many of its time-honored traditions in hopes of securing a place for itself in the future configuration of the industry. Meanwhile, the Big Three have invested vast sums of money in such new technologies as robotics and programmable automation. They have also experimented extensively with worker participation schemes and other organizational changes.

The current situation of auto workers graphically illustrates both the historical legacy of the glory days of American industrial unionism and the consequences of the recent unravelling of the social contract between labor and management that crystallized in the aftermath of World War II. This [reading] explores current changes in the nature of work and unionism in the auto industry, drawing on historical evidence and on fieldwork in a recently modernized General Motors (GM) assembly plant in Linden, New Jersey. The analysis focuses particularly on the effects of new technology and the new, participatory forms of management. While it is always hazardous to generalize from any one industry to "the" workplace, the recent history of labor relations in the auto industry is nonetheless suggestive of broader patterns. The auto industry case is also of special interest because it figures so prominently in current theoretical debates about workplace change. . . .

Because so much of the recent behavior of automobile manufacturing managers and of the U.A.W. and its members is rooted in the past, the first step in understanding the current situation is to look back to the early days of the auto industry, when the system of mass production and the accompanying pattern of labor-management relations that is now unravelling first took shape.

Fordism and the History of Labor Relations in the U.S. Auto Industry

The earliest car manufacturers depended heavily on skilled craftsmen to make small production runs of luxury vehicles for the rich. But the industry's transformation into a model of mass production efficiency, led by the Ford Motor Company in the 1910s, was predicated on the systematic removal of skill from the industry's labor process through scientific management, or Taylorism (named for its premier theorist, Frederick Winslow Taylor). Ford perfected a system involving not only deskilling but also product standardization, the use of interchangeable parts, mechanization, a moving assembly line, and high wages. These were the elements of what has since come to be known as "Fordism," and they defined not only the organization of the automobile industry but that of modern mass production generally.

As rationalization and deskilling proceeded through the auto industry in the 1910s and 1920s, the proportion of highly skilled jobs fell dramatically. The introduction of Ford's famous Five Dollar Day in 1914 (then twice the going rate for factory workers) both secured labor's consent to the horrendous working conditions these innovations produced and helped promote the mass consumption that mass production required for its success. Managerial paternalism, symbolized by Ford's "Sociological Department," supplemented high wages in this regime of labor control. Early Ford management also developed job classification systems, ranking jobs by skill levels and so establishing an internal labor market within which workers could hope to advance.

Deskilling was never complete, and some skill differentials persisted among production workers. Even in the 1980s, auto body painters and welders had more skill than workers who simply assembled parts, for example. But these were insignificant gradations compared to the gap between production workers and the privileged stratum of craft workers known in the auto industry as the "skilled trades"—tool and die makers, machinists, electricians, and various other maintenance workers. Nevertheless, the mass of the industry's semiskilled operatives united with the skilled trades elite in the great industrial union drives of the 1930s, and in the U.A.W. both groups were integrated into the same local unions.

The triumph of unionism left the industry's internal division of jobs and skills intact, but the U.A.W. did succeed in narrowing wage differentials among production workers and in institutionalizing seniority (a principle originally introduced by management but enforced erratically in the pre-union era) as the basic criterion for layoffs and job transfers for production workers. For the first decade of the union era, much labor-management conflict focused on the definition of seniority groups. Workers wanted plantwide or departmentwide seniority to maximize employment security, while management sought the narrowest possible seniority classifications to minimize the disruptions associated with workers' movement from job to job. But once the U.A.W. won plantwide seniority for layoffs, it welcomed management's efforts to increase the number of job classifications for transfers, since this maximized opportunities for workers with high seniority to choose the jobs they preferred. By the 1950s, this system of narrowly defined jobs, supported by union and management alike, was firmly entrenched.

Management and labor reached an accommodation on many other issues as well in the immediate aftermath of World War II. But at the same time, the U.A.W. began to retreat from the broad, progressive agenda it had championed in the 1930s and during the war. The failure of the 1945–46 "open the books" strike, in which the union demanded

that GM raise workers' wages without increasing car prices, and the national resurgence of conservatism in the late 1940s and 1950s led the U.A.W. into its famous postwar "accord" with management. Under its terms, the union increasingly restricted its goals to improving wages and working conditions for its members, while ceding to management all the prerogatives involved in the production process and in economic planning. The shop steward system in the plants was weakened in the postwar period as well, and in the decades that followed, the U.A.W. was gradually transformed from the highly democratic social movement that *Life* magazine had profiled in 1945 into a more staid, bureaucratic institution that concentrated its energies on the increasingly complex technical issues involved in enforcing its contracts and improving wages, fringe benefits, and job security for its members.

The grueling nature of production work in the auto industry changed relatively little over the postwar decades, even as the U.A.W. continued to extract improvements in the economic terms under which workers agreed to perform it. High wages and excellent benefits made auto workers into the blue-collar aristocrats of the age. It was an overwhelmingly male aristocracy, since women had been largely excluded from auto assembly jobs after World War II; blacks, on the other hand, made up a more substantial part of the auto production work force than of the nation's population. In 1987, at the Linden GM assembly plant where I did my fieldwork, for example, women were 12 percent of the production work force and less than 1 percent of the skilled trades. Linden production workers were a racially diverse group: 61 percent were white, 28 percent were black, and 12 percent were Hispanic; the skilled trades work force, however, was 90 percent white.

While the union did little to ameliorate the actual experience of work in the postwar period, with the job classification system solidified, those committed to a long-term career in the industry could build up enough seniority to bid on the better jobs within their plants. Although the early, management-imposed job classification systems had been based on skill and wage differentials, the union eliminated most of the variation along these dimensions. Indeed, the payment system the U.A.W. won, which persists to this day, is extremely egalitarian. Regardless of seniority or individual merit, assembly workers are paid a fixed hourly rate negotiated for their job classification, and the rate spread across classifications is very narrow. Formal education, which is in any case relatively low (both production workers and skilled trades at Linden GM averaged twelve years of schooling), is virtually irrelevant to earnings. At Linden GM, production workers rates in 1987 ranged from a low of $13.51 per hour for sweepers and janitors to a high of $14.69 for metal repair work in the body shop. Skilled trades workers' hourly rates were only slightly higher, ranging from $15.90 to $16.80 (with a twenty-cent-an-hour "merit spread"), although their annual earnings are much higher than those of production workers because of their extensive overtime.[5]

Since wage differentials are so small, the informal *de facto* hierarchy among production jobs is based instead on what workers themselves perceive as desirable job characteristics. While individual preferences always vary somewhat, the consensus is reflected in the seniority required to secure any given position. One testament to the intensely alienating nature of work on the assembly line is that among the jobs auto workers prefer most are those of sweeper and janitor, even though these jobs have the *lowest* hourly wage rates. Subassembly, inspection, and other jobs where workers could pace themselves rather than be governed by the assembly line are also much

sought after. At Linden in 1987, the median seniority of unskilled workers in the material and maintenance departments, which include all the sweepers and janitors and where all jobs are "off the line," was 24 years—twice the median seniority of workers in the assembly departments! By contrast, jobs in particularly hot or dirty parts of the plant, or those in areas where supervision is especially hostile, are shunned by workers whose seniority gives them any choice. Such concerns are far more important to production workers than what have become marginal skill or wage differentials, although there is a group that longs to cross the almost insurmountable barrier between production work and the skilled trades.[6]

Such was the system that emerged from the post–World War II accord between the U.A.W. and management. It functioned reasonably well for the first three postwar decades. The auto companies generated huge profits in these years, and for auto workers, too, the period was one of unprecedented prosperity. Even recessions in this cyclically sensitive industry were cushioned by the supplementary unemployment benefits the union won in 1955. However, in the 1970s, fundamental shifts in the international economy began to undermine the domestic auto makers. As skyrocketing oil prices sent shock waves through the U.S. economy, more and more cars were imported from the economically resurgent nations of Western Europe and, most significantly, Japan. For the first time in their history, the domestic producers faced a serious challenge in their home market.

After initially ignoring these developments, in the 1980s the Big Three began to confront their international competition seriously. They invested heavily in computerization and robotization, building a few new high-tech plants and modernizing most of their existing facilities. GM alone spent more than $40 billion during the 1980s on renovating old plants and building new ones.[7] At the same time, inspired by their Japanese competitors, the auto firms sought to change the terms of their postwar accord with labor, seeking wage concessions from the union, reducing the number of job classifications and related work rules in many plants, and experimenting with new forms of "employee involvement" and worker participation, from quality circles to flexible work teams.

The U.A.W., faced with unprecedented job losses and the threat of more to come, accepted most of these changes in the name of labor-management cooperation. To the union's national leadership, this appeared to be the only viable alternative. They justified it to an often skeptical rank and file membership by arguing that resistance to change would only serve to prevent the domestic industry from becoming internationally competitive, which in turn would mean further job losses. Once it won job security provisions protecting those members affected by technological change, the union welcomed management's investments in technological modernization, which both parties saw as a means of meeting the challenge of foreign competition. Classification mergers and worker participation schemes were more controversial within the union, but the leadership accepted these, too, in the name of enhancing the domestic industry's competitiveness.

Most popular and academic commentators view the innovations in technology and industrial relations that the auto industry (among others) undertook in the 1980s in very positive terms. Some go so far as to suggest that they constitute a fundamental break with the old Fordist system. New production technologies in particular, it is widely argued, hold forth the promise of eliminating the most boring and dangerous jobs while upgrading the skill levels of those that remain. In this view, new technology potentially offers workers something the U.A.W. was never able to provide, namely, an end to the deadening monotony of repetitive, deskilled work. Similarly, many commentators applaud the introduction of Japanese-style quality circles and other forms of participative management, which they see as a form of work humanization complementing the new technology. By building on workers' own knowledge of the production process, it is argued, participation enhances both efficiency and the quality of work experience. The realities of work in the auto industry, however, have changed far less than this optimistic scenario suggests.

New Technology and the Skill Question

Computer-based technologies are fundamentally different from earlier waves of industrial innovation. Whereas in the past automation involved the use of special-purpose, or "dedicated," machinery to perform specific functions previously done manually, the new information-based technologies are flexible, allowing a single machine to be adapted to a variety of specific tasks. As Shoshana Zuboff points out, these new technologies often require workers to use "intellective" skills. Workers no longer simply manipulate tools and other tangible objects, but also must respond to abstract, electronically presented information. For this reason, Zuboff suggests, computer technology offers the possibility of a radical break with the Taylorist tradition of work organization that industries like auto manufacturing long ago perfected, moving instead toward more skilled and rewarding jobs, and toward workplaces where learning is encouraged and rewarded. "Learning is the new form of labor," she declares.[8] Larry Hirschhorn, another influential commentator on computer technology, makes a similar agreement. As he puts it, in the computerized factory the "deskilling process is reversed. Machines extend workers' skill rather than replace it."[9]

As computer technology has transformed more and more workplaces, claims like these have won widespread public acceptance. They are, in fact, the basis for labor market projections that suggest a declining need for unskilled labor and the need for educational upgrading to produce future generations of workers capable of working in the factory and office of the computer age. Yet it is far from certain that workplaces are actually changing in the ways that Zuboff and Hirschhorn suggest.

The Linden GM plant is a useful case for examining this issue, since it recently underwent dramatic technological change. In 1985–86, GM spent $300 million modernizing the plant, which emerged from this process as one of the nation's most technologically advanced auto assembly facilities and as the most efficient GM plant in the United States. There are now 219 robots in the plant, and 113 automated guided vehicles (AGVs), which carry the car bodies from station to station as they are assembled. Other new technology includes 186 programmable logic controllers (PLCs), used to program the robots. (Before the plant modernization there was only one robot, no AGVs, and eight PLCs.)[10]

Despite this radical technological overhaul, the long-standing division of labor between skilled trades and production workers has been preserved intact. Today, as they did when the plant used traditional technology, Linden's skilled trades workers maintain the plant's machinery and equipment, while production workers perform the unskilled and semi-skilled manual work involved in assembling the cars. However, the number of production workers has been drastically reduced (by over 1,100 people, or 26 percent), while the much smaller population of skilled trades workers has risen sharply (by 190 people, or 81 percent). Thus the overall proportion of skilled workers increased—from 5 percent to 11.5 percent—with the introduction of robotics and other computer-based production technologies. In this sense,

the plant's modernization did lead to an overall upgrading in skill levels.

However, a closer look at the impact of the technological change on GM-Linden reveals that pre-existing skill differentials among workers have been magnified, leading to skill *polarization* within the plant rather than across-the-board upgrading. After the plant modernization, the skilled trades workers enjoyed massive skill upgrading and gained higher levels of responsibility, just as Zuboff and Hirschhorn would predict. In contrast, however, the much larger group of production workers, whose jobs were already extremely routinized, typically experienced still further deskilling and found themselves subordinated to and controlled by the new technology to an even greater extent than before.

The skilled trades workers had to learn how to maintain and repair the robots, AGVs, and other new equipment, and since the new technology is far more complex than what it replaced, they acquired many new skills. Most skilled trades workers received extensive retraining, especially in robotics and in the use of computers. Linden's skilled trades workers reported an average (median) of forty-eight full days of technical training in connection with the plant modernization, and some received much more. Most of them were enthusiastic about the situation. "They were anxiously awaiting the new technology," one electrician recalled. "It was like a kid with a new toy. Everyone wanted to know what was going to happen." After the "changeover" (the term Linden workers used for the plant modernization), the skilled trades workers described their work as challenging and intellectually demanding:

> We're responsible for programming the robots, troubleshooting the robots, wiping their noses, cleaning them, whatever. . . . It's interesting work. We're doing something that very few people in the

world are doing, troubleshooting and repairing robots. It's terrific! I don't think this can be boring because there are so many things involved. There are things happening right now that we haven't ever seen before. Every day there's something different. We're always learning about the program, always changing things to make them better—every single day. [an electrician]

With high technology, skilled trades people are being forced to learn other people's trades in order to do their trade better. Like with me, I have to understand that controller and how it works in order to make sure the robot will work the way it's supposed to. You have to know the whole system. You can't just say, "I work on that one little gear box, I don't give a damn about what the rest of the machine does." You have to have a knowledge of everything you work with and everything that is related to it, whether you want to or not. You got to know pneumatics, hydraulics—all the trades. Everything is so interrelated and connected. You can't be narrow-minded anymore. [a machine repairman]

However, the situation was quite different for production workers. Their jobs, as had always been the case in the auto industry, continued to involve extremely repetitive, machine-paced, unskilled or semi-skilled work. Far from being required to learn new skills, many found their jobs were simplified or further deskilled by the new technology:

It does make it easier to an extent, but also at the same time they figure, "Well, I'm giving you a computer and it's going to make your job faster, so instead of you doing this, this, and this, I'm going to have you do this and eight other things, because the time I'm saving you

on the first three you're going to make it up on the last." Right now I'm doing more work in less time, the company's benefiting, and I am bored to death—more bored than before! [a trim department worker with nineteen years seniority]

I'm working in assembly. I'm feeding the line, the right side panel, the whole right side of the car. Myself and a fellow worker, in the same spot. Now all we do, actually, is put pieces in, push the buttons, and what they call a shuttle picks up whatever we put on and takes it down the line to be welded. Before the changeover my job was completely different. I was a torch solderer. And I had to solder the roof, you know, the joint of the roof with the side panel. I could use my head more. I like it more. Because, you know, when you have your mind in it also, it's more interesting. And not too many fellow workers could do the job. You had to be precise, because you had to put only so much material, lead, on the job. [a body shop worker with sixteen years seniority]

Not only were some of the more demanding and relatively skilled traditional production jobs—like soldering, welding, and painting car bodies—automated out of existence, but also many of the relatively desirable off-the-line jobs were eliminated. "Before there were more people working subassembly, assembling parts," one worker recalled. "You have some of the old-timers working on the line right now. Before, if you had more seniority, you were, let's say, off the line, in subassembly."

Even when they operate computers—a rarity for production workers—they typically do so in a highly routinized way. "There is nothing that really takes any skill to operate a computer," one production worker in the final inspection area said. "You just punch in the numbers, the screen will tell you what to do, it will tell you when to race the engine and when to turn the air conditioner off, when to do everything. Everything comes right up on the screen. It's very simple."

The pattern of skill polarization between the skilled trades and production workers that these comments suggest is verified by the findings of an in-plant survey. Skilled trades workers at Linden, asked about the importance of twelve specific on-the-job skills (including "problem solving," "accuracy/ precision," "memory," and "reading/spelling") to their jobs before and after the plant was modernized, reported that all but one ("physical strength") increased in importance. In contrast, a survey of the plant's production workers asking about the importance of a similar list of skills found that all twelve declined in importance after the introduction of the new technology. The survey also suggested that boredom levels had increased for production workers; 45 percent stated that their work after the changeover was boring and monotonous "often" or "all the time," compared to 35 percent who had found it boring and monotonous before the changeover. Similarly, 96 percent of production workers said that they now do the same task over and over again "often" or "all the time," up from 79 percent who did so before the changeover.

In the Linden case, the plant modernization had opposite effects on skilled trades and production workers, primarily because no significant job redesign was attempted. The boundary between the two groups and the kinds of work each had traditionally done was maintained, despite the radical technological change. While management might have chosen (and the union might have agreed) to try to transfer some tasks from the skilled trades to production workers, such as minor machine maintenance, or to redesign jobs more extensively in keeping with the potential of the new technology, this was not seriously attempted. Engineers limited their efforts to conventional "line balanc-

ing," which simply involves packaging tasks among individual production jobs so as to minimize the idle time of any given worker. In this respect they treated the new technology very much like older forms of machinery. The fundamental division of labor between production workers and the skilled trades persisted despite the massive infusion of new technology, and this organizational continuity led to the intensification of the already existing skill polarization within the plant.

GM-Linden appears to be typical of U.S. auto assembly plants in that new technology has been introduced without jobs having been fundamentally redesigned or the basic division of labor altered between production workers and the skilled trades. Even where significant changes in the division of labor— such as flexible teams—have been introduced, as in the new Japanese transplants, they typically involve rotating workers over a series of conventionally deskilled production jobs, rather than changing the basic nature of the work. While being able to perform eight or ten unskilled jobs rather than only one might be considered skill upgrading in some narrow technical sense, it hardly fits the glowing accounts of commentators who claim that with new technology "the deskilling process is reversed." . . .

Perhaps work in the auto industry *could* be reorganized along the lines Zuboff and Hirschhorn suggest, now that new technology has been introduced so widely. However, a major obstacle to this is bureaucratic inertia on the management side, for which GM in particular is legendary. As many auto industry analysts have pointed out, the firm's investments in new technology were typically seen by management as a "quick fix," throwing vast sums of money at the accelerating crisis of international competitiveness without seriously revamping the firm's organizational structure or its management strategies to make the most efficient possible use of the new equipment. As MaryAnn Keller put it, for GM "the goal of all the technology push has been to get rid of hourly workers. GM thought in terms of automation rather than replacing the current system with a better system."[11] The technology was meant to replace workers, not to transform work.

Reinforcing management's inertia, ironically, was the weakness of the U.A.W. The union has an old, deeply ingrained habit of ceding to management all prerogatives on such matters as job design. And in the 1980s, faced with unprecedented job losses, union concerns about employment security were in the forefront. The U.A.W. concentrated its efforts on minimizing the pain of "downsizing," generally accepting the notion that new technology and other strategies adopted by management were the best way to meet the challenge of increased competition in the industry. After all, if the domestic firms failed to become competitive, U.A.W. members would have no jobs at all. This kind of reasoning, most prominently associated with the U.A.W.'s GM Department director Donald Ephlin, until his retirement in 1989, also smoothed the path for management's efforts to transform the industrial relations system in the direction of increased "employee involvement" and teamwork, to which we now turn.

Worker Participation and the "New Industrial Relations"

Inspired by both the non-union manufacturing sector in the U.S. and by the Japanese system of work organization, the Big Three began to experiment with various worker participation schemes in the 1970s. By the end of the 1980s, virtually every auto assembly plant in the United States had institutionalized some form of participation. Like the new technologies that were introduced in the same period, these organizational innovations—the "new industrial relations"—

were a response to the pressure of international competition. And even more than the new technologies, they signaled a historic break with previous industrial practices. For both the Taylorist organization of work in the auto industry and the system of labor relations that developed around it had presumed that the interests of management and those of workers were fundamentally in conflict. In embracing worker participation, however, management abandoned this worldview and redefined its interests as best served by cooperation with labor, its old adversary.

For management, the goal of worker participation is to increase productivity and quality by drawing on workers' own knowledge of the labor process and by increasing their motivation and thus their commitment to the firm. Participation takes many different forms, ranging from suggestion programs, quality circles, and quality-of-work-life (QWL) programs, which actively solicit workers' ideas about how to improve production processes, to "team concept" systems, which organize workers into small groups that rotate jobs and work together to improve productivity and quality on an ongoing basis. All these initiatives promote communication and trust between management and labor, in the name of efficiency and enhanced international competitiveness. Like the new technologies with which they are often associated, the various forms of worker participation have been widely applauded by many commentators who see them as potentially opening up a new era of work humanization and industrial democracy.

In the early 1970s, some U.A.W. officials (most notably Irving Bluestone, then head of the union's GM department) actively supported experimental QWL programs, which they saw as a means for improving the actual experience of work in the auto industry, a long-neglected part of the union's original agenda. But many unionists were more skeptical about participation in the 1980s, when QWL programs and the team concept became increasingly associated with union "give-backs," or concessions. In a dramatic reversal of the logic of the postwar labor-management accord, under which economic benefits were exchanged for unilateral management control over the production process, now economic concessions went hand-in-hand with the promise of worker participation in decision making. However, QWL and the team concept were introduced largely on management's terms in the 1980s, for in sharp contrast to the period immediately after World War II, now the U.A.W. was in a position of unprecedented weakness. In many Big Three plants, participation schemes were forced on workers (often in the face of organized opposition) through what auto industry analysts call "whipsawing," a process whereby management pits local unions against one another by threatening to close the least "cooperative" plants. Partly for this reason, QWL and the team concept have precipitated serious divisions within the union, with Ephlin and other national union leaders who endorse participation facing opposition from a new generation of union dissidents who view it as a betrayal of the union's membership.

The New United Motor Manufacturing, Inc., plant (NUMMI) in Fremont, California, a joint venture of Toyota and GM, is the focus of much of the recent controversy over worker participation. The plant is run by Toyota, using the team concept and various Japanese management techniques. (GM's responsibility is limited to the marketing side of the operation.) But unlike Toyota's Kentucky plant and the other wholly Japanese-owned transplants, at NUMMI the workers are U.A.W. members. Most of them worked for GM in the same plant before it was closed in 1982. Under GM, the Fremont plant had a reputation for low productivity and frequent wildcat strikes, but when it re-opened as NUMMI two years later, with the same work force and even the same local union officers, it became an overnight success story. NUMMI's productivity and quality ratings are comparable to those of Toyota plants in Japan, and higher than any other U.S. auto plant. Efforts to emulate its success further accelerated the push to establish teams in auto plants around the nation.

Many commentators have praised the NUMMI system of work organization as a model of worker participation; yet others have severely criticized it. The system's detractors argue that despite the rhetoric of worker control, the team concept and other participatory schemes are basically strategies to enhance *management* control. Thus Mike Parker and Jane Slaughter suggest that, far from offering a humane alternative to Taylorism, at NUMMI, and at plants that imitate it, workers mainly "participate" in the intensification of their own exploitation, mobilizing their detailed firsthand knowledge of the labor process to help management speed up production and eliminate wasteful work practices. More generally, "whether through team meetings, quality circles, or suggestion plans," Parker and Slaughter argue, "the little influence workers do have over their jobs is that in effect they are organized to time-study themselves in a kind of super-Taylorism."[12] They see the team concept as extremely treacherous, undermining unionism in the name of a dubious form of participation in management decisions.

Workers themselves, however, seem to find intrinsically appealing the idea of participating in what historically have been exclusively managerial decision-making processes, especially in comparison to traditional American managerial methods. This is the case even though participation typically is limited to an extremely restricted arena, such as helping to streamline the production process or otherwise raise productivity. Even Parker and Slaughter acknowledge that at NUMMI, "nobody says they want to return to the days when GM ran the plant."[13] Unless one wants to believe that auto workers are simply dupes of managerial manipulation, NUMMI's enormous popularity with the work force suggests that the new industrial relations have some positive features and cannot simply be dismissed as the latest form of labor control.

Evidence from the GM-Linden case confirms the appeal of participation to workers, although reforms in labor relations there were much more limited than at NUMMI. Linden still has over eighty populated job classifications, and although 72 percent of the production workers are concentrated in only eight of them, this is quite different from NUMMI, where there is only one job classification for production workers and seniority plays a very limited role. Nor has Linden adopted the team system. However, when the plant reopened after its 1985–86 modernization, among its official goals was to improve communications between labor and management, and both parties embraced "jointness" as a principle of decision making. At the same time, "employee involvement groups" (EIGs) were established. Production workers were welcomed back to the plant after the changeover with a jointly (union-management) developed two-week (eighty-hour) training program, in the course of which they were promised that the "new Linden" would be totally different from the plant they had known before. In particular, workers were led to expect an improved relationship with management, and a larger role in decision making and problem solving on the shop floor.[14]

Most workers were extremely enthusiastic about these ideas—at least initially. The problem was that after the eighty-hour training program was over, when everyone was back at work, the daily reality of plant life failed to live up to the promises about the "new Linden." "It's sort of like going to college," one worker commented about the training program. "You learn one thing, and then you go into the real world. . . . " Another agreed:

> It sounded good at the time, but it turned out to be a big joke. Management's attitude is still the same. It hasn't changed at all. Foremen who treated you like a fellow human being are still the same—no problems with them. The ones who were arrogant bastards are still the same, with the exception of a few who are a little bit scared, a little bit afraid that it might go to the top man, and, you know, make some trouble. Everyone has pretty much the same attitude.

Indeed, the biggest problem was at the level of first-line supervision. While upper management may have been convinced that workers should have more input into decision making, middle and lower management (who also went through a training program) did not always share this view. Indeed, after the training raised workers' expectations, foremen in the plant, faced with the usual pressures to get production out, seemed to quickly fall back into their old habits. The much-touted "new Linden" thus turned out to be all too familiar. As the workers pointed out:

> You still have the management that has the mentality of the top-down, like they're right, they don't listen to the exchange from the workers, like the old school. So that's why when you ask about the "new Linden," people say it's a farce, because you still . . . do not feel mutual respect, you feel the big thing is to get the jobs out. This is a manufacturing plant; they do have to produce. But you can't just tell this worker, you know, take me upstairs [where the training classes were held], give me this big hype, and then bring me downstairs and then have the same kind of attitude.

With management, they don't have the security that we have. Because if a foreman doesn't do his job, he can be replaced tomorrow, and he's got nobody to back him up. So everybody's a little afraid of their jobs. So if you have a problem, you complain to your foreman, he tries to take care of it without bringing it to his general foreman; or the general foreman, he don't want to bring it to his superintendent, because neither of them can control it. So they all try to keep it down, low level, and under the rug, and "Don't bother me about it—just fix it and let it slide." And that is not the teachings that we went through in that eighty-hour [training] course!

Many Linden workers expressed similar cynicism about the EIGs. "A lot of people feel very little comes out of the meetings. It's just to pacify you so you don't write up grievances," one paint department worker said, articulating a widespread sentiment. "It's a half-hour's pay for sitting there and eating your lunch," he added.

Research on other U.S. auto assembly plants suggests that Linden, where the rhetoric of participation was introduced without much substantive change in the quality of the labor-management relationship, is a more representative case than NUMMI, where participation (whatever its limits) is by all accounts more genuine. Reports from Big Three plants around the nation suggest that typical complaints concern not the *concept* of participation—which workers generally endorse—but management's failure to live up to its own stated principles. Gerald Horton, a worker at GM's Wentzville, Missouri, plant "thinks the team concept is a good idea if only management would abide by it." Similarly, Dan Maurin of GM's Shreveport, Louisiana, plant observes, "it makes people resentful when they preach participative management and then come in and say, 'this is how we do it.'"[15]

Betty Foote, who works at a Ford truck plant outside Detroit, expressed the sentiments of many auto workers about Employee Involvement (EI): "The supposed concern for workers' happiness now with the EI program is a real joke. It looks good on paper, but it is not effective. . . . Relations between workers and management haven't changed."[16]

At NUMMI, workers view participation far more positively. Critics of the team concept suggest that this is because workers there experienced a "significant emotional event" and suffered economically after GM closed the plant, so that when they were recalled to NUMMI a few years later they gratefully accepted the new system without complaint. But, given the uncertainty of employment and the history of chronic layoffs throughout the auto industry, that this would sharply distinguish NUMMI's workers from those in other plants seems unlikely. Such an explanation for the positive reception of the team concept by NUMMI workers is also dubious in light of the fact that even the opposition caucus in the local union, which criticizes the local U.A.W. officials for being insufficiently militant in representing the rank and file, explicitly supports the team concept.

Instead, the key difference between NUMMI and the Big Three assembly plants may be that workers have *more* job security at NUMMI, where the Japanese management has evidently succeeded in building a high-trust relationship with workers. When the plant reopened, NUMMI workers were guaranteed no layoffs unless management first took a pay cut; this promise and many others have (so far) been kept, despite slow sales. In contrast, the Big Three (and especially GM) routinely enrage workers by announcing layoffs and then announcing executive pay raises a few days later; while at the plant level, as we have seen, management frequently fails to live up to its rhetorical commitments to participation. On the one hand, this explains why NUMMI workers are so much more enthusiastic about participation than their counterparts in other plants. On the other hand, where teamwork and other participatory schemes have been forced on workers through "whipsawing," the result has been a dismal failure on its own terms. Indeed, one study found a negative correlation between the existence of participation programs and productivity.

Insofar as the U.A.W. has associated itself with such arrangements, it loses legitimacy with the rank and file when management's promises are not fulfilled. Successful participation systems, however, can help strengthen unionism. It is striking that at NUMMI, with its sterling productivity and quality record, high management credibility, and relatively strong job security provisions, the U.A.W. is stronger than in most Big Three plants. For that matter, the local union at NUMMI has more influence than do enterprise unions in Japanese auto plants, where teamwork systems are longstanding. But here, as in so many other ways, NUMMI is the exceptional case. In most U.S. auto plants, the weakness of the U.A.W.—in the face of industry overcapacity and capital's enhanced ability to shift production around the globe—has combined with management's inability to transform its own ranks to undermine the promise of participation.

NOTES

1. "U.A.W.: World's Largest Union Is Facing Troubled Times," *Life*, 19 (September 10, 1945): 103–11.

2. . . . [T]he quote is from Nelson Lichtenstein, "From Corporatism to Collective Bargaining: Organized Labor and the Eclipse of Social Democracy in the Postwar Era," in *The Rise and Fall of the New Deal Order, 1930–1980*, ed. Steve Fraser and Gary Gerstle (Princeton, N.J.: Princeton University Press, 1989), 126.

3. These figures are for private sector manufacturing wage and salary workers as a proportion of all employed civilian wage and salary workers, and are computed from U.S. Bureau of Labor Statistics, *Labor Force Statistics Derived from the Current Population Survey, 1948–87*, Bulletin No. 2307 (Washington, D.C.: Government Printing Office, 1988), 383, 386.

4. Figures for 1989 are from U.S. Bureau of Labor Statistics, *Employment and Earnings* 37 (January 1990): 231–32. Enumeration methods are different from those used in 1945 (see note 2 for sources for 1945 data), so that the figures are not strictly comparable; yet there can be no doubt as to the magnitude and direction of the change.

5. *1987 Agreement between Chevrolet—Pontiac—GM of Canada, Linden Plant, General Motors Corporation and Local No. 595, United Auto Workers, Region 9* (privately published), 37–42.

6. Author's field interviews with GM workers in Linden, New Jersey.

7. Maryann Keller, *Rude Awakening: The Rise, Fall and Struggle for Recovery of General Motors* (New York: William Morrow, 1989), 204.

8. Shoshana Zuboff, *In the Age of the Smart Machine: The Future of Work and Power* (New York: Basic Books, 1988), 395.

9. Larry Hirschhorn, *Beyond Mechanization: Work and Technology in a Postindustrial Age* (Cambridge, Mass.: MIT Press, 1984), 97.

10. Data supplied by local management. The finding that Linden is the most efficient GM plant in the United States is from *The Harbour Report*, 139.

11. Keller quoted in Amal Nag, "Tricky Technology: Auto Makers Discover 'Factory of the Future' Is Headache Just Now," *Wall Street Journal* (May 13, 1986), 1.

12. Parker and Slaughter, *Choosing Sides*, 19.

13. Parker and Slaughter, *Choosing Sides*, 111.

14. The data on job classification are computed from rosters supplied by local management. Other information is from the author's fieldwork. The quotes in the paragraphs that follow are from interviews with Linden workers.

15. Horton quoted in Peter Downs, "Wentzville: Strangest Job Training Ever," in Parker and Slaughter, *Choosing Sides*, 190; Maurin quoted in *Choosing Sides*, 130.

16. Foote quoted in Richard Feldman and Michael Betzold, *End of the Line: Autoworkers and the American Dream* (New York: Weidenfeld & Nicolson, 1988), 178–79.

14

The Transformation of Work Revisited
The Limits of Flexibility in American Manufacturing

Steven P. Vallas and John P. Beck

Introduction

In recent years social scientists concerned with the nature of work have increasingly spoken of an emerging "post-Fordist" pattern of work organization within the industrial capitalist nations. Advocates of this view typically argue that as large-scale shifts have occurred in both product markets and process technologies, large corporations have begun to shed their traditional reliance on centralized bureaucracy and standardized tasks, adopting a new set of work arrangements that answers to many names: "flexible specialization" (Piore and Sabel 1984; Sabel 1991), "the post-hierarchical workplace" (Zuboff 1988), and the "learning organization" (Senker 1992), to cite a few. Regardless of the precise formulation, the general argument has been that the organizational models appropriate to mechanized, mass production processes can no longer suffice in a technologically advanced, post-industrial economy.

Such bold assertions have succeeded in winning the ears of managerial personnel, public policy analysts, trade union officials, and others concerned with the changing structure of work. Yet despite its sweeping claims of the obsolescence of mass production techniques, post-Fordist theory remains afflicted by abiding ambiguities and conflicting formulations. Disagreements persist as to which factors seem to drive organizational change, with some theorists stressing factors exogenous to the work organization (such as volatile product demand), while others fasten on factors endogenous to the workplace (mainly, the dynamics of technological change). There is also significant uncertainty regarding the coordinates of the post-Fordist work organization: Some theorists anticipate a rehabilitation of the craft tradition within new economic contexts (Piore and Sabel 1984), while others speak of entirely "new production concepts" that synthesize mental and manual skills (Kern and Schumann 1992). Moreover, few accounts have shown how large, bureaucratic firms can shed their traditionally rigid modes of operation and embrace the new post-Fordist arrangements (see Kelley 1990). Mindful of these and other difficulties we will discuss further, many commentators have remained sharply critical of the degree to which post-Fordist theory can provide an empirically useful guide to workplace transformation in the advanced capitalist world today (Hyman 1988; Penn and Sleightholme 1995; Taplin 1995).

This [article] addresses the continuing debate over post-Fordism by exploring the transformation of work at four large manufacturing plants in the U.S. pulp and paper industry, all of which are owned by the same

Excerpts from "The Transformation of Work Revisited: The Limits of Flexibility in American Manufacturing" by Steven P. Vallas and John P. Beck in *Social Problems*, Vol. 43, No. 3, August 1996, pp. 339–361. Copyright © 1995 by The Society for the Study of Social Problems. Reprinted by permission.

multinational corporation. The study's goal is two-fold: first, to contribute to the larger task of assessing the empirical validity of post-Fordist claims; and second, to open up for discussion aspects of workplace change that advocates of post-Fordism have tended to neglect. Our research strategy is to focus upon a small number of establishments in one industry, in effect trading breadth of analysis for greater depth (see Wilkinson 1983; Child 1972; Child et al. 1984; Thomas 1994). Although this paper involves merely one dimension of a larger research project, it does point toward an important aspect of the current work restructuring that has gone largely unnoticed—the often-conflictual relations between technical experts and manual workers—and that calls for important qualifications within post-Fordist theory as typically construed. . . .

Post-Fordism Re-Examined

While sociologists of work have long studied the relationship between organizations and technologies, the area has gained greater prominence in recent years with the spread of what many refer to as a new scientific-technological revolution, often compared in magnitude to the first industrial revolution unleashed in late 18th-century England. Most analysts agree that massive changes are under way in the organization of manufacturing, but sharp differences remain as to which facets of work are likely to be recast, precisely how the structure of work (especially the management function) is likely to change, and why.

Adler (1992) usefully distinguishes four generations of post-war thinking about the relation between technological change and the structure of work. The first, "upgrading" approach is associated in the United States with the work of Blauner (1964), and in England with that of Joan Woodward (1958). Reflecting broader theories of modernization and the logic of industrial society, this gener-

ation of analysts concluded that the automation of manufacturing tended to free workers from highly standardized tasks and to give them a fuller, more integrated view of the work process, thus easing capitalism's endemic problems of alienation and industrial conflict. The second, "deskilling" approach of Braverman (1974) and his followers contested these upgrading claims and in some respects stood them on their head. For this second generation of scholars, the pressures of capital accumulation relentlessly forced employers to simplify the labor of skilled manual and "mental" occupations, using new technologies to place production knowledge into the hands of managerial employees.

The conflict between these two perspectives until recently has occupied much of the existing research, as analysts have sought to adjudicate their competing claims (see Spenner 1983, 1990; Vallas 1990, 1993; Smith 1994). Yet by the early 1980s, a third generation of theorists had explicitly renounced the search for a single dominant tendency in the evolution of work, arguing instead that "the quest for general trends about the development of skill levels, or general conclusions about the impact of technologies, is likely to be in vain and misleading" (Wood 1989:4). This third, "contingent" view has more modestly sought to identify the social conditions that help account for the varied consequences of technological change (e.g., Cornfield 1987; Kelley 1990; Child et al. 1984; Barley 1986; Form et al. 1988).

Frustrated with this contingent view of technological change, a loose assemblage of theorists (including Adler himself) has sought to articulate the elements of a fourth approach. Despite variations in its precise formulation, proponents of this last school of thought broadly agree on the contemporary emergence and spread of a "post-Taylorist" or post-Fordist model of work (e.g., Sabel and Zeitlin 1985; Piore and Sabel 1984; Sabel

1991; Hirschhorn 1984; Kern and Schumann 1992). Their claims can quickly be recited. During an earlier period of capitalism, machine designs were largely consonant with rigid, standardized job structures that accorded workers little responsibility and demanded of them few skills. Organizational structures under this regime reflected a sharp division between managers and the "managed," as the former sought to rule by command. Steady growth in mass consumption, stabilized by Keynesian economic policies, undergirded the Fordist paradigm. Yet now, dramatic shifts in process technologies and consumer markets have combined to generate a crisis of mass production throughout the advanced capitalist nations. To begin with, information technologies have transformed the structure of production in at least two respects: the spread of microprocessor technologies has made small-batch production more economically feasible than before, while at the same time requiring the use of greater analytic or "intellective" skills for the best use of new machines. Equally important, consumption patterns are more subject to rapid and volatile change, inducing firms to favor more flexible, general-purpose production systems over highly specialized (and therefore rigid) ones. What transpires, say post-Fordists, is a heightened level of skills required of manual workers; more generally, an expansion of craft discretion, presaging a synthesis of "mental" and manual functions within the automated plant; and a broader shift from bureaucratic "control" to organizational "commitment" as the principle that undergirds the new structure of work (R. Walton 1986; Zuboff 1988). Ironically, some theorists contend, the "project of liberated, fulfilling work, originally interpreted as an *anti*-capitalist project," is now "likely to be staged by capitalist management itself" (Kern and Schumann 1992: 111). . . .

The Study

. . . We conducted an intensive study of a single branch of production: the pulp and paper industry. This branch of production has historically made widespread use of continuous-process work methods, which have figured so prominently in the debate over the evolution of industrial work that one flexibility theorist has termed them "the paradigmatic settings of post-industrial manufacturing" (Hirschhorn 1984:99; cf. Blauner 1964; Nichols and Beynon 1977; Halle 1984; and Zuboff 1988). Because the industry relies heavily on workers employed as control room operators called "machine tenders"— highly skilled jobs at the center of production control systems—it provides an especially good terrain on which to apply Kern and Schumann's (1992) expectations about the role of the "systems controller" (a position they believe epitomizes the emerging synthesis of theoretical and practical knowledge).

Equally important, the major corporations in this industry have witnessed a massive wave of organizational and technological changes, beginning in the late 1970s and early '80s, which has only now begun to recede. In less than a single decade, micro-electronic controls and mill-wide information systems have transformed this terrain from a traditionally organized craft industry into a major outpost of automated manufacturing. Moreover, as the leading corporations in this industry have embraced the "quality movement" in general, and Total Quality Management (TQM) approaches in particular, new organizational principles have rippled throughout the industry, with many suppliers and contractors now formally constrained to demonstrate their application of TQM principles. Because the industry has been marked by the rapid adoption of these and other process innovations, then, it provides an especially opportune site for research on the transformation of work in U.S. industry (cf. Penn and Scattergood 1988; Penn, Lilja, and Scattergood 1992).

The evidence we present has been gathered from four pulp and paper mills located in different regions of the United States, all of which have been acquired in the last 10 years by the same multinational corporation with a reputation for its relatively cooperative labor relations policies. While not a leader in the implementation of team systems, the firm has sought to incorporate such principles into its labor management approach, providing each mill with resources and support toward this end. Our focus on a relatively progressive, forward-looking firm should provide a research context that is relatively favorable to the newer and more flexible production concepts that are so commonly discussed in the literature.

The selection of mills for inclusion in the study was guided by two considerations: the desire to include a broadly representative mix of plants that vary in their size, age, product mix, and locale; and our interest in plants that have adopted the most recent generation of information technologies and process controls. During the early stages of our fieldwork at a large southeastern mill, we encountered job training seminars that were part of the company's plan to introduce new mill-wide information systems at several of its plants. In as much as we were particularly eager to explore workplace relations within technologically advanced settings, we sought and received research access at three other plants that had recently introduced the new systems (although in a slightly different form). The four mills we ultimately selected are broadly representative of the company's production facilities and employ methods that are parallel to the pulp and paper establishments we have toured within the industry at large. The smallest of the mills in our research employs 700 workers in all positions, while the largest employs

in excess of 2,000. Two of the mills are in the Southeast and two are in the Northwest. Two are located near urban areas, while two are in outlying rural areas. The oldest of the four mills was built in 1882 and has been repeatedly expanded and modernized; the other three (including both Southern mills) are more modern establishments, built in the late 1950s. All four mills produce a mixture of consumer products such as tissue and paper towels, combined with commercial products such as photocopying paper and coated paper for magazines. Hourly workers at all four mills are unionized, as is the great majority of workers in the industry.

The remarks reported here are based on two periods of study conducted between 1992 and 1995. An initial phase of the research grew out of an exploratory study of work commitment and job satisfaction at one of the mills; this pilot phase of the research ultimately included semistructured interviews with a strategic sample of 50 managers and workers. An additional wave of data collection was then conducted by the first author, who conducted approximately 200 hours of fieldwork and an additional 65 open-ended interviews with roughly equal proportions of process engineers, manual workers, and plant managers. During both waves of research, the authors were granted free rein to sit in with production crews during their shifts, observing their routine activities and work culture while participating in their ongoing conversations. Interviews were conducted under conditions deemed least inhibiting to respondents: for manual workers, in their control rooms, as the rhythm of production allowed; for engineers and managers, in their offices. Finally, for purposes of comparison, we jointly conducted a small number of interviews and observations at three older mills in New England and the South, to understand the nature of the traditional methods of production that predominated during the manual era of production. In many respects these traditional mills served as living museums, showcasing craft-based tricks of the trade that have all but faded from human memory.

The Case of Pulp and Paper

The Labor Process Before Automation

The pulp and paper mills we studied are massive industrial complexes that daily ingest tons of logs, wood chips, water, and chemicals at one end and spew out truckloads of packaged paper products at the other. The process begins when trucks (sometimes railroad cars or river barges) deliver wood and chemicals to the mill. The wood is mechanically debarked and reduced to chips that are then automatically fed into the mill's digesters. These are vertical towers that use either chemical compounds ("white liquor") or mechanical grinding stones to produce liquid pulp, called brown stock. Workers in chemical processing areas are responsible for producing white liquor, other caustic agents, and bleaching compounds used in the pulping stages of production. Other workers oversee the bleaching, washing, and refining of the brown stock and add any necessary dyes or additives before furnishing the pulp to the appropriate paper machines—huge mechanical complexes in their own right. At the wet end of a paper machine, the pulp moves first to a head box, which evenly disperses it onto flat screens called "wires," which press and heat the stock to reduce its moisture content, until it rolls out as a continuous paper sheet at the dry end of the machine. Workers routinely oversee the accumulation of paper onto large, 10-foot-wide reels that often weigh more than 20 tons each. At this point, the process enters a number of final stages, which may include the coating, supercalendering (receiving a glossy finish), and eventual conversion into a shippable, packaged product by being cut into smaller rolls or sheets. Up until the dry end of the paper machine, the process is essentially a chemical production process. At the dry end, however, where the paper is formed, the process becomes a mechanical one, with more immediate contact between workers, product, and machines.

Each of the production areas we studied was closely dependent upon the others in the mill. As workers at a paper machine know only too well, slight variations in the bleaching and digesting process "upstream" from their work can and often do have huge effects on the quality of their output and even on the intensity of their work effort: slight variations in fiber length, for example, may result in frequent "breaks" on the paper machine, forcing workers to engage in arduous and sometimes dangerous efforts to rethread the machines and bring production back on line. Conversely, variations in the behavior of the paper machines can ripple upward, affecting work in bleaching and digesting areas. Frequently, we watched failures on a paper machine force workers in the bleaching and brown stock area to slow down the chemical reactions they controlled, only to have to speed them back up again once their co-workers brought the paper machines back on line. These changes are difficult and sometimes dangerous to control and can result in major spills and wastage of costly stock or white liquor.

Such tight coupling among different production areas requires frequent communication among workers in different areas of the mill who must learn to anticipate the decisions made by their co-workers in other departments. Despite the spread of portable phones, digital pagers, and radio intercoms, communication across production areas, shifts, and organizational ranks is often difficult. Seemingly minor changes in production methods—for example, adjustments in the specifications for particular grades of paper—are often not effectively transmitted. Intensifying this problem among workers in the mill is the fact that seniority rules and promotion sequences are typically intra-departmental. On the one hand, this rewards workers for the slow and patient accumulation of knowledge concerning their area's processes and machines. But on the other hand it has important social effects: It isolates hourly workers from their counterparts in other production areas and spawns departmental allegiances and identities that limit broader forms of cohesion among workers. Despite claims made by Blauner (1964) and some flexibility theorists, the organization of the production process provides little opportunity for workers to glimpse the production process as a whole.

Until the early 1980s, the consoles of most control rooms were equipped with pneumatic controls that provided workers with only a limited set of readings and process control capabilities. Typically, control rooms also contained panel boards—essentially, wall-mounted maps of each production area located above the pneumatic consoles and equipped with flashing indicators that displayed the status of valves, pumps, and tanks out on the shopfloor. Given the paucity of information these process controls provided, workers had to rely on direct physical or sensate means of collecting information about the process, much as Zuboff (1988) has described. Thus the workers we interviewed recalled spitting tobacco juice onto the winder (to gauge its take-up speed), and using wooden sticks to bang on the logs of the finished product (listening for signs of variation in their product's weight). Several recalled having to run their hands over the stock at the dry end of the mill (too much dust or static electricity told workers that their output was too dry). In pulping areas, workers would often take samples of bleached pulp directly from their dryers,

judging the fiber length and acidity of the stock on the basis of its look, feel, and even taste. Reflecting the primacy of sensory knowledge during the manual era, respondents often could not describe older forms of production knowledge without referring to one or more of the human senses: Thus workers and supervisors routinely recalled the workers' need to have a good "feel for the machinery," "an eye for the process," and a "nose for trouble."

To accumulate the repertoire of manual skills they needed to perform their jobs, operators had to serve long years of a *de facto* apprenticeship, moving from jobs as fifth or fourth hands to backtender, and (perhaps) even to the most senior job on a paper machine, the machine tender. During the years needed to move through this career progression, workers amassed a stock of knowledge that became an important form of intellectual property, qualifying them for promotion into more rewarding positions and giving them a critical source of power in relation to their supervisors and fellow workers (Halle 1984; Kusterer 1978). One worker we interviewed recalled a machine tender who stopped work whenever his fourth hand was nearby, explaining that such guarding of work knowledge "was his personal job security program." Even today, some workers carefully record vital information gained while making particular grades of paper, rarely offering to share the content of their "black books" with others in the mill.

Remaking the Labor Process

This portrait of paper making would be familiar to virtually all the workers in the mills we studied, but increasingly as an historical representation. For since the early 1980s, craft control over the production process has experienced a profound transformation, brought about by three distinct but interrelated changes in both the technology and the organization of production: Chronologically, these include (1) the introduction of Distributed Control Systems (DCS)—automated process controls that interpose symbolic, computer-mediated representations between machine tenders and the production process; (2) the adoption of Total Quality Management principles, which have dramatically altered decision-making methods and procedures within production areas; and (3) the introduction of a mill-wide information system that supplements the automated process controls with an array of analytic and communications tools. In the following pages we briefly describe these changes, and then analyze their effects on the structure and culture of shopfloor life.

Distributed Control Systems   Beginning in the late 1970s, the company began to follow an economic strategy based on the acquisition of undervalued capital assets. By the early 1980s it had accumulated significant numbers of older mills and began to modernize many of its key production facilities with an eye toward achieving greater stability in its operations and appreciable reductions in crew sizes. With these ends in mind, top management elected to introduce new, automated process controls—especially within the larger mills producing consumer goods. The result has involved massive changes in operators' working lives.

Especially in their most advanced incarnations, Distributed Control Systems employ computer terminals to provide visual depictions of the production process, using diagrams, graphs, and maps to represent the functioning of myriad pipes, valves, and pumps operators must oversee. In some respects, it is as if the old panel boards had sprung to electronic life. By using computer keyboards and touchscreen monitors, workers can peer into and adjust the most remote details of the process. Patiently moving through dozens of computerized screens of graphical maps and data, workers track key process variables—the acidity, fiber length, and brightness of the pulp, or the thickness, weight, and tensile strength of the paper—monitoring even minor changes during the course of their shifts. It is true that workers can sometimes put their systems on "cascade"—an automatic state of functioning in which the process controls become self-adjusting, and change in one variable triggers appropriate actions in other process variables. Yet even when workers leave the process on cascade, they must continue to track the state of their operations, lest the machine make inappropriate changes with potentially costly or even disastrous results.

The coming of DCS has granted operators access to a wealth of production data, but it has also placed workers at much greater distance from the process they control. Time on the floor checking the process has been replaced with time in the control room tending DCS controls and video monitors showing key bottlenecks in the process outside. Now, workers directly engage the machines only when they are down—e.g., during scheduled maintenance or when a "break" occurs in the flow of paper coming off the machines. In the latter case, workers must hurriedly intervene, feverishly cooperating to bring production back up. During "normal" periods of their working day, however, workers are now largely isolated from the material objects of their labor and work mainly with symbolic representations of the production process: a development that Zuboff (1988:58–96) has appropriately termed the increasing "abstraction" of industrial work.

Most workers recall having great difficulty in adapting to the new work methods. The new processes intimidated many workers, especially those with less education, and left them fearful of the consequences of a personal failure to master them. In one mill where trade union consciousness is fairly well developed, the introduction of DCS in the mid-1980s prompted workers to slash the tires of an engineer's car and to ostracize the technical implementation team. Workers remain wary even now, checking and double-checking the truth of computer-mediated data—as one worker put it, "to make sure the machine ain't lyin' to you." Workers often experience an enduring tension between two conflicting dispositions toward the machines: *hope* that they are correct (reflecting the workers' concern for the product, and their wish to avoid hard physical labor), and *fear* that the machines (and therefore a process that had relied on their personal skills) have grown beyond their control. Most find that the capacities of the new machines—their ability to enhance the system's stability—gain for the whole system (and therefore for management) a greater control at the expense of individual workers who must accept an end to their craft knowledge in the process. Many workers seem to have reconciled themselves to the loss of individual creativity and discretion in their jobs by focusing on the material benefits of the new technologies, such as the reduction of physical labor. This trade-off is perfectly expressed in one worker's comment that "I'd rather be bored to death than worked to death."

Total Quality Management   As top management began to introduce DCS technology into the company's larger mills, it also set about rethinking its organizational strategies. After having experimented with other innovations, by the mid-1980s it elected to incorporate many of the principles of Total Quality Management into its operations (for discussion see Appelbaum and Batt 1994; Hill 1991; Walton 1986). Viewing TQM against the background of previous management efforts at reform, many of which were both superficial and short-lived, production workers have commonly adopted a cynical

view of TQM as the latest "program of the month." Yet TQM seems to comprise more than just another managerial fad. Unlike earlier forms of workplace reform, TQM is directly tied to the technical methods and procedures of the work process itself (Hill 1991). Indeed, subsequent developments in process technology that we will discuss have begun to build TQM principles into their very design.

One of the key elements of TQM is its emphasis on Statistical Process Control (SPC), a heavily quantitative system of interpreting fluctuations in production outcomes that uses probability theory to distinguish between random and systematic variations. Production areas, led by engineers, have established target values (called "centerlines") for each critical process variable and have defined confidence intervals at given distances above and below these centerlines. Managers have directed the workers on each shift to take scheduled readings of key measures, plot the datapoints on control charts, and inspect the resulting patterns of deviation from the centerline value. Workers are trained to alter key process variables only when the observed pattern violates a rule, indicating that a "special" (or non-random) cause of variation has upset the equilibrium of the production process. Management has posted the rules governing centerlining on the walls of most control rooms, and workers who defy the rules must justify their actions. Although workers often comply in a ritualistic fashion (completing control charts only at the end of their shifts, rather than as an active tool during the work itself), the effect of centerlining and SPC has been to standardize production methods, removing a considerable degree of autonomy from workers' hands (Klein 1994).

Most of the managers we interviewed seemed quite aware of the potentially alienating effects that SPC can have and are often at pains to remind workers that they drew on workers' knowledge when defining centerline values. Moreover, in training sessions many technical staff have tried to translate quantitative concepts into more colloquial language that will be less off-putting from the workers' point of view. Thus one engineer liked to use a highway metaphor to explain centerlining and confidence intervals:

> Imagine you're riding down the highway on a motorcycle. If you get too far from the center stripe, you're gonna wind up in the ditch, right?

Regardless of the rhetorical devices managers employ, the reality is that centerlining has constrained workers' customary methods of process control. One departmental manager who had previously been a process engineer observed:

> It's tightened output up around the standard deviation, but it's eliminated a lot of individuality. Workers used to set things the way they liked to, with lots of variability. That's gone now.

In addition to the introduction of SPC methods, the shift toward Total Quality has also involved an increasing reliance on team systems of management, which the company hopes will foster greater cooperation across departments and levels in the organizational hierarchy. Often composed of both workers and supervisory personnel, teams vary widely in the breadth of their mission. One relatively pedestrian example concerned an *ad hoc* team composed of maintenance craftworkers, whom management had charged with designing a system for the storage of technical manuals and documents that are vital to expeditious machine repair. A somewhat more substantively important case was that of a small group of senior craftworkers who were invited to design a training and certification program for highly skilled operators. Regardless of the particular task that teams have been assigned, their effects have

been fairly limited: Decisions to authorize the work of each team remain in the hands of departmental managers; the hierarchical chain of command has remained in place; and production standards continue to distinguish between the performance of each bureaucratic unit. In short, despite an overlay of cross-functional teams, the logic of bureaucratic hierarchy has been left largely intact.

Information Systems   A last and most recent set of changes began during the late 1980s, when process engineers in the company's technical center developed a generation of information systems that have been introduced into several key plants, including all four of the mills in our study. The most important of these is the Mill-wide Information Network on Economics (MINE). Initially intended as a tool for middle managers to control production costs, it was designed for use on minicomputer systems and incorporated few user-friendly features. Since then, the company's development team has rewritten the system's software, incorporating a graphical user-interface and PC compatibility to make it more accessible to non-technical employees. MINE does not have operational functions: The task of controlling production remains the province of the DCS equipment. Instead, MINE provides a set of communications and analytic functions that even the most advanced DCS controls lack. The new information system provides for on-line bulletin boards, e-mail systems, and shift reports, all of which can now be accessed from any work station in the mill. Moreover, MINE enables workers to "see" into remote production areas— even into areas at mills elsewhere in the country—thus providing information that may have bearing on their own operations. The intent of the designers has clearly been to break down the pattern of departmental isolation that characterizes even the most advanced DCS-equipped production area.

In so doing, MINE provides a broader, more inclusive overview of the mills' operations, rendering the process more transparent, both to workers and to managers, than was possible before.

MINE also provides an array of programs that support the analysis of data on the causes of downtime, variations in quality, and fluctuations in production costs, most of which make explicit use of SPC terminology. In theory, operators who want to understand why significant deviations from certain centerline values have occurred in the past can access MINE's database and construct bivariate bar charts that show the proportion of such deviations attributable to each cause. Although many mill managers expressed the hope that not only technical personnel but also manual workers would share in the use of MINE, participation has been almost entirely limited to managerial and engineering personnel, for reasons that will be discussed.

The Changing Nature of Shopfloor Life

The changes just described make clear that there has indeed been ample opportunity for the transcendence of Fordist work structures. The profusion of information about the work process, the spread of team systems, and the availability of analytic tools like MINE render post-Fordist work structures more conceivable than ever before. The question to be addressed is how these technological and organizational developments have combined to reconfigure the structure and culture of the shopfloor. The answer that emerges from our research centers on three decisive shifts: the increasing centrality of process engineers within the production process; the redefinition of what constitutes legitimate work knowledge; and the growing standardization of decisions made by non-expert workers, in accordance with quantitative expertise. We discuss these shifts in turn.

Process Engineers   The first and most obvious change in shopfloor life is the increasingly decisive role played by process engineers in the day-to-day operations of the mill. The simplest manifestation of this trend is the disproportionate growth in the number of process engineers now directly involved in each mill's production process. This growth partly is due to the hiring of engineers into newly created positions such as that of the "shift engineer"—technical employees assigned to work alongside production crews more closely than before. It also stems from the creation of new technical positions that center on the monitoring of production standards in various departments. A final and perhaps most important source of growth in the ranks of the process engineers has stemmed from their increasing representation in supervisory and second-line management jobs that had traditionally been filled from the ranks of hourly personnel. The experience of one of the mills is representative of this latter development. As recently as 1986, 48 percent of all first- and second-level supervisors at this mill held B.S. degrees in an engineering field; only nine years later this proportion had increased by more than a third, rising to 62 percent. The superintendent of this mill has since declared that *all* supervisory openings will be filled with applicants with engineering degrees. When we inquired into this decision, the mill manager articulated an organizational strategy predicated on the expansion of technically qualified expertise. To hammer his point home he held up an organizational chart with the names of all salaried personnel. The names of degree-holding engineers had been marked with a yellow highlighter, indicating each department's relative strength at a glance.

The increasingly prominent role played by process engineers has had important effects on the structure of opportunity within the mills, as many manual employees have experienced a narrowing of their promotion prospects. For one thing, supervisors who have come up through the ranks no longer enjoy reasonable chances of promotion into jobs as second-line managers. Because these supervisors find themselves stuck in their present positions, and because technical education is increasingly required for even first-line supervisory jobs, hourly workers too find their opportunities reduced. These changes have erected or (in some cases) solidified a credential barrier between expert and non-expert labor (see Burris 1993).

Legitimate Work Knowledge As technically trained personnel have grown more prominent, more subtle changes have occurred in the social context in which manual workers are employed. Especially during day shifts, when salaried employees are most strongly represented, the numbers of engineers sometimes begins to approach those of the hourly personnel, especially when grade changes are introduced. This has brought engineers and hourly workers into much closer contact, as Blauner (1964) anticipated some decades ago; the results, however, have been at odds with what Blauner expected.

Bolstered by their increasing prominence in the mill and by the spread of sensors and other instruments that displace manual functions, engineers have set in motion a process that might be termed an "epistemological revolution" within mill life: an inversion in the criteria that define legitimate knowledge of the work process. Implied here is an overturning of traditional craft methods for generating knowledge about production and their replacement by a newer set based on scientific and engineering discourse—a process that has symbolically devalued craft expertise. In lunch-room discussions or meetings now, one sometimes hears engineers portray workers' knowledge in derisive terms: as either amateurish ("sandlot baseball") or else as a form of superstition ("black magic" or "voodoo"). The general thrust of such portrayals is that craft

knowledge is indicative of a backward, pre-scientific approach toward work that is steeped in the dogma of tradition. As one process engineer told us:

> It drives me *crazy* when operators say you can't control the whole process with the computers. They'll stand there and scrape the stock with their thumbnail, and say they can tell me more about the stock than the $40 million Accuray nuclear instruments we just installed! They're just feeling threatened by us, like all their secrets are being taken away, and they don't like that at all.

This engineer is convinced of the inherent superiority of the new equipment; he rejects the argument that craft knowledge might perceive things that sophisticated measurement instruments cannot detect. In this respect, his views are shared by many of his fellow process engineers. Another engineer said:

> I get frustrated whenever people talk about the "art" of papermaking . . . From my standpoint, it's a lot better if I put another control loop and some calibrated instrumentation on a paper machine, and just put out a memo telling the operators to leave the system on cascade, not to touch it. I'd rather have things that way than depend on a 50-year-old man filling out control charts and applying complex rules by himself.

The dominant view, as expressed here, is that nothing makes it harder to achieve consistency in the quality of output than workers who feel they must change production values on the basis of their own experience. This is precisely why control loops are often installed: to overcome what we have termed the "surplus creativity" of the operators.

In most of the production areas we studied, this shift in mill epistemology unfolded gradually. Yet, in a few cases, the process found expression in a single defining event, as occurred in the brown-stock area of one mill in the South. The following incident was related by a widely respected machine tender whose experience is especially noteworthy, for he has been extremely accommodating toward management during the restructuring of mill operations.

> I used to put my hands in and take out a handful of brown stock, squeeze it, tell you whether it was good quality Kraft [pulp], good pine stock or what. I'd tell you about fiber lengths. But then they started bringing in these sensors and machines and whatnot. I still used to put my hands in the dryer, see what I could tell. One day when I did, I said to myself, "that's not right, that's not good quality Kraft." So I told my superintendent. They got the lab testers to work and got the engineers down here. But the lab tests came out OK. So the question was, who they gonna go with? This went on for some time, until finally, this was two years ago, my superintendent said, "J.W., we're gonna go with the lab tests." See, they didn't trust my way of knowin' anymore.

It later turned out that J.W. was right: He had detected an impurity in the white liquor used to digest the wood that had gone unnoticed by the laboratory tests. In this case the result was not serious, but the event was significant in J.W.'s eyes; for to him it symbolized the end of an era. Asked how he felt, he said simply, "I don't put my hands in the brown stock anymore." At this point, he knew that the language of engineering had gained hegemony over its craft equivalent.

Despite these shifts in the definition of legitimate production knowledge, one sometimes hears evidence of a dissenting world view among engineers that breaks with the newly dominant epistemology and seeks to acknowledge the legitimacy of craft knowledge. Such engineers sometimes become defenders of traditional forms of working knowledge within highly automated control

rooms. Consider for example the words of one process engineer in his early 20s, born and raised near the Southern mill at which he now worked:

> I've been told to idiot-proof things, to lock people out. I've been told to put in [automatic feedback] loops that locked people out. But I'm not comfortable with people sitting back in their chairs, waiting for an alarm.

The same sentiments were put even more clearly by an engineer in one of the Northwestern mills, who explicitly challenged his peers' emphasis on electronic sensors and computer-mediated process controls.

> Some of our engineers think everything can be characterized in technical terms, and that if it can't, then it doesn't make sense. They just aren't able to listen to an hourly person talk about paper making. I mean, sometimes I think we get hooked on control rooms. It helps from the process point of view. It's quiet, so we can talk and use the computers to play "what if" games. But it takes you away from the process, isolates you. Out there, you can smell it, hear it, taste it. We have lots of sensors, but there's a lot of things that we don't have sensors for, and some of them can be extremely important for keeping the process on line.

Engineers who subscribe to this latter, more worker-centered view are in the minority. Yet they play an important role in shopfloor relations, often serving to maintain the fabric of trust among occupational groups that would otherwise be at odds.

Standardization of Decisions A further way in which shopfloor life has been reconfigured centers on the ways in which analytic functions and decision-making powers have been distributed. Recall that post-Fordist theory expects the process of work restructuring to reallocate a portion of these tasks downward, blurring or even transcending the traditional division between mental and manual labor. We find little evidence of such a trend. Instead, our research indicates that the dominant tendency has involved a pattern of *tightened* constraints upon manual workers' judgment rather than the "*relaxation* of constraints" that flexibility theory foresees (Hirschhorn 1984).

The point is clearly manifest in the workings of Statistical Process Control. In essence, SPC involves the effort to define expected values for key process variables and to formulate detailed rules that govern how workers respond to deviations from centerline values. A key issue here, which managers and engineers have rarely considered in any depth, concerns the process through which centerline values themselves are established. When we asked managers and engineers to explain how particular centerlines were chosen, many referred somewhat vaguely to "collective experimentation" or "inherited wisdom"—as if the target values were a consensual product of shopfloor history. Occasionally, managers would sense a contradiction here, even stopping in mid-sentence to reformulate their thoughts, as in the case of one quality engineer who oversaw tissue production. After he spoke somewhat critically of top management's effort to direct his *own* behavior, we asked him whether he thought that workers ever resented the imposition of centerlines on *their* routines:

> Yeah. And I can understand that. It's the same thing as we're being told [by headquarters] what starch we should use. *We're* telling *them* [hourly workers] . . . [Pauses]. We're not . . . I mean, it can come across that way, that we're telling them how we want them to run the machine, and to a certain point that's true. But actually, if we do our job right, we should be able to explain to them that

we're *not* telling them how to run the machines, but rather, this is where we *want* them to run it, and if they can't run it there, they need to understand why they can't and be able to explain that.

Displeased with the imposition of rigid, centralized patterns of authority on his own work situation, this man was reluctant to acknowledge participating in the standardization of craftworkers' jobs. Other respondents spoke more bluntly. Asked if the practice of centerlining made operators feel they were being told how to run their machines, a young engineer replied:

> Sure. That's natural. And you *are* telling them how to run. You're saying, in the collective opinion of the people who are good at running this process, it runs best at X. Therefore, we're gonna run it at X. When we deviate from X, it'll be under experimental, controlled conditions, and *we'll* determine if the deviation is in fact better than the old one. If it is better, we're gonna move to that one. So you *are* in fact telling them how to run.

This statement accords quite closely with our own field observations: The definition of centerline values has typically been defined as a technical question best left to the judgement of formally trained engineers.

There were of course dissenting voices among managers and engineers. Asked whether workers might play a more active role in establishing parameters for the process, some engineers felt that it would be both possible and desirable. Said one business manager with long experience as a mill engineer:

> We just don't . . . We tend to think only technically trained people can understand SPC. We're missing the boat in the formation of centerlines.

Other engineers acknowledge that centerlining was "largely a management program," expressing their regret at this turn of events. But again, such dissent was exceptional. Most engineers felt that workers had sufficient powers of consultation, and that any efforts to involve workers more fully would only magnify the problem of inconsistency and instability (surplus creativity) they had long sought to transcend. A high-ranking engineer in the company's technical center who himself oversaw the design of the new information systems said:

> We've got to get over *to* the boring stage. *We've got to make workers' jobs more boring.* We have to go from the chaos we have now to the stability that makes us money. I don't know how to deal with that [the social consequences of boredom]. Teams, or whatever. But this is where we have to go.

In this view, workers' discretion is equivalent to "chaos." Only a standardized work regime, achieved via the coupling of SPC and automation, can deliver the stability the company needs.

Discussion

It is clear that the structure of work in these mills has been evolving in a direction that departs in certain important respects from the expectations of post-Fordist theory. It is true that, with respect purely to skill requirements, manual workers have indeed encountered a rising set of skill demands, as they have had to learn the use of DCS equipment and to cope with the wealth of process information it makes available. In addition, workers have had to learn when to accept computer-provided directions, and when to intervene. Yet even as workers' *skill* requirements have apparently increased, we find little evidence of any expansion of craft *discretion* or *autonomy,* or any imminent synthesis of mental and manual labor, as post-Fordists predict. Before

we can address the larger implications of this finding, however, the question must be asked: Why has the hierarchical, Fordist structure of work proved so tenacious throughout the mills in our research?

Advocates of post-Fordist theory might point to the external market environments of these plants, and suggest that the structure of product demand has limited the development of alternative work structures. The argument here is that since much of the demand for pulp and paper products involves mass consumer markets for towel and tissue products—commodity items most economically produced through standardized work structures—the ingredients necessary for the cultivation of flexibility are largely absent from this case. While this thesis is plausible, we are compelled to reject it on a number of empirical grounds.

To begin, all of the mills in our study are complex, multi-product mills supplying heterogeneous markets that range from mass consumer products (towel and tissue, napkins) to smaller, specialty niches (unbleached coffee filters, specialty coated papers). There was no difference in work organization across mills or production areas oriented toward one or another product type. Smaller, specialty product lines whose paper machines undergo more frequent grade changes were no more disposed to adopt flexible work methods than their counterparts supplying larger, commodity markets. Indeed, of the company's two major product divisions—consumer products and communications paper (which includes such items as coated paper)—support for self-directed teams was appreciably stronger in the former division, which is more fully oriented toward mass production for commodity markets. We therefore doubt that the structure of product markets can suffice to explain the limits of flexibility in these mills.

While our observations are somewhat tentative, we believe that the limits of flexibility can be traced to two alternative influences. First, and at a macrosocial level of analysis, is the nature of the wider culture and society, whose institutional structure confers relatively little legitimacy on craft knowledge and provides relatively few resources for vocational training, certification, or recruitment (Lane 1988). Although we have not interviewed corporate managers, indirect evidence (such as directives expressing their desire to "catch up" with rival firms' technical strengths) indicates that corporate managers view the engineering composition of each mill's personnel as a symbol of its modernity. A second set of influences operates on the shopfloor itself, involving the distribution of resources among engineers and manual workers, affecting which groups are able to benefit from the restructuring of work. The following remarks are confined to the latter, organizational influences.

Recall that manual workers are typically embedded within intra-departmental seniority systems and progression ladders that anchor them within particular production areas. This system, codified in collective bargaining agreements, serves important functions for the company and its workers alike: It encourages workers to accumulate specialized knowledge of their immediate production locale, while it establishes a system of job security that protects the position of skilled workers in particular. At the same time, however, it perpetuates a pattern of local identification and occupational rivalry that often constrains workers' capacity to view the production process as a whole. Thus, one worker on a paper machine had been employed at the same Northwestern mill for more than 30 years, but he had never set foot in the pulping area that furnished his machines with its raw materials—a situation that leads pulp workers to comment that "it's like they think their furnish arrives through a magic pipe in the wall." Moreover,

the use of computerized process-controls has meant a shift toward fewer control rooms and sharp reductions in crew sizes, expanding the production areas that workers must oversee, increasing the pressure they feel to keep production on-line. Workers thus find themselves even more tightly confined within their traditionally defined job duties than before. Finally, although many workers are critical of formal, theoretically based knowledge and expertise, which they sometimes view as a tool of self-aggrandizement, they typically lack more than the rudiments of formal education and often seem intimidated by the cultural capital their superiors can wield (Bourdieu and Passeron 1977; Lamont and Lareau 1988). All these factors combine to limit craftworkers' capacity to compete for larger, more autonomous roles within the mills.

It is important to point out that despite the new-found dominance that engineering discourse enjoys, manual workers have nonetheless preserved a residue of informal, experiential knowledge that remains vital to production. As one worker on a paper machine admitted, "the knowledge stays, but in the cracks. We like to keep it hidden" (cf. Halle 1984; cf. Hodson 1991a, b). The question thus arises: If workers' knowledge has in effect been driven underground, can they not use this hidden knowledge as a strategic resource with which to weaken the hegemony of the engineers? At times, the workers we have studied did indeed employ their knowledge as a weapon, typically to retaliate against assaults upon their own dignity. In one representative case, workers suffered a series of insults at the hands of the same engineer. Led by their machine tender, they withheld their knowledge during a production change, rendering the engineer helpless as pulp eventually began to spill out (as one worker recalled), "looking like oatmeal all over the shopfloor." Workers refused to intervene until the engineer had retreated to his office, enabling them publicly to reaffirm their own competence.

Such instances prompt two observations. First and most obvious is the fact that open resistance like this is quite rare, in no small part because it represents a double-edged sword: it involves costly and often laborious disruptions in production, and it can damage workers' own performance records. Second and more important is the fact that even when such resistance occurs, it is almost always aimed at the *"abuse"* of engineering authority—as in the above example, an assault upon their dignity—leaving untouched the engineers' normal claim to superior expertise. We believe that such acts of resistance represent part of a broader process of informal negotiation, through which workers impose certain limits on engineers' interpersonal practices. Such tactics enable workers to exact a modicum of respect from their superiors—in workers' terms, ensuring that engineers "learn to play ball"—but in ways that rarely if ever challenge the hegemony of engineering knowledge itself.

Process engineers, for their part, are far better situated to benefit from the process of workplace change. Although they are also divided by their engineering specialties and their attendant levels of prestige—electrical engineers are "top dog," while civil engineers are merely "the concrete guys"—these differences seem to have little material effect. For the most part, process engineers constitute a relatively cohesive occupational group whose members spontaneously feel a shared sense of mission in relation to the production process. One major reason, we surmise, lies in the structure of mobility established for technical personnel within all of the mills. In contrast to the situation of hourly employees, engineers are expected to progress through a number of distinct positions within far-flung areas of the mill. (A newly hired engineer might be assigned to a tech-

nical group in a given department, to gain hands-on experience in technical support. After a few years, he or she commonly moves into a job as a technical specialist on a paper machine, and then into a position as a first-line supervisor in production. He or she would then be poised to assume a position with substantial authority within an engineering department.) Such mobility patterns make possible the accumulation of knowledge regarding the production process as a whole, which management increasingly values. These patterns also equip engineers with shared organizational experiences, enabling them to sustain a common sense of purpose in relation to the mill as a whole. Coupled with the generalized authority conferred on technical expertise by the wider culture and organizational environment and the traditional presumption that analytic functions are properly lodged in the engineers' hands, these factors quite naturally position engineers to reap the benefits of workplace change (cf. Wilkinson 1983; Child et al. 1984).

Conclusion

This [reading] has explored the transformation of work under conditions that should be relatively favorable to the flexibility thesis. These mills all employ continuous-process methods of production that make widespread use of programmable control systems and sophisticated information technologies. All four mills are owned by a large multinational corporation with a reputation as an innovative, forward-looking firm. Opportunities for the adoption of flexible, post-Fordist structures are therefore present in abundance. Yet our research has uncovered only partial support for the flexibility thesis. Indeed, the thrust of this [reading] has drawn attention to a set of obstacles to flexibility—centering on the power of engineering knowledge and its symbolic devaluation of skilled manual labor—that post-Fordist theory has ignored.

We do indeed find some halting developments that lead beyond the rigid bureaucratic structure of industrial organization. For one, management has sought to cultivate workers' normative commitment to the mill, especially through the articulation of cross-functional teams in all of the mills. Moreover, the evidence does indeed suggest that the complexities of new process technologies brought about an increasing level of skill requirements among manual employees, who must learn to master an increasing array of data generated by the computerized machine. This latter point effectively refutes Braverman's (1974:224) characterization of continuous-process work as involving little more complexity than "learning to tell time." Finally, a number of managers have expressed the hope that new methods of skill deployment could take root and would empower production workers as full citizens within the labor process. Yet these tendencies have been overwhelmed by a different set of influences that have imposed a rigid, hierarchical pattern founded on the language of technical expertise. As we have seen, process engineers play an increasingly salient role within mill operations, multiplying in relative numbers and importance, and by implication placing limits on manual workers' career opportunities. The definition of legitimate knowledge at work has shifted in ways that increasingly favor scientific discourse over local or experiential knowledge, rendering craft skill a frequent object of derision among salaried personnel. Finally, as management has introduced Statistical Process Control and other elements of Total Quality Management, work methods have been subject to increasing levels of standardization, as centerline values have come to be defined on the basis of formal expertise.

These developments, it seems clear, are not easily reconciled with the concept of post-Fordism. Indeed, there may be some virtue in speaking of the prevalence of important *neo*-Fordist tendencies in these mills, or of a neo-Taylorist search for the "one best way" to run the production process. . . .

REFERENCES

Adler, Paul. 1992. "Introduction." In *Technology and the Future of Work*, ed. Paul Adler. New York: Oxford.

Appelbaum, Eileen and Rosemary Batt. 1994. *The New American Workplace: Transforming Work Systems in the United States.* Ithaca, NY: ILR Press.

Barley, Steven. 1986. "Technology as an Occasion for Structuring." *Administrative Science Quarterly* 31:78–108.

Blauner, Robert. 1964. *Alienation and Freedom: The Factory Worker and His Job.* Chicago: University of Chicago Press.

Bourdieu, Pierre and Jean-Claude Passeron. 1977. *Reproduction: In Education, Society and Culture.* Thousand Oaks, CA: Sage.

Braverman, Harry. 1974. *Labor and Monopoly Capital: The Degradation of Work in the Twentieth Century.* New York: Monthly Review.

Burris, Beverly. 1993. *Technocracy at Work.* Albany, NY: SUNY Press.

Child, John. 1972. "Organizational Structure, Environment and Performance: The Role of Strategic Choice." *Sociology* 6:2–22.

Child, John, R. Loveridge, J. Harvey, and A. Spencer. 1984. "Microelectronics and the Quality of Employment in Services." Pp. 163–190 in *New Technology and the Future of Work and Skills*, ed. P. Marstrand. London: Pinter.

Cornfield, Daniel. 1987. *Workers, Managers and Technological Change: Emerging Patterns of Labor Relations.* New York: Plenum.

Form, William, Robert L. Kaufman, Toby Parcel, and Michael Wallace. 1988. "The Impact of Technology on Work Organization and Work Outcomes: A Conceptual Framework and Research Agenda." Pp. 303–330 in *Industries, Firms and Jobs: Sociological and Economic Approaches*, eds. G. Farkas and P. England. New York: Plenum.

Halle, David. 1984. *America's Working Man.* Chicago: University of Chicago Press.

Hill, Stephen J. 1991. "Why Quality Circles Failed, but Total Quality Management Might Succeed." *British Journal of Industrial Relations* 29:4.

Hirschhorn, Larry. 1984. *Beyond Mechanization.* Cambridge, MA: MIT Press.

Hodson, Randy. 1991a. "The Active Worker: Compliance and Autonomy at the Workplace." *Journal of Contemporary Ethnography* 20:47–78.

_____. 1991b. "Workplace Behaviors: Good Soldiers, Smooth Operators, and Saboteurs." *Work and Occupations* 18:271–290.

Hyman, Richard. 1988. "Flexible Specialization: Miracle or Myth?" Pp. 48–60 in *New Technology and Industrial Relations,* eds. R. Hyman and W. Streeck. Oxford: Basil Blackwell.

Kelley, Maryellen. 1990. "New Process Technology, Job Design and Work Organization: A Contingency Model." *American Sociological Review* 55:191–208.

Kern, Horst and Michael Schumann. 1992. "New Concepts of Production and the Emergence of the Systems Controller." Pp. 111–148 in *Technology and the Future of Work,* ed. Paul Adler. New York: Oxford.

Klein, Janice. 1994. "The Paradox of Quality Management: Commitment, Ownership, and Control." Pp. 178–194. In *The Post-Bureaucratic Organization: New Perspectives on Organizational Change,* eds. C. Heckscher and A. Donnellon. Thousand Oaks CA: Sage.

Kusterer, Kenneth. 1978. *Know-How on the Job: The Important Working Knowledge of Unskilled Workers.* Boulder, CO: Westview.

Lamont, Michele and Annette Lareau. 1988. "Cultural Capital: Allusions, Gaps and Glissandos in Recent Theoretical Developments." *Sociological Theory* 6:153–168.

Lane, Christel. 1988. "Industrial Change in Europe: The Pursuit of Flexible Specialization in Britain and West Germany." *Work, Employment and Society,* 2:141–168.

Nichols, T. and H. Beynon. 1977. *Working for Capitalism.* London: RKP.

Penn, Roger and Hilda Scattergood. 1988. "Continuities and Change in Skilled Work: A Comparison of Five Paper Manufacturing Plants in the UK, Australia and the USA." *British Journal of Sociology* 39:69–81.

Penn, Roger, Kari Lilja, and Hilda Scattergood. 1992. "Flexibility and Employment Patterns in the Contemporary Paper Industry: A Comparative Analysis of Mills in Britain and Finland." *Industrial Relations Journal* 23:214–223.

Penn, Roger and David Sleightholme. 1995. "Skilled Work in Contemporary Europe: A Journey into the Dark." Pp. 187–202 in *Industrial Transformation in Europe: Process and Con-texts,* eds. E. J. Dittrich, G. Schmitdt, and R. Whitley. London: Sage.

Piore, Michael and Charles F. Sabel. 1984. *The Second Industrial Divide: Possibilities for Prosperity.* New York: Basic.

Sabel, Charles. 1991. "Moebius-Strip Organizations and Open Labor Markets: Consequences of the Reintegration of Conception and Execution in a Volatile Economy." Pp. 23–53 in *Social Theory for a Changing Society,* eds. P. Bourdieu and J. Coleman. New York: Russell Sage.

Sabel, Charles and Jonathan Zeitlin. 1985. "Historical Alternatives to Mass Production: Politics, Markets and Technology in Nineteenth Century Industrialization." *Past and Present* 108:133–176.

Senker, Peter. 1992. "Automation and Work in Great Britain." Pp. 89–110 in *Technology and the Future of Work,* ed. Paul Adler. New York: Oxford University Press.

Smith, Vicki. 1994. "Braverman's Legacy: The Labor Process Tradition at 20." *Work and Occupations* 21:403–421.

Spenner, Kenneth. 1983. "Deciphering Prometheus: Temporal Change in the Skill Level of Work." *American Sociological Review* 48:824–837.

_____. 1990. "Skill: Meanings, Methods and Measures." *Work and Occupations* 17:399–421.

Taplin, I. 1995. "Flexible Production, Rigid Jobs: Lessons from the Clothing Industry." *Work and Occupations* 22:412–438.

Thomas, Robert J. 1994. *What Machines Can't Do: Politics and Technology in the Industrial Enterprise.* Berkeley: University of California Press.

Vallas, Steven. 1990. "The Concept of Skill: A Critical Review." *Work and Occupations* 17:379–398.

_____. 1993. *Power in the Workplace: The Politics of Production at AT&T.* Albany: State University of New York Press.

Walton, Mary. 1986. *The Deming Management Method.* New York: Perigee.

Walton, R. E. 1986. "From Control to Commitment in the Workplace." *Harvard Business Review* 63:77–84.

Wilkinson, Barry. 1983. *The Shopfloor Politics of New Technology.* London: Gower.

Wood, Stephen. 1989. "Introduction." In *The Transformation of Work? Skill, Flexibility and the Labour Process,* ed. Stephen Wood. London: Unwin Hyman.

Woodward, Joan. 1958. *Management and Technology.* London: HMSO.

Zuboff, Shoshana. 1988. *In the Age of the Smart Machine.* New York: Basic.

15

Employee Involvement, Involved Employees
Participative Work Arrangements in a White-Collar Service Occupation

Vicki Smith

Throughout the U.S. economy, employers and managers are promoting a new ethos of participation for their workers. The spread of a paradigm of participation—comprised of extensive discussion about the merits of worker involvement as well as actual transformation of production methods and staffing practices—may indeed be one of the most significant trends sweeping across postindustrial, late twentieth-century workplaces (Appelbaum and Batt 1994; Harrison 1994; Heckscher 1988; Hodson 1995; U.S. Department of Labor 1994). As Appelbaum and Batt (1994:5) note in their exhaustive study of emergent U.S. work systems, "In the 1990s, a new *vision* of what constitutes an effective production system appears to dominate management's views, if not yet its actions."

Sociologists, industrial relations researchers, organizational scientists, and policymakers who have studied this trend agree that leaders and managers of U.S. companies are climbing aboard the bandwagon of worker participation in their urgent attempts to maintain competitiveness under changing economic circumstances. Employers believe that when workers participate in making decisions, when they gain opportunities to apply their tacit knowledge to problem solving, and when they acquire responsibility for design-

ing and directing production processes, they feed into an infrastructure enabling firms to respond to shifting market and product demands in a rapid and timely way.

The introduction of management-initiated employee involvement programs (EIPs) has inspired a significant body of research by sociologists who study work, the labor process, organizations, and industrial relations. By and large, these researchers have been skeptical about workers' commitments and consent to such participative programs, suggesting that demands for participation thinly veil a reality of harder work with fewer resources, leaving workers themselves suspicious of such reform (Hodson 1995). Yet, as I will discuss, most research has focused on participative arrangements that are subject to collective bargaining in unionized, industrial work settings that employ a homogeneous and declining fraction of the U.S. labor force. As a result, our knowledge about the causes of, negotiations over, and outcomes associated with EIPs does not extend to the white-collar service work settings in which a vast number of Americans are employed in the late twentieth-century postindustrial U.S. . . .

Employee Involvement Programs in the U.S. Economy

The data on employee involvement or participation programs in the United States are overlapping, murky, sometimes contradictory, occasionally reported to be scientific but

Abridgment of "Employee Involvement, Involved Employees: Participative Work Arrangements in a White-Collar Service Occupation" by Vicki Smith, reprinted from *Social Problems*, Vol. 43, No. 2, May 1996, by permission. © 1996 by the Society for the Study of Social Problems, Inc.

generally believed not to be entirely reliable. Thus, estimates vary about how extensively employers have adopted such programs, ranging from claims that the proportion of Fortune 1000 companies with at least one employee involvement practice had reached about 85 percent in 1990 (Appelbaum and Batt 1994:60), to more cautious projections that a smaller number (37 percent) have "*significant* (my emphasis) involvement . . . (in which) a majority of core employees (are) covered by two or more forms of workplace innovation" (U.S. Department of Labor 1994:34-35).

As Fantasia, Clawson, and Graham (1988:469) point out, "Everything from a suggestion box to a worker-controlled economy has been included under the rubric" of worker participation. Despite the wide-ranging nature of these data, few sociologists who study work dispute that at the very least a *discourse* of involvement, but very often its practice, has become a common approach to work in the postindustrial workplace.

Part of the difficulty in pinning down precisely what employee involvement is and how far it has entered the corporate workplace is that many different participative schemes are included in the definition. Nevertheless, it is possible to categorize these schemes into two clusters, one geared toward the macro-level, power structure of the firm, and one geared toward micro-level work systems, toward improving and changing the way goods and services are produced.

In the first cluster of EIPs, workers negotiate and shape firm-level policies. Including representation on boards of directors (Stern 1988), joint labor/management committees (Bate and Murphy 1981), and ownership by workers (Tucker, Nock, and Toscano 1989), these organizational modes of participation are formal, structured, and nearly completely pertain to goods-producing, manufacturing workers who are represented by unions.

The second cluster contains participative approaches, varied in their depth, duration, and transformative potential, that oversee, coordinate, direct, and manage work systems. Some *consultative* practices, such as intermittently organized quality circles, or daily, weekly or monthly problem-solving and communicational meetings involving workers and managers, exist apart from everyday work routines.

Other participative innovations are comparatively more integrated into the labor process, enabling workers to participate on a permanent rather than sporadic, consultative basis. In theory, they reorganize how workers produce goods and services. They create opportunities for workers to learn new skills, acquire greater amounts of organizational/production information, use their judgement, provide meaningful input, and to make on-the-spot decisions. Particular innovations include job rotation, job enrichment, and self-managed teams and can be found across the occupational and industrial spectrum.

This paper addresses the latter cluster of EIPs—involvement at the point of production—but looks at a work setting that is different from those typically studied. Although all evidence suggests that these programs can be found across the spectrum of occupations and industries, to date we know much more about how they work in unionized, goods-producing firms (Appelbaum and Batt 1994; Fantasia, Clawson, and Graham 1988; Harrison 1994; Heckscher 1988; Hodson et al. 1993; Kochan, Katz, and McKersie 1986; Wells 1987). This limited framework universalizes the experiences of a relatively small proportion of the U.S. workforce, and implicitly suggests that innovations reshaping unionized, blue-collar workplaces are a harbinger of things to come for all U.S. workers.

Because we lack a well-developed body of research about participative forms in white-collar, service, non-union firms, our model of worker participation in the U.S. economy, and our knowledge about control, skill, and autonomy, is incomplete. Moreover, our explanation for why workers' responses to EIPs range from "cynicism and active resistance to grudging acceptance and even enthusiasm" (Hodson 1995:101) is partial. Most studies focus on the cynicism, resistance, or grudging acceptance that follows when workers feel they have no choice but to participate. They either have to comply with management's request for worker involvement and intensified effort or they lose their jobs and perhaps their plant. Sociologists and industrial relations researchers have well documented U.S. workers' weakened bargaining power as employers have shipped their jobs overseas, have downsized and laid off workers, forcing workers to accept management's terms for greater involvement. Such disadvantageous conditions can well explain why much of the labor movement has resisted or only grudgingly gone along with the new participatory agenda.

But those conclusions apply to a limited set of historically specific institutional work settings. Firms that are restructuring both entrenched production processes and industrial relations systems presumably will vary significantly from firms in which labor processes have not been as firmly institutionalized and bound by rules, which have never been characterized by adversarial labor/management relations, and whose workers demographically are comparatively new to core-sector, white-collar employment. We must ask whether, under the latter set of conditions, workers might be less likely to resist and will perhaps even embrace work reforms. And, if they embrace them, is it because they are uncritical dupes of managerial control, or is their endorsement linked in some fundamental way to the demands, constraints, and opportunities presented in their work? One purpose of the following analysis is to demonstrate that production workers' "enthusiastic effort" was explained by their belief that EI gave them new competencies in simultaneously handling and deflecting stressful work relations.

A secondary claim here is that endorsement was conditioned by the prevailing class, gender, and race hierarchy in the postindustrial United States. What we *do* know about why workers have appropriated or struggled over participation programs is limited to the experiences of male, primarily white workers, workers who have held historically secure positions in the labor market and who make up the overwhelming majority of the industrial, unionized workforce. Their institutionalized interests in regulating work, their definition of advantages gained and privileges lost, their willingness to adopt a new ethos of production, will most likely differ from the interests of relatively new workforce entrants, white women, and men and women of color who have struggled recently to make strides in an expanding, white-collar service economy.

Case Study Participants and Methods

The data analyzed here, drawn from interviews with and observations of white-collar service workers, were gathered in the course of studying an employee involvement program in a division of a large U.S. service firm: Reproco, a pseudonym for a company that manufactures photocopy and computer equipment and sells copying and other business services. These data illuminate the subjective side of a structural innovation as experienced by nonmanagerial employees.

I observed (in 10 of 40 worksites in this division), used company and business publications to do archival research, and conducted 26 in-depth, semistructured interviews (ranging from 1 to 2½ hours) with 10 supervisors and managers and 16 nonmanagerial employees. Of the managers and supervisors, 5 were men and 5 were women (8 white women and men, 2 women of color); of the nonmanagerial employees 11 were women and 5 were men (6 white, 10 nonwhite [African American and Hispanic]).

I interviewed Reproco employees about the programmatic aspects of employee involvement and explored their work biographies, job requirements, and experiences with the program. In particular, I explored their interpretations of employee involvement and their organizational interests in participation. Interview data were then coded to mine the subjective experiences of corporate workers at different organizational levels. This paper focuses on an unsolicited, serendipitous finding, in which workers delved at length into personal transformations that they felt had occurred as a result of training and participation. Finally, I distributed a survey to everyone I interviewed that collected data on salary, job experience, educational background, age, and family status.

The Jobs and the Workers: Skill, Compensation, Training

Reproco's employee involvement scheme was introduced to white-collar service workers who labored in an unpredictable, continually changing, low-status, and socially variegated job environment. To understand the meaning of employee involvement to workers, then, requires understanding the work conditions, job rewards, and human capital of the job holders; and how the EIP attempted to smooth possible friction between these features.

First, this division of Reproco had successfully marketed a flexible service by subcontracting out business-service workers to perform photocopy work in "facilities" on the premises of other companies. Taking advantage of an economic climate in which an increasing number of U.S. firms are downsizing the total number of their permanent employees and hiring others to work for a delimited period of time (Callaghan and Hartmann 1992; Harrison 1994), Reproco subcontracted the photocopy function to companies that no longer wished to organize and manage this service themselves. Reproco employees set up photocopy rooms in other companies, staffing them with two to five machine operators; company managers trained the photocopiers and provided, in Reproco's own centralized office, backup staff and machines to accommodate changing, unpredictable photocopy loads.

This arrangement meant that while employed by Reproco, machine operators performed their work in diverse organizational settings; they were "organizational boundary spanning" workers (Wharton 1993) who continually and simultaneously had to be cognizant of their own employers' demands (Reproco) and those of the employing company in which they physically worked. They were accountable to diverse sets of "corporate clients" (who differed with respect to professional and industry status, and race and gender) as well as to their off-site supervisors.

They moved from one type of organizational setting to another over time, receiving little forewarning about when and where they would work when a contract expired. They could perform quite routine photocopy work (photocopying 8.5" × 11" documents day in and day out for an insurance company) or they could perform highly complex photocopy work, quality production of which could be urgent (photocopying plant blueprints for trouble-shooting engineers in a nuclear power facility, for example). They learned the specifications for each organization on the job.

During any given day, the machine operators' work load was unpredictable and potentially stressful: "Corporate clients," those employees bringing jobs to the machine operators, rarely knew in advance when they would need something photocopied, and they felt no compunction to try and coordinate with or subordinate their needs to the needs of others, often demanding immediate turnaround for their job. The machine operators had to use their own judgement continually, whether about scheduling copy jobs, deciding upon specifications they could provide for a client, or sending jobs they couldn't accommodate to the divisional center.

The tone of these "unscriptable" interactions could be problematic because corporate clients often viewed Reproco machine operators as low-status workers: "just button pushers," or "just copiers" (epithets reported by copiers). In this highly uncertain, social-relationally complex environment, machine operators had no official supervisor or managers; a lead operator, designated as head worker without formal managerial status or compensation, took informal responsibility for coordinating the group as a whole. This reflected Reproco's agenda to cut back layers of management (typical of many large firms [Smith 1990]); supervisors and managers from the division's center periodically visited the facilities to gather information and evaluate work performance. In significant ways, corporate clients were as much agents of control as were Reproco managers.

The job carried with it a bundle of characteristics typical of white-collar service sector jobs in the U.S. postindustrial occupational structure (Sullivan 1989). Like other white-collar working-class jobs, it offered modest pay (the typical income category checked off by machine operators on a survey was the $15,000–$19,000 category), low status in the

organizational hierarchy, required only a high school degree (only one machine operator of the 16 I interviewed possessed a college degree), offered limited mobility to management, and did not demand or develop complex technical skills. But it also had characteristics of a white-collar middle-class job: Job holders developed social-relational skills and unique kinds of organizational knowledge, the work was unpredictable rather than routine, and semiautonomous rather than directed by others.

The machine operator position was highly race stratified although surprisingly gender balanced. Nearly 40 percent of the machine operators were African American and Hispanic, and these aggregate company statistics covered up much deeper regional stratification—in urban facilities there was much higher representation of men and women of color. Most men in machine operator positions were African American and Hispanic, while white men were found primarily in supervisory and management positions.

Like many other U.S. companies, Reproco's top management had formulated a new work system to increase the ability of its workforce to handle both the complexities of decentralized production and occupationally and demographically diverse work relations. To level its own organizational hierarchy, to iron out disparate work conditions and the potential tensions that might occur at their intersection, corporate-level management had implemented an employee involvement program. Reproco was attempting to manage the unpredictable work environment and to equip new workers to accommodate this unpredictability.

Reproco's EIP taught an in-depth approach to understanding the social relations of work, couched in conventional individualistic and psychologistic terms. Employees learned new communication techniques, taking turns, for example, playing different roles, simulating attack and defend situations, and learning to identify different kinds of statements and types of dialogues. They learned how to respond to aggressive and/or hostile individuals in an "appropriate" manner, in a way that supported the adage that "the customer is always right" but that allowed the worker to remain self-possessed.

The communications skills tied into the techniques they learned for determining the production of services independently of management. Employees were trained to initiate and lead problem-solving groups, for example, using their newfound communications skills to facilitate them. They learned group process procedures, such as running the meetings, identifying, describing, analyzing, and solving problems. Round-robin techniques, which gave everyone a chance to talk and which enabled the suppression of constant talkers, formally opened up the opportunity for all to participate.

Communications, problem solving, and group process techniques were used for myriad purposes. Workers and managers used them, casually and more formally, to figure out how to work more cost effectively, to open up bottlenecks in production processes, and adjudicate conflicts between fellow employees, or between Reproco employees and clients. The whole package of techniques was designed to enhance flexibility at work, to give company employees a chance to act on their own accumulated knowledge about the best way to conduct work tasks, to depend on co-workers to get them through difficult and unanticipated situations in the absence of formal management: in other words, to self-manage through the often choppy waters of flexible work life. Thus, despite the low level of these jobs in the overall hierarchy, there was a structural basis for involvement, for autonomous decision making, job planning, and limited self-management albeit under conditions clearly established by management.

Participating in Participation: Workers' Perceptions

Machine operators were expected to accommodate to shifting work loads and organizational contexts and to assume responsibility for basic supervisorial tasks without the formal recognition and compensation for being a manager. I anticipated, when I started interviewing the service workers in these settings, to find significant evidence of stress, noncompliance, or at least, cynicism about the conditions under which they worked. But I found instead something quite unanticipated: workers' expression of what Hodson (1991) calls "enthusiastic effort," wherein workers not only were willing to fine tune their efforts to unpredictable work loads, but they routinely praised the EIP, articulating their perceptions of benefits they received from their preparation and training for EI.

I argue that white-collar business-service workers in Reproco endorsed employee involvement because they saw it as providing a set of interpretive skills that enabled them to negotiate complex social relations in a decentralized organizational context. Working autonomously, building and using tacit knowledge, and working across the boundaries of multiple organizations implicated them in exacting and stressful work encounters. The EIP, according to my informants, had offered a means for reflecting on these encounters and to interpret them, thus increasing workers' feelings of efficacy in controlling them. In other words, workers viewed the EIP as critical to on-the-job survival.

Their interpretations of these advantages are situated within a larger context of class and race stratification. Most people hired as machine operators had limited educational backgrounds and occupational histories and had experienced rocky transitions into even this low level of the corporate work world.

Their chances for upward mobility into professional and managerial occupations were statistically narrow. I argue that their responses to Reproco's EIP were thus conditioned by the prevailing institutional sources of race, class, and gender inequality constraining their labor market choices. The EIP training and skills positioned them with a new cultural capital (Lamont and Lareau 1988), a body of knowledge about and awareness of interactions in the corporate world; workers believed this would help them succeed in their current position but also with long-term professional goals.

It is impossible to say with certainty that what workers identify as a new set of skills would genuinely lead to new opportunity, or that their perceptions of control translate into real control over interactions; nevertheless their impression of opportunity and advantage is an important ingredient in their willingness to accommodate themselves to the chaotic job of machine operator.

Building the Self, Learning Interaction

Machine operators repeatedly emphasized the sharpening of four skills: interpreting others' actions and meaning; taking the role of others; "depersonalizing" or transcending particular conflicts; and gaining confidence to participate to a greater degree.

Anita, a pseudonym for a 33-year-old African American woman who had worked for Reproco as a machine operator in various sites for 11 years, described her experiences and thoughts in painstaking terms that were echoed by many of the machine operators. Anita started working for Reproco as a temporary worker when, after a year of college, she was told that she would not be allowed to return due to poor grades.

Reproco's EIP had required her to participate in meetings and problem-solving groups for the first time in her life, a process that appeared to have been personally difficult. She said she had had to become involved:

> One step at a time. It's, ah, 'cause I don't want to get out there and fall flat on my face. But people are like taking numbers. "Oh god, there she is. She was never here before. What's she doing back there?" 'Cause you're seen, you know, you become more focused, you know, they can see it. "Gosh, she's in view."

Even though major life experiences such as having children and raising them as a single parent had forced her to be a "leader" (her word) in her family, it was only recently, in the course of participating in a few problem-solving groups, that she felt other people had "brought her into focus," recognizing about her, "Oh, she *does* have a mouth, and, oh, she *does* have thought."

When I asked Anita how EI might be useful to her in the way she performed her job—serving professional "clients" in a facility in a large architectural firm—she reflected that:

> There's a way that you want to be perceived. There's a way that you want people to respond to you. You don't want people snapping at you. You don't want people, ah, just tuning you out. You want people to try and understand what's going on with you and where you're coming from.
>
> I have to try and understand what the other person's point is. And to understand the other person's point you have to step out of your shoes for a moment and step in theirs. What they want. What they require . . . I come to work, put myself in the customer's position. Well, you don't want nobody snapping at you. Because if you snap at someone too much, it's a snap back attitude. But you have to remove yourself and think about the other person. So, yes, I've taken it and put it into everyday life.

Learning to detect and gaining the ability to deflect the "snap back attitude" of other people had been eye opening for Anita; she spoke of becoming "voiced" (her word) and visible in her facility work group when she gained the ability to interpret the needs of clients and co-workers, and to more successfully manage perceptions of herself.

The notion of stepping into someone else's shoes was echoed by Sally, a white re-entry woman in her fifties, who commented that she had learned new tools to

> . . . look at their [her clients'] perspective as well as your own and how you're trying to solve the problem. So, I try to . . . get their perspective of it and see if I can work around it.

This growing awareness of interpersonal dynamics and their implications for work was reported by men as well, who noted similar processes that had occurred in both training and in on-the-job deployment of new communications skills at Reproco. Ralph, for example, emphasized how he felt his ability to interpret others' behavior, to gain some control over interactions with others, had grown and that he felt mentally better equipped to control his reactions to others' behavior.

Ralph was an ex-Marine and Vietnam veteran, one of 10 children raised in a Hispanic family in the Bronx who had moved through a series of working-class, white-collar jobs, and had unsuccessfully tried to establish a small business, before working for Reproco. He emphasized that he had never had professional role models in his family and that he ultimately wished to run his own small business (a goal he felt he was getting closer to because of his experience with Reproco as a machine operator in the engineering division of a nuclear power plant facility). When I asked Ralph whether EIP had assisted him in any way he answered:

Yeah, the communicative skills impressed me. They showed me how I could get information from the customer in a clear way, *taught me how to read body language.* I used to say "Here's your copies, now get out of here." Now I have to make sure I'm communicating, *to understand their needs.* The customer is important and I have to figure out what they need and I'm trying to have more sensitivity to their needs.

In Ralph's eyes, the ability to interpret others' needs and to avoid overreacting to people had enabled him to master his ability to avoid and/or manage crisis, an ability he claimed was newfound. He spoke of avoiding "chain reactions and repetition of problems" (referring to business misfortunes in the past), and how the problem identifying and solving process had "organized his problem solving" ability (as did a number of other respondents, he elaborated in some detail how he used this in church and family affairs). In his thinking, these skills had very tangible outcomes: he saw them as necessary for eventually having his own business. He remarked:

> I don't want to reach the point where I'll have multiples of problems. I don't want to make the mistakes others have made. I want to be able to identify and solve before problems turn into a big crisis. I always wanted to have my own business but I've always been insecure *about my knowledge of people,* customers.

Having dropped out of Howard University and then community college for financial reasons, and having worked at two temporary clerical positions before joining Reproco, James, a 29-year-old African American man, was understandably committed to the company: The job security, the benefits package, the training he had undergone, and prospects for diverse job opportunities, were attractive even if limited. He started as a machine operator and at the time of our interview was working as a lead operator, coordinating seven operators. James's facility was one of the few that was not located inside another company; it was in a regional center and accepted copy jobs from firms in the area. This entailed a more complex set of negotiations with people from a range of diverse organizations.

He felt that training in group process and communications had changed his work life and his ability to effectively work in a job that was de facto a supervisorial job. Moreover, he emphasized that he had imported the tools and insights into other realms of his life, a claim mentioned by nearly all of my respondents. He spontaneously described his feeling that clear and undefensive communication enabled him to coordinate the work of the machine operators and deal with clients more authoritatively:

> . . . like I said, what I've learned here and dealing with people, I've taken outside. And I transfer what I learned and put it into my daily life and it helped me to, I learned how to, like I said before, *how to listen, and how to make sure that I understand exactly what someone is telling me* . . . just to listen and see if I'm able to do as someone is instructing me to do or if I'm able to do that . . .

Using the technique of getting people to clarify their statements, confusion about which could evoke the wrath of customers (and had, on occasion), enabled him to

> . . . test my understanding, make sure I understand exactly what someone was telling me. (I get them) to repeat it, to clarify it. That way, you won't cause any problems at the end because I . . . if I asked you again to repeat it, to clarify, then we won't have any problems at the

end. I find that it helps me to avoid conflict, helps me to resolve conflict . . . I find I help a lot of other people resolve conflicts and issues in their lives . . . It gives me a way of helping them see things from another perspective and in a nonthreatening way, it's kinda weird.

New to him, learning to pay attention to the dynamics of conversation and interaction added to his belief that he was better able to organize and accomplish complex jobs. In one recent job for which he could take credit, a leading chemical company had contracted the services of this facility to photocopy volumes of material for a federal investigation. James had not only had to organize the entire production process, but he also had to coordinate dozens of temporary workers brought in solely for this purpose and negotiate extensively with Reproco divisional-level management and with representatives of the federal government.

Being trained in communication and involvement, acquiring knowledge about work relations, I argue, built workers' perception of greater efficacy in interaction. The formal techniques of EI also provided openings for people to experience validation of different kinds of verbal participation by the organization. Gaining the confidence to talk, and thus not feeling completely at the mercy of others who could monopolize interaction, was another outcome of the EIP identified by nearly all my respondents.

For example, linguistic competence itself can be an important barrier for individuals who wish to deal effectively with co-workers and clients. For one Hispanic woman—for whom English was her second, extremely well-spoken language—differences in language competency translated, in her mind, to inferior thought itself.

Hilda's experience shows how one of the techniques followed in EI groups—the round-robin approach, wherein everyone around the room has to verbally contribute—helped her overcome genuine terror over language inadequacies and to place her own insights and contributions on a par with those she perceived as being "smarter," "more impressive" (who happened to be experienced male co-workers). She described her introduction to an EI group in the following way:

> I remember when we were first trained in leadership through quality, that you do the meetings and we were learning the lingo—seeking information, giving information—normally in a crowd full of people I would not talk because I'd figure—I would feel—the barrier of language would come up, the barriers of, well, these are men that have been doing this for years, maybe they know better than I do so let me shut up and not get involved . . .
>
> *They were more impressive.* And then once the employee involvement makes everybody get involved and the best thing about it, which I loved was that nobody is—when you're brainstorming, no one is allowed to criticize your idea. Even if it's weird, even if it's the worst idea you could ever make and you know it and it sorta comes out of your lips—nobody is allowed to make a comment because that's what brainstorming is. *Free ideas without an evaluation on them.* So the facilitator was, "No, no, no, you can't make a comment" (Author's note: Her facilitator stopped people from interrupting her). And he makes you feel better because you can say anything and you don't feel like, intimidated by the boys network.

Her insights about how public involvement and visibility rattled her were vivid in equating language mastery with competency itself:

> . . . in meetings, as soon as you said a meeting—I would have a fit. My palms

would sweat. I would start sweating and I would be like, "Please God, don't let them ask me anything." *Because my accent would automatically get very heavy and my brain was not translating at the pace that it normally does.* So my thoughts were coming in two languages . . . You know that I had a stomach ache. But I had to think real good because I wanted to say something that was intelligent. But it made me say something and it made me open up a little bit more in meetings and things like that.

These insights and experiences were seconded by others. Hillary, a 48-year-old African American woman, identified the importance of understanding hidden principles of communication, which she learned in her in-depth training session, for independently organizing cooperative relations in the course of working. She appreciated the participative approach to problem solving because it meant that groups had to "acknowledge that a person has made a proposal instead of *just ignoring it and going on,"* a kind of silencing process in which she felt herself to have been on the receiving end.

Speaking especially of one communication technique (learning how to clarify statements and requests) she pointed out the virtues of using this technique for helping people better understand cultural complexity and smoothing out tensions incurred in the process of accomplishing work tasks:

> These are all behaviors that this training helped us to identify, and that's part of the first step of being able to change anybody's behavior, *is to recognize it.* And once you are aware of it then you can begin to change it, address it. One of the areas that they taught and I was unaware of this until this training so this is very key for me, was the—what they call, clarifying, the clarifying behavior. To ask

a clarifying question as opposed to making an assumption that is wrong. Because our language can be very, ah, ah, *can have many meanings,* depending on voice inflection and ah, you know, a person can say something and they can mean something totally different from what you understand.

Pondering meaning, interpreting action, and taking the perspective of others; using the communication tools and an interpretive framework to strengthen one's voice and efficacy in a complex work setting; to become more involved in group processes and decision making, were themes raised over and over and spontaneously in interviews with machine operators. The perceived benefits that service workers identified cemented their commitments to Reproco, even when it was questionable whether these benefits lent themselves to meaningful upward mobility or wage improvement. In these informants' minds, new interactional insights and skills were meaningful if intangible assets.

"Procedural Resistance": Using Employee Involvement Techniques to Resist Clients

Workers' beliefs about how they benefited were bolstered in additional and comparatively concrete ways by the EI training. The EIP provided the techniques for "procedural resistance," a means for machine operators to coopt unreasonably insistent, contemptuous and otherwise difficult corporate clients, many of them professionals who could be a more immediate, intense, and stressful source of control than off-site supervisors or managers. Machine operators appropriated these simple techniques to enlist clients themselves as partners in the participative agenda and to set limits on their demands.

Machine operators reported having talked clients into helping finish copy jobs

that operators couldn't complete themselves (for example, collating particularly complex documents); drawing clients into the process of planning the work flow; getting clients to take joint responsibility for decisions about working overtime to complete urgently needed jobs; and using simple surveys to solicit feedback about machine operators' job performance as well as ideas about improving the service.

Using communications skills with the goal of sharing information with clients, encouraging them to participate in brainstorming about techniques for completing work, and eliciting feedback about service production and improvement of service delivery gave machine operators a way to negotiate competing demands and defuse potentially hostile client-operator interactions within the terms of the new participative program. This ability to use authorized procedures as tools of resistance, to establish parameters on their work loads, was an important defense mechanism for the operators. Importantly, workers didn't resist new techniques themselves, but they used the techniques to resist and coopt negative, antagonistic clients.

Conclusion

In many ways, Reproco's EIP is a stunning example of how contemporary managers draw on prevailing popular ideologies about participation to extract greater effort from workers. The machine operators in this study willingly directed their own work efforts day in and day out, engaged in group decision making, took risks in using their own judgement for production decisions, and represented the interests of Reproco by absorbing conflict and dispute in relations with corporate clients. In other words, this program coordinated workers' and management's goals, a participative system of control (Dickson 1981) highly successful in "securing yet obscuring" (Burawoy 1979:30) workers' consent.

Living up to the gravest concerns that observers have about EIP in U.S. workplaces, Reproco's system has intensified everyday work life for poorly compensated workers. The findings presented here confirm one pessimistic claim that has been made by those studying EIP: that these innovations may strengthen management's capacity to extract additional effort from workers by concealing job speedups and work intensification behind the language of enrichment (cf. O'Reilly 1994).

But what this research makes clear is that some workers have compelling reasons to participate in new systems and may consent to the conditions described throughout this paper because they perceive unanticipated payoffs and opportunities. For one thing, low-level, white-collar service workers endorsed Reproco's EIP precisely because the program and its micro-level techniques, in their eyes, heightened their sense of greater efficacy in managing those conditions. Their endorsement, then, was conditioned by the structural arrangements and the social relations of their jobs.

For another, workers saw these new skills as part of a process of career building. They envisioned taking these skills and applying them to their own small businesses, to different positions in other large corporations, and to higher level positions inside Reproco. Thus, while Reproco's participative arrangements entailed significant intensity of work effort and commitment, they also created a context for workers to develop new skills, seen by workers as relevant to future opportunity. They were not technological skills, much emphasized by the literature on involvement and worker participation; rather they were social-relational skills that were potentially transferable to other white-collar, service contexts, and perhaps to low levels of supervision and management. Participation in participation,

then, ostensibly represented a new step on a constrained mobility ladder.

Broadly, the acquisition of these skills is important for workers who have historically been excluded from core-sector, permanent job opportunities. Much research has been done on the difficulty African American and Hispanic youth, for example, have in making the transition from school to paid work (see Powers, forthcoming, for an overview of this transition). Neckerman and Kirshenman's (1991) important article on the way racist assumptions circumscribe employers' recruitment, selection, and hiring practices similarly underscores the achievement of those African Americans and Hispanics who have made it into the secure, albeit lowest employed, ranks of large, urban, white-collar firms. Neckerman and Kirschenman emphasize the significance of the very skills, identified by my informants, that employers use to screen out many people of color in the hiring process: Employers look for "appropriate interaction and conversational style—in short, shared culture" (1991:442); "job applicants must be sensitive to verbal and nonverbal cues and to the hidden agenda underlying interviewers' questions" (1991:442). These "social skills and cultural compatibility" are used to make future promotion decisions.

These conclusions are echoed by Moss and Tilly (1995), who analyze the way employers discriminate against African American men in their hiring practices. Employers feel that African American men lack the appropriate "soft" skills (communication and people skills, teamwork skills, demeanor and so forth) that are crucial to successful outcomes in the post-industrial workplace.

My respondents have made it past this screening process, laden with negative assumptions about race and class, and are now struggling to survive—to do their jobs on terms acceptable to the corporation, to achieve some degree of personal and occupational efficacy in order to work with others. They have found success in Reproco's white-collar ranks, doing work that is unskilled technically, but that builds white-collar interpersonal skills that can be transferred to other corporate contexts; in a position that pays low wages but offers a benefits package and secure employment; working in demographically and occupationally heterogeneous settings that build their interactional skill set.

Even if these new skills don't lead directly to upward mobility, even if structural reorganization flattens hierarchies and runs counter to the expansion of vertical opportunities (a structural trend affecting workers across the occupational spectrum [Smith 1993]), lower-level workers can compete for new lateral opportunities and learn to more effectively manipulate their work environments to defend their own interests and existing status, an important skill noted recently by sociologists studying other work settings (Paules 1991). They can learn to better negotiate the day-to-day operations of workplaces and to exercise authority in relations with co-workers. Although a beginning, such individual paths of change may have the long-term effect of transforming the workplace hierarchies that have consolidated around race, gender, and class.

REFERENCES

Appelbaum, Eileen and Rosemary Batt. 1994. *The New American Workplace*. Ithaca: ILR Press.

Bate, S. P. and J. Murphy. 1981. "Can Joint Consultation Become Employee Participation?" *Journal of Management Studies* 18:389–409.

Burawoy, Michael. 1979. *Manufacturing Consent*. Chicago: University of Chicago Press.

Callaghan, Polly and Heidi Hartmann. 1992. *Contingent Work: A Chart Book on Parttime and Temporary Employment*. Washington, D.C.: Institute for Women's Policy Research/ Economic Policy Institute.

Dickson, John. 1981. "Participation as a Means of Organizational Control." *Journal of Management Studies* 18:159–176.

Edwards, Richards. 1979. *Contested Terrain*. New York: Basic Books.

Fantasia, Rick, Dan Clawson, and Gregory Graham. 1988. "A Critical View of Worker Participation in American Industry." *Work and Occupations* 15:468–488.

Harrison, Bennett. 1994. *Lean and Mean*. New York: Basic Books.

Heckscher, Charles. 1988. *The New Unionism*. New York: Basic Books.

Hodson, Randy. 1991. "The Active Worker: Compliance and Autonomy at the Workplace." *Journal of Contemporary Ethnography* 20:47–78.

———. 1995. "Worker Resistance: An Underdeveloped Concept in the Sociology of Work." *Economic and Industrial Democracy* 16:79–110.

Hodson, Randy, Sean Creighton, Cheryl Jamison, Sabine Rieble, and Sandy Welsh. 1993. "Is Worker Solidarity Undermined by Autonomy and Participation? Patterns from the Ethnographic Literature." *American Sociological Review* 58:398–416.

Kochan, Thomas, Harry Katz, and Robert McKersie. 1986. *The Transformation of American Industrial Relations*. New York: Basic Books.

Lamont, Michelle and Annette Lareau. 1988. "Cultural Capital: Allusions, Gaps, and Glissandos in Recent Theoretical Developments." *Sociological Theory* 6:153–168.

Leidner, Robin. 1993. *Fast Food, Fast Talk*. Berkeley: University of California Press.

Moss, Philip, and Chris Tilly. 1995. " 'Soft' Skills and Race: An Investigation of Black Men's Employment Problems." *Russell Sage Foundation* Working Paper #80.

Neckerman, Kathryn and Joleen Kirschenman. 1991. "Hiring Strategies, Racial Bias, and Inner-City Workers." *Social Problems* 38: 433–447.

O'Reilly, Jacqueline. 1994. *Banking on Flexibility*. Aldershot: Avebury.

Paules, Greta. 1991. *Dishing it Out*. Philadelphia: Temple University Press.

Powers, Brian. Forthcoming. *Shadowed Passages: Remaking Inequality from High School to the Workplace*.

Smith, Vicki. 1990. *Managing in the Corporate Interest*. Berkeley: University of California Press.

———. 1993. "Flexibility in Work and Employment: The Impact on Women." *Research in the Sociology of Organizations* 11:195–216.

Stern, Robert. 1988. "Participation by Representation: Workers on Boards of Directors in the United States and Abroad." *Work and Occupations* 15:396–422.

Sullivan, Teresa. 1989. "Women and Minority Workers in the New Economy." *Work and Occupations* 16:393–415.

Tausky, Curt and Anthony Chelte. 1988. "Workers' Participation." *Work and Occupations* 15:363–373.

Tucker, James, Steven Nock, and David Toscano. 1989. "Employee Ownership and Perceptions of Work: The Effect of an Employee Stock Ownership Plan." *Work and Occupations* 16:26–42.

U.S. Department of Labor. 1994. *Fact Finding Report: Commission on the Future of Worker-Management Relations.*

Wells, Donald. 1987. *Empty Promises: Quality of Working Life Programs and the Labor Movement.* New York: Monthly Review Press.

Wharton, Amy. 1993. "The Affective Consequences of Service Work: Managing Emotions on the Job." *Work and Occupations* 20:205–232.

THE GLOBAL ECONOMY

16

Net-Working for a Living
Irish Software Developers in the Global Workplace

Seán Ó Riain

It is 4:15 in the afternoon. On the wall of the software test group in the Irish offices of USTech, a prominent Silicon Valley computer company, there are four clocks. At the moment they show that it is 8:15 A.M. in Silicon Valley, California, 10:15 in Austin and Fort Worth, Texas, and 11:15 in Montreal, Canada. Silicon Valley has just "opened for business," and the software developers and managers in Ireland begin a hectic few hours of discussion with their American counterparts. The row of clocks evokes a smoothly working global economy, held back only by time zones, and a software operation which seamlessly manages a variety of transnational connections.

I hurry downstairs, as I have a conference call to the United States at 4:30 p.m. Irish time (8:30 a.m. their time in Silicon Valley). Thirty minutes later I am sitting in an open-plan cubicle, along with five members of a software development team. Employed by USTech, they are developing a software product for a Silicon Valley start-up company called Womble Software. I have been writing a user guide for the product and am deep in discussion with Jane, the technical-writing editor in Silicon Valley, and Ramesh, an immigrant to the United States from India and the "chief architect" of the program, who is in St. Louis in the heart of middle-America. As my manager comes into the team area, I put the conference call on the speaker phone. Now the whole "Womble team" can hear the conversation.

As the conversation unfolds, so does the mime drama around me, as the team reacts

"Net-Working for a Living" by Seán Ó Riain in *Global Ethnography: Forces, Connections and Imaginations in a Postmodern World,* edited by Michael Burawoy. Copyright © 2000 The Regents of the University of California. Reprinted by permission.

to the flow of global communication into this cubicled "local" space. When Ramesh suggests adding new features (creating more work for the developers around me), there is an explosion of displeased sign language, including a variety of abusive gestures directed at the speaker phone. Since Ramesh can hear everything on our end, this pantomime is conducted in complete silence. I have a hard time not bursting out laughing. When Jane points out to Ramesh that it is difficult to write a user guide when the final screen designs for the software program have not been decided upon (a common complaint within the development team two weeks before the product is released), there is an explosion of mimed cheering and barely controlled laughter around me.

This is just another day in the global informational workplace, a workplace which is home to increasing numbers of employees around the world. The dominant image of these workplaces is that of places lifted out of time and space, places where communication and innovation are free from the drag of local cultures and practices and untainted by power relations. Robert Reich argues that new information and communication technologies make it possible and even necessary to reorganize firms into "global webs" and employees into global telecommuters.[1] For Reich these webs operate smoothly, destroying constraints of space and social structure, moving in conjunction with the ever-circling hands of the clocks on the USTech wall. The global workplace is "lifted out" of its temporal and spatial contexts and becomes a "pure" space for communication based on shared rules of interaction and understanding.[2]

Others argue that this perspective is too benign. The speeding up of the global economy destroys local space—the fact that Ramesh and the Womble team can participate in the same conversation at the same time means that they essentially share the same social and economic space, despite the physical distance between them. Time annihilates space, melting away "solid" local places into the "air" of the global economy. This is not a neutral process, however, as the once autonomous local space of the worker is increasingly dominated by global corporations and the ever more rapid pace of economic life under capitalism. Ramesh's presence—a phone call, e-mail message, or plane trip away—undermines the autonomy provided these workers by their local space.

The Womble team is certainly connected to other global workplaces—including Silicon Valley and St. Louis on this particular afternoon. They also experience the pressure of the global economy through the demands of Ramesh for new features. However, local space is not destroyed by these global connections. The Womble cubicle takes on a culture of its own, manifested in the mimed hostility to Ramesh's suggestions, but also in the information-sharing, problem-solving, and solidarity-building within the team on an everyday basis. In fact, the demands of the global economy for increased flexibility and specialized learning actually make the local context and interactions of the global workplace even more critical. Efficient production and constant innovation require the construction of shared physical spaces where workers can interact and communicate on a face-to-face basis and where shared goals and meanings can be created and maintained.

Global connections bring the pressures of the world economy into the heart of workplaces such as the Womble team cubicle. However, these pressures actually make local space and social context all the more important. The speed-up of time and the extension of social space across physical distance in the global economy do not destroy space but in fact intensify the impact of space in constituting successful global workplaces.

However, this does not herald a return to an era of workplaces dominated by localized social relations. This is because the importance of local social relations to innovation creates a dilemma for the global corporations that rely on this innovation. The local character of their work teams is essential to their efficiency but also poses a problem of regulating such localized relations from a distance. Ramesh may be aware that his proposals are not meeting with happy grins on the other end of the phone, but he is also unable to directly regulate the team's behavior because of his distance from the team and his only partial incorporation into the social space of the team. The typical managerial answer to this dilemma of control in the global workplace is to attempt to control the instrument of speed-up and pressure within the global economy—time itself. The politics of the contemporary workplace is increasingly the politics of time.

The most important instrument used to control time in the global workplace is the project deadline. Although Ramesh cannot control the everyday behavior of the Womble team, the parameters within which the team can operate are set by the demands of the deadline: the team members have a great deal of autonomy in how they work, but the supervisor looking over their shoulder is time itself, with every decision measured against its impact on meeting the deadline. Ramesh's requests for new features are not considered on their technical merits but on the basis of their impact on the team's ability to meet the deadline. Even as the importance of space is intensified in the global workplace, so too is time, in its manifestation as the dominant mode of control in these workplaces. Global workplaces are subject to a process of what I call time-space intensification. . . .

This [reading] argues . . . that as the workplace stretches out across national bor-

ders local spaces such as the Womble team cubicle become all the more crucial to the operation of the global economy. Overcoming the constraints of international time differences allows organization across time and space, but poses new problems of control from a distance—problems which are solved by the intensification of time through work-team deadlines. Global informational workplaces are characterized not by the disappearance of time and space as realities of work life, but by their increasing importance and intensification.

Dilemmas of the Global Workplace

Neither do these workplaces emerge tabula rasa onto the global stage, as a response to the prompting of the global market. In fact, the Womble team is the outcome of state development strategies, changing corporate structures and strategies, and the emergence of new industries organized around knowledge creation. Indeed, the routine phone and e-mail arguments between Ramesh and the Womble team would bring a glow to the heart of many industrial development agency officials in Ireland. The formation of connections to the global economy by attracting foreign high-technology investment has been the cornerstone of Ireland's industrial policy since the late 1950s. The connection to the United States has been particularly crucial—over four hundred United States companies have located in Ireland, and some three-quarters of jobs in electronics and software in Ireland are in foreign-owned companies. Through the 1970s and 1980s, transnational electronics and computer hardware firms located primarily low-level functions in Ireland and developed few links to the local economy.[3] Many of the transnational corporations used Ireland as an "export processing zone" within the European market, taking advantage of low tax and wage rates and Ireland's position within European Union tariff barriers. Irish plants were at best weakly integrated into the core activities of the corporate parents, as the typical Irish operation's activities were routine and relations with the parent hierarchical.

However, the past five to ten years have seen a shift in the nature of the activities and the character of some of the foreign investment in Ireland. Encouraged by the state industrial development agencies, many hardware operations began to grow software development centers as the information technology industry moved toward a focus on software and software became the strategic technology for these corporations. Local managers, usually Irish-born, were able to carve out strategic positions for their operations within the parent companies, although their position always remained precarious. In cases such as USTech, local managers often developed relationships with customers well before discussing these new lines of business with their colleagues at headquarters. In recent years, subcontracting and business partnership relationships between United States and Irish firms have expanded and the two economies have become increasingly closely integrated. Indeed, the apparent shortage of computer skills in Silicon Valley was one of the reasons why the Womble software contract went to the USTech Ireland office. Companies such as USTech Ireland were still limited by their place in the international corporate structure and often still concentrated on testing, support, and consulting software work rather than on the strategic software development tasks. However, many were able to develop small- to medium-sized software development teams, closely integrated with the parent's operations.

USTech is well established in Ireland, having located there over fifteen years ago and becoming one of the early success stories of Irish industrial policy. For many years it was one of Ireland's primary computer hardware production operations, with a reputation for high quality. The hardware manufacturing operations of USTech Ireland were dismantled, with massive layoffs, in the early 1990s, leaving local management scrambling for the operation's survival and turning to a complete reliance on the local pool of software skills. Their links to the global economy have subsequently diversified, with a proliferation of customers, partners, and internal corporate sponsors replacing their previous model of reporting directly to a single office in the United States. The software development contract for Womble reflects this change, as there was little opportunity within the previous corporate structure for such arrangements.

Womble Software itself is a perfect example of the "global web" corporate structure, which Reich argues is becoming the norm. Formed as a spin-off from a large hierarchical corporation, the company is partly owned by the four founders, partly by USTech itself, partly by a major customer, and the rest by a venture capital fund in Silicon Valley. It has no more than fifteen employees of its own. The development team is based in Ireland and is officially contracted to provide software development services to Womble. The screens for the program are conceptualized by Ramesh, but all the development work necessary to turn them into computer graphics is done in a small graphic-design house just outside San Francisco. The helpdesk staff, which users reach if they call with a problem, is staffed by the trained employees of a helpdesk contracting company. The technical writers who write the on-screen help for users are all hired on a contract basis. In place of more rigid, hierarchical organizational structures, we have a shifting web of connections forged into a relatively fleeting alliance.

Mobility and Connections in the Global Labor Market

Womble is not only, however, the prototype of the "global web" organization but also conforms to a new model of computer-industry careers. In this model, the dominant metaphor of IBM's promise of lifetime employment has been replaced by the image of the freewheeling Silicon Valley engineers who expect little from their employers and will jump ship for more money or more challenging work at the drop of a hat. Both of course are stereotypes, but there is more than a grain of truth in the emergence of cross-firm careers as the dominant pattern in software companies in Silicon Valley and in Ireland. These trends are intensified by a shortage of experienced personnel in most countries' software industries.[4] Certain skills are in particularly high demand—including the Unix, C++, database, and Java skills of the employees in the Womble team. The variety of local and global connections of the team reinforces the tendency toward mobility by providing the channels of information about new opportunities and the social contacts for facilitating moves to those emerging areas. Negotiating the commitment of highly mobile employees becomes the critical dilemma facing software firms, a dilemma which is addressed in the following sections of this [reading].

In industries such as software, the typical career pattern now involves a number of moves between organizations, and there has been a clear shift from internal labor markets to job-hopping between firms. When employees stay with the same firm, their tasks and level of responsibility change on a regular basis. Furthermore, professional migration into both the United States and Ireland has been increasing, with transnational intrafirm and interfirm careers expanding. As can be seen from the career histories described above, the high mobility career pattern, with employees feeling little attachment to the employer (or, conversely, the firm to the employee), has become a reality for these particular software developers. Even in a still "semiperipheral" region like Ireland, the careers of such software developers have converged quite significantly with those of their counterparts in the leading high-technology regions such as Silicon Valley or global cities such as New York and London. A survey of 250 software firms in Ireland in 1997 revealed that a quarter of the firms had had employee turnover of 25 percent or more in the previous year.[5]

These trends were evident in the experience of the Womble software team members. Including myself, the team consisted of six people during the time I was there. Séamus, the team leader, had been at USTech for seven years. In that time he had held four completely different positions—working as a computer test engineer, software systems test engineer, information systems support, and software development team leader. The rest of the team had been assembled over the prior six to eighteen months. Conor, six months out of college, still received job postings from his college career-counseling service every two weeks. If he follows the industry pattern he will most likely leave USTech after eighteen months or so, when another software company will be glad to pay him well for his skills and experience.

Jim and Paul were employed on a contract basis. Dan had also been a contractor and took a pay cut of almost 50 percent when he accepted a permanent post in order to get a mortgage from the bank. Paul's history is one of a "software cowboy," using a series of lucrative short-term contracts to see the world without being tied down by business, social, or personal obligations. Jim and Dan have pursued a different path, having at times been employees, contractors, entrepreneurs, or several of these at the same time. The lines between employer, self-employed, and employee begin to blur in such careers.

Transnational experience is a major part of the developers' careers. Dan is originally from Hong Kong and came to Ireland to study, subsequently pursuing a career in software. Almost all the contractors who worked with the team while I was there had emigrated at one point or spent a significant amount of time working on contracts abroad. Indeed, it is the contractors who are most openly dependent on mobility for their career advancement. They are usually brought in for their quite specialized skills and are often given tasks working on relatively self-contained parts of the system being designed. Their need to communicate with other team members may be minimal, although their ability to do so remains a critical part of their effectiveness. Sometimes, contractors stay with a team for a relatively long time. Jim, a contractor, had been with the team for longer than the two permanent staff and had successfully resisted efforts to make him take a permanent position. Indeed, he was the *de facto* deputy team leader. Mobility across organizational, employer/employee, and national boundaries has therefore been central to these workers' careers and is understood by all to be the background to workplace interactions and relationships.

Mobility is also the team members' key bargaining chip with their employers. One lunchtime, Conor, Michael, the group manager, and I ended up sitting together. We had somehow got onto the topic of the difficulty of getting people for the jobs that were available within USTech. Conor went into great detail on the job offers he had received on leaving college and on the ever-improving job market for graduates, until Michael quietly finished his lunch and left. Conor turned to me and asked: "What did you make of that? I wanted him to know there are plenty of other jobs out there. What I didn't say is that I've been getting job offers every two weeks through the college."

Mobility is the dominant career strategy within the software industry as a whole and within the Womble software team. There are also, however, constraints on the mobility system for both the firm and the employee. The firm will sometimes try to get contractors with crucial product knowledge to become permanent employees so that their knowledge is kept within the organization. In the Womble team, Dan had gone permanent because he had to get a mortgage, whereas Jim, already having a mortgage, was able to resist the efforts of the project managers to have him become a permanent employee. Nor are employees completely free to exercise their mobility. Companies are reluctant to pay employees if they threaten to leave, as they are likely to set a series of threats in train which may spiral out of control. However, companies will make exceptions on occasion as long as they can avoid having other employees learn about them. In general, the threat of mobility serves as a latent possibility, which keeps the company's attention focused on getting training for key employees, increasing their pay, and so on, in order to forestall ideas of leaving.

Employees must also be careful not to get a reputation for being unlikely to stay at a company. "If you look at a CV and see that someone has moved every nine months or so, you have to wonder if they'll stay here any longer than that. But if they stay two or three years, then you know they will contribute something" (Séamus). The degree of demand for a developer's particular skills is the critical factor that affects his or her bargaining power through mobility. "When I was in Belfast, you would be on contract if you couldn't get a permanent job. Here, you would be permanent if you couldn't go on contract. It's just a question of how many jobs there are" (Paul). This can even override the threat of lost reputation if the demand is high enough: "They mightn't think you'll stay, but if they need you badly enough they'll hire you anyway!" (Paul). Industry norms have developed around the "proper" forms of mobility—mobility between jobs is not unlimited but requires a strategy that must be carefully managed.

Mobility is therefore taken for granted as an element of the composition of software teams such as the Womble team. Relations with coworkers develop in the context of a constant awareness that the members of the team might be dispersed at short notice. This can happen either by corporate decision (the team beside us was disbanded overnight when USTech in Silicon Valley halted development of the product on which they were working) or through the decision of individuals to leave the team. Mobility, then, is a double-edged sword—the advantage to employees of being able to leave with few repercussions is balanced against the lack of constraints on companies' changing employees' responsibilities and even getting rid of them (within the bounds of the law). Indeed, the Womble team was itself largely disbanded when development work was moved back to the United States and fully disbanded when Womble itself went out of business. These advantages and dangers are all the more significant for contract employees, given their complete lack of formal job security. These highly fluid conditions threaten the ability of software developers to work together in a cohesive way on a common project. The intensification of space in the global workplace provides some of the critical elements of the answer to this organizational dilemma.

Putting Work in Its Place

While software developers may move quite regularly from job to job, they have an intense relationship with each other once in a particular job. In informational and design work, the labor process is usually organized in the form of teams working closely together on specific projects. Some see these as "virtual" teams interacting purely through cybertechnologies—the process of generating cooperation among employees is assumed to be unproblematic.[6] Indeed, Ramesh himself subscribed to the theory of the virtual economy in a "Thank You" e-mail message he sent to the contract graphic-design firm in California:

> Our project team was truly an international virtual-team, with up to 8 hours of time-zone difference among the different team members. We expected you to work at such a hectic pace, yet, we also demanded extreme flexibility from you in all respects. It is very rare that anybody of your caliber would be able to excel on both these fronts.

However, Ramesh had misread his own organization. Members of such teams are usually located in close proximity to one another, as this allows the team to handle the complex interdependencies among them through easy and constant communication and allows them to build a coherent collective identity, which becomes the basis of cooperation within the team.

The sheer volumes of information and the dependence of each member of the team on the design decisions of the others makes the easy interaction of the team members critical. As Jim at USTech worked on the user interface screens he would intermittently call over to Paul two desks away: "What did you call the course number variable, Paul? I can't find it," "Are you working on the database at the moment? It's a bit slow," "Who's doing the security screens?" The questions and answers are discussed on the way to and from breakfast and lunch, although by common consent rarely during the meal itself.

By contrast, information flows to the United States can be patchy and tend to be limited to broad strategic decisions. A developer in Silicon Valley would have great difficulty in developing this product with the team around me in Ireland. Indeed, my own easy ability to ask the developers around me for information fifteen times a day contrasts with the difficulties I have sharing information with Jane in Silicon Valley, a process that sometimes left me idle for mornings or afternoons as I waited to be able to call her in the United States to clear up some minor misunderstandings. Where such transnational "virtual" relationships work, they are constantly supplemented by travel to meet the team or teams in the other country. Ramesh was a regular visitor to the USTech Ireland office. Distance also clearly limits how much employees can learn from their colleagues. The experience of working in close physical proximity with the more experienced and skilled developers teaches others the skills and tricks that turn a computer science graduate into an effective and innovative programmer.

The accountability of team members to one another is also much more easily sustained in face-to-face interactions than in "virtual" communications. Problems can arise even in the most apparently "flat" and nonhierarchical of organizations. I was caught in a bind during the conference call when Ramesh asked me, an untrained technical writer with a long and largely irrelevant training in sociology, "Seán, are you happy with the proposal to put the toolbar in the help box?" While I was being formally asked to participate in a design decision, the social structure of this global organization made me think first not of the implications of my decision for the system itself but of my loyalties to the fuming developers around me. Even the periodical visits of Ramesh to Ireland did not solve the problems of miscommunication and alienation felt by the Irish team. As Michael, the business manager of the group, said, "Having a remote manager has made getting a process of communication in place a lot more difficult." Problems

which would require solution in a face-to-face context can be swept under the carpet or become a figure of fun in a context where communication is by phone and the Internet.

The issues that can be resolved in a daily phone call to the United States are those relating to the strategic technical decisions, which were hotly debated with Ramesh every day by Séamus, the team leader, and even by the other members of the team. E-mail was generally used within the team to pass on relatively routine information to one another—whether that was between the team members or between Séamus, the team leader, and Ramesh. On one occasion, although we sat fewer than ten feet apart, Conor and I exchanged a series of e-mails about problems I had found with the program and the fixes he had made—without ever turning around to speak to one another. Only when it became clear that one of the problems was more complex than it appeared did we discuss the issue face to face. E-mail also appeared to be a valuable tool for allowing the team members to stay in touch with their friends throughout the industry. I was able to combine my membership in the "global ethnography group" with participation in the Womble team, largely unbeknownst to anyone else on the team. Other team members seemed to use e-mail similarly—every now and then someone would read out a joke they had been sent by a friend or tell us about the bonuses being offered at other companies for recruiting a new employee. Overall, while face-to-face interactions were critical to conveying complex information or to building and sustaining trust, computer-supported communication seemed "especially suited to maintaining intermediate strength ties between people who cannot see each other frequently.[7]

USTech is situated in one of the areas best known for information technology in Ireland. In a city that is attractive to the young people who dominate the software industry, USTech also benefits from access to a large pool of local skilled labor and from the connections of the Womble team members to the broader "culture of innovation" within the region. The Womble team members, especially those who have had more mobile career patterns, have many connections to people throughout the local industry and often recount stories of people they know in common, people who could be hired by the team, other developers they met around the city and discussed their work with, and so on. Their high-mobility careers are also sustained through social ties to others in the industry who can provide the team members with information on job opportunities and can provide formal or informal recommendations to employers regarding the team members' competence. It turns out that both the high-mobility careers and the face-to-face interactions which mitigate the corrosive effect of that mobility on workplace cohesion are supported by the emergence of this regional "innovative milieu."

Face-to-face interaction, localized social relations, and electronic networks each structure the global workplace in important but different ways. Clearly face-to-face interaction does not guarantee good communication or cooperative working relationships. However, it makes it a lot easier than trying to achieve these across eight time zones and numerous digital interactions. Ease of communication and mutual accountability at "work" ensure that spaces defined by face-to-face interaction remain a critical component of the global workplace, even as virtual spaces proliferate.

A Globalized Local Culture

These globalized workplaces also take on a distinct culture, which reinforces the cooperation and cohesion produced by the organization of work itself. In many ways even these human paradigms of the global economy are "global locals" bringing distinct "lo-

cal" cultures to the global stage and remaking both global and local social relations in the process. This small open-plan team area may be a globalized space but it is one that has a clearly defined local identity and that interacts with the global economy with caution and at times with difficulty. Some have argued that such tensions between the local and the global are born out of a traditionalist resistance by the local to the cosmopolitanism of the global. However, the Womble team does not resist the global in and of itself but contests how the global should operate, showing disdain for the mismanagement of the global by the remote managers.

This can be seen most clearly in their perceptions of American software developers and managers. As an Irish manager at USTech told me:

> The test group here was the best in the corporation and they were really saving USTech with their customers in the field. So we had all these American managers coming over telling them they were the greatest and how they were the best thing since sliced pan. That's OK the first time, but after a while the people here started saying among themselves "Quit the bullshit—if you think we're so great, give us a raise or at least buy us a few pints."

This disjunction was shown up dramatically after one particular bout of complaining about the United States managers of the team. Séamus, the team leader, summed up the relationship to the United States parent ironically:

> *Séamus:* It's not as if there's "us and them" or anything. . . . It's not even that, it's just "them" really!
>
> *Jim (wearily):*   Yep, they're the enemy!

Nonetheless, the Irish managers and developers tended to work very successfully with their American counterparts, accepting some aspects of United States corporate culture while maintaining a clear rejection of many aspects of the Americanized environment in which they find themselves.

The developers themselves regard their team culture as homogenous, despite the fact that Dan is from Hong Kong:

Jim: What would we do if a black guy joined the group? Who would we pick on?

Conor: Or a woman?

Jim: Séamus, you can't ever hire a black woman!

Seán: There's always Americans to pick on. . . .

Séamus: Yeah, but they're too easy. There's no challenge in that. [Laughter.]

The mention of a "black guy" was largely rhetorical, as I never heard any comment within the team directed against "black guys." The team culture was clearly masculine, and there is no doubt that this culture could be self-perpetuating. "American" is also somewhat ambiguous in this context, as Ramesh, the "American" with whom the Womble team members have the most interaction, is originally from India. On a different occasion, three members of a different team discussed their Indian boss in the United States with Conor and me:

Pat: We have one too—Ranjit.

Conor: Ranjit—that sounds like something out of Aladdin.

Peter: [Says something imitating Ramesh's accent.] That's racist, that is. [Criticizing himself, very serious about it.]

Bob: Yeah, that's an "ism," that is. That's racism.

Pat: They're [Indian software developers] probably over there saying "those bloody Micks."

Aidan: Yeah, saying "drinking pints of Guinness over their computers."

"Difference" on a global scale is an everyday part of these software developers' milieu, although it is negotiated within a strong, homogenous local culture. This was evident in the team's relationship to Dan (from Hong Kong). In fact, while the culture of the team was strongly male and Irish, members of the team were highly aware of this global culture, and most would criticize racism and sexism that they saw elsewhere. On one occasion, two other team members and I were both shocked and amused on hearing Dan racially slander a visiting technical trainer who was Pakistani. "The other" was accepted as an everyday part of life for Irish software developers and helped to define the team identity. When Dan revealed his own criticisms of another Asian ethnic group, this disrupted our assumption of a single "other" and was both surprising and funny to Dan's team members. It revealed that Dan's behavior and attitudes regarding race were subject to different rules than those of the Irish-born team members.

While the team members worked relatively easily with people of a variety of national, ethnic, and racial backgrounds, they consciously maintained a strong local team culture. Operating in the global workplace required them to work with and around "difference" but, by the same token, the less hierarchical forms of economic domination in the global workplace allowed them to maintain their local culture within these global connections. There is also a strong pragmatic element in this ability of people from different backgrounds to work together in the global workplace. One of the Womble Software managers took us out for a meal when she was visiting from the United States. Halfway through the evening I commented to Pat, a contractor, "She seems OK, decent enough," to which Pat replied, "Well, when you come to discover the jungle you have to play with the natives."

Not only are the Womble developers "global locals," but they also think of themselves as such. Their highly mobile careers and relatively fleeting association with one another in the workplace demand an intense experience of a shared space and culture in order for them to create a cohesive work team. The team members use elements of a shared culture from outside the team to create this solidarity but are also able to accommodate aspects such as Dan's non-Irish racial and ethnic background into the team through the overriding emphasis on work and technical competence. While these local team cultures can be exclusionary of women and other ethnic groups, as indicated in the quotes above, they are also flexible enough to accommodate the presence of such others within the dominant team culture when necessary. Place, mobility, and the global workplace are not necessarily in tension with one another, as they might appear to be on first glance, but are in fact symbiotic, underpinning one another's importance and sustainability.

In short, globalization does not mean the end of place. Instead, it creates places which are increasingly "between" other places and have ever-deepening connections to other places. The high-mobility career pattern that is typical of the software industry poses a threat to the work team cooperation, commitment, and cohesion necessary for innovation. What I have called the intensification of space through the dense social networks of the team and the region provides a solution of sorts to this dilemma. However, local networks also serve to reproduce mobility, as developers use their connections to engineer their next career moves. Mobility and place sustain one another but also remain in tension within the structure of the global workplace. . . .

Time-Space Intensification

The emergence of a global information economy has transformed the character of the workplace for many employees, including those within informational industries such as software. Many authors argue that the globalization of work destroys place and locality, creating placeless "virtual" work. Against this view, this [reading] has argued for a concept of globalization that emphasizes the organization of the global economy through particular places and regions and the critical importance of patterns of mobility of people, information, and resources within and between these regions. These changes in the territorial organization of capitalism interact with an organizational restructuring characterized by the decentralization of work and firms. While some authors argue that these organizational changes will bring relative equality and a rough and ready economic democracy, this [reading] has shown that new forms of power operate within these new organizational forms. Ethnography reveals that we cannot simply deduce concrete social practices and power relations from a particular organizational and territorial work structure. Instead, we find that a new ground is emerging upon which the struggles of the global informational economy will be waged—a new set of social identities, resources, interests, and issues is created, which will be the basis of the politics of the global workplace in the years to come.

This new "contested terrain" of the global workplace is a system of time-space intensification where workers experience not the "end of time and space" but their ascent to a new level of intensity. Space is intensified by the necessity of local cooperation and the increased use of project teams in the face of the challenges posed by the global economy. Time becomes an ever more pressing reality in the deadline-driven workplace. This time-space intensification shapes the structure of both work and careers in the global workplace. Careers are built using mobility between firms to bargain for improved wages and access to technical learning, and these mobile careers only increase the importance of close interactions and strong local cooperation while working on any particular project. Out of these underlying structures emerges a set of dynamics, organized around the project deadline, which give the global workplace its dynamism but also generate certain costs and dilemmas for the participants. Conflicts over these dilemmas of time-space intensification constitute the new politics of the globalization of knowledge work.

What will be the central controversies on this new contested terrain? The two phases of time-space intensification create characteristic advantages and dilemmas for knowledge workers such as the software developers in this [reading], for firms such as USTech and Womble Software, and for workers' families, software users, and the other (largely invisible) social actors beyond the industry with an interest in its social organization. While these dynamics and dilemmas have been recognized for some time in the information industries, globalization intensifies them.

Certain characteristic organizational problems are likely to emerge: these are the internal organizational dilemmas of time-space intensification. In the pre-release phase, the introversion of the team, the intensification of time, and the pressures imposed by the deadline create the conditions that lead to employee burnout—manifested in the case I have described in the exhaustion

of the team members up to and after the deadline and also in the decision made by Ramesh (some five months after I left the team) to resign due to overwork. This creates problems for the organization, as the team's introversion cuts it off from the rest of the organization and raises the danger of organizational involution and the distancing of teams from one another, even teams working on related technical or business issues. For the Womble team this can be seen in the antagonistic attitude to the graphics team in California, a set of relationships which, if more cooperative, could have been very valuable in improving the product under development.

In the post-deadline phase, the solidarity fragments and team members begin to look elsewhere for future opportunities. The extroverted phase is when employees can turn to the labor market to gain the rewards of their new-found expertise and the organization can assemble a new group of employees with new sets of skills and resources into a project team for the next phase of the development effort. However, there is also a significant cost associated with the high levels of employee turnover within the industry. The accumulated knowledge derived from the development of the Womble software product, which has built up within the team, is now dissipated throughout the industry. This constitutes a significant loss of firm-specific knowledge from Womble's point of view and also a loss of the effort put into developing effective working relationships within the team. There are therefore clear organizational costs attached to failure to address these internal dilemmas.

Time-space intensification also causes certain external social dilemmas. The pressure and introverted character of the pre-deadline phase, and the resulting insulation of workers and the organization of their work from any kind of broader social accountability make it difficult to reconcile the team structure and team culture with broader social concerns. This is manifested in at least two areas. The most directly obvious is the work-family nexus, where work demands come to dominate family life, leaving very little space for workers to negotiate alternative work and family time arrangements. Secondly, as technology increasingly penetrates our everyday social practices, the involvement of users in decisions regarding these technologies becomes more and more crucial. But the isolation and insulation of the developers during their most creative and innovative phase militates strongly against any meaningful interaction with prospective users of the product from outside the team. To the extent that we might fear the arrival of the Weberian "iron cage" in the form of a society dominated by large, centralized organizations, there is some promise in the decentralized organizational forms compatible with this high-mobility system. However, although organizations no longer have the same rigid bureaucratic structures insulating them from social accountability, the intensification of time ultimately results in a similar outcome.

The post-deadline phase of high mobility creates a very high degree of volatility and insecurity in the labor market so that employees lack strong employment guarantees. This is not currently a major issue in the Irish industry, given the generally very high demand for software skills. Even in the current tight labor market, "employment security" gives way to "employability security." However, when career gains are based on the threat of mobility, this seems inevitably to lead to increased labor market inequality, as the threat to leave is only effective when replacing the employee is difficult. As it is inherently based on scarcity, the limits of mobility as a universal career strategy are clear.

This seems likely to be a contributing factor to the spiraling wage inequality in Ireland over the past ten years.

These internal and external dilemmas of time-space intensification are all the more crucial given that the economic success of the Republic of Ireland over the past ten years has been built upon the success of industries such as software. The politics of the conference call became the new politics of the global workplace—distant yet closely integrated into operations in the core, less hierarchical but nonetheless subject to new forms of power relations. As these global workplaces spread through economies such as Ireland's, the dilemmas of time-space intensification will become central economic and social issues for societies incorporated into new, deeper processes of globalization. The value of global ethnography is its ability to reveal these dilemmas as aspects of a "contested terrain" of globalization, rather than as inevitable outcomes of an apolitical process.

NOTES

1. Robert Reich, *The Work of Nations.*
2. Anthony Giddens, *The Consequences of Modernity.* Giddens argues that globalization occurs in a process of *time-space distanciation,* as space and time are "distanciated" from (lifted out of) their local contexts. There are two main mechanisms through which this happens: the use of *symbolic tokens* (universal media of exchange/ interaction such as money) and of *expert systems* (shared bodies of technical knowledge that can be applied in a wide variety of contexts).
3. Eoin O'Malley, *Industry and Economic Development.*
4. Office of Technology Policy, *America's New Deficit.*
5. Seán Ó Riain, "Remaking the Developmental State."
6. Reich, *The Work of Nations.*
7. Barry Wellman et al., "Computer Networks as Social Networks," p. 231.

REFERENCES

Giddens, Anthony. 1990. *The Consequences of Modernity*. Stanford, CA: Stanford University Press.

Office of Technology Policy. 1997. *America's New Deficit: The Shortage of Information Technology Workers*. Washington, DC: U.S. Department of Commerce, Technology Administration. On the World Wide Web at www.ta.doc.gov/reports/itsw/itsw.pdf.

O'Malley, Eoin. 1989. *Industry and Economic Development*. Dublin: Gill and Macmillan.

Ó Riain, Seán. 1999. "Remaking the Developmental State: The Irish Software Industry in the Global Economy." Ph.D. dissertation, University of California, Berkeley.

Reich, Robert B. 1991. *The Work of Nations*. New York: Vintage.

Wellman, Barry, Janet Salaff, Dimitrina Dimitrova, Laura Garton, Milena Gulia, and Caroline Haythornthwaite. 1996. "Computer Networks as Social Networks." *Annual Review of Sociology* 22:213–38.

17

The Global Economy and the Privileged Class

Robert Perrucci and Earl Wysong

Unbridled capitalism is an awesome force that creates new factories, wealth, and opportunities that go first to society's risk takers and holders of capital. But unbridled capitalism is also an awesome destructive force. It makes men and women obsolete as rapidly as it does the products they produce and the plants that produce them.

—Patrick Buchanan, *The Great Betrayal*, 1998

On December 1, 1982, an RCA television cabinet-making factory in Monticello, Indiana, closed its doors and shut down production. Monticello, a town of five thousand people in White County (pop-ulation twenty-three thousand), had been the home of RCA since 1946. The closing displaced 850 workers who were members of Local 3154 of the United Brotherhood of Carpenters and Joiners. Officials at RCA cited high manufacturing costs and foreign competition as key factors leading to the closing.

Reactions of displaced workers from RCA were varied, with most expressing either a general sense of despair or a feeling of confidence that they would survive. One worker was hopeful, stating: "Losing one's job is a serious jolt to your attitude of security, preservation, and well-being. However, I feel strongly that we must look forward to hope and faith in our country and its people. Deep inside I want to believe that tough times won't last, but tough people do. This will mean a lot of sacrifice, determination, and change in those people affected by losing one's job." Less hopeful views are revealed in the following remarks:

> We are down to rock bottom and will probably have to sell the house to live or exist until I find a job here or somewhere else. I have been everywhere looking in Cass, White, and Carroll counties. We have had no help except when the electric company was going to shut off the utilities in March and the Trustee [County Welfare] paid that $141. My sister-in-law helps us sometimes with money she's saved back or with food she canned last summer. The factories have the young. I've been to all the factories. (Authors' personal interviews with RCA workers.)

Whether the personal response to the closing was faith, fear, or anger, the common objective experience of the displaced workers was that they had been "dumped" from the "middle class." These displaced factory workers viewed themselves as middle class because of their wages and their lifestyles (home ownership, cars, vacations). Most had worked at RCA for two decades or more. They had good wages, health care benefits, and a pension program. They owned their homes (with mortgages), cars, recreational vehicles, boats, and all the household appliances of the middle class. All the trappings of the American Dream were threatened, and their stable jobs and secure incomes were gone. In the space of a few months these workers and their families would join the growing new working class—the 80 percent of Americans without stable resources for living.

The severity of this jolt to their sense of well-being and their "downward slide" are also revealed in the bleak picture displaced workers have of their future and the future of their children: "I'm afraid it will be years before I get up the courage to buy a car, appliance, or anything on a long-term note, regardless of how good the pay is in a new job"; "I have a National Honor Society daughter with one more year of high school. If she can't get aid there's no way she can go to college." (Authors' personal interviews with RCA workers.)

The experiences of the 850 RCA workers from Monticello, Indiana, were part of a national wave of plant closings that swept across the land a decade ago. Between the late 1970s and mid-1980s more than 11 million workers lost jobs because of plant shutdowns, relocation of facilities to other countries, or layoffs.[1] When these displaced workers found new jobs, it was often in the expanding service sector, where wages were significantly lower than what they had earned and jobs were often part-time and lacked health insurance and other benefits.

During this period, from the mid-1970s to the mid-1980s, the American class structure was being reshaped from the layer-cake "middle-class" society into the double-diamond society. . . . The first step in this reshaping was an attack on higher-wage unionized workers, eliminating their jobs in the auto industries, steel mills, rubber plants, and textile mills. The reshaping continued through the late 1980s to mid-1990s, when the strategy changed from plant closings and relocations to "restructuring and downsizing," often directed at eliminating white-collar jobs.

The rush to downsize in some of America's largest and most prestigious corporations became so widespread in the 1990s that a new occupation was needed to handle the casualties. The "outplacement professional" was created to put the best corporate face on a decision to downsize, that is, to terminate large numbers of employees—as many as ten thousand. The job of these new public relations types is to get the general public to accept downsizing as the normal way of life for corporations who have to survive in the competitive global economy. Their job is also to assist the downsized middle managers to manage their anger and to get on with their lives.

The *Human Resources Development Handbook* of the American Management Association provides the operating philosophy for the outplacement professional: "Unnecessary personnel must be separated from the company if the organization is to continue as a viable business entity. To do otherwise in today's globally competitive world would be totally unjustified and might well be a threat to the company's future survival."[2]

The privileged 20 percent of the population is hard at work telling the other 80 percent about the harsh realities of the changing global economy. "Lifetime employment" is out. The goal is "lifetime employability," which workers try to attain by accumulating skills and being dedicated and committed employees. Even Japan's highly touted commitment to lifetime employment (in some firms) is apparently unraveling, as reported in a prominent feature article in the *New York Times*.[3] It should be no surprise that an elite media organization like the *Times,* whose upper-level employees belong to the privileged class, should join in disseminating the myth of the global economy as the "hidden hand" behind the downsizing of America. The casualties of plant closings and downsizings are encouraged to see their plight as part of the "natural laws" of economics.

This enormous transformation of the U.S. economy over a twenty-year period has been described by political leaders and media as the inevitable and therefore normal workings of the emerging global economy. Some, like former president Reagan, even applauded the changes as a historic opportunity to revitalize the economy. In a 1985 report to Congress, he stated, "The progression of an economy such as America's from the agricultural to manufacturing to services is a natural change. The move from an industrial society toward a postindustrial ser-

vice economy has been one of the greatest changes to affect the developed world since the Industrial Revolution."[4]

A contrasting view posits that the transformation of the U.S. economy is not the result of natural economic laws or the "hidden hand" of global economic changes but is, rather, the result of calculated actions by multinational corporations to expand their profits and power. When corporations decide to close plants and move them overseas where they can find cheap labor and fewer government regulations, they do so to enhance profits and not simply as a response to the demands of global competition. In many cases, the U.S. multinationals themselves are the global competition that puts pressure on other U.S. workers to work harder, faster, and for lower wages and fewer benefits.

The Global Economy and Class Structure

Discussion about the new global economy generally focuses on three things. First is the appearance of many new producers of quality goods in parts of the world that are normally viewed as less developed. Advances in computer-based production systems have allowed many countries in Southeast Asia and Latin America to produce goods that compete with those of more advanced industrial economies in Western Europe and North America. Second is the development of telecommunication systems that permit rapid economic transactions around the globe and the coordination of economic activities in locations separated by thousands of miles. The combination of advances in computer-based production and telecommunications makes it possible for large firms, especially multinationals, to decentralize their production and locate facilities around the globe. Third is the existence of an international division of labor that makes it possible for corporations to employ engineers, technicians, or production workers from anywhere in the world. This gives corporations great flexibility when negotiating with their domestic workforce over wages and benefits.

These three conditions are often used as evidence of a "new global economy" *out there* constraining the actions of all corporations to be competitive if they hope to survive. One concrete indicator of this global economy *out there* is the rising level of international trade between the United States and other nations. In the 1960s, the United States was the dominant exporter of goods and services, and the imports of foreign products played a small part in the U.S. economy. Throughout the 1970s foreign imports claimed an increasing share, and by 1981 the United States "was importing almost 26 percent of its cars, 25 percent of its steel, 60 percent of its televisions, tape recorders, radios, and phonographs, 43 percent of its calculators, 27 percent of its metal-forming machine tools, 35 percent of its textile machinery, and 53 percent of its numerically controlled machine tools."[5] Imports from developing nations went from $3.6 billion in 1970 to $30 billion in 1980.

Throughout the 1980s, the United States became a debtor nation in terms of the balance between what we exported to the rest of the world and what we import. By 1997, the trade deficit indicated that the import of goods and services exceeded exports by $113.7 billion. This is the largest deficit since the previous high in 1987 of $153.4 billion. But what do these trade figures tell us? On the surface, they appear to be a function of the operation of the global economy, because the figures indicate that we have a $55.7 billion deficit with Japan, $49.7 billion with China, and $14.5 billion with Mexico.[6] It appears that Japanese, Chinese, and Mexican companies are doing a better job of producing goods than the United States and thus we import products rather than producing

them ourselves. But is this the correct conclusion? The answer lies in how you count imports and exports.

Trade deficit figures are based on balance-of-payment statistics, which tally the dollar value of U.S. exports to other countries and the dollar value of foreign exports to the United States; if the dollar value of Chinese exports to the United States exceeds the dollar value of U.S. exports to China, the United States has a trade deficit with China. This would appear to mean that Chinese companies are producing the goods being exported to the United States. But that is not necessarily the case. According to the procedures followed in calculating trade deficits, "the U.S. balance of payments statistics are intended to capture the total amount of transactions between U.S. *residents* and *residents* of the rest of the world."[7] If "resident" simply identifies the geographical location of the source of an import, then some unknown portion of the U.S. $49.7 billion deficit with China could be from U.S.-owned firms that are producing goods in China and exporting them to the United States. Those U.S. firms are residents of China, and their exports are counted as Chinese exports to the United States. Thus, the global economy that is *out there* forcing U.S. firms to keep wages low so we can be more competitive might actually be made up of U.S. firms that have located production plants in countries other than in the United States. Such actions may be of great benefit to the U.S. multinational firms that produce goods around the world and export them to the U.S. market. Such actions may also benefit U.S. consumers, who pay less for goods produced in low-wage areas. But what about the U.S. worker in a manufacturing plant whose wages have not increased in twenty years because of the need to compete with "foreign companies"? What about the worker who may never get a job in manufacturing because U.S. firms have been opening plants in other countries rather than in the United States? As the comic strip character Pogo put it: "We have met the enemy and it is us."

American multinational corporations' foreign investments have changed the emphasis in the economy from manufacturing to service. This shift has changed the occupational structure by eliminating high-wage manufacturing jobs and creating a two-tiered system of service jobs. There have been big winners and big losers in this social and economic transformation. The losers have been the three out of four Americans who work for wages—wages that have been declining since 1973; these American workers constitute the new working class. The big winners have been the privileged classes, for whom jobs and incomes have expanded at the same time that everyone else was in decline. Corporate executives, managers, scientists, engineers, doctors, corporate lawyers, accountants, computer programmers, financial consultants, health care professionals, and media professionals have all registered substantial gains in income and wealth in the last twenty years. And the changes that have produced the "big losers" and "big winners" have been facilitated by the legislative actions of the federal government and elected officials of both political parties, whose incomes, pensions, health care, and associated "perks" have also grown handsomely in the last two decades.

This [reading] demonstrates that the privileged classes have benefited at the expense of the working classes. The profits of corporations and stockholders have expanded because fewer workers produce more goods and services for lower wages. The profits of corporations are distributed to executives, managers, and professionals in higher salaries and benefits because they are able either to extract more work from workers while paying them less or to justify inequality, provide distracting entertainment

for the less fortunate, or control them, if necessary. The privileged class is able to maintain its position of advantage because its members control the jobs and incomes of other Americans. They also control the mass media and education, which are the instruments of ideological domination. If all of this is not enough, they also control the means of violence (military, national guard, police, and the investigative and security apparatus) that are used to deal with large-scale dissent.

Creating the Global Economy: The Path to Corporate Profits

When World War II ended in 1945, all but one of the industrial nations involved had experienced widespread destruction of their industrial system and the infrastructure that is necessary for a healthy economy to provide sufficient food, shelter, and clothing for its people. Although all nations that participated in the war suffered terrible human losses, the United States alone emerged with its economic system stronger than it was at the start of the war.

For nearly thirty years following World War II, the United States dominated the world economy through its control of three-fourths of the world's invested capital and two-thirds of its industrial capacity. At the close of the war, there was concern in the United States that the high levels of production, profits, and employment stimulated by war mobilization could not be sustained. The specter of a return to the stagnation and unemployment experienced only a decade earlier during the Great Depression led to the search for a new economic and political system that would maintain the economic, military, and political dominance of the United States.

The postwar geopolitical-economic policy of the United States was designed to provide extensive foreign assistance to stimulate the recovery of Western Europe. This policy would stimulate U.S. investment in Europe and provide the capital for countries to buy U.S. agricultural and industrial products. The policy was also designed to "fight" the creation of socialist governments and socialist policies in Western Europe, governments that might not be sympathetic to U.S. capital, trade, and influence. The foreign assistance policy known as the Marshall Plan was instituted to provide $22 billion in aid over a four-year period and to bring together European nations into a global economic system dominated by the United States.[8]

This system was the basis for U.S. growth and prosperity during the 1950s, the 1960s, and the early 1970s. By the mid-1970s, steady improvements in the war-torn economies of Western Europe and Asia had produced important shifts in the balance of economic power among industrialized nations. The U.S. gross national product was now less than twice that of the Soviet Union (in 1950 it was more than three times), less than four times that of Germany (down from nine times in 1950), and less than three times that of Japan (twelve times in 1950). With many nations joining the United States in the production of the world's goods, the U.S. rate of growth slowed. As England, France, Germany, and Japan produced goods for domestic consumption, there was less need to import agricultural and industrial products from the United States.

The profits of U.S. corporations from the domestic economy were in a steady decline through the late 1960s and into the 1970s. In the early 1960s the annual rate of return on investment was 15.5 percent. In the late 1960s it was 12.7 percent. In the early 1970s it was 10 percent, and after 1975 it slipped below 10 percent, where it remained.

The privileged classes in the United States were concerned about declining prof-

its. This affected their accumulation of wealth from stocks, bonds, dividends, and other investments. It affected corporate, managerial, and professional salaries indirectly, through the high rate of inflation that eroded the purchasing power of consumption capital (i.e., salaries) and the real value of investment capital (i.e., value of stocks, bonds, etc.). The usual list of suspects was rounded up to account for the U.S. decline. The leading "explanation" was that U.S. products could not compete in the global economy because of the power of organized labor. This power was reflected in the high labor costs that made products less competitive and in cost-of-living adjustments that increased wages at the rate of inflation (which was sometimes at double digits). Union control of work rules also made it difficult for management to adopt new innovations to increase productivity and reduce dependence on labor.

Next on the list was the American worker, who was blamed for a decline in work ethic, resulting in products of lower quality and higher cost. Our workers were seen as too content and secure and as unwilling to compete with the ambitious workers of the rapidly developing economies. The third suspect was the wide array of new regulations on business that had been adopted by the federal government to protect workers and the environment. Corporate executives complained about the increased cost of doing business that came from meeting the workplace standards of the Occupational Safety and Health Administration (OSHA) or the air and water pollution standards of the Environmental Protection Agency (EPA).

These explanations for declining profits, blaming workers and government regulations for making American products less competitive in the global economy, provided the basis for an attack on unions and on workers' wages and helped to justify the plant closings and capital flight to low-wage areas. They also served to put the government on the defensive for its failure to be sensitive to the "excessive" costs that federal regulations impose on business.

What was rarely discussed on the business pages of the *New York Times* or the *Wall Street Journal* was the failure of corporate management in major U.S. firms to respond to the increasing competition to the once U.S.-dominated production of autos, steel, textiles, and electronics. In the early 1960s, imports of foreign products played a small part in the American economy, but by 1980 things had changed. In the early 1960s, imports accounted for less than 10 percent of the U.S. market, but by 1980 more than 70 percent of all the goods produced in the United States were actively competing with foreign-made goods.[9]

American corporations failed to follow the well-established management approach to the loss of market share, competitive advantage, and profits. Instead of pursuing long-term solutions, like investing in more efficient technology, new plants, research and development, and new markets, corporate executives chose to follow short-term strategies that would make the bottom line of profits the primary goal. The way was open for increased foreign investment, mergers, and downsizing.

When Your Dog Bites You

With industrial jobs shrinking in the United States, and so much of what we buy, from clothing to electronics to automobiles, now made abroad, a common perception is that "globalized" production is a primary cause of falling living standards for American workers.
    —Richard B. DuBoff, *Dollars and Sense*,
        September–October 1997

While corporate profits from the domestic U.S. economy were declining steadily from the mid-1970s, investment by U.S. corporations abroad showed continued growth. The share of corporate profits from direct foreign investment increased through the 1970s, as did the amount of U.S. direct investment abroad. In 1970, direct investment by U.S. firms abroad was $75 billion, and it rose to $167 billion in 1978. In the 1980–85 period it remained below $400 billion but thereafter increased gradually each year, reaching $716 billion in 1994. The one hundred largest U.S. multinational corporations reported foreign revenue in 1994 that ranged from 30 to 70 percent of their total revenue: IBM had 62 percent of total revenue from foreign sources, Eastman Kodak 52 percent, Colgate-Palmolive 68 percent, and Johnson and Johnson, Coca Cola, Pepsi, and Procter and Gamble each 50 percent.[10]

American multinational corporations sought to maintain their profit margins by increasing investments in affiliates abroad. This strategy may have kept stockholders happy and maintained the price of corporate stocks on Wall Street, but it would result in deindustrialization—the use of corporate capital for foreign investment, mergers, and acquisitions rather than for investment in domestic operations.[11] Instead of investing in the U.S. auto, steel, and textile industries, companies were closing plants at an unprecedented rate and using the capital to open production facilities in other countries. By 1994, U.S. companies employed 5.4 million people abroad, more than 4 million of whom worked in manufacturing.[12] Thus, millions of U.S. manufacturing workers who were displaced in the 1980s by plant closings saw their jobs shifted to foreign production facilities. Although most criticism of U.S. investment abroad is reserved for low-wage countries like Mexico and Thailand, the biggest share of manufacturing investment abroad is in Germany and Japan—hardly low-wage countries. The United States has large trade deficits with Japan and Western Europe, where the hourly wages in manufacturing are 15–25 percent higher than in the United States.[13] This fact challenges the argument made by multinational corporations that if they did not shift production abroad, they would probably lose the sale of that product.

The movement of U.S. production facilities to foreign countries in the 1980s was not simply the result of a search for another home where they could once again be productive and competitive. It appeared as if RCA closed its plant in Monticello, Indiana, because its high-wage workers made it impossible to compete with televisions being produced in Southeast Asia. Saddened by having to leave its home of thirty-five years, RCA would now search for another home where, it was hoped, it could stay at least another thirty-five years, if not longer. Not likely: plants did not close in the 1980s to find other homes; the closures were the first step in the creation of the homeless and stateless multinational corporation—an entity without ties to place, or allegiances to people, communities, or nations.

Thus, the rash of plant closings in the 1970s and 1980s began as apparent responses to economic crises of declining profits and increased global competition. As such, they appeared to be rational management decisions to protect stockholder investments and the future of individual firms. Although things may have started in this way, it soon became apparent that what was being created was the *spatially decentered firm:* a company that could produce a product with components manufactured in a half-dozen different plants around the globe and then assembled at a single location for distribution and sale. This global production system was made possible by significant advances in computer-assisted design and manufacturing that made it unnecessary to produce a product at a single location. It was also made possible by advances in telecommunications that enabled management at corporate headquarters to coordinate re-

search, development, design, manufacturing, and sales decisions at various sites scattered around the world.

The homeless and stateless multinational firm is able to move its product as quickly as it can spot a competitive advantage associated with low wages, cheaper raw materials, advantageous monetary exchange rates, more sympathetic governments, or proximity to markets. This encourages foreign investment because it expands the options of corporations in their choice of where to locate, and it makes them less vulnerable to pressure from workers regarding wages and benefits.

The advantages of the multinational firm and foreign investments are also a product of the U.S. tax code. In addition to providing the largest firms with numerous ways to delay, defer, and avoid taxes, corporate profits made on overseas investments are taxed at a much lower rate than profits from domestic operations. Thus, as foreign investments by U.S. firms increased over the last two decades, the share of total taxes paid by corporations declined. In the 1960s, corporations in the United States paid about 25 percent of all federal income taxes, and in 1991 it was down to 9.2 percent. A 1993 study by the General Accounting Office reported that more than 40 percent of corporations with assets of more than $250 million either paid no income tax or paid less than $100,000.[14]

Creating the New Working Class

When the large multinational firm closes its U.S. facilities and invests in other firms abroad or opens new facilities abroad, the major losers are the production workers who have been displaced and the communities with lower tax revenues and increased costs stemming from expanded efforts to attract new businesses. But this does not mean that the firms are losers, for they are growing and expanding operations elsewhere. This growth creates the need for new employees in finance, management, computer operations, information systems, and clerical work. The total picture is one of shrinking production plants and expanding corporate headquarters; shrinking blue-collar employee rolls and two-tiered expansion of high-wage professional-managerial and low-wage clerical positions.

Having been extraordinarily successful in closing U.S. plants, shifting investment and production abroad, and cutting both labor and labor costs (both the number of production workers and their wage-benefit packages), major corporations now turned their attention to saving money by cutting white-collar employees. In the 1990s, there were no longer headlines about "plant closings," "capital flight," or "deindustrialization." The new strategy was "downsizing," "rightsizing," "reengineering," or how to get the same amount of work done with fewer middle managers and clerical workers.

When Sears, Roebuck and Company announced that it could cut 50,000 jobs in the 1990s (while still employing 300,000 people) its stock climbed 4 percent on the New York Stock Exchange. The day Xerox announced a planned cut of 10,000 employees, its stock climbed 7 percent. Eliminating jobs was suddenly linked with cutting corporate waste and increasing profits. Hardly a month could pass without an announcement by a major corporation of its downsizing plan. Tenneco Incorporated would cut 11,000 of its 29,000 employees. Delta Airlines would eliminate 18,800 jobs, Eastman Kodak would keep pace by eliminating 16,800 employees, and AT&T announced 40,000 downsized jobs, bringing its total of job cuts since 1986 to 125,000. Not to be outdone, IBM cut 180,000 jobs between 1987 and 1994.

Even the upscale, more prestigious banking industry joined in the rush to become "lean and mean." A total of ten bank mergers announced in 1995 would result in 32,400 jobs lost because of the new "efficiencies" that come with mergers. Even banks that were already successful in introducing "efficiencies" were not immune to continued pressure for more. Between 1985 and 1995, Chase Manhattan's assets grew by 38 percent (from $87.7 billion to $121.2 billion), and its workforce was reduced 28 percent, from 44,450 to 33,500 employees. Yet when Chase was "swallowed" by Chemical Banking Corporation in a merger, both banks announced further reductions, totaling 12,000 people.

Job loss in the 1990s appeared to hit hardest at those who were better educated (some college or more) and better paid ($40,000, or more). Job loss aimed at production workers in the 1980s was "explained" by the pressures of global competition and the opportunities to produce in areas with lower-wage workers. The "explanation" for the 1990s downsizing was either new technology or redesign of the organization. Some middle managers and supervisors were replaced by new computer systems that provide surveillance of clerical workers and data entry jobs. These same computer systems also eliminate the need for many middle managers responsible for collecting, processing, and analyzing data used by upper-level decision makers.

Redesign of organizations was achieved by eliminating middle levels within an organization and shifting work both upward and downward. The downward shift of work is often accompanied by new corporate plans to "empower" lower-level workers with new forms of participation and opportunities for career development. All of this redesign reduced administrative costs and increased the work load for continuing employees.

Investors, who may have been tentative about the potential of profiting from the deindustrialization of the 1980s because it eroded the country's role as a manufacturing power, were apparently delighted by downsizing. During the 1990s the stock market skyrocketed from below three thousand points on the Dow Jones Industrial Average to eighty-six hundred in March 1998—an almost 200 percent increase. The big institutional investors apparently anticipated that increasing profits would follow the broadly based actions of cutting the workforce.

Downsizing is often viewed by corporations as a rational response to the demands of competition and thereby a way to better serve their investors and ultimately their own employees. Alan Downs, in his book *Corporate Executions,* challenges four prevailing myths that justify the publicly announced layoffs of millions of workers.[15] First, downsizing firms do not necessarily wind up with a smaller workforce. Often, downsizing is followed by the hiring of new workers. Second, Downs questions the belief that downsized workers are often the least productive because their expertise is obsolete: according to his findings, increased productivity does not necessarily follow downsizing. Third, jobs lost to downsizing are not replaced with higher-skill, better-paying jobs. Fourth, the claim that companies become more profitable after downsizing, and that workers thereby benefit, is only half-true: many companies that downsize do report higher corporate profits and, as discussed earlier, often achieve higher valuations of their corporate stock. But there is no evidence that these profits are being passed along to employees in the form of higher wages and benefits.

After challenging these four myths, Downs concludes that the "ugly truth" of downsizing is that it is an expression of corporate self-interest to lower wages and increase profits. This view is shared by David Gordon, who documents the growth of executive, administrative, and managerial positions and compensation during the period when "downsizing" was at its highest.[16] Gordon describes bureaucratic "bloat" as part of a corporate strategy to reduce the wages of production workers and increase and intensify the level of managerial supervision. Slow wage growth for production workers and top-heavy corporate bureaucracies reinforce each other, and the combination produces a massive shift of money out of wages and into executive compensation and profits. This "wage squeeze" occurred not only in manufacturing (because of global competition) but also in mining, construction, transportation, and retail trade.[17] Although it is to be expected that foreign competition will have an impact on wages in manufacturing, it should not affect the nontrade sector to the same extent. Thus, the "wage squeeze" since the mid-1970s that increased income and wealth inequality in the United States is probably the result of a general assault on workers' wages and benefits rather than a response to global competition.

Thus, the result of more than a decade of plant closings and shifting investment abroad, and less than a decade of downsizing America's largest corporations, has been the creation of a protected privileged class and a divided working class. The three segments of the working class are core workers, temporary workers, and contingent workers.

Core Workers

These employees possess the skills, knowledge, or experience that are essential to the operation of the firm. Their income levels place them in the "comfort class." . . . They are essential for the firm, regardless of how well it might be doing from the point of view of profits and growth; they are simply needed for the firm's continuity. Being in the core is not the same as being in a particular occupational group. A firm may employ many engineers and scientists, only some of whom might be considered to be in the core. Skilled blue-collar workers may also be in the core. Core employees have the greatest job security with their employing organizations and also have skills and experiences that can be "traded" in the external labor market if their firm should experience an unforeseen financial crisis. Finally, core employees enjoy their protected positions precisely because there are other employees just like them who are considered temporary.

Temporary Workers

The employment of temporary workers is linked to the economic ups and downs that a firm faces. When sales are increasing, product demand is high, and profits match those of comparable firms, the employment of temporary workers is secure. When inventories increase, or sales decline sharply, production is cut back, and temporary employees are laid off or fired. The temporary workers' relationship to the firm is a day-to-day matter. There is no tacit commitment to these employees about job security and no sense that they "belong to the family."

A good example of the role of temporary workers is revealed in the so-called transplants—the Japanese auto firms like Toyota, Nissan, and Honda that have located assembly plants in Kentucky, Ohio, Michigan, Illinois, Indiana, and Tennessee. Each of these firms employs between two thousand and three thousand American workers in their plants, and they have made explicit no-layoff commitments to workers in return for high work expectations (and also as a way to discourage unionization). However, in a typical plant employing two thousand production workers, the no-layoff commitment was made to twelve hundred hires at start-up time; the other eight hundred hires being classified as temporary. Thus, when there is a need to cut production because of weak sales or excessive inventory, the layoffs come from the pool of temporary workers rather than from the core workers. Sometimes these

temporary workers are not even directly employed by the firm but are hired through an employment firm like Manpower. These temporary workers are actually contingent workers.

Contingent Workers

These workers, as noted above, are employees of an agency that contracts with a firm for their services. It is estimated that about one in four persons in the labor force is a contingent worker, that is, a temporary or part-time worker.[18] These workers can be clerk-typists, secretaries, engineers, computer specialists, lawyers, or managers. They are paid by the temp agency and do not have access to a company's benefit package of retirement or insurance programs. Many of the professionals and specialists who work for large firms via temp firms are often the same persons who were downsized by those same companies. The following experience of a downsized worker is an ironic example of how the contingent workforce is created.

> John Kelley, 48, had worked for Pacific Telesis for 23 years when the company fired him in a downsizing last December. Two weeks later, a company that contracts out engineers to PacTel offered him a freelance job.
>
> "Who would I work for?" Kelley asked.
>
> "Edna Rogers," answered the caller.
>
> Kelley burst out laughing. Rogers was the supervisor who had just fired him. "That was my job," he explained. "You're trying to replace me with myself."[19] . . .

Care and Feeding of the Privileged Class

The federal government of 1997 is a very different creature from that of, say, 1977—more egregiously corrupt and sycophantic toward wealth, more glaringly repressive, and even less responsive to the needs of low- and middle-income people.

—BARBARA EHRENREICH, *NATION*,
NOVEMBER 17, 1997

Most people who are in the privileged class are born there, as the sons, daughters, and relatives of high-paid executives, professionals, and business owners. Of course, they do not view their "achievements" that way. As some wag once said of former president George Bush, "He woke up on second base and thought he'd hit a double." But some members of the privileged class have earned their places, whether by means of exceptional talent, academic distinctions, or years of hard work in transforming a small business into a major corporation. Regardless of how much effort was needed to get where they are, however, the privileged class works very hard to stay where they are. Holding on to their wealth, power, and privilege requires an organized effort by businessmen, doctors, lawyers, engineers, scientists, and assorted political officials. This effort is often cited to convince the nonprivileged 80 percent of Americans that the privileged are deserving of their "rewards" and that, in general, people get out of life in direct proportion to what they put in. This effort is also used to dominate the political process so that governmental policies, and the rules for making policy, will protect and advance the interests of the privileged class.

However, before examining the organized effort of the privileged class to protect their privilege, it is first necessary to examine how members of the privileged class convince one another that they are deserving. Even sons and daughters from the wealthiest families need to develop biographical "accounts" or "stories" indicating they are deserving. This may involve accounts of how they worked their way up the ladder in the family business, starting as a clerk but

quickly revealing a grasp of the complexities of the business and obtaining recognition from others of their exceptional talent.

Even without the biographical accounts to justify exceptional rewards, justification for high income is built into the structure of the organizations they join. In every organization, whether an industrial firm, bank, university, movie studio, law firm, or hospital, there are multiple and distinct "ladders" that locate one's position in the organization. New employees get on one of these ladders based on their educational credentials and work experience. There are ladders for unskilled employees, for skilled workers, and for professional and technical people with specialized knowledge. Each ladder has its own distinct "floor" and "ceiling" in terms of what can be expected regarding salary, benefits, and associated "perks." In every organization, there is typically only one ladder that can put you in the privileged class, and this usually involves an advanced technical or administrative career line. This career line can start at entry levels of $70,000–80,000 annual compensation, with no upper limit beyond what the traffic will bear. These are the career ladders leading to upper executive positions providing high levels of consumption capital and opportunities for investment capital.

Claiming Turf

Many young attorneys, business school graduates, scientists, engineers, doctors, economists, and other professionals would like to get entry-level positions on these upper-level career ladders. In fact, there are probably many people who are qualified for entry positions in terms of their educational credentials and work experiences. So how are people selected from among the large number of qualified applicants for such desirable career opportunities? The answer is simple: Once qualifications and experience are used to define the pool of eligible applicants, the choice of who gets the job depends on the applicants' social capital. . . . We define *social capital* as the social ties that people have with members of their college, fraternity or sorority, ethnic group, or religious group. People get jobs through their social networks, which provide them with information about job openings and with references valuable to those doing the hiring.[20] These social networks are usually composed of persons with similar social backgrounds. A recent study examined the social backgrounds of persons in the highest positions in corporations, the executive branch of the federal government, and the military.[21] Although there is increased diversity among leaders today compared with 1950 with respect to gender, ethnicity, and race, the "core group continues to be wealthy white Christian males, most of whom are still from the upper third of the social ladder. They have been filtered through a handful of elite schools of law, business, public policy, and international relations."[22]

A good illustration of how social capital works is found in a study of 545 top position holders in powerful organizations in the United States.[23] Ten institutional sectors were studied, including *Fortune 500* industrial corporations, *Fortune 300* nonindustrial corporations, labor unions, political parties, voluntary organizations, mass media, Congress, political appointees in the federal government, and federal civil servants. Within each sector, fifty top position holders were interviewed—persons who may be considered "elites in the institutional sectors that have broad impact on policy making and political processes in the U.S."[24] Although we have no information on the incomes and wealth of the 545 elites, it is very likely they would fit our definition as members of the privileged class.

Table 1 provides some of the findings from this study, which identify the ethnic-religious composition of elites and their distribution across different institutional sectors. As can be seen from the first line of the table, 43 percent of all the elites in the study

TABLE 1 Ethnic Representation Among Elites

	WASPs	Other Protestants	Irish Catholics	Other Catholics	Jews	Minorities	Probably WASPs
1. Overall elite	43.0	19.5	8.5	8.7	11.3	3.9	5.0
2. Men born before 1932	22.9	22.5	4.2	17.2	2.9	14.4	13.4
3. College-educated men born before 1932	31.0	19.8	6.0	15.5	8.9	5.2	10.3
4. Institutional sectors							
Business	57.3	22.1	5.3	6.1	6.9	0.0	2.3
Labor	23.9	15.2	37.0	13.0	4.3	2.2	4.3
Political parties	44.0	18.0	14.0	4.0	8.0	4.0	8.0
Voluntary organizations	32.7	13.5	1.9	7.7	17.3	19.2	7.7
Mass media	37.1	11.3	4.8	9.7	25.8	0.0	11.3
Congress	53.4	19.0	6.9	8.6	3.4	3.4	5.2
Political appointments	39.4	28.8	1.5	13.6	10.6	3.0	3.0
Civil service	35.8	22.6	9.4	9.4	15.1	3.8	3.8

Source: Alba and Moore (1982), Table 1.

were WASPs (Protestants with ancestry from the British Isles), 19.5 percent were Protestants from elsewhere in Europe, 8.5 percent were Irish Catholics, 8.7 percent were Catholics from elsewhere in Europe, 11.3 percent were Jews, and 3.9 percent were minorities (nonwhites and Hispanics). The second line indicates the percentage of the national population of men born before 1932 from different ethnic-religious backgrounds. The third line indicates the percentage of the national population of college-educated men born before 1932 of each ethnic background. A comparison of line (1) with lines (2) and (3) shows the extent to which each ethnic-religious group may be overrepresented or underrepresented among the elites. Thus, WASPs and Jews are overrepresented among elites relative to their composition in the general population. The elite representation of other Protestants and Irish Catholics is comparable to their representation in the national population; and other Catholics and minorities are underrepresented among elites.

More interesting for our purposes is the overrepresentation and underrepresentation of elites in different institutional sectors. Overrepresentation would suggest the operation of social ties operating to get positions for persons with the same ethnic-religious background. White Anglo-Saxon Protestants are greatly overrepresented in business and in Congress. Irish Catholics are very overrepresented in labor and politics. Jews are sharply overrepresented in mass media, voluntary organizations, and federal civil service. This ethnic-religious overrepresentation indicates that social capital may be used to get access to career ladders leading to the privileged class. Moreover, there appears to be ethnic-religious specialization in the institutional sectors that they "colonize." People help to get jobs for relatives and friends, regardless of whether the job is for a Mexican immigrant in a Los Angeles sweat shop or a young Ivy League graduate in a Wall Street

law firm. Parents invest their capital in the Ivy League education for a son or daughter, who now uses the social capital of family or school ties to start on a career line in the privileged class. . . .

The Real Global Economy

. . . We have tried to provide a glimpse of the meaning of the "bogey-man" global economy. The term has been used to threaten workers and unions and to convince everyone that they must work harder if they want to keep their jobs. The global economy is presented as if it is "out there" and beyond the control of the corporations, which must continually change corporate strategies in order to survive in the fiercely competitive global economy. There is an aspect of the global economy that is real. More countries today are capable of producing consumer goods that compete with firms producing goods in the United States. The best example of the *real* global economy is the Japanese automobile companies that have captured a major segment of the U.S. auto market. Companies like Toyota, Honda, and Nissan have produced cars (in Japan and in the United States) of high quality and attractive design and have found buyers from among Americans who were used to buying cars from General Motors, Ford, or Chrysler.

The other aspect of the global economy is an accelerated version of what U.S. financial and industrial corporations have been doing since the end of World War II—roaming the globe in search of profits. The big change is that since the 1980s, U.S. firms have found it easier to invest overseas. They have used this new opportunity to attack organized labor and to threaten workers to keep their wage demands to a minimum. In this view, the global economy is composed primarily of U.S. companies investing abroad and exporting their products to the United States (as the largest consumer market in the world) and other countries. These multinational corporations have an interest in creating the fiction that the global economy is some abstract social development driven by "natural laws" of economics, when it is actually the product of the deliberate actions of one hundred or so major corporations.

The real problem posed by the global economy is that it has increased the influence of large corporations over the daily lives of most Americans. This influence is revealed in corporate control over job growth and job loss, media control of information, and the role of big money in the world of national politics. At the same time that this growing influence is revealed on a daily basis, it has become increasingly clear that the major corporations have abandoned any sense of allegiance to, or special responsibilities toward, American workers and their communities.

This volatile mix of increasing influence and decreasing responsibility has produced the double-diamond class structure, where one in five Americans is doing very well indeed, enjoying the protection that comes with high income, wealth, and social contacts. Meanwhile, the remaining four out of five Americans are exploited and excluded.

NOTES

1. Office of Technology Assessment, *Technology and Structural Unemployment* (Washington, D.C.: Congress of the United States, 1986).

2. Joel Bleifuss, "The Terminators," *In These Times*, March 4, 1996, 12–13.

3. Sheryl WuDunn, "When Lifetime Jobs Die Prematurely: Downsizing Comes to Japan, Fraying Old Workplace Ties," *New York Times*, June 12, 1996.

4. John Miller and Ramon Castellblanch, "Does Manufacturing Matter?" *Dollars and Sense*, October 1988, 6–8.

5. Robert B. Reich, *The Next American Frontier* (New York: Times Books, 1983).

6. Richard W. Stevenson, "Trade Deficits for 1997 Hit Nine-Year High," *New York Times*, February 20, 1998.

7. John Pomery, "Running Deficits with the Rest of the World—Part I," *Focus on Economic Issues*, West Lafayette, Ind.: Purdue Center for Economic Education, Fall 1987. (Emphasis added.)

8. For an extended discussion, see Michael Stohl and Harry R. Targ, *Global Political Economy in the 1980s* (Cambridge, Mass.: Schenkman, 1982).

9. Reich, *Next American Frontier*.

10. "The 100 Largest U.S. Multinationals," *Forbes*, July 17, 1995, 274–76.

11. Barry Bluestone and Bennett Harrison, *The Deindustrialization of America* (New York: Basic Books, 1982).

12. Louis Uchitelle, "U.S. Corporations Expanding Abroad at a Quicker Pace," *New York Times*, July 25, 1998.

13. David M. Gordon, *Fat and Mean: The Corporate Squeeze of Working Americans and the Myth of Managerial "Downsizing"* (New York: Free Press, 1996).

14. Richard J. Barnet and John Cavanagh, *Global Dreams: Imperial Corporations and the New World Order* (New York: Simon and Schuster, 1994).

15. Alan Downs, *Corporate Executions* (New York: AMACOM, 1995).

16. See Gordon, *Fat and Mean*, chap. 2.

17. Ibid., 191.

18. Charles Tilly, *Half a Job: Bad and Good Part-Time Jobs in a Changing Labor Market* (Philadelphia: Temple University Press, 1996); Kevin D. Henson, *Just a Temp* (Philadelphia: Temple University Press, 1996).

19. Ann Monroe, "Getting Rid of the Gray," *Mother Jones*, July–August 1996, 29.

20. Mark Granovetter, *Getting a Job: A Study of Contacts and Careers* (Cambridge: Harvard University Press, 1974).

21. Richard L. Zweigenhaft and G. William Domhoff, *Diversity in the Power Elite: Have Women and Minorities Reached the Top?* (New Haven: Yale University Press, 1998).

22. Ibid., 6.

23. Richard D. Alba and Gwen Moore, "Ethnicity in the American Elite," *American Sociological Review* 47 (June 1982): 373–83.

24. Ibid., 374.

18

McDonald's in Beijing

Yunxiang Yan

On April 23, 1992, the largest McDonald's restaurant in the world opened in Beijing. With 700 seats and 29 cash registers, the Beijing McDonald's served 40,000 customers on its first day of business.[1] Built on the southern end of Wangfujing Street near Tiananmen Square—the center of all public politics in the People's Republic of China—this restaurant had become an important landmark in Beijing by the summer of 1994, and the image of the Golden Arches appeared frequently on national television programs. It also became an attraction for domestic tourists, as a place where ordinary people could literally taste a bit of American culture. New McDonald's restaurants appeared in Beijing one after another: two were opened in 1993, four in 1994, and ten more in 1995; by the end of 1996, there were 29 outlets in Beijing.[2] According to Tim Lai, the company's general manager, the Beijing market is big enough to support 100 McDonald's restaurants, and McDonald's plans to open 600 outlets in China by century's end.[3]

The astonishing growth of the Beijing McDonald's has to be understood in the context of recent changes in Chinese society. There is a new tendency to absorb foreign cultural influences and transform them into local institutions, a trend that the Chinese political system resisted during the Maoist era (1949–78). In the case reviewed here, both the McDonald's management and staff

Reprinted from *Golden Arches East: McDonald's in East Asia,* edited by James L. Watson, with the permission of the publishers, Stanford University Press. Copyright © 1997 by the Board of Trustees of the Leland Stanford Junior University.

on the one hand and the Beijing customers on the other have been active participants in the localization process. To analyze this process, I first examine the image of McDonald's in the minds of ordinary Chinese people. Then I look at McDonald's efforts to fit into the Chinese market, as well as the ways in which Beijing consumers have appropriated McDonald's for their own use.

The Big Mac as a Symbol of Americana

On October 1, 1993, National Day in China, a couple in their early seventies had dinner at the McDonald's restaurant on Wangfujing Street. They had been invited to celebrate the holiday at McDonald's by their daughter and son-in-law, who spent almost 200 yuan for the dinner, an unimaginably large sum in the view of the elderly couple. The experience of eating in a foreign restaurant struck them as so significant they had their picture taken in front of the Golden Arches and sent it to their hometown newspaper, along with another photo they had had taken on October 1, 1949, in Tiananmen Square—celebrating the first National Day of the People's Republic of China. Their story was later published by the newspaper, with the two contrasting photographs. In the 1949 photo, the two young people appear in identical white shirts, standing slightly apart, their thin faces betraying undernourishment in hard times. In the 1993 photo, a portly woman proudly holds her husband's left arm, and the two are healthy looking and fashionably dressed. They took a taxi to McDonald's and, while crossing Tiananmen Square, they remembered how poor they had been in 1949 and realized how much China has changed in the interim.[4]

At first glance, this news story reads like the typical propaganda skit that one still finds in official Chinese media, with its constant play on "recalling the bitterness of old China and thinking of the sweetness of the new society" (*yiku sitian*). However, in this case it is McDonald's—a capitalist, transnational enterprise—that symbolizes the "sweetness" of current life. What is even more interesting, the headline of the story reads: "Forty-Four years: From *Tu* to *Yang*." The terms *tu* and *yang* have been paired concepts in the everyday discourse of Chinese political culture since the nineteenth century. In common usage, *tu* means rustic, uncouth, and backward, whereas *yang* refers to anything foreign (particularly Western), fashionable, and quite often, progressive. The juxtaposition of these common terms demonstrates how McDonald's and its foreign (*yang*) food have become synonymous with progressive changes that make life more enjoyable in contemporary China.

In the eyes of Beijing residents, McDonald's represents Americana and the promise of modernization. McDonald's highly efficient service and management, its spotless dining environment, and its fresh ingredients have been featured repeatedly by the Chinese media as exemplars of modernity. McDonald's strict quality control, especially regarding potatoes, became a hot topic of discussion in many major newspapers, again with the emphasis on McDonald's scientific management as reflected in the company's unwavering standards. According to one commentator who published a series of articles on McDonald's, the company's global success can be traced to its highly standardized procedures of food production, its scientific recipes, and its modern management techniques. As the title of his article ("Seeing the World from McDon-

ald's") suggests, each restaurant represents a microcosm of the transnational,[5] so much so that, according to another article by the same author, many American youths prefer to work at McDonald's before they leave home to seek work elsewhere. The experience of working at McDonald's, he continues, prepares American youth for any kind of job in a modern society.[6]

Other news items associate the success of transnational food chains with their atmosphere of equality and democracy. No matter who you are, according to one of these reports, you will be treated with warmth and friendliness in the fast food restaurants; hence many people patronize McDonald's to experience a moment of equality.[7] This argument may sound a bit odd to Western readers, but it makes sense in the context of Chinese culinary culture. When I asked my Beijing informants about the equality factor, they all pointed out that banquets in Chinese restaurants are highly competitive: people try to outdo one another by offering the most expensive dishes and alcoholic beverages. It is typical for the host at a banquet to worry that customers at neighboring tables might be enjoying better dishes, thus causing him or her to lose face. To avoid such embarrassment, many people prefer to pay the extra fees necessary to rent a private room within a restaurant. Such competition does not exist at McDonald's, where the menu is limited, the food is standardized, and every customer receives a set of items that are more or less equal in quality. There is no need to worry that one's food might be lower in status than a neighbor's. For people without a lot of money but who need to host a meal, McDonald's has become the best alternative.

During the autumn of 1994 I conducted an ethnographic survey of consumer behavior in Beijing. I discovered that the stories commonly told about McDonald's have taken on a surreal, even mythic tone. For instance, it is believed among a number of Beijing residents that the potato used by McDonald's is a cube-shaped variety. A 20-year-old woman working at McDonald's told me in all seriousness about McDonald's secret, cube-shaped potatoes, the key to the corporation's worldwide success. She was also fascinated by the foreign terms she had learned in the short time she had worked there, terms such as *weisi* (waste), *jishi* (cheese), and *delaisu* (drive-through). The first two are straight transliterations of the English terms, but the third is both a transliteration and a free translation: it means "to get it quickly." These half-Chinese, half-English terms are used by employees and customers alike, making their experiences at McDonald's restaurants exotic, American, and to a certain extent, modern.

In this connection the ways Beijing Mc-Donald's presents itself in public are also worth noting. By the autumn of 1994, McDonald's had not yet placed any advertisements on Beijing television. According to the general manager, it was pointless to advertise McDonald's on television because Chinese commercials, unlike their counterparts in the West, appear only during the interval between programs. After watching one program, audiences tend to switch to another channel, which means that advertisements have little chance of being seen. Newspapers and popular magazines were regarded as a better way to present McDonald's public image. In the Beijing region, McDonald's relied on Berson-Marsteller, a transnational public relations company, to deal with the Chinese news media. The main source of information about McDonald's in China is a short booklet that sketches the history of the American-based corporation and its famous business philosophy, QSC & V, or quality, service, cleanliness, and value. The absence of what might be called hard news has led Chinese reporters to repeat McDonald's corporate philosophy of QSC & V—which, inciden-

tally, reinforces the Chinese government's promotion of upgrading and modernizing the local business environment.

McDonald's local management has also made efforts to promote the corporation's image as an exemplar of modernity. For instance, a five-minute tour of the kitchen is provided upon request at each of the Beijing restaurants. I went on three such tours at different locations, and all were identical. My guides—McDonald's employees responsible for public relations—showed me all the machines, stoves, and other special equipment and explained how they work. I was then shown the place where employees wash their hands (following strict procedures) and the wastebins that contained food that was no longer fresh enough to meet the McDonald's standards. Throughout the five-minute tour, one message was emphasized repeatedly: McDonald's foods are cooked in accordance with strict scientific methods and are guaranteed fresh and pure.

In addition to the freshness and purity of its food, McDonald's management also emphasizes its nutritional value. In a published interview, a high-level manager maintains that the recipes for McDonald's foods are designed to meet modern scientific specifications and thus differ from the recipes for Chinese foods, which are based on cultural expectations. A central feature of this "scientifically designed" food is that it includes the main nutritional elements a human being needs daily: water, starch, protein, sugar, vitamins, and fat. Thus when one spends 10 to 15 yuan to have a standardized meal at McDonald's, one is guaranteed enough nutrition for half a day. The idea that McDonald's provides healthy food based on nutritional ingredients and scientific cooking methods has been widely accepted by both the Chinese media and the general public. In Japan, too, until the mid-1980s, McDonald's food was believed to be nutritious and healthy; it is only in recent years that the Japanese public has begun to worry about the negative effects of fast food.

Given the general eagerness for modernization, shared by both the government and ordinary people, and, in the realm of consumption, the growing appetite for all things foreign, or Western (*yang*), McDonald's has benefited greatly from the cultural symbolism it carries. Bolstering the "genuineness" of its food, the Beijing restaurant keeps its menu identical to that of its American counterpart. By 1994 the sale of Big Mac hamburgers accounted for 20 percent of local McDonald's sales, a figure higher than the comparable one for Taiwan. This figure has been interpreted by McDonald's management as an indicator that Beijing customers have no problem accepting American-style cuisine.

But what is it that the Beijing customers have accepted—the hamburgers or the ambience? My ethnographic inquiry reveals that whereas children are great fans of the Big Mac and french fries, most adult customers appear to be attracted to McDonald's by its American "style" rather than its food. Many people commented to me that the food was not really delicious and that the flavor of cheese was too strange to taste good. The most common complaint from adult customers was *chi bu bao*, meaning that McDonald's hamburgers and fries did not make one feel full; they are more like snacks than meals. I conducted a survey among students at a major university in Beijing and collected

97 completed questionnaires. Table 1 shows the informants' response to two questions: (1) Is McDonald's food a formal meal or a snack? (2) Does McDonald's food make you feel full?

Only one-fourth of my informants regarded McDonald's food as a formal meal, and most of these respondents were women students (18 out of 23). Accordingly, 24 of the 29 men students (83 percent) perceived McDonald's food as snacks (*xiaochi*). Regarding the sensation of fullness, 54 informants (56 percent) did not feel they had had a "satisfying" meal at McDonald's, and, not surprisingly, this sentiment appeared most commonly among young men—23 of the 29 male students (79 percent)—while fewer than half the women respondents found McDonald's food unsatisfying. Those who treated McDonald's food as a formal meal were more likely to feel full: only 3 of 23 such informants complained of *chi bu bao* (not feeling full). One implication of the findings is that the perception of McDonald's as a provider of meals or of snacks is largely determined by the capacity of the food to make one feel full. It seems that women are more likely to feel full, and hence a larger proportion of women are ready to accept McDonald's food as a formal meal.

The Chinese food system is based on a basic division of *fan* (grains and other starches) and *cai* (vegetable and/or meat dishes). "To prepare a balanced meal, it must have an appropriate amount of both

TABLE 1 Evaluation of McDonald's Food

Sensation after eating	Male (N = 29)		Female (N = 68)		Total
	"Filling"	"Unfilling"	"Filling"	"Unfilling"	
Perceived as formal meal	3	2	17	1	23
Perceived as snacks	3	21	20	30	74
Total	6	23	37	31	97

Source: Survey carried out by the author at Beijing University on Oct. 11 and 14, 1994.

fan and *ts'ai [cai]*, and ingredients are readied along both tracks."[8] According to these principles, the McDonald's hamburger—a patty of meat between layers of bread—is not a properly prepared meal. As a Beijing worker commented, at best a hamburger is the equivalent of *xianbing*, a type of Chinese pancake with meat inside, which no one would treat as a daily meal. In Chinese terms, foods like *xianbing* are classified as "small eats" (*xiaochi*), a term close to "snack." The logic is very clear: a McDonald's hamburger is reinterpreted as a foreign (*yang*) form of *xianbing* and thus as foreign "small eats" (*yang xiaochi*). No doubt this is why 75 percent of my informants classified McDonald's foods as snacks, and 55 percent of them did not feel full after eating at McDonald's restaurants.

It seems ironic that although people have reservations about the food at McDonald's, they are still keen on going there. Why? Most informants said that they liked the atmosphere of the restaurant, the style of eating, and the experience of being there. In other words, the attraction of McDonald's is that it offers, not filling food, but a fulfilling experience. Or, as a local writer says, it is the culture of fast food that draws Beijing consumers to these restaurants.[9]

In fact, before McDonald's entered the Beijing market, Kentucky Fried Chicken (KFC), followed by Pizza Hut, had aroused considerable consumer interest in imported fast foods. According to an early report on KFC, people did not go to KFC to eat the chicken; instead they enjoyed "eating" (consuming) the culture associated with KFC. Most customers spent hours talking to each other and gazing out the huge glass window that overlooks a busy commercial street—thereby demonstrating their sophistication to the people who passed by.[10] Some local observers have argued that the appeal of Chinese cuisine is the taste of the food itself, and that, by contrast, Western food relies on

its presentation. The popularity of imported fast food is thus taken as a demonstration that consumers are interested in the spectacle, the show, that this new form of eating permits.[11] Prior to McDonald's opening in Beijing, the company's name was already popular among trendy consumers and it was only natural that, when the first restaurant was opened in Beijing in April 1992, thousands lined up for hours in order to partake of the experience, along with the new cuisine offered by this famous restaurant. . . .

The representation of McDonald's as a symbol of American culture not only has drawn Beijing customers to new forms of dining but also has led them to accept new patterns of behavior. For instance, in 1992 and 1993 customers in Beijing (as in Hong Kong and Taiwan) usually left their rubbish on the table, letting the restaurant employees do the clean-up work. The main reason for this kind of behavior was that people regarded McDonald's as a formal restaurant where they had paid for full service. However, during the summer of 1994 I observed that about a fifth of the customers, many of them fashionably dressed youth, carried their own trays to the wastebins. From subsequent interviews I discovered that most of these people were regular customers, and they had learned to clean up their tables by observing what foreigners did. Interestingly enough, several informants told me that when they threw out their own rubbish, they felt they were more "civilized" (*wenming*) than other customers because they knew the proper behavior. It was also obvious that McDonald's customers spoke in lower tones than customers in other, Chinese-style eateries. They were also more careful not to throw rubbish on the ground or to spit near McDonald's outlets. Similarly, a comparison of customer behavior in McDonald's and that in comparably priced or more expensive Chinese restaurants shows that people in McDonald's were, on the whole, more self-restrained and polite toward one another. One possible explanation for this difference is that the symbolic meanings of the new food, along with customers' willingness to accept the exotic culture associated with fast food, has affected people's table manners in particular and social behavior in general. . . .

The Rise of Consumerism and McDonald's Instant Success

In the early 1980s, McDonald's started to negotiate with Chinese authorities, in the hope that the Golden Arches might eventually enter the largest consumer market in the world. Beginning in 1983, apples from China were bought for apple pies sold by McDonald's in Japan, and later, food distribution and processing facilities were developed in China. The actual opening of McDonald's restaurants in Beijing, however, did not occur until 1992. In the interim, there were revolutionary changes in Chinese consumption patterns. After fifteen years of economic reform and improvements in living standards, a large number of people in Beijing began to buy things simply out of the desire to possess things and the joy of shopping, instead of restricting their purchases to basic needs (as during the Maoist era). The reflection of this trend in the food culture is that people are now interested in different cuisines, and dining out has become a popular form of entertainment among those who have a little extra spending money. For these people, cleanliness and nutrition have superseded low prices as the main criteria for selecting a restaurant, because they can now afford to worry about their health. It is in this social context of mass consumption and consumerism that McDonald's appeals to so many Chinese customers.

Consumption has been an important feature of the political agenda underlying the government's promotion of economic re-

forms. In an effort to revitalize Chinese market forces, reformers encouraged consumer spending during the early 1980s. A famous slogan at that time was *nengzheng huihua*, which means "being able to make money and knowing how to spend it." This slogan was in direct conflict with the official ideology of Maoist socialism, which emphasized "hard work and simple living." Not surprisingly the Chinese mass media were filled with debates about the new consumerism. At the theoretical level, critiques of "premature consumption" (*chaoqian xiaofei*) and "hyperconsumption" (*gao xiaofei*) dominated these discussions. In practice, however, the rise of consumerism appears to be an irreversible trend. According to 1994 statistics released by the Chinese Consumers Society, the average expenditure per capita had increased fourfold in the previous decade. The ratio of "hard consumption" (of food, clothing, and other necessities of daily life) to "soft consumption" (of entertainment, tourism, fashion, and socializing) has changed from 3:1 in 1984 to 1:1.2 in 1994.[12] A new wave of mass consumption began in 1990, concentrating on interior decoration, private telephones and pagers, air conditioners, body building machines, and tourism. Stories of the conspicuous consumption of luxury items among the new rich and increasing demands for imported goods have become a dominant feature of Chinese popular culture.[13] Some Chinese scholars have argued that the growth of a luxury commodity market is the hallmark of a modern way of life and a phenomenon characteristic of postindustrial societies.[14] . . .

Conclusion: The Golden Arches in the Local-Global Nexus

McDonald's experience in Beijing is a classic case of the "localization" of transnational systems. Efficiency and economic value—the two most important features of McDonald's in the United States—appear to be far less significant in Beijing's cultural setting. When Chinese workers load their families into a taxi and take them to McDonald's, spending one-sixth of their monthly income in the process, efficiency and economy are the least of their concerns. When customers linger in McDonald's for hours, relaxing, chatting, reading, enjoying the music, or celebrating birthdays, they are taking the "fast" out of fast food. It is clear that McDonald's restaurants in Beijing have been transformed into middle-class family establishments, where people can enjoy their leisure time and experience a Chinese version of American culture.

This Chinese version of American culture, as stated at the beginning of this [reading], is a result of the interactions between the McDonald's management and staff, on the one hand, and Beijing customers on the other hand. As a symbol of Americana and modernity, McDonald's food became popular among the newly emerging middle class and also among ordinary citizens who were curious about American food. A consequence of the powerful appeal of representing Americana is the conversion of McDonald's hamburgers and fries, ordinary daily fare in America, into precious and stylish foreign cuisine in Beijing. Such a transformation, however, is not to the company's long-term advantage. Like other leading transnational corporations, McDonald's development relies on its capability to increase consumer demand and expand the fast food market. McDonald's foods are intended for large numbers of ordinary consumers and thus must be, as Sidney Mintz has noted, "transformed into the ritual of daily necessity and even into images of daily decency."[15] In other words, to build on their initial success, McDonald's restaurants must localize their foods (and some of their cultural associations as well), converting them into something that is routine and ordinary for Beijing residents, while somehow maintaining their image as the symbol of the American way of life. This is why McDonald's management has gone to such extraordinary lengths to fit into the local cultural setting.

The other side of the localization process has two dimensions: (1) Beijing consumers' appropriation of McDonald's food and culture; and (2) the responses of local catering businesses and the rise of Chinese-style fast foods. The first dimension has been examined earlier in this [reading] (one of the most obvious results of appropriation is the multifunctional use of McDonald's outlets). The notion of fast food (*kuaican*) itself is not new in Chinese culinary culture, which also has something to do with the way consumers have appropriated McDonald's food. I discovered that many informants regarded McDonald's, together with KFC and Pizza Hut, as but one of many cuisines available in the national capital. The real fast food, they said, is *hefan* (which literally means "boxed rice"), the various foods in styrofoam boxes sold at street stalls. When people sit at a table in a comfortable restaurant like McDonald's, they treat it as a formal event, and consequently spend as much time as possible over their food.

The success of foreign fast food chains posed a challenge to the local catering industry and, starting in 1990, many local restaurants met this challenge by creating their own versions of fast food. They started by imitating KFC, and several kinds of fried chicken soon appeared on the market, with names like Ronghua Chicken and Xiangfei Roast Chicken. The competition between local imitators and foreign fast food chains peaked in 1992 and early 1993. Beijing media termed it the "fast food war."[16] Since then, most local competitors have turned to Chinese-style fast food, such as noodles, rice dishes, and Chinese pancakes. The best known example is the Beijing Fast Food

Company, a corporation established in 1993 and comprising nearly a thousand local restaurants and street stalls. The company offered more than 50 varieties of food, including five set meals: roast duck, stir-fried rice, dumplings, noodles, and meat pancakes, all served with soup and an appetizer.[17] Several of the leading figures in this business, former employees of KFC or McDonald's who had learned management techniques on the job, claimed that, by combining modern methods of preparation and hygiene with traditional Chinese cuisine, they could recapture Beijing's fast food market from the control of foreign chains.[18] Interestingly enough, a key feature of this indigenization process is that McDonald's has been taken as a model of management and food hygiene by local imitators as well as by government officials. I was told by a public relations officer that every month McDonald's conducts several dozen tours of its restaurants for the benefit of local government officials or catering companies. The most famous restaurant in Beijing—Quanjude Roast Duck Restaurant—sent its management staff to McDonald's in 1993, and then introduced its own "roast duck fast food" in early 1994.[19]

This study demonstrates that analysts would be well advised to pay more attention to the responses of local people before drawing grand conclusions about the impact of transnational corporations. The emerging global culture is marked by diversity rather than uniformity, because local cultures, as Richard Adams notes, "continue to yield new emergent social entities, new adaptive forms brought into being in order to pursue survival and reproduction both through and in spite of the specific work of capitalism."[20] Daniel Miller's analysis of an American soap opera in Trinidad reveals, for instance, that Trinidadian audiences have positively appropriated this foreign product into their social life. The geographic origin of imported culture has be-

come increasingly less relevant; what really matters is its local consequence.[21]

In my view, the most significant contribution made by transnational institutions like McDonald's is that people can use them as bridges to other cultures. In the present case, it is American culture that makes the Beijing McDonald's ultimately attractive to Chinese consumers. The customers want a "taste" of America, and the outcome of their pursuit is the creation of a Chinese version of American fast food culture. McDonald's success in Beijing can therefore be understood only in the context of this localization process. Given the centuries-long development of Chinese cuisine, it is only natural that foreign foods have undergone the transformative process of localization. It is also tempting to predict that, twenty years from now, the "American" associations that McDonald's carries today will become but dim memories for older residents. A new generation of Beijing consumers may treat the Big Mac, fries, and shakes simply as local products.

NOTES

1. *New York Times* (NYT), Apr. 24, 1992.
2. *China Daily*, Sept. 12, 1994; *Shijie ribao* (World Journal), Dec. 2, 1966.
3. *Fuwu zhiqiao* (Service Bridge), Aug. 12, 1994.
4. Ibid., Aug. 19, 1994.
5. Xu Chengbei, "Cong maidanglao kan shijie" (Seeing the world from McDonald's), *Zhongguo pengren* (Chinese Culinary Art) 8:3 (1993).
6. *Fazhi ribao* (Legal System Daily), Sept. 9, 1992.
7. *Gaige daobao* (Reform Herald) 1:34 (1994).
8. K. C. Chang, "Introduction," in K. C. Chang, ed., *Food in Chinese Culture: Anthropological and Historical Perspectives* (New Haven, Conn.: Yale Univ. Press, 1997), p. 7. See also E. N. Anderson, *The Food of China* (New Haven, Conn.: Yale Univ. Press, 1988), p. 25.
9. Xu Chengbei, "Kuaican wenhua yu wenhua kuaican" (The culture of fast food and the "cultural fast food"), *Zhongguo pengren* 10:15–16 (1991).

10. *Zhongguo ripin bao* (Chinese Food News), Nov. 6, 1991.

11. *Jingji ribao*, Sept. 15, 1991.

12. *Zhongguo xiaofeizhe bao* (China Consumer News), Sept. 12, 1994.

13. Gong Wen, "Guonei gaoxiaofei daguan" (Hyperconsumption in China), *Xiaofei zhinan* (Consumption Guide) 2:1–12 (1993); and Zhao Bo, "Xingxing sese yang xiaofei" (Varieties of consumption of foreign goods), *Market Price* 3:9 (1994).

14. Luo Jufen, "Gaoxiaofei: buke yizhi de chaoliu" (Luxury consumption: an irresistible trend), *Shangpin pingjie* 6:5 (1993).

15. Sidney Mintz, "Time, Sugar and Sweetness," *Marxist Perspectives* 2:65 (1979). In his well-known book *Sweetness and Power: The Place of Sugar in Modern History* (New York: Penguin Books, 1985), Mintz offers an excellent analysis of how sugar, which was initially an imported foreign luxury good, was transformed by capitalism into an everyday necessity for working-class Europeans during the seventeenth and eighteenth centuries.

16. See *Beijing wanbao*, Sept. 13, 1992; and Mar. 15, 1993.

17. You Zi, "Jingcheng zhongshi kuaican re qi lai le!" (Chinese-style fast food is getting hot in Beijing!), *Jingji shijie* 6:60–61 (1994).

18. See *Beijing wanbao*, Mar. 15, 1993.

19. See *Jingji ribao*, Sept. 17, 1994. For a detailed study of the responses of the local restaurant industry to the challenge posed by foreign fast food chains, see Yan Yunxiang, "Beijing de kuaican re jiqi dui chuantong yinshi wenhua de yingxiang" (The fast food fever and its impact on local dietary culture in Beijing), in Lin Qinghu, ed., *Di si jie yingshi xueshu wenhua yantaohui lunwenji* (Proceedings of the 4th symposium on Chinese dietary culture) (Taipei: Foundation of Chinese Dietary Culture, 1996), pp. 47–63.

20. See R. N. Adams, "The Dynamics of Societal Diversity: Notes from Nicaragua for a Sociology of Survival," *American Ethnologist* 8:2 (1981).

21. See Daniel Miller, "The Young and the Restless in Trinidad: A Case of the Local and the Global in Mass Consumption," in Roger Silverstone and Eric Hirsch, eds., *Consuming Technologies: Media and Information in Domestic Spaces* (London: Routledge, 1992), pp. 163–82.

PART III
Work and Inequality

There are rewards and costs attached to all forms of work. The fact that some jobs pay more and some less is an obvious way in which the rewards attached to jobs differ. Jobs can be rewarding for other reasons—such as allowing for creativity or autonomy—and access to these rewards also varies from job to job. The costs of work, such as exposure to stress, harassment, or dangerous chemicals, are also variable. Because jobs vary in the rewards and costs associated with them, inequality is an inevitable aspect of work in American society. What factors determine the rewards or costs associated with a particular job? To what extent is access to rewarding jobs a function of a worker's race and gender? These questions are among those addressed in Part III.

Work, Wages, and Inequality

The economic fates of most people in the United States are tied to paid work. Children's livelihoods depend upon their parents' or caretakers' access to jobs and wages. The vast majority of adults either work for pay or are supported by someone who does. When jobs are unavailable, the consequences for individuals, their families, and their communities are devastating (Wilson 1996). Moreover, as debates about poverty and welfare policy make clear, unemployed adults in American society who are perceived as "able to work" (and who are not supported by another paid worker) are viewed negatively by many (Katz 1989). Thus, not only is access to paid work important for economic survival, but it has come to define one's worth as a person. Under these circumstances, it becomes important to understand how wages are assigned to jobs, the factors that determine how wages are distributed to workers, and the broader trends in wages and wage inequality.

These issues are addressed in the opening reading in this section. In answering the question "Can the Economy Still Produce Good Jobs and, If So, Who Gets Them?" Frank Levy provides readers with a careful look at how American jobs have changed since the end of World War II. In the process, he examines the consequences of these changes for different racial and gender groups in the workplace. Levy's analysis avoids simple explanations and all-or-nothing conclusions about trends in work and wages.

Whereas Levy examines wage inequality among employed workers, the next reading addresses another form of labor market disadvantage: the lack of a job (and hence, a wage). As William Julius Wilson argues, "the disappearance of work" has disproportionately affected lower-skilled men in inner cities, many of whom are African American. Wilson shows how patterns of industrial restructuring on a national level have contributed to increased joblessness in inner-city areas. When employment prospects are dim, increased poverty and neighborhood decline are two inevitable results.

Race, Gender, and Sexuality on the Job

The increasing demographic heterogeneity of the U.S. workforce is a well-documented trend (Johnston and Packer 1987). The implications of this trend are clear: "More and more individuals are likely to work with people who are demographically different from them in terms of age, gender, race, and ethnicity" (Tsui, Egan, and O'Reilly 1992, p. 549). This transformation has inspired numerous studies of the experiences of workers from numerically underrepresented and numerically overrepresented groups. The selections in this section offer a sampling of these studies.

The lead article, by Barbara Reskin, focuses on the demographics of the workplace from a more macro-historical perspective. Tracing historical changes in the gender composition of book editors, Reskin identifies some of the factors that have contributed to the feminization of this occupation. She shows that changes in the publishing industry, such as the shift to outside ownership, made publishing a less attractive field for men, while other societal changes increased the supply of women available for these jobs. Although women's movement into publishing desegregated this once predominantly male domain, Reskin suggests this change has not necessarily produced equality between women and men in this industry. Reskin's argument is important, as it implies that women's entrance into predominantly male occupations may coincide with declining rewards and diminishing opportunities for advancement in those fields.

Gender and race are highly salient social categories in America and operate in every sphere of social life. Because members of different social categories occupy different places in the world, both inside and outside the workplace, their perceptions and experiences of work are likely to vary. These dynamics and their consequences for how workers identify sexual harassment are the focus of Reading 22 by Patti Giuffre and Christine Williams. These authors' finding that the "gender, race, status, and sexual orientation of the assailant" enter into workers' decision to label a behavior sexual harassment underscores the ways in which work life is structured by the dynamics of difference.

Expressions of sexuality have generally been considered taboo in the professional workplace—and, indeed, in most workplaces. As James Woods and Jay Lucas explain: "We imagine that work is a rational activity and that workplaces depend on order. Sexuality, in contrast, is perceived as a threat to all that is rational and ordered, the antithesis of organization" (Woods and Lucas 1993, p. 33). These assumptions may be especially pervasive in professional jobs, where the appearance of objectivity and the avoidance of excessive emotion help maintain professionals' authority over clients. These pressures for processionals to be "asexual" require them to constantly manage and monitor their sexuality. Furthermore, Woods and Lucas suggest that gay men and lesbians are especially sensitive to these pressures and may be ambivalent about the need to deny their sexuality on the job.

In the final selection, Karen Hossfeld explores the work experiences of immigrant women in California's Silicon Valley. Immigrant women represent a cheap source of labor for microelectronics firms, and Hossfeld argues that managers foster divisions by gender, race, and immigrant status to prevent workers from organizing collectively to contest their employment conditions. Labor unions in the twenty-first century thus face both the challenge and the potential of a demographically diverse workforce.

REFERENCES

Johnston, William B. and Arnold E. Packer. 1987. *Workforce 2000: Work and Workers for the 21st Century.* Indianapolis, IN: The Hudson Institute, Inc.

Katz, Michael B. 1989. *The Undeserving Poor: From the War on Poverty to the War on Welfare.* New York: Pantheon Books.

Tsui, Anne S., Terry D. Egan, and Charles O'Reilly III. 1992. "Being Different: Relational Demography and Organizational Attachment." *Administrative Science Quarterly* 37: 549–579.

Wilson, William Julius. 1996. *When Work Disappears: The World of the New Urban Poor.* New York: Knopf.

Woods, James D. with Jay H. Lucas. 1993. *The Corporate Closet: The Professional Lives of Gay Men in America.* New York: The Free Press.

WORK, WAGES, AND INEQUALITY

19

Occupational Change
Can the Economy Still Produce Good Jobs and, If So, Who Gets Them?

Frank Levy

In this [reading], we examine trends in American jobs since World War II—the nature of the work, how much a job pays, the job's security. We will look at the progress of different groups—for example, black women or white men—within this occupational structure. Finally, we will examine the evidence for [a] picture of today's job market that [has] received substantial attention . . . that we have entered a winner-take-all market in which the very highest incomes grow enormously while all other incomes stagnate.

What Is a Good Job?

To tell this story, we need to define a good job. A starting point is a joke told forty-five years ago by the comedian Sam Levinson. Two young women, casual friends, meet by chance for the first time in several years. One of the women is pushing a stroller with two young children. The other woman asks the children's ages. The first woman replies: "The doctor is one and a half. The lawyer is six months old."

In the 1950s, Levinson could tell this joke knowing that his audience would equate doctors and lawyers with success. The question is, why? At that time, people saw both doctoring and lawyering as noble professions—saving lives, upholding the law. People respected schoolteachers too, yet Levinson (a former schoolteacher) never would have said, "The schoolteacher is six months old." In addition to their nobility, the doctor and the lawyer were perceived as successful because each performed well-paid, clean, steady

---

Excerpts from *The New Dollars and Dreams* by Frank Levy. 1998. New York: The Russell Sage Foundation. Reprinted with permission.

work in pleasant surroundings where they largely could be their own bosses. Each job also required significant education.

These characteristics—good pay, clean work, job security, autonomy—are what make a job good. They do not necessarily come together in any one job. One artist may be autonomous and eat well, while another is autonomous and starves. A bond trader with an extravagant income may be fired at a moment's notice. A good job in 1950 might not be a good job forever. In March 1995, the *Wall Street Journal* profiled the problems of Patrick Kwan, a new medical school graduate in anesthesiology. After years of training, Kwan was piecing together several part-time assignments because tighter health insurance reimbursements were eliminating anesthesiologist positions.[1] Kwan was not the only doctor to feel such pressure. Two years later, the American Medical Association (AMA) issued a joint statement with other medical groups calling on the United States to train fewer doctors. As the organization said, "The current rate of physician supply—the number of physicians entering the work force each year—is clearly excessive." The solution proposed by the AMA was to limit the number of foreign medical school graduates accepted into U.S. internships.

To an economist, Kwan's situation is part of normal economic life. Even in a very strong economy, the supply of people entering a particular occupation can catch up with demand. When this happens, openings are harder to come by, wages start to fall, and the occupation has fewer good jobs. Or the opposite can happen: demand leaps ahead of supply, creating new opportunities. If Levinson had said, "The software engineer is six months old," his 1950s audience would have been mystified, but in January 1998 good software engineers were as much in demand as good football quarterbacks.

At the same time, occupational markets are part of the broader economy and are also shaped by broad economic trends, [including:]

- The post-1973 slowdown in wage growth.
- The post-1979 surge in skill bias that lowered demand for high school graduates and high school dropouts.
- The long-term employment shift away from agriculture and goods production and toward the service sector.
- An increasingly competitive environment and a shift in power away from employees and toward a firm's shareholders.

Because these trends work in various directions—more "clean" work in the service sector, lower wages for semiskilled work—their net impact on the number of good jobs is not clear. We will see some evidence, however, that the public believes that "good" jobs are harder to come by, even for college graduates. This anxiety helps to explain several social trends and provides one justification for the growth of big salaries at the top of the earnings distribution. We discuss both the anxiety and winner-take-all salaries [in this reading]. . . .

Occupations and Earnings: White Men

. . . Many occupations require at least some training, and even in an era of downsizing, most people do not change careers often. It follows that the occupational structure evolves slowly as each new cohort of workers chooses a different set of careers.

Within the slow evolution of the occupational structure, the major occupational trend among white men has been the shift into white-collar work. In the 1950 census, 32 percent of white men were in white-collar occupations (Table 1). By 1980 the proportion had

TABLE 1 Occupational Distribution of White Male Workers, 1949 and 1979, and Non-Hispanic White Male Workers, 1996

Occupational Group	Percentage of All White Men in Group	Percentage of All White Men in Group	Percentage of All Non-Hispanic White Men in Group
	1949	1979	1996
Professional and managerial workers			
Executives, administrators, and managers	10.5%	9.8%	12.8%
Management-related occupations	1.4	2.8	2.8
Engineers and natural scientists	1.9	3.5	5.5
Doctors, dentists, and other health diagnostic occupations	0.7	0.9	0.9
Elementary and secondary-school teachers	0.9	2.0	2.0
Post-secondary-school teachers	0.2	0.7	0.8
Lawyers and judges	0.4	0.8	0.8
Miscellaneous professional specialties (ministers, social workers, and so on)	1.3	2.4	3.0
Other white-collar workers			
Health aides and technicians	0.4	0.7	1.1
Technicians other than health technicians	1.0	2.7	2.5
Sales-related occupations	7.0	8.9	11.4
Administrative support workers	6.8	6.4	5.5
Blue-collar workers			
Craftsmen and precision workers	20.8	21.5	19.7
Machine operators	13.4	9.5	6.6
Transport equipment operators	6.7	7.3	6.9
Handlers, laborers, and so on	6.7	6.1	5.3
Service workers			
Household workers	0.1	0.0	0.0
Protective service workers (police, fire, and so on)	1.5	2.2	2.6
Food services, building services (except household), childcare, restaurant, and personal services workers	3.4	5.5	5.5
Farmers and farm-related occupations	12.7	4.1	2.9
Armed forces	2.4	2.3	1.2
Total	100%	100%	100%

Sources: Author's tabulations using the 1950 and 1980 Decennial Census Public Use Microdata Sample files and 1997 March Current Population Survey.
Note: Data restricted to males aged eighteen to sixty-five with positive earnings.

climbed to 43 percent.[2] The shift was a broad-based trend and included well-paid lawyers and engineers, midlevel technicians, and lower-paid workers in retail sales and administrative support.

To a large extent, more white-collar jobs were the occupational equivalent of employment growth in the service sector. The government expansion of the 1950s and 1960s was concentrated in white-collar employment, as was the growth in health care and business services, but even in manufacturing, employment was becoming more white-collar as more managers, engineers, and accountants were hired. Bureau of Labor Statistics data show that within durable goods manufacturing nonproduction (white-collar) workers constituted 17 percent of employment in 1948, rising to 31 percent by 1980.[3]

In the years since 1980, the growth of white-collar employment for all workers—not just for white men—has centered on two occupational categories: managers and administrators, and sales occupations. Both have grown at astounding speed. In 1979 managerial and administrative positions accounted for about 10 percent of all jobs in the economy, but they accounted for 18 percent of the net jobs added from 1979 to 1989. Sales occupations accounted for 10 percent of all jobs in 1979, and one-quarter of net jobs added over the next ten years. Some new sales positions were in the expanding financial sector—stockbrokers and bond traders are classified as sales occupations—but sales positions grew in most industries, reflecting the economic changes of the 1980s: deregulation, more foreign competition, a slow-growing customer base, and slow-growing average wages, all of which increased competitive pressure on firms to expand market share.

By 1996, 49 percent of white male workers were in white-collar jobs, up from 32 percent in 1950. In a related trend, white men increasingly acquired college educations. That second trend, however, was far from smooth.

Since many white-collar jobs require education beyond high school, the post–World War II economy put college graduates in demand. Claudia Goldin and Robert Margo show that in 1940, on the eve of World War II, young male college graduates had weekly earnings about 70 percent higher than those of young male high school graduates.[4] By 1950 World War II veterans were entering the labor force, their college educations financed by the GI Bill. Nonetheless, demand for college graduates remained well ahead of supply, and thirty-year-old white men with four or more years of college earned on average 27 percent per year more than thirty-year-old white men with high school diplomas.

This pattern continued through the 1950s. Among whites in their late twenties, the proportion with four or more years of college rose from 6 percent in 1947 to 12 percent in 1959. Demand grew as well, however, and the gap between college and high school earnings in 1960 was 30 percent, slightly higher than in 1950.

As illustrated by the story of Patrick Kwan, the young anesthesiologist, supply-and-demand gaps do eventually close. Among young college graduates, closure occurred in the 1970s. The principal reason was the continued increase in supply. In the early 1970s, large numbers of young men went to college, both to raise their earnings and to avoid being drafted into the Vietnam War. By 1979, 28 percent of twenty-five- to twenty-nine-year-old white males had four years of college (or more).[5] Richard Freeman calculates that in 1952 there were 2.2 managerial, administrative, and professional jobs for every college graduate (regardless of race and sex). By the early 1970s, the ratio had declined to 1.6 to 1.[6] The surge in supply increased job competition among college graduates and exerted downward pressure on their wages.

By itself, the downward pressure on college graduates' wages would have closed the educational earnings gap, but the gap was also closing from below: the 1970s was the decade when macroeconomic events were driving up the wages of high school graduates. The falling international value of the dollar was stimulating U.S. manufacturing, while crop failures abroad and the oil price shock were stimulating food and energy production. In each of these industries, higher production spelled higher demand for blue-collar workers.

By 1979, thirty-year-old white men earned about $36,200 with a bachelor's degree, and $33,300 with a high school diploma. In percentage terms, the gap was 9 percent, less than half of what it had been in 1960. As strange as it sounds today, Freeman and others could reasonably speculate that college might no longer be a good investment in purely economic terms.

Rapid productivity growth and wage growth can serve as a safety net for economic change. The 1970s surge in college graduates is a case in point. If productivity and wages had continued to grow rapidly during the 1970s, college graduates would have gotten richer and high school graduates would have gotten richer faster (beginning from a lower starting point). Because the surge in college graduates occurred after 1973, wage growth had slowed in all occupations (Table 2) and a relative wage decline could also become an absolute wage decline.

This was the beginning of the anxious perception that there were no longer enough good jobs to go around. In one sense, the perception was crazy. After all, a thirty-year-old white male with a bachelor's degree had average 1979 earnings of $36,200. Nevertheless, the bad economic news—the surge of graduates, the oil and food price shocks, slow productivity growth—had taken its toll: these earnings were about $4,000 less than what thirty-year-old white men with a bachelor's degree had made in 1969 (in 1997 dollars).

The anxiety was compounded by young workers' high expectations. In the 1970s, young men and women had grown up exclusively in the post–World War II economic boom. Unlike their parents, who had known the war and something of the Great Depression, these young people had very high expectations, and even a temporary pause in wage growth was a big comedown.

An early sign was the shift in attitudes among college freshmen, whose views had been surveyed since the late 1960s by the American Council on Education. In these surveys, students were asked to rank the importance of each of a series of values in their lives. Between 1968 and 1972, about 40 percent of all freshmen felt that "being very well off financially" was "essential" or "very important," the highest and second-highest ratings. In the fall of 1973, as oil prices were rising and wages stopped growing, this proportion jumped to 62 percent, and it continued to climb: by the late 1980s, it had reached 75 percent, about where it stands today.[7] We can say (with a smirk) that freshmen suddenly abandoned flower power for Datsun 240-Zs. It is more likely, however, that freshmen saw the face of a different economy. In the late 1960s, when wages were growing and the unemployment rate was below 4 percent, a white male college student could major in anything and know he would graduate with a well-paying job (by the standards of the time) provided he could avoid the draft. By the mid-1970s, the sense of effortless upward mobility had disappeared.

Anxiety surfaced in other ways. Since the early 1950s, the proportion of young persons who described themselves as middle-class had increased steadily, but after 1970 it began to decline modestly.[8] In the mid-1960s, when all careers paid well (by historical standards), only 10 to 12 percent of freshmen majored in business administration. As the economy stalled, business administration majors increased, reaching 25

TABLE 2   White Men's and Non-Hispanic White Men's Median Earnings by Occupation and by Year (in 1997 Dollars)

	1949	1979	1996
All white males	$16,833	$30,928	$30,606
Professional and managerial workers			
Executives, administrators, and managers	22,955	47,069	48,970
Management-related occupations	23,567	40,522	40,808
Engineers and natural scientists	26,627	49,051	52,030
Doctors, dentists, and other health diagnostic occupations	37,033	89,767	102,019
Elementary and secondary-school teachers	20,506	35,618	35,707
Post-secondary-school teachers	24,791	42,655	45,909
Lawyers and judges	32,748	61,848	76,515
Miscellaneous professional specialties (ministers, social workers, and so on)	18,670	27,729	30,606
Other white-collar workers			
Health aides and technicians	20,812	31,993	34,687
Technicians other than health technicians	19,894	34,664	36,727
Sales-related occupations	18,670	31,993	30,606
Administrative support workers	18,670	29,947	26,525
Blue-collar workers			
Craftsmen and precision workers	18,670	31,993	28,566
Machine operators	16,833	27,729	25,505
Transport equipment operators	17,445	29,861	25,709
Handlers, laborers, and so on	12,548	17,068	14,283
Service workers			
Household workers[a]	—	—	—
Protective service workers (police, fire, and so on)	18,670	31,993	32,646
Food services, building services (except household), childcare, restaurant, and personal services workers	12,548	14,904	12,753
Farmers and farm-related occupations	8,264	17,041	15,303
Armed forces	10,100	17,964	26,525

Sources: Author's tabulations of 1950 and 1980 Decennial Census Public Use Microdata Sample files and March 1997 Current Population Survey. Data inflation-adjusted using the personal consumption expenditure deflator.
Notes: Data restricted to white males ages eighteen to sixty-five with positive earnings in the previous year. The 1996 sample excludes Hispanic whites.
[a]Denotes too few observations for a meaningful estimate.

percent of all freshmen in 1987 before the proportion fell back modestly.[9] Pre-med and pre-law (Levinson's occupations), and later, computer science, enjoyed similar popularity.

Until 1980 financial anxiety did not automatically translate into college attendance. The gap between college and high school earnings had become too small for that, and by the end of the 1970s the proportion of male high school graduates enrolling in college had actually leveled off. But everything changed in the blue-collar recession of 1980 to 1982, when the educational earnings gap reopened dramatically. Between 1979 and 1985, the educational earnings gap among younger white men expanded from 9 percent to about 32 percent—about $36,200 for the college graduate and $27,500 for the high school graduate. The corresponding earnings gap for women expanded at a more moderate pace.

Young people saw these changes, and the fraction of high school graduates who went on to college began to rise. The response among some of the least-educated older male workers, however, was to drop out of the labor force entirely. Between 1970 and 1996, the labor-force participation rate of prime-age white men fell from 97 percent to 93 percent, and among high school dropouts in this group, the rate declined from 94 percent to 80 percent.[10] The growing educational-earnings gap redefined good jobs and bad jobs within the occupational distribution. In 1979 white male managers and administrators (of any age) averaged $47,100 annually, while white male machine operators and assemblers averaged $27,700, a difference of $19,400. By 1989 managers and administrators averaged $49,000, while machine operators (now a declining occupation) averaged $25,500, a difference of $23,500. These numbers did not receive the attention given to the extraordinary gaps that emerged between production workers and CEOs—a subject to which we will return—but they did serve to stretch the middle of the earnings distribution and so contributed to earnings inequality.

Beyond the educational earnings gap, a second, less discussed source of earnings inequality was the growing difference in earnings among men (and among women) with the same age, race, education, and other observable characteristics. We can see examples of both types of inequality in Figures 1 and 2 [page 206].

Figure 1 compares the earnings distributions for prime-age white men in 1979 (the last year before demand for high school graduates fell) and 1996. The two distributions have similar medians, reflecting the lack of growth in the average wage during the period. The 1996 distribution has greater fractions of men with earnings below $30,000 (including those not working) and above $60,000. Much of the widening difference occurred along educational lines.

Figure 2 compares the 1979 and 1996 earnings distributions of twenty-five- to thirty-four-year-old white males with exactly four years of college. Even within this apparently homogenous group, the distribution spreads out over time.

This "within group" earnings inequality—earnings inequality among apparently similar people—was not new. It had been growing since at least the late 1960s, and even today its causes are not well understood. We might suppose that these earnings differences reflect the fact that people of the same age and education have different levels of skill (as measured on standardized tests) or work in different occupations or industries. Such explanations have been tested, and none can explain why within-group earnings differences have grown. Because of this aspect of earnings inequality, total male earnings inequality through most of the 1970s was a kind of stand-off: earnings differences within groups of apparently similar men were increasing, but earnings differences between more- and less-educated men were falling. After 1979 both kinds of inequality were growing, and so overall earnings inequality increased sharply.

By the late 1980s, the concept of within-group earnings inequality (if not the term) had entered the media in stories about the growing "lower tail" of new college graduates who were forced to take "high school" jobs.[11] The stories resonated because many people knew a recent college graduate who was living at home while working as a waiter in a restaurant or (in Seattle) a latte bar. The market for college graduates, it was said, had collapsed.

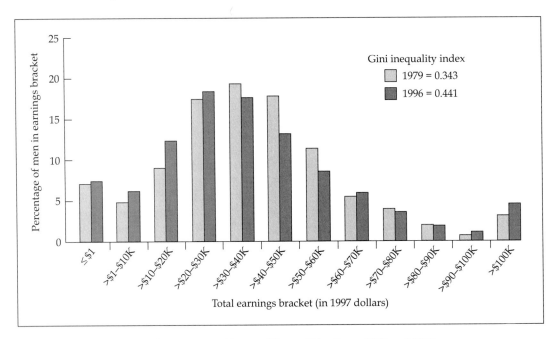

FIGURE 1   Earnings of White Men Age Twenty-Five to Fifty-Four, 1979 and 1996
Sources: Author's tabulations of the March 1980 and March 1997 Current Population Survey.

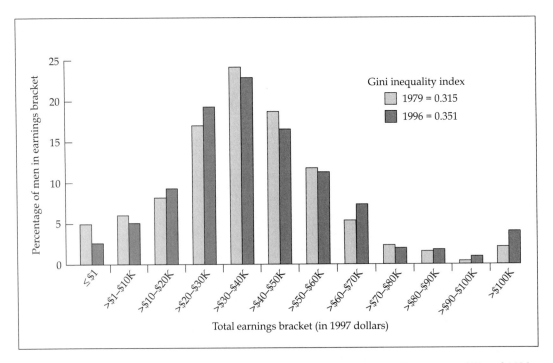

FIGURE 2   Earnings of White Male College Graduates Age Twenty-Five to Thirty-Four, 1979 and 1996
Sources: Author's tabulations of the March 1980 and March 1997 Current Population Survey.

The latte bar stories were exaggerated, but they held kernels of truth. The first thing to know about young college graduates is that in both the 1970s and the 1980s many started slowly. In 1989 the average twenty-three-year-old white male with a bachelor's degree earned $14,300 (in 1997 dollars). In that same year, the average twenty-nine-year-old white male with a bachelor's degree—someone who had found his niche—earned about $34,700, about the same as 1979. These slow starts reflect a softness in demand that enabled employers to enforce apprenticeship terms in journalism and other overcrowded occupations. More important, $34,700 was a median figure: higher within-group inequality meant that the fractions of graduates doing significantly better or worse than this median had both increased since the 1970s (Figure 2). Finally, a college graduate in the late 1980s carried more tuition debt than graduates in the 1970s. For most individuals, college was still the best game in town—but college per se could not guarantee protection against all economic change. This realization further increased anxiety and helped fuel the crush of students applying to Ivy League and other elite four-year colleges. It was as if good jobs were scarce prizes, like winning lottery tickets; perhaps "the right college" could provide a winning edge.[12]

In addition to the latte bars, a second change in the demand for white-collar labor was the slow reduction in job security. . . . Like the stories about college graduate waiters, the modest increase in white-collar job insecurity was news, and it received intense media attention. By focusing on layoffs (rather than on the people who kept their jobs), the stories often exaggerated the changes under way. In reality, white-collar workers reacted to the changes by becoming more cautious and less willing to quit jobs voluntarily. Thus, layoffs were up, quits were down, and the average worker's length of time on a job did not change much. In-creased caution was itself, however, a sign of a large psychological impact. . . .

We can make sense of the economy only by looking simultaneously at several different stories—there is no single punch line. White men's occupations show the same complexity. The shift into white-collar work—clean "brain" work—continues to improve job quality over time, but earnings for most occupations have not improved in recent years; indeed, earnings in occupations with low skill requirements have declined. In 1996 a typical white male in his fifties with a bachelor's degree had earnings of about $51,000, and he was almost certain to have health insurance. In the previous ten years, however, his earnings had grown by only 7 percent, and if he read the papers, he knew that there was a possibility, small but real, that he would soon be let go. He could be excused for thinking that comparable men two decades ago had it better. A white-male high school graduate of similar age had no doubts on this point. He was making about $31,300, about $2,000 to $3,000 less (in 1997 dollars) than he had made when he was forty, and there was an almost 10 percent chance that he did not have health insurance. As far as he could tell, his children would have to go to college to have a chance at the middle class.

Occupations and Earnings: Black Men

On the eve of World War II, half of all black men worked in the rural South, the poorest part of the country. Another quarter lived in southern cities. Only one-third had gone beyond the seventh grade (compared with three-quarters of whites). Black men were restricted to agriculture, service work, and low-level blue-collar jobs. In 1939, their nationwide earnings averaged $5,000 (in 1997 dollars), about two-fifths of the earnings of white men.

Beyond this was the pressure of legal and informal discrimination, not only in the South but in the North as well. Philly Joe Jones was a world-renowned jazz drummer who came to prominence in the Miles Davis Quintet of the late 1950s. In August 1944, Jones, then a World War II veteran, and seven other men were hired as the first black conductor-trainees for the Philadelphia Transportation Company (PTC). Six thousand white PTC conductors and motormen called a wildcat strike in protest. State liquor stores and bars were ordered closed to prevent racial violence. The strike was settled only after the secretary of war ordered military personnel to take over the system.[13]

In the years since then, black men as a group have passed through two distinct phases: substantial gains through the mid-1970s, and fragmented gains and declines since then. Through the mid-1970s, the civil rights movement and legal pressures to end discrimination were both important in the economic progress made by black men, but equally important was traditional upward mobility. As with white men, sons acquired more education than their fathers had, achieving some of the things the fathers could not. Through this difficult process of slowly and painfully changing its membership, a group thus improves its position in society. Occasionally, however, some larger event advances or retards the progress of most group members—not just the new ones. Over the postwar period, three such events affected black men: the movement out of agriculture, the 1960s boom, and industrial restructuring, which reached cities earlier than it reached the rest of the nation.

The movement out of southern agriculture reached its peak in the 1940s and 1950s. It was during that time that black men faced both the pull of manufacturing jobs in the North and the push of declining farm employment. Over these two decades, one-third of the southern black population migrated to cities in the North and, to a lesser extent, the Far West.

Migration did not lead to enormous occupational mobility. Once in cities, the migrants still faced extensive discrimination, and well under half had finished high school. They moved into blue-collar jobs and personal service jobs; white-collar jobs of any kind were out of reach. In 1960, only 12 percent of black men held white-collar jobs. This was one-third of the rate for white men, and the underlying disparity was greater because few of the black jobs were in the private sector. Most were in teaching, administrative support personnel, and other government positions, including large numbers of jobs in the postal service.[14]

Nevertheless, migration substantially increased black male incomes because southern agriculture had paid so little. In 1950 a black man in rural Georgia earned less than $3,000 (in 1997 dollars). When a man moved from agriculture to almost any blue-collar or service job, it was a big step up—an income jump comparable to the move from being a convenience store clerk to a computer technician.

Black men who could make the move and obtain full-time work were closing the gap with whites. By 1960 black men who worked full-time earned about 58 percent as much as their white counterparts. Many black men, however, were not finding full-time work. In the late 1950s, black men's unemployment rate averaged 10 percent, compared to 4 percent for white men. In terms of income, *all* black men (including men who worked less than full-time) had earned income equivalent to 47 percent as much as their white counterparts, a ratio lower than it had been in 1948 (Figure 3).[15]

The migration out of agriculture could boost black incomes, but the process had obvious limits. By 1960 the proportion of black men in agriculture had fallen to 11

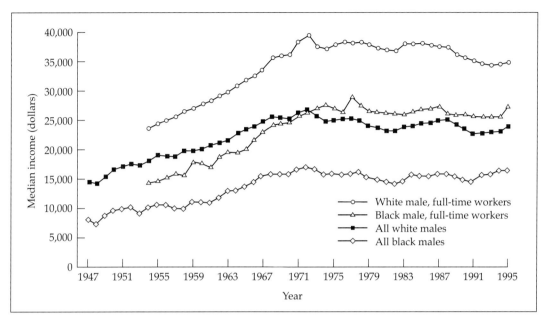

FIGURE 3   Median Individual Income of Black and White Men, 1948 to 1996 (in 1997 Dollars)

Sources: U.S. Department of Commerce, Bureau of the Census (1985) table 40 and author's tabulations of the Current Population Survey.

Note: Medians restricted to men with positive incomes.

percent, and there were few men left to migrate. At that point, a second event boosted black progress—the very low unemployment rates of the late 1960s.

The 1960s boom came at a good time. During the 1950s and 1960s, manufacturing jobs were rapidly leaving central cities, and in some cities the weakening economy left many black men stranded. By 1963 the national economy had recovered from the recession of 1958 to 1960, but the unemployment rate for black adult men still stood at 8 percent, more than twice the rate for white men. Then Keynesian tax cuts and Vietnam War deficit spending began to stimulate the economy. As high demand exhausted the white labor pool, increased demand focused on blacks.

Relative to earlier years, black men did well. In the last half of the 1960s, black men averaged 4.5 percent unemployment, their best

rate since unemployment statistics had been collected by race. Low unemployment translated into big relative income gains. By 1969 the black-white income ratio for full-time male workers stood at .67 (up from .58 in 1959), while the income ratio for all men stood at .57 (up from .47 in 1959).

Tight labor markets also led to modest occupational mobility. By 1969, 17 percent of black men were in white-collar jobs, up from 12 percent in 1960. Movement was still confined to the lower tier of white-collar jobs (administrative support positions, public school teachers); black men's white-collar employment still relied disproportionately on the public sector; and the proportion of black men in these jobs was still half that of white men. Nonetheless, it was progress.

It was also in the 1960s that the number of black families headed by women increased rapidly. How does this picture fit with the progress just described for black men? There is no single answer, but a part of the answer begins with the remark by W. E. B. Du Bois: "The conditions of life for men are much harder than for women." Du Bois was writing about Philadelphia in 1896; black men faced better conditions in cities in the 1960s. Nevertheless, a significant fraction of black men were simply dropping by the wayside. In 1969, a banner year for low unemployment, 6 percent of twenty-five- to fifty-four-year-old black men reported no earned income, while 32 percent reported total income below the federal poverty standard for a family of four.[16]

These statistics understate the true situation because they fail to adjust for the number of black men whom the census simply did not count. For example, in 1969 census statistics show 1.39 million black women but only 1.18 million black men aged twenty-five to thirty-four, a difference of 15 percent.[17] As the economist Robert Lerman notes, the Census Bureau had developed independent population estimates from birth and death certificates suggesting that only one-third of this gap was real, reflecting high rates of homicide and incarceration among black males. If we assume that most of these uncounted men had low earnings, the suggestion is that something over one-third of prime-age black men had very low earnings in a very tight labor market. There is more to the story of black female-headed families than black male joblessness, but the poor circumstances of many black males surely played a part.

The many black men who did progress in the 1960s and early 1970s benefited from more than tight labor markets. Discrimination was slowly eroding, and affirmative action also played an important role, particularly in the South and in firms with government contracts. Young blacks were closing the educational gap with whites in

terms of years of schooling, though differences in reading and mathematics test scores were closing more slowly. Low unemployment enhanced the impact of these changes, however, and when labor markets went slack after the 1973 OPEC price rise, most progress for black male workers stopped as well. The post-OPEC combination of sharp inflation and recession hurt many central city economies by accelerating the closing of older manufacturing plants and forcing cutbacks in municipal employment. Both kinds of job loss hurt less-educated black men. In the late 1970s, the incomes of black men who worked full-time were 71 percent of those of their white counterparts—up modestly from the late 1960s (69 percent). At the bottom of the distribution, the number of poorly educated black men who dropped out of the labor market continued to grow. In 1978, a fairly good year, 10 percent of prime-age black men reported no earned income from any source, a figure twice what it had been in the late 1960s. While some of these men may have actually had earnings from the underground economy, others were living on disability assistance or, more often, from the income of other family members.

Among all men (including those reporting no earnings), the early 1970s was the point of greatest black-white equality. Since that time, black-white male earnings differences have grown, but not for any single reason. . . .

Figure 3 looks at income equality between all black and white men with positive incomes. In terms of the labor market, we can argue that this measure of equality is too broad: we should expect income equality only among men of a similar age and education. Bound and Freeman show that since the mid-1970s earnings have become less equal under this narrower definition as well as under the broader one.

It is useful to take the comparison one additional step. Earlier, we noted that the gap in years of schooling between black and white young adults had narrowed substantially, but the gap in reading and math skills, as measured on standardized tests, was closing more slowly. Since a person's test scores directly measure what he or she knows, test scores may be better surrogates for job skills than years of education. Correspondingly, we should look at wage differences among black and white men with similar test scores. In exploring this difference, we assume that a test score at age seventeen or eighteen reflects a mix of the quality of an individual's education, the individual's innate ability, the individual's family background, and so on.

The economists Derek A. Neal and William R. Johnson have made such a comparison for younger workers (ages twenty to twenty-nine) in the early 1990s. Their analysis is based on the Department of Labor's National Longitudinal Survey of Youth in which all participants had been given the Armed Forces Qualification Test (AFQT) in 1980—a year in which the participants ranged in age from fifteen to age twenty-three. Neal and Johnson first estimate that the average earnings gap between black and white young men of the same age and education (regardless of AFQT score) was about 20 percent. Among black and white workers of the same age and same AFQT score (regardless of education), the earnings gap closes to 7 percent. Other studies suggest that similar test measures can explain some of the significant fraction of young black men who report no earnings from any source.

In sum, as education and skills have become more important in the economy, the poor quality of black education and disadvantaged family background can explain some, but not all, of the reemerging earnings differences between black and white men. Crime and arrest records also play a part in this gap, as does a mix of discrimination and the changing nature of work. In particular, we have seen that industrial restructuring has increased the demand for both hard skills—reading, math—and "soft" skills, such as the ability to market products to customers. In assessing soft skills, an individual's personal attributes—his accent, his understanding of a customer's frame of reference—can become confounded with employer prejudice or fears of customer prejudice. In the last decade, both employer interviews and experiments involving equally qualified black and white job applicants indicate that residual prejudice continues to hurt black men's employment chances.[18] Prejudicial attitudes have been declining over time—witness the growing number of black elected officials—but it is hard to imagine that they will disappear in day-to-day life very soon.

In 1997 several widely discussed books argued that blacks have made substantial progress over the last half century.[19] As we shall see, the description more accurately fits black women than black men, but it is undeniable that black men have made significant progress. In 1949 less than 2 percent of employed black men were managers or administrators; nearly 6 percent are today (Table 3). In 1949 more than one-fifth of black men worked in agriculture, mostly as farm laborers; less than 3 percent have such jobs today.

If we shift the frame of reference from the last fifty years to the last twenty years, the picture is cloudier. Since the mid-1970s, slow wage growth, the falling demand for less-skilled men, crime, and the end of affirmative action have combined to slow substantially the progress of black males. The year 1996 was a reasonably good one, with national unemployment averaging 5.6 percent. Yet in that year Current Population Survey data show that 22 percent of prime-age black males reported no earned income (Figure 4). Two-thirds of these men were high school dropouts. Assuming these statistics are exaggerated by unreported income, they remain startling.

TABLE 3   Occupational Distribution of Black Male Workers, 1949, 1979, and 1996

Occupational Group	Percentage of All Black Men in Group			Percentage of All Non-Hispanic White Men
	1949	1979	1996	1996
Professional and managerial workers				
Executives, administrators, and managers	2.0%	3.7%	5.7%	12.8%
Management-related occupations	0.1	1.5	2.0	2.8
Engineers and natural scientists	0.1	1.1	1.4	5.5
Doctors, dentists, and other health diagnostic occupations	0.1	0.2	0.3	0.9
Elementary and secondary-school teachers	0.7	1.6	1.6	2.0
Post-secondary-school teachers	0.1	0.4	0.3	0.8
Lawyers and judges	0.0	0.2	0.3	0.8
Miscellaneous professional specialties (ministers, social workers, and so on)	0.7	1.8	2.8	3.0
Other white-collar workers				
Health aides and technicians	0.1	0.8	1.0	1.1
Technicians other than health technicians	0.1	1.5	1.9	2.5
Sales-related occupations	1.2	3.5	6.5	11.4
Administrative support workers	3.3	8.6	8.2	5.5
Blue-collar workers				
Craftsmen and precision workers	9.3	15.1	15.8	19.7
Machine operators	14.4	14.6	9.8	6.6
Transport equipment operators	7.3	10.6	10.4	6.9
Handlers, laborers, and so on	24.3	11.7	11.4	5.3
Service workers				
Household workers	0.7	0.1	0.0	0.0
Protective service workers (police, fire, and so on)	0.4	2.8	4.2	2.6
Food services, building services (except household), childcare, restaurant, and personal service workers	12.9	12.3	12.6	5.5
Farmers and farm-related occupations	20.2	3.2	2.2	2.9
Armed forces	2.0	4.6	1.6	1.2
Total	100%	100%	100%	100%

Sources: Author's tabulations of the 1950 and 1980 Decennial Census Public Use Microdata Sample files and 1997 March Current Population Survey.
Note: Data restricted to workers ages eighteen to sixty-five with positive earnings.

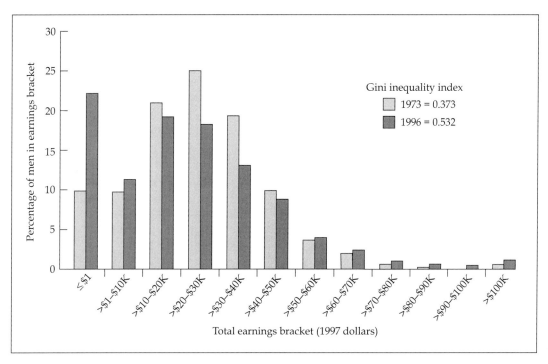

FIGURE 4 Earnings of Black Men Age Twenty-Five to Fifty-Four, 1973 and 1996
Sources: Author's tabulations of the March 1974 and March 1997 Current Population Survey.

It follows that the debate surrounding these recent books is not about their description of the past but about their uses of the past to project the future. Will future black male progress look like the last fifty years or the last twenty? Whatever else the answer depends on, it depends critically on the quality of education.

Occupations and Earnings: White Women

For white women, as for black men, the story of the last fifty years divides into two distinct subperiods. From World War II through the end of the 1970s, white women's occupational mobility was limited. Since 1980 white women have made significant gains. Progress was not spread evenly—as with other groups, progress among white women divided along educational lines. Nonetheless, white women's gains after 1979 stood out in a period when many other groups were at best staying even.

In the late 1970s, on the eve of this progress, the economic data for white women seemed to raise a paradox. Anyone could see that the number of women lawyers, doctors, and managers was growing, yet in 1979 white women who worked full-time had an average income of $22,700, 40 percent less than the earnings of white men who worked full-time (Figure 5). The percentage gap was almost as large as in 1955, the first year it was published.[20]

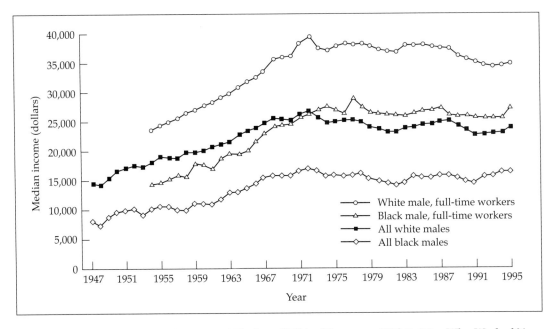

FIGURE 5   Median Individual Income of Black and White Women and White Men Who Worked Year Round and Full Time, 1955 to 1996 (in 1997 Dollars)

Sources: U.S. Department of Commerce, Bureau of the Census (1985) table 40 and author's tabulations of the Current Population Survey.

Note: Medians restricted to persons with positive incomes.

The paradox was reconciled by three facts:

- Over the postwar period, the number of white women in the labor force increased far more rapidly than the number of white men.
- The rapid increase in working women raised the number of women lawyers and managers, but also the number of women teachers, sales clerks, and secretaries. Thus, the overall occupational distribution of white women did not change very much.
- Within most occupations, women still earned less than men, even when age, education, and hours worked were held constant.

Even during World War II working women were an exception. In 1944, at the peak of the war, about 35 percent of all women over the age of fourteen were employed. It was a high rate for the time, but far less than today's rate of 58 percent of white women over the age of sixteen.

The low postwar labor-force participation rate for women reflected a straightforward career pattern: work for pay (if you work at all) before marriage and children, then stop. Among younger white women age eighteen to twenty-four, about one-half worked. Among prime-age white women (twenty-five to fifty-four), one-third worked. Women showed little tendency to return to work after their children were grown, but this would soon change. By the late 1950s, almost half of all white women age forty-five to fifty-four were working, and women in their late thirties were returning to work as well. The women most likely to have young children—those age twenty-five to thirty-four—still remained out of the labor market in large numbers.[21]

During the 1960s, labor-force participation grew moderately among women of all ages, but during the 1970s it exploded, particularly among women in their twenties and early thirties, the traditional child-raising years. Among women age twenty-five to thirty-four, labor-force participation rose from 46 percent in 1970 to 66 percent in 1979.

The huge influx of white women workers helped reshape the labor force. Between 1955 and 1980, the number of adult white male workers grew by twelve and a half million, while the number of adult white female workers increased by twenty million.[22] Since most of these women held white-collar jobs in the service sector, their large numbers accelerated the economy's transition to a service society. These numbers also created the paradox of women's economic position. Consider two questions:

- Among all employed white women in 1979, what proportion were managers and administrators?
- Among all managers and administrators in 1979, what proportion were white women?

In 1979 only 5 percent of employed white women worked as managers and administrators. This figure was not much larger than in 1949 (4 percent). To the contrary, in 1979 nearly half of all working white women were in three traditional occupations: administrative support and clerical (32 percent); sales (12 percent); and education (7 percent). Since the end of the war, white women's occupational distribution had advanced no more rapidly than the distribution for white men.

The proportion of managers and administrators who were white women was a different issue. Because the number of white women in the job market had grown so rapidly, women became more numerous and visible in every occupational category even without significant occupational mobility. Thus, the proportion of all managers and administrators who were white women rose from about 13 percent in 1950 to more than 27 percent in 1979. In this way, white women appeared to be making giant strides even as their occupational distribution improved only gradually.

Beyond occupational segregation, female-male earnings differences continued to exist *within* occupations. In the 1980 census, white women who worked full-time earned 20 to 30 percent less than white men of the same age, education, and occupational category.[23] Some of the difference was easily explained. At that time, women classified as year-round, full-time workers actually worked 10 percent fewer hours than men in the same category.[24] With the rapid growth in women's labor-force participation, many women (especially those above age thirty) were relatively new to the job, and their wages reflected their relative lack of experience.[25] Nevertheless, part of the earnings gap reflected simple discrimination. For example, the idea continued to prevail that married women could rely on their husbands' paycheck and did not need money as much as did men.

During the 1980s, these traditional patterns began to change. In a decade when many dimensions of inequality increased, the gap between women's and men's earnings closed, for both good and bad reasons. On the positive side was the continued erosion of occupational discrimination, a particular benefit for white women who had graduated from college. The fraction of white women who held managerial or administrative positions rose from 5 percent in 1979 to 10 percent in 1996 (Table 4), while the proportion in administrative support

TABLE 4 Occupational Distribution of White Female Workers, 1949, 1979, and 1996

Occupational Group	Percentage of All White Women in Group	Percentage of All White Women in Group	Percentage of Non-Hispanic White Women	Percentage of All Non-Hispanic White Men
	1949	1979	1996	1996
Professional and managerial workers				
Executives, administrators, and managers	4.1%	5.1%	9.8%	12.8%
Management-related occupations	0.6	2.3	4.7	2.8
Engineers and natural scientists	0.3	0.5	1.6	5.5
Doctors, dentists, and other health diagnostic occupations	0.1	0.2	0.4	0.9
Elementary and secondary-school teachers	6.4	6.5	7.4	2.0
Post-secondary-school teachers	0.2	0.6	0.8	0.8
Lawyers and judges	0.0	0.2	0.4	0.8
Miscellaneous professional specialties (ministers, social workers, and so on)	1.8	2.8	4.1	3.0
Other white-collar workers				
Health aides and technicians	4.4	5.3	6.9	1.1
Technicians other than health technicians	0.4	1.2	1.4	2.5
Sales-related occupations	10.1	11.9	13.5	11.4
Administrative support workers	32.0	31.7	24.1	5.5
Blue-collar workers				
Craftsmen and precision workers	2.3	2.4	1.9	19.7
Machine operators	20.8	8.9	4.1	6.6
Transport equipment operators	0.2	0.9	0.9	6.9
Handlers, laborers, and so on	0.6	2.2	1.5	5.3
Service workers				
Household workers	3.3	0.8	0.8	0.0
Protective service workers (police, fire, and so on)	0.1	0.4	0.6	2.6
Food services, building services (except household), childcare, restaurant, and personal services workers	10.7	15.1	14.4	5.5
Farmers and farm-related occupations	1.4	1.0	0.8	2.9
Armed forces	0.1	0.3	0.1	1.2
Total	100%	100%	100%	100%

Sources: Author's tabulations of the 1950 and 1980 Decennial Census Public Use Microdata Sample files and 1997 March Current Population Survey.

Note: Data restricted to workers ages eighteen to sixty-five with positive earnings.

(clerical) work fell. More generally, college-educated women (most of them white) were the only group to show consistent wage gains during the 1980s and 1990s. Between 1979 and 1995, the median earnings of twenty-five- to thirty-four-year-old white women with sixteen years of education rose from $23,400 to $26,500.

Earnings converged among less-educated women and men for a more negative reason: white women's earnings fell by less than white men's did. The earnings of male high school graduates and dropouts declined by 15 to 20 percent during the 1980s. While these earnings fell across all industries, the largest declines took place in high-wage durable goods manufacturing—industries that employed few women. When women worked in manufacturing at all, it was in textiles, apparel, or food processing, industries with lower pay scales. Coming into the 1980s, then, blue-collar women had less to lose than did blue-collar men. Over the decade, wages of high school-educated white women fell by only 3 to 5 percent, bringing men's and women's earnings closer.

A different dimension of convergence in men's and women's earnings was traceable through changing patterns in labor-force participation. As discussed earlier, during the 1970s and 1980s the least-educated prime-age men (with the weakest earnings prospects) began to drop out of the labor force. Among white women, labor-force participation rose among all education groups, but it rose highest among the well-educated. Among prime-age white women, college graduates' labor-force participation rose from 55 percent in 1970 to 83 percent in 1995. Among high school dropouts, labor-force participation rose from 44 percent in 1970 to 53 percent in 1995.

Converging earnings and converging labor-force participation were strong forces for income equality. Among year-round full-time workers, the ratio of median white

women's earnings to median white men's earnings rose from .59 in 1979 to .73 in 1996. Among younger men and women with at least some college, the ratio stood at .82. More generally, the hourly wage distribution for men and women, viewed as one group, showed little increase in inequality after the early 1980s. Taken separately, men's wage inequality and women's wage inequality continued to grow. When men's and women's wages were combined, however, the trend toward wage equality between the sexes offset growing inequality within each group.[26]

At the same time, the convergence of men's and women's earnings raised a second paradox. As Francine Blau and Lawrence Kahn point out, U.S. men and women are closer in education, labor market experience, and occupational status than men and women in many other industrialized countries.[27] Yet compared to other countries, the U.S. female-male earnings ratio is relatively low. Why?

As Blau and Kahn show, part of the answer involves the increasingly unequal wage structure among U.S. men. To see this, suppose that the education and work experience of the average working woman make her "equivalent" to men at the fortieth percentile of the male earnings distribution. If the male earnings distribution were very equal, earnings at the fortieth and fiftieth percentiles would be close in dollar terms, and so the female-male ratio of median earnings would be near 1.0. On the other hand, if the male earnings distribution were very unequal, earnings at the fortieth and fiftieth percentiles would be far apart in dollar terms, and the female-male ratio of median earnings would be lower.

We know that the U.S. male earnings distribution became substantially less equal during the 1980s. Working women were gaining on working men in both education and experience. The dollar penalty for being below average was growing, however, and so women were, in essence, swimming upstream. Blau and Kahn estimate that if male earnings inequality had not increased during the 1980s, the female-male earnings ratio for full-time workers would have risen to between .75 and .8.

A cynic would point to a second problem of timing: white women moved into higher-wage white-collar occupations just as those jobs became unstable. There is some truth to this. In the blue-collar recession of 1981 to 1983, a woman college graduate (regardless of age or occupation) had a job loss probability of about 2 percent per year, and the figure for a male college graduate was almost 3 percent per year. The difference reflected the concentration of women college graduates in teaching and other secure positions. By the mid-1990s, women's and men's occupations were more similar, and so women were more exposed to the risks of the wider economy. Between 1993 and 1995, a woman college graduate had a job loss probability of slightly over 3 percent per year, compared to 4 percent per year for male college graduates.

Despite these setbacks, the 1980s were a decade of substantial progress for white women. For better and worse—mostly for better—the market was treating women and men more as equals.

Occupations and Earnings: Black Women

Unlike white women, black women have always worked in large numbers. In the late 1940s, nearly half of all black women worked (compared to about one-third of white women). In those years, black working women shared many of the disadvantages faced by black men: geographic concentration in the low-wage South, limited education, and official and informal discrimination. These barriers could be seen in the jobs they held. In the 1950 census, two out of every five employed black women worked as a household domestic. Another one-fifth worked in cafeterias, on cleaning crews, and in other low-rung service jobs (Table 5). Low-rung occupations translated into low earnings. Even in the mid-1950s, a black woman who worked full-time had an income of $7,900 (in 1997 dollars), a figure about half as large as the income of her white counterpart (Figure 5).

With this starting point, it would be no surprise if black women's economic status paralleled that of black men: broad-based progress only through the mid-1970s. In fact, black women's progress was more sustained and their occupational status changed fairly rapidly.

In most ways, the forces behind black women's progress were similar to the forces affecting black men: migration out of the South, attitudes changed by the civil rights movement, the late 1960s Vietnam War–fueled boom. As important as any of these factors were rapid gains in education. In 1950 the average young white woman earned a high school diploma, while the average young black woman did not complete ninth grade. By the early 1970s, a majority of both black and white young women had graduated from high school though a greater fraction of white women were going on to college.[28]

Improved education allowed many black women to move into the expanding service sector. By the time of the 1980 census, the proportion of black women in domestic work had declined to less than 5 percent, while the proportion in clerical work, health care, and sales had grown from 7 percent to 37 percent. This progress occurred despite the growing number of black families headed by women. During the 1960s, as the number of black female-headed families was growing rapidly, 50 percent of black female

TABLE 5   Occupational Distribution of Black Female Workers, 1949, 1979, and 1996

Occupational Group	Percentage of All Black Women in Group			Percentage of All Non-Hispanic White Men
	1949	1979	1996	1996
Professional and managerial workers				
Executives, administrators, and managers	1.3%	2.9%	4.8%	12.8%
Management-related occupations	0.1	1.8	3.7	2.8
Engineers and natural scientists	0.0	0.3	0.9	5.5
Doctors, dentists, and other health diagnostic occupations	0.0	0.1	0.0	0.9
Elementary and secondary-school teachers	3.9	5.9	5.2	2.0
Post-secondary-school teachers	0.1	0.3	0.4	0.8
Lawyers and judges	—	0.1	—	0.8
Miscellaneous professional specialties (ministers, social workers, and so on)	0.4	2.2	3.0	3.0
Other white-collar workers				
Health aides and technicians	1.8	4.6	5.0	1.1
Technicians other than health technicians	0.1	0.9	0.8	2.5
Sales-related occupations	1.5	6.7	11.3	11.4
Administrative support workers	3.8	25.1	24.1	5.5
Blue-collar workers				
Craftsmen and precision workers	1.1	2.3	2.0	19.7
Machine operators	15.8	13.0	8.9	6.6
Transport equipment operators	0.2	0.9	1.4	6.9
Handlers, laborers, and so on	1.9	3.3	2.3	5.3
Service workers				
Household workers	41.2	4.3	1.2	0.0
Protective service workers (police, fire, and so on)	0.1	0.7	1.8	2.6
Food services, building services (except household), childcare, restaurant, and personal services workers	18.6	23.4	22.6	5.5
Farmers and farm-related occupations	8.1	0.8	0.3	2.9
Armed forces	0.2	0.6	0.4	1.2
Total	100%	100%	100%	100%

Sources: Author's tabulations of 1950 and 1980 Decennial Census Public Use Microdata Sample files and 1997 March Current Population Survey.

Note: Data restricted to workers ages eighteen to sixty-five with positive earnings.

family heads were in the labor force, a figure only slightly below the 58 percent participation rate of married black women.

As black women's occupational status improved, their earnings improved as well. By the mid-1970s, black and white women of similar age and education had approximate earnings parity.[29] As with men, the mid-1970s were a high point of earnings equality between black and white women (see Figure 5). In the years that followed, however, the experiences of black women and men diverged significantly.

During the mid-1970s, many central cities experienced the restructuring that the whole nation would experience after 1979: an accelerated loss of manufacturing jobs and losses in municipal employment, both of which reduced demand for semiskilled and unskilled workers. Where city employment was growing, it was in services that largely favored the better educated.

Black women and men were both vulnerable to the increased demand for better-educated workers, but black men were hurt by the loss of manufacturing jobs in a way that black women were not. Even in the booming 1960s a significant fraction of black men had low earnings or no earnings at all. The changing nature of central-city economies only compounded the situation. By contrast, the growing service sector created clerical, sales, and hospital jobs that favored women's soft skills over the skills of less-educated men. For women, this expansion of demand helped to cushion the falling demand for less-educated workers.

By the 1990s, the economy's shift toward better-educated workers had taken its toll, but black women continued to progress slowly. Black and white women were participating in the labor force at roughly equal rates. As a group, white women had an overall earnings and occupational advantage because of higher rates of college attendance, but racial differences in the labor market were narrowing.

Among younger black and white women of the same age and education, the racial gap in wages was 16 percent. Among younger women of the same age and AFQT score (regardless of education), the average racial gap in wages had disappeared.[30]

Occupation and Earnings: The Current Status of Hispanic Men and Women

[A] wave of legislation passed in Lyndon Johnson's second term: the Voting Rights Act, Medicare and Medicaid, the War on Poverty programs, and, less visible at the time, revisions to U.S. immigration law. Since the 1920s, the country's immigration policy had focused on limiting the number of immigrants and restricting their countries of origin to Britain and northern Europe—the countries from which the original U.S. settlers had migrated. The 1965 revisions allowed for increased numbers of immigrants and substantially expanded the countries from which they could come by emphasizing, for example, immigration that would reunite families.

By 1970 rapid inflows of immigrants were reshaping parts of the nation's population and labor force. The economists George J. Borjas, Richard B. Freeman, and Lawrence F. Katz have performed a careful analysis of these trends.[31] Table 6, reproduced from their work, shows the magnitudes involved.

In 1960, before the new law, foreign-born residents (immigrants) comprised 5 percent of the U.S. population. Four-fifths of these immigrants had been born in Europe or Canada. Between 1960 and the mid-1990s, the number of foreign-born citizens nearly tripled, from 9.7 million to 24.6 million. Immigrants now represented 9.3 percent of the U.S. population. At the same time, the European countries and Canada were no longer the main countries of origin; the immigrant flow from Asia and, in particular, from Latin

TABLE 6   The Foreign-Born Population of the United States and Its National Origins, 1960 to 1996

Item	Foreign-Born Population				
	1960	1970	1980	1990	1996
In millions	9.7	9.7	14.1	19.8	24.6
As percentage of entire population	5.4%	4.8%	6.2%	7.9%	9.3%
Distribution by origin (percent)					
Canada and Europe	84%	68%	43%	26%	21%
Caribbean and Latin America	9	19	31	43	50
Asia	5	9	18	25	25
Other	2	4	8	6	4

Sources: From Borjas, Freeman, and Katz (1997), reprinted with permission from the Brookings Institution. Authors' calculations. Data for 1960 are from U.S. Bureau of the Census, *Historical Statistics,* vol. 1 (1975). Data for 1970 to 1990 are from *Statistical Abstract of the United States* (various years). Data for 1996 are from the Census Bureau and are available on the bureau's worldwide Web page.

America and the Caribbean was increasing. While the change was enormous, it was not universally visible because most immigrants settled in one of a half-dozen states: California, New York, New Jersey, Illinois, Florida, and Texas. An issue like bilingual education could become politically charged in California because more than one-quarter of the California population is now foreign-born.

This history is important in discussing the occupational status of Hispanic Americans. Historical data for blacks and whites are, to an extent, pictures of successive generations of the same families interacting with the economy. Data for Hispanics are different. Between 1970 and 1996, the Hispanic American population grew from 14.7 million to 26.5 million, of whom 10.3 million were immigrants. When immigration changes a population to this extent, trends in occupational data depend a great deal on the immigrants' characteristics.

Immigrants to the United States tend to have either very low or very high levels of education—a bimodal distribution that differs sharply from the educational status of the native-born population. Hispanic Americans are themselves a diverse group, comprised of Cubans, Mexicans, Puerto Ricans, and Central and South Americans. Even among Cubans, the most educated of these groups, less than 70 percent have finished high school. Among all Hispanic American adults (native-born and foreign-born), roughly half have finished high school, a rate much lower than the 87 percent among non-Hispanic whites.

These numbers reflect both schooling in the immigrants' home countries and the problems of adapting to a new culture and language. These problems will ease with time, but for the present, limited education and poor educational quality significantly shape Hispanics' occupational status. Two-thirds of employed Hispanic men now work in blue-collar and service occupations (Table 7), a figure that compares to 47 percent among non-Hispanic white men. For Hispanic women, as with other women, clerical positions offer greater entry into white-collar occupations. Nevertheless, about 45 percent of Hispanic women currently work in blue-collar or service occupations.

The quantity and quality of Hispanic education can explain most of the earnings differences between Hispanics and non-Hispanic whites. Neal and Johnson show that among working young men of the same age and education, the average wage gap

TABLE 7   Occupational Distribution of Hispanic Female and Male Workers, 1996

Occupational Group	Percentage of All Hispanic Women	Percentage of All Hispanic Men	Percentage of All Non-Hispanic White Men
Professional and managerial workers			
Executives, administrators, and managers	5.2%	5.2%	12.8%
Management-related occupations	3.3	1.1	2.8
Engineers and natural scientists	0.3	1.5	5.5
Doctors, dentists, and other health diagnostic occupations	1.5	0.5	0.9
Elementary and secondary-school teachers	4.4	0.9	2.0
Post-secondary-school teachers	0.3	0.3	0.8
Lawyers and judges	0.3	0.2	0.8
Miscellaneous professional specialties (ministers, social workers, and so on)	2.5	1.7	3.0
Other white-collar workers			
Health aides and technicians	1.9	0.4	1.1
Technicians other than health technicians	1.2	1.2	2.5
Sales-related occupations	11.8	7.2	11.4
Administrative support workers	22.0	5.6	5.5
Blue-collar workers			
Craftsmen and precision workers	2.6	19.7	19.7
Machine operators	12.3	12.3	6.6
Transport equipment operators	0.5	7.1	6.9
Handlers, laborers, and so on	2.8	9.2	5.3
Service workers			
Household workers	3.7	0.0	0.0
Protective service workers (police, fire, and so on)	0.6	2.4	2.6
Food services, building services (except household), childcare, restaurant, and personal services workers	20.8	13.9	5.5
Farmers and farm-related occupations	2.0	8.8	2.9
Armed forces	0.1	0.9	1.2
Total	100%	100%	100%

Sources: Author's tabulations of 1997 March Current Population Survey.
Note: Data restricted to workers ages eighteen to sixty-five with positive earnings.

between Hispanics and white non-Hispanics is about 5 percent. Among working young men of the same age and AFQT score (regardless of education) the Hispanic-white wage gap disappears. Among young working women of the same age and education, Hispanics and non-Hispanic whites have similar wages. Among young working women of the same age and AFQT scores (regardless of education), Hispanic women have a 15 percent wage *premium.*

These estimates suggest that Hispanic Americans' job market success depends much more on the education they receive than on labor market discrimination once they have left school. As with blacks, the data point to education's central role in improving the economic status of future generations. At the same time, the large numbers of poorly educated immigrants have played a part in U.S. earnings inequality. Immigrants (from all countries) now comprise a significant fraction of U.S. high school dropouts. These workers have contributed to earnings inequality both through their own low wages and potentially by holding down the wages of less-educated, native-born workers. . . .

The Growth of Very High Incomes

To this point, we have focused on inequality in the broad middle of the earnings distribution. A different aspect of inequality—one that has received much media attention—is the growing share of all income at the very top of the distribution.

U.S. census data provide little guidance here. To preserve confidentiality and elicit the public's cooperation, the census imposes upper limits on the income data it records, and even stricter limits on the income data it releases for research analysis.

To examine very high incomes, the best data come from the U.S. Treasury's *Statistics of Income,* which annually reports adjusted gross incomes (AGIs) from a sample of tax returns. The Treasury maintains confidentiality by recording no information about the tax filers' personal characteristics—where they live, their gender or age, or education. Each observation does include the tax return's AGI and the sources of that income: wages and salaries, interest and dividends, capital gains, and so on.

The most thorough analyses of these data have been performed by Daniel Feenberg and James Poterba. Feenberg and Poterba estimate that in 1994 the top .5 percent of tax returns reported 10.7 percent of all AGI. The share is quite large and represents a sharp increase from the 6 percent of AGI reported by the top .5 percent of all tax returns in 1979. In 1994 the top .5 percent totaled 558,000 tax filers (out of 116 million) with income of at least $282,000 (in 1994 dollars, equivalent to $302,000 in 1997 dollars). Average income within the group was $718,000 and about 69,000 tax-filing units—one return out of every 1,700—had 1994 AGI over $1 million. Since the treasury data represent a fresh sample each year, it is possible that the top income recipients change substantially from year to year and so inequality is less than single-year statistics suggest. The economist Joel Slemrod has examined this question and finds that while there is turnover at the very top of the distribution, few persons who leave the very top fall very far.[32]

The political scientist Andrew Hacker has written a good book examining the people who earn this kind of money—athletes, CEOs, doctors, lawyers (Sam Levinson would be proud), and persons with very large inheritances.[33] Some of these people are well known—Michael Jordan, Warren Buffet, Oprah Winfrey. Some we know by the businesses they have founded—Frederick Smith's Federal Express, for example. Many others are totally unfamiliar to most of us.

Why has the income share of such people increased so much? Hacker provides one starting point by using the *Forbes* list of the four hundred wealthiest Americans[34] to construct a list of the twenty wealthiest Americans whose fortunes are largely self-made. Among these twenty fortunes, six were made in computers and computer software, a seventh was made in computer services (Ross Perot, formerly of Electronic Data Systems), four were made in media (for example, Rupert Murdoch and Ted Turner), four were made in investing and buyouts (Warren Buffet, George Soros, Ronald Perelman, and Kirk Kerkorian), and one was made in athletic shoes (Phil Knight of Nike). The remaining fortunes arose out of oil and chemicals (one each) and direct sales (Richard de DeVos and Jan Van Andel of Amway).

There are different stories here, but one economic factor—the growth of winner-take-all markets—helps explain the prominence of high technology on Hacker's list, as well as a growing number of very high-income surgeons, lawyers, athletes, and other professionals.

In a winner-take-all market, the best performers earn far more money than the runners-up, thereby increasing income concentration. These markets were first discussed at the beginning of this century by the economist Alfred Marshall, who was examining the effect of reputations on income.[35] An example of what Marshall had in mind is the difference between shopping for a banana and shopping for a surgeon to do a delicate eye operation. A person buying a banana usually looks for a low price. She would not be worried about buying a bad banana, both because she knows what a good banana looks like and because the consequences of a mistake are small. If the banana is bad, she can throw it away and buy another from a different store. Because most consumers think this way, no store can maintain banana prices far above the competition's prices.

A person requiring delicate eye surgery faces a different decision. She is purchasing a high-stakes, complicated service that can be done only once. As a nonsurgeon, she does not know how to judge a doctor's surgical ability. Therefore, she looks for an eye doctor with an outstanding reputation. Because most consumers think this way, a doctor who has a strong reputation does not face much price competition from a new doctor who says: "I have not done this operation before, but I received really good grades in medical school and I'll give you a great price." A celebrated defense attorney like Johnnie Cochran is in a similar position.

For winner-take-all theory to explain any *growth* in income concentration, winner-take-all markets must be growing as well. One source of growth was the high-stakes financial transactions that were part of the industrial restructuring that began in the 1980s. Corporate takeovers and mergers put strong investment banking houses in the same position as doctors and lawyers—they became producers of complex, onetime transactions that had to be done right the first time. The compensation of investment bankers rose correspondingly.

As Robert Frank and Philip Cook describe it, technology—particularly the media—gave a winner-take-all dimension to traditional occupations in other parts of the economy.[36] Consider professional tennis. Forty years ago, even the best tennis players spent much of their time playing in local tournaments before relatively small, live audiences. The modest size of these audiences set limits on what tennis players could earn. Today people interested in professional tennis can bypass local tournaments because television allows them to watch world-class players like Pete Sampras and Martina Hingis. As a result, Sampras and Hingis can command enormous earnings, and the earnings gap between the best and the near-best has grown much larger. In a similar example close to every author's heart, any book now featured on Oprah Winfrey's Book

Club sells far more copies than the runner-up books that did not quite make the cut to be on her show.

Winner-take-all theory affects computers and high technology through what economists call network externalities. Word-processing programs provide one example. Suppose we each had a computer, and it was the only computer we used for our written work. Each of us could use a different word-processing program and nobody would notice. But, of course, we do not work in this way. We work on projects with other people with whom we exchange disks (and viruses). We use each other's machines. Because of these exchanges, we put a premium on compatibility among word processors: the more widely a word-processing program is used, the more new users are compelled to buy it. One program can become a standard—the technology most people choose. If a few people can control that technology, they become very rich.

Controlling technology is not easy. The original standard for electronic spreadsheets, VisiCalc, was displaced by Lotus 123, which was largely displaced by Microsoft's Excel. IBM developed the dominant technology for personal computers but then lost control of the technology to Microsoft, which developed IBM's operating system, and to Intel, which developed the central processing units that now run most PCs. Bill Gates, Paul Allen, and Steve Ballmer, all of Microsoft, and Gordon Moore of Intel are on Andrew Hacker's list of the top twenty.

Winner-take-all theory can explain part of the increased concentration of income, but it obviously cannot account for it all. For example, most CEOs run corporations that do not compete in winner-take-all markets, and yet many have also done very well. *Forbes* also publishes a list of the eight hundred best-compensated CEOs. An executive near the bottom of this list, Raymond A. Johnson of Nordstrom, had 1996 compensation of $419,000—potentially well above the Feenberg-Poterba cutoff for the top .5 percent of taxpayers.

Similarly, Paul Joskow, Nancy Rose, and Andrea Sheppard tracked CEO compensation using a sample of about eight hundred firms per year from 1973 through 1991. Over the 1980s, average real compensation (including stock options) grew at 5.2 percent per year; by 1991 compensation in the sample averaged $2.25 million (in 1997 dollars).[37]

In other words, the average CEO now earns about seventy times as much as the average adult male, a ratio that has grown substantially over the 1980s. An explanation of this growing gap begins with the economy. We have seen how deregulation, technology, and trade create an increasingly competitive environment. In this environment, a CEO has to move more quickly to avoid being overtaken. Technology and trade have also given the CEO new strategic tools, and he is expected to use them. In the 1970s, financial markets would have viewed a firm's downsizing as a sign of trouble. Markets today view the absence of downsizing as a sign of potentially weak management.

A corporate board can argue that in this environment the CEO's job requires extraordinary talent, and talent costs money. The CEO himself can argue that in this environment his position is risky—he could be fired in a moment—so he needs high compensation for financial security.

As in most markets, however, these forces operate within man-made institutions. One institution is the corporate board's composition in which board members who approve the CEO's compensation are often beholden to the CEO for their appointment. A second we have already seen—the accounting standards that govern stock options. The awarding of stock options to a CEO addresses an important issue: A CEO paid only by salary may have weak incentives to maximize shareholder return. The awards' size has been magnified by the accounting standard in which options are not charged against the corporation's current income. Both institutions raise CEO compensation above its free-market level.

The result is a dynamic that has gone beyond the strategy of any individual firm and now prevails in the whole economy. Financial markets expect a firm's CEO to pursue cost reduction vigorously, often relying on downsizing and layoffs. The CEO's action not only affects his own firm but contributes to a general climate in which employees are cautious about pushing for higher wages. Low wage demands in the current recovery have raised the rate of corporate profit, higher profits have contributed to the stock market's remarkable recent performance, and until the summer of 1998 the stock market rise had substantially increased the value of most outstanding stock options.

We should not overstate the argument. The share of profits in gross domestic product has risen in recent years, but it remains lower today than it was in the 1950s and 1960s. Moreover, for any single corporation the immediate impact of downsizing may be to lower profits by incurring severance packages and related charges. Each firm's well-publicized downsizing, however, serves as a caution to workers in other firms and so helps to suppress wage demands throughout the economy.

In our discussion of these high incomes, we have assumed that those with market power—a CEO or a Barbra Streisand or a Henry Kravis—will use that power to maximize their income. This need not be true. Most of us are concerned about making money, but most of us are also concerned about our reputation, which depends in part on our conformance to community norms. A person who makes "too much money" runs a reputational risk, particularly when the money appears to be redistributed from others. Our definition of "too much money" rose considerably during the 1980s, and increased reliance on the market was one cause. Just as Schumpeter suggested, increased competition leads to more firms rising and falling and less stability of employment at all levels. When jobs no longer provide financial security, people see a greater need for financial assets, and reaching for the highest possible compensation becomes more socially acceptable.

In these ways, increased competition adds to economy-wide inequality. We can see why people who do well under these arrangements argue for even less government intervention in markets on the grounds that "everyone" will benefit. We can also see why people will try to bend the economy's rules to further enhance their position. . . .

The Shape of the Future

Having experienced the terrors of the Great Depression and World War II, the men and women of Sam Levinson's generation had already lived through a lot by the 1950s. But in those postwar years when Levinson's career was taking off, the U.S. economy was in an exceptionally strong position. American consumers had lots of unfilled demands and lots of money. Since foreign competition was weak, domestic producers could supply those demands, improving their productivity and wages as they grew, maintaining generally stable employment.

Today the situation is quite different. Partly in an effort to revive slow-growing productivity, we have increasingly turned to a deregulated, highly competitive environment. Compared to Levinson's time, competition, technology, and global markets have caused small but real reductions in job security. Because of the heightened competition, wages continue to grow slowly, in part because many workers see that they have less power to bargain for a piece of the economic gains. One by-product of these changes, the growing economic premium on education and skills, has slowed the assimilation of some minorities and increased inequality more generally.

The news is not all bad. Wages are higher now than in Levinson's time. Work itself is cleaner and less dangerous today. The lack of wage pressure has permitted the economy to sustain very low unemployment rates without succumbing to inflation. Nevertheless, some characteristics of a good job, as Sam Levinson would have defined the term, are gone for the foreseeable future. Both college freshmen and CEOs feel that they need the kind of money that offers financial security, but providing a large fraction of citizens with this kind of security will be an enormous challenge.

NOTES

1. Anders (1995).
2. Tabulations by the author of the 1950 and 1980 Census Public Use Microdata Samples.
3. U.S. Department of Labor (1982) table C-5.
4. See Goldin and Margo (1992). The statistics refer to young men of all races, and "young" refers to men with one to five years of work experience; thus, the high school graduates in this comparison are roughly four years younger than the college graduates.
5. See O'Neill and Sepielli (1985).
6. See Freeman (1976).
7. See American Council on Education (various years).
8. See Converse et al. (1980) table 1.24.
9. Richard Easterlin (1995) argues that this shift into business came from changing preferences (for making more money) as opposed to the weak economy.
10. See Blau (1998) table 1b. The statistics refer to the fraction of white men between twenty-five and fifty-four who were either employed or actively looking for work at a point in time.
11. See, for example, Hecker (1992).

12. For a discussion of this issue see Philip Cook and Robert Frank (1993), and the references cited therein.
13. See David (1986).
14. Based on tabulations by the author of the 1960 Census Public Use Microdata Sample files.
15. See U.S. Department of Commerce, Bureau of the Census (1985) table 40.
16. On the proportion of black men who report no earned income, see Levy (1980). On the distribution of black men's incomes in 1969, see U.S. Department of Commerce, Bureau of the Census (1970) table 45.
17. See U.S. Department of Commerce, Bureau of the Census (1970).
18. Moss and Tilly (1996); Kirschenman and Neckerman (1991); Holzer (1997); and the studies in Fix and Struyk (1993).
19. Thernstrom and Thernstrom (1997) and Patterson (1997).
20. See U.S. Department of Commerce, Bureau of the Census (1985) table 29.
21. For early data on women's labor-force participation, see U.S. Department of Commerce, Bureau of the Census (1975). For later data, see U.S. Department of Labor (1982) table A-3. For an excellent discussion of trends, see Bianchi and Spain (1986).
22. See U.S. Department of Labor (1982) table A-5.
23. See U.S. Department of Commerce, Bureau of the Census (1983) table 3.
24. See O'Neill (1984).
25. See O'Neill (1984) and Smith and Ward (1984).
26. See Lerman (1997) and Lee (1998).
27. Blau and Kahn (1992).
28. See U.S. Department of Commerce, Bureau of the Census (1974).
29. See, for example, Freeman (1973).
30. See Neal and Johnson (1996).
31. See Borjas, Freeman, and Katz (1997).
32. Slemrod (1991).
33. Hacker (1997).
34. See Conlin (1997).
35. Marshall (1961).
36. See Frank and Cook (1995).
37. Joskow, Rose, and Sheppard (1992). I base these calculations on the authors' fixed effects reported in table A.1.

REFERENCES

Anders, George. 1995. "Numb and Number: Once a Hot Specialty, Anesthesiology Cools as Insurers Scale Back." *Wall Street Journal,* March 17, 1995, p. 1.

Bianchi, Suzanne M., and Daphne Spain. 1986. *American Women in Transition.* The Population of the United States in the 1980s: A Census Monograph Series. New York: Russell Sage Foundation.

Blau, Francine D. 1998. "Trends in the Well-Being of American Women, 1970–1995." *The Journal of Economic Literature* 36(1):112–65.

Blau, Francine, and Lawrence Kahn. 1992. "The Gender Earnings Gap: Some International Evidence." *National Bureau of Economic Research Working Paper,* no. 4224. Cambridge, MA: National Bureau of Economic Research.

Borjas, George J., Richard B. Freeman, and Lawrence F. Katz. 1997. "How Much do Immigration and Trade Affect Labor Market Outcomes?" *Brookings Papers on Economic Activity,* no. 1. Washington, DC: Brookings Institution.

Conlin, Michelle. 1997. "When Billionaires Become a Dime a Dozen." *Forbes* (October 13):148ff.

Converse, Philip E., Jean Dodson, and Wendy J. Hoag. 1980. *American Social Attitudes Data Sourcebook, 1947–78.* Cambridge, MA: Harvard University Press.

David, Frances. 1986. "The Stories They Can Tell on Philly Joe." *Philadelphia Inquirer,* June 15, 1986, sect. H, p. 1.

Easterlin, Richard A. 1995. "Preferences and Prices in the Choice of a Career: The Switch to Business, 1972–87." *Journal of Economic Behavior and Organization* 27 (1):1–34.

Fix, Michael, and Raymond Struyk, eds. 1993. *Clear and Convincing Evidence: Measurement of Discrimination in America.* Washington, DC: The Urban Institute Press.

Frank, Robert H., and Philip J. Cook. 1995. *The Winner-Take-All Society.* New York: Martin Kessler Books.

Freeman, Richard B. 1973. "Changes in the Labor Market for Black Americans, 1948–72." *Brookings Papers on Economic Activity,* no. 1. Washington, DC: The Brookings Institution.

———. 1976. *The Over-Educated American.* New York: Academic Press.

Goldin, Claudia, and Robert Margo. 1992. "The Great Compression." *The Quarterly Journal of Economics* 57 (February):1–34.

Hacker, Andrew. 1997. *Money: Who Has How Much and Why?* New York: Scribner's.

Hecker, Daniel E. 1992. "Reconciling Conflicting Data on Jobs for College Graduates." *Monthly Labor Review* (July):3–12.

Holzer, Harry. 1997. *What Employers Want: Job Prospects for Less-Educated Workers.* New York: Russell Sage Foundation.

Joskow, Paul, Nancy Rose, and Andrea Shepard. 1993. "Regulatory Constraints on CEO Compensation." *Brookings Papers in Economic Activity, 1993,* no. 1. Washington, DC: The Brookings Institution.

Kirschenman, Joleen, and Katheryn M. Neckerman. 1991. " 'We'd Love to Hire Them, But . . .': The Meaning of Race for Employers." In *The Urban Underclass,* edited by Christopher Jencks and Paul E. Peterson. Washington, DC: Brookings Institution.

Lee, David S. 1998. "Wage Inequality in the U.S. during the 1980s: Rising Dispersion or Falling Minimum Wage?" Working Paper, no. 399. Princeton, NJ: Industrial Relations Section, Princeton University.

Lerman, Robert. 1997. "Reassessing Trends in U.S. Earnings Inequality." *Monthly Labor Review* (December):17–25.

Levy, Frank. 1980. "Changes in the Employment Prospects for Black Males." *Brookings Papers in Economic Activity,* no. 2. Washington, DC: The Brookings Institution.

Marshall, Alfred, ed. 1961. *Principles of Economics.* 9th (variorum) ed., with annotations by C. W. Guillebaud. New York: Macmillan for the Royal Economic Society.

Moss, Phil, and Chris Tilly. 1996. "Soft Skills and Race: An Investigation of Black Males' Employment Problems." *Work and Occupations* 23 (3):252–76.

Neal, Derek A., and William R. Johnson. 1996. "The Role of Premarket Factors in Black-White Wage Differences." *Journal of Political Economy* 5 (104):869–95.

O'Neill, Dave M., and Peter Sepielli. 1985. *Education in the United States: 1940–1983.* U.S. Bureau of the Census, Special Demographic Analyses, CDS-85-1. Washington: U.S. Government Printing Office.

Patterson, Orlando. 1997. *The Ordeal of Integration: Progress and Resentment in America's "Racial" Crisis.* Washington, DC: Civitas/Counterpoint.

Slemrod, Joel. 1991. "Taxation and Inequality: A Time-Exposure Perspective." In *Tax Policy and the Economy,* 6, edited by James Poterba. Cambridge, MA: MIT Press.

Smith, James P., and Michael P. Ward. 1984. *Women's Wages and Work in the Twentieth Century.* Santa Monica, CA: Rand Corporation.

Thernstrom, Abigail, and Stephen Thernstrom. 1997. *America in Black and White: One Nation, Indivisible.* New York: Simon and Schuster.

U.S. Department of Commerce, Bureau of the Census. 1970. "Income in 1969 of Families and Persons in the United States." *Current Population Reports,* ser. P-60, no. 75. Washington: U.S. Government Printing Office.

————. 1974. "Educational Attainment in the United States, March 1973 and March 1974." *Current Population Reports,* ser. P-20, no. 274. Washington: U.S. Government Printing Office.

————. 1975. *Historical Statistics of the United States: Colonial Times to 1970.* Washington: U.S. Government Printing Office.

————. 1983. *1980 Census of Population and Housing, Earnings by Occupation and Education,* Subject Report PC80-2-8B. Washington: U.S. Government Printing Office.

————. 1985. "Money Income of Households, Families, and Persons in the United States, 1983." *Current Population Reports,* ser. P-60, no. 146. Washington: U.S. Government Printing Office.

U.S. Department of Labor. 1982. *Employment and Training Report of the President: 1982.* Washington: U.S. Government Printing Office.

20

Jobless Poverty
A New Form of Social Dislocation in the Inner-City Ghetto

William Julius Wilson

In September 1996 my book, *When Work Disappears: The World of the New Urban Poor,* was published. In this chapter, I integrate some of the main arguments and conclusions presented in that book with social policy research in order to address current issues of welfare reform.

When Work Disappears describes a new type of poverty in our nation's metropolises: poor, segregated neighborhoods in which a majority of adults are either unemployed or have dropped out of the labor force altogether. What is the effect of these "jobless ghettos" on individuals, families, and neighborhoods? What accounts for their existence? I suggest several factors and conclude with policy recommendations: a mix of public and private sector projects is more effective than relying on a strategy of employer subsidies.

The Research Studies

When Work Disappears was based mainly on three research studies conducted in Chicago between 1986 and 1993. The first of these three studies included a variety of data: a random survey of nearly 2,500 poor and nonpoor African American, Latino, and white residents in Chicago's poor neighborhoods; a more focused survey of 175 participants who were reinterviewed and

---

Excerpts from "Jobless Poverty: A New Form of Social Dislocation in the Inner-City Ghetto" in *A Nation Divided: Diversity, Inequality, and Community in American Society,* edited by Phyllis Moen, Donna Dempster-McClain, and Henry A. Walker. 1999. Ithaca, NY: Cornell University Press. Used by permission of the publishers, Cornell University Press.

answered open-ended questions; a survey of 179 employers selected to reflect distribution of employment across industry and firm size in the Chicago metropolitan areas; and comprehensive ethnographic research, including participant-observation research and life-history interviews by ten research assistants in a representative sample of inner-city neighborhoods.

The first of the two remaining projects also included extensive data: a survey of a representative sample of 546 black mothers and up to two of their adolescent children (aged eleven to sixteen—or 887 adolescents) in working-class, middle-class, and high-poverty neighborhoods; a survey of a representative sample of 500 respondents from two high-joblessness neighborhoods on the South Side of Chicago; and six focus-group discussions involving the residents and former residents of these neighborhoods.

Jobless Ghettos

The jobless poverty of today stands in sharp contrast to previous periods. In 1950, a substantial portion of the urban black population was poor but they were working. Urban poverty was quite extensive but people held jobs. However, as we entered the 1990s most adults in many inner-city ghetto neighborhoods were not working. For example, in 1950 a significant majority of adults held jobs in a typical week in the three neighborhoods that represent the historic core of the Black Belt in Chicago—Douglas, Grand Boulevard, and Washington Park. But by 1990, only four in ten in Douglas worked in a typical week, one in three in Washington Park, and one in four in Grand Boulevard.[1] In 1950, 69 percent of all males aged fourteen and older who lived in these three neighborhoods worked in a typical week, and in 1960, 64 percent of this group were so employed.

However, by 1990 only 37 percent of all males aged sixteen and over held jobs in a typical week in these three neighborhoods.

The disappearance of work has had negative effects not only on individuals and families, but on the social life of neighborhoods as well. Inner-city joblessness is a severe problem that is often overlooked or obscured when the focus is mainly on poverty and its consequences. Despite increases in the concentration of poverty since 1970, inner cities have always featured high levels of poverty. But the levels of inner-city joblessness reached during the first half of the 1990s were unprecedented.

Joblessness versus Informal Work Activity

I should note that when I speak of "joblessness" I am not solely referring to official unemployment. The unemployment rate represents only the percentage of workers in the *official* labor force—that is, those who are *actively* looking for work. It does not include those who are outside of or have dropped out of the labor market, including the nearly six million males aged twenty-five to sixty who appeared in the census statistics but were not recorded in the labor market statistics in 1990 (Thurow 1990).

These uncounted males in the labor market are disproportionately represented in the inner-city ghettos. Accordingly, in *When Work Disappears,* I use a more appropriate measure of joblessness, a measure that takes into account both official unemployment and non–labor-force participation. That measure is the employment-to-population ratio, which corresponds to the percentage of adults aged sixteen and older who are working. Using the employment-to-population ratio we find, for example, that in 1990 only one in three adults aged sixteen and older held a job in the ghetto poverty areas of Chicago, areas representing roughly 425,000 men, women, and children. And in the ghetto tracts of the nation's one hundred largest cities, for every ten adults who did not hold a job in a typical week in 1990 there were only six employed persons (Kasarda 1993).

The consequences of high neighborhood joblessness are more devastating than those of high neighborhood poverty. A neighborhood in which people are poor but employed is much different than a neighborhood in which people are poor and jobless. *When Work Disappears* shows that many of today's problems in the inner-city ghetto neighborhoods—crime, family dissolution, welfare, low levels of social organization, and so on—are fundamentally a consequence of the disappearance of work.

It should be clear that when I speak of the disappearance of work, I am referring to the declining involvement in or lack of attachment to the formal labor market. It could be argued that, in the general sense of the term, "joblessness" does not necessarily mean "nonwork." In other words, to be officially unemployed or officially outside the labor market does not mean that one is totally removed from all forms of work activity. Many people who are officially jobless are nonetheless involved in informal kinds of work activity, ranging from unpaid housework to work that draws income from the informal or illegal economies.

Housework is work, baby-sitting is work, even drug dealing is work. However, what contrasts work in the formal economy with work activity in the informal and illegal economies is that work in the formal economy is characterized by, indeed calls for, greater regularity and consistency in schedules and hours. Work schedules and hours are formalized. The demands for discipline are greater. It is true that some work activities outside the formal economy also call for discipline and regular schedules. Several studies reveal that

the social organization of the drug industry is driven by discipline and a work ethic, however perverse. However, as a general rule, work in the informal and illegal economies is far less governed by norms or expectations that place a premium on discipline and regularity. For all these reasons, when I speak of the disappearance of work, I mean work in the formal economy, work that provides a framework for daily behavior because of the discipline, regularity, and stability that it imposes.

Effect of Joblessness on Routine and Discipline

In the absence of regular employment, a person lacks not only a place in which to work and the receipt of regular income but also a coherent organization of the present—that is, a system of concrete expectations and goals. Regular employment provides the anchor for the spatial and temporal aspects of daily life. It determines where you are going to be and when you are going to be there. In the absence of regular employment, life, including family life, becomes less coherent. Persistent unemployment and irregular employment hinder rational planning in daily life, a necessary condition of adaptation to an industrial economy (Bourdieu 1965).

Thus, a youngster who grows up in a family with a steady breadwinner and in a neighborhood in which most of the adults are employed will tend to develop some of the disciplined habits associated with stable or steady employment—habits that are reflected in the behavior of his or her parents and of other neighborhood adults. These might include attachment to a routine, a recognition of the hierarchy found in most work situations, a sense of personal efficacy attained through the routine management of financial affairs, endorsement of a system of personal and material rewards associated with dependability and responsibility, and so on. Accordingly, when this youngster enters the labor market, he or she has a distinct advantage over the youngsters who grow up in households without a steady breadwinner and in neighborhoods that are not organized around work—in other words, a milieu in which one is more exposed to the less disciplined habits associated with casual or infrequent work.

With the sharp recent rise of solo-parent families, black children who live in inner-city households are less likely to be socialized in a work environment for two main reasons. Their mothers, saddled with childcare responsibilities, can prevent a slide deeper into poverty by accepting welfare. Their fathers, removed from family responsibilities and obligations, are more likely to become idle as a response to restricted employment opportunities, which further weakens their influence in the household and attenuates their contact with the family. In short, the social and cultural responses to joblessness are reflected in the organization of family life and patterns of family formation; there they have implications for labor-force attachment as well.

Given the current policy debates that assign blame to the personal shortcomings of the jobless, we need to understand their behavior as responses and adaptations to chronic subordination, including behaviors that have evolved into cultural patterns. The social actions of the jobless—including their behavior, habits, skills, styles, orientations, attitudes—ought not to be analyzed as if they are unrelated to the broader structure of their opportunities and constraints that have evolved over time. This is not to argue that individuals and groups lack the freedom to make their own choices, engage in certain conduct, and develop certain styles and orientations; but I maintain that their decisions and actions occur within a context of constraints and opportunities that are drastically different from those in middle-class society.

Explanations of the Growth of Jobless Ghettos

What accounts for the growing proportion of jobless adults in inner-city communities? An easy explanation would be racial segregation. However, a race-specific argument is not sufficient to explain recent changes in such neighborhoods. After all, these historical Black Belt neighborhoods were *just as segregated by skin color in 1950* as they are today, yet the level of employment was much higher then. One has to account for the ways in which racial segregation interacts with other changes in society to produce the recent escalating rates of joblessness. Several factors stand out: the decreasing demand for low-skilled labor, the suburbanization of jobs, the social deterioration of ghetto neighborhoods, and negative employer attitudes. I discuss each of these factors next.

Decreasing Demand for Low-Skilled Labor

The disappearance of work in many inner-city neighborhoods is in part related to the nationwide decline in the fortunes of low-skilled workers. The sharp decline in the relative demand for unskilled labor has had a more adverse effect on blacks than on whites because a substantially larger proportion of African Americans are unskilled. Although the number of skilled blacks (including managers, professionals, and technicians) has increased sharply in the last several years, the proportion of those who are unskilled remains large, because the black population, burdened by cumulative experiences of racial restrictions, was overwhelmingly unskilled just several decades ago (Schwartzman 1997).[2]

The factors involved in the decreased relative demand for unskilled labor include changes in skilled-based technology, the rapid growth in college enrollment that increased the supply and reduced the relative cost of skilled labor, and the growing internationalization of economic activity, including trade liberalization policies, which reduced the price of imports and raised the output of export industries (Schwartzman 1997). The increased output of export industries aids skilled workers, simply because they are heavily represented in export industries. But increasing imports, especially those from developing countries that compete with labor-intensive industries (for example, apparel, textile, toy, footwear, and some manufacturing industries), hurts unskilled labor (Schwartzman 1997).

Accordingly, inner-city blacks are experiencing a more extreme form of the economic marginality that has affected most unskilled workers in America since 1980. Unfortunately, there is a tendency among policy makers, black leaders, and scholars alike to separate the economic problems of the ghetto from the national and international trends affecting American families and neighborhoods. If the economic problems of the ghetto are defined solely in racial terms they can be isolated and viewed as only requiring race-based solutions as proposed by those on the left, or as only requiring narrow political solutions with subtle racial connotations (such as welfare reform), as strongly proposed by those on the right.

Overemphasis on Racial Factors

Race continues to be a factor that aggravates inner-city black employment problems as we shall soon see. But the tendency to overemphasize the racial factors obscures other more fundamental forces that have sharply increased inner-city black joblessness. As the late black economist Vivian Henderson put it several years ago, "[I]t is as if racism having put blacks in their economic place steps aside to watch changes in the economy destroy that place" (Henderson 1975, 54). To repeat, the concentrated joblessness of the inner-city poor represents the most dramatic form of the growing economic dislocations among the unskilled stemming in large measure from changes in the organization of the economy, including the global economy.

Suburbanization of Jobs

But inner-city workers face an additional problem: the growing suburbanization of jobs. Most ghetto residents cannot afford an automobile and therefore have to rely on public transit systems that make the connection between inner-city neighborhoods and suburban job locations difficult and time consuming.

Although studies based on data collected before 1970 showed no consistent or convincing effects on black employment as a consequence of this spatial mismatch, the employment of inner-city blacks relative to suburban blacks has clearly deteriorated since then. Recent research (conducted mainly by urban labor economists) strongly shows that the decentralization of employment is continuing and that employment in manufacturing, most of which is already suburbanized, has decreased in central cities, particularly in the Northeast and Midwest (Holzer 1996).

Blacks living in central cities have less access to employment (as measured by the ratio of jobs to people and the average travel time to and from work) than do central-city whites. Moreover, unlike most other groups of workers across the urban-suburban divide, less-educated central-city blacks receive lower wages than suburban blacks who have similar levels of education. And the decline in earnings of central-city blacks is related to the decentralization of employment—that is, the movement of jobs from the cities to the suburbs—in metropolitan areas (Holzer 1996).

Social Deterioration of Ghetto Neighborhoods

Changes in the class, racial, and demographic composition of inner-city neighborhoods have also contributed to the high percentage of jobless adults in these neighborhoods. Because of the steady out-migration of more advantaged families, the proportion of nonpoor families and prime-age working adults has decreased sharply in the typical inner-city ghetto since 1970 (Wilson 1987). In the face of increasing and prolonged joblessness, the declining proportion of nonpoor families and the overall depopulation has made it increasingly difficult to sustain basic neighborhood institutions or to achieve adequate levels of social organization. The declining presence of working- and middle-class blacks has also deprived ghetto neighborhoods of key structural and cultural resources. Structural resources include residents with income high enough to sustain neighborhood services, and cultural resources include conventional role models for neighborhood children.

On the basis of our research in Chicago, it appears that what many high jobless neighborhoods have in common is a relatively high degree of social integration (high levels of local neighboring while being relatively isolated from contacts in the broader mainstream society) and low levels of informal social control (feelings that they have little control over their immediate environment, including the environment's negative influences on their children). In such areas, not only are children at risk because of the lack of informal social controls, they are also disadvantaged because the social interaction among neighbors tends to be confined to those whose skills, styles, orientations, and habits are not as conducive to promoting positive social outcomes (academic success, pro-social behavior, employment in the formal labor market, etc.) as those in more stable neighborhoods. Although the close interaction among neighbors in such areas may be useful in devising strategies, disseminating information, and developing styles of behavior that are helpful in a ghetto milieu (teaching children to avoid eye-to-eye contact with strangers and to develop a tough demeanor in the public sphere for self-protection), they may be less effective in promoting the welfare of children in society at large.

Despite being socially integrated, the residents in Chicago's ghetto neighborhoods shared a feeling that they had little informal social control over the children in their environment. A primary reason is the absence of a strong organizational capacity or an institutional resource base that would provide an extra layer of social organization in their neighborhoods. It is easier for parents to control the behavior of the children in their neighborhoods when a strong institutional resource base exists and when the links between community institutions such as churches, schools, political organizations, businesses, and civic clubs are strong or secure. The higher the density and stability of formal organizations, the less illicit activities such as drug trafficking, crime, prostitution, and the formation of gangs can take root in the neighborhood.

Few Community Institutions

A weak institutional resource base is what distinguishes high jobless inner-city neighborhoods from stable middle-class and working-class areas. As one resident of a high jobless neighborhood on the South Side of Chicago put it, "Our children, you know, seems to be more at risk than any other children there is, because there's no library for them to go to. There's not a center they can go to, there's no field house that they can go into. There's nothing. There's nothing. There's nothing at all." Parents in high jobless neighborhoods have a much more difficult task controlling the behavior of their adolescents and preventing them from getting involved in activities detrimental to pro-social development. Given the lack of organizational capacity and a weak institutional base, some parents choose to protect their children by isolating them from activities in the neighborhood, including avoiding contact and interaction with neighborhood families. Wherever possible, and often with great difficulty when one considers the problems of transportation and limited financial resources, they attempt to establish contacts and cultivate relations with individuals, families, and institutions, such as church groups, schools, and community recreation programs, outside their neighborhood. A note of caution is necessary, though. It is just as indefensible to treat inner-city residents as super heroes who overcome racist oppression as it is to view them as helpless victims. We should, however, appreciate the range of choices, including choices representing cultural influences, that are available to inner-city residents who live under constraints that most people in the larger society do not experience.

Effect of Joblessness on Marriage and Family

It is within the context of labor-force attachment that the public policy discussion on welfare reform and family values should be couched. The research that we have conducted in Chicago suggests that as employment prospects recede, the foundation for stable relationships becomes weaker over time. More permanent relationships such as marriage give way to temporary liaisons that result in broken unions, out-of-wedlock pregnancies, and, to a lesser extent, separation and divorce. The changing norms concerning marriage in the larger society reinforce the movement toward temporary

liaisons in the inner city, and therefore economic considerations in marital decisions take on even greater weight. Many inner-city residents have negative outlooks toward marriage, outlooks that are developed in and influenced by an environment featuring persistent joblessness.

The disrupting effect of joblessness on marriage and family causes poor inner-city blacks to be even more disconnected from the job market and discouraged about their role in the labor force. The economic marginality of the ghetto poor is cruelly reinforced, therefore, by conditions in the neighborhoods in which they live.

Negative Employer Attitudes

In the eyes of employers in metropolitan Chicago, the social conditions in the ghetto render inner-city blacks less desirable as workers, and therefore many are reluctant to hire them. One of the three studies that provided the empirical foundation for *When Work Disappears* included a representative sample of employers in the greater Chicago area who provided entry-level jobs. An overwhelming majority of these employers, both white and black, expressed negative views about inner-city ghetto workers, and many stated that they were reluctant to hire them. For example, a president of an inner-city manufacturing firm expressed a concern about employing residents from certain inner-city neighborhoods:

> If somebody gave me their address, uh, Cabrini Green I might unavoidably have some concerns. *Interviewer:* What would your concerns be? *Respondent:* That the poor guy probably would be frequently unable to get to work and . . . I probably would watch him more carefully even if it wasn't fair, than I would with somebody else. I know what I should do though is recognize that here's a guy

that is trying to get out of his situation and probably will work harder than somebody else who's already out of there and he might be the best one around here. But I, I think I would have to struggle accepting that premise at the beginning. (Wilson 1996, field notes)

In addition to qualms about the neighborhood milieu of inner-city residents, the employers frequently mentioned concerns about applicants' language skills and educational training. An employer from a computer software firm in Chicago expressed the view "that in many businesses the ability to meet the public is paramount and you do not talk street talk to the buying public. Almost all your black welfare people talk street talk. And who's going to sit them down and change their speech patterns?" (Wilson 1996, field notes). A Chicago real estate broker made a similar point:

A lot of times I will interview applicants who are black, who are sort of lower class. . . . They'll come to me and I cannot hire them because their language skills are so poor. Their speaking voice for one thing is poor . . . they have no verbal facility with the language . . . and these . . . you know, they just don't know how to speak and they'll say "salesmens" instead of "salesmen" and that's a problem. . . . They don't know punctuation, they don't know how to use correct grammar, and they cannot spell. And I can't hire them. And I feel bad about that and I think they're being very disadvantaged by the Chicago Public School system. (Wilson 1996, field notes)

Another respondent defended his method of screening out most job applicants on the telephone on the basis of their use of "grammar and English":

I have every right to say that that's a requirement for this job. I don't care if you're pink, black, green, yellow or orange, I demand someone who speaks well. You want to tell me that I'm a bigot, fine, call me a bigot. I know blacks, you don't even know they're black. (Wilson 1996, field notes)

Finally, an inner-city banker claimed that many blacks in the ghetto "simply cannot read. When you're talking our type of business, that disqualifies them immediately, we don't have a job here that doesn't require that somebody have minimum reading and writing skills" (Wilson 1996, field notes).

How should we interpret the negative attitudes and actions of employers? To what extent do they represent an aversion to blacks *per se* and to what degree do they reflect judgments based on the job-related skills and training of inner-city blacks in a changing labor market? I should point out that the statements made by the African American employers concerning the qualifications of inner-city black workers did not differ significantly from those of the white employers. Whereas 74 percent of all the white employers who responded to the open-ended questions expressed negative views of the job-related traits of inner-city blacks, 80 percent of the black employers did so as well.

This raises a question about the meaning and significance of race in certain situations—in other words, how race intersects with other factors. A key hypothesis in this connection is that given the recent shifts in the economy, employers are looking for workers with a broad range of abilities: "hard" skills (literacy, numerical ability, basic mechanical ability, and other testable attributes) and "soft" skills (personalities suitable to the work environment, good grooming, group-oriented work behaviors, etc.). While hard skills are the product of education and training—benefits that are apparently in short supply in inner-city schools—soft skills are strongly tied to culture, and are therefore shaped by the harsh environment of the inner-city ghetto.

For example, our research revealed that many parents in the inner-city ghetto neighborhoods of Chicago wanted their children not to make eye-to-eye contact with strangers and to develop a tough demeanor when interacting with people on the streets. While such behaviors are helpful for survival in the ghetto, they hinder successful interaction in mainstream society.

Statistical Discrimination

If employers are indeed reacting to the difference in skills between white and black applicants, it becomes increasingly difficult to discuss the motives of employers: are they rejecting inner-city black applicants out of overt racial discrimination or on the basis of qualifications?

Nonetheless, many of the selective recruitment practices do represent what economists call "statistical discrimination": employers make assumptions about the inner-city black workers *in general* and reach decisions based on those assumptions before they have had a chance to review systematically the qualifications of an individual applicant. The net effect is that many black inner-city applicants are never given the chance to prove their qualifications on an individual level because they are systematically screened out by the selective recruitment process.

Statistical discrimination, although representing elements of class bias against poor workers in the inner city, is clearly a matter of race both directly and indirectly. Directly, the selective recruitment patterns effectively screen out far more black workers from the inner city than Hispanic or white workers from the same types of backgrounds. But indirectly, race is also a factor, even in those decisions to deny employment to inner-city black workers on the basis of objective and thorough evaluations of their qualifications. The hard and soft skills among inner-city blacks that do not match the current needs of the labor market are products of racially segregated communities, communities that have historically featured widespread social constraints and restricted opportunities.

Thus the job prospects of inner-city workers have diminished not only because of the decreasing relative demand for low-skilled labor in the United States economy, the suburbanization of jobs, and the social deterioration of ghetto neighborhoods, but also because of negative employer attitudes. This combination of factors presents a real challenge to policy makers. Indeed, considering the narrow range of social policy options in the "balance-the-budget" political climate, how can we immediately alleviate the inner-city jobs problem—a problem which will undoubtedly grow when the new welfare reform bill takes full effect and creates a situation that will be even more harmful to inner-city children and adolescents?

Public Policy Dilemmas

What are the implications of these studies on public policy? A key issue is public-sector employment. If firms in the private sector cannot hire or refuse to hire low-skilled adults who are willing to take minimum-wage jobs, then policy makers should consider a policy of public-sector employment-of-last-resort. Indeed, until current changes in the labor market are reversed or until the skills of the next generation of workers can be upgraded before they enter the labor market, many workers, especially those who are not in the official labor force, will not be able to find jobs unless the government becomes an employer-of-last-resort (Danziger and Gottschalk 1995). This argument applies especially to low-skilled inner-city black workers. It is bad enough that they face the problem of shifts in labor-market demand shared by all low-skilled workers; it is even worse that they confront negative employer perceptions about their work-related skills and attitudes.

For all these reasons, the passage of the 1996 welfare reform bill, which did not include a program of job creation, could have very negative social consequences in the inner city. Unless something is done to enhance the employment opportunities of inner-city welfare recipients who reach the time limit for the receipt of welfare, they will flood a pool already filled with low-skilled, jobless workers. . . .

The Need for Action

At the same time that the new welfare law has generated a greater need for work opportunities, high jobless urban and rural areas will experience more difficulty in placing individuals in private-sector jobs. To create work opportunities for welfare recipients, these areas will therefore have to "rely more heavily upon job creation strategies in the public and private non-profit sectors" (Center on Budget and Policy Priorities 1996, 4). Although the placement of disadvantaged workers in private-sector jobs can help contain the overall costs in some communities (including many jobless ghetto areas and depressed rural areas) a mainly private-sector initiative will not be sufficient to generate enough jobs to accommodate the large oversupply of low-skilled individuals.

West Virginia, a state that has been plagued with a severe shortage of work opportunities, has provided community service jobs to recipients of welfare for several years. In Wisconsin, Governor Thompson's welfare reform plan envisions community service jobs for many parents in the more depressed areas of the state, and the New Hope program in Milwaukee provides community service jobs for those unable to find employment in the private sector (Center on Budget and Policy Priorities 1996). It is especially important that this mixed strategy include a plan to make *adequate* monies available to localities or communities with high jobless

and welfare dependency rates. Three billion dollars for this purpose is hardly sufficient.

Obviously, as more people become employed and gain work experience, they will have a better chance of finding jobs in the private sector when jobs become available. The attitudes of employers toward inner-city workers could change, in part because they would be dealing with job applicants who have steady work experience and who could furnish references from their previous supervisors. Children are more likely to be socialized in a work-oriented environment and to develop the job readiness skills that are seen as important even for entry-level jobs.

Thus, given the recent welfare reform legislation, *adequate* strategies to enhance the employment opportunities of inner-city residents should be contemplated, strategies that would be adequately financed and designed to address the employment problems of low-skilled workers not only in periods of tight labor markets, but, even more important, in periods when the labor market is slack. With the sharp reduction in the federal deficit and the talk about an economic surplus in the near future, now is an ideal time to urge the president and to press Congress to develop such strategies. If steps are not taken soon to enhance the job prospects of hundreds of thousands of inner-city residents, including welfare recipients who reach their time limit for receipt of welfare, we could be facing major social dislocations in many urban areas, especially if the current economic recovery ends in the near future.

NOTES

1. The figures on adult employment are based on calculations from data provided by the 1990 U.S. Bureau of the Census (1993) and the *Local Community Fact Book for Chicago—1950* (1953) and the *Local Community Fact Book for Chicago—1960* (1963). The adult employment rates represent the number of employed individuals (aged fourteen and older in 1950 and sixteen and older in 1990) among the total number of

adults in a given area. Those who are not employed include both the individuals who are members of the labor force but are not working and those who have dropped out or are not part of the labor force.

2. The economist David Schwartzman defines "unskilled workers to include operators, fabricators, and laborers, and those in service occupations, including private household workers, those working in protective service occupations, food service, and cleaning and building service." On the basis of this definition he estimates that 80 percent of all black workers and 38 percent of all white workers were unskilled in 1950. By 1990, 46 percent of black workers and 27 percent of white workers were employed in unskilled occupations (Schwartzman 1997).

REFERENCES

Bourdieu, Pierre. 1965. *Travail et Travailleurs en Algerie.* Paris: Editions Mouton.

Center on Budget and Policy Priorities. 1996. *The Administration's $3 Billion Jobs Proposal.* Washington, DC: Center on Budget and Policy Priorities.

Danziger, Sheldon H., and Peter Gottschalk. 1995. *America Unequal.* Cambridge, MA: Harvard University Press.

Henderson, Vivian. 1975. "Race, Economics, and Public Policy." *Crisis* 83(Fall):50–55.

Holzer, Harry J. 1987. "Informal Job Search and Black Youth Unemployment." *American Economic Review* 77:446–52.

———. 1996. *What Employers Want: Job Prospects for Less-Educated Workers.* New York: Russell Sage.

Kasarda, John D. 1993. "Inner-City Concentrated Poverty and Neighborhood Distress: 1970–1990." *Housing Policy Debate* 4(3):253–302.

Local Community Fact Book for Chicago—1950. 1953. Chicago: Community Inventory, University of Chicago.

Local Community Fact Book for Chicago—1960. 1963. Chicago: Community Inventory, University of Chicago.

Schwartzman, David. 1997. *Black Unemployment: Part of Unskilled Unemployment.* Westport, CT: Greenwood.

Thurow, Lester. 1990. "The Crusade That's Killing Prosperity." *American Prospect* March/April: 54–59.

U.S. Bureau of the Census. 1993. *Census of Population: Detailed Characteristics of the Population.* Washington, DC: U.S. Government Printing Office.

Wilson, William Julius. 1987. *The Truly Disadvantaged: The Inner City, The Underclass, and Public Policy.* Chicago: University of Chicago Press.

———. 1996. *When Work Disappears: The World of the New Urban Poor.* New York: Alfred A. Knopf.

21

Culture, Commerce, and Gender
The Feminization of Book Editing

Barbara F. Reskin

For centuries book editing was a "gentlemen's profession" (Tebbel, 1972: 207), yet in the 1970s women made such large gains in the occupation that some have speculated that editing is becoming a women's ghetto (Geracimos, 1974:25). How can we explain women's gains? This [reading] examines the changes in the publishing industry and the editorial role that have led to women's increasing representation among editors. . . .

Women in Publishing

Until the 1960s, publishing was "predominantly a business of middle-aged and older men" (Tebbel, 1975:101), but between 1963 and 1968, women accounted for 62 percent of employment growth in publishing (compared with 52 percent for the printing and publishing industry overall and 35 percent for all manufacturing), and during this period the numbers of men and women employed in the industry rose by 19 percent and 41 percent, respectively (U.S. Bureau of Labor Statistics, cited in *Publishers Weekly,* 1971:69). By 1980, publishing's sex composition had changed (Tebbel, 1981:728), and observers were calling it a "women's business" (Caplette, l982a:148). By the late 1970s and early 1980s, estimates put women's employment share at about two-thirds of the industry's workforce (Association of American Publishers, 1977:27; Cornelius, 1983:34; U.S. Bureau of the Census, 1984: Table 4).

Sex Segregation in Publishing

Even when men dominated the industry, publishing employed women for some jobs. While college publishing was predominantly male, scholarly publishing was so to a lesser degree (university presses could take advantage of the captive labor market that faculty wives represented). Women were concentrated in children's publishing, in mass-market paperbacks (Coser et al., 1982)—which enjoyed little status and lacked a "cultural" image because these houses reissued hard-cover editions and published lightly edited genre books, such as mysteries and historical romances—and in certain jobs in trade publishing.

Men dominated marketing and management, the highest-paying jobs in the industry, and except in paperback publishing the majority of editors—particularly acquisitions editors—were men (Strainchamps, 1974:133; Caplette, 1982a:157). Women were typically relegated to lower-level editorial jobs (copyeditor, editorial assistant), normally behind-the-scenes positions (Caplette, 1982a:154). Most began their careers as manuscript readers, secretaries, or editorial assistants, jobs whose low pay and clerical duties could attract few men (Tebbel, 1981:728).

Other female ghettos were the noneditorial "service" jobs of publicity and subsidiary rights (Geracimos, 1974:27; Caplette, 1982a:158). Selling subsidiary rights is complex, detailed work but—until recently—not especially profitable (Tebbel, 1975:140). A former subsidiary-rights director described it as "a pro forma job: . . . sending out notes, keeping track of things, and then the [male] editor-in-chief would step in to do the razzle-dazzle deal" (*Publishers Weekly*, 1979). Publicity, according to a former publicity director, "was naturally a female job" because it involved "lots of handholding, nurturing, socializing," and like subsidiary rights it was not considered a moneymaking function until the 1970s.

Until 1970, publishers rarely hired women as sales representatives, the traditional entry-level job for college editors; before that, "it was almost inconceivable that a woman should go on the road alone" (Strainchamps, 1974:159–60). Publishers feared, informants explained, that women would find the books too heavy, would not be able to find the colleges, or would get raped—or that professors would feel insulted if a woman called on them (Strain-champs, 1974:155). One editor recounted that a university press denied her a sales job in 1964, although she had six years editorial experience, because they "couldn't allow a pretty young lady to travel alone" even two or three days a month. Another interviewee recalled that when her employer transferred a woman to college sales in the mid-1960s, the male representatives "tormented her" until she quit. She added, "It was an object lesson to us all."

The Sex Composition of Editors

Although women were underrepresented in editorial jobs until the late 1960s and early 1970s, they have held some editorial positions since early in the century. About the time of World War I a survey of 82 publishing firms revealed that 14 percent of the 1,400 female employees were working in editorial jobs (Tebbel, 1975:177). Yet a world war later, publisher Henry Holt still described editors as male (Bechtold, 1946:14). Industry histories (Cerf, 1977; Tebbel, 1978) rarely mentioned women editors. Bechtold (1946:14) noted that women editors earned less than men and had to wait longer and work harder to succeed. Women with editorial titles usually copyedited or styled manuscripts for publication. Only in children's books was editing fully open to women (Laskey, 1969:13); indeed, men rarely held these jobs through the early 1960s (Tebbel, 1978).

Many female secretaries and editorial assistants did editorial work without the title, including screening the thousands of unsolicited manuscripts that swamped publishers (see, e.g., Caplette, 1982a:152–54). The secretarial and editorial assistant jobs were in a secondary labor market with a nonexistent or weakly defined career ladder to full editorial positions (Caplette, 1979), though finding a promising book in the "slushpile" of unsolicited manuscripts sometimes meant a step up the editorial ladder. Moreover, the ratio of aspirants to openings was—and remains—enormous. It took women extraordinary effort to get out of the secretarial–assistant ghetto, and few female editorial assistants became editors (Caplette, 1982a:161; Tebbel, 1987). In contrast, the few men who began as assistants moved up rapidly (Caplette, 1982a:154). Thus, the considerable sex segregation across editorial jobs revealed in a survey made by Chicago Women in Publishing (1973:2) probably reflected the industry as a whole.

The educational sector of the industry did not resemble trade publishing with respect to women's access to editorial jobs. College publishers required sales experience of editors because of the importance of marketing in college sales; sales representatives acted as "field editors" who scouted out potential authors (Coser et al., 1982:20, 102). As a result, men's monopoly over sales jobs ensured that editing was also their preserve (Caplette, 1979:5). No large college firms employed women as acquisitions editors in major disciplines until early in the 1970s, and late in the decade three-quarters of college editors were still men (Coser et al., 1982). In school publishing the sex ratio was more balanced because firms hired former teachers as editors. Scholarly—particularly university—presses employed relatively more women than did other sectors (Powell, 1985:30).

Women's Increased Representation Among Editors

By 1970 just under half the editors employed in book and periodical publishing were women (U.S. Bureau of the Census, 1972: Table 8), but only 5,025 of these 26,745 workers edited books (Association of American Publishers, 1977:24). Unfortunately, no data enumerate book editors by sex, but by all accounts women were underrepresented, and female editors were concentrated in school and paperback publishing or in low-level editorial positions in trade, college, and scholarly houses. During the 1970s women made considerable strides in editing in most sectors of the industry; by mid-decade their number had increased so much that a *Publishers Weekly* article (Geracimos, 1974:25) called 1974 "the year of the woman" in trade publishing (see also Tebbel, 1975:101), and in 1978 a survey of 117 publishing employees showed women outnumbering men two to one in editorial acquisitions and manuscript editing (Caplette, 1982a:155). However, the wage gap in one large publishing house, in which women editors averaged 54 cents for each dollar men received, indicates that although two-thirds of its 195 ed-

itors were female, they either held lower-level positions or were paid less than male editors in the same jobs (Osterman, 1979). Nonetheless, by 1980 women made up more than 57 percent of the 36,161 editors employed in book and periodical publishing (U.S. Bureau of the Census, 1984: Table 4), although again we do not know their proportion among the approximately 10,000 *book* editors (Wright, 1984:589). Caplette (1982b:158) observed that "the gradual increase of women editors in the last decade has, within the last few years, become an upsurge—nearly half of trade and mass-market paperback editors are now women." Confirming her impressions are those of more than forty industry informants who agreed that the 1970s brought dramatic progress for women in editing and other publishing jobs.

Explaining Women's Progress in Editing

Although women advanced in many occupations in the 1970s, their gains in editing outstripped those in most other occupations. To account for their progress, I used a variety of documentary data and published sources, including memoirs of editors and publishers, scholarly analyses of the publishing industry, articles from *Publishers Weekly* between 1968 and 1987, and forty-one interviews, including eleven that Michele Caplette (1981) conducted in 1978. I found that changes in the publishing industry and the editorial role set the stage for women's gains by altering both the supply of male would-be editors and the demand for women.

Industrial Growth and Change

First in the chain of events that transformed publishing was its pronounced growth over fifteen to twenty years, beginning about

1960 (Lofquist, 1970:6, 9; Powell, 1985:5). Rising personal income and educational levels, unprecedented federal investments in public education, and the information explosion (Powell, 1982:33) stimulated record book sales. Profits led existing firms to expand their lists and attracted new firms to the industry (Altbach, 1975:11; Dessauer, 1982:34). At least three hundred new firms set up shop between 1967 and 1978 (Noble, 1978:35); between 1972 and 1977 the number of firms increased by almost half (Gilroy, 1980:8, 11), and between 1954 and 1977 the number more than doubled (Powell, 1985:213). Both title output and sales volume showed increases of 50 to 100 percent between 1959 and 1980 (Powell, l985:4).

These two decades of expansion set the stage for dramatic changes in the culture of publishing. Rapid growth and solid profits led to a spate of mergers in the late 1960s and again in the late 1970s and middle 1980s (Gilroy, 1980:12) and inevitably drew the interest of nonpublishing firms and conglomerates looking for profitable acquisitions (Tebbel, 1981:733). Conglomerization, which hit publishing in the early 1970s, transformed the industry (Navasky, 1973b); it "became less of a gentleman's industry and more of a business" that emphasized "the bottom line" (Galassi, 1980:28).

Although concern with profits was not new, according to industry analyst John Dessauer (1982:36), "it has become more virulent [as] opportunities for making a quick buck have increased with a growing market, and the big-money ownership that has entered the field is more easily tempted by the quick buck than were the other-worldly types that used to constitute the industry's core." As Powell (1985:6) noted, "Outside ownership brought modern management practices that fundamentally altered the craftlike nature of book publishing." Commercialization eroded publishing's reputation as an industry outside the fray, and

in so doing, transformed editorial work. As a result, it also transformed the publishing workforce.

Changes in Editorial Work

To understand the changes in the role of editor that figure importantly in women's gains in the occupation, I begin by examining the traditional editorial role. The predecessors of modern editors were readers— often established writers or academicians (Lane, 1975:38)—whom publishers paid to evaluate manuscripts and help writers improve their work (Sifton, 1985:43). Twentieth-century editors perform similar functions: acquisitions editors select manuscripts and work with authors in completing them, and manuscript editors concentrate on the production side (Lane, 1975:35). Of the two functions, producing books enjoys less status and lower wages than the more exciting job of acquiring them (Carter, 1984:24). However, acquisitions can be demanding work in many sectors of the industry. Editors typically handle upward of forty books a year, a few of which are culled from thousands of unsolicited manuscripts (Rawson and Dolin, 1985:28). A book's existence and ultimate success depend on its editor's efforts to sell the manuscript to the editorial board and the marketing people (Rawson and Dolin, 1985:25). As the publishers' representatives, editors work closely with authors to negotiate contracts, monitor progress, suggest revisions (Sifton, 1985:43–45), and offer encouragement. The last function may extend to serving as friend, cheerleader, confessor, and psychotherapist (Giroux, 1982:55; Dong, 1984:22); some (Canfield, 1969:27; Rawson and Dolin, 1985:23) have characterized editors as surrogate parents. "You hear from authors on weekends, . . . they may even end up living in your house" (Dong, 1984:26). Editorial responsibilities include looking out for an author's interests within the firm: translating royalty statements, arranging advances, touting the book. Some editors also emphasize the importance of subordinating their egos to "literature" and to authors: "An editor . . . must be willing to play second fiddle" (Lehman, 1987:89; also see Evans, 1979:31).

Editors have written extensively about the qualifications their work demands. Common themes depict the ideal editor as charming, sophisticated, and willing to take risks; as a person with taste, intuition, and empathy who can be persuasive yet tactful in dealing with "difficult" authors and who is willing to make her- or himself an "agreeable nuisance" (Association of American Publishers, 1977:22; Galassi, 1980:29; Giroux, 1982:55; Carter, 1984:24–25). Besides all this, in most sectors of the industry, editors must be willing to work long hours for sometimes notoriously low salaries.

The shift to outside ownership strained the traditionally amiable relations between publishers and editors and profoundly altered editorial work. The pursuit of the blockbuster in large trade houses sharply circumscribed editorial autonomy in acquisition decisions (Wendroff, 1980): "Editors could no longer simply sign a book and then tell their house to sell it" (Powell, 1982:47). By 1973, "fewer and fewer editors [had] the right to commission books without first securing the approval of a Publishing Committee, and most often it [was] the editor-in-chief who [made] the presentation to the committee rather than the editor" (Navasky, 1973a). The new emphasis on packaging and sales gave publicity, marketing, and subsidiary-rights people much more sway in editorial decisions (Phalon, 1981:253; Powell, 1982:47), thereby eroding editorial autonomy. Bringing the views of the corporate boardroom into the editorial side also discouraged creative risk taking (Tebbel, 1981:733), an important source of satisfaction in editorial work. Instead, edi-

tors were under pressure to sign up best sellers or, in the smaller and still-independent houses, to acquire more books (Powell, 1982). An editor who noted that publication committees' choices are based largely on budget considerations wondered "whether editors have as much power as they once did, whether their power is more circumscribed, and . . . who controls what editors do" (Geracimos, 1974:25).

A second consequence of outside ownership was the deterioration of the traditional close relationship between editors and their authors. With more money at stake, authors changed houses frequently in pursuit of better deals and hired agents or lawyers to represent them in negotiating with editors (Powell, 1982). The growing role of literary agents in getting books published (Bannon, 1972:102; Doebler, 1978:27) further circumscribed editor–author contacts. Agents are more influential than editors in acquiring books and have assumed other traditional editorial functions in the publication process (Gabriel, 1989). Besides having less close contact with authors, editors interact less with other editors, thus fragmenting "the old sense of a community of bookmen" (Powell 1982:49).

The absorption of book publishing by other media also altered editors' duties. Arranging the fat subsidiary-rights agreements or movie tie-ins essential for big trade profits meant that editors "had to change their habits and spend more time working on deals." In his insightful analysis of the impact of outside ownership on book publishing, Powell (1982:48–49) quoted an editor whose small firm had been acquired by a large diversified publishing corporation: "After-[ward] I never had time to see authors. I spent all my time in meetings with various corporate executives and 'selling' our imprint within the parent company." After being promoted to head the trade department in a large house, another editor Powell interviewed, who had formerly helped his authors develop their work, said that he was "in danger of becoming simply a well-paid retailer of ideas and entertainment."

New ownership patterns also threatened editors' job security, the only economic compensation for publishing's low wages. The frequent mergers of the 1960s and 1970s often precipitated corporate shake-ups that cost editors their jobs (Evans, 1978:45; Carter, 1983:8). The corporate focus on performance further eroded job security (Tebbel, 1981:733) and forced editors to compete with corporate executive staff from outside the publishing industry for the only top-level positions to which senior editors could aspire—publisher and director.

Changes in the Supply of Would-Be Editors

For most of this century, publishing's glamour and its image as a "gentlemen's profession" were sufficient to attract more than enough qualified recruits. Then, although industrial expansion heightened the demand for editorial workers, the concomitants of that growth reduced the industry's attractiveness to its traditional workforce: talented young men from high socioeconomic backgrounds.

Dwindling Attraction for Men Publishing's primary draw for such men had been entree into the world of culture without the taint of commerce. But commerce is exactly what outside ownership meant. At the same time, as we have seen, editorial work lost many of the features that had compensated non-wealthy workers for low wages. To make matters worse, commerce was supplanting culture without conferring the usual economic incentives of commercial careers. Although editorial wages had always been low, there were other compensations. One editor said, "I consider the right to publish books which don't make money a part of my salary" (Navasky, 1973a). Just as some edi-

tors lost that right, wages may have actually declined (Tebbel, 1981:728; Rosenthal et al., 1986). In 1982, entry-level pay for editorial assistants was as low as $9,000 a year (Powell, 1985:225), and several people I interviewed noted that it is increasingly difficult, perhaps impossible, to survive—much less support a family—in Manhattan on editorial wages. An industry expert said, only partly in jest: "Only college graduates with rich parents willing to subsidize them can afford to work in editorial jobs any more" (Tebbel, 1981:728). In the face of society's growing emphasis on a fashionable life-style and the increasing tendency to use income as "the measure of a man," publishing's low wages further deterred men from pursuing editorial jobs (Tebbel, 1987). Better-paying media jobs (technical writing for high-tech companies, corporate public relations, film) and graduate school lured away talented men interested in communications.

With declining opportunities for mobility (Coser et al., 1982:112) and challenges to the traditional promotion practices that had given men a fast track to the top (Strainchamps, 1974), little remained to draw men to editorial work. A woman editor whom Caplette interviewed in 1978 remarked, "The average man thinks that he has a God-given right to start in as an editor." To the extent that this was true, entry-level jobs as editorial assistants (often a euphemism for secretary when these were women's jobs) attracted few men, and the industry increasingly relied on women as editorial assistants.

Increasing Supply of Women The gentility that had rendered publishing jobs appropriate for upper-status men did so too for "respectable" women whom traditional values encouraged to pursue cultural and aesthetic pursuits (Veblen, 1899). As a long-time assistant at Harper & Brothers said, "Young women getting out of college were so anxious to get a job in something they could be proud of that they would go into publishing and work for practically nothing" (Caplette, 1982a:151). Gender-role socialization further enhanced women's qualifications for publishing by schooling them in verbal and communications skills that equipped them with the facility and inclination to work with words and predisposed them toward the interpersonal work that editing often involved. One female holder of a master's degree said of her secretarial job in the mid-1950s, "I thought it was an honor to read books and write . . . flap copy" (Caplette, 1982a:169). Working in an intellectual and cultural industry situated in one of the metropolitan publishing "capitals" offered an added incentive to women graduating from prestigious eastern colleges, particularly before the 1970s, when few alternatives presented themselves to career-minded women.

The massive influx of women into the labor force during the 1970s expanded the pool of women available for editorial jobs, and the women's liberation movement encouraged women to consider occupations customarily reserved for men. Publishing attracted women also because it reputedly presented fewer obstacles than many other industries. Moreover, male occupations in predominantly female industries—particularly growing industries—tend to be more hospitable and hence more attractive to women (O'Farrell and Harlan, 1984). Thus, although women knew they faced discrimination in publishing, they probably realized that other commercial fields were worse (Dessauer, 1974:42). Publishing's low wages were less likely to deter women than men because their socialization had not encouraged them to maximize income. Because women lacked access to many better-paying jobs, they did not have to forgo more lucrative opportunities for jobs as assistants or editors, and their limited alternatives presum-

ably also explained their willingness to accept the changes that were making editorial work less desirable to men. As a result, the supply of female applicants remained unabated or grew, while that of males declined. Moreover, several interviewees contended that because publishing could no longer attract the most qualified men, female applicants often had better credentials than the males who did apply. If publishers chose the best applicant (as the new emphasis on profits dictated), it would probably be a woman.

The operation of the publishing labor market enhanced women's gains in editing. Several prestigious colleges close to the industry's centers in New York and Boston generated a supply of qualified women eager to work in publishing. The proliferation of publishing training programs (the first was established at Radcliffe) augmented that supply—by 1980 the director of the popular Denver Publishing Institute estimated that three-quarters of its students were women (Caplette, 1982a:169)—and helped women make contacts with employers. Most women began in entry-level positions on the editorial ladder. For years, sex discrimination and the high ratio of assistants to editors kept most secretaries and assistants from advancing. When the barriers to women began to crumble, however, most houses had a large number of talented, experienced women ready and able to edit books (Geracimos, 1974:25).

Even in college publishing, in the 1970s women successfully challenged both their exclusion from sales and the job ladder that made sales the only route to acquisitions (Association of American Publishers, 1977:16). Some companies began hiring women sales representatives, and others promoted to acquisitions one or two women who lacked sales experience. An early female sales representative speculated halfjokingly that her activity in a women's caucus at her firm may have won her a sought-after transfer to sales. The success of these first saleswomen who, as she said, "tore up the territory" eased the way for others, as well as putting women on the editorial ladder. Once college sales and acquisitions were recast as jobs to which women could aspire and the career ladder was restructured, a supply of women became available to work as acquisitions editors.

The Growing Demand for Women Editors

Two decades of growth in the publishing industry created a demand for additional personnel; nonproduction (white-collar) employment increased by approximately 50 percent during the 1970s. High turnover generated further demand for new editorial assistants and editors (Dong, 1980; Dessauer, 1982:34). Previously, publishing had never had trouble finding "eager bodies" to fill openings (Association of American Publishers, 1977:19), but as editing became less attractive to men, the demand for women grew. Publishing had long relied on women for many jobs, for reasons that are easy to understand. For one thing, gender-role socialization and a liberal-arts education qualified women for editorial jobs by encouraging literacy, deftness in interpersonal relations, and attention to detail—skills valued in an industry whose stock in trade is communicating ideas. As editor Elizabeth Sifton put it, "We all knew how to type, we were good work horses, and we were willing to learn the ropes" (quoted in Lehman, 1987:43). Moreover, their low profit margin restricted publishers to workers who would settle for low wages because either they had another source of income, placed low priority on earnings, or lacked better-paying alternatives. In fact, industry analyst John Dessauer (1974:64) contended that women won managerial-level jobs partly because publishers knew they could pay them less than men.

In addition to across-the-board growth, several traditionally female sectors grew disproportionately. The growth of subsidiary rights particularly benefited women. Long confined in a female ghetto, women who had developed expertise in rights rose to positions of power when rights directors began making million-dollar movie and paperback deals in the 1970s (*Publishers Weekly*, 1979). Editors consulted them in acquisition decisions, opening a path from subsidiary rights to editorial positions (Coser et al., 1982:104) and later to top management jobs. The detailed, technical nature of the work probably prevented inexperienced men from invading this "empty field" (Tuchman and Fortin, 1984), although Powell (1988) has pointed out that men with legal degrees are now entering subsidiary rights.

When the paperback industry exploded in the late 1960s and the 1970s (Benjamin, 1981:42; Tebbel, 1981:738) and paperback publishers began to acquire and publish original manuscripts, they needed more editors. Massive federal spending on education led to the expansion of school publishing, a sector in which the sexes were already integrated at the editorial level. Public interest in social issues spurred growth in the social sciences, a disproportionately female specialty in both college and mass-market houses. The women's movement gave birth to women's studies, creating jobs for editors knowledgeable about the women's movement and sympathetic to it. Finally, in order to cut costs, the industry increasingly contracted work out, fueling the demand for freelance editors—a predominantly female specialty.

A highly sex-differentiated society creates a demand for workers (such as coaches, counselors, and prison guards) who are the same sex as their occupational role partners (Bielby and Baron, 1984). Once women made up the majority of the fiction-reading and buying public (*Publishers Weekly,* 1974:25), publishers sought female editors for insight into women's taste (Geracimos, 1974:23). Women also compose a growing percentage of authors and the majority of the literary agents who are playing an increasingly important role in getting books published (Lane, 1975:41-42; Doebler, 1978:27), so the likelihood that the editor's role partners will be female has increased. To the extent that authors or literary agents prefer same-sex editors, the demand for female editors may have grown accordingly.

In other words, women became attractive to publishers because of their literary and interpersonal skills, their presumed ability to read for a largely female readership, and their expertise in growing segments of the industry—and because they would work cheap. These factors, combined with their availability as a surplus labor pool that could be readily drawn into the workforce, made women an acceptable solution to publishing's economic fluctuations (Caplette, 1982a:151).

Declining Sex Discrimination

Early in this century the feminist movement prompted publishing "to open its doors to [women], however reluctantly" (Tebbel, 1975:176). This process was repeated on a larger scale in the 1970s. Inspired by the women's liberation movement to reject the low-level jobs to which most women had been relegated, some women mobilized against sex discrimination and pressed for better opportunities in publishing (Dessauer, 1974:42; Strainchamps, 1974). Their efforts included both pressure from within and litigation.

By 1970 a group of women had formed Women in Publishing, an organization that carried out actions against some publishing houses, partly in conjunction with labor-organizing issues (*Publishers Weekly,* 1970),

and women's groups soon emerged at publishing houses (Strainchamps, 1974:154; Caplette, 1987). When these groups confronted their employers with evidence of wage and job discrimination, some houses began to rectify disparities. For example, after a year-long campaign for job posting by Boston Women in Publishing, five houses posted openings (Reuter, 1976:18). In 1974 the president of Harper & Row, in a letter to *Publishers Weekly* (Knowlton, 1974:12), described that firm's efforts to provide equal opportunities for women, including salary reviews and broader job posting. The industry reclassified secretaries as "editorial assistants"—although their duties did not change (Coser et al., 1982:108); and many firms eliminated separate career ladders for men and women, giving women greater access to senior-level editorial jobs and tempering their preference for men in certain jobs.

Other firms were less receptive. In 1974 New York state's attorney general challenged several companies privately and brought suit against Macmillan (Geracimos, 1974:27; Maryles, 1974; *Publishers Weekly,* 1975a), which subsequently established an affirmative-action plan (*Publishers Weekly,* 1976b). In 1975 a sex-discrimination suit by women editors in Houghton Mifflin's school division led to a cash settlement and to Houghton Mifflin's expansion of its job-representation goals (Smith, 1981:19). In the same year the publishing committee of the Boston chapter of the women's rights organization called 9to5 charged Addison-Wesley and Allyn & Bacon with race and sex discrimination (*Publishers Weekly,* 1975b; 1976a). As a result of these suits, "wages [rose] and management practices . . . changed," according to Massachusetts Attorney General Francis X. Bellotti (Mello, 1980; Reuter, 1980).

The spate of actions against other media giants, including *Newsday,* Time-Life, and NBC, heightened the impact of the suits against book publishing firms. A former editor at Holt, Rinehart & Winston claimed that a three-million-dollar suit against NBC prompted CBS (Holt's parent company) to implement a broad program to recruit and promote women and minorities: "You cannot imagine the amount of [management activity] there was around here [right after the NBC suit] in getting women up to speed."

A minority publisher claimed that no enforcement agency "is really after book publishers" and added, "If somebody zeroed in, there'd be a difference" (Weyr, 1980:31). However, most observers claimed that pressure from women's groups, litigation, and the risk of government intervention had companies running scared and that the pressure from women's groups had led publishers to curtail sex discrimination (Geracimos, 1974:25). For example, according to an editor in college publishing, "The threat of litigation made a difference. One major responsibility of the personnel director at [a large firm] that especially feared being sued was to keep the company out of trouble by encouraging the hiring of blacks and women."

Another observer commented, "They were worried primarily about the legal cost—not the loss of creative input, because they had gotten along without that." Educational publishers were especially vulnerable to government action in the early 1970s because they held large government contracts. A Harper & Row vice-president for personnel confirmed that affirmative action occurred because publishers—especially large trade and educational houses—had to implement affirmative-action regulations in order to get or keep government contracts (*Publishers Weekly*, 1980).

The women's liberation movement in conjunction with changing social values helped to alert gatekeepers who "consider[ed] themselves *avant garde*" to the contradiction between their behavior and their liberal values. One school publishing editor recalled that after the National Organization for Women (NOW) protested sex stereotyping in some materials she had developed, she and her male boss found stereotyped material in many of their other books. She said, "To have [NOW] protest has a consciousness-raising effect—whether you're a man or a woman." She believed that such experiences had helped men to recognize sex inequality in publishing employment.

The opening of management positions to women further enhanced women's access to editorial jobs. When men dominate management, hiring decisions for desirable jobs tend to favor men (Kanter, 1977). My interviews with women in top-level positions suggest that women's attaining organizational power fostered opportunities for women in lower ranks without necessitating preferential treatment of women. The presence of a few women who had finally attained top-level positions encouraged decision makers to ignore sex in filling lower-level editorial positions (see also Caplette, 1979:17). It also conveyed to women below that they could hope to advance. For example, Sherry Arden (quoted in Geracimos, 1974:23) recalled how moved the secretaries were when she was made a vice-president: "They felt . . . they had a chance at this point." Thus, "the notion that women [couldn't] be acquisitions editors gave way before the insistence of women" (Strainchamps, 1974:159–60; also see Tebbel, 1981:728), and the knowledge that opportunities existed generated a supply of applicants for them (Reskin and Hartmann, 1986).

Conclusions

In sum, the factors that facilitated women's increased representation in editing and the decline in sex segregation across editorial roles began with outside ownership and conglomeration, which tarnished the industry's image and reshaped the editor's role—especially that of the trade editor—robbing it of autonomy and the chance for creative risk taking. Job security declined, and wages failed to rise and may have declined. As a result of these changes, publishing could no longer attract the caliber of men it desired because they had better alternatives.

The decline in the number of qualified men seeking editorial careers paired with industrial growth to increase the ever present demand for editors, and the growth of several female-dominated specialties led the industry to turn to the large number of women who continued to seek work as editors. Women's availability at lower wages than men commanded no doubt contributed to their attractiveness to publishers. By the time these changes were under way, publishing was already a predominantly female industry, with women monopolizing the lower rungs on the editorial ladder. Pressure by women's groups and fear of government action encouraged publishers to modify their personnel practices to eliminate sex discrimination, creating opportunities for women in editorial jobs. Although sometimes women simply got titles to match the jobs they had been doing all along, many were promoted into senior editorships in trade and college houses. Publishing historian John Tebbel (1987) concluded, "Corporations were virtually forced to give women more opportunities, and women took advantage of [them]." Indeed, women now hold some of the top jobs in the industry (McDowell, 1987)—although they still report to the men who run the corporations that have come to control publishing.

In 1981 Michael and Susan Carter subtitled an article on women in the professions "Women get a ticket to ride after the gravy train has left the station." Although book editing has never been a gravy train, for most of this century its nonmonetary rewards compensated practitioners for low wages. Now, as many of those rewards have diminished, so too has the pool of male would-be editors on whom the industry formerly drew. The result has been both a higher proportion of female editors and a breakdown of sex segregation among editors. Most editors with whom I spoke indicated that male and female assistant editors now do the same jobs. A few expressed concern that editing is becoming resegregated as a female job (e.g., Geracimos, 1974:25). . . . But as Powell (1982) and others have pointed out, trends in publishing are fickle: mergers were common at the turn of the century, then ceased, only to reappear in the 1960s and 1970s; some conglomerates have sold their publishing houses, and others may look for greener pastures; firms may effectively resist takeovers (see, e.g., Glabberson, 1987). In short, the changes in the editorial role need not be irreversible. The data are not all in, and the final chapter remains to be written. What seems likely is that women will edit it.

REFERENCES

Altbach, Philip G. 1975. "Publishing and the Intellectual System." *Annals of the American Academy of Political and Social Science* 421 (September):1–13.

Association of American Publishers, Education for Publishing Committee. 1977. *The Accidental Profession: Education, Training, and the People of Publishing.* New York: Association of American Publishers.

Bannon, Barbara A. 1972. "Writers and Editors, the Publishing Lifeline." *Publishers Weekly* 201 (April 10):100–106.

Bechtold, Grace. 1946. *Book Publishing.* Vocational and Professional Monographs. Boston: Bellman.

Benjamin, Curtis G. 1981. "The Weaving of a Tangled Economic Web." *Publishers Weekly* 219 (April 24):41–45.

Bielby, Denise D., and William T. Bielby. 1987. "Writing for the Screen: Gender, Jobs, and Stereotypes in the Entertainment Industry." Paper presented at the meeting of the American Sociological Association, Chicago, August.

Bielby, William T., and James N. Baron. 1984. "A Woman's Place Is with Other Women: Sex Segregation within Organizations." In Barbara F. Reskin, ed., *Sex Segregation in the Workplace: Trends, Explanations, Remedies,* 27–55. Washington, DC: National Academy Press.

Bingley, Clive. 1972. *The Business of Book Publishing.* Oxford: Pergamon Press.

Canfield, Cass. 1969. "The Real and the Ideal Editor." *Publishers Weekly* 195 (March 31):24–27.

Caplette, Michele. 1979. "Editorial Career Paths in College Textbook Publishing." Paper presented to the annual meeting of the American Sociological Association, Boston.

———. 1981. "Women in Publishing: A Study of Careers in Organizations." Ph.D. diss., State University of New York at Stony Brook.

———. 1982a. "Women in Book Publishing: A Qualified Success Story." In Lewis Coser, Charles Kadushin, and Walter Powell, eds., *Books: The Culture and Commerce of Publishing,* 148–74. Chicago: University of Chicago Press.

———. 1982b. "Women in Book Publishing: Common Denominators in the Careers of Twelve Successful Women." Presented to the Women's National Book Association.

Carter, Robert A. 1984. "Acquiring Books for Fun and Profit." *Publishers Weekly* 225 (March 23): 24–26.

Cerf, Bennett. 1977. *At Random.* New York: Random House.

Chaney, Bev, ed. 1984. *The First Hundred Years: Association of Book Travelers, 1884–1984.* New York: Association of Book Travelers.

Charnizon, Marlene. 1987. "Women at the Top." *Publishers Weekly* 231 (January 23):27–31.

Chicago Women in Publishing. 1973. "Survey II: Comparative Status of Women and Men in Chicago Area Book Publishing." Unpublished report, Fall.

Cornelius, James. 1983. "Staying Alive—Young People in Publishing." *Publishers Weekly* 25 (November):32–35.

Coser, Lewis, Charles Kadushin, and Walter Powell. 1982. *Books: The Culture and Commerce of Publishing.* Chicago: University of Chicago Press.

Dong, Stella. 1980. "Publishing's Revolving Door." *Publishers Weekly* 218 (December 18):20–23.

———. 1984. "What Authors Look for in Editors." *Publisher's Weekly* 226 (December 14):22–27.

Gabriel, Trip. 1989. "Call My Agent!" *New York Times Magazine,* February 19, pp. 45–80.

Galassi, Jonathan W. 1980. "Double Agent: The Literary Editor in the Commercial House." *Publishers Weekly* 217 (March 7):28–30.

Geracimos, Ann. 1974. "Women in Publishing: Where Do They Feel They're Going?" *Publishers Weekly* 206 (November 11):22–27.

Gilroy, Angele A. 1980. "An Economic Analysis of the U.S. Domestic Book Publishing Industry." *Printing and Publishing* 21(4):8–11.

Giroux, Robert. 1982. "The Education of an Editor." *Publishers Weekly* 221 (January 8):54–60.

Glabberson, William. 1987. "Will Takeovers Be Bad for Books?" *New York Times,* April 5, p. 3.

Grannis, Chandler B. 1985. "The Structure and Function of the Book Business." In Elizabeth Geiser et al., eds., *The Business of Book Publishing,* 12–20. Boulder, CO: Westview Press.

James, Caryn. 1987. "New York's Spinning Literary Circles." *The World of New York, New York Times Magazine* supplement, April 26, pp. 40, 50–53.

Kanter, Rosabeth Moss. 1977. *Men and Women of the Corporation.* New York: Basic Books.

Laskey, Burton. 1969. "Who'll Do the Work?" *Publishers Weekly* 196 (December 15):13–14.

McDowell, Edwin. 1987. "Women Move to Top in Publishing." *New York Times,* October 25, p. E24.

Maryles, Daisy. 1974. "Macmillan Charged with Sex Bias in Hiring." *Publishers Weekly* 206 (September 30):19.

Mello, John P., Jr. 1980. "Allyn and Bacon Settles in Sex Discrimination Suit." *Publishers Weekly* 217 (May 23):23.

Much, Kathleen. 1988. Personal communication.

Navasky, Victor S. 1973a. "In Cold Print: What Is an Editor Worth?" *New York Times Book Review,* April 15, p. 2.

———. 1973b. "In Cold Print: Selling Out and Buying In." *New York Times Book Review,* May 20, p. 2.

Noble, Kendrick. 1978. "Assessing the Merger Trend." *Publishers Weekly* 214 (July 31):35–42.

O'Farrell, Brigid, and Sharon Harlan. 1984. "Job Integration Strategies: Today's Programs and Tomorrow's Needs." In Barbara F. Reskin, ed., *Sex Segregation in the Workplace: Trends, Explanations, Remedies,* 267–91. Washington, DC: National Academy Press.

Osterman, Paul. 1979. "Sex Discrimination in Professional Employment: A Case Study." *Industrial and Labor Relations Review* 32(4):451–64.

Phalon, Richard. 1981. "Publishing." *Forbes* 5 (January):253–54.

Powell, Walter. 1982. "From Craft to Corporation: The Impact of Outside Ownership on Book Publishing." In J. S. Ettema and D. C. Whitney, eds., *Individuals in Mass Media Organizations,* 33–52. Beverly Hills, CA: Sage.

———. 1985. *Getting into Print.* Chicago: University of Chicago Press.

———. 1988. Personal communication.

Publishers Weekly. 1969. "Who's Who among the Travelers?" 195 (March 10):3.

———. 1970. "McGraw-Hill Picketed by Women in Publishing." 198 (July 6):35.

———. 1971. "The Rise of Women in Publishing." 199 (February 15):66, 69.

———. 1974. "Some Harsh Words on How Women Fare in Publishing." 205 (March 25):25.

———. 1975a. "Women Editors File Suit against HM for Sex Bias." 208 (November 24):18.

———. 1975b. "News Brief." 208 (December 8):13.

———. 1976a. "Mass. Attorney General Joins Sex Bias Suit against HM." 209 (March 8):27.

———. 1976b. "Sex Bias Complaint Settled at Macmillan." 200 (April 19):28.

———. 1979. "Why Are Women So Successful in Sub Rights?" 215 (June 18):58–62.

———. 1980. "Affirmative Action and Inaction." 218 (August 8):25–26.

Rawson, Hugh, and Arnold Dolin. 1985. "The Editorial Process: An Overview." In Elizabeth Geiser et al., eds., *The Business of Book Publishing,* 21–42. Boulder, CO: Westview Press.

Reskin, Barbara F., and Heidi I. Hartmann. 1986. *Women's Work, Men's Work: Sex Segregation on the Job.* Washington, DC: National Academy Press.

Reuter, Madalynne. 1976. "Boston Women in Publishing Hails Job Posting Efforts." *Publishers Weekly* 210 (October 11):18.

———. 1980. "Addison-Wesley Agrees to $360,000 Sex-Bias Accord." *Publishers Weekly* 217 (April 11):10.

Roos, Patricia A., and Barbara F. Reskin. 1984. "Institutional Factors Contributing to Sex Segregation in the Workplace." In Barbara F. Reskin, ed., *Sex Segregation in the Workplace: Trends, Explanations, Remedies,* 235–60. Washington, DC: National Academy Press.

Rosenthal, Ellen, Carter Smith, Hope Steele, Clifford Crouch et al. 1986. "My Say." *Publishers Weekly* 230 (August 29):392.

Sifton, Elisabeth. 1985. "The Editor's Job in Trade Publishing." In Elizabeth Geiser et al., eds., *The Business of Book Publishing,* 43–61. Boulder, CO: Westview Press.

Smith, Wendy. 1981. "Houghton Reaches Accord in Sex Bias Suit." *Publishers Weekly* 219 (January 16):19.

Strainchamps, Ethel. 1974. *Rooms with No View: A Woman's Guide to the Man's World of Publishing.* New York: Harper & Row.

Tebbel, John. 1972. *A History of Book Publishing in the United States.* Vol. 1, *The Creation of an Industry.* New York: Bowker.

———. 1975. *A History of Book Publishing in the United States.* Vol. 2, *The Expansion of an Industry.* New York: Bowker.

———. 1978. *A History of Book Publishing in the United States.* Vol. 3, *The Golden Age between Two Wars, 1920–1940.* New York: Bowker.

———. 1981. *A History of Book Publishing in the United States.* Vol. 4, *The Great Change, 1940–1980.* New York, Bowker.

———. 1987. Personal communication.

Tuchman, Gay, and Nina Fortin. 1984. "Women Writers and Literary Tradition." *American Journal of Sociology* 90 (July):72–96.

U.S. Bureau of the Census. 1972. *1970 Census of Population: Occupation by Industry.* Subject Reports, PC(2)-7C. Washington, DC: Government Printing Office.

———. 1984. *1980 Census of Population: Subject Reports.* Vol. 2, *Occupation by Industry.* PC80-2-7C. Washington, DC: Government Printing Office.

U.S. Bureau of Labor Statistics. 1972. *Occupational Outlook Handbook.* 1972–73 ed. Bulletin 1700. Washington, DC: Government Printing Office.

———. 1984. *Occupational Outlook Handbook.* 1984–85 ed. Bulletin 2205. Washington, DC: Government Printing Office.

U.S. Department of Commerce. 1977. *Census of Manufacturing.* Subject Statistics, vol. 2, pt. SIC Major Groups 37–34. Washington, DC: Government Printing Office.

Weber, Max. 1978. *Economy and Society.* Vol. 2. Berkeley: University of California Press.

Wendroff, Michael. 1980. "Should We Do the Book?" *Publishers Weekly* 218 (August 15): 24–30.

Weyr, Thomas. 1980. "Minorities in Publishing." *Publishers Weekly* 218 (October 17):31–35.

Wright, John W. 1984. *The American Almanac of Jobs and Salaries.* New York: Avon Books.

22

Boundary Lines
Labeling Sexual Harassment in Restaurants

Patti A. Giuffre and Christine L. Williams

Sexual harassment occurs when submission to or rejection of sexual advances is a term of employment, is used as a basis for making employment decisions, or if the advances create a hostile or offensive work environment (Konrad and Gutek 1986). Sexual harassment can cover a range of behaviors, from leering to rape (Ellis, Barak, and Pinto 1991; Pryor 1987; Reilly et al. 1992; Schneider 1982). Researchers estimate that as many as 70 percent of employed women have experienced behaviors that may legally constitute sexual harassment (MacKinnon 1979; Powell 1986); however, a far lower percentage of women claim to have experienced sexual harassment. Paludi and Barickman write that "the great majority of women who are abused by behavior that fits legal definitions of sexual harassment—and who are traumatized by the experience—do not label what has happened to them 'sexual harassment' " (1991, 68).

Why do most women fail to label their experiences as sexual harassment? Part of the problem is that many still do not recognize that sexual harassment is an actionable offense. Sexual harassment was first described in 1976 (MacKinnon 1979), but it was

not until 1986 that the U.S. Supreme Court included sexual harassment in the category of gender discrimination, thereby making it illegal (Paludi and Barickman 1991); consequently, women may not yet identify their experiences as sexual harassment because a substantial degree of awareness about its illegality has yet to be developed.

Many victims of sexual harassment may also be reluctant to come forward with complaints, fearing that they will not be believed, or that their charges will not be taken seriously (Jensen and Gutek 1982). As the Anita Hill–Clarence Thomas hearings demonstrated, women who are victims of sexual harassment often become the accused when they bring charges against their assailant.

There is another issue at stake in explaining the gap between experiencing and labeling behaviors "sexual harassment": many men and women experience some sexual behaviors in the workplace as pleasurable. Research on sexual harassment suggests that men are more likely than women to enjoy sexual interactions at work (Gutek 1985; Konrad and Gutek 1986; Reilly et al. 1992), but even some women experience sexual overtures at work as pleasurable (Pringle 1988). This attitude may be especially strong in organizations that use and exploit the bodies and sexuality of the workers (Cockburn 1991). Workers in many jobs are hired on the basis of their attractiveness and solicitousness—including not only sex industry workers, but also service sector workers such as receptionists, airline attendants, and servers in trendy restaurants. According to Cockburn (1991), the sexual exploitation is not completely forced: many people find this dimension of their jobs appealing and reinforcing to their own sense of identity and pleasure; consequently, some men and women resist efforts to expunge all sexuality from their places of work.

This is not to claim that all sexual behavior in the workplace is acceptable, even to some people. The point is that it is difficult to label behavior as sexual harassment because it forces people to draw a line between illicit and "legitimate" forms of sexuality at work—a process fraught with ambiguity. Whether a particular interaction is identified as harassment will depend on the intention of the harasser and the interpretation of the interchange by the victim, and both of these perspectives will be highly influenced by workplace culture and the social context of the specific event. . . .

Methods

The occupation of waiting tables was selected to study the social definition of sexual harassment because many restaurants have a blatantly sexualized workplace culture (Cobble 1991; Paules 1991). According to a report published in a magazine that caters to restaurant owners, "Restaurants . . . are about as informal a workplace as there is, so much so as to actually encourage—or at the very least tolerate—sexual banter" (Anders 1993, 48). Unremitting sexual banter and innuendo, as well as physical jostling, create an environment of "compulsory jocularity" in many restaurants (Pringle 1988, 93). Sexual attractiveness and flirtation are often institutionalized parts of a waitperson's job description; consequently, individual employees are often forced to draw the line for themselves to distinguish legitimate and il-

legitimate expressions of sexuality, making this occupation an excellent context for examining how people determine what constitutes sexual harassment. In contrast, many more sexual behaviors may be labeled sexual harassment in less highly sexualized work environments.

Eighteen in-depth interviews were conducted with male and female waitstaff who work in restaurants in Austin, Texas. Respondents were selected from restaurants that employ equal proportions of men and women on their wait staffs. Overall, restaurant work is highly sex segregated: women make up about 82 percent of all waitpeople (U.S. Department of Labor 1989), and it is common for restaurants to be staffed only by either waitresses or waiters, with men predominating in the higher-priced restaurants (Cobble 1991; Hall 1993; Paules 1991). We decided to focus only on waitpeople who work in mixed-sex groups for two reasons. First, focusing on waitpeople working on integrated staffs enables us to examine sexual harassment between co-workers who occupy the same position in an organizational hierarchy. Co-worker sexual harassment is perhaps the most common form of sexual harassment (Pryor 1987; Schneider 1982); yet most case studies of sexual harassment have examined either unequal hierarchical relationships (e.g., boss-secretary harassment) or harassment in highly skewed gender groupings (e.g., women who work in nontraditional occupations) (Benson and Thomson 1982; Carothers and Crull 1984; Gruber and Bjorn 1982). This study is designed to investigate sexual harassment in unequal hierarchical relationships, as well as harassment between organizationally equal co-workers.

Second, equal proportions of men and women in an occupation implies a high degree of male-female interaction (Gutek 1985). Waitpeople are in constant contact with each other, help each other when the restaurant is busy, and informally socialize during slack periods. In contrast, men and women have much more limited interactions in highly sex-segregated restaurants and, indeed, in most work environments. The high degree of interaction among the wait staff provides ample opportunity for sexual harassment between men and women to occur and, concomitantly, less opportunity for same-sex sexual harassment to occur.

The sample was generated using "snowball" techniques and by going to area restaurants and asking waitpeople to volunteer for the study. The sample includes eight men and ten women. Four respondents are Latina/o, two African American, and twelve white. Four respondents are gay or lesbian; one is bisexual; thirteen are heterosexual. (The gay men and lesbians in the sample are all "out" at their respective restaurants.) Fourteen respondents are single; three are married; one is divorced. Respondents' ages range from 22 to 37. . . .

Findings

Respondents agreed that sexual banter is very common in the restaurant: staff members talk and joke about sex constantly. With only one exception, respondents described their restaurants as highly sexualized. This means that 17 of the 18 respondents said that sexual joking, touching, and fondling were common, everyday occurrences in their restaurants. For example, when asked if he and other waitpeople ever joke about sex, one waiter replied, "about 90 percent of [the jokes] are about sex." According to a waitress, "at work . . . [we're] used to patting and touching and hugging." Another waiter said, "I do not go through a shift without someone . . . pinching my nipples or poking me in the butt or grabbing my crotch. . . . It's just what we do at work."

These informal behaviors are tantamount to "doing heterosexuality," a process analogous to "doing gender" (West and Zimmerman 1987). By engaging in these public flirtations and open discussions of sex, men and women reproduce the dominant cultural norms of heterosexuality and lend an air of legitimacy—if not inevitability—to heterosexual relationships. In other words, heterosexuality is normalized and naturalized through its ritualistic public display. Indeed, although most respondents described their workplaces as highly sexualized, several dismissed the constant sexual innuendo and behaviors as "just joking," and nothing to get upset about. Several respondents claimed that this is simply "the way it is in the restaurant business," or "just the way men are."

With only one exception, the men and women interviewed maintained that they enjoyed this aspect of their work. Heterosexuality may be normative, and in these contexts, even compulsory, yet many men and women find pleasure in its expression. Many women—as well as men—actively reproduce hegemonic sexuality and apparently enjoy its ritual expression; however, in a few instances, sexual conduct was labeled as sexual harassment. Seven women and three men said they had experienced sexual harassment in restaurant work. Of these, two women and one man described two different experiences of sexual harassment, and two women described three experiences. . . .

We analyzed these 17 accounts of sexual harassment to find out what, if anything, these experiences shared in common. With the exception of two episodes (discussed later), the experiences that were labeled "sexual harassment" were not distinguished by any specific words or behaviors, nor were they distinguished by their degree of severity. Identical behaviors were considered acceptable if they were perpetrated by some people, but considered offensive if perpetrated by others. In other words, sexual behavior in the workplace was interpreted differently depending on the context of the interaction. In general, respondents labeled their experiences sexual harassment only if the offending behavior occurred in one of three social contexts: (1) if perpetrated by someone in a more powerful position, such as a manager; (2) if perpetrated by someone of a different race/ethnicity; or (3) if perpetrated by someone of a different sexual orientation.

Our findings do not imply that sexual harassment did not occur outside of these three contexts. Instead, they simply indicate that our respondents *labeled* behavior as "sexual harassment" when it occurred in these particular social contexts. We will discuss each of these contexts and speculate on the reasons why they were singled out by our respondents.

Powerful Position

In the restaurant, managers and owners are the highest in the hierarchy of workers. Generally, they are the only ones who can hire or fire waitpeople. Three of the women and one of the men interviewed said they had been sexually harassed by their restaurants' managers or owners. In addition, several others who did not personally experience harassment said they had witnessed managers or owners sexually harassing other waitpeople. This finding is consistent with other research indicating people are more likely to think that sexual harassment has occurred when the perpetrator is in a more powerful position (e.g., Ellis et al. 1991).

Carla describes being sexually harassed by her manager:

> One evening, [my manager] grabbed my body, not in a private place, just grabbed my body, period. He gave me

like a bear hug from behind a total of four times in one night. By the end of the night I was livid. I was trying to avoid him. Then when he'd do it, I'd just ignore the conversation or the joke or whatever and walk away.

She claimed that her co-workers often give each other massages and joke about sex, but she did not label any of their behaviors sexual harassment. In fact, all four individuals who experienced sexual harassment from their managers described very similar types of behavior from their co-workers, which they did not define as sexual harassment. For example, Cathy said that she and the other waitpeople talk and joke about sex constantly: "Everybody stands around and talks about sex a lot. . . . Isn't that weird? You know, it's something about working in restaurants and, yeah, so we'll all sit around and talk about sex." She said that talking with her co-workers about sex does not constitute sexual harassment because it is "only joking." She does, however, view her male manager as a sexual harasser:

> My employer is very sexist. I would call that sexual harassment. Very much of a male chauvinist pig. He kind of started [saying] stuff like, "You can't really wear those shorts because they're not flattering to your figure. . . . But I like the way you wear those jeans. They look real good. They're tight." It's like, you know [I want to say to him], "You're the owner, you're in power. That's evident. You know, you need to find a better way to tell me these things." We've gotten to a point now where we'll joke around now, but it's never ever sexual, ever. I won't allow that with him.

Cathy acknowledges that her manager may legitimately dictate her appearance at work, but only if he does so in professional—and not personal—terms. She wants him "to find a better way to tell me these things," implying that he is not completely out-of-line in suggesting that she wear tight pants. He "crosses the line" when he personalizes his directive, by saying to Cathy "*I like* the way you wear those jeans." This is offensive to Cathy because it is framed as the manager's personal prerogative, not the institutional requirements of the job.

Ann described a similar experience of sexual harassment from a restaurant owner:

> Yeah, there's been a couple of times when a manager has made me feel real uncomfortable and I just removed myself from the situation. . . . Like if there's something I really want him to hear or something I think is really important there's no touching. Like, "Don't touch me while I'm talking to you." You know, because I take that as very patronizing. I actually blew up at one of the owners once because I was having a rough day and he came up behind me and he was rubbing my back, like up and down my back and saying, you know, "Oh, is Ann having a bad day?" or something like that and I shook him off of me and I said, "You do not need to touch me to talk to me."

Ann distinguishes between legitimate and illegitimate touching: if the issue being discussed is "really important"—that is, involving her job status—she insists there be no touching. In these specific situations, a back rub is interpreted as patronizing and offensive because the manager is using his powerful position for his *personal* sexual enjoyment.

One of the men in the sample, Frank, also experienced sexual harassment from a manager:

> I was in the bathroom and [the manager] came up next to me and my tennis shoes were spray-painted silver so he knew it was me in there and he said something about, "Oh, what do you have in your hand there?" I was on the other side of a wall and he said, "Mind if I hold it for a while?" or something like that, you know. I just pretended like I didn't hear it.

Frank also described various sexual behaviors among the waitstaff, including fondling, "joking about bodily functions," and "making bikinis out of tortillas." He said, "I mean, it's like, what we do at work. . . . There's no holds barred. I don't find it offensive. I'm used to it by now. I'm guilty of it myself." Evidently, he defines sexual behaviors as "sexual harassment" only when perpetrated by someone in a position of power over him.

Two of the women in the sample also described sexual harassment from customers. We place these experiences in the category of "powerful position" because customers do have limited economic power over the waitperson insofar as they control the tip (Crull 1987). Cathy said that male customers often ask her to "sit on my lap" and provide them with other sexual favors. Brenda, a lesbian, described a similar experience of sexual harassment from women customers:

> One time I had this table of lesbians and they were being real vulgar towards me. Real sexual. This woman kind of tripped me as I was walking by and said, "Hurry back." I mean, gay people can tell when other people are gay. I felt harassed.

In these examples of harassment by customers, the line is drawn using a similar logic as in the examples of harassment by managers. These customers acted as though the waitresses were providing table service to satisfy the customers' private desires, instead of working to fulfill their job descriptions. In other words, the customers' demands were couched in personal—and not professional—terms, making the waitresses feel sexually harassed.

It is not difficult to understand why waitpeople singled out sexual behaviors from managers, owners, and customers as sexual harassment. Subjection to sexual advances by someone with economic power comes closest to the quid pro quo form of sexual harassment, wherein employees are given the option to either "put out or get out." Studies have found that this type of sexual harassment is viewed as the most threatening and unambiguous sort (Ellis et al. 1991; Fitzgerald 1990; Gruber and Bjorn 1982).

But even in this context, lines are drawn between legitimate and illegitimate sexual behavior in the workplace. As Cathy's comments make clear, some people accept the employers' prerogative to exploit the workers' sexuality, by dictating appropriate "sexy" dress, for example. Like airline attendants, waitresses are expected to be friendly, helpful, and sexually available to the male customers (Cobble 1991). Because this expectation is embedded in restaurant culture, it becomes difficult for workers to separate sexual harassment from the more or less accepted forms of sexual exploitation that are routine features of their jobs. Consequently, some women are reluctant to label blatantly offensive behaviors as sexual harassment. For example, Maxine, who claims that she has never experienced sexual harassment, said that customers often "talk dirty" to her:

> I remember one day, about four or five years ago when I was working as a cocktail waitress, this guy asked me for a "Slow Comfortable Screw" [the name of a drink]. I didn't know what it was. I didn't know if he was making a move or something. I just looked at him. He said, "You know what it is, right?" I said, "I bet the bartender knows!" (laughs). . . . There's

another one, "Sex on the Beach." And there's another one called a "Screaming Orgasm." Do you believe that?

Maxine is subject to a sexualized work environment that she finds offensive; hence her experience could fit the legal definition of sexual harassment. But because sexy drink names are an institutionalized part of restaurant culture, Maxine neither complains about it nor labels it sexual harassment: Once it becomes clear that a "Slow Comfortable Screw" is a legitimate and recognized restaurant demand, she accepts it (although reluctantly) as part of her job description. In other words, the fact that the offensive behavior is institutionalized seems to make it beyond reproach in her eyes. This finding is consistent with others' findings that those who work in highly sexualized environments may be less likely to label offensive behavior "sexual harassment" (Gutek 1985; Konrad and Gutek 1986).

Only in specific contexts do workers appear to define offensive words and acts of a sexual nature as sexual harassment—even when initiated by someone in a more powerful position. The interviews suggest that workers use this label to describe their experiences only when their bosses or their customers couch their requests for sexual attentions in explicitly personal terms. This way of defining sexual harassment may obscure and legitimize more institutionalized—and hence more insidious—forms of sexual exploitation at work.

Race/Ethnicity

The restaurants in our sample, like most restaurants in the United States, have racially segregated staffs (Howe 1977). In the restaurants where our respondents are employed, men of color are concentrated in two positions: the kitchen cooks and bus personnel (formerly called busboys). Five of the white women in the sample reported experiencing sexual harassment from Latino men who worked in these positions. For example, when asked if she had ever experienced sexual harassment, Beth said:

> Yes, but it was not with the people . . . it was not, you know, the people that I work with in the front of the house. It was with the kitchen. There are boundaries or lines that I draw with the people I work with. In the kitchen, the lines are quite different. Plus, it's a Mexican staff. It's a very different attitude. They tend to want to touch you more and, at times, I can put up with a little bit of it but . . . because I will give them a hard time too but I won't touch them. I won't touch their butt or anything like that.

> [Interviewer: So sometimes they cross the line?]

> It's only happened to me a couple of times. One guy, like, patted me on the butt and I went off. I lost my shit. I went off on him. I said, "No. Bad. Wrong. I can't speak Spanish to you but, you know, this is it." I told the kitchen manager who is a guy and he's not . . . the head kitchen manager is not Hispanic. . . . I've had to do that over the years only a couple of times with those guys.

Beth reported that the waitpeople joke about sex and touch each other constantly, but she does not consider their behavior sexual harassment. Like many of the other men and women in the sample, Beth said she feels comfortable engaging in this sexual banter and play with other waitpeople (who were predominantly white), but not with the Mexican men in the kitchen.

Part of the reason for singling out the behaviors of the cooks as sexual harassment may involve status differences between waitpeople and cooks. Studies have suggested that people may label behaviors as sexual ha-

rassment when they are perpetrated by people in lower status organizational positions (Grauerholz 1989; McKinney 1990); however, it is difficult to generalize about the relative status of cooks and waitpeople because of the varied and often complex organizational hierarchies of restaurants (Paules 1991, 107–10). If the cook is a chef, as in higher-priced restaurants, he or she may actually have more status than waitpeople, and indeed may have the formal power to hire and fire the waitstaff. In the restaurants where our respondents worked, the kitchen cooks did not wield this sort of formal control, but they could exert some informal power over the waitstaff by slowing down food orders or making the orders look and/or taste bad. Because bad food can decrease the waitperson's tip, the cooks can thereby control the waitperson's income; hence servers are forced to negotiate and to some extent placate the wishes and desires of cooks to perform their jobs. The willingness of several respondents to label the cooks' behavior as sexual harassment may reflect their perception that the cooks' informal demands had become unreasonable. In such cases, subjection to the offensive behaviors is a term of employment, which is quid pro quo sexual harassment. As mentioned previously, this type of sexual harassment is the most likely to be so labeled and identified.

Because each recounted case of sexual harassment occurring between individuals of different occupational statuses involved a minority man sexually harassing a white woman, the racial context seems equally important. For example, Ann also said she and the other waiters and waitresses joke about sex and touch each other "on the butt" all the time, and when asked if she had ever experienced sexual harassment, she said,

> I had some problems at [a previous restaurant] but it was a communication problem. A lot of the guys in the kitchen

did not speak English. They would see the waiters hugging on us, kissing us and pinching our rears and stuff. They would try to do it and I couldn't tell them, "No. You don't understand this. It's like we do it because we have a mutual understanding but I'm not comfortable with you doing it." So that was really hard and a lot of times what I'd have to do is just sucker punch them in the chest and just use a lot of cuss words and they knew that I was serious. And there again, I felt real weird about that because they're just doing what they see go on every day.

Kate, Carla, and Brenda described very similar racial double standards. Kate complained about a Mexican busser who constantly touched her:

This is not somebody that I talk to on a friendly basis. We don't sit there and laugh and joke and stuff. So, when he touches me, all I know is he is just touching me and there is no context about it. With other people, if they said something or they touched me, it would be funny or . . . we have a relationship. This person and I and all the other people do not. So that is sexual harassment.

And according to Brenda:

The kitchen can be kind of sexist. They really make me angry. They're not as bad as they used to be because they got warned. They're mostly Mexican, not even Mexican-American. Most of them, they're just starting to learn English.

[Interviewer: What do they do to you?]

Well, I speak Spanish, so I know. They're not as sexual to me because I think they know I don't like it. Some of the other girls will come through and they will touch them like here [points to the lower part of her waist]. . . . I've had some pretty bad arguments with the kitchen.

[Interviewer: Would you call that sexual harassment?]

Yes. I think some of the girls just don't know better to say something. I think it happens a lot with the kitchen guys. Like sometimes, they will take a relleno in their hands like it's a penis. Sick!

Each of these women identified the sexual advances of the minority men in their restaurants as sexual harassment, but not the identical behaviors of their white male co-workers; moreover, they all recognize that they draw boundary lines differently for Anglo men and Mexican men: each of them willingly participates in "doing heterosexuality" only in racially homogamous contexts. These women called the behavior of the Mexican cooks "sexual harassment" in part because they did not "have a relationship" with these men, nor was it conceivable to them that they *could* have a relationship with them, given cultural and language barriers—and, probably, racist attitudes as well. The white men, on the other hand, can "hug, kiss, and pinch rears" of the white women because they have a "mutual understanding"— implying reciprocity and the possibility of intimacy.

The importance of this perception of relationship potential in the assessment of sexual harassment is especially clear in the cases of the two married women in the sample, Diana and Maxine. Both of these women said that they had never experienced sexual harassment. Diana, who works in a family-owned and -operated restaurant, claimed that her restaurant is not a sexualized work environment. Although people occasionally make double entendre jokes relating to sex, according to Diana, "there's no contact whatsoever like someone pinching your butt or something." She said that she has never experienced sexual harassment:

Everybody here knows I'm married so they're not going to get fresh with me because they know that it's not going to go anywhere, you know so . . . and vice versa. You know, we know the guys' wives. They come in here to eat. It's respect all the way. I don't think they could handle it if they saw us going around hugging them. You know what I mean? It's not right.

Similarly, Maxine, who is Colombian, said she avoids the problem of sexual harassment in her workplace because she is married:

The cooks don't offend me because they know I speak Spanish and they know how to talk with me because I set my boundaries and they know that. . . . I just don't joke with them more than I should. They all know that I'm married, first of all, so that's a no-no for all of them. My brother used to be a manager in that restaurant so he probably took care of everything. I never had any problems anyway in any other jobs because, like I said, I set my boundaries. I don't let them get too close to me.

[Interviewer: You mean physically?]

Not physically only. Just talking. If they want to talk about, "Do you go dancing? Where do you go dancing?" Like I just change the subject because it's none of their business and I don't really care to talk about that with them . . . not because I consider them to be on the lower levels than me or something but just because if you start talking with them that way then you are just giving them hope or something. I think that's true for most of the guys here, not just talking about the cooks. . . . I do get offended and they know that so sometimes they apologize.

Both Maxine and Diana said that they are protected from sexual harassment because

they are married. In effect, they use their marital status to negotiate their interactions with their co-workers and to ward off unwanted sexual advances. Furthermore, because they do not view their co-workers as potential relationship "interests," they conscientiously refuse to participate in any sexual banter in the restaurant.

The fact that both women speak Spanish fluently may mean that they can communicate their boundaries unambiguously to those who only speak Spanish (unlike the female respondents in the sample who only speak English). For these two women, sexual harassment from co-workers is not an issue. Diana, who is Latina, talks about "respect all around" in her restaurant; Maxine claims the cooks (who are Mexican) aren't the ones who offend her. Their comments seem to reflect more mutual respect and humanity toward their Latino co-workers than the comments of the white waitresses. On the other hand, at least from Maxine's vantage point, racial harassment is a bigger problem in her workplace than is sexual harassment. When asked if she ever felt excluded from any groups at work, she said:

Yeah, sometimes. How can I explain this? Sometimes, I mean, I don't know if they do it on purpose or they don't but they joke around you about being Spanish. . . . Sometimes it hurts. Like they say, "What are you doing here? Why don't you go back home?"

Racial harassment—like sexual harassment—is a means used by a dominant group to maintain its dominance over a subordinated group. Maxine feels that, because she is married, she is protected from sexual harassment (although, as we have seen, she is subject to a sexualized workplace that is offensive to her); however, she does experience racial harassment where she works, and she feels vulnerable to this because she is one of very few non-whites working at her restaurant.

One of the waiters in the sample claimed that he had experienced sexual harassment from female co-workers, and race may have also been a factor in this situation. When Rick (who is African American) was asked if he had ever been sexually harassed, he recounted his experiences with some white waitresses:

> Yes. There are a couple of girls there, waitpeople, who will pinch my rear.
>
> [Interviewer: Do you find it offensive?]
>
> No (laughs) because I'm male. . . . But it is a form of sexual harassment.
>
> [Interviewer: Do you ever tell them to stop?]
>
> If I'm really busy, if I'm in the weeds, and they want to touch me, I'll get mad. I'll tell them to stop. There's a certain time and place for everything.

Rick is reluctant about labeling this interaction "sexual harassment" because "it doesn't bother me unless I'm, like, busy or something like that." In those cases where he is busy, he feels that his female co-workers are subverting his work by pinching him. Because of the race difference, he may experience their behaviors as an expression of racial dominance, which probably influences his willingness to label the behavior as sexual harassment.

In sum, the interviews suggest that the perception and labeling of interactions as "sexual harassment" may be influenced by the racial context of the interaction. If the victim perceives the harasser as expressing a potentially reciprocal relationship interest, they may be less likely to label their experience sexual harassment. In cases where the harasser and victim have a different race/ethnicity and class background, the possibility of a relationship may be precluded because of racism, making these cases more likely to be labeled "sexual harassment."

This finding suggests that the practices associated with "doing heterosexuality" are profoundly racist. The white women in the sample showed a great reluctance to label unwanted sexual behavior sexual harassment when it was perpetrated by a potential (or real) relationship interest—that is, a white male co-worker. In contrast, minority men are socially constructed as potential harassers of white women: any expression of sexual interest may be more readily perceived as nonreciprocal and unwanted. The assumption of racial homogamy in heterosexual relationships thus may protect white men from charges of sexual harassment of white women. This would help to explain why so many white women in the sample labeled behaviors perpetrated by Mexican men as sexual harassment, but not the identical behaviors perpetrated by white men.

Sexual Orientation

There has been very little research on sexual harassment that addresses the sexual orientation of the harasser and victim (exceptions include Reilly et al. 1992; Schneider 1982, 1984). Surveys of sexual harassment typically include questions about marital status but not about sexual orientation (e.g., Fain and Anderton 1987; Gruber and Bjorn 1982; Powell 1986). In this study, sexual orientation was an important part of heterosexual men's perceptions of sexual harassment. Of the four episodes of sexual harassment reported by the men in the study, three involved openly gay men sexually harassing straight men. One case involved a male manager harassing a male waiter (Frank's experience, described earlier). The other two cases involved co-workers. Jake said that he had been sexually harassed by a waiter:

> Someone has come on to me that I didn't want to come on to me. . . . He was another waiter [male]. It was laughs and

jokes the whole way until things got a little too much and it was like, "Hey, this is how it is. Back off. Keep your hands off my ass." . . . Once it reached the point where I felt kind of threatened and bothered by it.

Rick described being sexually harassed by a gay baker in his restaurant:

> There was a baker that we had who was really, really gay. . . . He was very straightforward and blunt. He would tell you, in detail, his sexual experiences and tell you that he wanted to do them with you. . . . I knew he was kidding but he was serious. I mean, if he had a chance he would do these things.

In each of these cases, the men expressed some confusion about the intentions of their harassers—"I knew he was kidding but he was serious." Their inability to read the intentions of the gay men provoked them to label these episodes sexual harassment. Each man did not perceive the sexual interchange as reciprocal, nor did he view the harasser as a potential relationship interest. Interestingly, however, all three of the men who described harassment from gay men claimed that sexual banter and play with other *straight* men did not trouble them. Jake, for example, said that "when men get together, they talk sex," regardless of whether there are women around. He acceded, "people find me offensive, as a matter of fact," because he gets "pretty raunchy" talking and joking about sex. Only when this talk was initiated by a gay man did Jake label it as sexual harassment.

Johnson (1988) argues that talking and joking about sex is a common means of establishing intimacy among heterosexual men and maintaining a masculine identity. Homosexuality is perceived as a direct challenge and threat to the achievement of masculinity and consequently, "the male homo-

sexual is derided by other males because he is not a real man, and in male logic if one is not a real man, one is a woman" (p. 124). In Johnson's view, this dynamic not only sustains masculine identity, it also shores up male dominance over women; thus, for some straight men, talking about sex with other straight men is a form of reasserting masculinity and male dominance, whereas talking about sex with gay men threatens the very basis for their masculine privilege. For this reason they may interpret the sex talk and conduct of gay men as a form of sexual harassment.

In certain restaurants, gay men may in fact intentionally hassle straight men as an explicit strategy to undermine their privileged position in society. For example, Trent (who is openly gay) realizes that heterosexual men are uncomfortable with his sexuality, and he intentionally draws attention to his sexuality in order to bother them:

> [Interviewer: Homosexuality gets on whose nerves?]
>
> The straight people's nerves. . . . I know also that we consciously push it just because, we know, "Okay. We know this is hard for you to get used to but tough luck. I've had my whole life trying to live in this straight world and if you don't like this, tough shit." I don't mean like we're shitty to them on purpose but it's like, "I've had to worry about being accepted by straight people all my life. The shoe's on the other foot now. If you don't like it, sorry."
>
> [Interviewer: Do you get along well with most of the waitpeople?]
>
> I think I get along with straight women. I get along with gay men. I get along with gay women usually. If there's ever going to be a problem between me and somebody it will be between me and a straight man.

Trent's efforts to "push" his sexuality could easily be experienced as sexual harassment by straight men who have limited experience negotiating unwanted sexual advances. The three men who reported being sexually harassed by gay men seemed genuinely confused about the intentions of their harassers, and threatened by the possibility that they would actually be subjected to and harmed by unwanted sexual advances. But it is important to point out that Trent works in a restaurant owned by lesbians, which empowers him to confront his straight male co-workers. Not all restaurants provide the sort of atmosphere that makes this type of engagement possible; indeed, some restaurants have policies explicitly banning the hiring of gays and lesbians. Clearly, not all gay men would be able to push their sexuality without suffering severe retaliation (e.g., loss of job, physical attacks).

In contrast to the reports of the straight men in this study, none of the women interviewed reported sexual harassment from their gay or lesbian co-workers. Although Maxine was worried when she found out that one of her co-workers was lesbian, she claims that this fact no longer troubles her:

Six months ago I found out that there was a lesbian girl working there. It kind of freaked me out for a while. I was kind of aware of everything that she did towards me. I was conscious if she walked by me and accidentally brushed up against me. She's cool. She doesn't bother me. She never touches my butt or anything like that. The gay guys do that to the [straight] guys but they know they're just kidding around. The [straight] guys do that to the [straight] girls, but they don't care. They know that they're not supposed to do that with me. If they do it, I stop and look at them and they apologize and they don't

do it anymore. So they stay out of my way because I'm a meanie (laughs).

Some heterosexual women claimed they feel *more* comfortable working with gay men and lesbians. For example, Kate prefers working with gay men rather than heterosexual men or women. She claims that she often jokes about sex with her gay co-workers, yet she does not view them as potential harassers. Instead, she feels that her working conditions are more comfortable and more fun because she works with gay men. Similarly, Cathy prefers working with gay men over straight men because "gay men are a lot like women in that they're very sensitive to other people's space." Cathy also works with lesbians, and she claims that she has never felt sexually harassed by them.

The gays and lesbians in the study did not report any sexual harassment from their gay and lesbian co-workers. Laura, who is bisexual, said she preferred to work with gays and lesbians instead of heterosexuals because they are "more relaxed" about sex. Brenda said she feels comfortable working around all of her male and female colleagues—regardless of their sexual orientation:

The guys I work with [don't threaten me]. We always run by each other and pat each other on the butt. It's no big deal. Like with my girlfriend [who works at the same restaurant], all the cocktailers and hostesses love us. They don't care that we're gay. We're not a threat. We all kind of flirt but it's not sexual. A lesbian is not going to sexually harass another woman unless they're pretty gross anyway. It has nothing to do with their sexuality; it has to do with the person. You can't generalize and say that gays and lesbians are the best to work with or anything because it depends on the person.

Brenda enjoys flirtatious interactions with both men and women at her restaurant, but distinguishes these behaviors from sexual harassment. Likewise, Lynn, who is a lesbian, enjoys the relaxed sexual atmosphere at her workplace. When asked if she ever joked about sex in her workplace, she said:

> Yes! (laughs) All the time! All the time—everybody has something that they want to talk about on sex and it's got to be funny. We have gays. We have lesbians. We have straights. We have people who are real Christian-oriented. But we all jump in there and we all talk about it. It gets real funny at times. . . . I've patted a few butts . . . and I've been patted back by men, and by the women, too! (laughs).

Don and Trent, who are both gay, also said that they had never been sexually harassed in their restaurants, even though both described their restaurants as highly sexualized.

In sum, our interviews suggest that sexual orientation is an important factor in understanding each individual's experience of sexual harassment and his or her willingness to label interactions as sexual harassment. In particular, straight men may perceive gay men as potential harassers. Three of our straight male respondents claimed to enjoy the sexual banter that commonly occurs among straight men, and between heterosexual men and women, but singled out the sexual advances of gay men as sexual harassment. Their contacts with gay men may be the only context where they feel vulnerable to unwanted sexual encounters. Their sense of not being in control of the situation may make them more willing to label these episodes sexual harassment.

Our findings about sexual orientation are less suggestive regarding women. None of the women (straight, lesbian, or bisexual) reported sexual harassment from other female co-workers or from gay men. In fact, all but one of the women's reported cases of sexual harassment involved a heterosexual man. One of the two lesbians in the sample (Brenda) did experience sexual harassment from a group of lesbian customers (described earlier), but she claimed that sexual orientation is *not* key to her defining the situation as harassment. Other studies have shown that lesbian and bisexual women are routinely subjected to sexual harassment in the workplace (Schneider 1982, 1984); however, more research is needed to elaborate the social contexts and the specific definitions of harassment among lesbians.

The Exceptions

Two cases of sexual harassment were related by respondents that do not fit in the categories we have thus far described. These were the only incidents of sexual harassment reported between co-workers of the same race: in both cases, the sexual harasser is a white man, and the victim, a white woman. Laura—who is bisexual—was sexually harassed at a previous restaurant by a cook:

> This guy was just constantly badgering me about going out with him. He like grabbed me and took me in the walk-in one time. It was a real big deal. He got fired over it too. . . . I was in the back doing something and he said, "I need to talk to you," and I said, "We have nothing to talk about." He like took me and threw me against the wall in the back. . . . I ran out and told the manager, "Oh my God. He just hit me," and he saw the expression on my face. The manager went back there . . . and then he got fired.

This episode of sexual harassment involved violence, unlike the other reported cases. The threat of violence was also present in the other exception, a case described by Carla. When asked if she had ever been sexually harassed, she said,

> I experienced two men, in wait jobs, that were vulgar or offensive and one was a cook and I think he was a rapist. He had the kind of attitude where he would rape a woman. I mean, that's the kind of attitude he had. He would say totally, totally inappropriate [sexual] things.

These were the only two recounted episodes of sexual harassment between "equal" co-workers that involved white men and women, and both involved violence or the threat of violence. . . .

Discussion and Conclusion

We have argued that sexual harassment is hard to identify, and thus difficult to eradicate from the workplace, in part because our hegemonic definition of sexuality defines certain contexts of sexual interaction as legitimate. The interviews with waitpeople in Austin, Texas, indicate that how people currently identify sexual harassment singles out only a narrow range of interactions, thus disguising and ignoring a good deal of sexual domination and exploitation that take place at work.

Most of the respondents in this study work in highly sexualized atmospheres where sexual banter and touching frequently occur. There are institutionalized policies and practices in the workplace that encourage—or at the very least tolerate—a continual display and performance of heterosexuality. Many people apparently accept this ritual display as being a normal or natural feature of their work; some even enjoy this behavior. In the in-depth interviews, respondents labeled such experiences as sexual harassment in only three contexts: when perpetrated by someone who took advantage of their powerful position for personal sexual gain; when the perpetrator was of a different race/ethnicity than the victim—typically a minority man harassing a white woman; and when the perpetrator was of a different sexual orientation than the victim—typically a gay man harassing a straight man. In only two cases did respondents label experiences involving co-workers of the same race and sexual orientation as sexual harassment—and both episodes involved violence or the threat of violence.

These findings are based on a very small sample in a unique working environment, and hence it is not clear whether they are generalizable to other work settings. In less sexualized working environments, individuals may be more likely to label all offensive sexual advances as sexual harassment, whereas in more highly sexualized environments (such as topless clubs or striptease bars), fewer sexual advances may be labeled sexual harassment. Our findings do suggest that researchers should pay closer attention to the interaction context of sexual harassment, taking into account not only gender but also the race, occupational status, and sexual orientation of the assailant and the victim. . . .

REFERENCES

Anders, K. T. 1993. "Bad Sex: Who's Harassing Whom in Restaurants?" *Restaurant Business,* 20 January, pp. 46–54.

Benson, Donna J. and Gregg E. Thomson. 1982. "Sexual Harassment on a University Campus: The Confluence of Authority Relations, Sexual Interest and Gender Stratification." *Social Problems* 29:236–51.

Britton, Dana M. and Christine L. Williams. Forthcoming. "Don't Ask, Don't Tell, Don't Pursue: Military Policy and the Construction of Heterosexual Masculinity." *Journal of Homosexuality.*

Carothers, Suzanne C. and Peggy Crull. 1984. "Contrasting Sexual Harassment in Female- and Male-Dominated Occupations." In *My Troubles Are Going to Have Trouble with Me: Everyday Trials and Triumphs of Women Workers,* edited by K. B. Sacks and D. Remy. New Brunswick, NJ: Rutgers University Press.

Cobble, Dorothy Sue. 1991. *Dishing It Out: Waitresses and Their Unions in the Twentieth Century.* Urbana: University of Illinois Press.

Cockburn, Cynthia. 1991. *In the Way of Women.* Ithaca, NY: I.L.R. Press.

Crull, Peggy. 1987. "Searching for the Causes of Sexual Harassment: An Examination of Two Prototypes." In *Hidden Aspects of Women's Work,* edited by Christine Bose, Roslyn Feldberg, and Natalie Sokoloff. New York: Praeger.

Ellis, Shmuel, Azy Barak, and Adaya Pinto. 1991. "Moderating Effects of Personal Cognitions on Experienced and Perceived Sexual Harassment of Women at the Workplace." *Journal of Applied Social Psychology* 21:1320–37.

Fain, Terri C. and Douglas L. Anderton. 1987. "Sexual Harassment: Organizational Context and Diffuse Status." *Sex Roles* 17:291–311.

Fitzgerald, Louise F. 1990. "Sexual Harassment: The Definition and Measurement of a Construct." In *Ivory Power: Sexual Harassment on Campus,* edited by Michele M. Paludi. Albany: State University of New York Press.

Grauerholz, Elizabeth. 1989. "Sexual Harassment of Women Professors by Students: Exploring the Dynamics of Power, Authority, and Gender in a University Setting." *Sex Roles* 21:789–801.

Gruber, James E. and Lars Bjorn. 1982. "Blue-Collar Blues: The Sexual Harassment of Women Auto Workers." *Work and Occupations* 9:271–98.

Gutek, Barbara A. 1985. *Sex and the Workplace.* San Francisco: Jossey-Bass.

Hall, Elaine J. 1993. "Waitering/Waitressing: Engendering the Work of Table Servers." *Gender & Society* 7:329–46.

Howe, Louise Kapp. 1977. *Pink Collar Workers: Inside the World of Women's Work.* New York: Avon.

Jensen, Inger W. and Barbara A. Gutek. 1982. "Attributions and Assignment of Responsibility in Sexual Harassment." *Journal of Social Issues* 38:122–36.

Johnson, Miriam. 1988. *Strong Mothers, Weak Wives.* Berkeley: University of California Press.

Konrad, Alison M. and Barbara A. Gutek. 1986. "Impact of Work Experiences on Attitudes Toward Sexual Harassment." *Administrative Science Quarterly* 31:422–38.

MacKinnon, Catherine A. 1979. *Sexual Harassment of Working Women: A Case of Sex Discrimination.* New Haven, CT: Yale University Press.

McKinney, Kathleen. 1990. "Sexual Harassment of University Faculty by Colleagues and Students." *Sex Roles* 23:421–38.

Paludi, Michele and Richard B. Barickman. 1991. *Academic and Workplace Sexual Harassment.* Albany: State University of New York Press.

Paules, Greta Foff. 1991. *Dishing It Out: Power and Resistance Among Waitresses in a New Jersey Restaurant.* Philadelphia: Temple University Press.

Powell, Gary N. 1986. "Effects of Sex Role Identity and Sex on Definitions of Sexual Harassment." *Sex Roles* 14:9–19.

Pryor, John B. 1987. "Sexual Harassment Proclivities in Men." *Sex Roles* 17:269–90.

Reilly, Mary Ellen, Bernice Lott, Donna Caldwell, and Luisa DeLuca. 1992. "Tolerance for Sexual Harassment Related to Self-Reported Sexual Victimization." *Gender & Society* 6:122–38.

Schneider, Beth E. 1982. "Consciousness about Sexual Harassment Among Heterosexual and Lesbian Women Workers." *Journal of Social Issues* 38:75–98.

———. 1984. "The Office Affair: Myth and Reality for Heterosexual and Lesbian Women Workers." *Sociological Perspectives* 27:443–64.

U.S. Department of Labor, Bureau of Labor Statistics. 1989, January. *Employment and Earnings.* Washington, DC: Government Printing Office.

West, Candace and Don H. Zimmerman. 1987. "Doing Gender." *Gender & Society* 1:125–51.

23

The Corporate Closet
The Professional Lives of Gay Men in America

James D. Woods with Jay H. Lucas

In 1980 it was revealed that Mary Cunningham, then vice president of strategic planning at Joseph E. Seagram & Sons, was having an affair with the chairman of its parent company, William Agee. The result was an unprecedented flurry of speculation and criticism in the national press. Although she was an honors graduate of the Harvard Business School, Cunningham was portrayed as a sexual opportunist. She had won a string of promotions and raises since joining the company in 1979, and these were now subject to intense scrutiny. Why had she been promoted so quickly? Had she been rewarded for professional performance or for her extraprofessional dealings with her boss? Agee, meanwhile, was accused of behavior unbefitting a chief executive officer. The relationship with Cunningham wasn't the issue, according to his critics; the problem was the lapse in judgment it reflected. Dogged by these accusations, her credibility in question, Cunningham resigned.

The Agee-Cunningham affair, like countless others that attract less attention, highlights one of our most cherished beliefs about the workplace: that it is, or at least should be, asexual. Whether it's a company, law office, hospital, or charity, an organization is usually described as a structure, as a hierarchy of abstract "slots" to be filled by generic, asexual "workers." Activity within is organized around getting something done—managing an activity, manufacturing a commodity, providing a service—and behavior not relating to that central endeavor is kept at the fringes. Sexuality, when acknowledged at all, is assigned one of several labels: It's a friendly social diversion, an imprudent distraction, or an unwanted (and in the case of harassment, illegal) intrusion. Whatever it is, it's not official business.

Indeed, the legitimacy of bureaucratic authority is grounded in its apparent asexuality. Bureaucratic principles emphasize formal chains of command and official channels through which power and influence are presumed to flow. Few circumstances invite more resentment or are more discrediting to a manager than the appearance that he or she acquired a position of power "unfairly"—that is, by establishing romantic or sexual ties to those above. "Even when decision-makers actually remain uninfluenced by personal loyalties, the appearance of impartiality that a bureaucracy must maintain to preserve its legitimacy can be threatened if intimate relationships are publicized."[1]

Because they appear to short-circuit formal lines of authority, relationships like the one that developed between Agee and Cunningham are seen as threats to the organization. Eleven years after the liaison was made public, Standley H. Hoch's resignation as president of the General Public Utilities Corporation suggests that the rules have changed very little. In the summer of 1991, word traveled through the company that Hoch was having an affair with Susan Schepman, the company's vice president of communications. The only difference this time was who paid the penalty: It was the senior officer, Hoch, who was forced to resign. As the *New York Times* noted in its headline to the story, "The Boss Who Plays Now Pays."[2]

The Asexual Imperative

Our most powerful metaphor for the workplace is the machine, a comparison that encourages us to judge organizations according to their efficiency, productivity, and the smoothness of their output. We imagine that work is a rational activity and that workplaces depend on order. Sexuality, in contrast, is perceived as a threat to all that is rational and ordered, the antithesis of organization. It is part of an animal nature— biologically or psychodynamically driven, irrational, innate—that exists prior to (and is at war with) civilization, society, and the forces that would repress or tame it.

With their emphasis on the rational, goods-producing side of work, organizational theorists have traditionally ignored sexuality in the workplace. As a topic of study, sex is largely neglected in textbooks and journals concerned with organizational theory. Except when it can be commodified and made part of the output (as it is, for example, by models, entertainers, and others for whom physical appeal is explicitly part of the job), sexuality has no place in traditional organizational theory. In most cases this means that sexuality is viewed as an external threat to an organization, something that interferes with its primary purpose— something that must be regulated, prohibited, or otherwise held at the company gates. Our dominant ideologies and images of organization make sexuality an outsider.

Indeed, one can identify an array of policies and informal rules designed to eliminate "personal" considerations like sexuality from business. Most organizations have official or unofficial rules against nepotism, and some forbid fraternizing with clients. Managers are usually expected to absent themselves from decisions involving coworkers who are also friends, just as judges routinely disqualify themselves from trials involving people to whom they have personal ties. Employment statutes distinguish private and professional roles by prohibiting an interviewer from asking questions about an applicant's ancestry, national origin, marital status, parental status, birthplace, spouse, children, or other relatives. Implicit in these restrictions is the assumption that such matters have no impact on a candidate's ability to do the job; an employer presumably cares only about the "worker" who lies beneath the various "personal" characteristics on the surface. Even when violated, these rules establish an ideal type, an expectation about the proper way of doing business.

When sex does appear, the informal policy in most organizations is to look the other way. A 1987 survey of thirty-seven Fortune 500 companies found, for example, that only two had formal policies on romantic relationships at work (though sixteen had policies on nepotism).[3] When personnel managers were asked how they handled relationships in the office, most replied that they either "tried to overlook them" (36 percent) or "felt the problem [would] resolve itself" (18 percent). Only two (6 percent) gave new employees any kind of orientation or instruction on the matter of romantic involvements at work. Asked at what point they would have "a sense of responsibility" for their subordinates' sexual behavior, the managers replied that they would step in only when it "blatantly interfere[d] with their credibility with other employees," "[became] a source of gossip so that others might avoid the person," or "became offensive to others or disrupted the normal flow of business."[4] Likewise, when asked by *Business Week* to describe his company's policy on in-house romance, a senior manager at Leo Burnett Co., an advertising agency, explained that his company didn't have one: "As long as the relationship doesn't affect our ability to get out ads, it is none of our damn business."[5]

As a result, sexual liaisons in the office are more often governed by informal custom and taboo than by company policy. Explaining the absence of a formal etiquette on sex between coworkers, for example, Letitia Baldrige advises in her *Complete Guide to Executive Manners:* "There is no book of sexual manners in the office, because sex simply doesn't belong in the office. It exists, in lesser and greater degrees, but the greater the degree becomes, the closer the situation approaches disaster."[6] Indeed, when sexuality is acknowledged in employee manuals and hiring policies, it is usually to guard the organization against it. Policies that prohibit nepotism, fraternizing with clients, and immodest clothing all take the form of organizational prophylaxis; office romances can be stopped before they start (an implicit purpose of most dress codes) or firmly escorted outside company doors. When coworkers marry, for example, one of them is usually asked to leave.

Most often, however, sexuality goes unacknowledged until someone files a charge of sexual harassment, a matter on which most companies now have an explicit policy. The prescribed solution is usually the same: The sexual offender is simply expelled from the organization. Consequently, while some researchers have explored the definition of what constitutes harassment, most have attempted only to gauge the frequency and effect of particular harassing behaviors: "There is little systematic description of non-harassing sexual behavior at work and few attempts to understand sexuality at work aside from determining whether some particular class of behavior is or is not harassment."[7] While useful for policymakers and law enforcement officials, this approach scarcely suggests the protean role sexuality plays at work.

Sexuality is thus seen as the transgression of asexual actors into sexual territory, not as an inherent component of organizational behavior. The official, top-down view of a company classifies sexuality as an extra-organizational phenomenon. Formal and informal policies acknowledge it only when it seems to trespass on company grounds. When organizations do acknowledge sexuality, they define it narrowly, as a category of discrete "acts" (innuendos, affairs, flirtations), not as a broad subtext to all organizational behavior (sexual identities and sex-appropriate behaviors and assumptions). Indeed, if sexuality were rightly seen as an inherent component of all human interaction—something constitutive of, rather than threatening to, a professional relationship—formal policies on the matter might serve very different ends. Rather than simplistic prohibitions on sexuality, we might have an etiquette that sought to shape and police it.

The resulting sex-work dichotomy means that when professionals step into their offices, they cross an important cultural boundary. They leave the private world and assume their public roles as bankers and doctors, lawyers and teachers; sexuality stays behind in the realm of pleasure and emotion. They imagine that sex and work utilize different skills and satisfy different appetites. Each is given its characteristic time slots (the workday versus evenings and weekends) and its intended spaces (offices versus bedrooms). Geographically, temporally, and ideologically, we keep them apart. Social space is partitioned accordingly, permitting us to distinguish professional and social friends, work and leisure clothing, official and unofficial business. However it is expressed, the dichotomy implies that there is a public, work-producing, professional "self," one that can be shorn of its sexuality during office hours.

And that's how it *should* be, according to most professionals, both gay and straight. When asked to describe the role their sexuality plays at work, gay men often volunteer the conclusion that it is entirely fair and proper that the two be kept apart. In addition to formal policies that ignore or attempt to expel sexuality, they cite informal rules and normative beliefs that define sexuality as marginal, inappropriate organizational behavior. In office hallways one hears the familiar remarks: Sexuality is a private matter and doesn't belong in the office; it isn't relevant to the task at hand; people shouldn't be that intimate at work; it's impolite, a breach of office etiquette. Office decor is expected to be in "good taste," and off-color jokes are usually off limits. The cumulative message is loud and clear.

Taken together these entwined beliefs about privacy, professionalism, and office etiquette comprise an "asexual imperative," a multilayered argument that sexuality doesn't belong in the workplace at all. Gay men did not invent the imperative; on the contrary, their defense of conventional notions about privacy and professionalism merely echoes the values of the larger culture, which have a long and tangled history. But if they did not invent the imperative, they make special and insistent use of it. Like their straight peers, they often believe that sexuality has no place at work; unlike them, however, they use the imperative to protect themselves, to rationalize their own visibility. Recognizing the penalties they might pay for being openly gay at work—fearing they cannot be candid about their sexuality—they embrace the idea that they should not be, that it would be unprofessional, rude, disruptive, or tacky. The asexual imperative, although voiced by gay and straight professionals alike, is therefore most meaningful to those whose sexuality has been a source of stigma.

"My Sex Life Is Private"

Without thinking, we often use the terms *sex* and *private life* interchangeably. When asked if they've come out at work, for example, gay men often answer in euphemisms: "My boss doesn't know about my private life," or, "I haven't told her about my personal situation." Steve, an accountant with a Houston firm, remembers his dismay when a coworker moved into the same apartment complex. "He used the stairwell that runs right up to my front door," Steve recalls. "So I had to be careful. I kept my personal life—my personal life didn't come to my apartment. I went out for my personal life." Because romantic encounters were now arranged off site, Steve felt that his "personal life" no longer took place at home.

Offices, by contrast, are defined as public places, and the result is a familiar syllogism: Sexuality is private; offices are public; therefore sexuality doesn't belong in the office. When asked why he was reluctant to tell coworkers about his lover, Martin invoked the same binary logic: "Sex belongs in the bedroom, not the boardroom." Brent, a Houston manager in his late twenties, attributes the same thinking to his employer: "I think management would probably look at my coming out as a conflict of interests, in other words, that I'm bringing my personal life to work and I shouldn't be." Brent expects to be promoted within the next few years, provided "my life isn't becoming a problem with the job I'm doing."

Sexual secrecy can thus be justified as a matter of boundary maintenance, as gay men try to keep private behavior in its proper domain. In a 1992 survey by *Out/Look,* 36 percent of lesbians and gay men cited the "desire for privacy" as a reason they have remained secretive with one or more coworkers.[8] "There are lines you don't cross," says Carter, a sales representative with Hilton Hotels. "Personal matters, private matters, just don't belong in the office. You have to be aware of those boundaries." Glen, the general counsel at a large Houston company, agrees. "I need to have balance," he says. "I don't need to be socializing more with the people I work with. Likewise, I don't particularly need for my parents to know more of the details of my private life than they already know. It's *mine*. Privacy has a function, it seems to me. I've got an equilibrium that I'm comfortable with." Glen's "private life" is thus posed as something distinct from (and opposed to) his work, something that can be balanced against the counterweight of work. As he explains it, one must seek "equilibrium."

Sometimes it may be an influential boss or coworker who draws the boundaries. Jeff is one of three analysts in a small Philadelphia investment firm. Though he considers his coworkers liberal and open minded, he is reluctant to talk about sexuality at work. "I don't think they'd have any problem with it," he says. "I think about telling my boss sometimes. I'm just not sure what the reason would be. I know his attitude is that he really keeps his private life private. He doesn't talk much about his wife and kids. I'd be bringing my private life into the office, to a degree." In keeping his sexuality a secret, Jeff feels he's merely taking his cue from his boss. "We all keep our social lives pretty separate," Jeff says.

With this conceptual framework in place, even the most elaborate efforts to mislead coworkers can be justified in the interest of privacy. Louis, a lawyer in his mid-forties, recalls his first few years at one of Boston's most prestigious firms. With a growing client base and considerable expertise in tax law, Louis was considered one of the firm's rising stars. Other associates found him easy to work with, and in a few years he was considered a likely candidate for partner. The word in the hallways was that Louis was going places.

There were others, however, who considered him something of an enigma. He rarely attended office social events, and although invitations were often extended, no one at the firm had met his wife and family. She never called him at work. One Christmas Louis had invited several of the partners to a holiday party for which a lavish meal had been prepared, but even then his wife had been unexpectedly called away and was unable to meet the guests. An otherwise friendly, sociable man, Louis avoided conversations about his home life and would sometimes protest that he "wanted to keep private matters private" or that it was "unprofessional" to bring family concerns to work. When a secretary asked where Louis and his wife would be spending a summer vacation, he replied, half jokingly, that it was a secret.

His notion of privacy seems somewhat strict until one learns—as the partners ultimately did, after Louis made partner—that the wife in question was actually a man, a lover of many years who had been carefully kept out of sight, disguised in countless conversations, and excluded from office gatherings and parties. Louis's wedding ring was a family heirloom, and the photographs on his desk were of a college girlfriend long since married to someone else. At the mysterious dinner party, Louis's lover had dutifully prepared the meal and hidden in the garage until the guests were gone. While the other attorneys were surprised by the news, Louis says that they understood his reasons for doing what he did. The scheme had been an attempt, Louis explains, "to set up some boundaries and mark off a little space for my private life."

"I Don't Want to Be That Intimate with Coworkers"

Most of us learn early on to associate sexuality with intimacy. Sex, we are taught, is to be shared by those who are emotionally or conjugally attached; sex between strangers, even when morally condoned, is considered an indulgence, a substitute for the real thing. The same can be said about conversations on the subject. We are usually reluctant to discuss our sexual lives with strangers and are encouraged to reserve the topic for chats with lovers, close friends, or therapists of one sort or another.

As a result, explicit sexual conversations often serve as milestones in the development of an intimate friendship. By withholding information about our sexuality, we place limits on the growth of a relationship. Terry, a Houston attorney, feels that being secretive about his sexuality has made him "a bit colder than I might otherwise be at work." Tony, who works for a Philadelphia financial services firm, is also somewhat distant at work. "Coming out might make us closer," he says. "It might open up the opportunity for us to become close friends. In fact, I might be blocking it." The converse is also true. By coming out at work, men invite coworkers to treat them as intimates, sometimes without intending to. Sean, who works for a large public relations firm in New York, remembers coming out to his secretary. "Suddenly she assumed she knew me really well, that we were really close friends, just because she knew that I was gay."

Professional asexuality is often justified on precisely these grounds. Gay men imagine that relationships with coworkers are categorically different from friendships. A "strictly professional" relationship encompasses only the work at hand, which means that when confidences are exchanged, they should be of a business nature. "It's not as if I have a personal friendship with most of these people," says Randy. "I've socialized once with three or four of them, but we're not close friends." Work relationships that grow more intimate, as many do, are said to have "crossed over" from one category to another. As Charles, a travel agent in Virginia, explains: "After a

while, somebody's not your coworker, they're your friend—someone who's stepped over the boundary from coworker to friend. They have a new definition in your life."

To keep their distance, some men avoid all mention of sexuality at work. "I just don't think it's proper behavior in the office," says Roland, an art director for a small Manhattan advertising agency. "I don't come here to socialize with everybody. I work with these people, and if I like them, fine. And if we get along, great. But I'm not going to do it on a regular basis." Many fear that if the lines are blurred, if professional relationships become too intimate, they won't be able to do their jobs. "I have too many other things on my mind during the course of the day," says Arthur, who insists: "It isn't appropriate to get that involved in other people's personal lives." Dan warns: "There's the potential for it to get too loose, too comfortable, too friendly," when coworkers are open with one another. "It's real nice to have that comfortable feeling," he says, "but you can't cross the line. People start personalizing and not being objective."

Often they fear that their judgment will be compromised by intimate knowledge of a coworker's life. Glen refers to office friendships as a form of "modified nepotism." Brent avoids even casual lunches with coworkers. "I just think you have a better workplace if people keep their private lives to themselves," he says. "If they bring too much of it to the office, if I know too much about a person's social life, it's going to influence my decisions on merit increases or disciplinary actions, that sort of thing. Specifically, if I know that someone has gone through a divorce, and it's an unpleasant divorce and there are children involved, I'm going to be more sympathetic in my treatment of that person. And that really shouldn't impact what goes on in the office. You leave that outside the door at 8 A.M." Les, the business manager of a technical high school in Pennsylvania, lives by the same rule. "There's an old adage," he says. "You never dip your pen in the company inkwell. There must have been half a dozen times in my life when I wanted to. But I'm always glad that I didn't, because eventually I'd have to fire someone, or there'd be some static or something."

"Professionalism" is the term often invoked in defense of these boundaries. In the survey of *Out/Look* readers, 15 percent of lesbian and gay respondents said they would consider it "unprofessional" to come out at work.[9] Dan insists that the gay men on his staff be discreet about their sexuality in the presence of clients, and last year threatened to fire a male therapist who came to work wearing an earring, attire that Dan considered "unprofessional." When asked if female therapists were allowed to wear earrings in the clinic, Dan confessed that there was a double standard. The problem wasn't the earring per se but the message it might send to patients. "On a man an earring will arouse suspicion that he's gay, and that poses a problem from a professional point of view," according to Dan. "A mental health professional has to be a blank screen, so that a client can project whatever they have on you. If you disclose something inappropriate about yourself, that makes the process less clean and effective than it could be. I try to maintain the professional atmosphere you need in this society." Patrick's boss has a similar rule. Herself a lesbian, she heads a small staff of personnel trainers, including Patrick, at a large teaching hospital in Washington. "She thinks that trainers should be anonymous," Patrick says. "It would be inappropriate to come out at work, because that draws attention to yourself." Brent agrees. "It could become dangerously unprofessional around here if people found out that I'm gay," he says.

Chip, who manages the information system in a Houston company, received a harsh lesson in professionalism. Several years ago, he confronted a former coworker when she made a negative remark about gay people and AIDS. In the ensuing argument, Chip revealed that he is gay. Although he thought the disagreement had ended amicably, he received notice several days later that he had been fired. The official explanation: "unprofessional behavior."

"My Sexuality Isn't Relevant to Work"

Like arguments about privacy and intimacy, the relevance argument is grounded in the notion that "work" and "sexuality" are distinct classes of activity. It assumes that the separation of spheres is natural and normal, that the boundary between them should be breached only when there is a compelling reason. "I don't think that personal knowledge about one's sexuality is necessary for working relationships," says George, a senior airline executive, and "if there's no reason to bring it up, then why go to all the trouble?" Roland offers a similar explanation. "I'm not one of those people to go around advertising my sexuality because I don't think it's necessary. What's necessary is what I do for a living, and the job is not who I sleep with or who I date."

Typical of this view is an emphasis on the job itself and the insistence that all other matters, including sexuality, are of secondary importance. When asked if coworkers know that he is gay, Les assured me that it makes no difference. "I do my job. I'm competent. I treat them fairly. My sexuality is irrelevant." Matt, an executive at Ford, says that his boss "doesn't care if people come to work in their fucking pajamas, as long as they do the job." Jerry, a securities trader, is even more adamant. "On Wall Street, a place of work, it really isn't a place to discuss sexuality. With your friends, on nonwork time, it's perfectly fine to discuss sexuality. And if your friends happen to be coworkers, when you're not on work time, if you want to discuss sexuality, that's fine.

But in a business setting there really isn't any reason to gossip." "You want to be judged on your accomplishments," says Grey, the public relations director for a Houston mall, "not on your relationships."

In saying that sex has nothing to do with work, these men imagine that asexuality is a man's natural, initial state of being. Asexuality is his status by default, the role he assumes passively. Until he indicates otherwise, he simply *remains* asexual. Jason, a senior executive at Johnson & Johnson, remembers speaking to a friend at a meeting of the gay physicians' group in Philadelphia. The woman asked if Jason thought she should tell a potential employer, a local hospital, that she is a lesbian. "I told her that if somebody came into my office with that information, applying for a job in our organization, I would wonder, 'Why are you telling me this?' I would question their judgment. People don't come in and tell me they're heterosexual or bisexual or homosexual. That's not a part of the employment interview." Implicit in Jason's advice is the notion that workers are asexual—not heterosexual, bisexual, or homosexual—until they affirm otherwise. In a working environment, he says, such affirmations are a sign of poor judgment.

If sexuality is indeed irrelevant to work, then "coming out" can be made to appear trivial, even laughable. Milton says that "if someone ever said to me 'Are you gay?' my immediate response would be, 'Well, why on earth are you asking me?'" Jim imagined this scenario: "I've thought about it a couple of times—actually coming out at work—but I don't see how it's relevant. I don't need to go round saying, 'I'm gay, I'm gay,' and write a memo to everyone saying, 'Oh, by the way, I'm gay.' It doesn't seem like it's really important." Others described equally unlikely situations. "Unless you're a prostitute or a porn actor," asks Martin, "what does your sexuality have to do with work?"

Joel, who runs his own consulting firm in Washington, says that the same applies to most of his friendships. "Sometimes people need to know everything about you to be your friend, but I don't feel that that's the basis for friendship. My friends are not Republicans, or Lutherans, or rich people, or gay people. They're *all* people. I have lots of minorities, straights, non-Lutherans as friends. So it won't enhance our relationship for them to know that I'm gay." Only under unusual circumstances, Joel says, does he reveal his sexuality to any but close friends. As an example he describes an encounter that took place several years ago. A member of a local church organization, Joel frequently hosts dinners for students from Georgetown, American, and other universities in the Washington area. "They come in and have dinner here and socialize," he explains. After one of these dinners, one student in particular seemed eager to talk. "He said to me, as he discussed his life, that he was gay. He wanted to talk to me. He was a graduate student, and he taught Bible studies. And as I listened to him, my sense was that he needed a gay friend. He was really reaching out for help."

For Joel this at last was ample "reason" to reveal himself. "So I told him that I was also gay and invited him to go with me to get a broader range of experience in gay life in Washington." Joel admits that he rarely finds himself in situations like this, but says that "when there's a need, I'm happy to address my sexuality. But if there's no need, I'm not prepared to take the risk."

"It's Rude to Talk about Sex"

It can also be objected that sexual disclosures constitute a breach in office etiquette, that they are rude or tacky. Talking about sex, gay or otherwise, is potentially offensive, intrusive, or rude. Coworkers may find the subject distasteful, and their sensitivities must be taken into account.

Gay men are aware that sexual topics are often unwelcome, that coworkers may be upset by even the intimation of sex. "I put a joke on the messaging system once," says Chip. "The question was, 'What has a thousand teeth and eats weenies?' The answer is 'a zipper.' One of the guys called me and said he didn't think that was appropriate, because women were on the system." Arthur feels that "lawyerly etiquette" prohibits such jokes at his firm. "I think lawyers have it easier than any other profession," he says. "It's just not an inquisitive profession. We're paid to ask questions, and when it comes to our intramural relations, we just don't. It would be unseemly for me to ask another single associate—I might ask what he did over the weekend, and he'd say, 'I saw *Postcards from the Edge.*' But it would be unseemly to say, 'Well, did you go with a girl with big tits, and did you, you know, *do it?*'"

Conversations about homosexuality, in particular, are off limits. "I always find them—because of my southern background—to be a bit crass," explains Chris, an arts management consultant in New York. "You know, as southerners we don't talk about things like that. We just do them." Dave, likewise, is certain that his secretary knows his secret. "But she would *never* bring it up. She knows that it would make me uncomfortable, so she wouldn't do it. She would consider it inappropriate."

The list of examples could go on. The asexual imperative is a central, pervasive feature of professional culture, and some version of it was reported by all of the men to whom we spoke. It was defended in different ways, sometimes as a matter of privacy, productivity, or professionalism, sometimes as plain "good manners."

However it is articulated, asexuality becomes the model against which professionals judge their own behavior, a norm they observe even in the breach. The particular arguments made on its behalf differ in certain respects but are joined at the base in the shared assumption that "work" (and its corollaries "organization," "professional," and so forth) and "sexuality" (or "personal life") are inherently distinct.

Marginalizing Sex

But what happens when sexuality *does* find its way through the office door? How do professionals respond to behavior, at work, that they *do* interpret as being sexual?

One need not look far to find countless work situations that involve sexuality in one way or another. As we've already seen, sexuality suffuses the workplace. At the personal, social, and symbolic levels of organizational life, one invariably finds sexual attractions and impulses, roles and appearances, flirtations and jokes, expectations and assumptions. They range from sexual feelings, fantasies, and innuendos right through to sexual relationships, sexual acts, violations, and harassment.

On a day-to-day basis, few of these activities are categorized as sex. When they are, however, the asexual imperative supplies the conceptual framework with which we label, evaluate, and make sense of them. The imperative ensures, in particular, that while we may sometimes acknowledge sexuality in work settings, we never see it as an inherent component of work. We recognize that sexual and professional activities may at times overlap—temporarily, accidentally, illegally—but believe that we can nonetheless tell them apart, disentangling them when necessary. Indeed, even in work environments that are overtly and explicitly sexual, the imperative encourages us to see sex as the perpetual visitor, external to the true life and purpose of the organization. As workers, we signal one another that sex is (or should be) marginal to work.

One tactic is to trivialize sexual displays. We devalue work environments in which physical attractiveness is emphasized and are reluctant to assign "professional" status to those whose jobs require them to be physically attractive. Recent efforts to "professionalize" some jobs, for example by turning "stewardesses" into "flight attendants" or "secretaries" into "office managers," are often little more than campaigns to desexualize them. Professional women, especially, find it insulting to be told that their appearance is part of the job. Because we imagine a distinction between "real work" and sex appeal, such compliments are seen as a trivialization of their professional skills. Workers who do acknowledge their use of sexuality are usually deemed nonprofessional or are criticized for being unprofessional.

We frame sexual discussions as jokes or distractions and use special labels to distinguish sexuality from the flow of "real" work. When sex is the subject of conversation, we are trading "gossip" or "just kidding around." "We joke about it, you know," according to Ralph, an executive with an oil and gas exploration company in Houston. "We'll say, 'So, did you get any sex this weekend?' Or, 'I'm gonna go out and get some sex this weekend.' I'll ask Perry, this guy at work, when's the last time he and his girlfriend Jackie had sex. You know, we joke about that a lot."

Sometimes the discussion is accompanied by a disclaimer, a protestation of surprise that denotes its forbidden status. "It's *amazing* what people will tell you if you ask them," says Peter, a Philadelphia realtor who claims to know "a lot" about the private lives of his coworkers. Matt adds, "I'm always *astounded* that people will engage in that sort of locker-room talk" about their sexual conquests. Others confess a sort of guilty pleasure in talking about sex while at work. "It's terrible," Peter says, "but we shock each other by saying outrageous things, just to

pass the time when the market is slow." Scott, who works for Blue Cross in Philadelphia, agrees. "You'd be amazed—or maybe you wouldn't—at what people will ask after they've had a couple of beers or a couple of drinks. And how forward people will get!"

When work environments are especially matter-of-fact about sexuality, they are usually described as being "unusual" in this respect. George feels that his company is unique because most of its senior executives are Scandinavian. "People talk about sex in Scandinavia like they talk about going to the store. They just don't have the hangups we have in America. It took some getting used to." Others say they don't appreciate the sexual candor. Burt, a paralegal for a large Philadelphia firm, has no patience for the "constant heterosexual jokes" he hears at work. "As I'm taking notes, my boss will say things like, 'Did you see the piece of ass on that chick?' To me that's just gross. There's no place for that kind of talk in the office." Whether they are deemed amusing or offensive, trivial or inappropriate, sexual conversations are thus seen as a sort of lived exception to the asexual imperative. They are considered surprising or shocking, an indulgence or a distraction. By labeling sex in these ways, professionals signify its tenuous status in the organization.

Professionals also tend to limit their discussion of sex to those below or beside them in the hierarchy. Like other discrediting or "unprofessional" behavior, sex talk travels downward along the chain of command. Of the men we interviewed, only one felt that he could discuss sexual matters openly with his superior. "With people below you in the hierarchy, no problem," Burt adds, to clarify his earlier comment. "You can joke and have a good time, you can do whatever you want. But there are lines of demarcation about what you say to people above you." The result is a tendency to save one's sexual puns or confidences for those who are less powerful, those who share one's status, or those who are discredited. Steve shares a series of "secret nicknames" with the other junior accountants in his Houston firm (like "The FF Look," for the "fresh-fucked look"). Grey regularly "cruises" the aisles of the mall during his lunch hour, usually with the women in his secretarial pool.

Some men even suggest that sexual conversations are typical of a category of person, usually those of lower status within the organization. "My boss is a professional, and my colleagues are somewhat professional," according to Brent. "Everyone else is clerical, so it's a different kind of person. They tend to be busybodies, discussing people's personal—you know, gossiping and that sort of thing, not as serious about their work." Like most men, Brent says that sex talk isn't something a rising executive should indulge in.

The formal hierarchy is further supplemented in most organizations by a gender hierarchy, which makes it easier for gay men to confide in women than in other men. Gay professionals sometimes accumulate a coterie of female subordinates (nurses, secretaries, and so forth) with whom they share their secrets. Tip has this sort of relationship with the support staff at his hospital. Though he avoids sexual topics with his various supervisors, Tip is close to several of the female nurses. "Because of the intensity of the emergency room and operating room, you bond with everyone," he explains. "The nurses that I run into know that I'm gay—I seek them out. I go down there when I have nothing to do and visit. We chat and discuss relationships."

In short, sexual banter is considered a trivial activity and is generally reserved for trivial people. Professionals feel they are being casual or frivolous when talking about sex, and are reluctant to take this tone with those who are more senior. "A lot of flirting goes on at our office," says Darren, whose clinic employs a number of young, female dental hygienists. "As you can imagine, there are so many young women in our office, and I'm the only unmarried man there. So you have a lot of women between twenty and thirty, and flirting with me is a big part of their lives."

The asexual imperative further compels professionals to marginalize sexuality, to grant it the sort of limited access one accords any visitor: only to certain physical areas and at certain times, usually when "normal" office activities have been temporarily suspended (during lunches, breaks, travel, or special events). Overtly sexual behaviors are thus confined to the temporal and spatial margins of "work," permitted only in personal spaces or during specks of personal time.

In the most obvious sense, personal time commences when the workday ends, during the transition from business hours to social or leisure time. The restraint that coworkers show during the day dissolves over drinks or dinner, and after-work outings often raise sexual or romantic possibilities (for many gay men, a compelling reason to avoid them). "If you want to talk about sex, you should talk about it after work or some other time," says Roland. "If a coworker said to me, 'Can we go out after work and talk about X, Y or Z?', I'd say 'Sure'," Jerry makes the same distinction. "With your friends, on nonwork time, it's perfectly fine to discuss sexuality. It's also fine if your friends happen to be coworkers, when you're not on work time."

Blocks of personal time or space can also be snatched at other times during the day, provided official duties have been temporarily suspended. Sometimes, a verbal cue signals the transition. Martin remembers feeling a "pang of fear" when his boss at Ogilvy & Mather suggested that they "have a friendly chat." "I knew that meant he wanted to talk about personal stuff, which made me uncomfortable." Other men chuckle at the tendency of their coworkers to whisper when talking about personal matters, as if they were sharing a dirty secret. "They don't say, 'She works in respiratory therapy and she happens to be gay,'" according to Patrick. "It's more like [he whispers and points], 'She's gay.'" Verbal ("Let's get back to work") or nonverbal cues (withdrawing eye contact, shuffling papers) can signal the end of a personal moment.

At other times the transition is spatial. Coworkers may seek the refuge of a private office or call one another "aside" in the hallways before trafficking in sexual information. Men's restrooms become "personal space," in which the usual restrictions on sex talk are suspended. Business travel occupies a hazy gray area, bringing coworkers together in settings (hotels, airports) that mingle the personal and the professional. Company picnics, dinners, and outings are in fact designed for this purpose, to encourage social relationships between those who might otherwise know each other only on a limited, professional basis. As any corporate caterer knows, nothing kills a company party more quickly than the decision to hold it on company grounds. Perhaps because the spatial location (work space) is at odds with its temporal location (after work) and purpose (nonwork), the frequent result is ambiguity about appropriate social behavior and a lousy time for all. The move from company space signals a transition to personal time.

When coworkers encounter one another unexpectedly in such settings, the boundaries can become fuzzy. Martin ran into his secretary at a gay disco, and was distressed the following Monday when she complimented him on "the shirt I was wearing on Saturday night." Though no one else overheard their exchange, he felt she had "intruded" on his social life. Arthur remembers running into Robert, one of the firm's paralegals, at a concert. "I've known for a long time that Robert is gay," says Arthur. "You know, I see him sitting on the Long Island Railroad, getting off at the right stops, that kind of stuff. He's seen me with all-male groups; I've seen him with all-male groups, having dinner or going to the movies. We

never really talked about it. Then I went to a performance of the Gay Men's Chorus, and there he was, singing baritone. At first I was afraid to congratulate him on a wonderful concert, but then I realized that that's a very public sort of thing, to get up there on stage. I mean, Carnegie Hall, that's pretty public. And so I told him I enjoyed the concert, and since then we've been friendly."

The distinction between personal and company time is further eroded in those exceptional institutions that establish no such boundaries. Most organizations permit some segregation of professional and personal lives, however vague or shifting the boundary. It is a different matter, however, when the "total" quality of an organization precludes such distinctions. "My boss has this view of officers as representatives, twenty-four hours per day, of the company," says Jeff. As evidence of this he cites a story he heard about the director of human resources, a man named Greg, shortly after he joined the company. "I've never asked Greg whether this is true or not, but somebody told me that the president of the company told Greg that he didn't want him seen coming out of the all-male theater, the Tom Cat bookstore. Apparently Greg had been seen going in there a couple of times."

Tip complains that he has no personal time. As a surgical resident he is accustomed to long hours and frequent nights on call. Even when not at the hospital, he is at the beck and call of the hospital—practically and symbolically affirmed by the pager he wears. "My boss doesn't like you to take vacations," he says, "even though it's allowed. He feels you're wasting your time. If you come in with a tan, he'll give you grief about the fact that you weren't at home reading." Other organizations, like churches and the military, argue that their members are always on the job, that one simply *is* a soldier or priest. In dismissing thousands of lesbian and gay men, the military has argued that their sexual behavior falls within its broad jurisdiction, even when it takes place off site and after hours.

But such organizations are unusual. In most cases the question is not if but *where* the boundary between the public and private shall be placed. The asexual imperative, having insisted that such a divide is possible, ensures that work and sex will be on opposite sides of it. The imperative is neither unconditional nor universally imposed (or self-imposed); indeed, it varies in strength from one setting to the next, even within the same organization. Yet virtually all gay men articulate it—and quite often defend it—in one form or another.

It is easy to see why the asexual imperative might appeal to gay men. Describing it, they are sometimes emotional, often passionate. They adopt a tone of voice reserved for sensitive subjects, and it is clear that they have used these same words before. In their comments one often hears what appear to be contradictions, as they articulate their wishes (the hortatory "Sexuality *shouldn't* matter") in the form of observations or statements of fact (the declarative "Sexuality *doesn't* matter"). Yet the repeated insistence—that sexuality *doesn't* matter, *doesn't* belong in the workplace, *is* a private matter—scarcely conceals the men's recognition that it is not always so.

The asexual imperative insists that workers be judged on the quality of their work, that professional interactions be stripped of their sexual component. For men whose sexuality has been stigmatized, criminalized, medicalized, morally condemned, and subjected to interpersonal penalties of all sorts, this is a powerful idea. Seen in this way, the invocation of the imperative is an appeal for fairness; it demands that "work" be defined narrowly, that it not be confused with the social or sexual characteristics of the individual doing it. "It's not a perfect world," says Terry. "Sexuality should have no impact on the people you work with, on clients, or on business development and all of that." But Terry knows that this isn't the case. "I know some people in town who have that situation, but there are damn few."

The imperative is appealing for another reason. By demanding that workers be asexual, it permits gay men to rationalize the painful efforts they sometimes make to misrepresent themselves at work. As they worry about the necessity of misleading coworkers, as they speak to them of imaginary lovers or take pains to disguise actual ones, they often believe that they are acting on principle. Strict beliefs about privacy and professionalism are comforting; they supply a justification, other than self-protection, for sexual secrecy. "Even if coming out were easier, if you weren't worried about losing your job or something, I don't think I would do it," says Glen. "Even if gay people were in the majority, I would want a certain amount of privacy. I don't think I'd want everyone at work to know my business." But beneath his statement of principle lies another motive. "It would be nice," he adds, "to have the choice."

NOTES

1. David F. Greenberg, *The Construction of Homosexuality* (Chicago: University of Chicago Press, 1988), pp. 437–38. See also pp. 434–54.
2. *New York Times,* June 13, 1991, p. D1.
3. Andrea Warfield, "Co-Worker Romances: Impact on the Work Group and on Career-Oriented Women," *Personnel,* May 1987, pp. 22–35.
4. Ibid., p. 30.
5. "Romance in the Workplace: Corporate Rules for the Game of Love," *Business Week,* June 18, 1984, pp. 70–71.
6. Letitia Baldrige, *Letitia Baldrige's Complete Guide to Executive Manners* (New York: Rawson, 1985), p. 53.
7. Barbara Gutek, "Sexuality in the Workplace: Key Issues in Research and Organizational Practice," in Hearn et al., *The Sexuality of Organization,* p. 57.
8. Woods, James D., "Self-Disclosure at Work." Results of a questionnaire distributed in *Out/Look,* vol. 16 (Spring 1992), pp. 87–88.
9. Woods, "Self-Disclosure at Work," pp. 87–88.

24

"Their Logic Against Them"
Contradictions in Sex, Race, and Class in Silicon Valley

Karen J. Hossfeld

The bosses here have this type of reasoning like a seesaw. One day it's "you're paid less because women are different than men," or "immigrants need less to get by." The next day it's "you're all just workers here—no special treatment just because you're female or foreigners."

Well, they think they're pretty clever with their doubletalk, and that we're just a bunch of dumb aliens. But it takes two to use a seesaw. What we're gradually figuring out here is how to use their own logic against them.

—FILIPINA CIRCUIT BOARD ASSEMBLER IN SILICON VALLEY (EMPHASIS ADDED)

This [reading] examines how contradictory ideologies about sex, race, class, and nationality are used as forms of both labor control and labor resistance in the capitalist workplace today. Specifically, I look at the workplace relationships between Third World immigrant women production workers and their predominantly white male managers in high-tech manufacturing industry in Silicon Valley, California. My findings indicate that in workplaces where managers and workers are divided by sex and race, class struggle can and does take gender- and race-specific forms. Managers encourage women immi-

grant workers to identify with their gender, racial, and national identities when the managers want to "distract" the workers from their *class* concerns about working conditions. Similarly, when workers have workplace needs that actually *are* defined by gender, nationality, or race, managers tend to deny these identities and to stress the workers' generic class position. Immigrant women workers have learned to redeploy their managers' gender and racial tactics to their own advantage, however, in order to gain more control over their jobs. As the Filipina worker quoted at the beginning of the [reading] so aptly said, they have learned to use managers' "own logic against them." . . .

This [reading] draws from a larger study of the articulation of sex, race, class, and nationality in the lives of immigrant women high-tech workers (Hossfeld 1988b). Empirical data draw on more than two hundred interviews conducted between 1982 and 1986 with Silicon Valley workers; their family members, employers, and managers; and labor and community organizers. Extensive in-depth interviews were conducted with eighty-four immigrant women, representing twenty-one Third World nationalities, and with forty-one employers and managers, who represented twenty-three firms. All but five of these management representatives were U.S.-born white males. All of the workers and managers were employed in Santa Clara County, California, firms that engaged in some aspect of semiconductor "chip" manufacturing. I observed production at nineteen of these firms. . . .

Silicon Valley

The Prototype

"Silicon Valley" refers to the microelectronics-based high-tech industrial region located just south of San Francisco in Santa Clara County, California. The area has been heralded as an economic panacea and as a regional prototype for localities around the globe that seek rapid economic growth and incorporation into the international market. Representatives from more than two thousand local and national governments, from People's Republic of China delegations to the queen of England, have visited the valley in search of a model for their own industrial revitalization. They have been awed by the sparkling, clean-looking facilities and the exuberant young executives who claim to have made riches overnight. But the much-fetishized Silicon Valley "model" that so many seek to emulate implies more than just the potential promise of jobs, revenue, growth, and participation in the technological "revolution." . . .

Class Structure and the Division of Labor

Close to 200,000 people—one out of every four employees in the San Jose Metropolitan Statistical Area labor force—work in Silicon Valley's microelectronics industry. There are more than 800 manufacturing firms that hire ten or more people each, including 120 "large" firms that each count over 250 employees. An even larger number of small firms hire fewer than ten employees apiece. Approximately half of this high-tech labor force—100,000 employees—works in production-related work: at least half of these workers—an estimated 50,000 to 70,000—are in low-paying, semiskilled operative jobs (Siegel and Borock 1982; *Annual Planning Information* 1983).

The division of labor within the industry is dramatically skewed according to gender and race. Although women account for close to half of the total paid labor force in Santa Clara County both inside and outside the industry, only 18 percent of the managers, 17 percent of the professional employees, and 25 percent of the technicians are female. Conversely, women hold at least 68 percent and by some reports as many as 85 to 90 percent of the valley's high-tech operative jobs. In the companies examined in my study, women made up an average of 90 percent of the assembly and operative workers. Only rarely do they work as production managers or supervisors, the management area that works most closely with the operatives.

Similar disparities exist vis-à-vis minority employment. According to the 1980 census, 26.51 percent of the civilian work force of Santa Clara County was composed of racial minorities. Fifteen percent were Hispanic (all races); 7.5 percent were Asian–Pacific Islanders; 3 percent were Black; 0.5 percent were Native American; and 0.2 percent were listed as "other races—not Hispanic" (*Annual Planning Information* 1983:96–97). Over 75 percent of the Hispanics were of Mexican descent. Of the 102,000 Asian–Pacific Islanders counted in the 1980 census as living in the area, roughly 28 percent were Filipino or of Filipino descent; 22 percent each were Japanese and Chinese; 11 percent were Vietnamese; 6 percent were Korean; 5 percent were Asian Indian; and less than 2 percent each were of other national origins (*Annual Planning Information* 1983:64).

Since the census was taken, influxes of refugees from Indochina have quadrupled the number of Vietnamese, Laotians, and Cambodians in the area: as of early 1984, there were an estimated forty-five thousand Southeast Asian refugees in Santa Clara County, as well as a smaller but growing number of refugees from other regions such as Central America. I have talked with Silicon Valley production workers from at least thirty Third World nations. In addition to the largest groups, whose members are from Mexico,

Vietnam, the Philippines, and Korea, workers hail from China, Cambodia, Laos, Thailand, Malaysia, Indonesia, India, Pakistan, Iran, Ethiopia, Haiti, Cuba, El Salvador, Nicaragua, Guatemala, and Venezuela. There are also small groups from southern Europe, particularly Portugal and Greece.

Within the microelectronics industry, 12 percent of the managers, 16 percent of the professionals, and 18 percent of the technicians are minorities—although they are concentrated at the lower-paying and less powerful ends of these categories. An estimated 50 to 75 percent of the operative jobs are thought to be held by minorities. My study suggests that the figure may be closer to 80 percent.

Both employers and workers interviewed in this study agreed that the lower the skill and pay level of the job, the higher the percentage of Third World immigrant women who were employed. Thus assembly work, which is the least skilled and lowest-paid production job, tends to be done predominantly by Third World women. Entry-level production workers, who work in job categories such as semiconductor processing and assembly, earn an average of $4.50 to $5.50 an hour; experienced workers in these jobs earn from $5.50 to $8.50. At the subcontracting assembly plants I observed, immigrant women accounted for 75 to 100 percent of the production labor force. At only one of these plants did white males account for more than 2 percent of the production workers. More than 90 percent of the managers and owners at these businesses were white males, however.

This occupational structure is typical of the industry's division of labor nationwide. The percentage of women of color in operative jobs is fairly standardized throughout various high-tech centers; what varies is *which* minority groups are employed, not the job categories in which they are employed.

Obviously, there is tremendous cultural and historical variation both between and within the diverse national groups that my informants represent. Here I emphasize their commonalities. Their collective experience is based on their jobs, present class status, recent uprooting, and immigration. Many are racial and ethnic minorities for the first time. Finally, they have in common their gender and their membership in family households.

Labor Control on the Shop Floor

Gender and Racial Logic

In Silicon Valley production shops, the ideological battleground is an important arena of class struggle for labor control. Management frequently calls upon ideologies and arrangements concerning sex and race, as well as class, to manipulate worker consciousness and to legitimate the hierarchical division of labor. Management taps both traditional popular stereotypes about the presumed lack of status and limited abilities of women, minorities, and immigrants and the workers' own fears, concerns, and sense of priorities as immigrant women.

But despite management's success in disempowering and devaluing labor, immigrant women workers have co-opted some of these ideologies and have developed others of their own, playing on management's prejudices to the workers' own advantage. In so doing, the workers turn the "logic" of capital against managers, as they do the intertwining logics of patriarchy and racism. . . .

From interviews with Silicon Valley managers and employers, it is evident that high-tech firms find immigrant women particularly appealing workers not only because they are "cheap" and considered easily "expendable" but also because management can draw on and further exploit preexisting patriarchal and racist ideologies and arrangements that have affected these women's consciousness and realities. In their dealings with the women, managers fragment the women's multifaceted identities into falsely separated categories of "worker," "ethnic," and "woman." The effect is to increase and play off the workers' vulnerabilities and splinter their consciousness. But I also found limited examples of the women drawing strength from their multifaceted experiences and developing a unified consciousness with which to confront their oppressions. These instances of how the workers have manipulated management's ideology are important not only in their own right but as models. To date, though, management holds the balance of power in this ideological struggle.

I label management's tactics "gender-specific" and "racial-specific" forms of labor control and struggle, or gender and racial "logic." I use the term *capital logic* to refer to strategies by capitalists to increase profit maximization. Enforcement by employers of a highly stratified class division of labor as a form of labor control is one such strategy. Similarly, I use the terms *gender logic* and *racial logic* to refer to strategies to promote gender and racial hierarchies. Here I am concerned primarily with the ways in which employers and managers devise and incorporate gender and racial logic in the interests of capital logic. Attempts to legitimate inequality form my main examples.

I focus primarily on managers' "gender-specific" tactics because management uses race-specific (il)logic much less directly in dealing with workers. Management clearly draws on racist assumptions in hiring and dealing with its work force, but usually it makes an effort to conceal its racism from workers. Management recognizes, to varying degrees, that the appearance of blatant racism against workers is not acceptable, mainly because immigrants have not sufficiently internalized racism to respond to it positively. Off the shop floor, however, the managers' brutal and open racism toward workers was apparent during "private" interviews. Managers' comments demonstrate that racism is a leading factor in capital logic but that management typically disguises racist logic by using the more socially ac-

ceptable "immigrant logic." Both American and immigrant workers tend to accept capital's relegation of immigrants to secondary status in the labor market.

Conversely, "gender logic" is much less disguised: management uses it freely and directly to control workers. Patriarchal and sexist ideology is *not* considered inappropriate. Because women workers themselves have already internalized patriarchal ideology, they are more likely to "agree" with or at least accept it than they are racist assumptions. This [reading] documents a wide range of sexist assumptions that management employs in order to control and divide workers. . . .

The Logic of "Secondary" Work

Central to gender-specific capital logic is the assumption that women's paid work is both secondary and temporary. More than 70 percent of the employers and 80 percent of the women workers I interviewed stated that a woman's primary jobs are those of wife, mother, and homemaker, even when she works full time in the paid labor force. Because employers view women's primary job as in the home, and they assume that, prototypically, every woman is connected to a man who is bringing in a larger paycheck, they claim that women do not need to earn a full living wage. Employers repeatedly asserted that they believed the low-level jobs were filled only by women because men could not afford to or would not work for such low wages.

Indeed, many of the women would not survive on what they earned unless they pooled resources. For some, especially the nonimmigrants, low wages did mean dependency on men—or at least on family networks and household units. None of the women I interviewed—immigrant or nonimmigrant—lived alone. Yet most of them would be financially better off without their menfolk. For most of the immigrant women, their low wages were the most substantial and steady source of their family's income. *Eighty percent of the immigrant women workers in my study were the largest per annum earners in their households.*

Even when their wages were primary—the main or only family income—the women still considered men to be the major bread-winners. The women considered their waged work as secondary, both in economic value and as a source of identity. Although most agreed that women and men who do exactly the same jobs should be paid the same, they had little expectation that as women they would be eligible for higher-paying "male" jobs. While some of these women—particularly the Asians—believed they could overcome racial and class barriers in the capitalist division of labor, few viewed gender as a division that could be changed. While they may believe that hard work can overcome many obstacles and raise their *families'* socioeconomic class standing, they do not feel that their position in the gender division of labor will change. Many, of course, expect or hope for better jobs for themselves—and others expect or hope to leave the paid labor force altogether—but few wish to enter traditional male jobs or to have jobs that are higher in status or earn-ings than the men in their families.

The majority of women who are earn-ing more than their male family members view their situation negatively and hope it will change soon. They do not want to earn less than they currently do; rather, they want their menfolk to earn more. This was true of women in all the ethnic groups. The exceptions—a vocal minority—were mainly Mexicanas. Lupe, a high-tech worker in her twenties, explained:

Some of the girls I work with are ridiculous—they think if they earn more than their husbands it will hurt the men's pride. They play up to the machismo. . . . I guess it's not entirely ridiculous, because some of them regu-larly come in with black eyes and bruises, so the men are something they have to reckon with. But, my God, if I had a man like that I would leave. . . .

My boyfriend's smart enough to real-ize that we need my paycheck to feed us and my kids. He usually brings home less than I do, and we're both damn grateful for every cent that either of us makes. When I got a raise he was very happy—I think he feels more relieved, not more resentful. But then, he's not a very typical man, no? Anyway, he'd probably change if we got married and had kids of his own—that's when they start wanting to be the king of their castle.

A Korean immigrant woman in her thir-ties told how her husband was so adamant that she not earn more than he and that the men in the household be the family's main supporters that each time she cashed her paycheck she gave some of her earnings to her teenaged son to turn over to the father as part of the earnings from his part-time job. She was upset about putting her son in a po-sition of being deceitful to his father, but both mother and son agreed it was the only alternative to the father's otherwise danger-ous, violent outbursts.

As in the rest of America, in most cases, the men earned more in those households where both the women and men worked reg-ularly. In many of the families, however, the men tended to work less regularly than the women and to have higher unemployment rates. While most of the families vocally blamed very real socioeconomic conditions for the unemployment, such as declines in "male" industrial sector jobs, many women also felt that their husbands took out their resentment on their families. A young Mexi-cana, who went to a shelter for battered women after her husband repeatedly beat her, described her extreme situation:

He knows it's not his fault or my fault that he lost his job: they laid off almost his whole shift. But he acts like I keep my job just to spite him, and it's gotten so I'm so scared of him. Sometimes I think he'd rather kill me or have us starve than watch me go to work and bring home pay. He doesn't want to hurt me, but he is so hurt inside because he feels he has failed as a man.

Certainly not all laid-off married men go to the extreme of beating their wives, but the majority of married women workers whose husbands had gone through periods of unemployment said that the men treated other family members significantly worse when they were out of work. When capitalism rejects male workers, they often use patriarchal channels to vent their anxieties. In a world where men are defined by their control over their environment, losing control in one arena, such as that of the work world, may lead them to tighten control in another arena in which they still have power—the family. This classic cycle is not unique to Third World immigrant communities, but as male unemployment increases in these communities, so may the cycle of male violence.

Even some of the women who recognize the importance of their economic role feel that their status and identity as wage earners are less important than those of men. Many of the women feel that men work not only for income but for respect and dignity. They see their own work as less noble. Although some said they derive satisfaction from their ability to hold a job, none of the women considered her job to be a primary part of her identity or a source of self-esteem. These women see themselves as responsible primarily for the welfare of their families: their main identity is as mother, wife, sister, and daughter, not as worker. Their waged work is seen as an extension of caring for their families. It is not a question of *choosing* to work—they do so out of economic necessity.

When I asked whether their husbands' and fathers' waged work could also be viewed as an extension of familial duties, the women indicated that they definitely perceived a difference. Men's paid labor outside the home was seen as integral both to the men's self-definition and to their responsibility vis-à-vis the family; conversely, women's labor force participation was seen as contradictory both to the women's self-image and to their definitions of female responsibility.

Many immigrant women see their wage contribution to the family's economic survival not only as secondary but as *temporary,* even when they have held their jobs for several years. They expect to quit their production jobs after they have saved enough money to go to school, stay home full time, or open a family business. In actuality, however, most of them barely earn enough to live on, let alone to save, and women who think they are signing on for a brief stint may end up staying in the industry for years.

That these workers view their jobs as temporary has important ramifications for both employers and unions, as well as for the workers themselves. When workers believe they are on board a company for a short time, they are more likely to put up with poor working conditions, because they see them as short term. A Mexican woman who used to work in wafer fabrication reflected on the consequences of such rationalization:

I worked in that place for four years, and it was really bad—the chemicals knocked you out, and the pay was very low. My friends and me, though, we never made a big deal about it, because we kept thinking we were going to quit soon anyway, so why bother. . . . We didn't really think of it as our career or anything—just as something we had to do until our fortune changed. It's not exactly the kind of work a girl dreams of herself doing.

My friend was engaged when we started working there, and she thought she was going to get married any day, and then she'd quit. Then, after she was married, she thought she'd quit as soon as she got pregnant. . . . She has two kids now, and she's still there. Now she's saying she'll quit real soon, because her husband's going to get a better job any time now, and she'll finally get to stay home, like she wants.

Ironically, these women's jobs may turn out to be only temporary, but for different reasons and with different consequences than they planned. Industry analysts predict that within the next decade the majority of Silicon Valley production jobs may well be automated out of existence (Carey 1984). Certainly for some of the immigrant women, their dreams of setting aside money for occupational training or children's schooling or to open a family business or finance relatives' immigration expenses do come true, but not for most. Nonetheless, almost without exception, the women production workers I interviewed—both immigrant and nonimmigrant—saw their present jobs as temporary.

Employers are thus at an advantage in hiring these women at low wages and with little job security. They can play on the women's *own* consciousness as wives and mothers whose primary identities are defined by home and familial roles. While the division of labor prompts the workers to believe that women's waged work is less valuable than men's, the women workers themselves arrive in Silicon Valley with this ideology already internalized.

A young Filipina woman, who was hired at a walk-in interview at an electronics production facility, experienced a striking example of the contradictions confronting immigrant women workers in the valley. Neither she nor her husband, who was hired the same day, had any previous related work experience or degrees. Yet her husband was offered an entry-level job as a technician, while she was offered an assembly job paying three dollars per hour less. The personnel manager told her husband that he would "find [the technician job] more interesting than assembly work." The woman had said in the interview that she wanted to be considered for a higher-paying job because she had two children to support. The manager refused to consider her for a different job, she said, and told her that "it will work out fine for you, though, because with your husband's job, and you *helping out* [emphasis added] you'll have a nice little family income."

The same manager told me on a separate occasion that the company preferred to hire members of the same families because it meant that workers' relatives would be more supportive about their working and the combined incomes would put less financial strain on individual workers. This concern over workers and their families dissipated, however, when the Filipino couple split up, leaving the wife with only the "helping-out" pay instead of the "nice little family income." When the woman requested a higher-paying job so she could support her family, the same manager told her that "family concerns were out of place at work" and did not promote her.

This incident suggests that a woman's family identity is considered important when it is advantageous to employers and irrelevant when it is disadvantageous. Similarly, managers encourage women workers to identify themselves primarily as workers or as women, depending on the circumstances. At one plant where I interviewed both managers and workers, males and females were openly separated by the company's hiring policy: entry-level jobs for females were in assembly, and entry-level jobs for males were as technicians. As at the plant where the Filipino couple worked, neither the "male" nor the "female" entry-level jobs required previous experience or training, but the "male" job paid significantly more.

Apparently, the employers at this plant *did* see differences between male and female workers, despite their claims to the contrary. Yet, when the women workers asked for "special treatment" because of these differences, the employers' attitudes rapidly changed. When the first quality circle was introduced in one production unit at this plant, the workers, all of whom were women, were told to suggest ways to improve the quality of work. The most frequently mentioned concern of all the women production workers I met was the lack of decent child-care facilities. The company replied that child care was not a quality of work–related issue but a "special women's concern" that was none of the company's business.

A Portuguese worker succinctly described the tendency among employers to play on and then deny such gender logic:

> The boss tells us not to bring our "women's problems" with us to work if we want to be treated equal. What does he mean by that? I am working here *because* of my "women's problems"— because I am a woman. Working here *creates* my "women's problems." I need this job because I am a woman and have children to feed. And I'll probably get fired because I am a woman and need to spend more time with my children. I am only one person—and I bring my whole self to work with me. So what does he mean, don't bring my "women's problems" here?

As this woman's words so vividly illustrate, divisions of labor and of lives are intricately interwoven. Any attempts to organize the women workers of Silicon Valley—by unions, communities, political or social groups and by the women themselves— must deal with the articulation of gender, race, and class inequalities in their lives. . . .

Racial and Ethnic Logic

Typically, high-tech firms in Silicon Valley hire production workers from a wide spectrum of national groups. If their lack of a common language (both linguistically and culturally) serves to fragment the labor force, capital benefits. Conversely, management may find it more difficult to control workers with whom it cannot communicate precisely. Several workers said they have feigned a language barrier in order to avoid taking instructions; they have also called forth cultural taboos— both real and feigned—to avoid undesirable situations. One Haitian woman, who took a lot of kidding from her employer about voodoo and black magic, insisted that she could not work the night shift because evil spirits were out then. Because she was a good worker, the employer let her switch to days. When I tried to establish whether she believed the evil spirits were real or imagined, she laughed and said, "Does it matter? The result is the same: I can be home at night with my kids."

Management in several plants believed that racial and national diversity minimized solidarity. According to one supervisor, workers were forbidden from sitting next to people of their own nationality (i.e., language group) in order to "cut down on the chatting." Workers quickly found two ways to reverse this decision, using management's own class, racial, and gender logic. Chinese women workers told the supervisor that if they were not "chaperoned" by other Chinese women, their families would not let them continue to work there. Vietnamese women told him that the younger Vietnamese women would not work hard unless they were under the eyes of the older workers and that a group of newly hired Vietnamese workers would not learn to do the job right unless they had someone who spoke their language to explain it to them. Both of these arguments could also be interpreted as examples of older workers wanting to control younger ones in a generational hierarchy, but this was not the case. Afterwards both the Chinese and the Vietnamese women laughed among themselves at their cleverness. Nor did they forget the support needs of workers from other ethnic groups: they argued with the supervisor that the same customs and needs held true for many of the language groups represented, and the restriction was rescinded.

Another example of a large-scale demonstration of interethnic solidarity on the shop floor involved workers playing off supervisors' stereotypes regarding the superior work of Asians over Mexicans. The incident was precipitated when a young Mexicana, newly assigned to an assembly unit in which a new circuit board was being assembled, fell behind in her quota. The supervisor berated her with racial slurs about Mexicans' "laziness" and "stupidity" and told her to sit next to and "watch the Orientals." As a group, the Asian women she was stationed next to slowed down their production, thereby setting the average quota on the new boards at a slower than usual pace. The women were in fits of laughter after work because the supervisor had assumed that the speed set by the Asians was the fastest possible, since they were the "best" workers.

Hispanic workers also turn management's anti-Mexican prejudices against them, as a Salvadorean woman explained:

First of all, the bosses think everyone from Latin America is Mexican, and they think all Mexicans are dumb. So, whenever they try to speed up production, or give us something we don't want to do, we just act dumb. It's not as if you act smart and you get a promotion or a bonus anyway.

A Mexicana operative confided, "They [management] assume we don't understand much English, but we understand when we want to."

A Chinese woman, who was under five feet tall and who identified her age by saying she was a "grandmother," laughingly told how she had her white male supervisor "wrapped around [her] finger." She consciously played into his stereotype that Asian women are small, timid, and obedient by frequently smiling at and bowing to him and doing her job carefully. But when she had a special need, to take a day or a few hours off, for example, she would put on her best guileless, ingratiating look and, full of apologies, usually obtained it. She also served as a voice for co-workers whom the supervisor considered more abrasive. On one occasion, when three white women in her unit complained about poor lighting and headaches, the supervisor became irritated and did not respond to their complaint. Later that week the Chinese "grandmother" approached him, saying that she was concerned that poor lighting was limiting the workers' productivity. The lighting was quickly improved. This incident illustrates that managers can and do respond to workers' demand when they result in increased productivity.

Some workers see strategies to improve and control their work processes and environments as contradictory and as "Uncle Tomming." Two friends, both Filipinas, debated this issue. One argued that "acting like a China doll" only reinforced white employers' stereotypes, while the other said that countering the stereotype would not change their situation, so they might as well use the stereotype to their advantage. The same analysis applies to women workers who consciously encourage male managers to view women as different from men in their abilities and characteristics. For women and minority workers, the need for short-term gains and benefits and for long-term equal treatment is a constant contradiction. And for the majority of workers, short-term tactics are unlikely to result in long-term equality.

Potential for Organizing

Obviously, the lesson here for organizing is contradictory. Testimonies such as the ones given in these pages clearly document that immigrant women are not docile, servile people who always follow orders, as many employers interviewed for this study claimed. Orchestrating major actions such as family migration so that they could take control of and better their lives has helped these women develop leadership and survival skills. Because of these qualities, many of the women I interviewed struck me as potentially effective labor and community organizers and rank-and-file leaders. Yet almost none of them were interested in collective organizing, because of time limitations and family constraints and because of their lack of confidence in labor unions, the feminist movement, and community organizations. Many were simply too worn out from trying to make ends meet and caring for their families. And for some, the level of inequality and exploitation on the shop floor did not seem that bad, compared to their past experiences. A Salvadorean woman I interviewed exemplified this predicament. Her job as a solderer required her to work with a microscope all day, causing her to develop severe eye and back strain. Although she was losing her eyesight and went home exhausted after working overtime, she told me she was still very happy to be in the United States and very grateful to her employer. "I have nothing to

complain about," she told me. "It is such a luxury to know that when I go home all of my children will still be alive." After losing two sons to government-backed terrorist death squads in El Salvador, her work life in Silicon Valley was indeed an improvement.

Nonetheless, their past torment does not reduce the job insecurity, poor working conditions, pay inequality, and discrimination so many immigrant workers in Silicon Valley experience in their jobs. In fact, as informants' testimonies suggest, in many cases, past hardships have rendered them less likely to organize collectively. At the same time, individual acts of resistance do not succeed on their own in changing the structured inequality of the division of labor. Most of these actions remain at the agitation level and lack the coordination needed to give workers real bargaining power. And, as mentioned, individual strategies that workers have devised can be contradictory. Simultaneous to winning short-run victories, they can also reinforce both gender and racial stereotypes in the long run. Further, because many of these victories are isolated and individual, they can often be divisive. For workers to gain both greater workplace control *and* combat sexism and racism, organized *collective* strategies hold greater possibilities.

Neither organized labor nor feminist or immigrant community organizations have prioritized the needs of the Silicon Valley's immigrant women workers. As of 1989, for example, not a single full-time paid labor union organizer was assigned to the local high-tech industry. Given that Silicon Valley is the center of the largest and fastest-growing manufacturing industry in the country, this is, as one long-time local organizer, Mike Eisenscher, put it, "a frightening condemnation of the labor movement" (1987). That union leadership has also failed to mark for attention a work force that is dominated by women of color is equally disheartening.

My findings indicate that Silicon Valley's immigrant women workers have a great deal to gain from organizing, but also a great deal to contribute. They have their numeric strength, but also a wealth of creativity, insight, and experience that could be a shot in the arm to the stagnating national labor movement. They also have a great deal to teach—and learn from—feminist and ethnic community movements. But until these or new alternative movements learn to speak and listen to these women, the women will continue to struggle on their own, individually and in small groups. In their struggle for better jobs and better lives, one of the most effective tactics they have is their own resourcefulness in manipulating management's "own logic against them."

REFERENCES

Annual Planning Information: San Jose Standard Metropolitan Statistical Area, 1983–1984. 1983. Sacramento: California Department of Employment Development.

Carey, Pete. 1984. "Tomorrow's Robots: A Revolution at Work." *San Jose Mercury News,* February 8–11.

Eisenscher, Mike. 1987. "Organizing the Shop in Electronics." Paper presented at the West Coast Marxist Scholars Conference, November 14, Berkeley, California.

Hossfeld, Karen. 1988a. "Divisions of Labor, Divisions of Lives: Immigrant Women Workers in Silicon Valley." Ph.D. diss., University of California, Santa Cruz.

———. 1988b. "The Triple Shift: Immigrant Women Workers and the Household Division of Labor in Silicon Valley." Paper presented at the annual meetings of the American Sociological Association, Atlanta.

Siegel, Lenny and Herb Borock. 1982. *Background Report on Silicon Valley.* Prepared for the U.S. Commission on Civil Rights. Mountain View, CA: Pacific Studies Center.

Types of Work

How do medical students learn to be doctors? How do workers in routine production jobs avoid boredom and make the workday interesting? How do restaurant workers whose jobs require them to interact with the public cope with angry customers? Although some forces shaping the workplace are relevant for virtually all types of workers (e.g., technological change, race and gender dynamics), answering these questions requires us to narrow our focus and examine particular occupational groups. The five sections in Part IV are designed to address some of these occupation-specific topics.

Industrial Work

For the purposes of this anthology, industrial work refers to "blue-collar" occupations—craft, operative, and laborer positions. These occupations may have received more attention from sociologists than any other type of work. In fact, what is now called "the sociology of work" used to be known more narrowly as "industrial sociology" (or, in Thompson's (1989, p. 14) words, "plant sociology"). The historical importance of industrial work for sociologists stemmed from several factors. First, a relatively large segment of the labor force was employed in these occupations. In the immediate post-WWII era, for example, approximately 40 percent of the labor force held blue-collar jobs (Tausky 1996, p. 48). More important than their numbers, however, was the fact that industrial workers were a major force in labor unions. Industrial workers' ability and willingness to collectively challenge their employers was apparent even in the early stages of industrialization. As modern industry developed, industrial conflict increased, inspiring the efforts of people like Frederick Taylor, as well as the attention of sociologists. Industrial sociology tended to be heavily focused on workers' behavior inside the workplace, and this concern continues to be expressed in participant observation–based studies of blue-collar jobs.

In the lead article of this section, Michael Burawoy examines the "art of making out" among operators in a machine shop. In contrast to those who view industrial workers as tightly controlled by management and technology, Burawoy argues that operators retain a degree of autonomy that they use to pursue their own objectives. In particular, by manipulating the rules that regulated the organization of their work, machine shop operators increased their production levels and thus earned higher pay.

Workers' ability to "self-organize" and thus to expand their control over production is also a theme of Tom Juravich's reading, "Women on the Line." Like Burawoy's, Juravich's analysis of assembly line labor is based on participant observation. Juravich challenges accepted accounts of industrial work, especially that traditionally performed by women. He argues that this work is often portrayed as deskilled, menial, and routine. Instead, however, Juravich reveals women workers' hidden "craft knowledge" and shows how this knowledge can be used to subvert management directives.

Personal Service Work

By all accounts, the United States has become a service society. The vast majority of new jobs being created are service occupations, while goods-producing occupations are in decline (Kutscher 1987). What counts as a service job? Definitions vary, but at the most general level, service jobs are those in which "face-to-face or voice-to-voice interaction is a fundamental element of the work" (Macdonald and Sirianni 1996, p. 3). Because they involve interaction, these jobs also typically require workers to perform emotional labor (see Reading 10).

There are many different types of service jobs, and they vary widely in their earnings and organization. The three service jobs described in this section represent a type of service employment known as "personal services." These are services that are produced primarily for individuals and families, and hence involve the worker directly in service delivery. Two additional factors differentiate the occupations discussed in this section from professionals and other higher-level service workers. The first is the degree of control workers exercise over their interactions and, hence, emotions. Unlike professionals, who monitor their own behavior, the workers described in these readings tend to be closely supervised by others. In addition, the *clients* of professionals have less power in the interaction than do the *customers* of service workers. The authority relations in the two types of occupations thus are somewhat different, with professionals having much greater authority over their clients than service workers have over customers.

The fast-food industry has become a symbol of a service economy, and McDonald's is undoubtedly one of the most well known American corporations (see Reading 18). Part of what has made McDonald's so successful is its ability to produce a highly standardized product: "Not only is the food supposed to taste the same every day everywhere in the world, but McDonald's promises that every meal will be served quickly, courteously, and with a smile" (Leidner 1993, p. 45). As this quote reveals, standard-

ization of the product also implies a certain standardization of workers' behavior. This theme is developed in more detail by Robin Leidner, whose reading is drawn from her 1993 study, *Fast Food, Fast Talk: Service Work and the Routinization of Everyday Life.* As a participant-observer working in a Chicago-area McDonald's, Leidner gained a first-hand account of McDonald's efforts to routinize service interactions.

Whereas McDonald's workers have relatively little opportunity to improvise or tailor their interactions with customers, restaurant wait staff are not quite so restricted. At the same time, however, since workers in this occupation depend heavily on tips, they face pressures to interact with customers in ways that will maximize their earnings and preserve their dignity. The tipping relationship underscores the service worker's subordinate position vis-à-vis customers. As Greta Foff Paules describes in Reading 28, a tip is a "unilateral gift," which signifies the higher status of the donor over the recipient. She shows that while tipping places the balance of power in the customers' hands, female servers pursue strategies to challenge this power imbalance and resist the negative symbolism of service work.

Service work—like other forms of work—is racially and gender stratified. Racial and gender distinctions have played a particularly important role in domestic service. Historically, domestic service in the United States has been performed by subordinate racial and ethnic groups; African American and Hispanic women continue to be overrepresented in this occupational category. In the final reading in this section, "Maid to Order," Barbara Ehrenreich examines the work experiences of paid house-cleaners employed by a domestic cleaning service. Ehrenreich also raises larger questions about the meaning and significance of "outsourcing" domestic work.

Professional and Knowledge Work

By most accounts, professional and knowledge workers constitute the most privileged sector of the labor force. Higher average earnings, lower average rates of unemployment, and greater access than other workers to job autonomy are a few examples of these privileges. In addition, as the core of the "new middle class," professional and knowledge workers occupy an important role in the larger society (Ehrenreich 1989; Gouldner 1979).

What are the professions? Although the term "profession" is often used synonymously with "occupation," sociologists prefer to reserve the former label for occupations with a distinct set of characteristics. As Ehrenreich (1989, pp. 260–261) observes: "Professions, as opposed to *jobs,* are understood to offer some measure of intrinsic satisfaction, some linkage of science and service, intellect and conscience, autonomy and responsibility. No one has such expectations of a mere *job;* and it is this, as much as anything, which defines the middle-class advantage over the working-class majority."

Medicine, engineering, and law—the topics covered in this section's readings—are among the oldest professions. In "Working on (and Around) the Unborn Patient," Monica Casper examines the social construction of work in fetal surgery. Operating on unborn patients is a new and controversial area of medicine, and Casper examines the processes of cooperation and conflict as they play out in this surgical arena. Of particular interest to Casper is the varying ways that participants define "the work object" and the factors that account for those different definitions.

In Reading 31, we turn our attention to law. Like other professions, law involves the mastery of highly abstract, specialized knowledge. Prospective lawyers thus must undergo a lengthy training period. During this time, students are expected not only to acquire technical knowledge, but also to take on the persona of their profession. Becoming a professional thus involves the acquisition of a distinct occupational identity, culture, and behavioral style.

Jennifer Pierce examines the emotional demands and expectations associated with being a litigator. These legal professionals must display a particular emotional demeanor in order to elicit cooperation from others in the courtroom and to achieve their broader objectives. Pierce suggests that the "gamesmanship" that is at the center of the litigator's presentation of self is a highly gendered style. Definitions of good lawyering and expectations for professional behavior in this historically male-dominated profession have come to be expressed in masculine terms. Pierce thus shows how gender can become embedded in occupational expectations for behavior, which can create different dilemmas for male and female professionals.

Professionals—like other workers—are often employed by large organizations. In Reading 32, Gideon Kunda examines the relations between the self and the organization in a large engineering firm. He explores how engineering professionals at "Tech" construct and manage their organizational selves. Kunda finds that these professionals continually struggle to balance their organizational selves with who they believe they "really" are. Kunda's research demonstrates the power of organizational cultures to shape members' lives.

Managerial Work

The two readings in this section focus on managers. This occupational group covers a variety of jobs—from supervisors to chief executives—and thus is difficult to easily characterize. Robert Jackall's focus in "The

Social Structure of Managerial Work" is the ranks of "middle managers," whose authority puts them above first-line supervisors and below the chief executive. Managers at this level must learn to operate within a complex, hierarchical system where relations of authority must be constantly negotiated. For example, as Jackall shows, details are "pushed down" the hierarchy and credit is "pushed up." More generally, Jackall reveals the uncertainty and ambiguity that permeate managerial work and the ways managers cope with these features of managerial life.

Managerial hierarchies are also the topic of Sharon Collins's reading, "Black Corporate Executives." Collins shows that despite increased numbers of blacks in managerial positions, racial segregation within managerial ranks persists. In particular, Collins suggests that black managers often find themselves in racialized positions that are highly vulnerable to changing economic and social policies. At a more general level, Collins's reading is important for two related reasons. First, she underscores the earlier claim that management occupations differ widely in their authority, pay, and security. Hence, we must resist the temptation to generalize about managerial work. In addition, Collins shows that rising numbers of African Americans in management does not necessarily imply a move toward greater racial equality in managerial ranks.

Marginal, Contingent, and Low-Wage Jobs

A major trend affecting work organization is the growth of contingent or temporary work. In their desire to cut costs and increase flexibility, employers in many industries have begun to shrink their permanent workforces and rely on workers subcontracted from a temporary agency. Reading 35, drawn from Kevin Henson's 1996 book, *Just a Temp*, exam-

ines what it means to be a temporary worker. Henson pays particular attention to the stigma attached to temporary work and the ways temp workers cope with this stigma.

Jobs in fast food, as Katherine Newman observes, "are notoriously stigmatized and denigrated. 'McJob' has become a common epithet for work without much redeeming value." Under these conditions, how do workers in these jobs overcome this stigma and maintain their dignity and self-respect? In Reading 36, Newman examines this question by looking at the experiences of mostly young, mostly minority workers living in central Harlem. For these workers, a low-wage job in fast food is a job nevertheless. Newman shows that in a work-centered society like the United States, even a stigmatized job confers more honor and dignity than being without work.

This point is also brought home in the final reading in this section, which examines workers in the informal or "underground" economy. In many people's eyes, scavenging for recyclables does not count as "work"; instead, sifting through city dumpsters and garbage cans—by those other than "garbage collectors" employed by city government—may be viewed as an act of deviance motivated by economic desperation. In her study of homeless recyclers, Teresa Gowan shows that homeless men derive meaning and dignity from scavenging, despite its marginalized status. Her research underscores the centrality of work—even marginal and stigmatized work—in people's lives.

REFERENCES

Ehrenreich, Barbara. 1989. *Fear of Falling: The Inner Life of the Middle Class.* New York: Pantheon.

Gouldner, Alvin J. 1979. *The Future of the Intellectuals and the Rise of the New Class.* London: Macmillan Press.

Henson, Kevin. 1996. *Just a Temp.* Philadelphia: Temple University Press.

Hochschild, Arlie Russell. 1983. *The Managed Heart.* Berkeley: University of California Press.

Kutscher, Ronald E. 1987. "Projections 2000: Overview and Implications of the Projections to 2000." *Monthly Labor Review* (September): 3–9.

Leidner, Robin. 1993. *Fast Food, Fast Talk: Service Work and the Routinization of Everyday Life.* Berkeley: University of California Press.

MacDonald, Cameron Lynne and Carmen Sirianni. 1996. "The Service Society and the Chang-ing Experience of Work." Pp. 1–26 in *Working in the Service Society,* edited by Cameron Lynne MacDonald and Carmen Sirianni. Philadelphia: Temple University Press.

Tausky, Curt. 1996. *Work and Society.* Itasca, IL: F. E. Peacock Publishers, Inc.

Thompson, Paul. 1989. *The Nature of Work.* London: Macmillan.

INDUSTRIAL WORK

25

Thirty Years of Making Out

Michael Burawoy

Making Out—A Game Workers Play

. . . In this section I propose to treat the activities on the shop floor as a series of games in which operators attempt to achieve levels of production that earn incentive pay, in other words, anything over 100 percent. The precise target that each operator aims at is established on an individual basis, varying with job, machine, experience, and so on. Some are satisfied with 125 percent, while others are in a foul mood unless they achieve 140 percent—the ceiling imposed and recognized by all participants. This game of making out provides a framework for evaluating the productive activities and the social relations that arise out of the organization of work. We can look upon making out, therefore, as comprising a sequence of stages—of

encounters between machine operators and the social or nonsocial objects that regulate the conditions of work. The rules of the game are experienced as a set of externally imposed relationships. The art of making out is to manipulate those relationships with the purpose of advancing as quickly as possible from one stage to the next.

At the beginning of the shift, operators assemble outside the time office on the shop floor to collect their production cards and punch in on the "setup" of their first task. If it has already been set up on the previous shift, the operator simply punches in on production. Usually operators know from talking to their counterpart, before the beginning of the shift, which task they are likely to receive. Knowing what is available on the floor for their machine, an operator is sometimes in a position to bargain with the scheduling man, who is responsible for distributing the tasks. . . . the scheduling man's duties [did not] end with the distribution of work, but . . . he also assumed some responsibility for ensuring that the department turned out the

From *Manufacturing Consent,* by Michael Burawoy. Reprinted by permission of the University of Chicago Press and the author.

requisite parts on time. Therefore, he is often found stalking the floor, checking up on progress and urging workers to get a move on. Because he has no formal authority over the operators, the scheduling man's only recourse is to his bargaining strength, based on the discretion he can exert in distributing jobs and fixing up an operator's time. Operators who hold strategic jobs, requiring a particular skill, for example, or who are frequently called upon to do "hot jobs" are in a strong bargaining position vis-à-vis the scheduling man. He knows this and is careful not to upset them. . . .

After receiving their first task, operators have to find the blueprint and tooling for the operation. These are usually in the crib, although they may be already out on the floor. The crib attendant is therefore a strategic person whose cooperation an operator must secure. If the crib attendant chooses to be uncooperative in dispensing towels, blueprints, fixtures, etc., and, particularly, in the grinding of tools, operators can be held up for considerable lengths of time. Occasionally, operators who have managed to gain the confidence of the crib attendant will enter the crib themselves and expedite the process. Since, unlike the scheduling man, the crib attendant has no real interest in whether the operator makes out, his cooperation has to be elicited by other means. For the first five months of my employment my relations with the crib attendant on second shift were very poor, but at Christmas things changed dramatically. Every year the local union distributes a Christmas ham to all its members. I told Harry that I couldn't be bothered picking mine up from the union hall and that he could have it for himself. He was delighted, and after that I received good service in the crib. . . .

While I was able to secure the cooperation of the crib attendant, I was not so fortunate with the truck drivers. When I was being broken in on the miscellaneous job, I was told repeatedly that the first thing I must do was to befriend the truck driver. He or she was responsible for bringing the stock from the aisles, where it was kept in tubs, to the machine. Particularly at the beginning of the shift, when everyone is seeking their assistance, truck drivers can hold you up for a considerable period. While some treated everyone alike, others discriminated among operators, frustrating those without power, assisting those who were powerful. Working on the miscellaneous job meant that I was continually requiring the truck driver's services, and, when Morris was in the seat, he used to delight in frustrating me by making me wait. There was nothing I could do about it unless I was on a hot job; then the foreman or scheduling man might intervene. To complain to the foreman on any other occasion would only have brought me more travail, since Morris could easily retaliate later on. It was better just to sit tight and wait. Like the crib attendants, truckers have no stake in the operator's making out, and they are, at the same time, acutely conscious of their power in the shop. All they want is for you to get off their backs so that they can rest, light up, chat with their friends, or have a cup of coffee—in other words, enjoy the marginal freedoms of the machine operator. As one of the graffiti in the men's toilet put it, "Fuck the company, fuck the union, but most of all fuck the truckers because they fuck us all." Operators who become impatient may, if they know how, hop into an idle truck and move their own stock. But this may have unfortunate consequences, for other operators may ask them to get their stock too. . . .

As they wait for the stock to arrive, each operator sets up his machine, if it is not already set up. This can take anything from a few minutes to two shifts, but normally it takes less than an hour. Since every setup has a standard time for completion, operators try to make out here, too. When a setup is unusually rapid, an operator may even be able to make time so that, when he punches in on production, he has already turned out a few pieces. A setup man is available for assistance. Particularly for the inexperienced, his help is crucial, but, as with the other auxiliary personnel, his co-operation must be sought and possibly bargained for. He, too, has no obvious stake in your making out, though the quicker he is through with you, the freer he is. Once the machine is set up and the stock has arrived, the operator can begin the first piece, and the setup man is no longer required unless the setup turns out to be unsatisfactory.

The quality and concern of setup men vary enormously. For example, on day shift the setup man was not known for his cooperative spirit. When I asked Bill, my day man, who the setup man was on day shift, he replied, "Oh, he died some years ago." This was a reference to the fact that the present one was useless as far as he was concerned. On second shift, by contrast, the setup man went about his job with enthusiasm and friendliness. When he was in a position to help, he most certainly did his best, and everyone liked and respected him. Yet even he did not know all the jobs in the shop. Indeed, he knew hardly any of my machines and so was of little use to me. . . .

The assigned task may be to drill a set of holes in a plate, pipe, casting, or whatever; to mill the surface of some elbow; to turn an internal diameter on a lathe; to shave the teeth on a gear; and so on. The first piece completed has to be checked by the inspector against the blueprint. Between inspector and operator there is an irrevocable conflict of interest because the former is concerned with quality while the operator is concerned with quantity. Time spent when an operation just won't come right—when piece after piece fails, according to the inspector, to meet the specifications of the blueprint—represents lost time to the operator. Yet the inspector wants to OK the piece as quickly as possible and doesn't want to be bothered with checking further pieces until the required tolerances are met.

When a piece is on the margin, some inspectors will let it go, but others will enforce the specifications of the blueprint to the nth degree. In any event, inspectors are in practice, if not in theory, held partly responsible if an operator runs scrap. Though formally accountable only for the first piece that is tagged as OK, an inspector will be bawled out if subsequent pieces fall outside the tolerance limits. Thus, inspectors are to some extent at the mercy of the operators, who, after successfully getting the first piece OK'd, may turn up the speed of their machine and turn out scrap. An operator who does this can always blame the inspector by shifting the tag from the first piece to one that is scrap. Of course, an inspector has ample opportunity to take revenge on an operator who tries to shaft him. Moreover, operators also bear the responsibility for quality. During my term of employment, charts were distributed and hung up on each machine, defining the frequency with which operators were expected to check their pieces for any given machine at any particular tolerance level. Moreover, in the period immediately prior to the investigation of the plant's quality-assurance organization by an outside certifying body, operators were expected to indicate on the back of the inspection card the number of times they checked their pieces. . . .

When an inspector holds up an operator who is working on an important job but is unable to satisfy the specifications on the blueprint, a foreman may intervene to persuade the inspector to OK the piece. When this conflict cannot be resolved at the lowest level, it is taken to the next rung in the management hierarchy, and the superintendent fights it out with the chief inspector. . . . [P]roduction management generally defeated quality control in such bargaining . . . which reflects an organizational structure in which quality control is directly subordinated to production. Not surprisingly, the function of quality control has become a sensitive issue and the focus of much conflict among the higher levels of Allied's engine division. Quality control is continually trying to fight itself clear of subordination to production management so as to monitor quality on the shop floor. This, of course, would have deleterious effects on levels of production, and so it is opposed by the production management. Particularly sensitive in this regard is control of the engine test department, which in 1975 resided with production management. The production manager naturally claimed that he was capable of assessing quality impartially. Furthermore, he justified this arrangement by shifting the locus of quality problems from the shop floor to the design of the engine, which brought the engineers into the fray. Engineering management, not surprisingly, opposes the trend toward increasing their responsibility for quality. Therefore, the manager of engineering supported greater autonomy for quality control as a reflection of his interest in returning responsibility for quality to the shop floor. . . .

After the first piece has been OK'd, the operator engages in a battle with the clock and the machine. Unless the task is a familiar one—in which case the answer is known, within limits—the question is: Can I make out? It may be necessary to figure some angles, some short cuts, to speed up the machine, make a special tool, etc. In these undertakings there is always an element of risk—for example, the possibility of turning out scrap or of breaking tools. If it becomes apparent that making out is impossible or quite unlikely, operators slacken off and take it easy. Since they are guaranteed their base earnings, there is little point in wearing themselves out unless they can make more than the base earnings—that is, more than 100 percent. That is what Roy refers to as

goldbricking. The other form of "output restriction" to which he refers—quota restriction—entails putting a ceiling on how much an operator may turn in—that is, on how much he may record on the production card. In 1945 the ceiling was $10.00 a day or $1.25 an hour, though this did vary somewhat between machines. In 1975 the ceiling was defined as 140 percent for all operations on all machines. It was presumed that turning in more than 140 percent led to "price cuts" (rate increases), and this was indeed the case.

In 1975 quota restriction was not necessarily a form of restriction of *output,* because operators *regularly* turned *out* more than 140 percent, but turned *in* only 140 percent, keeping the remainder as a "kitty" for those operations on which they could not make out. Indeed, operators would "bust their ass" for entire shifts, when they had a gravy job, so as to build up a kitty for the following day(s). Experienced operators on the more sophisticated machines could easily build up a kitty of a week's work. There was always some discrepancy, therefore, between what was registered in the books as completed and what was actually completed on the shop floor. Shop management was more concerned with the latter and let the books take care of themselves. Both the 140 percent ceiling and the practice of banking (keeping a kitty) were recognized and accepted by everyone on the shop floor, even if they didn't meet with the approval of higher management.

Management outside the shop also regarded the practice of "chiseling" as illicit, while management within the shop either assisted or connived in it. Chiseling (Roy's expression, which did not have currency on the shop floor in 1975) involves redistributing time from one operation to another so that operators can maximize the period turned in as over 100 percent. Either the time clerk cooperates by punching the cards in and out at the appropriate time or the operators are allowed to punch their own cards.

In part, because of the diversity of jobs, some of them very short, I managed to avoid punching any of my cards. At the end of the shift I would sit down with an account of the pieces completed in each job and fiddle around with the eight hours available, so as to maximize my earnings. I would pencil in the calculated times of starting and finishing each operation. No one ever complained, but it is unlikely that such consistent juggling would have been allowed on first shift. . . .

The Organization of a Shop-Floor Culture

So far we have considered the stages through which any operation must go for its completion and the roles of different employees in advancing the operation from stage to stage. In practice the stages themselves are subject to considerable manipulation, and there were occasions when I would complete an operation without ever having been given it by the scheduling man, without having a blueprint, or without having it checked by the inspector. It is not necessary to discuss these manipulations further, since by now it must be apparent that relations emanating directly from the organization of work are understood and attain meaning primarily in terms of making out. Even social interaction not occasioned by the structure of work is dominated by and couched in the idiom of making out. When someone comes over to talk, his first question is, "Are you making out?" followed by "What's the rate?" If you are not making out, your conversation is likely to consist of explanations of why you are not: "The rate's impossible," "I had to wait an hour for the inspector to check the first piece," "These mother-fucking drills keep on burning up." When you are sweating it out on the machine, "knocking the pieces out," a passerby may call out "Gravy!"—suggesting that the job is not as difficult as you are making it appear. Or, when you are "goofing off"—visiting other workers or gossiping at the coffee machine—as likely as not someone will yell out, "You've got it made, man!" When faced with an operation that is obviously impossible, some comedian may bawl out, "Best job in the house!" Calling out to a passerby, "You got nothing to do?" will frequently elicit a protest of the nature, "I'm making out. What more do you want?" At lunchtime, operators of similar machines tend to sit together, and each undertakes a postmortem of the first half of the shift. Why they failed to make out, who "screwed them up," what they expect to accomplish in the second half of the shift, can they make up lost time, advice for others who are having some difficulty, and so on—such topics tend to dominate lunchtime conversations. As regards the domination of shop-floor interaction by the culture of making out . . . the idiom, status, tempo, etc., of interaction at work continue to be governed by and to rise out of the relations in production that constitute the rules of making out.

In summary, we have seen how the shop-floor culture revolves around making out. Each worker sooner or later is sucked into this distinctive set of activities and language, which then proceed to take on a meaning of their own. Like Roy, when I first entered the shop I was somewhat contemptuous of this game of making out, which appeared to advance Allied's profit margins more than the operators' interests. But I experienced the same shift of opinion that Roy reported:

> . . . attitudes changed from mere indifference to the piecework incentive to a determination not to be forced to respond, when failure to get a price increase on one of the lowest paying operations of his job repertoire convinced him that the company was unfair. Light scorn for the incentive scheme turned to bitterness. Several months

later, however, after fellow operator Mc-Cann had instructed him in the "angles on making out," the writer was finding values in the piecework system other than economic ones. He struggled to attain quota "for the hell of it," because it was a "little game" and "keeps me from being bored."[1]

Such a pattern of insertion and seduction is common. In my own case, it took me some time to understand the shop language, let alone the intricacies of making out. It was a matter of three or four months before I began to make out by using a number of angles and by transferring time from one operation to another. Once I knew I had a chance to make out, the rewards of participating in a game in which the outcomes were uncertain absorbed my attention, and I found myself spontaneously cooperating with management in the production of greater surplus value. Moreover, it was only in this way that I could establish relationships with others on the shop floor. Until I was able to strut around the floor like an experienced operator, as if I had all the time in the world and could still make out, few but the greenest would condescend to engage me in conversation. Thus, it was in terms of the culture of making out that individuals evaluated one another and themselves. It provided the basis of status hierarchies on the shop floor, and it was reinforced by the fact that the more sophisticated machines requiring greater skill also had the easier rates. Auxiliary personnel developed characters in accordance with their willingness to cooperate in making out: Morris was a lousy guy because he'd always delay in bringing stock; Harry was basically a decent crib attendant (after he took my ham), tried to help the guys, but was overworked; Charley was an OK scheduling man because he'd try to give me the gravy jobs; Bill, my day man, was "all right" because he'd show me the angles on making out, give me some kitty if I needed it, and sometimes cover up for me when I made a mess of things. . . .

What we have observed is the expansion of the area of the "self-organization" of workers as they pursue their daily activities. We have seen how operators, in order to make out at all, subvert rules promulgated from on high, create informal alliances with auxiliary workers, make their own tools, and so on. In order to produce surplus value, workers have had to organize their relations and activities in opposition to management, particularly middle and senior management. . . . For Cornelius Castoriadis, this represents the fundamental contradiction of capitalism:

> In short, it [the deep contradiction] lies in the fact that capitalism . . . is obliged to try and achieve the simultaneous exclusion and participation of people in relation to their activities, in the fact that people are forced to ensure the functioning of the system half of the time *against* the system's own rules and therefore in struggle against it. This fundamental contradiction appears constantly wherever the process of management meets the process of execution, which is precisely (and par excellence) the social moment of production.[2]

But if the self-organization of workers is necessary for the survival of capitalism, it also questions the foundations of capitalism.

> When the shop-floor collective establishes norms that informally sanction both "slackers" and "speeders," when it constantly constitutes and reconstitutes itself in "informal" groups that respond to both the requirements of the work process and to personal affinities, it can only be viewed as actively opposing to capitalist principles new principles of productive and social organization and a new view of work.[3]

But is making out as radical as Castoriadis claims? Or is it, as Herbert Marcuse would argue, a mode of adaptation that reproduces "the voluntary servitude" of workers to capital? Are these freedoms and needs, generated and partially satisfied in the context of work and harnessed to the production of surplus value, a challenge to "capitalist principles"? Does making out present an anticipation of something new, the potential for human self-organization, or is it wholly contained within the reproduction of capitalist relations?[4] . . .

NOTES

1. Donald Roy, "Work Satisfaction and Social Reward in Quota Achievement," *American Journal of Sociology* 57 (1953): 509–10.

2. Paul Cardan (alias Cornelius Castoriadis), *Redefining Revolution* (London: Solidarity Pamphlet 44, n.d.), p. 11.

3. Cornelius Castoriadis, "On the History of the Workers' Movement," *Telos* no. 30 (Winter 1976–77): 35.

4. See, for example, Herbert Marcuse, *One Dimensional Man* (Boston: Beacon Press, 1964), chap. 1; *An Essay on Liberation* (Boston: Beacon Press, 1969); *Eros and Civilization* (Boston: Beacon Press, 1955), chap. 10.

26

Women on the Line

Tom Juravich

Until recently, the role played by women in the industrial labor force has been severely underestimated. Although the postwar bias emphasized the extent to which women remained in the home, women have played fundamental roles in American industry; as Barbara Wertheimer has written, "We Were There" (Wertheimer, 1977). We tend to forget that it was women who first left the New England farms (leaving the men behind) to work in the new industrial centers of Lawrence, Massachusetts and Manchester, New Hampshire. In addition, entire industries, such as the garment industry, hired primarily female workers.

It is important, however, to characterize the nature of women's participation in the industrial labor force. Despite great shifts in American industry (textiles in New England have been replaced by high-tech, for example), "women's work" has remained essentially the same. For the most part women have occupied the lowest paid, most tedious "handwork" positions. In the textile industry women nimbly replaced spools of thread and tied swift weavers' knots as well as similar handwork. In today's high-tech industry they assemble electrical components and micro chips. As in the garment industry, women hold the majority of assembly positions (Grossman, 1980).

Thus the women at National are part of a continuing American tradition, one that our conventional view of the industrial workplace has generally downplayed. In what follows we will observe assembly work at National—

and see that in addition to low pay and repetition, it is characterized by a considerable degree of chaos.

Women's Work

On the average there were twenty women working on the second floor at National. The number fluctuated greatly while I was there. It plummeted to a low of eight during two different lay-offs, and rose to forty during peak production (for about two months when a four-hour second shift was added). The women were extremely young. A handful were in their forties and fifties, but most were in their early twenties. At least eight were under twenty.

There were ten to fifteen small machines on the floor that were used sporadically for a variety of jobs. Two or three might be running at any given time. But most of the women worked on the three-wire assembly, the major product of the floor. The production of these assemblies was broken down into six separate tasks.

The process began at the SELM, where terminals were placed on various lengths of wire. It was the operator's job to inspect these leads (wires) as they came off the machine. They were then stacked in cardboard boxes and put in a shelf near the SELM at the back of the floor.

The assembly itself began in the next phase. Between four and eight women took three different colors (and lengths) of wire and inserted them into a small plastic block an inch square and a quarter of an inch deep. This was by far the hardest and most tedious job. Each lead had a square terminal on the end which had to be pushed into a square channel in the plastic block until it locked. It was not an easy task. It took a certain amount of force and some finesse as well. If you held the lead too far back you bent the terminal. If you held the lead too close you banged your fingers.

You could always tell who was new on the job by their bandaged fingers. Without exception, new employees were assigned to "blocking," as this job was called, and without exception their hands bled. If they lasted beyond the first few weeks, which most did not, they developed the calluses necessary to do the job.

Besides being physically difficult, "blocking" demanded speed. The women were expected to block close to two hundred assemblies per hour, although we had no bonus system (where workers can earn extra money by being more productive). If after a training period that rate was not met, the women would be called into the office repeatedly and threatened with dismissal, although to my knowledge that never happened. Usually they quit long before that.

From the blockers the assemblies moved down the line to be sewed. Although I use the phrase "down the line," the assemblies were not moved down a belt or automatic assembly line. They were stacked in boxes which the women shifted from station to station. At any given time the floor was stacked with a variety of boxes containing assemblies at different stages of production. The sewers took assemblies that had been blocked and on specially designed machines sewed around the three wires. Sewing was the most favored job on the line, and it was usually assigned to women who had been at National the longest. The younger women competed hard for these positions.

The assemblies then passed to the singers (singe-ers) and trimmers. The actual stitching of the assemblies was fairly loose, and it was the singer's job to pass a heat gun (which looked like a large hair dryer) over the stitching to shrink the thread around the wires. After singeing, the loose end of the thread was cut off by the trimmers. In many ways the easiest job, trimming, was often held back as a reward or to be done when there was little else to do.

These five steps—making the leads on the SELM, blocking, sewing, singeing, and trimming—produced the assembly. The sixth and final stage was to inspect and pack the finished product. The inspectors checked the length of the wire, the sewing, the blocks (to see that they were not scratched in the blocking process), and a variety of other characteristics. Depending on the work load, one or two women worked as inspectors.

For a while my knowledge of the women's work was only that of an outsider. I had observed them repeating their tasks over and over, but my attention had been focused on the SELMs. Their work seemed straightforward, and although boring, appeared to present little confusion. Yet in the coming months, as I spent more time with the women, I began to understand that their work was quite different. Although these six tasks appeared so simple that one would expect the process to be automatic, it was actually the source of much confusion, conflict, and disagreement. A careful look at the production process reveals why women on the line were beset with their own kind of chaos.

The Craft Knowledge of Deskilled Workers

Much has been written about the deskilling of labor in the twentieth century. Perhaps the best example is Harry Braverman's *Labor and Monopoly Capital* (1974). Throughout the book, as well as in related volumes (see Zimbalist, 1979), we are given numerous examples of how technology has taken away the skill from a job, leaving only routine to the workers.

If there ever were an example of this degradation of labor, it was the kind of work performed by the women at National. There is no way that their work could be seen as exciting, satisfying, or rewarding. It was tolerable at best. Even Carroll recognized this. He once told me, "It takes a special kind of girl [sic] to do this kind of work. The guys could never do it, they don't have the patience. We like the neat ones, the ones who like this close work."

One comes away from Braverman convinced that little skill is necessary to perform most factory jobs. This conviction is very much shared as a conventional wisdom. Yet these "simple" tasks often look quite different from the shop floor.

One of my first jobs working closely with the women involved changing the belts on the sewing machines. The belts were made of leather and stretched or broke over time. Installing a new belt involved cutting a new piece of leather to the proper length and fastening it together with a metal staple. This took about half an hour (until much later when I discovered a special tool which was designed to punch the holes and fasten the staple). The women poked fun at my somewhat clumsy style (the task actually was quite difficult), especially Carol (not to be confused with Carroll), whose machine I started on. She was a large woman in her late thirties with a hot temper but also a good sense of humor.

After replacing the belt, I sat down at her machine and asked her to show me how to sew. I never heard such laughter. The other women thought that a man sewing was the funniest thing they ever saw. It took me five minutes to sew a single assembly, and it came out completely wrong. "You'll never make your rate that way, honey," said Carol. "You think your job is hard," said one of the other sewers. Carroll would also sew while repairing or testing a machine. He was a little better at it than me, but not much. The women used the opportunity to give him all the grief they could. "See if you can keep that up all day," one of the women used to say.

It was clear to me, and to anyone else watching, that a worker could not walk in off the street, sit down at the machine, and make her rate. Yet despite his own experience, this is how Carroll often threatened the women: "Why, I could get somebody right off the street who could do that job faster than you." Perhaps Carroll believed it. The usual explanation is that these jobs require a certain manual dexterity, though no real skill, and some people simply lack the physical coordination. Yet this explanation is not adequate. As I found out, many of our assembly positions required more than deftness.

At one point I was called over to adjust a small press. It applied a spade terminal (like the one on your television antenna) to an already cut and stripped length of wire. The repair amounted essentially to cleaning out the applicator with the air line and some lubricant, but in the process I discovered that Betty, the operator of the machine, had perfected an ingenious technique.

The wire was approximately sixteen inches long, and terminals had to be placed on each end parallel to each other. I had seen other women struggle with this job, placing a terminal on one end, turning the wire around, lining it up and applying the other terminal. Betty, however, had found another way to do it. As I was checking the machine, I saw her pick up a handful of wires and bounce them in her hand. When I asked what she was doing, she said she was finding the "bend" in the wire. This "bend" she referred to was due to the fact that the wire had originally been coiled on a spool. Although the machine that stripped and cut the wire included a mechanical device called a straightener, it was impossible to remove the bend entirely, and when lined up in a tray, the wires bent one way or the other.

Once Betty had bounced the wires and they lined up the same way (with the ends bending down as she held them), still holding them as a bunch, she put a terminal on one end of all of them. She then turned the bundle around and put terminals on the other end. Because she let the memory of the wire keep the ends turned the same way, the terminals were easily applied in the proper parallel fashion.

I was impressed. This was hardly a deskilled worker performing routine procedures. When I asked her how she learned to do it, she responded casually that she had figured it out doing the job. As I began to see the women's work from the inside, I noticed a host of skills like Betty's that facilitated production. In fact, I was surprised how fundamental this "craft knowledge" was to the day-to-day operation of the mill. By "craft knowledge," most people think of skills possessed by someone like a violin maker. It is knowledge that cannot be rigidly systematized or reduced to procedural rules but is developed through years of experience. I would argue that the women on the line possessed skills very much akin to those of a craftsman.

Even so, I would hardly argue that working in National was anything like making violins. Indeed, as we have seen, the work itself was menial. Yet contrary to Braverman, a job that involves repetitive, boring tasks is not necessarily devoid of skill or craft. As Manwaring and Wood conclude, the recognition of "working knowledge does not in and of itself refute the deskilling thesis, but it does provide a different vantage point, one in which the central notion is that work is both degrading and constructive, both crippling and enriching" (Manwaring and Wood, 1984: 56).

It is not that craft knowledge at National merely facilitated speedier production. Rather, it was integral to getting the job done at all. Based on research in a paper cone factory, Ken Kusterer (1978) implies this point in his distinction between basic and supplemental (craft) knowledge.

Basic knowledge includes all the procedures necessary to routinely carry out their work tasks: how to start and stop the machine, clean it in a prescribed manner, "bridge the cones," label the case, etc. Supplemental knowledge includes all the know-how necessary to handle obstacles to this routine work performance that arise from time to time: how to keep the machinery running, overcome "bad paper," diagnose the cause of the defects. (Kusterer, 1978: 45)

Thus, when Carroll told the women that he could replace them with "somebody off the street," what he really meant was, "Provided that all the materials are perfect, the machines are running well, and with constant supervision," then "somebody off the street" would do. But as we have seen, National hardly ever ran under those conditions. The machines were in constant disrepair, the materials were inconsistent, and most of the actual decisions on the floor were made by the women themselves, not by Carroll or June. If the managers had to make every decision themselves, production schedules would never be met.

The high labor turnover at National always threatened production. A new assembler would be trained for a day or two and then left on her own. This worked fine as long as things went smoothly. But a problem could spell disaster. For example, one new blocker was doing fine until she blocked 5,000 assemblies with wire that was too heavy. A more experienced blocker would have detected the overly heavy gauge simply by feeling the wire, and could have avoided the lost time and materials. (In a way Carroll was right about taking workers directly off the street. This blocker had made her rate all right, but her work had to be tossed in the scrap pile.)

Thus, the day-to-day operation of the mill required more than mere routine assembly. Yet the constant need for decision-making had mixed implications for the women on the line.

Chaos on the Line

As Kusterer demonstrates in *Know-How on the Job* (1978), all jobs from bank teller to longshoreman demand an insider's knowledge, without which the job cannot be done effectively. This craft knowledge is important to workers in a number of ways. First, it is an important source of pride and dignity. That jobs involve more than menial tasks contributes in fundamental ways to workers' self-esteem. Second, craft knowledge can be an important source of power for workers. Because for the most part it is hidden from management, it can become a tool for workers to assert power in the workplace.

Yet the degree to which this kind of decision-making was constantly needed on the line indicates how confused production really was. The women did not really mind making decisions—it was by far the most interesting part of their day—but making the right decision was not always clear, and the wrong decision often carried strong sanctions.

For example, the leads produced by the SELM were supposed to be measured on an ongoing basis by the operator and once an hour by an inspector. They checked the overall length of the wire, the length of the strip, and how the wire was placed in the terminal. The specifications for these leads were extremely rigid, with the tolerance on each measure plus or minus one-sixty-fourth of an inch. Given the condition of the machines, the quality of the materials, and the experience of the workers, this tolerance was nearly impossible to achieve. In fact, the manual for the machine specified that it would work only to a one-thirty-second of an inch tolerance. In actuality, the machines were running plus or minus one-sixteenth of an inch.

Everyone in the mill, from the operator Alice to the inspectors, was aware of this. They knew that by official specifications most of the leads were beyond tolerance. Yet they also knew that the leads were probably acceptable to the purchaser, and that if they rejected too many items Carroll would be on their backs. Thus everyone was in an ambiguous position that required a constant negotiation of the rules.

From my experience, this goes on in other mills, where official specifications only serve as general guidelines, and where actual specifications are actually much looser. Yet I never witnessed anywhere near the negotiation that occurred daily at National. If the women actually obeyed the specifications, they would do no work. Yet if they accepted (or produced) something beyond an acceptable tolerance, they ran the risk of being held responsible for producing "bad" items.

This uncertainty led to endless "crises" at National. Every two or three weeks, management shut down the production line and called everyone into the cafeteria. Carroll or June would show us some assemblies and ask us what was wrong with them. It was a test. It was amazing how much we could find wrong if we looked hard enough, although what we found was often not what they had in mind. One time the blocks were scratched, another time the tab on the end of the terminals was bent, and once the sewing pulled out. They would chew us out and send us back to the line, usually with some new procedure or inspection to eliminate the problem.

However, if we focused on one detail or aspect of production, the line would immediately slow down. As long as the women stuck close to specifications, the production rate dropped. Interestingly, most of these crises ended the same way. For a week or two the women were very careful, but before long they went back to their old ways. The new inspection or procedure was usually forgotten, and the uncertainty in the production line remained essentially the same. It was amazing to me that despite a series of these crises, the line ran basically the same when I left National as when I arrived.

Much More Than Just a Routine Job

From this in-depth look at the women on the line at National, we have discovered that what they do is much more than just routine work. Not denying that it was boring and repetitive, working at National required constant decision-making and precarious negotiation of what was expected. At first glance, it might be argued that the women at National were "lucky" to have this high level of decision-making, to the extent that it relieved them of the boredom they would otherwise experience. Yet upon further analysis, this constant decision-making cannot be seen as relieving boredom. Decision-making took place in such a confusing and contradictory context that in fundamental ways it added to the pressure.

Workers have a number of ways of dealing with monotony. For some it is dreams of summer vacations or a new car, for others it is the beer at lunch, while others try radios and singing on the job. If you observe a mill carefully, you will notice all kinds of routines that appear pointless at first glance. For example, one of the older women on the floor had a routine she followed religiously. Every day at morning coffee break she went to the corner store and bought a newspaper. She brought it to her table and then went to the bathroom for a paper towel that she spread on her table. She then proceeded to eat half of her sandwich, no more, no less, every working day. There were numerous other examples of women "setting up" their meager possessions—radio, cigarettes, and coffee cup—in similar fashion.

At first you wonder if these routines are the product of working too long in an alienating workplace. Yet over time you see the purpose behind these rituals. Most of what the workers at National did was out of their control. They knew they would produce thousands of assemblies each day, yet had no control over the conditions under which that production occurred. These rituals, then, in important and fundamental ways served to impose some, if only a small amount, of personal impact on the day. The woman who eats just half a sandwich at the same time each day in her own way is imposing some order on the day's events. Although these jobs are clearly "too small for people," it is through this imposition of order that they somehow become "enough."

Jobs become less boring to the extent that workers control their daily activities. For example, if workers' rates were computed by the day instead of by the hour, workers could work harder in the morning when they were fresh, and slower in the afternoon when tired. A break in the work routine, however, when not tied to an increase in control, does not necessarily make a job less boring. For instance, when management stopped production at National because of problems with tolerances, it did not alleviate boredom. Since constant decision-making made the workday more unpredictable, the women felt less in control than if their jobs were utterly routine.

Psychologists agree that random punishment is the worst kind because it threatens an individual's sense of control and order. A punishment that follows from a certain behavior or occurs at some fixed interval is much easier to deal with than one that occurs at random times. In a similar fashion, the ongoing decision-making and the confu-

sion that resulted made the work at National difficult to bear.

Especially confusing times (during one of our "crises," for instance) had an obvious effect on the women who worked on the line. Tempers flared, arguments were more common, people took more days off, and some worked as slowly as they could. They complained as well. "I wish they'd make up their damn minds," said one of the blockers to me. "It's bad enough having such boring work, and then there's so much confusion all the time. One day it'll pass, the next day it won't." As another woman said to me, "All I want to do is to be able to do my job without anyone bothering me, and then go home."

REFERENCES

Braverman, Harry. 1974. *Labor and Monopoly Capital: The Degradation of Work in the Twentieth Century.* New York: Monthly Review Press.

Grossman, Rachael. 1980. "Women's Place in the Integrated Circuit." *Radical America* 14: 29–50.

Kusterer, Ken C. 1978. *Know-How on the Job: The Important Working Knowledge of "Unskilled" Workers.* Boulder, Colo.: Westview Press.

Manwaring, T. and S. Wood. 1984. "The Ghost in the Machine: Tacit Skills in the Labor Process." *Socialist Review*, no. 74 (14), 55–83, 94.

Wertheimer, Barbara Mayer. 1977. *We Were There: The Story of Working Women in America.* New York: Pantheon.

Zimbalist, Andrew, ed. 1979. *Case Studies on the Labor Process.* New York: Monthly Review Press.

PERSONAL SERVICE WORK

27

Over the Counter
McDonald's

Robin Leidner

McDonald's

No one ever walks into a McDonald's and asks, "So, what's good today?" except satirically. The heart of McDonald's success is its uniformity and predictability. Not only is the food supposed to taste the same every day everywhere in the world, but McDonald's promises that every meal will be served quickly, courteously, and with a smile. Delivering on that promise over 20 million times a day in 54 countries is the company's colossal challenge (*McDonald's Annual Report* for 1990: 2). Its strategy for meeting that challenge draws on scientific management's most basic tenets: find the One Best Way to do every task and see that the work is conducted accordingly.

To insure that all McDonald's restaurants serve products of uniform quality, the company uses centralized planning, centrally designed training programs, centrally approved and supervised suppliers, automated machinery and other specially designed equipment, meticulous specifications, and systematic inspections. To provide its customers with a uni-

formly pleasant "McDonald's experience," the company also tries to mass-produce friendliness, deference, diligence, and good cheer through a variety of socialization and social control techniques. Despite sneers from those who equate uniformity with mediocrity, the success of McDonald's has been spectacular.

McFacts

By far the world's largest fast-food company, McDonald's has over 11,800 stores worldwide (*McDonald's Annual Report* for 1990: 1), and its 1990 international sales surpassed those of its three largest competitors combined (Berg 1991: sec. 3, 6). In the United States, consumer familiarity with McDonald's is virtually universal: the company estimates that 95 percent of U.S. consumers eat at a McDonald's at least once a year (Koepp 1987: 58). McDonald's 1990 profits were $802.3 million, the third highest profits of any retailing company in the world (*Fortune* 1991: 179). At a time when the ability of many U.S. businesses to compete on the world market is in question, McDonald's continues to expand around the globe—most recently to Morocco—everywhere remaking consumer demand in its own image.

As politicians, union leaders, and others concerned with the effects of the shift to a service economy are quick to point out, McDonald's is a major employer. McDonald's restaurants in the United States employ about half a million people (Bertagnoli 1989: 33), including one out of fifteen first-time job seekers (Wildavsky 1989: 30). The company claims that 7 percent of all current U.S. workers have worked for McDonald's at some time (Koepp 1987: 59). Not only has McDonald's directly influenced the lives of millions of workers, but its impact has also been extended by the efforts of many kinds of organizations, especially in the service sector, to imitate the organizational features they see as central to McDonald's success.

For a company committed to standardization, McDonald's inspires strikingly varied reactions, both as an employer and as a cultural icon. On one side, Barbara Garson (1988), for instance, presents work at McDonald's as so systematized, automated, and closely monitored that all opportunity for thought, initiative, and human contact, let alone self-development, has been removed. To other critics, the ubiquity and uniformity of McDonald's epitomize the homogenization of U.S. culture and its imperialist export. At McDonald's, they point out, local culture is invisible and irrelevant, personal interactions are flattened into standardized patterns, and individual preferences are subordinated to efficient production processes. Nutritionists scorn McDonald's menu, environmentalists its packaging.

However, McDonald's has been as widely admired as reviled. To its supporters, McDonald's represents efficiency, order, familiarity, good cheer, and good value. Many business writers hold McDonald's up as an example of excellence in service management (see, e.g., Heskett, Sasser, and Hart 1990; Peters and Austin 1985; Zemke with Schaaf 1989). A pioneer in the standardization and mass-production of food and service, the company is often represented as emblematic of American capitalist knowhow. It is a company whose phenomenal growth has resulted from steadfast commitment to its basic promise to customers of fast service, hot food, and clean restaurants.

The relentless standardization and infinite replication that inspire both horror and admiration are the legacy of Ray Kroc, a salesman who got into the hamburger business in 1954, when he was fifty-two years old, and created a worldwide phenomenon.[1] His inspiration was a phenomenally successful hamburger stand owned by the McDonald brothers of San Bernardino, California. He believed that their success could be reproduced consistently through carefully controlled franchises, and his hamburger business succeeded on an unprecedented scale. The basic idea was to serve a very few items of strictly uniform quality at low prices. Over the years, the menu has expanded somewhat and prices have risen, but the emphasis on strict, detailed standardization has never varied.

Kroc set out to achieve the kind of tight control over work routines and product quality that centralized production in factories makes possible, although the fast-food business is necessarily highly decentralized. Not only are the stores geographically dispersed, but approximately 75 percent of McDonald's outlets are owned by individual franchisees rather than by the corporation (*McDonald's Annual Report* for 1989: i). In his autobiography, Kroc describes how he approached the problem of combining standardization with decentralization (Kroc with Anderson 1977: 86):

> Our aim, of course, was to insure repeat business based on the system's reputation rather than on the quality of a single store or operator. This would require a continuing program of educating and assisting operators and a constant review of their performance. It would also require a full-time program of research and development. I knew in my bones that the key to uniformity would be in our ability to provide techniques of prepara-

tion that operators would accept because they were superior to methods they could dream up for themselves.

McDonald's franchise owners retain control over some matters, including pay scales, but the company requires that every store's production methods and products meet McDonald's precise specifications. The company encourages and enforces compliance with its standards in a variety of ways. The franchise agreements detail the obligations of both the owners and the corporation; the corporation requires that all potential owners go through its rigorous store-management training program; the corporation provides training materials for crew people and managers that include step-by-step instructions for every task in the store; raters from the corporation regularly visit franchises to evaluate their quality, service, and cleanliness; and owners must purchase their equipment and food products from suppliers approved by the corporation. For those aspects of store operation not specifically covered by the franchise agreement, the corporation must persuade franchisees that they will maximize their profits by following the recommendations of the corporation. Given McDonald's phenomenal success, this persuasive power is considerable, as Kroc intended.

Luxenberg (1985: 77) writes that "Kroc introduced an extreme regimentation that had never been attempted in a service business." This regimentation is not limited to food-preparation techniques. McDonald's has standardized procedures for bookkeeping, purchasing, dealing with workers and customers, and virtually every other aspect of the business. But it is the assembly-line techniques used to produce and serve identical products in every McDonald's that are most salient for workers and most relevant to customers. These are the procedures designed to ensure that the food served to customers will be up to McDonald's standards

and that customers will not have to wait more than a few minutes for their meal. The most comprehensive guide to corporate specifications for producing and serving "McDonald's quality" food is the "Operations and Training Manual"—McDonald's managers call it "the Bible"—which describes company procedures and standards in painstaking detail. Its 600 pages include, for instance, full-color photographs illustrating the proper placement of ketchup, mustard, and pickle slices on each type of hamburger on the menu. McDonald's stresses that these specifications are not arrived at arbitrarily, but are the accumulated fruits of years of experience and research. Franchise owners are kept up-to-date on corporate specifications by means of regularly issued bulletins.

Enforcement of McDonald's standards has been made easier over the years by the introduction of highly specialized equipment. Every company-owned store in the United States now has an "in-store processor," a computer system that calculates yields and food costs, keeps track of inventory and cash, schedules labor, and breaks down sales by time of day, product, and worker (*McDonald's Annual Report* for 1989: 29). In today's McDonald's, lights and buzzers tell workers exactly when to turn burgers or take fries out of the fat, and technologically advanced cash registers, linked to the computer system, do much of the thinking for window workers. Specially designed ketchup dispensers squirt exactly the right amount of ketchup on each burger in the approved flower pattern. The french-fry scoops let workers fill a bag and set it down in one continuous motion and help them gauge the proper serving size.

The extreme standardization of McDonald's products, and its workers, is closely tied to its marketing. The company advertises on a massive scale—in 1989, McDonald's spent $1.1 billion system-wide on advertising and promotions (*McDonald's Annual Report* for 1989: 32). In fact, McDonald's is the single most advertised brand in the world (*Advertising Age* 1990: 6). The national advertising assures the public that it will find high standards of quality, service, and cleanliness at every McDonald's store. The intent of the strict quality-control standards applied to every aspect of running a McDonald's outlet, from proper cleaning of the bathrooms to making sure the hamburgers are served hot, is to help franchise owners keep the promises made in the company's advertising.

The image of McDonald's outlets promoted in the company's advertising is one of fun, wholesomeness, and family orientation. Kroc was particularly concerned that his stores not become teen-age hangouts, since that would discourage families' patronage. To minimize their attractiveness to teenage loiterers, McDonald's stores do not have jukeboxes, video games, or even telephones. Kroc initially decided not to hire young women to work behind McDonald's counters for the same reason: "They attracted the wrong kind of boys" (Boas and Chain 1976: 19). . . .

One McDonald's Franchise

I was assigned to a McDonald's in the downtown area of a small city near Chicago. It was a new store, only about fifteen months old when I began my fieldwork, but an exemplary one; it had recently won a major McDonald's award. The store was far more elegant than the average McDonald's. Adjacent to an expensive hotel, the restaurant was designed to seem "high-class," not garish or tacky. The interior decor included marble walls, a mahogany dining counter, black Art Deco fixtures, and mauve draperies. Outside were window boxes filled with flowers or greenery, and a relatively small Golden Arches sign, since the city council would not permit a large one.

This McDonald's differed from most in that it had neither a parking lot nor a drive-thru [*sic*] service window. It depended on pedestrian traffic for business, and its clientele included business people, college students, senior citizens, and shoppers. Fewer families came in than is typical for a McDonald's, and more people ordered just coffee or ice cream rather than a full meal; the average check size was accordingly smaller than at most McDonald's stores. At the time of my research in 1986, the store served 1,700 customers on an average day. In the course of a year, those customers collectively spent about one and a half million dollars. (The average McDonald's store brought in $1.34 million in 1985, half of it in drive-thru sales [training center lecture].)

The franchisee who owned the store owned three other McDonald's stores in the Chicago suburbs. The business had made him wealthy, and he proudly showed off a "new toy" to me, a Corvette convertible, complete with telephone. He also had a yacht. He, his wife, and some of their grown children were closely involved in running the store, coming in several times a week, planning improvements, and overseeing the operation. Such involvement is encouraged by the corporation, which wants all of its franchisees to be "owner/operators," not just investors.

This McDonald's store had five salaried managers, all male, three white and two black. The owner's son, another white, also worked as a manager on occasion. In addition, there were as many as five hourly swing managers at a time (all female; three black, one white, one Native American). During my fieldwork, two crew people, a black woman and an Asian man, were promoted to that level of management.

The store's crew fluctuated in size between sixty-five and about one hundred people in the course of six months; the store manager believed that eighty-five was optimal. There were about equal numbers of window workers and grill workers.

Personnel policies at McDonald's franchises, including pay scales, are determined by the franchise owners, not by the corporation. Many press reports have described fast-food franchises raising wages and offering benefits to compete for the declining number of teenage workers, but the crew at this franchise, both grill and window workers, started work at the federal minimum wage, $3.35 in 1986, and they received no benefits such as health insurance, paid holidays, or paid sick days. Merit raises of five or ten cents per hour were granted quarterly, when job performance reviews were made, and crew people promoted to crew trainer or crew chief received raises of five to fifteen cents per hour as well. The pay remained quite low, however. One crew trainer who had worked at the franchise for about a year and a half was earning $3.75.

Most, though not all, male crew members worked on the grill and most female crew members worked on the window. This pattern was usually based on managers' decisions when hiring workers. Some crew people reported having been given a choice about where they would start out, but more than half said that they had been assigned to their first job. A couple of crew people reported that the first women to be cross-trained to work on the grill had to persuade managers that they should be allowed to do so. In my interview sample of window people, 75 percent of the workers were women; according to the store's manager, this proportion accurately approximated the actual gender composition of the job category.

Salaried managers were expected to work forty-six to fifty hours per week. Officially, all of McDonald's crew workers are part-time, but 25 percent of my interview sample of window crew said that they usually worked thirty-five hours or more per week. The number of hours worked by crew people varied greatly, since many of them were students who only wished to work a few hours per week. Those who did want longer hours were expected to compete

for them, proving themselves deserving through conscientious job performance. In practice, a core group of about twenty steady workers was sure to get its preferred hours, but cutting back an employee's hours was a standard way the managers showed their displeasure over poor job performance or attitude. The usual strategy for getting rid of poor workers, the store manager told me, was to decrease the hours they were scheduled to work until they got the message.

Through its scheduling practices McDonald's attempted to minimize labor costs without sacrificing speedy service for customers. As in almost all restaurants, McDonald's business normally came in waves rather than in a steady stream, with big rushes at meal times. On the one hand, managers did not want to have to pay crew people for hours they were not needed, since crew labor productivity is one of the main criteria by which managers are judged (Garson 1988: 32). On the other hand, they wanted to be sure to have enough people to keep lines moving quickly when business was brisk. The computerized cash-register system analyzed sales by hour of the day and day of the week, and managers used these figures to schedule work crews.

Since, however, computer projections are never entirely accurate, the schedules at this McDonald's were designed so that workers bore much of the burden of uncertainty. On the work schedule, posted one week in advance, a line for each crew person showed the hours she or he was scheduled to work. A solid line indicated hours the employee could count on working, and a zigzag line marked an additional hour or so. If the store was busy when a worker's guaranteed hours were finished, she or he would be required to work that extra time; if it was not busy, she or he would be asked to leave. In addition, it was quite common at unexpectedly quiet times for managers to tell workers they could leave before their scheduled hours were completed or even to pressure them to leave when they would rather have kept on working. I heard one manager say, "Come on, can't I make a profit today?" when a crew person resisted being sent home fifteen minutes early. Conversely, when the store was busy, managers were reluctant to let workers go when their scheduled hours, including the optional time, were done. When lines of people were waiting to be served, workers—I was one of them— would often have to ask repeatedly to be "punched out" (off the time clock) at the end of their shift.

Workers' preferences for longer or shorter hours varied; some wanted to earn as much as possible, others preferred to have more time for other activities. Whatever their preferences, the scheduling practices made it difficult for workers to plan ahead. Arrangements for transportation, social activities, child care, and so on could be disrupted by unexpected changes in the schedule, and workers could not accurately predict how much money they would earn in a given week. Furthermore, one of the most common complaints among the workers was that they had been scheduled to work at times they had said they were not available. Once on the schedule, they were held responsible for finding a replacement (see Garson 1988: 32–33). Since the McDonald's schedule was made up of such small units of time, however, it was usually relatively easy for workers to arrange hours for their convenience, an advantage McDonald's emphasized in recruitment. For example, workers who played on a high school team could cut down their hours during the sports season, and workers who needed to take a particular day off could usually arrange it if they gave sufficient notice.

The Interview Sample

Thirty-five percent of my sample was of high school age. (It is possible that I undersampled high school students simply because, since they were less likely to work many hours, I had less opportunity to meet them.) Although the majority of my sample (65 percent) were eighteen years old or over, 60 percent of the crew people told me that this was their first job.

The great majority of the crew people in the store were black, although blacks are a minority, albeit a large one, of the city's population. In my interview sample, 80 percent were black (including three Caribbean immigrants), one person was Hispanic-American, one was an Asian immigrant, and the rest were American-born white. A sizable minority of the workers commuted long distances, from the South Side and the West Side of Chicago. A full 25 percent of my sample had one-way commutes that took at least an hour and required at least one change of train, and I knew of several other workers with commutes at least that long. Given that the crew people started work at McDonald's at minimum wage, this pattern strongly suggests that these workers had been unable to find work near their homes or better-paying jobs elsewhere.

About two-thirds of the store's crew people were trained to work at the window. My sample of twenty-six window workers was not completely representative of all of the employees who worked behind the counter during the months I was there. Since my sampling method depended on my meeting the worker in the crew room, I probably oversampled those who worked relatively long or relatively steady hours and missed both those who worked only a few hours per week and those who worked for only a short time before quitting. I oversampled crew trainers and crew chiefs—30 percent of my sample had been promoted to one of these jobs. However, according to the store's manager, my sample was fairly representative of the store's population of customer-service workers in its gender, race, and age distributions. . . .

The Routine

McDonald's had routinized the work of its crews so thoroughly that decision making had practically been eliminated from the jobs. As one window worker told me, "They've tried to break it down so that it's almost idiot-proof." Most of the workers agreed that there was little call for them to use their own judgment on the job, since there were rules about everything. If an unusual problem arose, the workers were supposed to turn it over to a manager.

Many of the noninteractive parts of the window workers' job had been made idiot-proof through automation. The soda machines, for example, automatically dispensed the proper amount of beverage for regular, medium, and large cups. Computerized cash registers performed a variety of functions handled elsewhere by human waitresses, waiters, and cashiers, making some kinds of skill and knowledge unnecessary. As a customer gave an order, the window worker simply pressed the cash register button labeled with the name of the selected product. There was no need to write the orders down, because the buttons lit up to indicate which products had been selected. Nor was there any need to remember prices, because the prices were programmed into the machines. Like most new cash registers, these added the tax automatically and told workers how much change customers were owed, so the window crew did not need to know how to do those calculations. The cash registers also helped regulate some of the crew's interactive work by reminding them to try to increase the size of each sale. For example, when a customer ordered a Big Mac, large fries, and a regular Coke, the cash register buttons for cookies, hot apple pies, ice cream cones, and ice cream sundaes would light up, prompting the worker to suggest dessert. It took some skill to operate the relatively complicated cash register, as my difficulties during my first work shift made clear, but this organizationally specific skill could soon be acquired on the job.

In addition to doing much of the workers' thinking for them, the computerized cash registers made it possible for managers to monitor the crew members' work and the store's inventory very closely. For example, if the number of Quarter Pounder with Cheese boxes gone did not match the number of Quarter Pounders with Cheese sold or accounted for as waste, managers might suspect that workers were giving away or taking food. Managers could easily tell which workers had brought in the most money during a given interval and who was doing the best job of persuading customers to buy a particular item. The computerized system could also complicate what would otherwise have been simple customer requests, however. For example, when a man who had not realized the benefit of ordering his son's food as a Happy Meal came back to the counter to ask whether his little boy could have one of the plastic beach pails the Happy Meals were served in, I had to ask a manager what to do, since fulfilling the request would produce a discrepancy between the inventory and the receipts. Sometimes the extreme systematization can induce rather than prevent idiocy, as when a window worker says she cannot serve a cup of coffee that is half decaffeinated and half regular because she would not know how to ring up the sale.[2]

The interactive part of window work is routinized through the Six Steps of Window Service and also through rules aimed at standardizing attitudes and demeanors as well as words and actions. The window workers were taught that they represented McDonald's to the public and that their attitudes were therefore an important component of service quality. Crew people could be reprimanded for not smiling, and often were. The window workers were supposed to be cheerful and polite at all times, but they were also told to be themselves while on the job. McDonald's does not want its workers to seem like robots, so part of the emotion work asked of the window crew is that they act naturally. "Being yourself" in this situation meant behaving in a way that did not seem stilted. Although workers had some latitude to go beyond the script, the short, highly schematic routine obviously did not allow much room for genuine self-expression.

Workers were not the only ones constrained by McDonald's routines, of course. The cooperation of service-recipients was crucial to the smooth functioning of the operation. In many kinds of interactive service work . . . constructing the compliance of service-recipients is an important part of the service worker's job. The routines such workers use may be designed to maximize the control each worker has over customers. McDonald's window workers' routines were not intended to give them much leverage over customers' behavior, however. The window workers interacted only with people who had already decided to do business with McDonald's and who therefore did not need to be persuaded to take part in the service interaction. Furthermore, almost all customers were familiar enough with McDonald's routines to know how they were expected to behave. For instance, I never saw a customer who did not know that she or he was supposed to come up to the counter rather than sit down and wait to be served. This customer training was accomplished through advertising, spatial design, customer experience, and the example of other customers, making it unnecessary for the window crew to put much effort into getting customers to fit into their work routines.

McDonald's ubiquitous advertising trains consumers at the same time that it tries to attract them to McDonald's. Television commercials demonstrate how the service system is supposed to work and familiarize customers with new products. Additional cues about expected customer behavior are provided by the design of the restaurants. For example, the entrances usually lead to the service counter, not to the dining area, making it unlikely that customers will fail to realize that they should get in line, and the placement of waste cans makes clear that customers are expected to throw out their own trash. Most important, the majority of customers have had years of experience with McDonald's, as well as with other fast-food restaurants that have similar arrangements. The company estimates that the average customer visits a McDonald's twenty times a year (Koepp 1987: 58), and it is not uncommon for a customer to come in several times per week. For many customers, then, ordering at McDonald's is as routine an interaction as it is for the window worker. Indeed, because employee turnover is so high, steady customers may be more familiar with the work routines than the workers serving them are. Customers who are new to McDonald's can take their cue from more experienced customers.

Not surprisingly, then, most customers at the McDonald's I studied knew what was expected of them and tried to play their part well. They sorted themselves into lines and gazed up at the menu boards while waiting to be served. They usually gave their orders in the conventional sequence: burgers or other entrees, french fries or other side orders, drinks, and desserts. Hurried customers with savvy might order an item "only if it's in the bin," that is, ready to be served. Many customers prepared carefully so that they could give their orders promptly when they got to the counter. This preparation sometimes became apparent when a worker interrupted to ask, "What kind of dressing?" or "Cream and sugar?", flustering customers who could not deliver their orders as planned.

McDonald's routines, like those of other interactive service businesses, depend on the predictability of customers, but these businesses must not grind to a halt if customers are not completely cooperative. Some types of deviations from standard customer behavior are so common that they become routine themselves, and these can be handled through subroutines (Stinchcombe 1990: 39). McDonald's routines work most efficiently when all customers accept their products exactly as they are usually prepared; indeed, the whole business is based on this premise. Since, however, some people give special instructions for customized products, such as "no onions," the routine allows for these exceptions. At the franchise I studied, workers could key the special requests into their cash registers, which automatically printed out "grill slips" with the instructions for the grill workers to follow. Under this system, the customer making the special order had to wait for it to be prepared, but the smooth flow of service for other customers was not interrupted. Another type of routine difficulty was customer dissatisfaction with food quality. Whenever a customer had a complaint about the food—cold fries, dried-out burger—window workers were authorized to supply a new product immediately without consulting a supervisor.

These two kinds of difficulties—special orders and complaints about food—were the only irregularities window workers were authorized to handle. The subroutines increased the flexibility of the service system, but they did not increase the workers' discretion, since procedures were in place for dealing with both situations. All other kinds of demands fell outside the window crew's purview. If they were faced with a dispute about money, an extraordinary request, or a furious customer, workers were instructed to call a manager; the crew had no authority to handle such problems.

Given the almost complete regimentation of tasks and preemption of decision making, does McDonald's need the flexibility and thoughtfulness of human workers? As the declining supply of teenagers and legislated increases in the minimum wage drive up labor costs, it is not surprising that McDonald's is experimenting with electronic replacements. So far, the only robot in use handles behind-the-scenes work rather than customer interactions. ARCH (Automated Restaurant Crew Helper) works in a Minnesota McDonald's where it does all the frying and lets workers know when to prepare sandwich buns, when supplies are running low, and when fries are no longer fresh enough to sell. Other McDonald's stores (along with Arby's and Burger King units) are experimenting with a touch-screen computer system that lets customers order their meals themselves, further curtailing the role of the window worker. Although it requires increased customer socialization and cooperation, early reports are that the system cuts service time by thirty seconds and increases sales per window worker 10–20 percent (Chaudhry 1989: F61).

Getting Workers to Work

The extreme routinization does not mean that McDonald's work is undemanding. I found that the company asked a lot of its workers, and the stresses of the job could be considerable. Especially when the store was busy, window work was extraordinarily hectic. From the grill area came the sounds of buzzers buzzing and people shouting instructions. Workers dashed from side to side behind the counter to pick up the various products they needed. Just getting around was extremely difficult. There might be six window workers, a manager or two overseeing the flow of food from the grill and backing up window workers, and another worker in charge of french fries, all trying to maneuver in a very small area, all hurrying, often carrying drinks, ice cream cones, stacks of burgers. Workers with pails of soapy water would frequently come to mop up the greasy floor, leaving it slippery and treacherous even for workers in the regulation nonskid shoes. Traffic jams formed around the soda machines and the salad cases.

In the course of a shift various supplies would run out, and there would be no lids for the large cups, no clean trays, no Italian dressing, no ice, until someone found a moment to replenish the stock. Food products were frequently not ready when needed, frustrating window workers' efforts to gather their orders speedily—the supply of Big Macs in the food bin could be wiped out at any moment by a worker with an order for four of them, forcing several other workers to explain to their customers that they would have to wait for their food. The customers, of course, could be a major source of stress themselves. All in all, McDonald's work may be regarded as unskilled, but it was by no means easy to do well. Window workers had to be able to keep many things in mind at once, to keep calm under fire, and to exhibit considerable physical and emotional stamina.

Even when the store was not crowded, workers were expected to keep busy, in accordance with the McDonald's slogan "If there's time to lean, there's time to clean." I was struck by how hard-working most of the crew people were:

> Matthew moves very fast, sweeps up whenever he has a spare moment. In fact, all of the crew people work like beavers—backing each other up, cleaning, etc.

Considering workers' low wages and limited stake in the success of the enterprise, why did they work so hard? Their intensity of effort was produced by several kinds of pressures. First, it seemed to me that most workers did conceive of the work as a team effort and were loath to be seen by their peers as making extra work for other people by not doing their share. Even workers who had what managers would define as a "bad attitude"—resentment about low wages, disrespectful treatment, or any other issue—might work hard in order to keep the respect of their peers.

Naturally, managers played a major role in keeping crew people hard at work. At this store, managers were virtually always present behind the counter and in the grill area. During busy periods several managers would be there at once, working side by side with the crew as well as issuing instructions. Any slacking off by a worker was thus very likely to be noticed. Managers insisted on constant effort; they clearly did not want to pay workers for a moment of nonproductive time. For instance, I heard a manager reprimand a grill worker for looking at the work schedule: "Are you off work? No? You look at the schedule on your time, not on my time." A handwritten sign was posted recommending that window workers come in fifteen minutes early to count out the money in their cash-register drawers on their own time so that, if the amount was wrong, they would not later be held responsible for a shortage. Crew trainers and crew chiefs were encouraged to let managers know about any workers who were shirking or causing problems.

The presence of customers on the scene was another major factor in intensifying workers' efforts. When long lines of people were waiting to be served, few workers had to be told to work as swiftly as possible. The sea of expectant faces provided a great deal of pressure to keep moving. Window workers in particular were anxious to avoid antagonizing customers, who were likely to take out any dissatisfactions on them. The surest way to keep people happy was to keep the lines moving quickly. The arrangement of the workplace, which made window workers clearly visible to the waiting customers as they went about their duties, and customers clearly visible to workers, was important in keeping crew people hard at work. This pressure could have an effect even if customers did not complain. For example, on the day I was to be trained to work window during breakfast, I spent quite a while standing behind the counter, in uniform, waiting to be given instructions and put to work. I was acutely aware that customers were likely to wonder why I did not take their orders, and I tried to adopt an air of attentive expectancy rather than one of casual loitering, in the hope that the customers would assume there was a good reason for my idleness.

These sorts of pressures were not the only reasons crew people worked hard and enthusiastically, however. Managers also tried to motivate them to strenuous efforts through positive means. The managers' constant presence meant that good work would not go unnoticed. McDonald's Corporation stresses the importance of acknowledging workers' efforts, and several workers mentioned that they appreciated such recognition. Indeed, I was surprised at how much it cheered me when a manager complimented me on my "good eye contact" with customers. Various incentive systems were in place as well, to make workers feel that it was in their individual interest to work hard. Free McDonald's meals (instead of the usual half-priced ones) and free record albums were some of the rewards available to good workers. Contests for the highest sales totals or most special raspberry milk shakes sold in a given hour encouraged window workers to compete in speed and pushiness. The possibility of promotion to crew trainer, crew chief, or swing manager also motivated some workers to work as hard as possible.

Group incentives seemed to be especially effective in motivating the crew. As part of a national advertising effort stressing service, all of the stores in McDonald's Chicago region competed to improve their speed. The owner of the store where I worked promised that if one of his stores came out near the top in this competition, the entire crew would be treated to a day at a large amusement park and the crew trainers would be invited for a day's outing on his yacht. The crew trainers and many other workers were very excited about this possibility and were willing to try to

achieve unprecedented standards of speed. (They did not win the prize, but the crew of one of the owner's other stores did.) Some workers, though, especially the more disaffected ones, had no desire for either promotions or the low-cost rewards available and spoke derisively of them.

Managers also tried to make workers identify with the interests of the store, even when it clearly resulted in harder work for the same pay. At a monthly meeting for crew trainers, a manager acknowledged that workers were always asking why the store would not pay someone for an extra fifteen minutes to sweep up or do other such tasks not directly related to production, instead of making workers squeeze these tasks in around their main duties. He explained the importance to management of keeping labor costs down:

> "Say we use four extra hours a day—we keep extra people to [wash] the brown trays" or some other tasks. He reels off some calculations—"that's 120 hours a month, times—let's pay them the minimum wage—times twelve months. So that's 1,440 hours times \$3.35, equals \$4,825." There are oohs and ahs from the trainers—this sounds like a lot of money to them. I don't think it sounds like that much out of \$1.5 million (which he had just said the store brought in annually). The manager went on, "So how do we get extra labor? By watching how we schedule. A \$200 hour [an hour with \$200 in sales], for instance, will go smoother with four window people, but three good people could do it. We save money, and then we can use it on other things, like training, for instance."

The crew trainers were willing to agree that it was only reasonable for the store to extract as much labor from them as possible, though resentments about overwork certainly did not disappear. The manager was also successful enough in getting the crew trainers to identify with management that they were willing to give the names of crew people who were uncooperative. . . .

For the most part, it seemed that sticking to corporate directives on proper management produced good results, while, predictably, more authoritarian and arbitrary interactions with staff produced resentment. The apparently respectful, even-handed, psychologistic management style that McDonald's encourages helped make the repetitive, fast-paced, low-autonomy, low-paid jobs tolerable to workers. Workers learned to accept even rules that were quite disadvantageous to them when they perceived those rules to be fairly administered by people who regarded them as human beings. The official McDonald's stance was likely to anger workers, however, when, faced with customers who did not treat the crew as human beings, managers felt it was more important to satisfy the paying public than to defend the workers' dignity. . . .

Overview

. . . Most McDonald's work is organized as low-paying, low-status, part-time jobs that give workers little autonomy. Almost every decision about how to do crew people's tasks has been made in advance by the corporation, and many of the decisions have been built into the stores' technology. Why use human workers at all, if not to take advantage of the human capacity to respond to circumstances flexibly? McDonald's does want to provide at least a simulacrum of the human attributes of warmth, friendliness, and recognition. For that reason, not only workers' movements but also their words, demeanor, and attitudes are subject to managerial control.

Although predictability is McDonald's hallmark, not all factors can be controlled by management. One of the most serious irregularities that store management must deal with is fluctuation in the flow of customers, both expected and unexpected. Since personnel costs are the most manipulable variable affecting a store's profitability, managers want to match labor power to consumer demand as exactly as possible. They do so by paying all crew people by the hour, giving them highly irregular hours based on expected sales—sometimes including split shifts—and sending workers home early or keeping them late as conditions require. In other words, the costs of uneven demand are shifted to workers whenever possible. Since most McDonald's crew people cannot count on working a particular number of hours at precisely scheduled times, it is hard for them to make plans based on how much money they will earn or exactly what times they will be free. Workers are pressured to be flexible in order to maximize the organization's own flexibility in staffing levels. In contrast, of course, flexibility in the work process itself is minimized.

Routinization has not made the crew people's work easy. Their jobs, although highly structured and repetitive, are often demanding and stressful. Under these working conditions, the organization's limited commitment to workers, as reflected in job security, wages, and benefits, makes the task of maintaining worker motivation and discipline even more challenging. A variety of factors, many orchestrated by the corporation, keeps McDonald's crew people hard at work despite the limited rewards. Socialization into McDonald's norms, extremely close supervision (both human and electronic), individual and group incentives, peer pressure, and pressure from customers all play their part in getting workers to do things the McDonald's way. . . .

NOTES

1. Information about McDonald's history comes primarily from Boas and Chain 1976; Kroc with Anderson 1977; Love 1986; Luxenberg 1985; and McDonald's training materials. Rei-

ter's (1991) description of Burger King reveals numerous parallels in the operation of the two companies, although Burger King, unlike McDonald's, is a subsidiary of a multinational conglomerate.

2. Thanks to Charles Bosk for this story.

REFERENCES

Advertising Age. 1990. "Adman of the Decade: McDonald's Fred Turner: Making All the Right Moves." (January 1): 6.

Bertagnoli, Lisa. 1989. "McDonald's: Company of the Quarter Century." *Restaurants and Institutions* (July 10): 32–60.

Boas, Max and Steve Chain. 1976. *Big Mac: The Unauthorized Story of McDonald's.* New York: New American Library.

Chaudhry, Rajan. 1989. "Burger Giants Singed by Battle." *Nation's Restaurant News* (August 7): F36.

Fortune. 1991. "Fortune Global Service 500: The 50 Largest Retailing Companies." (August 26): 179.

Garson, Barbara. 1988. *The Electronic Sweatshop: How Computers Are Transforming the Office of the Future into the Factory of the Past.* New York: Simon and Schuster.

Heskett, James L., W. Earl Sasser, Jr., and Christopher W. L. Hart. 1990. *Service Breakthroughs: Changing the Rules of the Game.* New York: Free Press.

Koepp, Stephen. 1987. "Big Mac Strikes Back." *Time* (April 13): 58–60.

Kroc, Ray, with Robert Anderson. 1977. *Grinding It Out: The Making of McDonald's.* Chicago: Contemporary Books.

Love, John F. 1986. *McDonald's: Behind the Arches.* New York: Bantam Books.

Luxenberg, Stan. 1985. *Roadside Empires: How the Chains Franchised America.* New York: Viking.

McDonald's Annual Report. Various years. Oak Brook, Ill.

Peters, Tom and Nancy Austin. 1985. *A Passion for Excellence: The Leadership Difference.* New York: Random House.

Reiter, Ester. 1991. *Making Fast Food: From the Frying Pan into the Fryer.* Montreal: McGill-Queen's University Press.

Stinchcombe, Arthur L. 1990. *Information and Organizations.* Berkeley: University of California Press.

Wildavsky, Ben. 1989. "McJobs: Inside America's Largest Youth Training Program." *Policy Review* 49: 30–37.

Zemke, Ron, with Dick Schaaf. 1989. *The Service Edge: 101 Companies That Profit from Customer Care.* New York: NAL Books.

28

"Getting" and "Making" a Tip

Greta Foff Paules

The waitress can't help feeling a sense of personal failure and public censure when she is "stiffed."

—WILLIAM F. WHYTE, "WHEN WORKERS AND CUSTOMERS MEET"

They're rude, they're ignorant, they're obnoxious, they're inconsiderate. . . . Half these people don't deserve to come out and eat, let alone try and tip a waitress.

—ROUTE WAITRESS

Making a Tip at Route

A common feature of past research is that the worker's control over the tipping system is evaluated in terms of her efforts to con, coerce, compel, or otherwise manipulate a customer into relinquishing a bigger tip. Because these efforts have for the most part proven futile, the worker has been seen as having little defense against the financial vicissitudes of the tipping system. What these studies have overlooked is that an employee can increase her tip income by controlling the number as well as the size of tips she receives. This oversight has arisen from the tendency of researchers to concentrate narrowly on the relationship between server and served, while failing to take into account

the broader organizational context in which this relationship takes place.

Like service workers observed in earlier studies, waitresses at Route strive to boost the amount of individual gratuities by rendering special services and being especially friendly. As one waitress put it, "I'll sell you the world if you're in my station." In general though, waitresses at Route Restaurant seek to boost their tip income, not by increasing the amount of individual gratuities, but by increasing the number of customers they serve. They accomplish this (a) by securing the largest or busiest stations and working the most lucrative shifts; (b) by "turning" their tables quickly; and (c) by controlling the flow of customers within the restaurant.

Technically, stations at Route are assigned on a rotating basis so that all waitresses, including rookies, work fast and slow stations equally. Station assignments are listed on the work schedule that is posted in the office window where it can be examined by all workers on all shifts, precluding the possibility of blatant favoritism or discrimination. Yet a number of methods exist whereby experienced waitresses are able to circumvent the formal rotation system and secure the more lucrative stations for themselves. A waitress can trade assignments with a rookie who is uncertain of her ability to handle a fast station; she can volunteer to take over a large station when a *call-out* necessitates reorganization of station assignments;[1] or she can establish herself as the only waitress capable of handling a particularly large or chaotic station. Changes in station assignments tend not to be formally recorded, so inconsistencies in the rotation system often do

---

not show up on the schedule. Waitresses on the same shift may notice of course that a co-worker has managed to avoid an especially slow station for many days, or has somehow ended up in the busiest station two weekends in a row, but the waitresses' code of noninterference . . . inhibits them from openly objecting to such irregularities.

A waitress can also increase her tip income by working the more lucrative shifts. Because day is the busiest and therefore most profitable shift at Route, it attracts experienced, professional waitresses who are most concerned and best able to maximize their tip earnings. There are exceptions: some competent, senior-ranking waitresses are unable to work during the day due to time constraints of family or second jobs. Others choose not to work during the day despite the potential monetary rewards, because they are unwilling to endure the intensely competitive atmosphere for which day shift is infamous.

The acutely competitive environment that characterizes day shift arises from the aggregate striving of each waitress to maximize her tip income by serving the greatest possible number of customers. Two strategies are enlisted to this end. First, each waitress attempts to *turn* her tables as quickly as possible. Briefly stated, this means she takes the order, delivers the food, clears and resets a table, and begins serving the next party as rapidly as customer lingering and the speed of the kitchen allow. A seven-year veteran of Route describes the strategy and its rewards:

> What I do is I prebus my tables. When the people get up and go all I got is glasses and cups, pull off, wipe, set, and I do the table turnover. But see that's from day shift. See the girls on grave-yard . . . don't understand the more times you turn that table the more money you make. You could have three tables and still make a hundred dollars. If you turn them tables.

As the waitress indicates, a large part of turning tables involves getting the table cleared and set for the next customer. During a rush, swing and grave waitresses tend to leave dirty tables standing, partly because they are less experienced and therefore less efficient, partly to avoid being given parties, or *sat*, when they are already behind. In contrast, day waitresses assign high priority to keeping their tables cleared and ready for customers. The difference in method reflects increased skill and growing awareness of and concern with money-making strategies.

A waitress can further increase her customer count by controlling the flow of customers within the restaurant. Ideally the hostess or manager running the front house rotates customers among stations, just as stations are rotated among waitresses.[2] Each waitress is given, or *sat,* one party at a time in turn so that all waitresses have comparable customer counts at the close of a shift. When no hostess is on duty, or both she and the manager are detained and customers are waiting to be seated, waitresses will typically seat incoming parties.

Whether or not a formal hostess is on duty, day waitresses are notorious for by-passing the rotation system by racing to the door and directing incoming customers to their own tables. A sense of the urgency with which this strategy is pursued is conveyed in the comment of one five-year veteran, "They'll run you down to get that person at the door, to seat them in their station." The competition for customers is so intense during the day that some waitresses claim they cannot afford to leave the floor (even to use the restroom) lest they return to find a co-worker's station filled at their expense. "In the daytime, honey," remarks an eight-year Route waitress, "in the daytime it's like pulling teeth. You got to stay on the floor to survive. To survive." It is in part because they do not want to lose customers and tips to their co-workers that waitresses do not take formal breaks. Instead, they rest and eat between waiting tables or during lulls in business, returning to the floor intermittently to check on parties in progress and seat customers in their stations.

The fast pace and chaotic nature of restaurant work provide a cover for the waitress's aggressive pursuit of customers, since it is difficult for other servers to monitor closely the allocation of parties in the bustle and confusion of a rush. Still, it is not uncommon for waitresses to grumble to management and co-workers if they notice an obvious imbalance in customer distribution. Here again, the waitress refrains from directly criticizing her fellow servers, voicing her displeasure by commenting on the paucity of customers in her own station, rather than the overabundance of customers in the stations of certain co-waitresses. In response to these grumblings, other waitresses may moderate somewhat their efforts to appropriate new parties, and management may make a special effort to seat the disgruntled server favorably.

A waitress can also exert pressure on the manager or hostess to keep her station filled. She may, for instance, threaten to leave if she is not seated enough customers.

> I said, "Innes [a manager], I'm in [station] one and two. If one and two is not filled at all times from now until three, I'm getting my coat, my pocketbook, and I'm leaving." And one and two was filled, and I made ninety-five dollars.

Alternatively, she can make it more convenient for the manager or hostess to seat her rather than her co-workers, either by keeping her tables open (as described), or by taking extra tables. If customers are waiting to be seated, a waitress may offer to pick up parties in a station that is closed or, occasionally, to pick up parties in another waitress's station.[3] In attempting either strategy, but especially the latter, the waitress must be adept not only at waiting tables, but in interpersonal restaurant politics. Autonomy and possession are of central concern to waitresses, and a waitress who offers to pick up tables outside her station must select her words carefully if she is to avoid being accused of invading her co-workers' territory. Accordingly, she may choose to present her bid for extra parties as an offer to help—the manager, another waitress, the restaurant, customers—rather than as a request.

The waitress who seeks to increase her tip income by maximizing the number of customers she serves may endeavor to cut her losses by refusing to serve parties that have stiffed her in the past. If she is a low-ranking waitress, her refusal is likely to be overturned by the manager. If she is an experienced and valuable waitress, the manager may ask someone else to take the party, assure the waitress he will take care of her (that is, pad the bill and give her the difference), or even pick up the party himself. Though the practice is far from common, a waitress may go so far as to demand a tip from a customer who has been known to stiff in the past.

> This party of two guys come in and they order thirty to forty dollars worth of food . . . and they stiff us. Every time. So Kaddie told them, "If you don't tip us, we're not going to wait on you." They said, "We'll tip you." So Kaddie waited on them, and they tipped her. The next night they came in, I waited on them and they didn't tip me. The third time they came in [the manager] put them in my station and I told [the manager] straight up, "I'm not waiting on them . . ." So he made Hailey pick them up. And they stiffed Hailey. So when they came in the next night . . . [they] said, "Are you going to give us a table?" I said, "You going to tip me? I'm not going to wait on you. You got all that money, you sell all that crack on the streets and you come here

and you can't even leave me a couple bucks?" . . . So they left me a dollar. So when they come in Tuesday night, I'm telling them a dollar ain't enough.

The tactics employed by waitresses, and particularly day-shift waitresses, to increase their customer count and thereby boost their tip earnings have earned them a resounding notoriety among their less competitive co-workers. Day (and some swing) waitresses are described as "money hungry," "sneaky little bitches," "self-centered," "aggressive," "backstabbing bitches," and "cutthroats over tables." The following remarks of two Route waitresses, however, indicate that those who employ these tactics see them as defensive, not aggressive measures. A sense of the waitress's preoccupation with autonomy and with protecting what is hers also emerges from these comments.

> You have to be like that. Because if you don't be like that, people step on you. You know, like as far as getting customers. I mean, you know, I'm sorry everybody says I'm greedy. I guess that's why I've survived this long at Route. Cause I am greedy. . . . *I want what's mine,* and if it comes down to me cleaning your table or my table, I'm going to clean my table. Because see I went through all that stage where I would do your table. To be fair. And you would walk home with seventy dollars, and I'd have twenty-five, cause I was being fair all night. (emphasis added)

> If the customer comes in the door and I'm there getting that door, don't expect me to cover your backside while you in the back smoking a cigarette and I'm here working for myself. You not out there working for me. . . . When I go to the door and get the customers, when I keep my tables clean and your tables are dirty, and you wonder why you only got

one person . . . then that's just tough shit. . . . You're damn right my station is filled. *I'm not here for you.* (emphasis added)

Whether the waitress who keeps her station filled with customers is acting aggressively or defensively, her tactics are effective. It is commonly accepted that determined day waitresses make better money than less competitive co-workers even when working swing or grave. Moreover Nera, the waitress most infamous for her relentless use of "money-hungry tactics," is at the same time most famous for her consistently high daily takes. While other waitresses jingle change in their aprons, Nera is forced to store wads of bills in her shoes and in paper bags to prevent tips from overflowing her pockets. She claims to make a minimum of five hundred dollars a week in tip earnings; her record for one day's work exceeds two hundred dollars and is undoubtedly the record for the restaurant.

Inverting the Symbolism of Tipping

It may already be apparent that the waitress views the customer—not as a master to pamper and appease—but as substance to be processed as quickly and in as large a quantity as possible. The difference in perspective is expressed in the objectifying terminology of waitresses: a customer or party is referred to as a *table,* or by table number, as *table five* or simply *five;* serving successive parties at a table is referred to as *turning the table;* taking an order is also known as *picking up a table;* and to serve water, coffee, or other beverages is to *water, coffee,* or *beverage* a table, number, or customer. Even personal acquaintances assume the status of inanimate matter, or tip-bearing plants, in the language of the server:

> I got my fifth-grade teacher [as a customer] one time. . . . I kept her coffeed. I kept her boyfriend coked all night. So-daed. . . . And I kept them filled up.

If the customer is perceived as material that is processed, the goal of this processing is the production or extraction of a finished product: the tip. This image too is conveyed in the language of the floor. A waitress may comment that she "got a good tip" or "gets good tips," but she is more likely to say that she "made" or "makes good tips." She may also say that she "got five bucks out of" a customer, or complain that some customers "don't want to give up on" their money. She may accuse a waitress who stays over into her shift of "tapping on" her money, or warn an aspiring waitress against family restaurants on the grounds that "there's no money in there." In all these comments (and all are actual), the waitress might as easily be talking about mining for coal or drilling for oil as serving customers.

Predictably, the waitress's view of the customer as substance to be processed influences her perception of the meaning of tips, and especially substandard tips. At Route, low tips and stiffs are not interpreted as a negative reflection on the waitress's personal qualities or social status. Rather, they are felt to reveal the refractory nature or poor quality of the raw material from which the tip is extracted, produced, or fashioned. In less metaphorical terms, a low tip or stiff is thought to reflect the negative qualities and low status of the customer who is too cheap, too poor, too ignorant, or too coarse to leave an appropriate gratuity. In this context, it is interesting to note that *stiff*, the term used in restaurants to refer to incidents of nontipping or to someone who does not tip, has also been used to refer to a wastrel or penniless man (Partridge 1984), a hobo, tramp, vagabond, deadbeat, and a moocher (Wentworth and Flexner 1975).

Evidence that waitresses assign blame for poor tips to the tipper is found in their reaction to being undertipped or stiffed. Rather than breaking down in tears and lamenting her "personal failure," the Route waitress responds to a stiff by announcing the event to her co-workers and managers in a tone of angry disbelief. Co-workers and managers echo the waitress's indignation and typically ask her to identify the party (by table number and physical description), or if she has already done so, to be more specific. This identification is crucial for it allows sympathizers to join the waitress in analyzing the cause of the stiff, which is assumed a priori to arise from some shortcoming of the party, not the waitress. The waitress and her co-workers may conclude that the customers in question were rude, troublemakers, or bums, or they may explain their behavior by identifying them as members of a particular category of customers. It might be revealed, for instance, that the offending party was a church group: church groups are invariably tightfisted. It might be resolved that the offenders were senior citizens, Southerners, or businesspeople: all well-known cheapskates. If the customers were European, the stiff will be attributed to ignorance of the American tipping system; if they were young, to immaturity; if they had children, to lack of funds.

These classifications and their attendant explanations are neither fixed nor trustworthy. New categories are invented to explain otherwise puzzling incidents, and all categories are subject to exception. Though undependable as predictive devices, customer typologies serve a crucial function: they divert blame for stiffs and low tips from the waitress to the characteristics of the customer. It is for this reason that it is "important" for workers to distinguish between different categories of customers, despite the fact that such distinctions are based on "unreliable verbal and appearance clues." In fact, it is precisely the unreliability, or more appropriately the flexibility, of customer typologies that makes them valuable to waitresses. When categories can be constructed and dissolved on demand, there is no danger that an incident will fall outside the existing system of classification and hence be inexplicable.

While waitresses view the customer as something to be processed and the tip as the product of this processing, they are aware that the public does not share their understanding of the waitress–diner–tip relationship. Waitresses at Route recognize that many customers perceive them as needy creatures willing to commit great feats of service and absorb high doses of abuse in their anxiety to secure a favorable gratuity or protect their jobs. They are also aware that some customers leave small tips with the intent to insult the server and that others undertip on the assumption that for a Route waitress even fifty cents will be appreciated. One waitress indicated that prior to being employed in a restaurant, she herself subscribed to the stereotype of the down-and-out waitress "because you see stuff on television, you see these wives or single ladies who waitress and they live in slummy apartments or slummy houses and they dress in rags." It is these images of neediness and desperation, which run so strongly against the waitress's perception of herself and her position, that she attacks when strained relations erupt into open conflict.

> Five rowdy black guys walked in the door and they went to seat themselves at table seven. I said, "Excuse me. You all got to wait to be seated." "We ain't got to do *shit*. We here to eat. . . ." So they went and sat down. And I turned around and just looked at them. And they said, "Well, I hope you ain't our waitress, cause you blew your tip. Cause you ain't getting nothing from us." And I turned around and I said, "You need it more than I do, baby."

This waitress's desire to confront the customer's assumption of her destitution is widely shared among service workers whose status as tipped employees marks them as needy in the eyes of their customers. Davis (1959:162–63) reports that among cabdrivers "a forever repeated story is of the annoyed driver, who, after a grueling trip with a Lady Shopper, hands the coin back, telling her, 'Lady, keep your lousy dime. You need it more than I do.'" Mars and Nicod (1984:75) report a hotel waitress's claim that "if she had served a large family with children for one or two weeks, and then was given a 10p piece, she would give the money back, saying, 'It's all right, thank you, I've got enough change for my bus fare home.'" In an incident I observed (not at Route), a waitress followed two male customers out of a restaurant calling, "Excuse me! You forgot this!" and holding up the coins they had left as a tip. The customers appeared embarrassed, motioned for her to keep the money, and continued down the sidewalk. The waitress, now standing in the outdoor seating area of the restaurant and observed by curious diners, threw the money after the retreating men and returned to her work. Episodes such as these allow the worker to repudiate openly the evaluation of her financial status that is implied in an offensively small gratuity, and permit her to articulate her own understanding of what a small tip says and about whom. If customers can only afford to leave a dime, or feel a 10p piece is adequate compensation for two weeks' service, they must be very hard up or very ignorant indeed.

In the following incident the waitress interjects a denial of her neediness into an altercation that is not related to tipping, demonstrating that the customer's perception of her financial status is a prominent and persistent concern for her.

> She [a customer] wanted a California Burger with mayonnaise. And when I got the mayonnaise, the mayonnaise had a

little brown on it. . . . So this girl said to me, she said, " What the fuck is this you giving me?" And I turned around, I thought, "Maybe she's talking to somebody else in the booth with her." And I turned around and I said, "Excuse me?" She said, "You hear what I said. I said, 'What the fuck are you giving me?'" And I turned around, I said, "I don't know if you're referring your information to *me*," I said, "but if you're referring your information to *me*," I said, "I don't *need* your bullshit." I said, "I'm not going to even take it. . . . Furthermore, I could care less if you eat or *don't* eat. . . . And you see this?" And I took her check and I ripped it apart. . . . And I took the California Burger and I says, "You don't have a problem anymore now, right?" She went up to the manager. And she says, "That black waitress"—I says, "Oh. By the way, what is my name? I don't have a name, [using the words] 'that black waitress'. . . . My name happens to be Nera. . . . That's N-E-R-A. . . . And I don't need your bullshit, sweetheart. . . . People like you I can walk on, because you don't know how to talk to human beings." And I said, "I don't need you. I don't need your quarters. I don't need your nickels. I don't need your dimes. So if you want service, be my guest. Don't you *ever* sit in my station, cause I won't wait on you." The manager said, "Nera, please. Would you wait in the back?" I said, "No. I don't take back seats no more for nobody."

In each of these cases, the waitress challenges the customer's definition of the relationship in which tipping occurs. By speaking out, by confronting the customer, she demonstrates that she is not subservient or in fear of losing her job; that she is not compelled by financial need or a sense of social hierarchy to accept abuse from customers; that she does not, in Nera's words, "take back seats no more for nobody." At the same time, she reverses the symbolic force of the low tip, converting a statement on her social status or work skills into a statement on the tipper's cheapness or lack of savoir faire.

Symbolic Dimensions of Tipping

Of 1.5 million restaurant servers employed in the United States, 90 percent are women who receive at least two-thirds of their earnings in the form of gratuities (Butler and Skipper 1980:489). For some waitresses the fact that tips have traditionally gone un- or underreported and therefore un- or undertaxed contributes to their economic appeal, despite the adverse consequences of underreporting for social security and unemployment benefits (L. Howe 1977:123). For others, the immediacy of tipping income is its central redeeming factor. "Waiting and waitressing is a MAC card," a Route waiter commented. "You walk in, you punch in your five hours of work, you walk out, you got forty bucks in your hand." For those whose financial needs are often small but urgent, the fast cash factor of the tipping system may be more valuable than the security of a steady weekly wage. This was the case for a seventeen-year-old hostess at Route who justified her demand to be trained for the floor partly on the grounds that if she were a waitress, whenever her baby needed something (Pampers, for example), she could come in and make the money by the end of her shift.

But a tip is more than payment for service rendered; it is a potent symbol capable of evoking a profound sense of triumph or provoking an angry blitz of expletives. It is, moreover, a symbol that embodies in coarse, even vulgar material form the myriad whisperings of power and control that pervade the server–served relationship. . . .

In drawing attention to the waitress's ability to subvert this complex and potentially degrading symbolism and moderate the financial risks of tipping, my purpose has been to demonstrate the waitress's power of resistance, her spirit of defiance, and her ability to manipulate her work environment to protect her interests. It has not been my intention to question the exploitive nature of a system of compensation that compels women to compete against one another to secure a fair wage, and absolves employers from responsibility for the economic security of workers from whose labor they profit. Nor has it been the aim of this discussion to suggest that waitresses are immune to the financial and emotional dangers of the tipping system. However skillfully the waitress maximizes her customer count, she remains vulnerable to the vicissitudes of the food service industry. Route servers suffered periodic drops in their tip income because of seasonal fluctuations in customer volume and unexpected slumps in business, as when the restaurant stood nearly empty for three weeks while road construction obscured the entrance to the parking lot. Likewise, though waitresses blame their customers and not themselves for low tips, being stiffed or undertipped remains an emotionally taxing experience. At Route as elsewhere, the failure of a customer to provide adequate compensation for service was the frequent cause of impassioned outbursts. Nonetheless, throughout the course of research and in five years' prior experience waiting tables, I never encountered a waitress who interpreted a bad tip as a "personal failure." What tears were shed were shed in anger, not in self-rebuke.

NOTES

1. *Call-out:* an employee calls the restaurant to say she will not be coming to work because of sickness, transportation problems, or a personal emergency. Employees often call out shortly before they are supposed to start work, or after their scheduled shift has begun, making it difficult for management to find replacements in time.

2. *Front house:* area of restaurant open to customers, including the floor, the register and waiting area, and the customer restrooms. The back house comprises all areas to which the public does not have access, including the kitchen, dish room, managers' office, stockroom, main waitresses' station, and employee break room and restrooms. To *run the front house* is primarily to perform the duties of hostess, though the expression carries supervisory connotations.

3. *Pick up:* to take the order from or wait on a party.

REFERENCES

Butler, Suellen, and James K. Skipper, Jr. 1980. "Waitressing, Vulnerability, and Job Autonomy: The Case of the Risky Tip." *Sociology of Work and Occupations* 7(4):487–502.

Davis, Fred. 1959. "The Cabdriver and His Fare: Facets of a Fleeting Relationship." *American Journal of Sociology* 65(2):158–65.

Howe, Louise K. 1977. *Pink Collar Workers: Inside the World of Women's Work.* New York: Putnam.

Mars, Gerald, and Michael Nicod. 1984. *The World of Waiters.* London: George Allen & Unwin.

Partridge, Eric. 1984. *A Dictionary of Slang and Unconventional English.* 8th ed., s.v. "stiff." New York: Macmillan.

Wentworth, Harold, and Stuart Berg Flexner, eds. and comps. 1975. *Dictionary of American Slang.* 2d supplemental ed., s.v. "stiff." New York: Thomas Y. Crowell Co.

29

Maid to Order
The Politics of Other Women's Work

Barbara Ehrenreich

In line with growing class polarization, the classic posture of submission is making a stealthy comeback. "We scrub your floors the old-fashioned way," boasts the brochure from Merry Maids, the largest of the residential-cleaning services that have sprung up in the last two decades, "on our hands and knees." This is not a posture that independent "cleaning ladies" willingly assume—preferring, like most people who clean their own homes, the sponge mop wielded from a standing position. In her comprehensive 1999 guide to homemaking, *Home Comforts,* Cheryl Mendelson warns: "Never ask hired housecleaners to clean your floors on their hands and knees; the request is likely to be regarded as degrading." But in a society in which 40 percent of the wealth is owned by 1 percent of households while the bottom 20 percent reports negative assets, the degradation of others is readily purchased. Kneepads entered American political discourse as a tool of the sexually subservient, but employees of Merry Maids, The Maids International, and other corporate cleaning services spend hours every day on these kinky devices, wiping up the drippings of the affluent.

I spent three weeks in September 1999 as an employee of The Maids International in Portland, Maine, cleaning, along with my fellow team members, approximately sixty houses containing a total of about 250 scrubbable floors—bathrooms, kitchens, and entryways requiring the hands-and-knees treatment. It's a different world down there below knee level, one that few adults voluntarily enter. Here you find elaborate dust structures held together by a scaffolding of dog hair; dried bits of pasta glued to the floor by their sauce; the congealed remains of gravies, jellies, contraceptive creams, vomit, and urine. Sometimes, too, you encounter some fragment of a human being: a child's legs, stamping by in disgust because the maids are still present when he gets home from school; more commonly, the Joan & David–clad feet and electrolyzed calves of the female homeowner. Look up and you may find this person staring at you, arms folded, in anticipation of an overlooked stain. In rare instances she may try to help in some vague, symbolic way, by moving the cockatoo's cage, for example, or apologizing for the leaves shed by a miniature indoor tree. Mostly, though, she will not see you at all and may even sit down with her mail at a table in the very room you are cleaning, where she would remain completely unaware of your existence unless you were to crawl under that table and start gnawing away at her ankles.

———

Housework, as you may recall from the feminist theories of the Sixties and Seventies, was supposed to be the great equalizer of women. Whatever else women did—jobs, school, child care—we also did housework, and if there were some women who hired others to do it for them, they seemed too privileged and rare to include in the theoretical calculus. All women were workers, and the home was their workplace—unpaid and unsupervised, to be sure, but a workplace no less than the offices and factories men repaired to every morning. If men thought of the home as a site of leisure and recreation—a "haven in a heartless world"—this was to ignore the invisible female proletariat that kept it cozy and humming. We were on the march now, or so we imagined, united against a society that devalued our labor even as it waxed mawkish over "the family" and "the home." Shoulder to shoulder and arm in arm, women were finally getting up off the floor. . . .

A couple of decades later, however, the average household still falls far short of that goal. True, women do less housework than they did before the feminist revolution and the rise of the two-income family: down from an average of 30 hours per week in 1965 to 17.5 hours in 1995, according to a July 1999 study by the University of Maryland. Some of that decline reflects a relaxation of standards rather than a redistribution of chores; women still do two-thirds of whatever housework—including bill paying, pet care, tidying, and lawn care—gets done. The inequity is sharpest for the most despised of household chores, cleaning: in the thirty years between 1965 and 1995, men increased the time they spent scrubbing, vacuuming, and sweeping by 240 percent—all the way up to 1.7 hours per week—while women decreased their cleaning time by only 7 percent, to 6.7 hours per week. The averages conceal a variety of arrangements, of course, from minutely negotiated sharing to the most clichéd division of labor, as described by one woman to the *Washington Post:* "I take care of the inside, he takes care of the outside." But perhaps the most disturbing finding is that almost the entire increase in male participation took place between the 1970s and the mid-1980s. Fifteen years after the apparent

cessation of hostilities, it is probably not too soon to announce the score: in the "chore wars" of the Seventies and Eighties, women gained a little ground, but overall, and after a few strategic concessions, men won.

Enter then, the cleaning lady as *dea ex machina,* restoring tranquillity as well as order to the home. Marriage counselors recommend her as an alternative to squabbling, as do many within the cleaning industry itself. A Chicago cleaning woman quotes one of her clients as saying that if she gives up the service, "my husband and I will be divorced in six months." When the trend toward hiring out was just beginning to take off, in 1988, the owner of a Merry Maids franchise in Arlington, Massachusetts, told the *Christian Science Monitor,* "I kid some women. I say, 'We even save marriages. In this new eighties period you expect more from the male partner, but very often you don't get the cooperation you would like to have. The alternative is to pay somebody to come in. . . .'" Another Merry Maids franchise owner has learned to capitalize more directly on housework-related spats; he closes between 30 and 35 percent of his sales by making follow-up calls Saturday mornings, which is "prime time for arguing over the fact that the house is a mess." The microdefeat of feminism in the household opened a new door for women, only this time it was the servants' entrance.

In 1999, somewhere between 14 and 18 percent of households employed an outsider to do the cleaning, and the numbers have been rising dramatically. Mediamark Research reports a 53 percent increase, between 1995 and 1999, in the number of households using a hired cleaner or service once a month or more, and Maritz Marketing finds that 30 percent of the people who hired help in 1999 did so for the first time that year. Among my middle-class, professional women friends and acquaintances, including some who made important contributions to the early feminist analysis of housework, the employment of a maid is now nearly universal. This sudden emergence of a servant class is consistent with what some economists have called the "Brazilianization" of the American economy: We are dividing along the lines of traditional Latin American societies—into a tiny over-class and a huge underclass, with the latter available to perform intimate household services for the former. Or, to put it another way, the home, or at least the affluent home, is finally becoming what radical feminists in the Seventies only imagined it was—a true "workplace" for women and a tiny, though increasingly visible, part of the capitalist economy. And the question is: As the home becomes a workplace for someone else, is it still a place where you would want to live?

Strangely, or perhaps not so strangely at all, no one talks about the "politics of housework" anymore. The demand for "wages for housework" has sunk to the status of a curio, along with the consciousness-raising groups in which women once rallied support in their struggles with messy men. In the academy, according to the feminist sociologists I interviewed, housework has lost much of its former cachet—in part, I suspect, because fewer sociologists actually do it. Most Americans, over 80 percent, still clean their homes, but the minority who do not include a sizable fraction of the nation's opinion-makers and culture-producers—professors, writers, editors, politicians, talking heads, and celebrities of all sorts. In their homes, the politics of housework is becoming a politics not only of gender but of race and class—and these are subjects that the opinion-making elite, if not most Americans, generally prefer to avoid.

Even the number of paid houseworkers is hard to pin down. The Census Bureau reports that there were 549,000 domestic workers in 1998, up 9 percent since 1996, but this may be a considerable underestimate, since so much of the servant economy is still un-

derground. In 1995, two years after Zoe Baird lost her chance to be attorney general for paying her undocumented nanny off the books, the *Los Angeles Times* reported that fewer than 10 percent of those Americans who paid a housecleaner reported those payments to the IRS. Sociologist Mary Romero, one of the few academics who retain an active interest in housework and the women who do it for pay, offers an example of how severe the undercounting can be: the 1980 Census found only 1,063 "private household workers" in El Paso, Texas, though the city estimated their numbers at 13,400 and local bus drivers estimated that half of the 28,300 daily bus trips were taken by maids going to and from work. The honesty of employers has increased since the Baird scandal, but most experts believe that household workers remain, in large part, uncounted and invisible to the larger economy.

One thing you can say with certainty about the population of household workers is that they are disproportionately women of color: "lower" kinds of people for a "lower" kind of work. Of the "private household cleaners and servants" it managed to locate in 1998, the Bureau of Labor Statistics reports that 36.8 percent were Hispanic, 15.8 percent black, and 2.7 percent "other." Certainly the association between housecleaning and minority status is well established in the psyches of the white employing class. When my daughter, Rosa, was introduced to the wealthy father of a Harvard classmate, he ventured that she must have been named for a favorite maid. And Audre Lorde can perhaps be forgiven for her intemperate accusation at the feminist conference . . . when we consider an experience she had in 1967: "I wheel my two-year-old daughter in a shopping cart through a supermarket . . . and a little white girl riding past in her mother's cart calls out excitedly, 'Oh look, Mommy, a baby maid.'" But the composition of the household workforce is hardly fixed and has changed with the life chances of the different ethnic groups. In the late nineteenth century, Irish and German immigrants served the northern upper and middle classes, then left for the factories as soon as they could. Black women replaced them, accounting for 60 percent of all domestics in the 1940s, and dominated the field until other occupations began to open up to them. Similarly, West Coast maids were disproportionately Japanese American until that group, too, found more congenial options. Today, the color of the hand that pushes the sponge varies from region to region: Chicanas in the Southwest, Caribbeans in New York, native Hawaiians in Hawaii, whites, many of recent rural extraction, in Maine.

The great majority—though again, no one knows exact numbers—of paid housekeepers are freelancers, or "independents," who find their clients through agencies or networks of already employed friends and relatives. To my acquaintances in the employing class, the freelance housekeeper seems to be a fairly privileged and prosperous type of worker, a veritable aristocrat of labor—sometimes paid $15 an hour or more and usually said to be viewed as a friend or even treated as "one of the family." But the shifting ethnic composition of the workforce tells another story: this is a kind of work that many have been trapped in—by racism, imperfect English skills, immigration status, or lack of education—but few have happily chosen. Interviews with independent maids collected by Romero and by sociologist Judith Rollins, who herself worked as a maid in the Boston area in the early Eighties, confirm that the work is undesirable to those who perform it. Even when the pay is deemed acceptable, the hours may be long and unpredictable; there are usually no health benefits, no job security, and, if the employer has failed to pay Social Security taxes (in some cases because the maid herself prefers to be paid off the books), no retirement benefits. And the pay is often far from

acceptable. The BLS found full-time "private household cleaners and servants" earning a median annual income of $12,220 in 1998, which is $1,092 below the poverty level for a family of three. Recall that in 1993 Zoe Baird paid her undocumented household workers about $5 an hour out of her earnings of $507,000 a year.

At the most lurid extreme there is slavery. A few cases of forced labor pop up in the press every year, most recently—in some nightmare version of globalization—of undocumented women held in servitude by high-ranking staff members of the United Nations, the World Bank, and the International Monetary Fund. Consider the suit brought by Elizabeth Senghor, a Senegalese woman who alleged that she was forced to work fourteen-hour days for her employers in Manhattan, without any regular pay, and was given no accommodations beyond a pull-out bed in her employers' living room. Hers is not a particularly startling instance of domestic slavery; no beatings or sexual assaults were charged, and Ms. Senghor was apparently fed. What gives this case a certain rueful poignancy is that her employer, former U.N. employee Marie Angelique Savane, is one of Senegal's leading women's rights advocates and had told *The Christian Science Monitor* in 1986 about her efforts to get the Senegalese to "realize that being a woman can mean other things than simply having children, taking care of the house."

Mostly, though, independent maids—and sometimes the women who employ them—complain about the peculiar intimacy of the employer-employee relationship. Domestic service is an occupation that predates the refreshing impersonality of capitalism by several thousand years, conditions of work being still largely defined by the idiosyncrasies of the employers. Some of them seek friendship and even what their maids describe as "therapy," though they are usually quick to redraw the lines once the maid is perceived as overstepping. Others demand deference bordering on servility, while a growing fraction of the nouveau riche is simply out of control. In August 1999, the *New York Times* reported on the growing problem of dinner parties being disrupted by hostesses screaming at their help. To the verbal abuse add published reports of sexual and physical assaults—a young teenage boy, for example, kicking a live-in nanny for refusing to make sandwiches for him and his friends after school.

————

But for better or worse, capitalist rationality is finally making some headway into this weird preindustrial backwater. Corporate cleaning services now control 25 to 30 percent of the $1.4 billion housecleaning business, and perhaps their greatest innovation has been to abolish the mistress-maid relationship, with all its quirks and dependencies. The customer hires the service, not the maid, who has been replaced anyway by a team of two to four uniformed people, only one of whom—the team leader—is usually authorized to speak to the customer about the work at hand. The maids' wages, their Social Security taxes, their green cards, backaches, and child-care problems—all these are the sole concern of the company, meaning the local franchise owner. If there are complaints on either side, they are addressed to the franchise owner; the customer and the actual workers need never interact. Since the franchise owner is usually a middle-class white person, cleaning services are the ideal solution for anyone still sensitive enough to find the traditional employer-maid relationship morally vexing.

In a 1997 article about Merry Maids, *Franchise Times* reported concisely that the "category is booming, [the] niche is hot, too, as Americans look to outsource work even at home." Not all cleaning services do well, and there is a high rate of failure among informal, mom-and-pop services. The "boom" is concentrated among the national and international chains—outfits like Merry Maids, Molly Maids, Mini Maids, Maid Brigade, and The Maids International—all named, curiously enough, to highlight the more antique aspects of the industry, though the "maid" may occasionally be male. Merry Maids claimed to be growing at 15 to 20 percent a year in 1996, and spokesmen for both Molly Maids and The Maids International told me that their firms' sales are growing by 25 percent a year; local franchisers are equally bullish. Dan Libby, my boss at The Maids, confided to me that he could double his business overnight if only he could find enough reliable employees. To this end, The Maids offers a week's paid vacation, health insurance after ninety days, and a free breakfast every morning consisting—at least where I worked—of coffee, doughnuts, bagels, and bananas. Some franchises have dealt with the tight labor market by participating in welfare-to-work projects that not only funnel employees to them but often subsidize their paychecks with public money, at least for the first few months of work (which doesn't mean the newly minted maid earns more, only that the company has to pay her less). The Merry Maids franchise in the city where I worked is conveniently located a block away from the city's welfare office.

Among the women I worked with at The Maids, only one said she had previously worked as an independent, and she professed to be pleased with her new status as a cleaning-service employee. She no longer needed a car to get her from house to house and could take a day off—unpaid of course—to stay home with a sick child without risking the loss of a customer. I myself could see the advantage of not having to deal directly with the customers, who were sometimes at home while we worked and eager to make use of their supervisory skills: criticisms of our methods, and demands that we perform unscheduled tasks, could simply be referred to the franchise owner.

But there are inevitable losses for the workers as any industry moves from the entrepreneurial to the industrial phase, probably most strikingly, in this case, in the matter of pay. At Merry Maids, I was promised $200 for a forty-hour week, the manager hastening to add that "you can't calculate it in dollars per hour" since the forty hours include all the time spent traveling from house to house—up to five houses a day—which is unpaid. The Maids International, with its straightforward starting rate of $6.63 an hour, seemed preferable, though this rate was conditional on perfect attendance. Miss one day and your wage dropped to $6 an hour for two weeks, a rule that weighed particularly heavily on those who had young children. In addition, I soon learned that management had ways of shaving off nearly an hour's worth of wages a day. We were told to arrive at 7:30 in the morning, but our billable hours began only after we had been teamed up, given our list of houses for the day, and packed off in the company car at about 8:00 A.M. At the end of the day, we were no longer paid from the moment we left the car, though as much as fifteen minutes of work—refilling cleaning-fluid bottles, etc.—remained to be done. So for a standard nine-hour day, the actual pay amounted to about $6.10 an hour, unless you were still being punished for an absence, in which case it came out to $5.50 an hour.

Nor are cleaning-service employees likely to receive any of the perks or tips familiar to independents—free lunches and coffee, cast-off clothing, or a Christmas gift of cash. When I asked, only one of my coworkers could recall ever receiving a tip, and that was a voucher for a free meal at a downtown restaurant owned by a customer. The customers of cleaning services are probably no stingier than the employers of independents; they just don't know their cleaning people and probably wouldn't even recognize them on the street. Plus, customers probably assume that the fee they pay the service—$25 per person-hour in the case of The Maids franchise I worked for—goes largely to the workers who do the actual cleaning.

But the most interesting feature of the cleaning-service chains, at least from an abstract, historical perspective, is that they are finally transforming the home into a fully capitalist-style workplace, and in ways that the old wages-for-housework advocates could never have imagined. A house is an innately difficult workplace to control, especially a house with ten or more rooms, like so many of those we cleaned; workers may remain out of one another's sight for as much as an hour at a time. For independents, the ungovernable nature of the home-as-workplace means a certain amount of autonomy. They can take breaks (though this is probably ill-advised if the homeowner is on the premises); they can ease the monotony by listening to the radio or TV while they work. But cleaning services lay down rules meant to enforce a factorylike—or even convent-like—discipline on their far-flung employees. At The Maids, there were no breaks except for a daily ten-minute stop at a convenience store for coffee or "lunch"—meaning something like a slice of pizza. Otherwise, the time spent driving between houses was considered our "break" and the only chance to eat, drink, or (although this was also officially forbidden) smoke a cigarette. When the houses were spaced well apart, I could eat my sandwich in one sitting; otherwise, it would have to be divided into as many as three separate, hasty snacks.

Within a customer's house, nothing was to touch our lips at all, not even water—a rule that, on hot days, I sometimes broke by drinking from a bathroom faucet. TVs and radios were off-limits, and we were never, ever, to curse out loud, even in an ostensibly deserted house. There might be a homeowner secreted in some locked room, we were told, ear pressed to the door, or, more likely, a tape recorder or video camera running. At the time, I dismissed this as a scare story, but I have since come across ads for devices like the Tech-7 "incredible coin-sized camera" designed to "get a visual record of your babysitter's actions" and "watch employees to prevent theft." It was the threat or rumor of hidden recording devices that provided the final capitalist-industrial touch—supervision.

What makes the work most factorylike, though, is the intense Taylorization imposed by the companies. An independent, or a person cleaning his or her own home, chooses where she will start and, within each room, probably tackles the most egregious dirt first. Or she may plan her work more or less ergonomically, first doing whatever can be done from a standing position and then squatting or crouching to reach the lower levels. But with the special "systems" devised by the cleaning services and imparted to employees via training videos, there are no such decisions to make. In The Maids' "healthy touch" system, which is similar to what I saw of the Merry Maids' system on the training tape I was shown during my interview, all cleaning is divided into four task areas—dusting, vacuuming, kitchens, and bathrooms—which are in turn divided among the team members. For each task area other than vacuuming, there is a bucket containing rags and the appropriate cleaning fluids, so the biggest decision an employee has to make is which fluid and scrubbing instrument to deploy on which kind of surface; almost everything else has been choreographed in advance. When vacuuming, you begin with the master bedroom; when dusting, with the first room off of the kitchen; then you move through the rooms going left to right. When entering each room, you proceed from left to right and top to bottom, and the same with each surface—top to bottom, left to right. Deviations are subject to rebuke, as I discovered when a team leader caught me moving my arm from right to left, then

left to right, while wiping Windex over a French door.

It's not easy for anyone with extensive cleaning experience—and I include myself in this category—to accept this loss of autonomy. But I came to love the system: First, because if you hadn't always been traveling rigorously from left to right it would have been easy to lose your way in some of the larger houses and omit or redo a room. Second, some of the houses were already clean when we started, at least by any normal standards, thanks probably to a housekeeper who kept things up between our visits; but the absence of visible dirt did not mean there was less work to do, for no surface could ever be neglected, so it was important to have "the system" to remind you of where you had been and what you had already "cleaned." No doubt the biggest advantage of the system, though, is that it helps you achieve the speed demanded by the company, which allots only so many minutes per house. After a week or two on the job, I found myself moving robotlike from surface to surface, grateful to have been relieved of the thinking process.

The irony, which I was often exhausted enough to derive a certain malicious satisfaction from, is that "the system" is not very sanitary. When I saw the training videos on "Kitchens" and "Bathrooms," I was at first baffled, and it took me several minutes to realize why: There is no water, or almost no water, involved. I had been taught to clean by my mother, a compulsive housekeeper who employed water so hot you needed rubber gloves to get into it and in such Niagaralike quantities that most microbes were probably crushed by the force of it before the soap suds had a chance to rupture their cell walls. But germs are never mentioned in the videos provided by The Maids. Our antagonists existed entirely in the visible world—soap scum, dust, counter crud, dog hair, stains, and smears—and were attacked by damp rag or, in hard-core cases, by a scouring pad. We scrubbed only to remove impurities that might be detectable to a customer by hand or by eye; otherwise, our only job was to wipe. Nothing was ever said, in the videos or in person, about the possibility of transporting bacteria, by rag or by hand, from bathroom to kitchen or even from one house to the next. Instead, it is the "cosmetic touches" that the videos emphasize and to which my trainer continually directed my eye. Fluff out all throw pillows and arrange them symmetrically. Brighten up stainless steel sinks with baby oil. Leave all spice jars, shampoos, etc., with their labels facing outward. Comb out the fringes of Persian carpets with a pick. Use the vacuum to create a special, fernlike pattern in the carpets. The loose ends of toilet paper and paper towel rolls have to be given a special fold. Finally, the house is sprayed with the service's signature air freshener—a cloying floral scent in our case, "baby fresh" in the case of the Mini Maids.

When I described the "methods" employed to housecleaning expert Cheryl Mendelson, she was incredulous. A rag moistened with disinfectant will not get a countertop clean, she told me, because most disinfectants are inactivated by contact with organic matter—i.e., dirt—so their effectiveness declines with each swipe of the rag. What you need is a detergent and hot water, followed by a rinse. As for floors, she judged the amount of water we used—one half of a small bucket—to be grossly inadequate, and, in fact, the water I wiped around on floors was often an unsavory gray. I also ran The Maids' cleaning methods by Don Aslett, author of numerous books on cleaning techniques and self-styled "number one cleaner in America." He was hesitant to criticize The Maids directly, perhaps because he is, or told me he is, a frequent speaker at conventions of cleaning-service franchise holders, but he did tell me how he would clean a countertop: first, spray it thoroughly with an all-purpose cleaner, then let it sit for three to four minutes of "kill time," and finally wipe it dry with a clean cloth. Merely wiping the surface with a damp cloth, he said, just spreads the dirt around. But the point at The Maids, apparently, is not to clean so much as it is to create the appearance of having been cleaned, not to sanitize but to create a kind of stage setting for family life. And the stage setting Americans seem to prefer is sterile only in the metaphorical sense, like a motel room or the fake interiors in which soap operas and sitcoms take place.

But even ritual work takes its toll on those assigned to perform it. Turnover is dizzyingly high in the cleaning-service industry, and not only because of the usual challenges that confront the working poor—child-care problems, unreliable transportation, evictions, and prior health problems. As my long-winded interviewer at Merry Maids warned me, and my coworkers at The Maids confirmed, this is a physically punishing occupation, something to tide you over for a few months, not year after year. The hands-and-knees posture damages knees, with or without pads; vacuuming strains the back; constant wiping and scrubbing invite repetitive stress injuries even in the very young. In my three weeks as a maid, I suffered nothing more than a persistent muscle spasm in the right forearm, but the damage would have been far worse if I'd had to go home every day to my own housework and children, as most of my coworkers did, instead of returning to my motel and indulging in a daily after-work regimen of ice packs and stretches. Chores that seem effortless at home, even almost recreational when undertaken at will for twenty minutes or so at a time, quickly turn nasty when performed hour after hour, with few or no breaks and under relentless time pressure.

So far, the independent, entrepreneurial housecleaner is holding her own, but there are reasons to think that corporate cleaning services will eventually dominate the industry.

New users often prefer the impersonal, standardized service offered by the chains, and, in a fast-growing industry, new users make up a sizable chunk of the total clientele. Government regulation also favors the corporate chains, whose spokesmen speak gratefully of the "Zoe Baird effect," referring to customers' worries about being caught paying an independent off the books. But the future of housecleaning may depend on the entry of even bigger players into the industry. Merry Maids, the largest of the chains, has the advantage of being a unit within the $6.4 billion ServiceMaster conglomerate, which includes such related businesses as TruGreen-ChemLawn, Terminix, Rescue Rooter, and Furniture Medic. Swisher International, best known as an industrial toilet-cleaning service, operates Swisher Maids in Georgia and North Carolina, and Sears may be feeling its way into the business. If large multinational firms establish a foothold in the industry, mobile professionals will be able to find the same branded and standardized product wherever they relocate. For the actual workers, the change will, in all likelihood, mean a more standardized and speeded-up approach to the work—less freedom of motion and fewer chances to pause.

The trend toward outsourcing the work of the home seems, at the moment, unstoppable. Two hundred years ago women often manufactured soap, candles, cloth, and clothing in their own homes, and the complaints of some women at the turn of the twentieth century that they had been "robbed by the removal of creative work" from the home sound pointlessly reactionary today. Not only have the skilled crafts, like sewing and cooking from scratch, left the home but many of the "white collar" tasks are on their way out, too. For a fee, new firms such as the San Francisco–based Les Concierges and Cross It Off Your List in Manhattan will pick up dry cleaning, babysit pets, buy groceries, deliver dinner, even do the Christmas shopping. With other firms and individuals offering to buy your clothes, organize your financial files, straighten out your closets, and wait around in your home for the plumber to show up, why would anyone want to hold on to the toilet cleaning?

Absent a major souring of the economy, there is every reason to think that Americans will become increasingly reliant on paid housekeepers and that this reliance will extend ever further down into the middle class. For one thing, the "time bind" on working parents shows no sign of loosening; people are willing to work longer hours at the office to pay for the people—house cleaners and baby-sitters—who are filling in for them at home. Children, once a handy source of household help, are now off at soccer practice or SAT prep classes; grandmother has relocated to a warmer climate or taken up a second career. Furthermore, despite the fact that people spend less time at home than ever, the square footage of new homes swelled by 33 percent between 1975 and 1998, to include "family rooms," home entertainment rooms, home offices, bedrooms, and often bathrooms for each family member. By the third quarter of 1999, 17 percent of new homes were larger than 3,000 square feet, which is usually considered the size threshold for household help, or the point at which a house becomes unmanageable to the people who live in it.

One more trend impels people to hire outside help, according to cleaning experts such as Aslett and Mendelson: fewer Americans know how to clean or even to "straighten up." I hear this from professional women defending their decision to hire a maid: "I'm just not very good at it myself" or "I wouldn't really know where to begin." Since most of us learn to clean from our parents (usually our mothers), any diminution of cleaning skills is transmitted from one generation to another, like a gene that can, in the appropriate environment, turn out to be disabling or lethal. Upper-middle-class children raised in the servant economy of the Nineties are bound to grow up as domestically incompetent as their parents and no less dependent on people to clean up after them. Mendelson sees this as a metaphysical loss, a "matter of no longer being physically centered in your environment." Having cleaned the rooms of many overly privileged teenagers in my stint with The Maids, I think the problem is a little more urgent than that. The American overclass is raising a generation of young people who will, without constant assistance, suffocate in their own detritus.

If there are moral losses, too, as Americans increasingly rely on paid household help, no one has been tactless enough to raise them. Almost everything we buy, after all, is the product of some other person's suffering and miserably underpaid labor. I clean my own house (though—full disclosure—I recently hired someone else to ready it for a short-term tenant), but I can hardly claim purity in any other area of consumption. I buy my jeans at The Gap, which is reputed to subcontract to sweatshops. I tend to favor decorative objects no doubt ripped off, by their purveyors, from scantily paid Third World craftspersons. Like everyone else, I eat salad greens just picked by migrant farm workers, some of them possibly children. And so on. We can try to minimize the pain that goes into feeding, clothing, and otherwise provisioning ourselves—by observing boycotts, checking for a union label, etc.—but there is no way to avoid it altogether without living in the wilderness on berries. Why should housework, among all the goods and services we consume, arouse any special angst?

And it does, as I have found in conversations with liberal-minded employers of maids, perhaps because we all sense that there are ways in which housework is different from other products and services. First, in its inevitable proximity to the activities that compose "private" life. The home that becomes a workplace for other people remains a home, even when that workplace has been minutely regulated by the corporate cleaning chains. Someone who has no qualms about purchasing rugs woven by child slaves in India or coffee picked by impoverished peasants in Guatemala might still hesitate to tell dinner guests that, surprisingly enough, his or her lovely home doubles as a sweatshop during the day. You can eschew the chain cleaning services of course, hire an independent cleaner at a generous hourly wage, and even encourage, at least in spirit, the unionization of the housecleaning industry. But this does not change the fact that someone is working in your home at a job she would almost certainly never have chosen for herself—if she'd had a college education, for example, or a little better luck along the way—and the place where she works, however enthusiastically or resentfully, is the same as the place where you sleep.

It is also the place where your children are raised, and what they learn pretty quickly is that some people are less worthy than others. Even better wages and working conditions won't erase the hierarchy between an employer and his or her domestic help, because the help is usually there only because the employer has "something better" to do with her time, as one report on the growth of cleaning services puts it, not noticing the obvious implication that the cleaning person herself has nothing better to do with her time. In a merely middle-class home, the message may be reinforced by a warning to the children that that's what they'll end up doing if they don't try harder in school. Housework, as radical feminists once proposed, defines a human relationship and, when unequally divided among social groups, reinforces preexisting inequalities. Dirt, in other words, tends to attach to the people who remove it—"garbagemen" and "cleaning ladies." Or, as cleaning entrepreneur Don Aslett told me with some bitterness—and this is a successful man, chairman of the board of an industrial cleaning service and frequent television guest—"The whole mentality out there is that if you clean, you're a scumball."

One of the "better" things employers of maids often want to do with their time is, of course, spend it with their children. But an underlying problem with post-nineteenth-century child-raising, as Deirdre English and I argued in our book *For Her Own Good* years ago, is precisely that it is unmoored in any kind of purposeful pursuit. Once "parenting" meant instructing the children in necessary chores; today it's more likely to center on one-sided conversations beginning with "So how was school today?" No one wants to put the kids to work again weeding and stitching; but in the void that is the modern home, relationships with children are often strained. A little "low-quality time" spent washing dishes or folding clothes together can provide a comfortable space for confidences—and give a child the dignity of knowing that he or she is a participant in, and not just the product of, the work of the home.

There is another lesson the servant economy teaches its beneficiaries and, most troublingly, the children among them. To be cleaned up after is to achieve a certain magical weightlessness and immateriality. Almost everyone complains about violent video games, but paid housecleaning has the same consequence-abolishing effect: you blast the villain into a mist of blood droplets and move right along; you drop the socks knowing they will eventually levitate, laundered and folded, back to their normal dwelling place. The result is a kind of virtual existence, in which the trail of litter that follows you seems to evaporate all by itself. Spill syrup on the floor and the cleaning person will scrub it off when she comes on Wednesday. Leave *The Wall Street Journal* scattered around your airplane seat and the flight attendants will deal with it after you've deplaned. Spray toxins into the atmosphere from

your factory's smokestacks and they will be filtered out eventually by the lungs of the breathing public. A servant economy breeds callousness and solipsism in the served, and it does so all the more effectively when the service is performed close up and routinely in the place where they live and reproduce.

Individual situations vary, of course, in ways that elude blanket judgment. Some people—the elderly and disabled, parents of new babies, asthmatics who require an allergen-free environment—may well need help performing what nursing-home staff call the "ADLs," or activities of daily living, and no shame should be attached to their dependency. In a more generous social order, housekeeping services would be subsidized for those who have health-related reasons to need them—a measure that would generate a surfeit of new jobs for the low-skilled people who now clean the homes of the affluent. And in a less gender-divided social order, husbands and boyfriends would more readily do their share of the chores.

However we resolve the issue in our individual homes, the moral challenge is, put simply, to make work visible again: not only the scrubbing and vacuuming, but all the hoeing, stacking, hammering, drilling, bending, and lifting that goes into creating and maintaining a livable habitat. In an ever more economically unequal culture, where so many of the affluent devote their lives to such ghostly pursuits as stock-trading, image-making, and opinion-polling, real work—in the old-fashioned sense of labor that engages hand as well as eye, that tires the body and directly alters the physical world—tends to vanish from sight. The feminists of my generation tried to bring some of it into the light of day, but, like busy professional women fleeing the house in the morning, they left the project unfinished, the debate broken off in midsentence, the noble intentions unfulfilled. Sooner or later, someone else will have to finish the job.

30

Working on (and Around) the Unborn Patient
Negotiating Social Order in a Fetal Treatment Unit

Monica J. Casper

Since 1981, when surgeons in the United States successfully operated on a fetus and galvanized the field of fetal medicine, fetal treatment programs have sprouted at hospitals around the world. Most emphasize closed-uterus forms of treatment, such as the placement of shunts (mechanical devices to divert fluid that has accumulated) or selective termination. Yet a few brave centers are forging ahead with research on open surgical techniques for a range of life-threatening congenital defects. One of these institutions is Capital Hospital, a large medical center in the western United States. A rich and diverse site, it has fostered the development of a Fetal Treatment Unit (FTU) focused on the clinical needs of the fetus. Here, medical workers have created an interdisciplinary center for diagnosis and treatment, where pregnant women and their fetuses are warmly welcomed and treated by a team of specialists. Here, too, medical workers struggle with and against each other in an emergent specialty with fuzzy boundaries, jockeying for professional control and access to new patients and health care markets. This [reading] explores the social organization of

the Fetal Treatment Unit at Capital Hospital, specifically the complex negotiations that occur in the everyday lives of medical personnel who work on and around the unborn patient.

. . . In this [reading] fetal surgery is examined as an intersection of multiple practitioners with different skills and interests. Fetal surgery, despite its dazzling array of instruments and procedures, is as much about people and their work as it is about technology. I show here that fetal surgery is characterized by a diverse organizational form in which a wide variety of interactions shape what fetal surgery looks like in practice. The most significant interactions revealed in my data are but two sides of the same variegated coin: *cooperation*, which makes the achievement of fetal surgery possible, and *conflict*, which threatens this achievement at every turn. Participants are well aware of their need to cooperate with each other to make the fetal surgery enterprise successful even while they may disagree loudly and consistently about how to accomplish this. They are equally aware of their many professional and political differences around which dissent erupts and which must be continually negotiated and managed. Understanding the social organization of the Fetal Treatment Unit, or how the medical personnel who inhabit it work together, sheds light on the hybrid interactional and institutional aspects of fetal surgery. Capital Hospital's ace fetal surgery

Excerpts from *The Making of the Unborn Patient: A Social Anatomy of Fetal Surgery* by Monica J. Casper. 1998. New Brunswick, NJ: Rutgers University Press. Copyright © 1998 by Monica J. Casper. Reprinted by permission of the publisher.

team is a microcosm of the broader world of fetal surgery, which is continually disrupted and reordered through work on and around fetuses.

In addition to the concept of work objects—material entities around which people make meaning and organize their work practices—this [reading] draws also on *negotiated order* (Strauss et al. 1964). Based on research in a psychiatric hospital, Strauss et al. (1964) argued that the structural life of an institution is constituted by "continual negotiative activity." Negotiations may be patterned, as for example within a web of institutional or organizational relationships, but they must be continually reconstituted through a variety of interactions as the basis for social order. Negotiations are emergent, contingent, constrained, and fluid—that is, they are ongoing, flexible, and do not exist in a vacuum—and they are essential to the coordination of medical work. The shapes of hospital wards, clinical and administrative arrangements, professional hierarchies, and institutional rules are all products of ongoing negotiations. These may achieve a relatively stable shape over time, but even stable social orders are continuously remade through commitments to certain routine interactions. Such arrangements can always be unmade if commitments flag and attention is diverted elsewhere. This [reading] focuses on two types of interactions that are especially germane to fetal surgery and its unique work objects: those centered on cooperation and those involved in the negotiation of conflict.

The emerging and controversial world of fetal surgery offers a particularly fitting site through which to examine the social organization of work. Drawing on interview and ethnographic data collected at Capital Hospital from 1991 to 1994, I first describe what goes on in the Fetal Treatment Unit, painting a multihued picture of this world and its inhabitants. I then turn to the heart of the analysis: how medical workers negotiate social order in the face of tremendous diversity and outright conflict. . . .

The Setting

Capital Hospital is a modern facility, outfitted with highly trained personnel and gleaming technologies. It is part of a large medical complex, where some buildings are steel and glass, and others a more antiquated yellow brick. Behind the hospital is an animal kennel where canine research animals bark loudly and frequently. Across the street is a medical bookstore where stethoscopes and skeletons hang on the walls; next door is a bustling café with striped umbrellas on the tables. Inside the hospital are long, brightly lit corridors leading to operating rooms with sterile, stainless steel equipment and to consulting rooms with subtle gray and mauve furniture designed to calm nervous patients. There is a persistent low hum in the air occasionally punctuated by announcements and calls for "Dr. Cart" (code blue) over the loudspeaker. Inside the flesh-toned walls of the hospital are people engaged in a variety of activities ranging from the mundane to the daring. The medical workers are recognizable by their crisp white lab coats and blue-green scrubs, while a worried, tired air hovers over the patients and their loved ones. Some patients, wearing revealing hospital gowns and paper slippers, slump in wheelchairs, while others shuffle along hospital corridors, dragging IVs behind them. Family members sit tensely in crowded waiting rooms, one eye on the television and the other on the door. Throughout, Capital Hospital is pervaded by an odd, familiar smell redolent of Mr. Clean, ether, and human bodies.

The Fetal Treatment Unit is located on an upper floor of the hospital, where the corridors are quieter and the view is better. It is spacious and elegantly decorated in muted shades of pink, mauve, and gray. A central reception area is dominated by a large desk and a bulletin board covered with photographs of fetal surgery's success stories—an appealing display of a dozen or more babies with rosy cheeks. There are offices behind the reception area for the fetal surgeons, nurses, and other FTU staff, and there is a medium-sized conference room with a table, chairs, projection screen, and small library. There are also several well-stocked laboratories in another area of the center. Medical workers come and go in this space, intent on the enormous, grave work of diagnosing and treating fetuses. Like cave paintings from a premodern time, fetal images abound in this space offering archaeological clues to the center's purpose. A small office is decorated with a certificate describing one of the fetal surgeons as a "Fetus Fixer," while on the wall of the conference room is an image of a fetus in a plastic bubble over the caption "Womb with a View." The FTU's logo, in black and white graphic design, depicts an outstretched hand with a tiny fetus nestled in the palm.

Unlike other parts of Capital Hospital, the main offices of the Fetal Treatment Unit are typically not chaotic. The FTU offices merely serve as headquarters for the fetal surgery team, while many activities take place elsewhere. Indeed, the quiet elegance of the FTU's reception area serves as a barrier of sorts to the noisy, bloody, controversial work that goes on behind closed doors. In addition to surgery on the fetus, the work involved in making the unborn patient occurs through meetings, consultations, telephone calls, conferences, and other sites and practices. Surgical procedures are done in the hospital's general operating rooms, and weekly fetal treatment meetings are held in a large conference room in the obstetrics department. The following are brief vignettes of the work of fetal surgery as it occurs both inside and outside the operating room. The first, a fragment from my fieldnotes recounting one of the many procedures that I watched, describes an operation on a young woman whose fetus was diagnosed with a diaphragmatic hernia:

> The surgeons sliced through [the patient's] abdomen. It was messy, and there were many layers of tissue, fat, muscle, and blood. The incisions were not neat and clean; surgeons would pull the layers apart as they ran a scalpel across [her] abdomen and the flesh and muscle would sort of rip apart slowly. As they worked their way through her body, they would pull parts of her abdomen aside and clamp them with big silver metal clips. After about eight minutes of cutting, they reached the uterus. Dr. ⸻ pulled the fetus partially out of the uterus and made two incisions on its left side, one about heart level and one about umbilical cord level in its abdomen. The lower incision was about two fingers wide. After making both incisions, Dr. ⸻ pushed the organs that had accumulated in the chest cavity downward. Immediately, a nurse placed a small device inside the fetus' chest to monitor its condition, while the organs came careening out of the lower incision and hung outside of the fetus' body.

The second vignette moves beyond the operating room to another, less visceral site where the unborn patient is crafted. The meeting described next took place in a small library located on the fifth floor of Capital Hospital; the room was crowded, noisy, and very hot, and tempers were running high following a spate of fetal deaths. Providers argued passionately about maternal management strategies and the need for better monitoring of pregnant women and fetuses both during and after fetal surgery. As we shall see, diversity is foregrounded in this vignette as multiple voices representing different specialties are heard together evaluating problems:

> A fetal physiologist remarked that the major issue in monitoring has to be umbilical blood flow reduction. An operating room nurse commented, somewhat testily, that the fetal team might "think about getting information from other operations and techniques in obstetrics and gynecology." An anesthesiologist responded that a major difference between fetal surgery and other obstetrical operations is the size of the uterine incision. Almost everyone present nodded at this, indicating wide agreement that fetal surgery is indeed different. The physiologist again took the floor and cautioned that "you should be careful about throwing things into the fetus without knowing what's going on." Speaking about a specific case, a nurse on the fetal surgery team suggested that they "need to figure out how to inhibit contractions without dangerous medications." All of a sudden, the room erupted and a number of people began talking at once. Somebody remarked, heatedly, that all procedures on the fetus are "insults." A neonatologist, with anger in his voice, asserted that "you can't compare normal labor with a woman who's had her uterus cut open and a fetus with its chest open!"

These examples provide an important backdrop for the analysis that follows. I analyze these and similar clusters of activity with an eye toward how social order is negotiated in fetal surgery through various types of patterned interactions. The remainder of this [reading] explores the interactional and institutional scaffolding of fetal surgery and its role in the making of the unborn patient in the contemporary era.

"A Spirit of Cooperation": Working Together in the Fetal Treatment Unit

Like Liley, Adamsons, Freda, and their many colleagues in the 1960s—and despite persistent conflicts—contemporary medical workers *do* cooperate with each other; their cooperation indeed is a source of pride and a foundation for claims of legitimacy. From its interdisciplinary roots three decades ago, fetal surgery has continued to attract and enroll numerous different specialists through a combination of professional needs and career goals. Providers recognize that cooperation is necessary in order to bring all of their different experiences and skills to bear on complicated fetal problems. It is certainly seen as integral to the "success" of fetal surgery, such as achieving fetal survival and ensuring that pregnant women do not die during the procedure. Cooperation may also be desired as an end in itself to make working conditions more pleasant or to satisfy certain institutional requirements related to fetal surgery. For example, attempting to secure funding for research or the approval of institutional review boards is far more expedient if medical workers are able to portray the fetal surgery enterprise as cooperative rather than as riddled with conflict. But while cooperation is an important building block for "doing things together" (Becker 1986) in fetal surgery, it is by no means a naturally occurring phenomenon. Rather, cooperation, like all other human interactions, must be achieved; its existence is something to be explained rather than taken for granted. The production of fetal surgery as a cooperative enterprise is characterized by numerous institutional activities, such as regular staff meetings designed to enable and encourage people to work together. According to key actors in the field, "the institutional setting, organization, and coordination of [fetal treatment units] are elements critical to [their] success" (Howell et al. 1993,

143). What follows is a description of the cooperative components of fetal surgery that make this nascent specialty possible.

The Fetal Treatment Unit at Capital Hospital originated in the early 1980s when a pediatric surgeon, a sonographer, and an obstetrician began working together on experimental fetal surgery. Obstetricians, with input from sonographers, had already been treating fetuses nonsurgically for a variety of conditions before pediatric surgeons began to focus on the fetus, beginning with transfusions for Rh disease based on Liley's work. But for the most part, pediatric specialists and neonatologists had been unsuccessful in saving babies whose diseases were too advanced for treatment. Echoing Liley and others from the 1960s, contemporary clinicians were dismayed that they could not save afflicted newborns who routinely died at birth or shortly thereafter. This frustration, coupled with important historical precedents in fetal diagnosis and treatment, prompted the trio at Capital Hospital to consider operating on fetuses *prenatally* in order to repair defects or to prevent life-threatening conditions from developing at birth. Open fetal surgery was used in one desperate case in which a fetal catheter inserted nonsurgically to treat a blocked urinary tract refused to stay in place; replacing the catheter in order to save the fetus necessitated surgically opening the pregnant woman's abdomen. However, once a new catheter was developed it proved easier to use than the old model, rendering subsequent open surgery unnecessary for this condition. By that time, however, the door to fetal surgery itself had been wedged open, and physicians had begun to consider applying this "new" technique to other diseases and conditions. Thus, a combination of concern for fetuses, technical innovation, professional goals, and institutional conditions revived interest in open fetal surgery almost twenty years after the pioneering but short-lived efforts of the 1960s.

As with the broader enterprise of fetal surgery, the Fetal Treatment Unit at Capital Hospital evolved through the interaction of professionals from many disciplines who shared an interest in the fetus. One fetal surgeon described the FTU as "a microcosm of the fetal treatment enterprise throughout the world." And like the clinical work settings of the 1960s in New Zealand and Puerto Rico, the FTU has remained multidisciplinary since its inception. From the initial triad of pediatric surgeon, sonographer, and obstetrician, the fetal surgery team at Capital has grown to include a range of practitioners with diverse skills, perspectives, and backgrounds. These include perinatologists skilled in fetal diagnosis, fetal blood sampling, and intrauterine transfusion; neonatologists, who must often intensively manage newborns after surgery and birth and during subsequent postnatal treatment; social workers who address psychosocial issues (including emotional, financial, employment, and social support issues) faced by pregnant women, their partners, and families; pediatric and obstetric anesthesiologists; nurses representing different specialties and levels of expertise; geneticists and genetic counselors; fetal physiologists knowledgeable in basic fetal biology; and medical ethicists. The feasibility of fetal surgery and the likelihood that it will become a routine rather than experimental medical practice are seen by participants as outcomes contingent upon cooperative interaction among the specialty's diverse practitioners. A successful fetal treatment center is, in the words of one fetal surgeon (Harrison 1991, 11), a "blend of skills and expertise," and there are increasing numbers of these centers appearing in the United States and in other nations.

Practitioners of fetal surgery are acutely aware of the diversity of skills and knowledges required to diagnose and treat the fetus. Every informant I spoke with talked at length about the necessity for cooperation and working together, an issue that has also received ample attention in the clinical literature. Such cooperation and collaboration is not unusual in medicine, but the novelty and extreme risks of fetal surgery make the need to work together especially compelling. As one fetal surgeon framed the problem, "This is the most complex undertaking in surgery. We've got to enlist the aid of every person who's involved in every stage of this." An obstetrician, speaking at a professional meeting, stressed that "it's important to have a well-rounded unit for fetal surgery, including neonatologists, pediatric surgeons, and so on." One of the sonographers agreed that there is a great degree of cooperation and remarked, "Considering some of the problems we've had, generally I would say it's a reasonably orderly group of people." Another fetal surgeon remarked, "It has to be a team approach. . . . The team approach is key." And a social worker declared, "I think the days of territorialism are long gone. Because there's so much to be done for these families, everybody sort of pitches in. And I think there is a spirit of cooperation on this team that makes it reasonable to work on."

As with the Rh group in Auckland, these last comments indicate that a "team" metaphor is often used to describe working arrangements in fetal treatment units. While many medical specialties are organized around the team concept, in fetal surgery this is especially crucial as a means of achieving both efficacy and legitimacy. According to practitioners, a number of general principles have evolved since the inception of contemporary fetal surgery to guide its development. Chief among these is that "fetal surgery is a team effort requiring varying amounts of input from all team members" (Harrison 1991, 9). As well as specifying all the requisite members of the team (e.g., obstetrician, perinatologist, geneticist, surgeon, nurse, and so forth), these principles also lay out additional rules underlying the organization of fetal sur-

gery. For example, "although all members of the team can contribute to any particular procedure, there must be a team leader" (Harrison 1991, 9). Who is selected as team leader may be a source of conflict and basis for negotiation, despite the rule that "the procedure is done by the team member who is most likely to produce the best outcome" (ibid.). Further, just as experimental fetal surgery is a proving ground for developing and implementing new procedures, it also provides "an invaluable opportunity to work out . . . the professional relationships that will enable the team to function smoothly. The lines of responsibility must be drawn clearly among team members before the choice of doing a procedure is offered to a patient" (ibid.). Here, team metaphors are seen as facilitating the formation of a division of labor.

At Capital Hospital, in particular, certain organizational conventions within the FTU indicate that cooperative teamwork is extremely important. At ongoing fetal treatment group meetings, all types of interested practitioners come together to discuss specific cases and strategies for treatment, evaluating past and current activities as well as planning for the future. These regular meetings, held in the same place at the same time each week, provide a forum for addressing the complexities of specific cases. Different specialists present their particular slant and, while there is much agreement, there is also much heated negotiation. In addition, regular "consensus meetings" are held among clinicians and researchers to discuss current basic scientific research as it relates to clinical practices. It is here that new fetal technologies and innovations, developed in a fetal treatment lab using animal models, are first introduced into a setting of clinicians. Fetal surgeons, obstetricians, genetics counselors, and social workers also routinely meet with potential patients, coordinating their schedules and agendas to coincide with a family's visit to the hospital. And there are ad hoc meetings on a variety of issues, such as a discussion of fetal and maternal management that took place following a rash of postoperative maternal health problems and fetal deaths. In introducing the topic of this ad hoc meeting, a fetal surgeon described those present as a "working group" convened to address the issue of maternal safety.

An illustration of the continual quest for cooperation was provided in a talk presented by one of the fetal surgeons for another group of practitioners at Capital Hospital. The presentation was given during grand rounds for obstetrics and gynecology, with most of the audience representing these two specialties. Focused on prenatal and perinatal management of anomalies, the talk was clearly designed to "enroll" (Latour 1987) obstetricians as allies, or members of the team, in the enterprise of fetal surgery. Many obstetricians are vocal critics of open fetal surgery; nonetheless, they possess the skills and expertise in maternal health issues that fetal surgeons may be lacking or seeking. For example, preterm labor is a major problem in fetal surgery, and obstetricians identify themselves as best equipped to resolve it. They are skeptical of surgeons' encroachment on this territory. The fetal surgeon strategically emphasized throughout his lecture that his team is very concerned about maternal safety. In a significant bid to establish cooperative working relationships, he invited the obstetricians to "talk about [fetal surgery] together, both its limitations and new approaches." He assured his audience that fetal surgeons are "looking to forge a new partnership." The speaker ended his talk by emphasizing that the success of the Fetal Treatment Unit at Capital Hospital "depends on people meeting in the hall, talking informally, and working together." An example of behind-the-scenes maneuvering, the presentation was a strategically delivered and polished invitation to obstetricians to participate in fetal surgery as a cooperative venture.

At Capital Hospital, then, there is an ongoing commitment to cooperation and teamwork among those who work on and around fetuses. To a large degree, any cooperation that is achieved is based in part on shared understandings of the work of fetal surgery. Regardless of what professional and political identities each medical worker brings to fetal surgery, the institutional shape of this practice situates the fetus as a primary focus of activities. Simply stated, the chief reason that people work together in fetal surgery is because a pregnant woman has been admitted to the hospital with a sick fetus requiring treatment. There are certainly many ancillary reasons for the collective nature of fetal surgery—including professional norms, organizational patterns, loyalty to colleagues, and the allure of challenging work—but these are overshadowed by the broad, public aim of "saving babies." The fetal surgery team at Capital Hospital is organized around the clinical requirements of diagnosing and treating fetuses in an experimental context. And those who work on the fragile fetus and on pregnant women made vulnerable by surgery need all the assistance, and legitimacy, they can muster.

However, given the consistent controversy surrounding human fetuses, the new and experimental status of fetal surgery, and the intersection of so many different specialties, the picture of harmony painted by medical workers in fetal surgery is too rosy. While there is certainly a great deal of cooperation, as displayed in staff meetings and in operating rooms and in the very longevity of the enterprise, it is often achieved despite profound differences between medical workers in this specialty. A prominent fetal surgeon (Harrison 1991, 9) has written that "a special problem arises with interventional fetal procedures, especially those that require the expertise of specialists from very different fields. . . . Because no single specialty training provides the total spectrum of skills and experience, this is an area in which 'turf' battles between medical specialties and 'ego' battles among team members may sabotage the fetal treatment enterprise." This was certainly the case at Capital Hospital during the period in which I conducted my research. As any chemist (or sociologist) knows, affinity is not the only possible reaction to mixing different elements; sometimes the end result is a volatile compound.

"Folks Are Always Rubbing Shoulders": Working Around Critical Differences

Although cooperation is necessary for fetal surgery to work, differences among practitioners in this domain are pervasive. There are both minor disagreements and major fights about how fetuses and pregnant women are talked about and worked on, about proper treatment plans, about postoperative procedures, about who is responsible for which work tasks, and so on. There is a seemingly infinite number of reasons why actors in the fetal surgery domain do not always "get along" with each other, some of which they themselves recognize and articulate. (They may also recognize other reasons but choose not to discuss these publicly.) Significantly, conflict is associated with failures in fetal surgery, including fetal deaths, harrowing cases with uncertain outcomes, and problems with pregnant women's health. One surgeon told me that "if everything worked right, everybody would get along fine." A sonographer stated, "If everything was red, white, and blue banners flying all the time about the successes, then believe me, there would be no conflict. Everybody would be so happy. The only conflicts would be who got to stand first in line for the laurels. We're more likely to have conflicts when we have failures." And another fetal surgeon remarked that "because things are new and things aren't worked out, folks are always rubbing shoulders. We've had terrible

conflicts, arguments, and things that were strictly differences of opinion medically."

This last comment suggests that while medical failures may be seen as contributing to dissension, differences in professional training may also form the basis for conflict. For example, an obstetrician had this to say about disagreements in the program: "I think that any time you have a group of people, sort of management by committee, there are going to be problems. People just have different views, particularly when you have groups of people from different backgrounds." Yet the differences between participants in fetal surgery may be considerably more complex. One of the social workers—a somewhat unique group because they are not clinicians and are more akin to social scientists—described this rich and complicated diversity in more detail: "It was a baptism by fire. Meaning that I was surprised at how, in some ways, unprepared I was for the politics of the program. We all have a slightly different vantage, orientation, perspective, and cultural agenda. There are so many subtle ways in which we are different from one another, both because of our professional training and because of who we are as human beings." The deep-seated differences between workers in this domain, pinpointed by a number of informants, affect the shape and trajectory of this practice in often highly consequential ways both locally at Capital Hospital and in terms of the broader fetal surgery enterprise. Examining diversity at the local level of work arrangements in the Fetal Treatment Unit, I next focus on ways in which these differences are made meaningful and are acted upon in the context of actual practices.

Negotiating the "What" of Fetal Surgery: Different Definitions of Work Objects

A major site at which differences emerge and coalesce in fetal surgery is in definitions of work objects. Because operating on fetuses

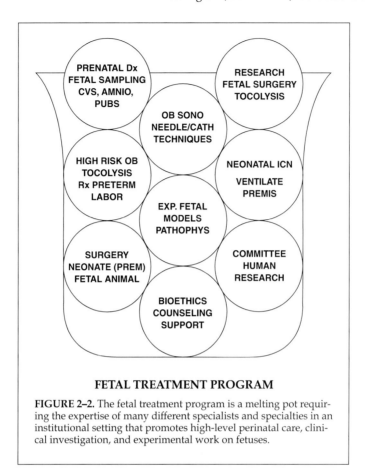

FETAL TREATMENT PROGRAM

FIGURE 2–2. The fetal treatment program is a melting pot requiring the expertise of many different specialists and specialties in an institutional setting that promotes high-level perinatal care, clinical investigation, and experimental work on fetuses.

FIGURE 1   A graphic depiction of a fetal treatment program as a "melting pot" of different specialists. Such interdisciplinarity requires extensive cooperation while also fostering conflict and dissent. It is interesting to note the placement of specialties, with prenatal diagnosis and fetal surgery at the top and bioethics counseling at the bottom, with other specialties in-between.

Source: M. R. Harrison, M. S. Golbus, and R. A. Filly. 1991. *The Unborn Patient: Prenatal Diagnosis and Treatment.* Philadelphia: W. B. Saunders Company, p. 12.

necessarily means surgically opening pregnant women's bodies, there would seem to be only one major human work object in fetal surgery: the pregnant woman. Yet medical workers draw a clear distinction, both in practice and discursively, between woman-as-work-object and fetus-as-work-object. Contestation centers around these often competing defini-

tions, as well as around how much and what kind of clinical and ethical consideration to accord each entity. Moreover, although there are two recognized work objects, the fetus is positioned as the primary work object—*the patient*—within this domain, while the pregnant woman is reduced to a nonessential feature of the clinical environment. A division of labor has emerged around these different work objects, with an entire specialty now devoted to the unique clinical needs of the unborn patient.

A variety of specific practices illustrate this phenomenon. For example, every fetal operation at Capital Hospital is videotaped for research and recording purposes. Taping begins after full anesthesia of the pregnant woman has occurred and after surgeons have opened her uterus; it ends when they are finished working on the fetus but before the woman's uterus and abdomen have been sutured closed. Visually erasing women from the frame, this practice illustrates graphically what/who is considered the important work object in fetal surgery. Surgeons at Capital Hospital also hope to create a Fetal Intensive Care Unit (FICU) in the future where fetuses (and presumably pregnant women) can be monitored postoperatively. Currently after surgery the pregnant women are monitored in the standard ICU by medical workers trained in both general and obstetrical acute care. If fetuses are abruptly transformed into fragile "newborns" during surgery and not replaced in their mothers' wombs, those that survive are immediately whisked away to the neonatal intensive care unit. But, according to surgeons I spoke to, neither the standard ICU nor the neonatal ICU focuses exclusively on the needs of the unborn patient. Some medical workers, in expressing concern about inadequate fetal monitoring after surgery, have proposed intensive care of the fetus as one solution. Ironically, the FICU as conceptualized by my informants gives no indication that a fetus would still be inside its mother's body during this postoperative period. In yet another example of the intensive focus on the fetus, Capital Hospital instituted a catchy toll-free number for referring physicians and potential patients who desire information about the program: 800-FETUSRx.

Among all medical workers in this domain, fetal surgeons especially view the fe-

tus as the primary work object. Many of them were trained in pediatric surgery and are already used to working with pint-sized bodies and doll-like body parts. They are also highly invested in building a new specialty (and a new health care market) organized around the unborn patient. A number of surgeons recounted their deep interest in learning more about the womb's tiny occupant with its own set of health problems. Echoing pro-life discourse—which defines fetal and postnatal existence as continuous—one surgeon told me that he had always understood the distinction between fetuses and infants "in geographic terms"; in his view, they are similar enough anatomically that surgeons can use similar techniques and tools to treat them. What is missing in this characterization is any sense that the fetus, unlike a newborn, is located inside a pregnant woman's body and thus much more difficult to access. Another surgeon, a resident interested in neurosurgery, explained that despite its rather obscure geographical location the fetus was a useful work object precisely because of its miniature size. Working out how to monitor and treat such a diminutive object inside an adult body is, according to this resident, excellent training for a career in heart or brain surgery, where a delicate touch is worth a great deal.

Yet as ubiquitous as constructions of the fetal patient are in this domain, not all of the actors define fetuses as their primary, or even secondary, work objects. In a number of ways, different participants attribute diverse, sometimes conflicting meanings to fetuses and pregnant women and thus organize their work activities differently. This diversity often leads to considerable strain between fetal surgeons, who define fetuses as central work objects, and other participants with different tasks and agendas. For example, most obstetricians generally consider pregnant women to be their primary work objects and are concerned with fetal health secondarily or only in relation to maternal health. Indeed, relations between fetal surgeons and obstetricians at Capital Hospital have become increasingly difficult in recent years, with the latter group, in one obstetrician's view, being "slowly pushed out" by the fetal surgeons. An obstetrician involved with the program for many years expressed her dissatisfaction with the direction of the FTU, stating, "We are having trouble with fetal surgery because we're seeing lots of complications in women. The obstetricians, of course, take care of the maternal patient." She later remarked, "Fetal surgeons don't take care of the woman afterward. We've had women who've not been able to leave the hospital, who've been in and out of labor for the rest of their pregnancies. And those are the successes!" This informant clearly foregrounds maternal health issues, which have long been paramount in obstetrics and gynecology but which are not the primary consideration in fetal surgery except as they affect and constrain fetal procedures.

One of the social workers confirmed these dynamics and described difficult relations between fetal surgeons and obstetricians: "The OBs are used to managing [maternal] patients. There is a lot of angry stuff between the OBs, such as who is going to be in attendance at these deliveries. You know, there are people who really didn't want to do it or believe in it. They think it's bad medicine to take a pregnant woman and cut her open." This is the same informant who remarked earlier that the days of territorialism in fetal surgery were now over, perhaps because much of this conflict occurs behind the scenes. Ironically, the Fetal Treatment Unit at Capital Hospital is often approached by other hospitals interested in starting fetal surgery units. One of the surgeons told me that the FTU advised a major East Coast hospital "*not* to include obstetricians from day one." As he explained, if obstetricians can be prevented from participating in new programs, then

some of the problems "plaguing" the FTU at Capital Hospital might be avoided at other institutions.

Comments of fetal surgeons are especially revealing about ongoing conflict between "baby doctors" and "mom doctors." For example, the proposed Fetal Intensive Care Unit described above has proved somewhat controversial and has yet to be implemented. According to a fetal surgeon, "Anytime you have new concepts like the FICU, you're bound to encounter some resistance. That was a new concept for many people and it led to friction." When I pressed him about the source of resistance, he remarked, "Well, you know, it's just a different way of dealing with things. I'm used to doing big operations and having patients in the ICU, and some of the obstetricians and OB nurses are not used to that. They view the postoperative period as the preterm labor problem. But it was clear that patient management went far beyond just management of preterm labor, and we couldn't *not* be responsible outside of monitoring. That led to friction." Suggesting that obstetricians are not used to "big operations" is a somewhat curious criticism; they have historically, and increasingly routinely, performed cesarean sections and must have at least a passing knowledge of major surgery.

Another fetal surgeon described in far more critical terms cardinal differences between pregnant women and fetuses as work objects: "The unfortunate part is that the obstetricians have been taking care of the fetal/maternal pair for so long it's driven into them. But our patients aren't like their patients. Our patients are mid-gestation fetuses, our mom has just undergone a major operation, our fetus has just undergone a major operation, there's been prolonged anesthesia, and now there are problems with pain control, volume fluctuations, and all the normal perioperative things. Obstetricians don't understand anything about perioperative management; they don't understand anything about management of a patient in the perioperative period." Particularly striking is the distinction this informant draws between *fetal* patients/work objects as constituting the territory of fetal surgeons, and *maternal* patients/work objects as part of the proprietary but increasingly narrow terrain of obstetricians. Indeed, in his final sentence it is not even clear which patient the surgeon is talking about. But regardless of who is in charge, managing the pregnant woman means that she must remain in or nearby the hospital after surgery, often for several weeks until she delivers her baby. Throughout this period, which is characterized by cooperative efforts to ensure a successful stay for the woman and her family, there are ample opportunities for tensions to erupt among medical workers.

One fetal surgeon ascribes such heated differences to professional training and background: "Basically every group of physicians has their own personality. Surgeons tend to be a little more aggressive, we tend to push harder, get things done. It's just a personality thing. The obstetricians now have seen enough problems with fetal surgery that they're absolutely opposed to it. They don't like it. They don't want it to happen. They're against it. The only reason they're going through the moves right now is because it's protocol driven." A fetal physiologist echoes these points: "Well, I think it's again a turf issue. Obstetricians feel that they should be responsible for all prenatal care—care of the fetus *and* mother. And surgeons feel that the fetus is their patient and have therefore assumed some responsibility for the mother." Yet, although professional training may be significant, it is the implementation of such training in local work arrangements that both shapes and reinforces crucial distinctions among specialists in this domain, particularly who has access to fetuses. The availability of direct access to fetuses is an important constraint on how, by

whom, and under what conditions fetuses and pregnant women are defined as meaningful work objects.

This dynamic is illustrated in a discussion in the major fetal surgery text, *The Unborn Patient* (Harrison et al. 1991), about which specialist should perform fetal surgery, or rather, which specialist should be the team leader. Harrison (1991) begins by stating that the most politically expedient solution would be to have each specialist do his or her part of the overall procedure. This means that obstetricians would open and close the uterus, and the pediatric surgeon would operate on the fetus. This easy solution is, according to Harrison (1991, 10), "likely to keep team members comfortable in their accustomed roles." Yet he goes on to state that this practice is not likely to yield the best outcomes because "it assumes that traditional skills will suffice; that is, that obstetricians can close the uterus as they do in the case of an empty uterus and that the pediatric surgeon can do with a fetus what he learned in a neonate. Neither is true." He argues that "tag-team surgery is never ideal," particularly where exposure of the fetus by hysterotomy is complicated by preterm labor problems. Thus, despite the rhetoric of teamwork, it seems that a division of labor by extant specialties may not work or be construed as ideal. Harrison's answer to this dilemma is that "fetal surgery cannot develop and will not succeed unless a few *surgeons* are willing to devote considerable time and effort to developing, practicing, and perfecting all aspects of this new procedure" (1991, 10; emphasis added). This passage is striking for the degree to which chief responsibility for this new procedure is appropriated by fetal surgeons, while the participation of obstetricians (and presumably other medical workers) is marginalized.

Another group with whom fetal surgeons struggle for territory is neonatologists, who view fetuses as potential work objects but with a very important geographical and anatomical difference. A relatively new medical specialty, neonatology provides intensive (and expensive) care for fragile newborns who are either premature or very ill. As Renée Anspach (1993) has documented, neonatologists are used to working in highly charged contexts where life-and-death decisions are made all the time. At fetal treatment meetings at Capital Hospital, neonatologists revealed themselves to be acutely interested in the fate of the unborn patient. If surgery is unsuccessful but the fetus survives—that is, if surgeons cannot replace the fetus in the pregnant woman's womb—neonatologists argue that they should then assume control over the fetus-cum-neonate. But fetal surgeons guard their work objects jealously and have demonstrated resistance to neonatologists' quest for professional control over the ambiguous fetal body. These tensions become more vivid when the fetuses in fetal surgery are the same gestational age—or older—than those being cared for in the neonatal intensive care unit (NICU). The dispute that ensued when this issue surfaced at one of the fetal treatment meetings illustrates some of the emotional and professional investments on all sides.

The fetal surgery team presented a case involving a pregnant woman carrying a 26-week-old fetus. A neonatologist suggested that resuscitation equipment be available in the operating room in the event that the fetus could not be replaced in the pregnant woman's body during or after surgery. This had only been necessary once before in the history of fetal surgery; most often, the fetuses are too young to warrant neonatal salvageability if an operation is not successful. One of the fetal surgeons responded negatively to this suggestion, declaring, "When we do our thing, it's all or nothing. We don't pull out live babies. We either put them back alive or pull them out dead." The neonatologist then demanded to know what circumstances would require removing a live fetus,

and the fetal surgeon responded by citing uncontrollable labor and a contracting uterus. The surgeon then went on to say that he saw two problems in making resuscitation equipment available: "explaining it to the mother" and "having it there logistically." In a flash of anger, the neonatologist replied that "there is also a problem in that you're doing something very few people in the world are doing and we don't know what will happen!" At this point, confronted with a blatant reminder about how deadly serious fetal surgery can be, the surgeon retreated and became quite accommodating (at least on the surface), agreeing with his colleague's assessment of the situation. Several other people joined in the negotiations, and it was eventually decided that the equipment would be made available for older fetuses (those at or near the viability marker of about twenty-three weeks) and that it would be set up in the hallway outside the operating room.

To further complicate the situation regarding work objects, other participants in the FTU define their patients/clients quite differently than do fetal surgeons, obstetricians, and neonatologists. For example, many of the social workers, nurses, and genetic counselors (almost all women) were deeply troubled by fetal surgery, especially during periods of failure. In the words of one nurse, "every baby was dying. Every step of the way we've been thwarted by consequences of surgery that have high morbidity and high mortality for these babies." Because negative outcomes often create or intensify conflict, one social worker decided that she would be "an advocate for the parent." Yet differences in status within the FTU, and in medicine more widely, between social workers and physicians often made this difficult. The social worker described being frustrated in her attempts to advocate for the pregnant women by surgeons more intently focused on fetuses. For example, her judgment about a particular patient who she felt was not psychologically equipped to deal with surgery was challenged by surgeons, leading her to remark: "I was incensed about it. At that point, my confidence was shaken and I felt that if I'm going to be the psychosocial person on this team, I'm going to have to have the support of the members of the team." While her recommendation was ultimately supported by an outside psychiatrist, she described the incident as "forcing me to look again at my role and my interactions with the team."

In sum, there are a number of divergent positions on who or what are, and are not, work objects in fetal surgery. As the examples above make clear, different participants ascribe different meanings to the bodies they work on in fetal surgery. For fetal surgeons, fetuses are first and foremost patients and objects of therapeutic practices such as surgery. For obstetricians, pregnant women are (usually) the first and most important patients and objects of maternity care, while fetuses are secondary work objects. Most obstetricians do not completely reject the notion of a fetal patient; indeed, one of the striking developments in medicine in recent years is the emergence of maternal-fetal medicine as a replacement for standard obstetrics (Creasy and Resnick 1994). Nor have specialists in obstetrics and gynecology always been valiant protectors of women's health (Arney 1982; Moscucci 1990; Rothman 1982). However, conflicts between obstetricians and fetal surgeons tend to center on other aspects of treatment, such as how to keep pregnant women healthy while operating on them solely for the benefit of their fetuses. For neonatologists, fetuses may become work objects when surgery is unsuccessful and the unborn patient is transformed into a neonatal patient. For social workers, genetic counselors, and nurses, fetuses are only work objects in an ancillary sense. The pregnant woman and her family are the primary locus of care, which is defined in terms of psychosocial and ongoing postoperative care rather than surgical intervention. Yet even these practitioners may be concerned about fetal outcomes; for example, the social worker quoted above who wanted to advocate for parents was also anguished that too many fetuses were dying.

These varied constructions of pregnant women and their fetuses are consequential, as work practices are organized around the meanings that each work object has for different actors. There is a certain "logic" at work here in terms of identifying what to do next in the clinical setting (Berg 1992). That is, if the fetus is a patient, then it must be treated. If the pregnant woman is a patient, then she (and secondarily her fetus) must be cared for. If a pregnant woman and her partner need psychosocial or postoperative care, it is to be provided by the appropriate person, generally a social worker or nurse. The definition of fetuses as primary work objects is negotiated and contested in practice, and there may be significant deviations from a straight course to the making of the unborn patient. For example, obstetricians, social workers, and nurses continue to assert the importance of women's health while questioning the overall enterprise of fetal surgery. Thus, the process of negotiating social order in fetal surgery is itself shaped by several factors, including professional training, work cultures and identities, institutional hierarchies, the materiality of work objects (e.g., fetuses may die), and control over the conditions of medical work, such as access to patients. Yet despite tensions surrounding different work objects and practices, the Fetal Treatment Unit, and fetal surgery more broadly, is collectively geared toward the diagnosis, treatment, and salvation of fetuses, which continue to be institutionally and culturally defined as the most significant work objects. Pregnant women, and the medical workers who care for and about them, may thus be relegated to a secondary status in this domain. . . .

REFERENCES

Arney, William Ray. 1982. *Power and the Profession of Obstetrics.* Chicago: University of Chicago Press.

Becker, Howard. 1986. *Doing Things Together.* Evanston, IL: Northwestern University Press.

Berg, Marc. 1992. "The Construction of Medical Disposals: Medical Sociology and Medical Problem Solving in Clinical Practice." *Sociology of Health and Illness* 14:151–180.

Creasy, Robert K. and Robert Resnick (eds.). 1994. *Maternal-Fetal Medicine: Principles and Practice.* Philadelphia: W. B. Saunders.

Harrison, Michael R. 1991. "Professional Considerations in Fetal Treatment." Pp. 8–13 in *The Unborn Patient: Prenatal Diagnosis and Treatment,* edited by Michael R. Harrison, Mitchell S. Golbus, and Roy A. Filly. Philadelphia: W. B. Saunders.

Harrison, Michael R., Mitchell S. Golbus, and Roy A. Filly (eds.). 1991. *The Unborn Patient: Prenatal Diagnosis and Treatment.* Philadelphia: W. B. Saunders.

Howell, Lori J., N. Scott Adzick, and Michael R. Harrison. 1993. "The Fetal Treatment Center." *Seminars in Pediatric Surgery* 2:143–146.

Moscucci, Ornella. 1990. *The Science of Woman: Gynecology and Gender in England, 1800–1929.* Cambridge, U.K.: Cambridge University Press.

Rothman, Barbara Katz. 1982. *In Labor: Women and Power in the Birthplace.* New York: Norton.

Strauss, Anselm, Leonard Schatzman, Rue Bucher, Danuta Erlich, and Melvin Sabshin. 1964. *Psychiatric Ideologies and Institutions.* Glencoe, IL: Free Press.

31

Rambo Litigators
Emotional Labor in a Male-Dominated Job

Jennifer L. Pierce

Late in the afternoon, I was sitting with Ben and Stan. . . . They were complaining about being litigators, or as they put it, how "litigation turns people into bastards—you don't have any real choices." Stan said that if you don't fit in, you have to get out because you won't be successful. And Ben added, "To be a really good litigator, you have to be a jerk. Sure you can get by being a nice guy, but you'll never be really good or really successful."

—FIELD NOTES

Excerpts from "Rambo Litigators," in *Gender Trials: Emotional Lives in Contemporary Law Firms,* by Jennifer L. Pierce. Copyright © 1995 by the Regents of the University of California. Reprinted by permission of the University of California Press and the author.

The comments made by these two young lawyers suggest that the legal profession often requires behavior that is offensive not only to other people, but to oneself: "To be a really good litigator, you have to be a jerk." In popular culture and everyday life, jokes and stories abound that characterize lawyers as aggressive, manipulative, unreliable, and unethical. This image is expressed in the joke about why the lawyer who falls overboard in shark-infested waters is not eaten alive—it's professional courtesy. Our popular wisdom is that lawyers are ruthless con artists who are more concerned with making money than they are with fairness (Post 1987; *National Law Journal* 1986). Few consider, as these two young men do, that the requirements of the profession itself support and reinforce this behavior. . . .

Gamesmanship and the Adversarial Model

Popular wisdom and lawyer folklore portray lawyering as a game, and the ability to play as gamesmanship (Fox 1978; Spence 1988). As one of the trial attorneys I interviewed said,

> The logic of gamesmanship is very interesting to me. I like how you make someone appear to be a liar. You know, you take them down the merry path and before they know it, they've said something pretty stupid. The challenge is getting them to say it without violating the letter of the law.

Lawyering is based on gamesmanship—legal strategy, skill, and expertise. But trial lawyers are much more than chess players; their strategies are not simply cerebral, rational, and calculating moves, but highly emotional, dramatic, flamboyant, shocking presentations that evoke sympathy, distrust, or outrage. In litigation practice, gamesmanship involves the utilization of legal strategy through a presentation of an emotional self that is designed specifically to influence the feelings and judgment of a particular legal audience—the judge, the jury, the witness, or opposing counsel. Furthermore, in my definition, the choices litigators make about selecting a particular strategy are not simply individual; they are institutionally constrained by the structure of the legal profession, by formal and informal professional norms, such as the American Bar Association's Model Code of Professional Responsibility (1982), and by training in trial advocacy, through programs such as those sponsored by the National Institute of Trial Advocacy.

The rules governing gamesmanship derive from the adversarial model that underlies the basic structure of our legal system. This is a method of adjudication in which two advocates (the attorneys) present their sides of the case to an impartial third party (the judge and the jury), who listens to evidence and argument and declares one party the winner (Luban 1988; Menkel-Meadow 1985). As Menkel-Meadow (1985) observes, the basic assumptions that underlie this set of arrangements are "advocacy, persuasion, hierarchy, competition and binary results (win/lose)." She writes: "The conduct of litigation is relatively similar . . . to a sporting event—there are rules, a referee, an object to the game, and a winner is declared after play is over" (1985: 51).

Within this system, the attorney's main objective is to persuade the impartial third party that his client's interests should prevail (American Bar Association 1982: 34). However, clients do not always have airtight, defensible cases. How then does the "zealous advocate" protect his client's interests and achieve the desired result? When persuasion by appeal to reason breaks down, an appeal to emotions becomes paramount (Cheatham 1955: 282–83). As legal scholar John Buchan writes, "the root of the talent is simply the power to persuade" (1939: 211–13). And in "Basic Rules of Pleading," Jerome Michael writes:

> The decision of an issue of fact in a case of closely balanced probabilities therefore, must, in the nature of things, be an emotional rather than a rational act; and the rules regulating that stage of a trial which we call the stage of persua-

sion, the stage when lawyers sum up to the jury. . . . The point is beautifully made by an old Tennessee case in which the plaintiff's counsel, when summing up to the jury began to weep. . . . The lawyer for the defendant objected and asked the trial judge to stop him from weeping. Weeping is not a form of argument. . . . Well, the Supreme Court of Tennessee said: "It is not only counsel's privilege to weep for his client; it is his duty to weep for his client." (1950: 175)

By appealing to emotions, the lawyer becomes a con man. He acts as if he has a defensible case; he puffs himself up; he bolsters his case. Thus, the successful advocate must not only be smart, but, as the famous turn-of-the-century trial lawyer Francis Wellman observed, he must also be a good actor (1986 [1903]: 13). In *The Art of Cross-Examination*, first published in 1903 and reprinted to the present, Wellman describes how carefully the litigator must present himself to the judge and jury:

The most cautious cross-examiner will often elicit a damaging answer. Now is the time for the greatest self-control. If you show by your face how the answer hurt, you may lose by that one point alone. How often one sees a cross-examiner fairly staggered by such an answer. He pauses, blushes, [but seldom regains] control of the witness. With the really experienced trial lawyer, such answers, instead of appearing to surprise or disconcert him, will seem to come as a matter of course, and will fall perfectly flat. He will proceed with the next question as if nothing happened, or else perhaps give the witness an incredulous smile, as if to say, "Who do you suppose would believe that for a minute." (1986 [1903]: 13–14)

More recently, teacher and lawyer David Berg (1987) advises lawyers to think of themselves as actors and the jury as an audience:

Decorum can make a difference, too. . . . Stride to the podium and exude confidence, even if there is a chance that the high school dropout on the stand is going to make you look like an idiot. Take command of the courtroom. Once you begin, do not grope for questions, shuffle through papers, or take breaks to confer with cocounsel. Let the jury know that you are prepared, that you do not need anyone's advice, and that you care about the case . . . because if you don't care, the jurors won't care. (1987: 28)

Wellman and Berg make a similar point: in the courtroom drama, attorneys are the leading actors. Appearance and demeanor are of utmost importance. The lawyer's manner, his tone of voice, and his facial expressions are all means to persuade the jury that his client is right. Outrageous behavior, as long as it remains within the letter of the law, is acceptable. Not only are trial lawyers expected to act, but they are expected to act with a specific purpose in mind: to favorably influence feelings of the judge and jurors.

This emphasis on acting is also evident in the courses taught by the National Institute for Trial Advocacy, where neophyte litigators learn the basics of presenting a case for trial. NITA's emphasis is on "learning by doing" (Kilpatrick quoted in Rice 1989). Attorneys do not simply read about cases but practice presenting them in a simulated courtroom with a judge, a jury, and witnesses. In this case, doing means acting. As one of the teachers/lawyers said on the first day of class, "Being a good trial lawyer means being a good actor. . . . Trial attorneys love to perform." Acting, in sociological terms, constitutes emotional labor, that is, inducing or suppressing feelings in order to produce the outward countenance that influences the emotions of others. The instructors discuss style, delivery, presentation of self, attitude, and professionalism. Participants, in turn, compare notes about the best way to "handle" judges, jurors, witnesses, clients, and opposing counsel. The efforts of these two groups constitute the teaching and observance of "feeling rules," or professional norms that govern appropriate lawyerly conduct in the courtroom. . . .

Intimidation

Litigation is war. The lawyer is a gladiator and the object is to wipe out the other side.

—CLEVELAND LAWYER QUOTED IN THE *NEW YORK TIMES,* AUGUST 5, 1988

The most common form of emotional labor associated with lawyers is intimidation. In popular culture, the tough, hard-hitting, and aggressive trial lawyer is portrayed in television shows such as *L.A. Law* and *Perry Mason* and in movies such as *The Firm, A Few Good Men,* and *Presumed Innocent.* The news media's focus on famous trial attorneys such as Arthur Liman, the prosecutor of Oliver North in the Iran-Contra trial, also reinforces this image. Law professor Wayne Brazil (1978) refers to this style of lawyering as the "professional combatant." Others have termed it the "Rambo litigator" (a reference to the highly stylized, super-masculine role Sylvester Stallone plays in his action movies), "legal terrorists," and "barbarians of the bar" (Margolick 1988; Sayler 1988; Miner 1988). Trial attorneys themselves call litigators from large law firms "hired guns" (Spangler 1986). And books on trial preparation, such as McElhaney's *Trial Notebook* (1987), endorse the litigator-as-gladiator metaphor by portraying the attorney on the book's dust jacket as a knight in a suit of armor ready to do battle (McElhaney 1987).

The recurring figure in these images is not only intimidating but strongly masculine. In the old West, hired guns were sharpshooters; men who were hired to kill other men. The strong, silent movie character Rambo is emblematic of a highly stylized, supermasculinity. The knight in shining armor preparing to do battle on the front cover of McElhaney's *Trial Notebook* is male, not female. Finally, most of the actors who play tough, hard-hitting lawyers in the television shows and movies mentioned above are men. Thus, intimidation is not simply a form of emotional labor associated with trial lawyers, it is a masculinized form of labor.

Intimidation is tied to cultural conceptions of masculinity in yet another way. In a review of the literature on occupations, Connell (1987) observes that the cult of masculinity in working-class jobs centers on physical prowess and sexual contempt for men in managerial or office positions (1987: 180). Like the men on the shop floor in Michael Burawoy's (1979) study who brag about how much they can lift or produce, lawyers in this study boast about "destroying witnesses," "playing hard-ball," and "taking no prisoners" and about the size and amount of their "win." In a middle-class job such as the legal profession, however, intimidation depends not on physical ability but on mental quickness and a highly developed set of social skills. Thus, masculinizing practices such as aggression and humiliation take on an emotional and intellectual tone in this occupation. . . .

In the sections on cross-examination at NITA, teachers trained lawyers to "act mean." The demonstration by the teachers on cross-examination best exemplified this point. Two male instructors reenacted an aggressive cross-examination in a burglary case. The prosecutor relentlessly hammered away until the witness couldn't remember any specific details about the burglar's appearance. At the end of his demonstration, the audience clapped vigorously. Three male students who had been asked to comment responded unanimously and enthusiastically that the prosecutor's approach had been excellent. One student commentator said, "He kept complete control of the witness." Another remarked, "He blasted the witness's testimony." And the third added, "He destroyed the witness's credibility." The fact that a destructive cross-examination served as the demonstration for the entire class underscores the desirability of aggressive behavior as a model for appropriate lawyer-like conduct in this situation. Furthermore, the students' praise for the attorney's tactics collectively reinforce the norm for such behavior.

Teachers emphasized the importance of using aggression to motivate oneself as well. Before a presentation on cross-examination, Tom, one of the students, stood in the hallway with one of the instructors trying to "psyche himself up to get mad." He repeated over and over to himself, "I hate it when witnesses lie to me. It makes me so mad!" The teacher coached him to concentrate on that thought until Tom could actually evoke the feeling of anger. He said later in an interview, "I really felt mad at the witness when I walked into the courtroom." In the actual cross-examination, each time the witness made an inconsistent statement, Tom became more and more angry: "First, you told us you could see the burglar, now you say your vision was obstructed! So, which is it, Mr. Jones?" The more irate he became, the more he intimidated and confused the witness, who at last completely backed down and said, "I don't know" in response to every question. The teacher characterized Tom's performance as "the best in the class" because it was "the most forceful" and "the most intimidating." Students remarked that he deserved to "win the case."

NITA's teachers also utilized mistakes to train students in the rigors of cross-examination. For example, when Laura cross-examined [a] witness . . . , a teacher commented on her performance:

Too many words. You're asking the witness for information. Don't do that in cross-examination. You tell them what the information is. You want to be destructive in cross-examination. When the other side objects to an answer, you were too nice. Don't be so nice! Next time, ask to talk to the judge, tell him, "This is crucial to my case." You also asked for information when you didn't know the answer. Bad news. You lost control of the witness.

By being nice and losing control of the witness, Laura violated two norms underlying the classic confrontational cross-examination. A destructive cross-examination is meant to impeach the witness's credibility, thereby demonstrating to the jury the weakness in opposing counsel's case. In situations that call for such an aggressive cross-examination, being nice implies that the lawyer likes the witness and agrees with her testimony. By not being aggressive, Laura created the wrong impression for the jury. Second, Laura lost control of the witness. Rather than guiding the witness through the cross with leading questions that were damaging to opposing counsel's case, she allowed the witness to make his own points. As we will see in the next section . . . , being nice can also be used as a strategy for controlling a witness; however, such a strategy is not effective in a destructive cross-examination.

Laura's violation of these norms also serves to highlight the implicitly masculine practices utilized in cross-examination. The repeated phrase, "keeping complete control of the witness," clearly signals the importance of dominating other women and men. Further, the language used to describe obtaining submission—"blasting the witness," "destroying his credibility," pushing him to "back down"—is quite violent. In addition, the successful control of the witness often takes on the character of a sexual conquest. One brutal phrase used repeatedly in this way is "raping the witness." Within this discursive field, men who "control," "destroy," or "rape" the witness are seen as "manly," while those who lose control are feminized as "sissies" and "wimps," or in Laura's case as "too nice."

The combative aspect of emotional labor carries over from the courtroom to other lawyering tasks, such as depositions, negotiations, communications with opposing counsel, and discovery. Attorneys "shred" witnesses not only in the courtroom but in depositions as well. When I worked at the private firm, Daniel, one of the partners, employed what he called his "cat and mouse game" with one of the key witnesses, Jim, in a deposition I attended. During the deposition, Daniel aggressively cross-examined Jim. "When did you do this?" "You were lying, weren't you?" Jim lost his temper in response to Daniel's hostile form of interrogation—"You hassle me, man! You make me mad!" Daniel smiled and said, "I'm only trying to get to the truth of the situation." Then he became aggressive again and said, "You lied to the IRS about how much profit you made, didn't you, Jim!" Jim lost his temper again and started calling Daniel a liar. A heated interchange between Daniel and opposing counsel followed, in which opposing counsel objected to Daniel's "badgering the witness." The attorneys decided to take a brief recess.

When the deposition resumed, Daniel began by pointing his index finger at John, the other attorney, and accusing him of withholding crucial documents. Opposing counsel stood up and started yelling in a high-pitched voice—"Don't you ever point your finger at me! Don't you ever do that to me! This deposition is over. . . . I'm leaving." With that he stood up and began to cram papers into his briefcase in preparation to leave. Daniel immediately backed down, apologized, and said, "Sit down John, I promise, I won't point my finger again." He went on to smooth the situation over and proceeded to tell John in a very calm and controlled voice what his objections were. John made some protesting noises, but he didn't leave. The deposition continued.

In this instance, the deposition, rather than the courtroom, became the "stage" and Daniel took the leading role. His cross-examination was confrontational, and his behavior with the witness and opposing counsel was meant to intimidate. After the deposition Daniel boasted to me and several associates about how mad he had made the witness and how he had "destroyed his credibility." He then proceeded to reenact the final confrontation by imitating John standing up and yelling at him in a falsetto voice. In the discussion that followed, Daniel and his associates gave the effects of his behavior on the "audience" utmost consideration. Hadn't Daniel done a good job forcing the witness to lose control? Hadn't he controlled the situation well? Didn't he make opposing counsel look like a "simpering fool"?

The reenactment and ensuing discussion reveal several underlying purposes of the deposition. First, they suggest that for the attorney the deposition was not only a fact-finding mission but a show designed to influence a particular audience—the witness. Daniel effectively flustered and intimidated the witness. Second, Daniel's imitation of John with a falsetto voice "as if" he were a woman serves as a sort of "degradation ceremony" (Garfinkel 1956). By reenacting the drama, he ridicules the man on the other side before an audience of peers, further denigrating him by inviting collective criticism and laughter from colleagues. Third, the discussion of the strategy builds up and elevates Daniel's status as an attorney for his aggressive, yet rational control of the witness and the situation. Thus, the discussion creates an opportunity for collectively reinforcing Daniel's intimidation strategy. . . .

Masculine images of violence and warfare—destroying, blasting, shredding, slaying, burying— are used repeatedly to characterize the attorney's relationship to legal audiences. They are also used to describe discovery tactics and filing briefs. Discovery tactics such as enormous document requests are referred to as "dropping bombs" or "sending missiles" to the other side. And at the private firm, when a lawyer filed fourteen pretrial motions the week before trial, over three hundred pages of written material, he referred to it as "dumping an avalanche" on the other side.

Strategic Friendliness

Mr. Choate's appeal to the jury began long before final argument. . . . His manner to the jury was that of a friend, a friend solicitous to help them through their tedious investigation; never an expert combatant, intent on victory, and looking upon them as only instruments for its attainment.

(WELLMAN 1986 [1903]: 16–17)

The lesson implicit in Wellman's anecdote about famous nineteenth-century lawyer Rufus Choate's trial tactics is that friendliness is another important strategy the litigator must learn and use to be successful in the courtroom. Like aggression, the strategic use of friendliness is a feature of gamesmanship, and hence, a component of emotional labor. As Richard, one of the attorney/teachers at NITA, stated, "Lawyers have to be able to vary their styles; they have to be able to have multiple speeds, personalities, and style." In his view, intimidation did not always work, and he proposed an alternative strategy, what he called "the toe-in-the-sand, aw-shucks routine." Rather than adopting an intimidating stance toward the witness, he advocated "playing dumb and innocent": "Say to the witness, 'Gee, I don't know what you mean. Can you explain it again?' until you catch the witness in a mistake or an in-

consistent statement." Other litigators such as Leonard Ring (1987) call this the "low-key approach." Ring describes how opposing counsel delicately handled the cross-examination of a child witness:

> The lawyer for the defendant . . . stood to cross-examine. Did he attack the details of her story to show inconsistencies? Did he set her up for impeachment by attempting to reveal mistakes, uncertainties and confusion? I sat there praying that he would. But no, he did none of the things a competent defense lawyer is supposed to do. He was old enough to be the girl's grandfather [and] the image came through. He asked her very softly and politely: "Honey, could you tell us again what you saw?" She told it exactly as she had on my direct. I felt relieved. He still wasn't satisfied. "Honey, would you mind telling us again what you saw?" She did again exactly as she had before. He still wasn't satisfied. "Would you do it once more?" She did. She repeated, again, the same story—the same way, in the same words. By that time I got the message. The child had been rehearsed by her mother the same way she had been taught "Mary Had a Little Lamb." I won the case, but it was a very small verdict. (1987: 35–36)

Ring concludes that a low-key approach is necessary in some situations and advises against adhering rigidly to the prototypical combative style.

Similarly, Scott Turow (1987), the lawyer and novelist, advises trying a variety of approaches when cross-examining the star witness. He cautions against adopting a "guerrilla warfare mentality" in cross-examination and suggests that the attorney may want to create another impression with the jury:

> Behaving courteously can keep you from getting hurt and, in the process, smooth

the path for a win. [In one case I worked on] the cross examination was conducted with a politesse appropriate to a drawing room. I smiled to show that I was not mean-spirited. The chief executive officer smiled to show that he was not beaten. The commissioners smiled to show their gratitude that everybody was being so nice. And my client won big. (1987: 40–42)

Being nice, polite, welcoming, playing dumb, or behaving courteously are all ways that a trial lawyer can manipulate the witness in order to create a particular impression for the jury. I term this form of gamesmanship strategic friendliness. Rather than bully or scare the witness into submission, this tactic employs friendliness, politeness and tact. Yet it is simply another form of emotional manipulation of another person for a strategic end—winning one's case. For instance, the attorney in Ring's account is gentle and considerate of the child witness for two strategic reasons. First, by making the child feel comfortable, he brings to light the fact that her testimony has been rehearsed. Second, by playing the polite, gentle grandfatherly role, he has made a favorable impression on the jury. In this way, he improves his chances for winning. As, in fact, he did. Although he didn't win the case, the verdict for the other side was "small."

Although strategic friendliness may appear to be a softer approach than intimidation, it carries with it a strongly manipulative element. Consider the reasoning behind this particular approach. Ring's attorney is nice to the child witness not because he's altruistically concerned for her welfare, but to achieve the desired result, as simply a means to an end. This end is best summed up by litigator Mark Dombroff: "So long as you don't violate the law, including the rules of procedure and evidence or do violence to the canons of ethics, winning is the only thing that matters" (1989: 13).

This emphasis on winning is tied to traditional conceptions of masculinity and competition. Sociologist Mike Messner (1989) argues that achievement in sporting competitions such as football, baseball, and basketball serve as a measure of men's self-worth and their masculinity. This can also be carried over into the workplace. For example, as I have suggested, by redefining production on the shop floor as a "game," Burawoy's factory workers maintain their sense of control over the labor process, and hence, their identity as men. In her research on men in sales, Leidner (1991) finds that defining the jobs as competition becomes a means for construing the work as masculine:

> The element of competition, the battle of wills implicit in their interactions with customers, seemed to be a major factor which allowed agents to interpret their work as manly. Virtually every step of the interaction was understood as a challenge to be met—getting in the door, making the prospect relax and warm up, being allowed to start the presentation . . . making the sale, and perhaps even increasing the size of the sale. (1991: 168)

For litigators, keeping score of wins in the courtroom and the dollar amount of damages or settlement awards allows them to interpret their work as manly. At Bonhomie Corporation and at Lyman, Lyman and Portia, the first question lawyers often asked others after a trial or settlement conference was "Who won the case?" or "How big were the damages?" Note that both Ring and Turow also conclude their pieces with descriptions of their win—"I won the case, but the verdict was small" and "I won big." Trial attorneys who did not "win big" were described as "having no balls," or as being "geeks" or "wimps." The fact that losing is associated with being less than a man suggests that the constant focus on competition and winning is an arena for proving one's masculinity.

One important area that calls for strategic friendliness and focuses on winning is jury selection or voir dire. The main purpose of voir dire is to obtain personal information about prospective jurors in order to determine whether they will be "favorably disposed to you, your client, and your case, and will ultimately return a favorable verdict" (Mauet 1980: 31). Once an attorney has made that assessment, biased jurors can be eliminated through challenges for cause and peremptory challenges. In an article on jury selection, attorney Peter Perlman maintains that the best way to uncover the prejudices of the jury "is to conduct voir dire in an atmosphere which makes prospective jurors comfortable about disclosing their true feelings" (1988: 5). He provides a checklist of strategies for lawyers to utilize which enable jurors to feel more comfortable. Some of these include:

> Given the initial intimidation which jurors feel, try to make them feel as comfortable as possible; approach them in a natural, unpretentious and clear manner.
>
> Since jurors don't relate to "litigants" or "litigation," humanize the client and the dispute.
>
> Demonstrate the sincere desire to learn of the jurors' feelings.
>
> The lawyer's presentation to the jury should be positive and radiate sincerity. (1988: 5–9)

Perlman's account reveals that the underlying goal of jury selection is to encourage the jury to open up so that the lawyer can eliminate the jurors he doesn't want and develop a positive rapport with the ones who appear favorable to his case.

This goal is supported not only by other writings on jury selection (Blinder 1978; Cartwright 1977; Mauet 1980; Ring 1983; Wagner 1981) but also through the training offered by NITA. As one teacher, a judge, said after the class demonstration on jury selection, "Sell your personality to the jury. Try to get liked by the jury. You're not working for a fair jury, but one favorable to your side." This fact is also recognized by a judge in Clifford Irving's best-selling novel *Trial:* "Assuming his case has some merit, if a lawyer gets a jury to like him and then trust him more than the son of a bitch who's arguing against him, he's home free" (1990: 64).

At NITA, teachers emphasized this point on the individual level. In their sessions on voir dire, students had to select a jury for a case which involved an employee who fell down the steps at work and severely injured herself. (Jurors for the case were classmates, including me.) Mike, one of the students, began his presentation by explaining that he was representing the woman's employer. He then went on to tell the jury a little bit about himself: "I grew up in a small town in Indiana." Then he began to ask each of the jurors where they were from, whether they knew the witness or the experts, whether they played sports, had back problems, suffered any physical injuries, and had ever had physical therapy. The instructor gave him the following comments:

> The personal comments about yourself seem forced. Good folksy approach, but you went overboard with it. You threw stuff out and let the jury nibble and you got a lot of information. But the main problem is that you didn't find out how people feel about the case or about their relatives and friends.

Another set of comments:

> Nice folksy approach, but a bit overdone. Listen to what jurors say, don't draw conclusions. Don't get so close to them, it makes them feel uncomfortable. Use body language to give people a

good feeling about you. Good personality, but don't cross certain lines. Never ask someone about their ancestry. It's too loaded a question to ask. Good sense of humor, but don't call one of your prospective jurors a "money man." And don't tell the jury jokes! You don't win them over that way.

The sporting element to voir dire becomes "winning over the jury." This theme also became evident in discussions student lawyers had before and after jury selection. They discussed at length how best "to handle the jurors," "how to get personal information out of them," "how to please them," "how to make them like you," and "how to seduce them to your side." The element of sexual seduction is apparent in the often used phrase "getting in bed with the jury." The direct reference to sexual seduction and conquest suggests, as did the intimidation strategy used in cross-examination, that "winning over the jury" is also a way to prove one's masculinity. Moreover, the desired result in both strategic friendliness and intimidation is similar: obtaining the juror's submission, and winning.

Strategic friendliness is also utilized in the cross-examination of sympathetic witnesses. In one of NITA's hypothetical cases, a woman dies of an illness related to her employment. Her husband sues his deceased wife's employer for her medical bills, lost wages, and "lost companionship." One of the damaging facts in the case, which could hurt his claim for "lost companionship," was the fact that he had a girlfriend long before his wife died. In typical combative, adversarial style, some of the student lawyers tried to bring this fact out in cross-examination to discredit his claims about his relationship with his wife. The teacher told one lawyer who presented such an aggressive cross-examination:

> It's too risky to go after him. Don't be so confrontational. And don't ask the judge

to reprimand him for not answering the question. This witness is too sensitive. Go easy on him.

The same teacher gave the following comments to another student who had "come on too strong":

> Too stern. Hasn't this guy been through enough already! Handle him with kid gloves. And, don't cut him off. It generates sympathy for him from the jury when you do that. It's difficult to control a sympathetic witness. It's best to use another witness's testimony to impeach him.

And to yet another student:

> Slow down! This is a dramatic witness. Don't lead so much. He's a sympathetic witness—the widower—let him do the talking. Otherwise you look like an insensitive jerk to the jury.

. . . Strategic friendliness carries over from the courtroom to depositions. Before deposing a particularly sensitive or sympathetic witness, Joe, one of the attorneys in the private firm, asked me whether "there is anything personal to start the interview with—a sort of warm-up question to start things off on a personal note?" I had previously interviewed the woman over the phone, so I knew something about her background. I told him that she was a young mother who had recently had a very difficult delivery of her first child. I added that she was worried about the baby's health because he had been born prematurely. At the beginning of the deposition later that afternoon, Joe said in a concerned voice that he understood the witness had recently had a baby and was concerned about its health. She appeared slightly embarrassed by the question, but with a slow smile and lots of encouragement from him, she began to tell him all about the baby and its health problems. By the time Joe began the formal part of the deposition, the witness had warmed up and gave her complete cooperation. Later, the attorney bragged to me and one of the associates that he had the witness "eating out of his hand."

After recording these events in my field notes, I wrote the following impressions:

> On the surface, it looks like social etiquette to ask the witness these questions because it puts her at ease. It lets her know he takes her seriously. But the "personal touch" is completely artificial. He doesn't care about the witness as a person. Or, I should say, only insofar as she's useful to him. Moreover, he doesn't even bother to ask the witness these questions himself the first time around. He asks me to do it. I'm to find the "personal hook" that he can use to manipulate her to his own ends.

Thus an innocuous personal remark becomes another way to create the desired impression with a witness and thereby manipulate him or her. Perhaps what is most ironic about strategic friendliness is that it requires a peculiar combination of sensitivity to other people and, at the same time, ruthlessness. The lawyer wants to appear kind and understanding, but that is merely a cover for the ulterior motive—winning. Although the outward presentation of self for this form of emotional labor differs from intimidation, the underlying goal is the same: the emotional manipulation of the witness for a favorable result.

Attorneys also employed strategic friendliness when dealing with clients. As I mentioned in the previous section, intimidation is rarely used with clients, particularly at the private firm, who are typically treated with a politesse, courtesy, and reassurance. The sensitivity to the client's needs and interests does not reflect genuine concern, however, but rather serves as a means to an

end—obtaining and maintaining the client's current and future business. The importance of clients to lawyers can be gauged by one of the criteria for determining partnership at private law firms: the ability to attract and maintain a client base (Nelson 1988; Smigel 1969). In this light, clients become another important legal audience for whom the lawyer performs and obtaining a client's business is construed as another form of "winning."

Articles in legal newspapers such as the *National Law Journal* address the importance of lawyers' efforts to attract new clients (O'Neil 1989; Foster and Raider 1988). These articles underscore the importance not only of obtaining business but of appealing to clients through "communication," "cultural sensitivity," and "creating good first impressions." Thus, "finding" new clients is not simply an instrumental role as Nelson (1988) suggests, it also carries with it an emotional dimension.

"Wooing clients" to the firm, or "making rain," as lawyers call it, is a common practice at the private firm. Partners were rewarded in annual bonuses for their ability to bring in new business. In informal conversations, partners often discussed the competition between firms for the clients' business. For example, when one of the partners procured a case from a large San Francisco bank that typically did business with another large firm in the city, he described it as a "coup." Attorneys boasted not only about bringing clients into the firm but about how much revenue "their client" brought into the firm's coffers. The constant focus on capturing clients, "making rain," and making big money betrays male lawyers' need to prove themselves through accomplishments and achievements. Further, those who lost big clients were considered "weak," "impotent," and no longer "in with the good old boys." In this way, winning clients' business is also associated with manly behavior. . . .

REFERENCES

American Bar Association. 1982. *Model Code of Professional Responsibility and Code of Judicial Conduct.* Chicago, Ill.: National Center for Professional Responsibility and the American Bar Association.

Berg, David. 1987. "Cross-Examination." *Litigation: Journal of the Section of Litigation, American Bar Association* 14, no. 1 (Fall):25–30.

Blinder, Martin. 1978. "Picking Juries." *Trial Diplomacy* 1, no. 1 (Spring):8–13.

Brazil, Wayne. 1978. "The Attorney as Victim: Toward More Candor about the Psychological Price Tag of Litigation Practice." *The Journal of the Legal Profession* 3:107–17.

Buchan, John. 1939. "The Judicial Temperament." In his *Homilies and Recreations.* 3d ed. London: Hodder and Stoughton.

Burawoy, Michael. 1979. *Manufacturing Consent: Changes in the Labor Process Under Monopoly Capitalism.* Chicago: University of Chicago Press.

Cartwright, John. 1977. "Jury Selection." *Trial* 28:13.

Cheatham, Elliott. 1955. *Cases and Materials on the Legal Profession.* 2d ed. Brooklyn: Foundation Press.

Connell, Robert. 1987. *Gender and Power: Society, the Person and Sexual Politics.* Stanford, Calif.: Stanford University Press.

Dombroff, Mark. "Winning Is Everything!" *National Law Journal,* 25 September 1989:13.

Foster, Dean and Ellen Raider. "Bringing Cultural Sensitivity to the Bargaining Table." *San Francisco Banner,* 17 October 1988:14.

Fox, Priscilla. 1978. "Good-bye to Game Playing." *Juris Doctor* (January):37–42.

Garfinkel, Harold. 1956. "Conditions of Successful Degradation Ceremonies." *American Journal of Sociology* 61, no. 11 (March):420–24.

Irving, Clifford. 1990. *Trial.* New York: Dell.

Leidner, Robin. 1991. "Serving Hamburgers and Selling Insurance: Gender, Work, and Identity in Interactive Service Jobs." *Gender & Society* 5, no. 2:154–77.

Luban, David. 1988. *Lawyers and Justice: An Ethical Study.* Princeton, N.J.: Princeton University Press.

Margolick, David. "At the Bar: Rambos Invade the Courtroom." *New York Times,* 5 August 1988:B5.

Mauet, Thomas. 1980. *Fundamentals of Trial Techniques.* Boston: Little Brown.

McElhaney, James. 1987. *McElhaney's Trial Notebook.* 2d ed. Chicago: Section of Litigation, American Bar Association.

Menkel-Meadow, Carrie. 1985. "Portia in a Different Voice: Speculations on a Women's Lawyering Process." *Berkeley Women's Law Review* 1, no. 1 (Fall):39–63.

Messner, Michael. 1989. "Masculinities and Athletic Careers." *Gender & Society* 3, no. 1 (March):71–88.

Michael, Jerome. 1950. "The Basic Rules of Pleading." *The Record: New York City Bar Association* 5:175–99.

Miner, Roger. "Lawyers Owe One Another." *National Law Journal,* 19 December 1988:13–14.

National Law Journal. "What America Really Thinks About Lawyers." October 1986:1.

Nelson, Robert. 1988. *Partners with Power: The Social Transformation of the Large Law Firm.* Berkeley and Los Angeles: University of California Press.

O'Neil, Suzanne. "Associates Can Attract Clients, Too." *National Law Journal,* 16 January 1989:17.

Perlman, Peter. 1988. "Jury Selection." *The Docket: Newsletter of the National Institute for Trial Advocacy* (Spring):1.

Post, Robert. 1987. "On the Popular Image of the Lawyer: Reflections in a Dark Glass." *California Law Review* 75, no. 1 (January):379–89.

Rice, Susan. "Two Organizations Provide Training, In-House or Out." *San Francisco Banner,* 24 May 1989:6.

Ring, Leonard. 1987. "Cross-examining the Sympathetic Witness." *Litigation: Journal of the Section of Litigation, American Bar Association* 14, no. 1 (Fall):35–39.

Sayler, R. "Rambo Litigation: Why Hardball Tactics Don't Work." *American Bar Association Journal,* 1 March 1988:79.

Smigel, Erwin. 1969. *The Wall Street Lawyer: Professional or Organizational Man?* 2d ed. New York: Free Press.

Spangler, Eve. 1986. *Lawyers for Hire: Salaried Professionals at Work.* New Haven, Conn.: Yale University Press.

Spence, Gary. 1989. *With Justice for None.* New York: Times Books.

Turow, Scott. "Crossing the Star." 1987. *Litigation: Journal of the Section of Litigation, American Bar Association* 14, no. 1 (Fall):40–42.

Wagner, Ward. 1981. *The Art of Advocacy: Jury Selection.* New York: Matthew Bender.

Wellman, Francis. 1986 [1903]. *The Art of Cross-Examination: with the Cross-Examinations of Important Witnesses in Some Celebrated Cases.* 4th ed. New York: Collier.

32

Engineering Culture
Self and Organization: In the Shadow of the Golden Bull

Gideon Kunda

"Built right into the social arrangements of an organization," Erving Goffman (1961: 180) says, "is a thoroughly embracing conception of the member—and not merely a conception of him qua member, but behind this a conception of him qua human being." If this is true of all forms of organization, it is particularly true at Tech. Here, as we have seen, the managerially sanctioned and enforced view of employees, which I have referred to as the "member role," includes explicit, detailed, wide-ranging, and systematically enforced prescriptions for what members in good standing are to think and feel about themselves, their work, and the social arrangements under which it is performed. What forms of experience are shaped in the glare of this ideological spotlight and in the shadows of its darker sides? What meanings do people attribute to their experience as members of an organization with such definite ideas about its members' experience? How, in short, do members construct a sense of self in the face of attempted normative control?

The nature of the relationship between the self—that ineffable source of subjective experience—and the social context within which it arises is, perhaps, the most enduring problem of social theory. If one generalization emerges from the enormous body of work on this issue, it is that self and society stand in a dialectical relationship: how one sees, thinks, and feels about the social world and about one's own place in it is the outcome of a continuing dialogue with the representatives of the social order into which one is born, its various forms of social organization, and the ready-made roles they offer.

What is the outcome of this dialogue? As Goffman (1961) suggests, a sense of self is formed both by the ways individuals identify with prescribed roles and the ways in which they distance themselves from them. In his words (p. 320), "the individual is best seen as a stance-taking entity, a something that takes up a position somewhere between identification with an organization and opposition to it, and is ready at the slightest pressure to regain its balance by shifting its involvement in either direction." The self, then, is a social product, constituted not only from spontaneous internal responses but from the processes of self-awareness, self-management, and self-display in the context of social interaction. Underlying this definition is a belief in the inherent freedom of individuals to interpret and make meaningful their situation and to create and recreate their sense of self within socially imposed constraints.

In complex societies, self-construction occurs in a variety of social settings. Consequently, individuals may be seen as possessors of "multiple selves," each defined and brought forth for a particular region of social life and the roles it offers. As Everett Hughes (1958) suggests, work life in general and organizational life in particular are central sources of self-definition. In this sense, one might speak of an "organizational self"—the subjective meanings attributed to the self arising out of balancing acceptance and rejection of the organizational ideology and the member role it prescribes.

So defined, however, the organizational self is an elusive subject. At Tech, as elsewhere, self-referent meanings are not easily come by, nor do they lend themselves to straightforward interpretation. Some of the data are by definition inaccessible; the rest are often complex, context-dependent, and purposeful interpretations by members, and, as such, their meanings are rarely as self-evident as they are made to appear. To capture the subjective experience of membership at Tech, it is necessary to cast a wide net: a comprehensive interpretation requires attention not only to ritual events, but also to mundane occasions, routine settings, and private—and sometimes reflective—moments where an individual's sense of self is enacted. To accomplish this, a number of sources of data are used in this [reading]: interviews in which members discuss their own experiences; observation-based descriptions of members' behavior; and analysis of self-display through the use of artifacts. It is worth noting that interviews are themselves a form of self-presentation, in this case to an audience of one—namely, the fieldworker. . . .

The Full Member

. . .

Managing the Organizational Self

The main theme of members' descriptions of their experience at Tech is the need to construct and manage an "organizational self"—first, by delineating the boundaries of a self relevant to the organizational context, and, second, by managing the organizational self's cognitive and affective responses to the requirements of the member role. The subjective meanings associated with each of these aspects of the self are analyzed in turn.

Managing Boundaries   Work at Tech is experienced as making great demands on time and energy. Members describe heavy workloads, scheduling pressures, competition, and the possibility of working at home, and they perceive these as factors that combine to blur the distinction between work and nonwork. In response, members suggest, it is necessary to put considerable efforts into establishing boundaries to one's involvement in work. These take two forms: boundaries around time dedicated to work, and boundaries around the social relationships that develop in the context of work.

Time boundaries are established by designating segments of time as work-related and allocating them to the organizational self, while others are considered a respite from work. Members carefully distinguish time at work from nonwork time. Many make an effort to adhere to prescribed working hours. Says a marketing manager:

> "My boss puts in eighteen hours a day, and you should hear his wife complain. I do fifty hours a week, and then I have time for my real estate deals. Sometimes I'm tempted to work longer hours, to turn on the terminal at home. I have to remind myself—there is no rush! We just bought a second home. My wife is over in Marketing. There is a lot of free time there. So she manages some of the deals, and in a few years we should be independently wealthy. I still want to be a VP, but there's no rush."

Work time is portrayed as both contaminated and attractive. It is "shit" and "crap," yet engrossing nevertheless. Enacting the boundary between work time and nonwork time is described by a product manager as a daily ritual of purification.

"During the day, I'm 'on' all the time. No time to stop and think. I drive home thirty-five miles a day, slowly, on the right-hand side of the road, and play Mozart on the stereo. It sort of buffers me from the shit here. At home Tech doesn't exist; just turn it off. Look at those junior engineers: they don't know any better; they read journals like *Byte* at home. I don't. And I *never* use my terminal at home. I don't smoke or abuse stuff, I do a lot of sports. I want to retire at the age of forty, but in the meanwhile it's a good place to work if you keep in mind that it is a large company; so you put up with all the shit, all the talk about Tech culture."

Vacations are a longer period of nonwork time. These, too, are equated with purity. Yet, as one manager describes it, the boundary is often hard to maintain.

"I'm going to Club Med for a week. It's tiring, all this head work, all this politics. I need to wash the culture out of my hair. It's almost a physical thing. Here you just sit and talk all day. But even there you meet Tech people. Last year I wound up spending a lot of time talking Tech. We're having a reunion soon."

Members also take breaks in the course of their workday. Breaks vary in length and utilization of space. Short ones may be momentary and personal. One manager describes these as respites from "bullshit" and being an "asshole":

"You have to keep your sanity somehow. You gotta laugh. I go out for lunch, leave this building even for forty-five minutes with someone, talk about basketball. People just walk into your office here. You can't close doors or hide. Finding a

few minutes for yourself is a problem. If I eat in the cafeteria, I'm caught up in business. People get caught up in this shit. It's not only the power. Maybe the growth. The times I want to leave are when there are too many things happening that are out of control. I can't take too much bullshit even though I'm paid to be an asshole."

Lunchtime leisure activities offer more extended communal breaks: daily basketball games, running, "Trivial Pursuit," bridge. Says one engineer:

"Without my daily bridge game I'm a wreck. Look at all those runners. What do you think they're running from?"

More extended breaks may be accomplished by defining "off days." As one manager describes it, this requires a considerable effort.

"The most important thing is keeping a boundary. Prioritize. You can't do everything. That is what I tell my people. My terminal is often shut all day and I don't take any calls. When I want to hide, I go sit in someone else's office. It takes a lot of energy to separate yourself. Discipline. People are after you all the time. Before you know it, your calendar is full. Luckily I don't get too much pressure from home, and the secretary has orders to let my wife through whenever she calls. Most people I know are just-married or divorced. It is incredible how many divorces there are. You can tell by looking at someone's calendar what the state of their marriage is."

Time segmentation may also be accomplished by constructing images of the more distant future and past. Hope and memory offer a fantasy of limits to involvement. One option is to see a future end to one's career at Tech. Many speak hopefully of the day they will leave—a benchmark beyond which the organizational self will cease to exist, thus making way for other forms of experience. Such images of future disassociation often carry overtones of purification. An engineer says:

> "You have to take a lot of crap here. It's rough, it's crazy. I want to slow down. It's not worth it, all the Tech crap. I've been considering leaving—maybe to a new discipline altogether: carpentry, plumbing. Take a cut in income—but kiss Tech goodbye. Perhaps when my kids grow up and go to college."

One often-posed alternative for the future is "meaningful work." A group manager, reputed to be highly successful and very involved with his work, nevertheless says:

> "I give myself five more years before I go back to teaching art. That was my major in college before I got caught up in this. It's still my first love, although I don't have too much time for it. But I promised myself that I was going to go back."

Another frequently mentioned alternative is affluent leisure. A thirty-one-year-old product manager, currently on the fast track, has clear plans:

> "I'm planning to retire at the age of forty. I had it all planned when I was still at school. By then I will be independently wealthy. I'll live on my yacht. By then I will have deserved it."

The past, nostalgically remembered, offers another time boundary. The company's early days, for those who can claim to have "been there," are recollected as purer, a time when, unlike the disappointing present, heavy involvement was justified. Says a product manager:

> "In the early days loyalty was real and strong. We had less than 20,000 people. I worked my butt off to make it a success.

I believed in the company. It was a moral force. People were behind that. You worked for a company that didn't deliberately lie to customers, you worked to keep commitments. We worked hard. Now that it's big, people are more concerned with their own welfare. With 20 people you can have a company spirit. In '72 we did. My badge number is 13705. There were 10,000 people then. I could call up a vice-president—there were only two or three. I could go around my boss and his boss. Today the open-door policy is not nearly as open as it is alleged to be. I can do it with my boss, maybe, but many others can't. And in '72 *they* would have been going around to speak to us."

In sum, most members find that work, by its nature, is not limited to a time or a place. Consequently, the construction of time boundaries for an organizational self is essential. In the recurring imagery, work is impure and crazy; nonwork is pure and sane. Work is at once seductive and repulsive; nonwork time must be protected. Maintaining a time boundary between the two is considered important and difficult and is thought to require discipline and effort: one has to combat both the company's demands and one's own impulses, not easily distinguishable, to allocate more time to work and to the organizational self that is formed in its context.

Also crucial for the maintenance of a successful organizational self is the active management of social relationships. This is considered necessary because of the frequent overlapping of work and nonwork relationships. As a development manager describes it, this may occur when nonwork relations are pulled into the sphere of work:

> "They needed a lab manager here and asked me if I knew anybody. I recommended a guy I sort of knew socially. It didn't work out. He couldn't operate on

his own. He was making rules, you had to go fight and scream to get anything. He turned into a little czar. It just didn't work out. I still saw him socially. I helped him get another job because I felt responsible."

More often, work encounters offer the opportunity for socializing. A project supervisor says:

"Socially there isn't much going on here, but there are connections. My two best friends work for me. It happens that these are the people you run into."

Consequently, work relationships often become personalized. For some—particularly those farther up in the hierarchy—this serves instrumental goals. Says a senior development manager:

"Over time you develop a series of personal/professional relationships. It is based on trust and can take years to develop. Without it, nothing can work for you. It requires a lot of work, including socializing."

Similarly, another manager mentions the importance of having Tech "confidants":

"You need someone you can trust, someone you can do reality testing with about what's going on. A lot of people have confidants: an ex-boss, a friend from somewhere else. Without reality testing, you can go crazy."

This potential for overlapping relationships is for many members a cause of considerable tension. Some attempt to separate, at least conceptually, different types of involvement with the same people. Thus, after-hours socializing with work acquaintances is labeled by some as work, as a duty, or as a political necessity that should be kept to a minimum. A development manager says:

"At Silicon I worked eighty hours a week. That's two weeks in one. Then I realized that you can walk away from your job but not your family. I decided that my family comes first. I've been married for twenty-two years now, and I keep my life *totally* separate. Look around and you'll see how unusual that is. We do no socializing. Nothing. It's an ironclad rule we have. I go to my boss's party every year, but that is work. I only socialize when it is political."

Many who do socialize with colleagues take care to distinguish a work relationship with someone from a social relationship with the same person. Thus, a supervisor says of her relationship with an engineer who reports to her:

"We go out together sometimes. But after work we have a rule never to talk about work. Every Thursday after work we drive to a ceramics class together. The company sponsors it. They are very good at that type of thing. We very consciously don't talk work. Once when there was a crisis, I said: 'I'm breaking the rule now because I forgot to tell you something, but it will never happen again!'"

Conversely, there are limits to the degree to which "personal" issues are allowed to surface when working. Another supervisor says of his engineers:

"I'm willing to listen to some of their problems. They come with all kinds of stuff. Some supervisors listen, but when it gets too personal I send them to EAP— the Employee Assistance Program—freelance shrinks the company hires. That's what the company pays them for."

An extreme case of overlap occurs when two members are married or live together. This requires a continued effort at social segmentation that is both public and private.

Says one supervisor, married to an engineer who works at the same facility:

> "My husband works here too. We work on separate sides of the building and try not to see each other. I don't want to hear his voice. And I don't want any finger pointing. People might not trust you if they know you have a special relation. Some things you might not hear. I know my boss is sometimes concerned about information flow. I ride home with my husband. But some things I just wouldn't tell him."

On the whole, however, work and nonwork aspects of social ties are experienced as hard to separate, requiring constant definition and redefinition and never fully resolved. Consider the following description of a manager's relationship with his boss:

> "His wife is unhappy. She complains a lot about his work involvement. I had them over one evening. You learn a lot that way. She is a potential ally. I should invite them again. But it is because they are OK. My wife likes them. It would never be only for politics. I would never do that! Social is separate from political—you have to draw the line. Somewhere. . . ."

In sum, members consider the management of social relationships an important complement to the management of time in creating and sustaining well-defined boundaries to an organizational self. It is not so much the success or failure of these efforts but the perceived importance and difficulty of engaging in them that is indicative of subjective experience. Drawing boundaries is experienced as a struggle to limit self-involvement in the face of organizational and internal pressures to merge work and nonwork aspects of life and thus to expand organizational influence over private experience.

Managing Role Responses   Members also construct an organizational self through the active management of thoughts and feelings prescribed by the member role. Such role responses, frequently enacted in rituals, take two forms: role embracement and role distancing.

Role embracement—expressing identification with aspects of the member role—is a widely shared and often-recurring feature of self-reports. Generally referred to as "being a Techie," role embracement is reportedly experienced as a general orientation to the company, a combination of beliefs and feelings glossed by the label "loyalty." A typical explication is offered by an engineering manager.

> "You know, I like Tech. I don't think of leaving. People might say that the culture swallowed me, but there really is a feeling of loyalty I have. We have a lot of that in the culture. We like working for Tech. It is a positive company. You get really involved. I get a real charge when Tech gets a good press. Or when people I knew from this other company were dumping on Tech, I was offended. I didn't like hearing it. They made millions with us! Because of us they got rich! They get all this free knowledge from us and say it with impunity! My husband works for Tech and he feels the same way. We spend time with friends talking about work; we're worse than doctors. I guess you can call me a Techie."

Note in particular the pervasive imagery of incorporation—"swallowing"—that underlies the language used to describe the relationship of self and company. . . .

Many members also acknowledge the validity and applicability to their own experience of specific aspects of the prescribed member role. An engineering supervisor combines beliefs and feelings in his acceptance of "individual responsibility and ownership"—a fundamental and oft-repeated ideological principle.

> "I'm a slow cultural learner. It took me two years to learn mainly that 'it is your own ownership.' You can do anything you want, but you have to push. The idea is that you are a professional and responsible. You gotta *feel* the ownership. Don't sit and wait. You're a grown-up. The onus is placed on you to live up to expectations. Don't bitch about problems; go do something about it. I buy that. You know, I'm trying to get my son into Tech—that should tell you something."

Role embracement is typically associated with Tech as a whole rather than with functional subgroup affiliations. Groups, if anything, are conceived of as stepping stones, temporary arrangements that do not require loyalty or identification. For example, a manager who thinks he is about to lose his job in one of the unfunded staff functions is openly disturbed and worried about his future. He is angry with his boss and his peers, whom he blames for the failure. He sees his commitment to the company, however, as overriding the commitment to the specific group.

> "I'll never leave Tech. I'm a Techie! But I want to leave this group; I came because I wanted to learn and watched it crumble and fall apart. I was insulted; I got upset and stayed home. My boss is crazy; he's nuts! The worst boss I've ever worked for. I have my resume out, and I'm speaking to all my friends. People come and go. Organizations change here. But you'll meet again if you're around for a while."

The meaning of role embracement may be gleaned also from the ways members discuss the experience of others in the company. This allows members to present themselves implicitly, by way of contrast, as possessors of culturally appropriate selves, or at least reveal their adherence to standards to which they—or others—might hold themselves. Hierarchical relations are a frequently observed basis for such contrast. Senior managers present themselves as agents of the company, "the culture," and its demands. They identify themselves through contrast with subordinates whom they wish to change "for the company's good." A senior vice-president says reproachfully of his "direct reports" (who, under different circumstances, might make similar claims about their own subordinates):

> "They come to the staff meetings and want to know what is in it for them, not for the company! That kind of responsibility does not exist. It is a question of maturity. Not everything is always immediately relevant, but what about the company good? They don't have it in their gut! I have to keep pounding away at them; I have to keep painting a vision. I told them I was at the executive staff meeting and I sat in on stuff that didn't concern me. I made a contribution for the company good! That is the mindset we have to create."

Embracing the member role, then, is seen as a developmental matter—a question of "maturity"—but this view of the self also carries connotations of a religious experience: conversion, total commitment to "the larger cause," and self-sacrifice. This is evident in a senior manager's views on his role in motivating people:

> "You know the old anthropological maxim: Get them in a survival mode. Convince them that survival is at stake, that there is a threat to survival, then make them see the light. I'm a missionary. I articulate the vision. Sure, careers can get hurt. It's often more than they bargained for. But they help others in

getting the religion. Give them the resources and point them in the right direction. They'll kill themselves."

Middle managers often assume a more pragmatic, macho style. The images of intense involvement and strong motivation are the same, but the explanations are less lofty. A development group manager says of a peer who is "in trouble":

"She's in the problem employee mode now. You saw the signs. She's an alcoholic. That is the nature of the industry. Constant change, high pressure, motivation to achieve. It results in burnout. That is the 'old Tech.' Sam has one primary criterion: success in the marketplace. Nothing else counts, no institution at Tech is holy. We'll try different things. Sociologists tell us the price is high. Bullshit! Get people really involved and motivated, and 20 percent burn out. But 80 percent work. And there are countless start-ups to employ people. I worked at Data Corp, and it was exactly the same."

Standards for evaluating appropriate embracement of the member role might be applied to one's peers and managers as well. For example, a lower-level manager says of her supervisor, with whom she has been feuding:

"He's a loser. He just can't handle the ambiguity. He wants someone to tell him what to do. He doesn't go out and get it done. Gets all scared when he doesn't get clear direction. You know the kind. He was out sick for a few days after one emotional meeting. A wimp. It doesn't work in the Tech culture."

Role embracement, then, means submitting to the company's definition of one's self. Such submission, however, is typically presented as a form of voluntary exchange with the company. A number of different attributes of the company are often cited as facilitating such an exchange. One is the image of the president, who has come to symbolize the "philosophy" and everything that is unique about Tech. A positive view of Sam Miller is frequently heard, particularly at middle and lower levels (more senior managers often tend to be critical; it is a sign of the insider to be close enough to know "the real story"). For example, a mid-level manager, speaking, as many do, in the first person plural, acknowledges his belief in the validity of the ideology, identified with the president. Emotional attachment is presented as a fair exchange:

"Maybe I've swallowed slogans, the party line, the whole Sam Miller 'do what's right' thing. But I *do* believe that Tech 'does what's right.' We don't lay off, even though some people deserve to be laid off. So you feel loyalty back. Sam Miller believes in 'taking care of your people,' and he gets paid back with loyalty. They've never done wrong by me."

A similar exchange is apparent in an engineering supervisor's description of the impact of a speech by Sam Miller:

"I trust the man. He means well. There is a lot of honesty at the top and the bottom of the company. I don't know about the middle. But he really means it when he says it's the company's duty to take care of employees and customers. I've never met him, but I've seen the videotapes. He can be very powerful. I got excited when I heard him say: 'It's our moral duty to give the customers what they want.' *Moral* duty!"

Frequently heard from engineers is support for "Sam Miller's philosophy":

"You can tell he's an engineer. His philosophy is give the workers the tools and they will do the job. He believes that their goal in life is not to rip off the company. That's the way it should be!"

A second factor facilitating the exchange is the perception of the company's positive treatment of its employees (often in comparison with other companies). Thus, an engineer compares Tech's tradition of job security to its competitors' approach:

"Tech is good because they grow to your weakness; other places, they milk your knowledge dry and then kill you. At Data they pay great, but they fire you as soon as the downturn comes. This company keeps people and retrains them. I just love this company. I would die for it! There is a tradition of job security here: you can have your neck chopped off and it'll grow back again. You take your risks and you're not hurt too bad. Take Henderson's group: they were responsible for Jupiter and now they're back again. 'Fail and you're history' is just hype."

Similarly, an engineer whose project is sinking is nonetheless positive:

"I don't want to leave Tech. I like the environment. These things happen elsewhere too. I wouldn't want to be at some other place. You know the stories, you've heard them so often. Some old engineers working on obsolete technology in the basement of Corporate. The project was canceled, and the company sent them to school for six months; they went on to become the biggest fans of the company. That's why I basically like it here; I certainly don't want to go into supervision, and I'm keeping the headhunters at bay in the meanwhile. It'll take time to evaluate—maybe a year or two—to see if the product makes money."

Many value the relative security of working for a large and stable corporation. Compared

with the high-risk life at start-ups, Tech is seen as a haven of stability. A consulting engineer says:

"In the start-ups and the small companies, things are much worse. I worked at one where the bank auctioned off the company and the paychecks were held up. In comparison, here the pressure is fairly low. The whole industry is high-pressure. Time is important. You've got to get things out before the competition. But in the small ones it is much more competitive. I tried a start-up for a while. The headhunters got to my head. It was a big mistake! Things were crazy there. I burnt out. Had to see a psychiatrist. I really needed help. I was lucky they took me back. I called my old boss. Except for a few 'I told you so's,' there was no problem."

Members also cite Tech's "corporate culture" in explaining their positive orientation to the company. They contrast its "informal environment" with beliefs about other companies. A manager says of his reasons for joining:

"I didn't want Chiptech. I have an irrational dislike of them. Suits, pinstripes, the whole corporate clown thing. And because they unfairly and unjustly dominate the market. They just don't deserve the sales they have. It's not right! It's only because the purchasers are morons. I took a lateral to come here and also lost some pay."

Another manager points to the freedom and opportunity he feels is characteristic of the company:

"When you join the company, people convince you that it is different, that it is a unique place: there is a lot of freedom from higher up; you have to be self-motivated in your work; and there are a lot of opportunities. It's partly true! You *can* be creative; I've seen cases where you can convince people; it *is* more open; they allow people to transfer freely in the company; they spend money on employees; I've done a lot of training. Even the fact that I was offered this position shows that they prefer to develop people. That's why I like it here."

Engineers often portray Tech as "a good environment for engineering," a "country club" or an "engineers' sandbox" where engineers who are supposedly addicted to their work and emotionally attached to their projects can "play." An engineer in Advanced Development explains:

"Tech has the best engineers. I'm an engineer, and I want state-of-the-art technology. At Chiptech they develop what Marketing tells them. I'm happy as long as you keep me away from marketing types. Tech caters to engineers. Its reputation in the industry is a country club for engineers. It's laid-back. Overall there are less fires, less stupid deadlines. They allow people to transfer freely, they put a lot of money into training, they give inexperienced people opportunity. Learning is the most important thing to me. If I gave it up, I'd become comatose. Right now I'm learning chip design. A totally new area for me. Some engineers love houses, others cars; engineers like details, how things work. I like to learn. And the environment here is open enough to let you get involved in anything you like."

Similarly, many engineers acknowledge attachment to Tech's technology, which they view as unique, and through that to the company. Says one:

"Once you've worked with Tech products in a Tech environment, it's hard to go to anything else. They are just so much better. It's an engineer's dream—if he's into technology."

Finally, some depict Tech's business practices and moral stance as worthy of one's commitment. Tech's way of doing business is often contrasted with the less than honest approaches presumably found elsewhere. One project manager contrasts Tech with "sleazy defense contractors"—the companies that develop products for the Department of Defense:

"I worked for a while for a company that was built on those contracts. I worked on the ABM radar. It's not so much that I mind what the products end up doing. No. But all the dishonesty—the excessive costs, the stupidity, the unnecessary work—it really got me down. The norm was: hide the basic specs, follow the letter of the law and produce garbage, then get another contract. Disgusting stuff. Like telling reliability engineers to cook figures. At Tech at least we give customers an honest product. They get what they pay for. Most of the time. I feel good about that."

In sum, role embracement is a recurring theme in members' description of their subjective experience. The rhetoric of role embracement is built around the imagery of immersion, incorporation, psychological maturity, and religion. The organizational self is presented as tightly coupled with the company: the "mature" self is bound by ties of belief, strong emotions, and even religious fervor, all of which, members seem to imply, are quite authentic. At the extreme, self-definitions merge (at least temporarily) with the shared definitions of the culture, suggesting the collapse of the boundaries between self and organization.

Unqualified role embracement, however, is felt by many to be undignified. This is evident in the self-conscious quality of the descriptions, and in the emphasis on a fair and, more crucially, on a controlled exchange with the company. Thus, members claim the right to control the extent and the degree to which role demands are embraced. This capacity for role distancing—one that we have seen enacted in the course of organizational rituals—is often made explicit and elaborated with regard to both the cognitive and the emotional dimensions of the member role.

Cognitive distancing—disputing popular ideological formulations—is manifested when one suggests that one is "wise" to what is "really" going on. Being "wise" implies that despite behaviors and expressions indicating identification, one is also fully cognizant of their underlying meaning, and thus free of control: autonomous enough to know what is going on and dignified enough to express that knowledge.

One frequently encountered mode of cognitive distancing is cynicism. This is usually expressed as a debunking assertion, cast as a personal insight, that reality is very different from ideological claims. For example, an engineer questions the meaning of Tech culture:

> "It's like a religion, a philosophy that the company expounds; Sam Miller says, 'Do what's right,' be on the up and up, satisfy the customer, do the right thing by them. He's a weird bird; pushes all this morality stuff. There is a whole Sam Miller subculture. His memos circulate on the technet. It's like a kind of morality thing. You can go into Sam's office if you're not happy about a supervisor. I've heard of someone who has done it. Of course, nothing might get done. In this group, 'do what's right' means 'make your manager visible.' [Laugh.] Aren't all organizations like that?"

A second mode of cognitive distancing is that of detached theoretical observation, often referred to as "Tech watching." Its essence is the ability to interpret Tech reality and view it with scientific detachment; observations are frequently cast in the language of various social scientific disciplines. Tech watching not only expresses a point of view that is distinct from ideology; it also reverses roles: members who are often the subjects of organizational research become knowledgeable students of organizations (and of organizational researchers). A senior manager who has since left the company says:

> " 'Tech culture' is a way to control people, to rationalize a mess, to get them to work hard, and feel good about it; it is really an ideology. Like all other ideologies it is part truth and part lie."

. . . Most Tech watchers . . . are . . . familiar with the style of analysis propagated by management theory and the popular business press. A development manager says:

> "I have a mixed reaction to layoffs. Sam Miller says things like 'moral obligation' to employees, but it isn't consistent with American culture. American culture is individualistic. No layoffs are suited to the Japanese. It's consistent with their culture: paternalism, traditions. It's a long time coming getting rid of poor performers. The question is: is it worth betting the company? He feels it is big enough to absorb the slack. He feels he has responsibility; I respect him for that. But I respectfully disagree. Making a profit and carrying the deadwood don't go together."

Similarly, a manager says of a consultants' report on the problems in a well-known project:

> "There was nothing surprising about the report for anyone who has been here for ten years. Every book will tell you the same thing—*Soul of a New Machine* or *Mythical Man-month:* you have to be

careful not to mix cultures, not to have just one technical guru. So we proved them right again—there is nothing specific to Tech about all that."

A third mode of cognitive distancing is the reference to "common sense," presented as a body of practical knowledge that describes the social attributes of Tech, yet is not part of the formally prescribed ideology. In some cases the difference between ideology and common sense seems more stylistic than substantive. A group manager distances himself from "the culture stuff" and contrasts it with independently gained pragmatic knowledge:

"They are making more out of this culture stuff than it's worth. You have to laugh. It's an instance of self-consciousness. 'Look at us enjoying ourselves, being good guys.' I never read that stuff, maybe see it in passing. It's the same nauseating stuff they print in *Business Week*. They have this intro course for new employees. They talk about culture, but I will never send anyone to it. It leads to circular thinking. It's a waste of time. You have to know how this place really works, how decisions get made at Tech. You pick it up as you go along. I tell my people how to get things done. We know that we want consensus, that power plays lose. I don't know what it's like at the top, how the big guys fight, or what they do. But the people who work for me, I brief them: 'Be tactful, don't beat 'em up, don't piss 'em off.' I train them explicitly and show them how. I'm a development engineer. I don't buy all that theology. If it works it's good; if it makes money it's good. Everything else—everything!—is bullshit."

. . . The three modes of cognitive distancing differ (no doubt influenced in part by the speaker's perception of the interviewer), but all demonstrate the felt ability and freedom to

reflect on the validity of ideological reality claims and to offer alternative formulations. This is manifested in the rich terminology used to refer to the managerial point of view: "religion," "philosophy," "song and dance," "ideology," "theology," and "bullshit."

It is not just in the domain of ideologically prescribed beliefs that members claim the right to some autonomy. Distancing also occurs with respect to the feelings prescribed by the member role or associated with the organizational self. Three types of such emotional distancing are apparent in members' discourse: denial, depersonalization, and dramatization. Denial is accomplished by presenting one's motives for membership as purely instrumental. The relationship with the company is construed as contractual and economically driven, and its emotional aspects denied. For an engineer, this means not only avoiding the "people and the politics," where "emotions" are likely to be found—a typical response—but also a denial that one "loves one's work." An engineer says:

"I wanted the security of working for a big company—no excitement and less pay. I don't identify with any organization. Those things are circles within circles; they come and go, but the job remains. I get green dollars, I do my best, I know my worth. I work flexible hours but *never* more than eight. Technology is *not* my hobby. I have no terminal at home, and I keep my social life separate. I'm a private person. I don't go to the workshops or to the meetings. That's for those who want to make an impression, those who want to get ahead. They can have it. None of the 'addicted to your work,' 'ego-involvement' bullshit. I do my job. All the weird political aspects of the project don't bother me. They fight all the time. They are defensive and paranoid. There is an 'ain't it awful' attitude. Finger pointing. Accusing each other of screwing up. But I stay away from all of that emotional stuff."

Managers, too, may engage in emotional denial. Says a group manager, considered a hard worker:

"Loyalty—they make a big deal about that—is old school. What is important is work. Some people feel a sense of belonging, but in my case it's not strong. It's a nice company, but it isn't my mother. I'm not a joiner; I never liked organizations or clubs. I just don't feel that way about organizations, even though I bust my ass here. Others get some satisfaction in belonging. 'Techies'! [Laughs.] At social gatherings they will talk about Tech, say: 'We do it this way, we do it better.' Some of them don't even work at Tech any more. Some started fifteen years ago, felt part of what was happening. But it isn't the same any more. Some moved on. Tech is just a thing. I find it amusing when I hear all that talk."

In both cases, denial of emotional involvement in work is contrasted both with recognized ideological role demands and with a caricatured depiction of those who accept them.

The second mode of emotional distancing is depersonalization. Here, the emotions experienced as part of the organizational self are presented as distinct from other aspects of emotional life and at some remove from one's "authentic" sense of self. Specific codes for such emotions are widely used in everyday discourse. The word "emotion" often refers to a recognized part of work-related interaction, a form of experience that is used to explain behavior but is isolated from other facets of one's emotional life. "Pain"—sometimes accompanied by a tap on the stomach to illustrate its location—refers to negative "emotions" of this sort. One manager describes a stormy staff meeting:

"It was an emotional meeting. We went through a lot of pain. But we did reorganize. Bill lost quite a bit of his project work, and Jim is going into a career-examination mode—he took the heat for the slips. But everybody took it professionally—you can't let those things get to you. Go home and forget about it till tomorrow."

. . . Terms for positive emotions also exist, as this comment by a manager illustrates:

"I'm very excited about the second-quarter figures! When they see the profit numbers and read the reports coming in on this project, management will get the warm fuzzies."

Successful depersonalization is seen as requiring a constant effort, captured by the recurring images of "ignoring crap" and "developing a thick skin." Says a development manager, temporarily on a staff assignment after his project was "unfunded":

"I've learned here that you can do your own job, but you have to let the waves flow over you; ignore them or you'll go crazy. There is a lot of shit coming down, people wandering around, consultants, studies; that's the way it is, but it isn't a bad place. On a scale of ten it's maybe a six or a seven; but they really stuff ten pounds of shit into five-pound bags. I have a Russian immigrant friend who says it reminds him of the USSR; all this shit about Big Brother."

In a similar fashion, a product manager, considered by many to be highly successful, explains his success:

"In this job we are self-motivated, internally driven. But you have to have a thick skin to survive. You must depersonalize; it's a rough environment. Take all this stuff professionally, not personally."

. . . Depersonalization, then, requires that one control and even suppress personal and spontaneous reactions to the work environment, thus purging them from the organizational self and leaving only appropriate "emotions." Failure to do this is noticed in others. A group manager says of a peer:

> "Rick gets too emotional; he takes it too personally. He's a good manager, but he gets carried away with his stuff. It's not bad, but sometimes I think he overdoes it, loses control. It's not professional, and it can harm you. Personally, and also career damage. Someone should tell him."

In the third mode of emotional distancing, dramatization, emotional expression is viewed as strategically driven: it is contrived and calculated in order to accomplish goals, and the authenticity of performances is therefore regarded with suspicion. In a typical statement, a development manager describes his view of members' underlying motivations:

> "Techies. We're all Techies. The whole goddamn industry. It's a type of individual who is aggressive and involved, looks loyal, puts in a lot of time, but underneath the surface is self-serving and owes allegiance only to himself. They are mobile and choose the projects as they see fit."

More specifically, a supervisor refers to the ability to manage and interpret the display of emotions as "people skills":

> "I'm developing a thick hide. Before I take anyone's advice, or react to yelling and screaming, I think about what their agenda is. The people skills are important here; I learned that the hard way. I'm suspicious. All of a sudden my boss is being a good guy, being nice. He's learning to put on that act. That means I have to be even more careful now."

Similarly, a manager of one of the staff functions suggests that emotional expression is a game that many recognize:

> "We went to this off-site meeting. A consultant led a session on 'how we feel toward each other.' People were talking. But it's not real. It's just an opportunity to see how you handle yourself in that kind of session. The only one who believed all that California bathtub crap was the consultant. I'd believe it too for fifteen hundred bucks a day."

Members often describe their own displays in a strategic light. For example, a supervisor reveals her approach to a discussion with her boss in which they reviewed her performance and decided on her future responsibilities:

> "Before I had a one-on-one with my boss, I read some advice in *Things They Never Taught Me at the Harvard Business School*. Good stuff. It says: 'Never show them that you're feeling anything; keep a straight face; confuse them.' It's exactly what I did. Worked, too."

An engineer says of his campaign for a promotion to senior consulting engineer:

> "I didn't get the promotion. Maybe my boss didn't support me enough, or maybe someone on the promotion committee was playing some game. So I'm in a career-evaluation mode now. I'm angry. I haven't signed on to any new projects. I'm too depressed and angry. The EAP therapist type—I met her at a workshop on stress—says I'm too dependent on external approval and should change jobs. I'll show them dependency."

. . . Inability to dramatize, and the ensuing perception of loss of control, is viewed as a serious problem, worthy of managerial attention. A development manager says of one of his project leaders:

"Jim has a people problem. He is gruff with people and says exactly what is on his mind. He gets angry in meetings. I want him to control himself. Next year he is going to be evaluated on that. I'm watching him. He knows it."

And a project manager says of a supervisor:

"He's a good manager, but a complainer. He's too negative about the company and constantly complains about too many levels of management, fucked-up decision making, and all that. It's a bad attitude."

In sum, cognitive and emotional distancing reflect the felt necessity of maintaining a controllable distance from the beliefs and feelings prescribed by the member role and displayed as part of the organizational self. A ludic metaphor underlies members' attempts to convey this experience: the construction of an organizational self is seen as drama or as a game. Notions of performing, playing a game, watching oneself, strategically designing roles, and, ultimately, assuming a calculative stance toward the management of one's own thoughts and feelings are deeply ingrained in experience and explicitly articulated by members. . . .

Conclusion: The Unstable Self

The extensive demands of the member role pose a fundamental dilemma. By seeking and accepting higher status, greater opportunity, increased centrality, and more rewards, . . . members have also exposed themselves to the organizational ideology—the codification of "Tech culture" and its cognitive and affective correlates. They are the targets of its formulations, "overlaid worlds," and attempts at mind and emotion description, prescription, and control. By choice they have entered into a contract that is more than eco-

nomic, one that must contend with overt external claims on self-definition. Behavioral conformity and evidence of a vaguely defined "loyalty" are not enough. A demonstration of "incorporation" of the culture, of adoption of an organizationally defined and sanctioned self, is required. Consequently, the appearance of personal autonomy—a condition naturally (and ideologically) associated with the high status they seek—is threatened. Although it is not immediately apparent, the price of power is submission: not necessarily to demands concerning one's behavior, as is typical of low-status work, but to prescriptions regarding one's thoughts and feelings, supposedly the most cherished belongings of autonomous beings.

In short, inherent in a system of normative control is a contradiction between the requirements of internal and external control of the self. This causes members to experience what Merton (1957: 6) refers to as "sociological ambivalence"—a condition that results from "incompatible normative expectations of attitudes, beliefs and behaviors assigned to a status or a set of statuses in society." Sociological ambivalence is manifested in numerous ways. It is articulated as confusion between the attractiveness and repulsiveness of the company and its demands, between the seductiveness of increased involvement and the desire and need to maintain personal autonomy. It is artistically expressed in office artifacts and publicly displayed in such central symbols as the "golden bull" and the "management model," which contrast "shit" and "glory." Perhaps its ultimate expression is found in the double meaning of "burnout" as both elevation and degradation—the contrast between being a casualty and engaging in self-sacrifice, between becoming a loser or a hero.

The organizational self that is formed under conditions of sociological ambivalence is founded on the carefully cultivated ability to control and manage an appropriate and often ambiguous or shifting balance of role embracement and role distancing. This balancing act may be observed in the ironic stance that permeates ritual performances and social interaction; in the self-consciousness that infuses the members' discourse; in the humor that at once highlights and denies ambivalence; in the rapid frame shifts in the course of presentations; and in the qualifiers that precede many statements and the escape clauses designed into them. More tellingly, perhaps, it is evident in the pervasiveness and centrality of the metaphor of

drama in the construction of experience, and the oft-repeated and widely shared insight that things are never as they seem. . . .

REFERENCES

Goffman, E. 1961. *Asylums*. Garden City, NY: Anchor.

Hughes, E. C. 1958. *Men and Their Work*. Glencoe, IL: Free Press.

Merton, R. K. 1957. *Social Theory and Social Structure*. Glencoe, IL: Free Press.

MANAGERIAL WORK

33

The Social Structure of Managerial Work

Robert Jackall

I

The hierarchical authority structure that is the linchpin of bureaucracy dominates the way managers think about their world and about themselves. Managers do not see or experience authority in any abstract way; instead, authority is embodied in their personal relationships with their immediate bosses and in their perceptions of similar links between other managers up and down the hierarchy. When managers describe their work to an outsider, they almost always first say: "I work for [Bill James]" or "I report to [Harry Mills]" or "I'm in [Joe Bell's] group," and only then proceed to describe their actual work functions. Such a personalized statement of au-

thority relationships seems to contradict classical notions of how bureaucracies function but it exactly reflects the way authority is structured, exercised, and experienced in corporate hierarchies.

American businesses typically both centralize and decentralize authority. Power is concentrated at the top in the person of the chief executive officer (CEO) and is simultaneously decentralized; that is, responsibility for decisions and profits is pushed as far down the organizational line as possible. For example, Alchemy Inc. is one of several operating companies of Covenant Corporation. When I began my research, Alchemy employed 11,000 people; Covenant had over 50,000 employees and now has over 100,000. Like the other operating companies, Alchemy has its own president, executive vice-presidents, vice-presidents, other executive officers, business area managers, staff divisions, and more than eighty manufacturing plants scattered throughout the country and indeed the world producing a wide range of specialty and commodity chemicals. Each operating company is, at least theoretically, an autonomous, self-sufficient organization, though they are all monitored and coordinated by a central corporate staff, and each president reports directly to the corporate CEO. Weft Corporation has its corporate headquarters and manufacturing facilities in the South; its marketing and sales offices, along with some key executive personnel, are in New York City. Weft employs 20,000 people, concentrated in the firm's three textile divisions that have always been and remain its core business. The Apparel Division produces seven million yards a week of raw, unfinished cloth in several greige (colloquially gray) mills, mostly for sale to garment manufacturers; the Consumer Division produces some cloth of its own in several greige mills and also finishes—that is, bleaches, dyes, prints, and sews—twelve million yards of raw cloth a month into purchasable items like sheets, pillowcases, and tablecloths for department stores and chain stores; and the Retail Division operates an import-export business, specializing in the quick turnaround of the fast-moving cloths desired by Seventh Avenue designers. Each division has a president who reports to one of several executive vice-presidents, who in turn report to the corporate CEO. The divisional structure is typically less elaborate in its hierarchical ladder than the framework of independent operating companies; it is also somewhat more dependent on corporate staff for essential services. However, the basic principle of simultaneous centralization and decentralization prevails and both Covenant and Weft consider their companies or divisions, as the case may be, "profit centers." Even Images Inc., while much smaller than the industrial concerns and organized like most service businesses according to shifting groupings of client accounts supervised by senior vice-presidents, uses the notion of profit centers.

The key interlocking mechanism of this structure is its reporting system. Each manager gathers up the profit targets or other objectives of his or her subordinates and, with these, formulates his commitments to his boss; this boss takes these commitments and those of his other subordinates, and in turn makes a commitment to his boss. At the top of the line, the president of each company or division, or, at Images Inc., the senior vice-president for a group of accounts, makes his commitment to the CEO. This may be done directly, or sometimes, as at Weft Corporation, through a corporate executive vice-president. In any event, the commitments made to top management depend on the pyramid of stated objectives given to superiors up the line. At each level of the structure, there is typically "topside" pressure to achieve higher goals and, of course, the CEO frames and paces the whole process by applying pressure for attainment of his own objectives. Meanwhile, bosses and subordinates down the line engage in a series of intricate negotiations—managers often call these "conspiracies"—to keep their commitments respectable but achievable.

This "management-by-objective" system, as it is usually called, creates a chain of commitments from the CEO down to the lowliest product manager or account executive. In practice, it also shapes a patrimonial authority arrangement that is crucial to defining both the immediate experiences and the long-run career chances of individual managers. In this world, a subordinate owes fealty principally to his immediate boss. This means that a subordinate must not overcommit his boss, lest his boss "get on the hook" for promises that cannot be kept. He must keep his boss from making mistakes, particularly public ones; he must keep his boss informed, lest his boss get "blindsided." If one has a mistake-prone boss, there is, of course, always the temptation to let him make a fool of himself, but the wise subordinate knows that this carries two dangers—he himself may get done in by his boss's errors, and, perhaps more important, other managers will view with the gravest suspicion a subordinate who withholds crucial information from his boss even if they think the boss is a nincompoop. A subordinate must also not circumvent his boss nor ever give the appearance of doing so. He must never contradict his boss's judgment in public. To violate the last admonition is thought to constitute a kind of death wish in business, and one who does so should practice what one executive calls "flexibility drills," an exercise "where you put your head between your legs and kiss your ass goodbye." On a social level, even though an easy, breezy, first-name informality is the prevalent style of American business, a concession perhaps to our democratic heritage and egalitarian rhetoric, the subordinate must extend to the boss a certain ritual deference. For instance, he must follow the boss's lead in conversation, must not speak out of turn at meetings, must laugh at his boss's jokes while not making jokes of his own that upstage his boss, must not rib the boss for his foibles. The shrewd subordinate learns to efface himself, so that his boss's face might shine more clearly.

In short, the subordinate must symbolically reinforce at every turn his own subordination and his willing acceptance of the obligations of fealty. In return, he can hope for those perquisites that are in his boss's gift—the better, more attractive secretaries, or the nudging of a movable panel to enlarge his office, and perhaps a couch to fill the added space, one of the real distinctions in corporate bureaucracies. He can hope to be elevated when and if the boss is elevated, though other important criteria intervene here. He can also expect protection for mistakes made, up to a point. However, that point is never exactly defined and depends on the complicated politics of each situation. The general rule is that bosses are expected to protect those in their bailiwicks. Not to do so, or to be unable to do so, is taken as a sign of untrustworthiness or weakness. If, however, subordinates make mistakes that are thought to be dumb, or especially if they violate fealty obligations—for example, going around their boss—then abandonment of them to the vagaries of organizational forces is quite acceptable.

Overlaying and intertwined with this formal monocratic system of authority, with its patrimonial resonance, are patron-client relationships. Patrons are usually powerful figures in the higher echelons of management. The patron might be a manager's direct boss, or his boss's boss, or someone several levels higher in the chain of command. In either case, the manager is still bound by the immediate, formal authority and fealty patterns of his position but he also acquires new, though more ambiguous, fealty relationships with his highest ranking patron. Patrons play a crucial role in advancement, a point that I shall discuss later.

It is characteristic of this authority system that details are pushed down and credit is pulled up. Superiors do not like to give detailed instructions to subordinates. The official reason for this is to maximize subordinates' autonomy. The underlying reason is, first, to get rid of tedious details. Most hierarchically organized occupations follow this pattern; one of the privileges of authority is the divestment of humdrum intricacies. This also insulates higher bosses from the peculiar pressures that accompany managerial work at the middle levels and below: the lack of economy over one's time because of continual interruption from one's subordinates, telephone calls from customers and clients, and necessary meetings with colleagues; the piecemeal fragmentation of issues both because of the discontinuity of events and because of the way subordinates filter news; and the difficulty of minding the store while sorting out sometimes unpleasant personnel issues. Perhaps more important, pushing details down protects the privilege of authority to declare that a mistake has been made. A high-level executive in Alchemy Inc. explains:

> If I tell someone what to do—like do A, B, or C—the inference and implication is that he will succeed in accomplishing the objective. Now, if he doesn't succeed, that means that I have invested part of myself in his work and I lose any right I have to chew his ass out if he doesn't succeed. If I tell you what to do, I can't bawl you out if things don't work. And this is why a lot of bosses don't give explicit directions. They just give a statement of objectives, and then they can criticize subordinates who fail to make their goals.

Moreover, pushing down details relieves superiors of the burden of too much knowledge, particularly guilty knowledge. A superior will say to a subordinate, for instance: "Give me your best thinking on the problem with [X]." When the subordinate makes his report, he is often told: "I think you can do better than that," until the subordinate has worked out all the details of the boss's predetermined solution, without the boss being specifically aware of "all the eggs that have to be broken." It is also not at all uncommon for very bald and extremely general edicts to emerge from on high. For example, "Sell the plant in [St. Louis]; let me know when you've struck a deal," or "We need to get higher prices for [fabric X]; see what you can work out," or "Tom, I want you to go down there and meet with those guys and make a deal and I don't want you to come back until you've got one." This pushing down of details has important consequences.

First, because they are unfamiliar with—indeed deliberately distance themselves from—entangling details, corporate higher echelons tend to expect successful results without messy complications. This is central to top executives' well-known aversion to bad news and to the resulting tendency to kill the messenger who bears the news.

Second, the pushing down of details creates great pressure on middle managers not only to transmit good news but, precisely because they know the details, to act to protect their corporations, their bosses, and themselves in the process. They become the "point men" of a given strategy and the potential "fall guys" when things go wrong. From an organizational standpoint, overly conscientious managers are particularly useful at the middle levels of the structure. Upwardly mobile men and women, especially those from working-class origins who find themselves in higher status milieux, seem to have the requisite level of anxiety, and perhaps tightly controlled anger and hostility, that fuels an obsession with detail. Of course, such conscientiousness is not necessarily, and is certainly not systematically, rewarded; the real organizational premiums are placed on other, more flexible, behavior.

Credit flows up in this structure and is usually appropriated by the highest ranking officer involved in a successful decision or resolution of a problem. There is, for instance, a tremendous competition for ideas in the corporate world; authority provides a license to steal ideas, even in front of those who originated them. Chairmen routinely appropriate the useful suggestions made by members of their committees or task forces; research directors build their reputations for scientific wizardry on the bricks laid down by junior researchers and directors of departments. Presidents of whole divisions as well are always on the lookout for "fresh ideas" and "creative approaches" that they can claim as their own in order to put themselves "out in front" of their peers. A subordinate whose ideas are appropriated is expected to be a good sport about the matter; not to balk at so being used is one attribute of the good team player. The person who appropriates credit redistributes it as he chooses, bound essentially and only by a sensitivity to public perceptions of his fairness. One gives credit, therefore, not necessarily where it is due, although one always invokes this old saw, but where prudence dictates. Customarily, people who had nothing to do with the success of a project can be allocated credit for their exemplary efforts. At the middle levels, therefore, credit for a particular idea or success is always a type of refracted social honor; one cannot claim credit even if it is earned. Credit has to be given, and acceptance of the gift implicitly involves a reaffirmation and strengthening of fealty. A superior may share some credit with subordinates in order to deepen fealty relationships and induce greater efforts on his behalf. Of course, a different system obtains in the allocation of blame.

Because of the interlocking character of the commitment system, a CEO carries enormous influence in his corporation. If, for a moment, one thinks of the presidents of operating companies or divisions as barons, then the CEO of the corporation is the king. His word is law; even the CEO's wishes and whims are taken as commands by close subordinates on the corporate staff, who turn them into policies and directives. A typical example occurred in Weft Corporation a few years ago when the CEO, new at the time, expressed mild concern about the rising operating costs of the company's fleet of rented cars. The following day, a stringent system for monitoring mileage replaced the previous casual practice. Managers have a myriad of aphorisms that refer to how the power of CEOs, magnified through the zealous efforts of subordinates, affects them. These range from the trite "When he sneezes, we all catch colds" to the more colorful "When he says 'Go to the bathroom,' we all get the shits."

Great efforts are made to please the CEO. For example, when the CEO of Covenant Corporation visits a plant, the most significant or-der of business for local management is a fresh paint job, even when, as in several cases, the cost of paint alone exceeds $100,000. If a paint job has already been scheduled at a plant, it is deferred along with all other cosmetic maintenance until just before the CEO arrives; keeping up appearances without recognition for one's efforts is pointless. I am told that similar anecdotes from other corporations have been in circulation since 1910, which suggests a certain historical continuity of behavior toward top bosses.

The second order of business for the plant management is to produce a book fully describing the plant and its operations, replete with photographs and illustrations, for presentation to the CEO; such a book costs about $10,000 for the single copy. By any standards of budgetary stringency, such expenditures are irrational. But by the social standards of the corporation, they make perfect sense. It is far more important to please the king today than to worry about the future economic state of one's fief, since, if one does not please the king, there may not be a fief to worry about or indeed vassals to do the worrying.

By the same token, all of this leads to an intense interest in everything the CEO does and says. In all the companies that I studied, the most common topic of conversation among managers up and down the line is speculation about their respective CEO's plans, intentions, strategies, actions, style, public image, and ideological leanings of the moment. Even the metaphorical temper of a CEO's language finds its way down the hierarchy to the lower reaches of an organization. In the early stages of my fieldwork at Covenant Corporation, for example, I was puzzled by the inordinately widespread usage of nautical terminology, especially in a corporation located in a landlocked site. As it happens, the CEO is devoted to sailboats and prefers that his aides call him "Skipper." Moreover, in every corporation that I studied, stories and rumors circulate constantly about the social world of the CEO and his immediate subordinates—who, for instance, seems to have the CEO's ear at the moment; whose style seems to have gained approbation; who, in short, seems to be in the CEO's grace and who seems to have fallen out of favor. In the smaller and more intimate setting of Images Inc., the circulation of favor takes an interesting, if unusual, tack. There, the CEO is known for attaching younger people to himself as confidants. He solicits their advice, tells them secrets, gets their assessments of developments further down in the hierarchy, gleans the rumors and gossip making the rounds about himself. For the younger people selected for such attention, this is a rare, if fleeting, opportunity to have a place in the sun and to share the illusion if not the substance of power. In time, of course, the CEO tires of or becomes disappointed with particular individuals and turns his attention to others. "Being discarded," however, is not an obstacle to regaining favor. In larger organizations, impermeable structural barriers between top circles and junior people prevent this kind of intimate interchange and circulation of authoritative regard. Within a CEO's circle, however, the same currying and granting of favor prevails, always amidst conjectures from below about who has edged close to the throne.

But such speculation about the CEO and his leanings of the moment is more than idle gossip, and the courtlike atmosphere that I am describing more than stylized diversion. Because he stands at the apex of the corporation's bureaucratic and patrimonial structures and locks the intricate system of commitments between bosses and subordinates into place, it is the CEO who ultimately decides whether those commitments have been satisfactorily met. The CEO becomes the actual and the symbolic keystone of the hierarchy that constitutes the defining point of the managerial experience. Moreover, the CEO and his trusted associates determine the fate of whole business areas of a corporation.

Within the general ambiance established by a CEO, presidents of individual operating companies or of divisions carry similar, though correspondingly reduced, influence within their own baronies. Adroit and well-placed subordinates can, for instance, borrow a president's prestige and power to exert great leverage. Even chance encounters or the occasional meeting or lunch with the president can, if advertised casually and subtly, cause notice and the respect among other managers that comes from uncertainty. Knowledge of more clearly established relationships, of course, always sways behavior. A middle manager in one company, widely known to be a very close personal friend of the president, flagged her copious memoranda to other managers with large green paperclips, ensuring prompt attention to her requests. More generally, each major division of the core textile group in Weft Corporation is widely thought to reflect the personality of its leader—one hard-driving, intense, and openly competitive; one cool, precise, urbane, and proper; and one gregarious, talkative, and self-promotional. Actually, market exigencies play a large role in shaping each division's tone and tempo. Still, the popular conception of the dominance of presidential personalities not only points to the crucial issue of style in business, a topic to be explored in depth later, but it underlines the general tendency to personalize authority in corporate bureaucracies.

Managers draw elaborate cognitive maps to guide them through the thickets of their organizations. Because they see and experience authority in such personal terms, the singular feature of these maps is their biographical emphasis. Managers carry around in their heads thumbnail sketches of the occupational history of virtually every other manager of their own rank or higher in their particular organization. These maps begin with a knowledge of others' occupational expertise and specific work experience, but focus especially on previous and present reporting relationships, patronage relationships, and alliances. Cognitive maps incorporate memories of social slights, of public embarrassments, of battles won and lost, and of people's behavior under pressure. They include as well general estimates of the abilities and career trajectories of their colleagues. I should mention that these latter estimates are not necessarily accurate or fair; they are, in fact, often based on the flimsiest of evidence. For instance, a general manager at Alchemy Inc. describes the ephemeral nature of such opinions:

> It's a feeling about the guy's perceived ability to run a business—like he's not a good people man, or he's not a good numbers man. This is not a quantitative thing. It's a gut feeling that a guy can't be put in one spot, but he might be put in another spot. These kinds of informal opinions about others are the lifeblood of an organization's advancement system. Oh, for the record, we've got the formal evaluations; but the real opinions—the ones that really count in determining people's fates—are those which are traded back and forth in meetings, private conferences, chance encounters, and so on.

Managers trade estimates of others' chances within their circles and often color them to suit their own purposes. This is one reason why it is crucial for the aspiring young manager to project the right image to the right people who can influence others' sketches of him. Whatever the accuracy of these vocabularies of description, managers' penchant for biographical detail and personal histories contrasts sharply with their disinclination for details in general or for other kinds of history. Details, as I have mentioned, get pushed down the ladder; and a concern with history, even of the short-run, let alone long-term, structural shifts in one's own organization, constrains the forward orientation and cheerful optimism highly valued in most corporations. Biographical detail, however, constitutes crucial knowledge because managers know that, in the rough-and-tumble politics of the corporate world, individual fates are made and broken not necessarily by one's accomplishments but by other people. . . .

II

. . . Here I want to highlight a few basic structures and experiences of managerial work, those that seem to form its essential framework. First of all, at the psychological level, managers have an acute sense of organizational contingency. Because of the interlocking ties between people, they know that a shake-up at or near the top of a hierarchy can trigger a widespread upheaval, bringing in its wake startling reversals of fortune, good and bad, throughout the structure. Managers' cryptic aphorism, "Well, you never know . . . ," repeated often and regularly, captures the sense of uncertainty created by the constant potential for social reversal. Managers know too, and take for granted, that the personnel changes brought about by upheavals are to a great extent arbitrary and depend more than anything else on one's social relationships with key individuals and with groups of managers. Periods of organizational quiescence and stability still managers' wariness in this regard, but the foreboding sense of contingency never entirely disappears. Managers' awareness of the complex levels of conflict in their world, built into the very structure of bureaucratic organizations, constantly reminds them that things can very quickly fall apart.

The political struggles at Covenant Corporation, for instance, suggest some immediately observable levels of conflict and tension.

First, occupational groups emerging from the segmented structure of bureaucratic work, each with different expertise and emphasis, constantly vie with one another for ascendancy of their ideas, of their products or services, and of themselves. It is, for instance, an axiom of corporate life that the greatest satisfaction of production people is to see products go out the door; of salesmen, to make a deal regardless of price; of marketers, to control salesmen and squeeze profits out of their deals; and of financial specialists, to make sure that everybody meets budget. Despite the larger interdependence of such work, the necessarily fragmented functions performed day-to-day by managers in one area often put them at cross purposes with managers in another. Nor do competitiveness and conflict result only from the broad segmentation of functions. Sustained work in a product or service area not only shapes crucial social affiliations but also symbolic identifications, say, with particular products or technical services, that mark managers in their corporate arenas. Such symbolic markings make it imperative for managers to push their particular products or services as part of their overall self-promotion. This fuels the constant scramble for authoritative enthusiasm for one product or service rather than another and the subsequent allocation or re-allocation of organizational resources.

Second, line and staff managers, each group with different responsibilities, different pressures, and different bailiwicks to protect, fight over organizational resources and over the rules that govern work. The very definition of staff depends entirely on one's vantage point in the organization. As one manager points out: "From the perspective of the guy who actually pushes the button to make the machine go, everyone else is staff." However, the working definition that managers use is that anyone whose decisions directly affect profit and loss is in the line; all others in an advisory capacity of some sort are staff. As a general rule, line managers' attitudes toward staff vary directly with the independence granted staff by higher management. The more freedom staff have to intervene in the line, as with the environmental staff at Alchemy or Covenant's corporate staff, the more they are feared and resented by line management. For line managers, independent staff represent either the intrusion of an unwelcome "rules and procedures mentality" into situations where line managers feel that they have to be alert to the exigencies of the market or, alternatively, as power threats to vested interests backed by some authority. In the "decentralized" organizations prevalent today in the corporate world, however, most staff are entirely dependent on the line and must market their technical, legal, or organizational skills to line managers exactly as an outside firm must do. The continual necessity for staff to sell their technical expertise helps keep them in check since line managers, pleading budgetary stringency or any number of other acceptable rationales, can thwart or ignore proffered assistance. Staff's dependent position often produces jealous respect for line management tinged with the resentment that talented people relegated to do "pine time" (sit on the bench) feel for those in the center of action. For instance, an environmental manager at Weft Corporation comments on his marginal status and on how he sees it depriving him of the recognition he feels his work deserves:

> I also want recognition. And usually the only way you get that is having a boss near you who sees what you do. It rubs me raw in fact. . . . For instance, you know they run these news releases when some corporate guy gets promoted and all? Well, when I do something, nothing

ever gets said. When I publish papers, or get promoted, and so on, you never see any public announcement. Oh, they like me to publish papers and I guess someone reads them, but that's all that's ever said or done. . . . I can get recognition in a variety of arenas, like professional associations, but if they're going to recognize the plant manager, why not me? If we walked off, would the plants operate? They couldn't. We're *essential.*

This kind of ambivalent resentment sometimes becomes vindictiveness when a top boss uses staff as a hammer.

Staff can also become effective pitchmen; line managers' anxious search for rational solutions to largely irrational problems, in fact, encourages staff continually to invent and disseminate new tactics and schemes. Alternatively, social upheavals that produce rapid shifts in public opinion—such as occurred in the personnel or environmental areas in the aftermath of the 1960s—may encourage proliferation of staff. In either circumstance, staff tend to increase in an organization until an ideological cycle of "organizational leanness" comes around and staff, at least those of lower rank, get decimated.

Third, powerful managers in Alchemy Inc., each controlling considerable resources and the organizational fates of many men and women, battle fiercely with one another to position themselves, their products, and their allies favorably in the eyes of their president and of the CEO. At the same time, high-ranking executives "go to the mat" with one another striving for the CEO's approval and a coveted shot at the top. Bureaucratic hierarchies, simply by offering ascertainable rewards for certain behavior, fuel the ambition of those men and women ready to subject themselves to the discipline of external exigencies and of their organization's institutional logic, the socially constructed, shared understanding of how their world works.

However, since rewards are always scarce, bureaucracies necessarily pit people against each other and inevitably thwart the ambitions of some. The rules of such combat vary from organization to organization and depend largely on what top management countenances either openly or tacitly.

Nor are formal positions and perquisites the only objects of personal struggle between managers. Even more important on a day-to-day basis is the ongoing competition between talented and aggressive people to see whose will prevails, who can get things done their way. The two areas are, of course, related since one's chances in an organization depend largely on one's "credibility," that is, on the widespread belief that one can act effectively. One must therefore prevail regularly, though not always, in small things to have any hope of positioning oneself for big issues. The hidden agenda of seemingly petty disputes may be a struggle over long-term organizational fates.

At the same time, all of these struggles take place within the peculiar tempo and framework each CEO establishes for an organization. Under an ideology of thorough decentralization—the gift of authority with responsibility—the CEO at Covenant actually centralizes his power enormously because fear of derailing personal ambitions prevents managers below him from acting without his approval. A top official at Alchemy comments:

What we have now, despite rhetoric to the contrary, is a very centralized system. It's [the CEO] who sets the style, tone, tempo of all the companies. He says: "Manage for cash," and we manage for cash. The original idea . . . was to set up free-standing companies with a minimum of corporate staff. But . . . we're moving toward a system that is really beyond what we used to have, let alone modeled on a small corporate staff and autonomous divisions. What we used to have was separate divisions reporting to a corporate staff. I think we're moving away from that idea too. I think what's coming is a bunch of separate businesses reporting to the corporation. It's a kind of portfolio management. This accords perfectly with [the CEO's] temperament. He's a financial type guy who is oriented to the bottom line numbers. He doesn't want or need intermediaries between him and his businesses.

In effect, the CEO of Covenant, who seems to enjoy constant turmoil, pits himself and his ego against the whole corporation even while he holds it in vassalage. Other CEOs establish different frameworks and different tempos, depending on self-image and temperament. The only firm rule seems to be that articulated by a middle-level Covenant manager: "Every big organization is set up for the benefit of those who control it; the boss gets what he wants."

Except during times of upheaval, the ongoing conflicts that I have described are usually hidden behind the comfortable and benign social ambiance that most American corporations fashion for their white-collar personnel. Plush carpets, potted trees, burnished oak wall paneling, fine reproductions and sometimes originals of great art, mahogany desks, polished glass tables and ornaments, rich leather upholstery, perfectly coiffured, attractive and poised receptionists, and private, subsidized cafeterias are only a few of the pleasant features that grace the corporate headquarters of any major company. In addition, the corporations that I studied provide their employees with an amazing range and variety of services, information, and social contacts. Covenant Corporation, for instance, through its daily newsletter and a variety of other internal media, offers information about domestic and international vacation packages; free

travelers' checks; discounted tickets for the ballet, tennis matches, or art exhibits; home remedies for the common cold, traveling clinics for diagnosing high blood pressure, and advice on how to save one's sight; simple tests for gauging automotive driving habits; tips on home vegetable gardening; advice on baby-sitters; descriptions of business courses at a local college; warning articles on open fireplaces and home security; and directions for income tax filing. The newsletter also offers an internal market for the sale, rental, or exchange of a myriad of items ranging from a Jamaican villa, to a set of barbells, to back issues of *Fantasy* magazine. Covenant offers as well intracompany trapshooting contests, round-robin tennis and golf tournaments, running clinics, and executive fitness programs. Weft Corporation's bulletin is even more elaborate, with photographic features on the "Great Faces" of Weft employees; regular reports on the company's 25- and 50-year clubs; personal notes on all retirees from the company; stories about the company's sponsorship of art exhibits; human-interest stories about employees and their families—from a child struggling against liver cancer to the heroics of a Weft employee in foiling a plane hijacker; and, of course, a steady drumbeat of corporate ideology about the necessity for textile import quotas and the desirability of "buying American."

My point here is that corporations are not presented nor are they seen simply as places to work for a living. Rather, the men and women in them come to fashion an entire social ambiance that overlays the antagonisms created by company politics; this makes the nuances of corporate conflict difficult to discern. A few managers, in fact, mistake the first-name informality, the social congeniality, and the plush exterior appointments for the entire reality of their collective life and are surprised when hard structural jolts turn their world upside down. Even battle-scarred veterans evince, at times, an ambivalent half-belief in the litany of rhetorics of unity and cohesive legitimating appeals. The latter are sometimes accompanied by gala events to underline the appeal. For instance, not long after the "big purge" at Covenant Corporation when 600 people were fired, the CEO spent $1 million for a "Family Day" to "bring everyone together." The massive party was attended by over 14,000 people and featured clowns, sports idols, and booths complete with bean bag and ring tosses, foot and bus races, computer games, dice rolls, and, perhaps appropriately, mazes. In his letter to his "Fellow Employees" following the event, the CEO said:

> I think Family Day made a very strong statement about the [Covenant] "family" of employees at [Corporate Headquarters]. And that is that we can accomplish whatever we set out to do if we work together; if we share the effort, we will share the rewards. The "New World of [Covenant]" has no boundaries only frontiers, and each and everyone can play a role, for we need what *you* have to contribute.

The very necessity for active involvement in such rituals often prompts semicredulity. But wise and ambitious managers resist the lulling platitudes of unity, though they invoke them with fervor, and look for the inevitable clash of interests beneath the bouncy, cheerful surface of corporate life. They understand implicitly that the suppression of open conflict simply puts a premium on the mastery of the socially accepted modes of waging combat.

The continuous uncertainty and ambiguity of managerial hierarchies, exacerbated over time by masked conflict, causes managers to turn toward each other for cues for behavior. They try to learn from each other and to master the shared assumptions, the complex rules, the normative codes, the underlying institutional logic that governs their world. They thus try to control the construction of their everyday reality. Normally, of course, one learns to master the managerial code in the course of repeated, long-term social interaction with other managers, particularly in the course of shaping the multiple and complex alliances essential to organizational survival and success.

Alliances are ties of quasiprimal loyalty shaped especially by common work, by common experiences with the same problems, the same friends, or the same enemies, and by favors traded over time. Although alliances are rooted in fealty and patronage relationships, they are not limited by such relationships since fealty shifts with changing work assignments or with organizational upheavals.

Making an alliance may mean, for instance, joining or, more exactly, being included in one or several of the many networks of managerial associates that crisscross an organization. Conceptually, networks are usually thought of as open-ended webs of association with a low degree of formal organization and no distinct criteria of membership. One becomes known, for instance, as a trusted friend of a friend; thought of as a person to whom one can safely refer a thorny problem; considered a "sensible" or "reasonable" or, especially, a "flexible" person, not a "renegade" or a "loose cannon rolling around the lawn"; known to be a discreet person attuned to the nuances of corporate etiquette, one who can keep one's mouth shut or who can look away and pretend to notice nothing; or considered a person with sharp ideas that break deadlocks but who does not object to the ideas being appropriated by superiors.

Alliances are also fashioned in social coteries. These are more clublike groups of friends that, in Weft Corporation, forge ties at the cocktail hour over the back fence on Racquet Drive, the road next to the company's tennis courts where all important and socially ambitious executives live; or in Friday night poker sessions that provide a bluff and hearty setting where managers can display their own and unobtrusively observe others' mastery of public faces, a clue to many managerial virtues. In other companies, coteries consist of "tennis pals" who share an easy camaraderie over salad and yogurt lunches following hard squash games or two-mile jogs at noon. They are also made up of posthours cronies who, in midtown watering holes, weld private understandings with ironic bantering, broad satire, or macabre humor, the closest some managers ever get to open discussion of their work with their fellows; or gatherings of the smart social set where business circles intersect with cliques from intellectual and artistic worlds and where glittering, poised, and precisely vacuous social conversation can mark one as a social lion. In one company, a group of "buddies" intertwine their private lives with their organizational fates in the most complete way by, for example, persuading an ambitious younger colleague to provide a woodsy cabin retreat and local girls for a collegial evening's entertainment while on a business trip. At the managerial and professional levels, the road between work and life is usually open because it is difficult to refuse to use one's influence, patronage, or power on behalf of another regular member of one's social coterie. It therefore becomes important to choose one's social colleagues with some care and, of course, know how to drop them should they fall out of organizational favor.

Alliances are also made wholly on the basis of specific self-interests. The paradigmatic case here is that of the power clique of established, well-placed managers who put aside differences and join forces for a "higher cause," namely, their own advancement or protection. Normally, though not always, as Brown's case at Covenant shows, one must be "plugged into" important networks and an active participant in key coteries in order to have achieved an organizational position where one's influence is actively counted. But the authority and power of a position matter in and of themselves. Once one has gained power, one can use one's influence in the organization to shape social ties. Such alliances often cut across rival networks and coteries and can, in fact, temporarily unite them. Managers in a power clique map out desired organizational tacks and trade off the resources in their control. They assess the strengths and weaknesses of their opponents; they plan coups and rehearse the appropriate rationales to legitimate them. And, on the other hand, they erect requisite barriers to squelch attempted usurpations of their power. Cliques also introduce managers to new, somewhat more exclusive networks and coteries. Especially at the top of a pyramid, these social ties extend over the boundaries of one's own corporation and mesh one's work and life with those of top managers in other organizations.

I shall refer to all the social contexts that breed alliances, fealty relationships, networks, coteries, or cliques, as circles of affiliation, or simply managerial circles. Now, the notion of "circles," as it has been used in sociological literature as well as colloquially, has some drawbacks for accurately delineating the important features of the web of managerial interaction. Specifically, a circle suggests a quasiclosed social group made up of members of relatively equal status without defined leadership and without formal criteria for membership or inclusion. In a bureaucratic hierarchy, nuances of status are, of course, extremely important. Moreover, since business cannot be conducted without formal authorization by appropriate authorities, one's formal rank always matters even though there is ample scope for more informal charismatic leadership. Finally, the most crucial feature of managerial circles of affiliation is precisely their establishment of informal criteria for admission, criteria that are, it is true, ambiguously defined and subject to constant, often arbitrary, revision. Nonetheless, they are criteria that managers must master. At bottom, all of the social contexts of the managerial world seek to discover if one "can feel comfortable" with another manager, if he is someone who "can be trusted," if he is "our kind of guy," or, in short, if he is "one of the gang." The notion of gang, in fact, insofar as it suggests the importance of leadership, hierarchy, and probationary mechanisms in a bounded but somewhat amorphous group, may more accurately describe relationships in the corporation than the more genteel, and therefore preferable, word "circle." In any event, just as managers must continually please their boss, their boss's boss, their patrons, their president, and their CEO, so must they prove themselves again and again to each other. Work becomes an endless round of what might be called probationary crucibles. Together with the uncertainty and sense of contingency that mark managerial work, this constant state of probation produces a profound anxiety in managers, perhaps the key experience of managerial work. It also breeds, selects, or elicits certain traits in ambitious managers that are crucial to getting ahead.

34

Black Corporate Executives

Sharon M. Collins

Tracking African American managers into racialized jobs was a strategy white companies developed during the 1960s and 1970s, when these executives' value became tinged with race-conscious political purposes. For example, ten of seventeen managers (59 percent) that I interviewed, all with highly technical skills as accountants, engineers, chemists, and so on, were asked to fill such jobs. Twenty-two of the forty-five people (49 percent) in my interview group who became affirmative-action and urban affairs managers started in line areas but were recruited for racialized jobs, twelve of them (55 percent) by senior level white management, usually either senior vice-presidents or chief executive officers. Nine (41 percent) turned down the first offer and were approached a second time by top management. Eleven (50 percent) were given salary increases, more prestigious job titles, and promises of future rewards. The push in companies to fill new administrative roles in employment and social policy areas cut across both personal preference and previous work experience. A midlevel manager in his forties comments: "It was during the early 1970s, and there weren't very many people around that could do anything for minorities. . . . I mean, . . . all the companies were really scrambling. All you saw was minorities functioning in [affirmative action and urban affairs] and it doesn't take much brain power to figure out that that's where

Excerpts from *Black Corporate Executives: The Making and Breaking of a Black Middle Class* by Sharon M. Collins. Copyright © 1997 by Temple University. All rights reserved. Reprinted with permission of Temple University Press.

most of us were going to end up." A white senior vice-president of human resources noted that top management deployed people from line jobs into affirmative-action jobs to signal the rank and file that the company was serious in its commitment. Transferring an experienced line manager into affirmative action increased the credibility of a collateral role and enhanced its effectiveness. From one perspective it would seem that employers either ignored these executives' education and experience or used it against them.

These executives are among those who rose to the top by managing affirmative-action, urban affairs, manpower-training, and technical assistance programs. Twenty-six of the seventy-six black managers I interviewed spent their entire careers in racialized jobs outside the corporate mainstream. Another twenty-five held one or more racialized jobs but eventually moved permanently into the mainstream. Only twenty-five had careers made up only of white corporate mainstream jobs.

This high concentration in racialized jobs is consistent with the notion of a politically mediated black middle class. It indicates the nature of pressures on corporations and shows the incentives for getting blacks into these areas. Conversely, this high concentration calls into question notions of a color-blind allocation of labor and of a color-blind market demand.

To obtain a rough comparative measure, I conducted an informal survey of top white executives by asking twenty CEOs of major Chicago companies if they ever held affirmative-action or urban affairs jobs. (I asked about these jobs specifically because they typify racialized jobs.) Some seemed startled by the question, and only one reported having worked in either area, a CEO whose tasks in urban affairs fell in a different category from those performed by my black interviewees. Although this man represented

the company on several citywide committees to improve race relations, his job, unlike the black executives I interviewed, was a part-time and temporary assignment, not a full-time and permanent position. The results of my informal survey suggested that among the managerial elite in Chicago, blacks are likely to have held racialized jobs, but whites are not. Moreover, just 5.9 percent of 698 respondents to Korn/Ferry's (1986) survey of corporate vice-presidents, senior vice-presidents, executive vice-presidents, chief financial officers, and group vice-presidents held positions in personnel or public relations departments, where companies tend to house affirmative-action and urban affairs jobs. More typically, the track to top jobs in companies includes profit-oriented positions such as sales, operations, and, more recently, finance (Korn/Ferry 1990).

African Americans in Mainstream Careers

Mainstream careers are grounded entirely in jobs with goals oriented to general (i.e., predominantly white) constituencies, not jobs produced in response to black protest and subsequent social policy. The career of a forty-year-old vice-president and regional sales manager for a Fortune 500 company in the manufacturing and retail food industry illustrates a mainstream work history. The executive holds a two-year college degree in natural sciences. When he entered the private sector in 1960 as a market researcher for a Fortune 500 East Coast oil company, his job involved marketing to the total (predominantly white) consumer market, not to "special" (predominantly black) markets. In 1968, he accepted a position as a salesman with his current employer, and, even in the midst of the civil rights era, he was never assigned to a black territory. He moved up through the sales hierarchy from salesman to sales manager, zone manager, district manager, area manager, division manager, and, eventually, to his present job in the company. Throughout his ascent, he was never responsible for a predominantly black sales force or for strategic marketing to the black community when he managed geographical areas. His current employer once offered him an affirmative-action job in personnel, but he declined the offer because of negative experiences in a similar, but unpaid, role thrust upon him by his first employer. Moreover, he perceived affirmative-action jobs as lacking power in the company.

Another illustration of a mainstream career executive is a highly recruited woman with an MBA from the University of Chicago who was a vice-president of investor relations. She entered the white private sector in 1968 and worked her way up in banking through a series of financial assignments. In 1984, she was recruited for an assistant vice-president and director's position with a leading food manufacturer in Chicago where, she said, she "could be a part of the management team." In 1985, she again was recruited, this time by her final employer in the private sector, and became a full vice-president and company officer. By 1993, she had left there to start her own business. This woman was never asked to implement, nor did she ever manage, programs related to blacks. (I asked, for instance, if she had participated in any bank program designed to give financial advice to black organizations, if she had ever consulted primarily with black consumers or investors, or if she had administered any Small Business Administration minority business start-up programs sponsored by the bank during her tenure.)

Mainstream executive careers represent the affirmative-action ideal, as opportunities for talented blacks to compete for power and prestige in business bureaucracies. Yet mainstream African American executives stand out as the exceptions. How were they able to avoid racialized assignments? One explanation is that their employers viewed them as too well trained to shift out of the mainstream. The banking executive's MBA from a prestigious school undoubtedly made her a unique commodity in 1968 relative to other black job candidates. Yet level of education has not proven a good predictor of career track. Executives I interviewed at each level—bachelor's, master's, and doctoral—had at least a fifty-fifty chance of getting a racialized job.

Another possible scenario is that companies filled affirmative-action and urban affairs jobs on an ad hoc basis. That is, when the need to develop programs arose, a company first looked in-house for black candidates to fill those positions. Conversely, if racialized jobs were already filled, mainstream people were more likely to stay mainstream. Each of the three firms the MBA worked in had affirmative-action and urban affairs programs in place when she came on board. Ten of twenty-five in mainstream competition also reported such programs in place when they were hired. In addition, the vice-president and regional sales manager offered his opinion that no pressure was exerted on him to manage affirmative action because another black professional in the company subsequently agreed to take the offer.

However, blacks' ability to move up in the mainstream of a company did not mean their careers evolved free of the influences of job discrimination (see Fernandez 1981; Jones 1986). Nevertheless, these two African American executives and others who built mainstream careers were extremely successful relative to most African Americans (and most whites). Both the MBA and the vice-president and regional sales manager made six-figure salaries. Both were officers in their respective companies in the 1980s.

The African American Mobility Trap

Most of the executives I interviewed (51 of 76) moved into and stayed in, or moved through, racialized jobs that also created barriers to corporate mobility. For example, a 46-year-old man who I'll refer to as the frustrated manager was initially hired by a major steel company in the 1960s for a job administering a federally funded in-house program for disadvantaged youth. Funded by the U.S. Department of Labor, the program was designed to train, or retrain, predominantly black Chicago youth in skills that would qualify them to work in Chicago's white private sector. The frustrated manager, who was a social worker employed by the city of Chicago before he was hired by the steel company, said the company identified him as a candidate for this position through his work with inner-city youth and gang members. He recalled being told during the initial interview with the personnel manager that his active ties to Chicago's inner-city youth, and the implication these ties had for program development, was a key reason the company was interested in hiring him. His response: "I told [the personnel manager] that I don't want a nigger job and I don't want to be dead ended. That's the job I didn't take. But I saw some value in the manpower training because it was an inroad for minorities and females."

The frustrated manager defined a "nigger job" as corporate "positions preidentified for blacks only. Those jobs have high-ranking titles and are highly visible but do not have any power in a company. Those jobs are not with the mainstream of [a] company [so they] would [not] turn into any kind of career with the company. [In contrast] real jobs [were positions by which] good performers could rise [in a company]." In other words, people in "real jobs," but not "nigger jobs," performed valued corporate

functions and were thereby able to move up the corporate ladder. This man seemed to be ambitious and intense; he punctuated his recollections about his job interview by pounding his fist on the boardroom table. He recounted his career with pride in his voice, but also a hint of ambivalence about how far he had been able to go. He believed that because manpower-training programs served the disadvantaged (i.e., black) population, they created a need for skilled black labor, which gave him a chance to move into the white private sector in an administrative slot and to develop, he said, a "different kind of work experience." But, although he was interested in the job, he negotiated, he said, "up front so that [the company] would not dead end" him. He did not want this to be one of those "jobs in companies [where blacks are left] to die on the vine."

He also observed that corporate jobs administering manpower-training programs, which sprang up in the wake of urban riots, were similar to the training programs themselves: Both were vehicles corporations used to bring blacks into the private work force. However, he took the job because he perceived it not as a dead-end position but as a valid step on a career path leading to personnel director. He aspired to a career in personnel over other functions such as production, because he believed that "black people [at that time] had no involvement in managing [other] parts of a corporation." He also said, "I'm a people person and I knew I wanted to be a director of personnel. This was a way to get there, [and] that was agreed upon in that interview with [the personnel manager]."

It is doubtful the personnel director of the steel company in this case seriously viewed the manpower-training job as a route to a director of personnel job. Although the company explicitly recruited this manager because of his networks in the black community, implicitly management may have chosen him because they needed to hire a black person. The company was based in a riot-torn community, and the manpower-training program was part of an effort to improve the company's poor record of employment and training of African Americans. According to this man the company at the time employed only one other black professional. Apparently no one on board would, or in the company's judgment could, fill the position of manpower program director.

After the frustrated manager had the manpower-training program for two years, "very successfully," the company created a job for him as a community relations representative, part of a move "to institutionalize the [minority] manpower-training program within the organization" after federal funding ended. Two and a half years later, he moved into a second newly created job, community relations director, a promotion in both title and salary. Still proudly, he attributed his career mobility to his success in employing residents from the surrounding black community.

Although, according to the frustrated manager, the company was willing to promote him and increase his salary because he was meeting a need, his promotion did not move him into a mainstream personnel career. When asked what his last promotion meant in light of his original career goals, he admitted he was aware, even then, that his future in the company might be limited. "You have a little stepladder . . . a logical progression [of positions] you have to go through if you are to ever become a personnel director. I wasn't doing any of that. As far as I could see, the company wanted black folks to be my only responsibility." The manager reminded his superiors that his career goals lay elsewhere, but he was not deployed into mainstream personnel. He therefore viewed his movement within the company as promotions "in place," evidence that he "was not re-ally experiencing mobility in [the corporate] structure." He also believed his ability to accomplish the job he was in was limited because of conflicts with the personnel director. He said, "My problem [in developing a good minority recruitment program] was not one of identifying qualified minorities, but of stopping discrimination among those with authority." An important part of his job, he pointed out, was to identify, and attempt to correct, irregular hiring patterns for which the regional director of personnel was ultimately responsible. "[Whites] were hired . . . who did not have high school diplomas, who could not speak English [and] could not pass any of those battery of tests that they give to the blacks or the women." When the program to improve minority hiring "worked out well, [the director of personnel] was the person who was embarrassed. He was the person who was made to change."

Believing his in-house options were limited, the frustrated manager volunteered to be a loaned executive on a citywide corporate project engaged in community and economic development. He felt this route "represented more training and [potential] mobility." In the early 1970s, after leading seminars on community relations for the steel company, he was courted for a personnel job in ten other companies. He decided to start over with a new computer firm and try, once again, for a director position. Yet, ironically, "community work" was involved even in his subsequent jobs in the computer field because those companies also were "not doing well in the recruitment of minorities."

I was unable to reinterview this man in 1992. However, the person who originally referred him to me reported that he had been transferred to California, was "still doing community affairs, and was ready for an early retirement." Secondhand reports are often suspect, but the two are friends, work for the same company, and talk with one another often. Our mutual acquaintance also said that their recent conversations about their current careers increasingly focus on personal disappointment and missed opportunities.

The frustrated manager, like one-third of the executives I interviewed, gained status in the private sector by filling corporate positions linked to black constituencies. At the same time, filling race-based roles effectively locked him out of conventional routes up the corporate ladder. Several facets of his career in the steel company converged to keep him out of the mainstream. First, he performed well in a position that, at that time, was valued in the company. Top management rewarded him with higher salaries and kept him assigned to that area. Consequently, he was excluded from experiences that would broaden his mastery of more generalized personnel functions. The lack of generalized experiences further undermined the legitimacy of his claims for promotion to a mainstream personnel job. Moreover, when he identified hiring biases in the company, intentionally or not, he criticized and alienated an important potential mentor, the regional personnel director. Finally, if he habitually used the word "nigger" in a conservative corporate environment it may have further minimized his chances for promotion. The provocative nature of that racial epithet could cause his image in the company to suffer and increase his chances of being left behind. He used the word often during our interview, and I wondered at the time if he used it with the personnel director.

Career-Enhancing Strategies

During the 1960s and 1970s, the executives studied here either began their careers in mainstream jobs or wanted to exchange racialized jobs for mainstream assignments. About half who wanted to move into the mainstream (25 of 51) achieved their goal. By 1986, executives who had left racialized areas

had been out about nine years on average. They were distinguished from those who remained in racialized jobs by falling into one of two categories. One group was able to decipher the rules of the game by seeking mentors and other sources of information about meaningful career routes. They used that knowledge to generate career-enhancing moves, which included requesting alternative assignments. In the second category are workers for whom racialized jobs inadvertently became a career springboard toward solid—mainstream—ground.

Reading the System

Fourteen of the twenty-five who escaped the racialized sphere during the 1960s and 1970s simply asked to be reassigned. In contrast, only seven of the twenty-six who stayed in racialized jobs during this time asked to be reassigned. Virtually all who requested reassignment perceived both the trend in corporations to have black managers fill affirmative-action and urban affairs jobs and their potential to limit opportunities in the long run of corporate life. The group's collective consciousness is summed up in an observation about people who turn [down] this type of job, made by a vice-president at a major electronics firm. This man started one affirmative-action program for a company and turned down several similar job offers from other companies. Referring to his stint in affirmative action, he said: "They would send me to some of these conferences [and] . . . you'd walk in and there would be a room full of blacks. . . . And I met titles, . . . directors and you name it, of equal employment opportunity. It was a terrible misuse at that time of some black talent. There were some black people in those jobs that were rather skilled, much like myself."

He recognized such job ghettoization as a race-related mobility trap for black managers. "During the 1960s and 1970s blacks in these jobs had fancy titles, but basically they were in dead-end positions," he said. Black executives approached to take such jobs faced a career dilemma. They believed they had to be committed team players to get ahead in the company, and at the same time they feared that if they succeeded in affirmative action or urban affairs, top management might never transfer them.

A forty-six-year-old sales vice-president expressed the first side of the dilemma when he explained, "In this company you don't turn down requests when they come from a senior vice-president, and especially when they look like a promotion." When he was asked to fill affirmative-action positions, however, he said he also "just wanted it to be up front" that he "didn't intend to keep that job forever," that he thought it necessary to set time limits on his transfer. Expressing the second side of the dilemma, he said, "You can do those [affirmative-action] jobs too well [or top management feels] . . . this is where you need to be." The sales vice-president mentioned earlier concurred with this observation. "All we had to do was to look at blacks around us to come to that conclusion."

Although they risked appearing recalcitrant, managers headed for mainstream careers stipulated time limits when taking racialized jobs and, once in these jobs, assertively requested reassignment. Many were eventually mainstreamed. The sales vice-president, for instance, transferred into an affirmative-action job from floor sales, but also set the stage for his mainstream reentry by negotiating a one-year limit on this placement before accepting the position. The company honored its promise and moved him out of affirmative action and into a buyer's position.

A current vice-president of human resources for a clothing manufacturer also requested a transfer from affirmative action because he recognized the limits of the job. This man transferred into affirmative action in 1967 when he worked for a federal contractor-operator of a huge munitions plant in southern Indiana. Although he was trained in and working as a research chemist, the personnel director approached him about transferring to personnel. He was the only black professional in an operating environment that was facing intense federal scrutiny. At the time he was approached, "the federal government had the big push on government contractors to do more for affirmative action," he explained. The plant was particularly vulnerable because it was wholly supported by millions of dollars in federal contracts. "A lot of the federal investigators were black," he observed, "and . . . so if anybody had a chance of staving off all kinds of repercussions, then a black probably had a better chance."

The job came with a salary this manager characterized as "a pretty good deal." Yet he agonized over taking the offer because he would be leaving "the laboratory," he said, for a job he "wasn't trained for."

To his surprise, personnel proved to be his true niche, and he went on to develop the plant's first affirmative-action program. But in 1970, he was worried about the vulnerability of his career track. He reasoned that affirmative action, as a field, was transient and did not offer technical skills that would allow him to branch out in a company. Affirmative action "is the kind of field where . . . a few laws might change, but the concept doesn't. Once you know those [laws], there's not an awful lot more to learn." Like the frustrated steel company manager, he realized that this avenue could diminish his ability to manage non-race-related personnel areas.

He also expressed the dilemma of becoming too successful. "My biggest concern was I was going to end up becoming the guy who handles all the EEO problems in the corporation. I'm thinking, [even] back in the early 1970s, . . . that if something ever happened to affirmative action, where it wasn't popular anymore, I wouldn't have any other marketable skills." Consequently, in 1972 he asked for, and moved laterally into, the mainstream job of personnel manager.

Twelve of the fourteen executives who asked to be reassigned to nonracialized positions pointed to the role of mentors and, more significantly, to their own fact-finding efforts as fundamental elements of their eventual transition into mainstream jobs. Those who stayed in racialized jobs read the business environment narrowly by observing blacks around them. But those who exited these jobs were more cognizant of the overall structure of a particular corporate hierarchy. They educated themselves, or found mentors, and assessed the corporate environment early in their careers, which enabled them to identify career-enhancing moves in their firm. For instance, a vice-president in a communications firm said that two years into his job, he knew "you can spend all the time you want . . . in personnel, and public relations, and that kind of stuff. But you aren't going to be a vice-president of this company, or president of this company without [going through] operations." Seventeen of twenty-five people who left racialized jobs specifically analyzed which routes led to the executive suites in their company. A vice-president in the communications industry told me, with a hint of condescension at having to state what to him appeared obvious, "All you had to do was look at who ran the company and see what areas they came from. I just observed who was sitting where. I looked at those yellow bulletins because they announced organization changes and because they also give personal bios."

Using Racialized Jobs as Springboards to the Mainstream

Executives I interviewed who had turned functionally segregated assignments to their advantage often found senior management mentors who trained and propelled them into core corporate positions. A vice-president of operations who has done post-graduate work in physics and engineering, for example, between 1968 and 1972 was an equal employment opportunity manager. The employee relations director at his first firm approached him to set up the company's affirmative-action program. He had been with the company eight years and, he said, "I wanted to get into management. That was the first and only opportunity that I felt I was going to get."

He said he believes he was approached for this role because "there was some concern that if you put the wrong guy in there that he would just raise all kinds of hell. And what safer guy could you get than someone who's sitting in the engineering department?" (Also, the company had only one or two blacks in professional jobs, and none in personnel.)

The company may have chosen this man merely because he seemed to have the requisite interests. During his off-hours he volunteered with black community agencies and often attempted to convince the company to donate funds to community projects in black areas. The firm, an aerospace company that subsisted on federal contracts, was extremely vulnerable to federal oversight. But in 1968, when the federal government's approach to contract compliance was relatively untested, the company was still unclear about affirmative-action mandates and its own direction in developing programs. As this executive put it, "Nobody knew how to do it, but everybody knew it would have to be good."

The company's dependence on federal contracts and its consequent emphasis on compliance with affirmative action made his job highly valued and anointed him with a status he knew no other black in the company had. He received "a job with a manager title, exposure to the company's inner works, and visibility to the corporation's top people." Yet he approached the job as if it were a stepping-stone rather than a permanent stopping place—a chance, as he put it, to "let me get my nose somewhere" and "to get something for myself." As he developed the affirmative-action program in conjunction with a senior vice-president in the company, he did get something for himself—a powerful and active mentor. Up to that point, he said, "essentially I lacked what most blacks lack . . . sponsorship. I was totally on my own." He credited the sponsorship of this executive vice-president with his ability to turn his career around. "He was a white guy who . . . got to know me. Supported a lot of things that I wanted to do. And said, 'You know you've got a lot of capability, and it's a waste to keep you here in EEO. So I want to send you back to [Massachusetts Institute of Technology] because I think when you come back we can get you ready for a senior management job.'"

After administering affirmative action for five years, this man entered MIT's Sloan School of Management executive-training program. Soon afterward his mentor retired. When he returned from MIT, he expected the company to reward his achievements. "I was looking for a position where I could eventually do something, where I had some power." But offers for that type of position were not forthcoming. "I had forgotten I was black." Moreover, his mentor's protection and advocacy were gone. Despite his postgraduate work and success as an MIT-Sloan executive fellow, the offers that he received from his employer and, he stressed, from "so many other companies were to direct affirmative-action programs."

He said he heard about "all those guys I'd been with [at Sloan], . . . and their promotions." He believed that, at minimum, he should have been promoted to company director. After a lengthy pause, he said "[I] was screaming inside my head; I was hurt terribly by the [job offers]." But in spite of his initial disappointment, the training at Sloan

(and, I would argue, the existence of federal anti-bias legislation) helped him to redirect his career. He told his employer, "No, hell no," he said. "I wouldn't even be interested in a job making decisions between black and white cars, let alone black and white people. I'm through with that. I've done my share." He demanded a line job, he said, because he "was no longer so naive to be seduced by title or salary." He subsequently became a project manager in his original company, staying with the firm for the next two years.

There is more bad news, however, and it is grounded in a by-now-familiar dilemma. In his efforts to achieve affirmative action as the company's EEO manager, the interviewee had alienated the man who later stepped into the executive vice-president position vacated by his mentor; he had "embarrassed" this person and "shoved something" he did not want "down his throat," he said. When he became a project manager, this adversary became his direct supervisor. His opportunities within the company stagnated once again.

One way to interpret the careers discussed thus far is to view them as blacks' struggles to succeed in a world where they are anomalies. In this context, blacks' unique status worked both for these people and against them. They were approached for racialized jobs because their visibility brought them to the attention of senior management. Such jobs were both potential springboards for, and hazards to, entering mainstream corporate training and competition. With an eye on both factors, they negotiated conditions for taking affirmative-action and urban affairs positions. In the case of the MIT-Sloan graduate, the racialized job was the vehicle that gave him a new chance—a mentor—and the year of additional specialized and prestigious training. Yet playing racialized roles also pigeonholed this man, inviting new affirmative-action job offers, creating a powerful enemy, and robbing him of a new mentor. Ultimately, however, occupying a racialized job created a window of opportunity, which this man used well. He eventually got other offers and went on to become a vice-president in a major firm.

In his first jobs, from 1963 to 1968, a vice-president and central region manager in a consumer goods industry, he developed special markets successfully for two Chicago companies.

Although these special markets directly addressed each firm's economic initiatives, they were not a springboard from which blacks were expected to gain organizational power. Nevertheless, by 1968 this man's outstanding sales and performance records prompted senior management to create a new position for him as a special-market sales manager. His upgrade, while earned, was considered a radical innovation for this employer. His new position made him the second black manager in the company; the black executive who predated him ran urban affairs. He said that during this time, "I always wanted to break into the mainstream market but . . . I didn't even try. I just tried to do the best I could in that particular area." In 1973, five years after becoming special-market manager, his aspirations to participate in the mainstream came to fruition when the vice-president of sales promoted him to central division manager. From that point on, he moved quickly and steadily up the mainstream corporate ladder.

When asked what he thought influenced his ability to enlarge his racialized career, he recalled learning "a host of bottom-line functions" that eventually led him out of special markets. "I thought it was positive," he said. "It allowed me to learn the business—distribution, pricing, taxation, expenditures, promotional activities." His optimistic view of his opportunities, however, obscures the hiring discrimination that influenced his assignment to sales territories dominated by black consumers. He gives his early placement the gloss of an apprenticeship when he would

have received similar—or possibly broader and better—training had he been given general-market assignments. But he was making his assessment based on what was possible for him at the time. When he was hired by this Chicago company, white companies simply did not offer blacks sales jobs in white-dominated geographic areas.

On the other hand, unlike the case of the frustrated manager in the steel industry, the same vision and skills this man demonstrated in special markets were recognized as valuable to the broader, mainstream sales territory. Although the timing of his recognition may have been an effect of governmental activity or some other race-related corporate considerations, his special-market assignment spotlighted his performance and prompted upper management to risk moving a black employee into a traditional (white) sales area. As he put it, "The vice-president of sales felt that I was good enough. He brought me in and really started teaching me the business."

The career path of a finance company's senior vice-president is a third example of converting a racialized job into a mainstream trajectory leading up the corporate hierarchy. In 1970, this man was transferred out of an entry level position and into a management role in the company's guaranteed loan program designed to assist small and minority businesses. The position had many pitfalls because it involved screening and lending capital to the most difficult, and economically vulnerable, customer base—owners of small black businesses. Thus when this manager generated profits, his success was both surprising and noteworthy. "We pulled it off," he said. "We made some good loans, and some folks became quite wealthy because of [them]. We had some real winners. We were doing so well that we got a pretty good reputation." As a result of his performance in lending, he was promoted into a commercial area he characterized as a "big hitter" and "for whites only."

When asked to give some background on this promotion, he said he viewed it as a natural progression in line with the job he had. His response assumes that his performance running the loan program created the perception among top management that he had the necessary skills to fill the higher position. Significantly, at about this time, a higher-placed executive took an interest in him and eventually became his lifelong mentor. In a tangible way, his racialized job in a profit-generating area gained him visibility and recognition that led to a permanent position in a formerly all-white domain.

Both this man and the special-markets manager discussed earlier became the first black members of all-white senior management teams. In both cases, their initial, and racialized, assignments became launching pads for mainstream careers. This man's client and business skills were perceived by top management as transferable to and, more important, better exploited in a mainstream profit-driven area. In addition, each had a mentor who played a crucial and active role in his ascent. Also, both mentors stepped forward after the workers excelled despite the limitations perceived to be inherent in their racialized assignments.

Golden Handcuffs and Social Obligations

Like the frustrated manager in the steel company, eighteen of the twenty-six workers who stayed in racialized jobs during the 1960s and 1970s aspired to mainstream positions at varying points in their private sector careers. Why, then, did only seven of the twenty-six request reassignment into core corporate functions? One theme among people who stayed in racialized jobs was that their ambitions were shaped, and sometimes thwarted, by their racial identity and a sense of racial solidarity. A second theme was that their ambition, compounded by their lack of practical knowledge about constructing corporate careers, made them easily seduced by racialized jobs and the corporate perquisites that often accompanied them. One manager who worked in sales before he took on affirmative-action responsibilities reminisced in a voice filled with irony that the move "was supposed to be an honor." . . .

In the 1960s and 1970s, these people thought racialized jobs were their best opportunities for social and economic advancement. As a fifty-three-year-old director of corporate contributions, then in his twenty-third year in a racialized job, told me, "That was the place for us to be." Many now see the downside of that decision. With the benefit of hindsight, the affirmative-action director explained, "I believe that had I stayed in operations [I would have] continued to move up, and that's where the clout is. But the opportunity just wasn't there [for blacks] when I first started with that company." After a slight pause he added, somewhat ruefully, "Things changed, and it is now."

Comments on Mentorship and Role Models

Role models and mentors may have changed the course of these men's careers. The white corporate milieu and collegial relationships with whites were new and mysterious to many people I interviewed. Only twenty-six of seventy-six came from families where at least one parent was a professional, managerial, or sales person. Moreover, only two of the twenty-six had a parent, close relative, or friend who had professional work experience in a major corporation. Half had graduated from all-black colleges or universities. Since these executives, like most blacks, had not been exposed to the white corporate world, they had no one to help them decipher the rules of the game. Thus, historical restrictions on blacks' access to white corporate culture played a role in shaping their managerial career preferences.

Those who stayed in racialized jobs were as ambitious as those who got out of them; indeed—and ironically—ambition was a large part of the reason they stayed where they were. During the civil rights era, racialized jobs made educated, ambitious blacks company stars. Paradoxically, the most attractive features of the jobs, such as starting titles and salary, freedom, and visibility, for some of them also diluted their desire to move into the companies' mainstream areas. But with black role models, aggressive mentors, or more knowledge about company hierarchies, would those who stayed have made different career choices? Did they need mentors and role models to perceive alternative career options as truly possible? The district personnel manager who spoke of representing a billion-dollar business may, in retrospect, be satisfied with his career choices, but he now also understands that visibility among white business elites was not the same as power. The longtime affirmative-action manager now knows that, for corporate success in the long run, social commitment must come second to business decisions, important only when they support a company's profit-generating function.

When confronted with racialized job offers, these executives lacked the experience, role models, and mentorship to assist them in reading company culture. And, in the absence of support, blacks who remained in racialized jobs in Chicago corporations turned to each other for help in making career decisions. The affirmative-action director said, "It was a case of the blind leading the blind. I was stupid. I remember the CEO saying . . . 'We want you to take this beautiful job. It's going to pay you all this money. It's going to make you a star.'"

A sense of disappointment comes through as these people look back on their careers. Middle age, regardless of race, is a period when people review their lives; some regret past choices, even if they are by objective standards successful. Among people who were firsts in history, expectations about making a difference and achieving economic success may run even higher than the norm, and their disappointment that much greater.

REFERENCES

Fernandez, John. 1981. *Racism and Sexism in Corporate Life: Changing Values in American Business.* Lexington, MA: Lexington Books.

Jones, Edward W. 1986. "Black Managers: The Dream Deferred." *Harvard Business Review,* May–June, 84–89.

Korn/Ferry. 1986. *Korn/Ferry International's Executive Profile: A Survey of Corporate Leaders in the Eighties.* New York: Korn/Ferry. Pamphlet.

35

Just a Temp

Kevin D. Henson

*Where I work on a long-term temporary assign-
ment there's a lot of people who I graduated
from college with on staff. And when they see
me, you know, they go, "What are you doing?
Why are you working as a temporary secretary?!" There's a lot of . . . I don't know. Maybe
it's all in my mind because I feel sort of inferior
to that because they're kind of established. I feel
really inadequate. (Bob)*

Occupation is one of the primary ways
in which we identify ourselves and
are identified by others. "What do
you do?" is the first thing we are likely to be
asked after introductions in most adult social settings. And most of us respond with an
explanation of our paid labor activity, giving
our job title, naming our employer, or describing our particular "bundle of tasks." As
Everett Hughes noted, "A man's work is one
of the more important parts of his social
identity, of his self, of his fate, in the one life
he has to live" (1984, 339).

This self-defining characteristic of work,
along with the relatively low status of their
own economic activity, is not lost on temporary workers. Nor is it lost on those with
whom they interact on or off the job. Temporaries are repeatedly confronted with the inadequacy of their occupational "choice"
(they may be asked, for example, "When are

you going to get a 'real' job?") and the alleged personal deficiencies their temporary
employment implies. Indeed, in this sense,
working as a temporary is a stigma, a stigma
that carries with it negative assumptions
about an individual's qualifications, abilities, and character.

When temporary workers interact with
others who perceive them as temporaries,
they are confronted with their deviance.
Temporaries cannot simply ignore the
stigma of their imputed social identity. Like
other stigmatized groups, temporaries can
either internalize the stigma, incorporating it
into their self-concept, or adopt strategies to
deny, deflect, or manage it (Goffman 1961,
1963; Scott 1969).

The Erosion of Self-Esteem

Temporaries, both on and off the job, must
face the inadequacy of their occupation and
the unfitness, ineptness, or undesirability
their temporary employment implies. Lillian,
for example, described the social embarrassment she felt when asked "What do you do?":

> The worst part about temping is proba-
> bly when people ask you what you do.
> It's, like, "Oh, you're doing temp work
> still, Lillian? Can't you get a job?" That's
> a big one. My parents are, like, "Lillian,
> let's get a job." They're really, like, "Why
> did you go to a private liberal arts col-
> lege? Why did we spend all this money
> for you to go to this school?"

Lillian was confronted with a status incongruity: she was college-educated yet still employed in low-status, low-wage work. Her position in the occupational structure, in the eyes of others, implied at best inadequacies or ineptitude in her job-seeking abilities and at worst that their perceptions of her had been false.

Kimberly also noted the difficulties of explaining why she was working as a temporary:

> When you meet somebody new who's your age and they say, "Oh, what do you do?" I kind of swallow and say, "I'm temping right now, but . . ." Because I think it very much is. . . . We're in a status society and what you do is very important. Talking to friends of mine that I went to college with about their jobs and "Oh, they've just been promoted to this and this. Now what are you doing?" "Well, I'm still temping now." "Oh. Well . . ." It's a kind of feeling that they're moving so far with their career and I'm just kind of staying temping. And yet I know that I don't want a career like theirs.

Although some temporaries know that they don't want a typical career and others, given current economic conditions and the changing occupational opportunity structure, can't find a "real" job, the social legitimacy automatically accorded full-time, permanent employees (normals) compared to temporaries' present circumstances is hard to deny to both self and others.

Similarly, their relative status in the workplace is made painfully clear to temporaries: they are "just the temp." Temporaries, like the occupants of other low-status roles prefaced with the qualifier "just," are identified exclusively with (or as) their devalued occupational category. As Steve said, "Well, they assume right away that you're a moron because you're a temp, rather than accepting that you just have something else going on." In other words, individuals involved in temporary work are assigned the deviant "master status" of temporary regardless of other possible social statuses they could take on (Hughes 1945; Becker 1963). Besides this conflation of the individual with the organizational category ("just the temp"), assumptions are made about workers' qualifications, abilities, and character generally ("just a temp"). These assumptions of deviance are expressed through face-to-face interactions, the organization of the work, and the physical layout of the workplace.

One marker of the extent to which "temporary worker" becomes an individual's master status in the workplace is the depersonalizing manner in which "co-workers" frequently fail to learn or use a temporary's name: "But you'd go to these places and people are always like, 'Temp. Temp. There's a temp.' And you'd get that, 'The temp.' You'd have a couple nice people, but for the most part in a big office people go, 'Where's the temp? What's the temp doing?' You know, you never had a name" (Pamela). Failing to learn someone's name, in many contexts, is a sign of disrespect or an indicator of unequal status. The successful completion of the temporary assignment requires temporaries to learn the permanent workers' names and faces, primarily for the performance of communication tasks, but "co-workers" often do not feel compelled, even out of courtesy, to learn and use the temporary's name. Although that may simply be an outgrowth of the relatively short duration of the temporary's tenure, temporary workers are denied their individuality as unique, interesting, and worthwhile persons when treated categorically as "just the temp."

In interactions with supervisors and co-workers, assumptions are made and communicated to temps about their ability (or inability) to handle even low-skill tasks. Bob, for example, found requests to set work aside "until so-and-so gets back" condescending: "People assume that you're just a temp. There's, like, this whole 'just a temp' attitude among the permanent employees. And it's kind of like 'Don't give him this because he probably won't know how to do it.' It's just really insulting." Similarly, Susan complained that she was treated "like a moron" by her co-workers on a temporary assignment:

> When I started temping at the real estate development corporation, I was sitting there and one of the guys came out and he said, "Here, would you make copies of this?" Tracy, a permanent secretary, goes, "Oh, here. I'll do that." Like I'm going to screw it up, you know? So every time someone came up, Tracy would go, "Here. I'll do that. I'll do that." So I sat there and I said, "Knock your socks off, bitch. If you want to run your legs off, you go right ahead. I'll sit here and make my *x* number of dollars per hour. If you want to do all the work, go ahead. I don't mind a bit." She did not think I was capable of doing the work they were giving me. But they do treat you like you're a moron, and that's the hard part.

Temporaries find themselves patronized and demeaned in a variety of ways, besides being asked to put aside work they know is well within their capabilities. Simple tasks are overexplained, intensely supervised, and effusively complimented when completed. I was particularly irritated by overdone praises for my work. On several occasions I was complimented on my typing speed, told that I did a "nice job on the memo," and left perky thank-you notes ("Mornin', Kevin—I've gone through all of our information. You're doing *a super job!* Thanks!"). These work episodes remind temporary workers of the low opinions others generally hold of temporaries and their work abilities.

The relatively low value of a temporary's time is evident in both their low wages and the way their time is controlled and used by others in the workplace. For example, temporaries not only often take their lunch alone; they also take it at everyone else's convenience (including permanent employees nominally at the same level):

> They felt free to be more abusive. You know, like you weren't human. "No, you can't go to eat lunch until so-and-so goes to lunch. You have to cover the phones while they're gone." So sometimes you end up eating . . . like, your lunch time was always weird compared to everybody else's. You were always the last. (Pamela)

Additionally, temporaries are, as part of their work, expected to screen callers (protecting the "valuable" time of permanent people in the organization) and generally do the bulk of time-consuming, low-status, and routine work, such as photocopying, opening mail, filing, fetching coffee, greeting guests, and office "housekeeping."

Exclusion from regular sociability routines, although usually done without malice, further reinforces the temporary's "otherness" and low standing in the workplace. Temporaries, for example, are rarely included when permanent employees break their work routine for a shared cup of coffee or a trip to the vending machine. Temporaries are also commonly left out of office birthday, holiday, retirement, and other celebrations. A temporary may in fact be used to facilitate office sociability by providing phone or other work coverage for permanent employees on these occasions. One temporary described an assignment in which her sole duty was to cover—with a less than truthful story—for the permanent office staff members while they enjoyed their holiday party.

Even the relative size, comfort, and privacy of their work settings and furnishings impress on temporaries that they are at the bottom of the corporate hierarchy. At one of my temporary assignments in a large Chicago law firm, for example, the clerical furniture (huddled in a common, public, windowless island toward the interior of the building) consisted of half-back, low chairs without arms, whereas the attorneys (in their private offices with expansive views of the city) had deep, reclining leather chairs with arms. Furthermore, the limited work space and layout of desks, typing tables, and computer stations enforced a position of holding in one's body, keeping the knees together, and generally taking up very little space. These setting-induced positions are powerless ("feminine") body postures (Henley 1977) and act as one more symbolic reminder to temporaries, and clerical workers in general, of their subordinate status within the corporation.

These continual verbal and nonverbal assaults on one's self-concept become increasingly difficult for temporaries to escape, deny, or deflect. Over time many temporaries begin to experience a loss of self-confidence, a painful erosion of self-esteem, as these unflattering views are (at least partially) internalized. Pamela, for example, commented:

> It was hard. It wasn't hard the way I thought it was going to be hard. I thought it was going to be hard because they were going to ask me to do some office thing that I didn't know how to do, till I found out that usually office things don't take that long to do. Although they usually think it takes a long time. But it was hard emotionally. Emotionally hard. It sounds so dramatic, but it was to me. It was really a drag. At the time I was a weeping, crying fool in parking lots all over. A lot of jobs. The way they treated me, I just felt like, "Lighten up, man. Be nice to me." People work a lot better when you're nice to them. So in that re-

spect, I didn't expect it to be such a traumatic thing. Because by the time I was done I was like . . . it took a while to bolster that self-confidence.

Helen described how the work assaulted her self-concept and how her lack of embeddedness and the way in which others evaluated, regarded, or failed to regard her were occasionally too much to bear:

> One morning I was walking to the train to go to my temporary job and I started to cry! You know, nobody gives a shit about you! You could drop dead and they wouldn't notice. They'd just get another temp. It's a little overdramatic, of course. You just feel like you're very wrapped up in this futile routine. And it's just too much. It's really upsetting. I've really dreaded going in some days.

Temporaries, confronted with assumptions about who they are and how they ought to behave, are forced to respond in some manner.

Passing as Normal

So that they may survive emotionally and protect their self-concept, temporaries devise ways of buttressing their sense of self from the stigma and assaults of temporary work. Particularly at the beginning of their tenure, temporaries may pursue a strategy of blurring the lines or boundaries of their temporary role in an attempt to "pass" as normals (Goffman 1963). In this strategy temporaries assimilate themselves into the organization and say, "I belong here. I am more and can do more than be just a temporary for you." Joanne, for example, described her strategy for fitting in on temporary assignments:

> It just takes five or ten minutes to give me the basics. And that's what I like about it too. It's very challenging mentally to go

into a place, to set up a rapport with people you've never seen before and you may never see again in life. And to instantly, just about, pick up what needs they have. Incorporate what knowledge you have of how businesses run. Put it all together and have the place operating fairly smoothly. My goal is so that people don't even know that there's a temp there. I want to be invisible to the point that I don't want a lot of mistakes and that, where people say, "Oh. That temp!" You know, that kind of negative thing. I want to portray myself in such a way that I'm here to help. I'm helping. And I'm a plus to your company and not a minus. And that's my personal goal.

Temporary workers who can fit in with the team, make themselves seem indispensable, and gain the respect of their co-workers conceal the stigma of their temporary status.

Seeking Continuity

Seeking placement in a known industry such as insurance, banking, or accounting allows temporaries to draw on previous work experiences to conceal the temporary status of their current employment and pass for normals or permanent employees of the organization. A comfortable setting with a familiar work lingo, as Ginny noted, can be an effective resource for a credible performance as a permanent employee:

> At AdvertLand it was wonderful, because I do know something about commercial production. I do know something about TV production and ads and copyrighting and everything. And I was able to make sense to these clients that would call in. And I knew what I was talking about. And it was wonderful. I would hate to be sent to, like, an accounting firm or a real estate firm or something like that. Because it would be, like, "What the hell is going on?"

Although the content of the work may be very different, at least the setting and lingo are congruent with a previous or preferred self.

Doing "Quality Work" and Bumping up the Skill

Temporaries can blur the lines of their temporary role by becoming a "super" employee. Through acting in the capacity of a computer consultant, computer trainer, or graphic designer, one can be more than just a temporary to both self and co-workers. Bobby Jean described how she took on extra tasks, framing herself more as a consultant than a temporary, on one of her assignments:

> I ended up automating their office. Because they were taking preprinted letters and trying to line them up on the typewriter to try to get the name and address right. And I'm looking at this like, "This is stupid." This is the computer age. And you have a computer sitting over there that can do this. And so I put, like, the letters . . . and I did it really easy for them. I didn't even do a merge. I just did "date" and "address." I said, "Just delete this. Type over it. Print it. And don't save it. Or save it under another name. But just leave your blank. And you can pull this up whenever you want it."

Pamela recounted how she adopted the role of computer trainer and teacher on an assignment:

> They had just bought computers for everybody. Nobody had had a computer before 1988. And all of a sudden the company said everyone must have a computer. And then I walked in and I knew all these different software packages. People were just popping software packages onto their machines. So even though I was there specifically to send out a form letter . . . that's why I was really there, because I knew how to do mail merge on

Displaywrite 4. But as it turned out, I did that really quickly. And I started to support all these secretaries on their PC packages. So they kept me because I was helping everybody. Actually, I did a class for these guys. And pretty soon everybody . . . like, the head of sales administration was like, "Who is that person?"

Through taking the role of a nonstigmatized but nonpermanent office worker, temporaries attempted to obscure the temporary status of their organizational role and pass as normal. By doing quality work or bumping up the skill level, temporaries, in effect, say, "I'm more than just a temporary—I'm a valuable player on your team."

Saving the Bosses

Temporaries may also blur the lines of their organizational role or status by engaging in a tactic of saving the bosses from their own errors. As Everett C. Hughes noted, a "common dignifying rationalization of people in all positions of a work hierarchy except the very top one is, 'We in this position save the people in the next higher position above from their own mistakes'" (Hughes 1984, 340–41). Aleshia, for example, attempted to keep her boss from overexplaining:

She basically wrote what basically could have been a merge letter with three variations. And instead of saying, "Here's a list of people. Everyone gets this information. That's stock. He gets insert A and B. He gets insert C," she wrote out every letter. And instead of just saying basically what I just said, "You'll notice that each letter is a little bit different. Make sure that you follow my letter," she said, "Now this letter has something different." She sat down and explained every letter. After about seven letters, I said, "Delia, I think I've got it." And I have a lot of work to do. I don't have time for bullshit like that. I don't get-

offended, because I know I'm intelligent and I don't need to prove that to her. How could a woman with this little logic, it's a basic logic function, pairing functions, saying the basic plus the variant. She doesn't have a grasp of that. Why is this woman in a management position? Well, maybe she has some other qualities that . . . this isn't one of them.

Similarly, Mary attempted to correct grammatical errors in her bosses' work:

Because I studied English I'll edit their, the bosses', work a lot and they'll notice that and they don't like it. It's an insult to them that someone would be doing this. And I'll say, "But I teach English. That's what I normally do." Which even bothers them more, I think. That they have an educated secretary on their hands. You know, a lot of these men are kind of insecure. But no, the men, they don't like their work to be edited. I think they just want someone to sit down and do the work.

While catching mistakes may improve one's own status within the organization, it can also be fraught with tension in actual usage. Operating on one-upmanship—publicly pointing out the ignorance or errors of those higher in the hierarchy—may not be a particularly endearing technique for passing as normal. Temporaries who can "help" their bosses correct errors without offending or publicly challenging the hierarchy (that is, framing corrections in a less assertive or confrontational style such as a suggestion, a question, or a comment with a tag question—"*Commitment* is spelled with two *m*'s, isn't it?"), may more successfully blur the boundaries of the temporary role.

Securing Long-Term Assignments

One of the most effective ways to obscure the boundaries of one's temporary role and pass as a normal is to secure long-term assignments. An extended stay of several weeks or months within a single client company (or return assignments) routinizes the presence of the temporary in the workplace to the point that he or she may be mistaken for a permanent employee. Susan, for example, noted that the difficulties of managing assumptions about self were reduced in long-term assignments: "It is truly tough to go to a new company and prove yourself. I was so glad that I was able to stay at the real estate development corporation and the law firm, because they knew that I wasn't a dummy." Daniel also noted the way in which longer-term assignments allowed one to "break through" (Davis 1961) the assumed stigma(s):

> When I walk into an office and they see me, they have certain expectations right away. I open my mouth, and I speak in a certain way, and they don't know how to handle it. Being treated as a black male, and then having a certain amount of intelligence, they don't know how to deal with you. If you're there for a week, that's fine. If you're there for a month, then they eventually get to know Daniel and I eventually get to know them. So it's that kind of thing.

Long-term assignments, then, allow individuation and differentiation from the category of just a temp. Temporaries in these assignments can reveal enough other social information eventually to break through and disavow their deviant identity. Whereas permanent workers may say that they've been someplace so long they're beginning to feel like part of the furniture, temporaries who stay on the same assignment say they begin to feel less like a piece of furniture and more like a person.

Telling the Cover Story

One of the most common strategies for managing the stigma of working as a temporary is to invoke the "cover story." The cover story, which is told to both self and others, presents an alternative identity and explains and legitimates one's presence in an otherwise stigmatizing situation. Through bringing in one's supporting props (providing additional social information) and reinterpreting and rationalizing narrative-disrupting or discordant elements, temporaries attempt to build a supporting and believing audience for their alternative identity performance. In short, temporaries, through the cover story, claim an alternative "master status" or basis for their identity—"Well, I'm working as a temporary, but I'm not really a temporary. I'm really this."

Verbally telling one's cover story to co-workers, providing social information about self not readily available in the workplace, was one common strategy temporaries employed in the effort to disavow or cover their stigma. Bob, for example, noted how temporaries without prompting would share their cover stories, revealing their "underlying reason" for presence in a stigmatic situation:

> I don't want to say that they're not proud of being temps, but they want you to know that there is another reason that they are temping. I mean, you don't have to ask, "So what's your story?" Well, "before I get a real job" or "in between shows." There's always that little subtlety. Even secretaries too, but not as much as temps, sort of let you know that there is a reason why they're doing this and that it's not a copout. An underlying reason. A more worthwhile underlying reason.

Steve, who used this strategy, told me that he always informed his co-workers that he was an actor:

> S: Oh, I always told them I was an actor. Immediately. Immediately. And they were, like, "Great! This is wonderful." So maybe that's what cut the ice, you know. They knew I wasn't just waiting

to get a "real job." "Why doesn't this guy have a real job yet?"

KH: So you told them right away?

S: Sure. I'm a temp. This is what I do. This is what I want to do because I'm an actor.

Through the telling of their personal circumstances and the articulation of their cover story for temping, temporary workers attempted to differentiate and distance themselves from the stigma of temporary work.

The opportunity to tell the cover story, however, does not always arise easily and naturally for temporaries. Consequently, some temporaries openly wished that their agencies would intervene to facilitate the individuation process, providing personalized introductions or placements in settings where the work would spontaneously allow revelations of more positive social information:

I'm fluent in German. And I have all these artistic skills. And I know a little bit of Moroccan Arabic and some French. And I go, like, "God. Why can't I temp in a German bank?" Or something like that. That would be really neat. These things are never even mentioned. The agency could mention to the person where you're being placed on assignment that you were in the Peace Corps or that you have an education. None of that seems to be conveyed at all. (Helen)

The extent to which temporaries desire and consciously seek opportunities to tell their cover story was revealed in an anecdote I was told by a temporary counselor:

I had a temporary once. Her name was Laura. And she was an executive secretary, and she had very good skills. I think she had low self-esteem from being a temporary. And she told me once, "Cindy, what I think I'm going to do is type up a letter about myself and just hand it to people. And say I'm Laura

Naiman, I am not just a temporary and da, da, da, da, da." I was, "Laura, no." She was so caught up, she was so embarrassed that she was a temporary. (Cindy)

Using Supporting Props

One way of creating appropriate openings in which to tell the cover story is to conspicuously carry alternative identity props or "prestige symbols" (Goffman 1963). Some temporaries are never seen without a "self"-revealing book; others wear lapel pins or carry their business cards, résumés, theatrical scripts, backpacks, or textbooks in support of an alternative self.

Sometimes they ask, "What are you doing?" Or I'll be reading a book on Windsor Castle. "Oh, what's that?" You know, that kind of thing. And I'll say, "Well . . ." I'm always eager to talk about my documentary project on Windsor Castle. You know, if you talk about it, it may happen. Sometimes I need that little opportunity to say, "Yes, I am really working for that. And not for six dollars and twenty-five cents." (Daniel)

A carefully chosen prop will often give the desired impression (Goffman 1959) or elicit questions creating an appropriate context in which to tell the cover story and reveal positive social information about one's self.

On one occasion when I found myself working near another temporary, I initiated a conversation (hoping to request a formal interview) by asking about her book bag, which bore the logo of a well-known Chicago theater company. She cheerfully told me that she interned at the theater and was currently looking for steady technical theater work. Over the course of the week that we worked together, I heard her repeat her story, almost verbatim, to several others who inquired about her ubiquitous book bag. Similarly, I relied heavily on my cover story: "I'm a graduate student." I carried my backpack and chose scholarly books as prestige symbols. Indeed, although I was teaching an introductory sociology course one night a week, I did not want to be seen with the textbook: it did not signify the desired prestige (I did not want to be mistaken for an undergraduate student).

Even when props do not directly elicit the opportunity to tell the cover story to others, they can be used to buttress one's chosen identity in a performance for the self. Like carefully chosen stage props, temporaries' props supported the enactment of their chosen character.

> I had a lapel pin at one of my really lax jobs. It says in Arabic, "We Are All One People." And it has a little picture of a globe. And people would notice that and I would tell them. So that was kind of cool. Sometimes I have my Morocco pictures and I look at them while I'm at lunch or something. Or I have it like a pile. You desperately want to preserve that connection. Like, yes, I do have a life outside of this. This is temporary, but . . . (Helen)

Reinterpreting and Rationalizing

Even elements of the work situation that at first appear constraining to the development or expression of an alternative self are creatively interpreted by temporaries as resources. I believed, for example, that temporaries, required to play the part of an office worker, were denied the opportunity for self-expression and characterization through costume. One temporary I interviewed, however, had reinterpreted her "corporate" or "temporary" look as consistent with her acting career:

> KH: Did you have to buy special clothes when you started temping?
>
> L: Yes! Only because I had no clothes. I didn't have any suits. That was another

thing. When I started temping and started applying for jobs and stuff, I had to get a suit. But I also had to get a suit for industrial acting auditions too. So what I would use for my industrial look . . . you know, at the same time because of the corporate look and things like that. Because my style of dress is not like that.

Others reinterpreted experiences on the job as being useful for other life projects: emotional material to draw on for stage portrayals, talents for dealing with others, or skills and experiences that could be helpful in selling oneself on the "real" job market. What might at first appear as frivolous hairsplitting is actually identity work, work that is useful to temporaries in closing the gap between a preferred identity and an assigned identity.

Some temporaries even reinterpreted their lowly position within the corporate hierarchy as a virtue: their low status is the admirable result of their rejection of injurious mainstream values and conceptions of success. If they wanted to play corporate America's game, they could win at it, but they are not interested:

> When you see the seamy sides of what you're doing, that's just really awful. Working for a company that developed regional shopping malls, I became alerted to articles about malls. I couldn't stop myself. They banned protesters against the Gulf War from demonstrating in the mall. "It's not a public place." They don't even let the Salvation Army in there. I guess you can see their point if you're a ruthless capitalist. There's just some sort of seedy things. I just hate that whole hierarchy. It's just so awful. I mean, the secretaries are mistreated. The politics are hideous. There's so much backstabbing. You don't approve of what they're doing in the first place. I guess I'm not even interested in being in the corporate

arena at all. I don't want any of it. I hate all of it together. It's just feeling very alienated. Hope it's over soon. (Helen)

By claiming to want no part of it at all, whether truthful or just sour grapes, temporaries can deflect the stigma of occupying one of the corporate sector's low-ranking positions.

Building a Supportive Audience

It doesn't matter terribly whether the cover story is "true" or not. It does matter, however, whether you can get others to believe and help support it. Plenty of people who call themselves actors, for example, rarely (or never) appear in a dramatic production. Telling the cover story to co-workers is one way of enlisting others in constructing an alternative conception of self—if others believe it, it may just come true.

> The people who I worked with were really sweet. They were infatuated with the fact that I was an actor, but they really couldn't understand it. So I was, like, in this situation where I was kind of my own entity among all these people. You know, it was real hard to fit in anywhere'. 'Cause it wasn't something that I would do as a career choice. (Sergei)

Audiences, on or off the job, that accept the enactment of alternative or "normal" selves are helpful to temporaries in denying their deviance, recuperating from the stresses of demeaning treatment on the job, and bolstering their preferred identity or self-concept.

The temporary who successfully asserts his or her cover story breaks through many of the stigmatizing assumptions associated with being "just a temp." Many temporaries, like Helen, reported that they went from being treated categorically and stereotypically as "just a temp" to being treated individually and given more respect when they divulged their cover story:

> Some places they ask you, "Oh, are you in school?" I guess because I'm relatively young or whatever. And I tell them I just was in the Peace Corps. And then, oh my God! It's like the floodgates open. And suddenly you were on an equal footing. And this other man brought in all these articles about Madagascar for me, because I said I might be going there. Yeah, and suddenly you were treated much differently. But as soon as they find out that you've had any education, or whatever, they really change.

Natalie also noted the change in interaction with others when social information was revealed and acknowledged:

> I think most people know that I've just finished this graduate program. And so I think . . . and if they didn't know . . . what I do notice is that when someone didn't know and they find out, there's a behavioral change toward me. Like all of a sudden, "Oh!" And there's a certain amount of respect accorded me that might have just . . . not that it wasn't accorded to me before, it just wasn't there. Like there's a certain amount of attention given to me as an individual when certain facts about my background come out.

"Suddenly, you were on an equal footing" and "There's a certain amount of attention given to me as an individual" are expressions of breaking through initial categorical and stereotypical treatment to recognition as an individual with a name, a personal history, and worth.

Constructing the Self in Opposition to Others

When asserting definitional control over one's identity through the strategies of passing as normal and telling the cover story is unsuccessful, temporaries may paradoxically attempt to maintain their alternative identity through a tactic of silence, avoidance, and stigmatization of others. By not revealing their alternative identity, by withholding the cover story, temporaries can preserve and nurture their preferred self both privately and in the company of known, safe audiences. Kirk, for example, pursued a strategy of protecting and controlling his social information: "Yeah, I pretty much prefer not talking too much or revealing much about myself at all at these places. I think it could be a pretty demeaning experience in lots of ways except that I think that you and I and people like us can really shrug off people saying things to us that might sort of insult our intelligence." Similarly, Pamela described attempts to maintain control over her personal information:

> There were the people who were like, "You have a degree. Why don't you get a job? What are you, a goof?" I'm like, "No, I'm not a goof. I want to write. I want to write in advertising, but there aren't any jobs." But, yeah, a lot of people were really curious why I was temping. I think I usually said I was interviewing and looking for full-time work. A lot of the times when they were asking me, it was the people who were, you know, "the temp" kind of people who were, "Why don't you . . . ?" And I really didn't want to answer their questions. You know what I mean? Because it wasn't like they were really interested in why you were a temp. They were more like, "Uh . . . [distaste sound]." Like that. It's because, like, "I'm broke."

Maintaining control over one's personal information maintained social distance from normals in the workplace. For temporaries to acknowledge that these others were worth talking to was also to acknowledge that their positive judgments were desired and sought.

Additionally, telling one's dreams and aspirations puts them out on the line for public inspection and exposes them to judgments, judgments that may be less than kind. Daniel, for example, sometimes attempted to protect his dream through a strategy of information control:

> If somebody asks, I tell them that I'm an independent film director. But I try not to because . . . you know, then you have to go back, it's a dream, but it's also a dream that I'm working on. But still it reinforces the fact that I'm working nine to five, whatever job it is that I need to work. So a lot of things come up other than my life as a closet movie director or producer. But I usually don't bring it up, because I just found that it's depressing at times.

Even simple questions ("Oh, you're an actor. What have you been in?"), asked in innocence, may challenge and threaten one's alternative conception of self. Experiences that are less than fully affirming, over time with many placements, may make one less willing to divulge personal information on the job.

At Least I'm Not a Secretary

Interactions with other temporary or permanent secretaries may also be avoided to minimize the stigma of association and the ever-present, ever-threatening fear that one might really belong. Natalie, for example, described how she avoided associating, at least at first, with permanent secretaries:

> When I first was starting to work here, I wouldn't want to go hang out with the secretaries. I thought like . . . one woman pulls, like, two people pull out their needlepoint. I'm just, like, appalled. And yet I think it's . . . I've gotten to know some of them better and I've sort of lost that attitude a little bit. I really like a lot of the women I work with and think they're really great human beings. They're doing

these jobs that aren't that great, but a lot of them are single mothers and this is it. The only way they can bring the money home.

Kimberly reported a similar strategy:

> It could just be me. But I do feel myself getting defensive about this is just something I'm doing, you know, to earn some money and fill in time until I figure out how to get to point *A* or I can get another interview. I want people to know that I'm not interested in being a secretary. I'm not interested in just doing this. And there have been a couple . . . especially in some of the larger companies where I was filling in for the secretaries. Some of the other female secretaries even try to pull you into their circles. "Oh, you don't have any, not higher ambitions, but other aspirations, than we do." "Oh, you're going to be a secretary too! Wouldn't you like to stay here and work with us?" "No, I'm sorry. I wouldn't."

Like the cover story, these avoidance patterns say, "I am different. I am not a temporary or secretary in training. I keep my distance because I have nothing in common with you."

The need for differentiation from and avoidance of permanent secretaries was particularly prominent among the college-educated female temporaries I interviewed. Aware of the large gap between their work expectations and work realities, and acutely conscious of the conflation of "traditional" femininity with the secretarial role, they found association with permanent secretaries threatening. Note, for example, how the stereotypical feminine activity of needlepoint is denigrated. Many of the women I interviewed did not want to end up in the pink-collar clerical army and consequently eschewed activities (at least in the workplace) that they found congruent or resonant with stereotypical images of femininity. The singly stigmatized female temporaries, then, may have been avoiding the double stigma of being both female and a secretary (see Kowalewski 1988). The fear of fitting in or belonging was far greater than the fear of being seen as other and isolated.

In addition to avoidance, temporaries sometimes appraised the permanent staff in ways that emphasized their own differences and superiority. Bobby Jean, for example, viewed the educational or intelligence level of permanent employees as lower than her own: "And a lot of them could hardly read and write. I really didn't feel that a lot of them were very well educated. I got along with them, but they weren't people I wanted to hang around with or anything." Temporaries also criticized the way the permanent staff dressed and completed their work. Through devaluing the permanent employees, temporaries attempted to increase the evaluation of their own merits and enhance their sense of personal worth.

At Least I'm Not a Lifer

Besides directly avoiding interactions with the permanent office inhabitants, temporaries, instead of bonding together, also often avoided one another. Other temporaries, presumed to be real temporaries or "lifers" who were truly deviant and lacked the maturity, ambition, or ability to secure and hold down a real job, were to be shunned. "People who just do this all their lives! I just want to say, 'You poor things. Where are you going with your life?' You know? If you have a husband or a wife who's bringing in the basis of the cash and this is just something fun for you, then great, great. But if this is your entire life" (Steve). Whether or not it exists, the lifer does fulfill the role of an oppositional other. Through comparison to this oppositional other who embodies and merits all the derision, stigma, and low status accorded temporaries generally, individual temporary workers can deny their own deviance. Temporaries, through articulating the stereotype of the lifer to self and others, highlight their individual differences and thus their individual worth.

It's Only for the Day

Forgoing the possibility of building a supportive audience, temporaries who pursue a strategy of avoidance and self-isolation must instead simply "grin and bear it" (see Eggleston 1990; Kanner 1990). Focusing on one's own cover story, the insignificance of the work to one's self-concept, and the finite nature of the assignment allows temporaries to "get through it." Kara, for example, articulated this approach:

> If I had my way in life, I would do commercials and film work and never have to do . . . lift my finger. So I take it with a grain of salt, because I know this isn't what I want to do. So when I'm folding envelopes and stuff and just feeling like a peon, you know, after a few days, going, "God, when am I going to get out of here?" I just realize that it's not my life's work and I really don't care. And I'm never going to have to see these people again.

Daniel recommended this strategy to me as a way of protecting the self:

> You cannot think of yourself as a lawyer or a doctoral candidate. You have to think of yourself as Kevin who is such-and-such and such-and-such. Because let's say you lose the job or you don't go through with . . . what are you? There's nothing. You have to rely on you, that inner you, that self, that's there. If you have a temporary job, you can't think of yourself as . . . you'll go batty. I'm a human being. This is what I'm doing this week. And you distance yourself as much as you can from the job, because you don't want to get involved. It's just stressful. And you don't want to play those games. You just want to go there, do your work, and get out.

"It's only for the day" or "it's only for another week" are the refrains temporaries repeat to themselves when the going gets rough. When the work is tedious and alienating, when the supervisor is condescending and rude, when the hours are long and the pay is low, temporaries can rest assured that things will change. Thus, by focusing on the "temporary" character of their work, their lack of personal commitment to it, and their alternative identity, temporaries can make it through assignments, collect their paychecks, and move on. . . .

REFERENCES

Becker, Howard S. 1963. *Outsiders: Studies in the Sociology of Deviance.* New York: Free Press.

Davis, Fred. 1961. "Deviance Disavowal: The Management of Strained Interaction by the Visibly Handicapped." *Social Problems* 9 (May): 120–32.

Eggleston, Kirk. 1990. "Working One Day at a Time: The Best Thing About a Job as a 'Temp' Is That It Doesn't Last." *Washington Post,* 2 September, 5(B).

Goffman, Erving. 1959. *The Presentation of Self in Everyday Life.* New York: Anchor Books.

———. 1961. *Asylums: Essays on the Social Situation of Mental Patients and Other Inmates.* New York: Anchor Books.

———. 1963. *Stigma: Notes on the Management of Spoiled Identity.* Englewood Cliffs, NJ: Prentice-Hall.

Henley, Nancy M. 1977. *Body Politics: Power, Sex, and Nonverbal Communication.* Englewood Cliffs, NJ: Prentice-Hall.

Hughes, Everett C. 1945. "Dilemmas and Contradictions of Status." *American Journal of Sociology* 50 (March):353–59.

———. 1984. *The Sociological Eye.* New Brunswick, NJ: Transaction Books.

Kanner, Bernice. 1990. "Peon for a Day." *New York,* 2 April, 41–44.

Kowalewski, Mark R. 1988. "Double Stigma and Boundary Maintenance: How Gay Men Deal with AIDS." *Journal of Contemporary Ethnography* 17 (July): 211–28.

Scott, Robert A. 1969. *The Making of Blind Men: A Study of Adult Socialization.* New York: Russell Sage Foundation.

36

No Shame in My Game

Katherine S. Newman

In the early 1990s, the McDonald's Corporation launched a television ad campaign featuring a young black man named Calvin, who was portrayed sitting atop a Brooklyn stoop in his Golden Arches uniform while his friends down on the sidewalk passed by, giving him a hard time about holding down a "McJob." After brushing off their teasing with good humor, Calvin is approached furtively by one young black man who asks, *sotto voce,* whether Calvin might help him get a job too. He allows that he could use some earnings and that despite the ragging he has just given Calvin, he thinks the uniform is really pretty cool—or at least that having a job is pretty cool.

Every fast food worker we interviewed . . . knew the Calvin series by heart: Calvin on the job, Calvin in the streets, Calvin helping an elderly woman cross the street on his way to work, Calvin getting promoted to management. And they knew what McDonald's was trying to communicate to young people by producing the series in the first place: that the stigma clings to fast food jobs, that it can be overcome, and that even your best friends will come to admire you if you stick with it—after they've finished dissing you in public.

Americans have always been committed to the moral maxim that work defines the person. We carry around in our heads a rough tally that tells us what kinds of jobs are worthy of respect and what kinds are to be disdained, a pyramid organized by the income a job carries, the sort of credentials it takes to secure a particular position, the qualities of an occupation's incumbents—and we use this system of stratification (ruthlessly at times) to boost the status of some and humiliate others. This penchant for ranking by occupation is more pervasive in the United States than in other societies, where there are different ways of evaluating the personal worth of individuals. In these societies, coming from a "good family" counts heavily in the calculus of social standing. Here in America, there is no other metric that matters as much as the kind of job you hold.

Given our tradition of equating moral value with employment, it stands to reason that the most profound dividing line in our culture is that separating the working person from the unemployed. Only after this canyon has been crossed do we begin to make the finer gradations that distinguish white-collar worker from blue-collar worker, CEO from secretary. We attribute a whole host of moral virtues—self-discipline, personal responsibility, maturity—to those who have found and kept a job, almost any job, and dismiss those who haven't as slothful or irresponsible.

We inhabit an unforgiving culture that is blind to the many reasons why some people cross that employment barrier and others are left behind. While we may remember, for a time, that unemployment rates are high, or that particular industries have downsized millions of workers right out of a job, or that racial barriers or negative attitudes toward teenagers make it harder to get a job at some times and for some people, in the end American culture wipes these background truths out in favor of a simpler dichotomy: the worthy and the unworthy, the working stiff and the lazy sloth.

These days, our puritanical attitudes owe some of their force to the resentment the employed bear toward the taxes they must pay to support those who cannot earn on their own. But it has deeper cultural dimensions. From the earliest beginnings of the nation, work has been the *sine qua non* of membership in this society. Adults who work are full-fledged citizens in the truest sense of the term—complete participants in the social world that is most highly valued. No other dimension of life—community, family, religion, voluntary organizations— qualifies Americans for this designation of citizen in the same way.

We express this view in a variety of ways in our social policies. Virtually all our benefits (especially health care but including unemployment insurance, life insurance, child care tax credits, etc.) are provided through the employment system. In Western Europe this is often not the case: health care is provided directly through the tax system and benefits come to people who are political "citizens" whether they work or not. In the United States, however, those outside the employment system are categorized as unworthy and made to feel it by excluding them from these systems of support. To varying degrees, we "take care" of the socially excluded by creating stigmatized categories for their benefits—welfare and Medicaid being prime examples. Yet we never confuse the approved, acceptable Americans with the undeserving, and we underscore the difference by separating them into different bureaucratic worlds.

For those on the positive side of the divide, those who work for a living, the rewards are far greater than a paycheck. The employed enter a social world in which their identities as mainstream Americans are shaped, structured, and reinforced. The workplace is the main institutional setting in which individuals become part of the collective American enterprise that lies at the heart of our culture: the market. We are so divided in other domains—race, geography, family organization, gender roles, and the like— that common ground along almost any other lines is difficult to achieve. Indeed, only in wartime do Americans tend to cleave to their national origins as a major feature of their self-concept. The French, by contrast, are French whether they work or not. But for our more diverse and divided society, participation in the world of work is the most powerful source of social integration.

It is in the workplace that we are most likely to mix with those who come from different backgrounds, are under the greatest pressure to subordinate individual idiosyncrasy to the requirements of an organization, and are called upon to contribute to goals that eclipse the personal. All workers have these experiences in common; even as segregation constrains the real mix of workers, conformity is expected to a greater degree for people who work in some kinds of jobs than in others, and the organizational goals to which they must subscribe are often elusive, unreachable, or at odds with personal desire.

The creation of an identity as a worker is never achieved by individuals moving along some preordained path. It is a transformation worked by organizations, firms, supervisors, fellow workers, and the whole long search that leads from the desire to find a job to the end point of landing one. This is a particularly dramatic transformation for ghetto youth and adults, for they face a difficult job market, high hurdles in convincing employers to take a chance on them, and relatively poor rewards—from a financial point of view—for their successes. But the crafting of an identity is an important developmental process for them, just as it is for their more privileged counterparts.

Powerful forces work to exclude minorities from full participation in American society. From a school system that provides a substandard education for millions of inner city kids, to an employment system rife with discrimination, to a housing market that segregates minority families, there is almost no truth to the notion that we all begin from the same starting line. Precisely because this is the case, blasting one's way through the job barrier and starting down that road of acquiring a common identity as a mainstream worker is of the greatest importance for the young. It may be one of the few available pipelines into the core of American society, and the one with the greatest payoff, symbolic and material.

The Social Costs of Accepting Low-Wage Work

Even though we honor the gainfully employed over the unemployed, all jobs are not created equal. Fast food jobs, in particular, are notoriously stigmatized and denigrated. "McJob" has become a common epithet for work without much redeeming value. The reasons for this are worth studying; [these] workers . . . have a mountain of stigma to overcome if they are to maintain their self-respect. Indeed, the organizational culture they join when they finally land a job at Burger Barn is instrumental in generating conditions and experiences that challenge a worker's self-esteem.

As Robin Leidner has argued, fast food jobs epitomize the assembly-line structure of de-skilled service positions: they are highly routinized and appear to the casual observer to be entirely lacking in discretion—almost military in their scripted nature. The symbolic capital of these assembly-line jobs can

be measured in negative numbers. They represent the opposite of the autonomous entrepreneur who is lionized in the popular culture, from *Business Week* to hip-hop.

Burger Barn workers are told that they must, at whatever cost to their own dignity, defer to the public. Customers can be unreasonably demanding, rude, even insulting, and workers must count backwards from a hundred in an effort to stifle their outrage. Servicing the customer with a smile pleases management because making money depends on keeping the clientele happy, but it can be an exercise in humiliation for teenagers. It is hard for them to refrain from reading this public nastiness as another instance of society's low estimation of their worth. But they soon realize that if they want to hold on to their minimum-wage jobs, they have to tolerate comments that would almost certainly provoke a fistfight outside the workplace.

It is well known among ghetto customers that crew members have to put up with whatever verbal abuse comes across the counter. That knowledge occasionally prompts nasty exchanges designed explicitly to anger the worker, to push him or her to retaliate verbally. Testing those limits is a favorite pastime of teenage customers in particular, for this may be the one opportunity they have to put a peer on the defensive in a public setting, knowing that there is little the victim can do in return.

It is bad enough to be on the receiving end of this kind of abuse from adults, especially white adults, for that has its own significance along race lines. It is even worse to have to accept it from minority peers, for there is much more personal honor at stake, more pride to be lost, and an audience whose opinion matters more. This, no doubt, is why harassment is a continual problem for fast food workers in Harlem. It burns. Their agemates, with plenty of anger bottled up for all kinds of reasons extraneous to the restaurant experience, find counterparts working the cash register convenient targets for venting.

Roberta is a five-year veteran of Burger Barn who has worked her way up to management. A formidable African-American woman, Roberta has always prided herself on her ability to make it on her own. Most of her customers have been perfectly pleasant; many have been longtime repeat visitors to her restaurant. But Roberta has also encountered many who radiate disrespect.

Could you describe some of the people who came into the store during your shift?

The customers? Well, I had alcoholics, derelicts. People that are aggravated with life. I've had people that don't even have jobs curse me out. I've dealt with all kinds. Sometimes it would get to me. If a person yelled out [in front of] a lobby full of people . . . "Bitch, that's why you work at [Burger Barn]," I would say [to myself], "I'm probably making more than you and your mother." It hurts when people don't even know what you're making and they say those things. Especially in Harlem, they do that to you. They call you all types of names and everything.

Natasha is younger than Roberta and less practiced at these confrontations. But she has had to contend with them nevertheless, especially from customers her age who at least claim to be higher up the status hierarchy. Though she tries, Natasha can't always control her temper and respond the way the firm wants her to.

It's hard dealing with the public. There are good things, like old people. They sweet. But the younger people around my age are always snotty. Think they better than you because they not working at [Burger Barn]. They probably work at something better than you.

How do you deal with rude or unfriendly customers?

They told us that we just suppose to walk to the back and ignore it, but when they in your face like that, you get so upset that you have to say something. . . . I got threatened with a gun one time. 'Cause this customer had threw a piece of straw paper in the back and told me to pick it up like I'm a dog. I said, "No." And he cursed at me. I cursed at him back, and he was like, "Yeah, next time you won't have nothing to say when I come back with my gun and shoot your ass." Oh, excuse me.

Ianna, who had just turned sixteen the summer she found her first job at Burger Barn, has had many of the same kinds of problems Natasha complains of. The customers who are rude to her are just looking for a place to vent their anger about things that have nothing to do with buying lunch. Ianna recognizes that this kind of thing could happen in any restaurant, but believes it is a special problem in Harlem, for ghetto residents have more to be angry about and fewer accessible targets. So cashiers in fast food shops become prime victims.

What I hate about [Burger Barn] is the customers, well, some of them that I can't stand. . . . I don't want to stereotype Harlem . . . but since I only worked in Harlem that's all I can speak for. Some people have a chip on their shoulders. . . . Most of the people that come into the restaurant are black. Most of them have a lot of kids. It's in the ghetto. Maybe, you know, they are depressed about their lifestyles or whatever else that is going on in their lives and they just . . . I don't know. They just are like, urff! And no matter what you do you cannot please them. I'm not supposed to say anything to the customer, but that's not like me. I have a mouth and I don't take no short from nobody. I don't care who it is, don't take anybody's crap.

Despite this bravado, Ianna knows well that to use her mouth is to risk her job. She has had to work hard to find ways to cope with this frustration that don't get her in trouble with management.

> I don't say stuff to people most of the time. Mostly I just look at them like they stupid. Because my mother always told me that as long as you don't say nothin' to nobody, you can't never get in trouble. If you look at them stupid, what are they going to do? If you roll your eyes at somebody like that, I mean, that's really nothing [compared to] . . . cursing at them. Most of the time I try to walk away.

As Ianna observes, there is enough free-floating fury in Harlem to keep a steady supply of customer antagonism coming the way of service employees every day of their work lives. The problem is constant enough to warrant official company policies on how crew members should respond to insults, on what managers should do to help, on the evasive tactics that will work best to quell an ugly situation without losing the business. Management tries to minimize the likelihood of incidents by placing girls on the registers rather than boys, in the apparent belief that young women attract less abuse and find it easier to quash their anger than young men.

Burger Barn does what it can to contend with these problems in the workplace. But the neighborhood is beyond their reach, and there, too, fast food workers are often met with ridicule from the people they grew up with. They have to learn to defend themselves against criticism that they have lowered themselves by taking these jobs, criticism from people they have known all their lives. As Stephanie explains, here too she leans on the divide between the worker and the do-nothing:

> People I hang out with, they know me since I was little. We all grew up together. When they see me comin', they laugh and say, "Here come Calvin, here come Calvin sister." I just laugh and keep on going. I say, "You're crazy. But that's okay 'cause I got a job and you all standing out here on the corner." Or I say, "This is my job, it's legal." Something like that. That Calvin commercial show you that even though his friends tease him he just brushed them off, then he got a higher position. Then you see how they change toward him.

Tiffany, also a teen worker in a central Harlem Burger Barn, thinks she knows why kids in her community who don't work give her such a hard time. They don't want her to succeed because if no one is "making it," then no one needs to feel bad about failing. But if someone claws her way up and it looks as if she has a chance to escape the syndrome of failure, it implies that everyone could, in theory, do so as well. The teasing, a thinly veiled attempt to enforce conformity, is designed to drag would-be success stories back into the fold.

> What you will find in any situation, more so in the black community, is that if you are in the community and you try to excel, you will get ridicule from your own peers. It's like the "crab down" syndrome. . . . If you put a bunch of crabs in a big bucket and one crab tries to get out, what do you think the other crabs would do now? According to my thinking, they should pull 'em up or push 'em or help 'em get out. But the crabs pull him back in the barrel. That's just an analogy for what happens in the community a lot.

Keeping everyone down protects against that creeping sense of despair which comes from believing things could be otherwise for oneself.

Swallowing ridicule would be a hardship for almost anyone in this culture, but it is particularly hard on minority youth in the inner city. They have already logged four or five years' worth of interracial and cross-class friction by the time they get behind a

Burger Barn cash register. More likely than not, they have also learned from peers that self-respecting people don't allow themselves to be "dissed" without striking back. Yet this is precisely what they must do if they are going to survive in the workplace.

This is one of the main reasons why these jobs carry such a powerful stigma in American popular culture: they fly in the face of a national attraction to autonomy, independence, and the individual's "right" to respond in kind when dignity is threatened. In ghetto communities, this stigma is even more powerful because—ironically—it is in these enclaves that this mainstream value of independence is most vigorously elaborated and embellished. Film characters, rap stars, and local idols base their claim to notoriety on standing above the crowd, going their own way, being free of the ties that bind ordinary mortals. There are white parallels, to be sure, but this is a powerful genre of icons in the black community, not because it is a disconnected subculture but because it is an intensified version of a perfectly recognizable American middle-class and working-class fixation.

It is therefore noteworthy that thousands upon thousands of minority teens, young adults, and even middle-aged adults line up for jobs that will subject them, at least potentially, to a kind of character assassination. They do so not because they start the job-seeking process with a different set of values, one that can withstand society's contempt for fast food workers. They take these jobs because in so many inner-city communities, there is nothing better in the offing. In general, they have already tried to get better jobs and have failed, landing at the door of Burger Barn as a last resort.

Social stigma has other sources besides the constraints of enforced deference. Money and mobility matter as well. Fast food jobs are invariably minimum-wage positions. Salaries rise very little over time, even for

first-line management. In ghetto areas, where jobs are scarce and the supply of would-be workers chasing them is relatively large, downward pressure on wages keeps these jobs right down at the bottom of the wage scale.

The public perception (fueled by knowledge of wage conditions) is that there is very little potential for improvement in status or responsibility either. Even though there are Horatio Algers in this industry, there are no myths to prop up a more glorified image. As a result, the epithet "McJob" develops out of the perception that fast food workers are not likely to end up in a prestigious job as a general manager or restaurant owner; they are going to spend their whole lives flipping burgers.

As it happens, this is only half true. The fast food industry is actually very good about internal promotion. Workplace management is nearly always recruited from the ranks of entry-level workers. Carefully planned training programs make it possible for employees to move up, to acquire transferable skills, and to at least take a shot at entrepreneurial ownership. McDonald's, for example, is proud of the fact that half of its board of directors started out as crew members. One couldn't say as much for the rest of the nation's Fortune 500 firms.

However, the vast majority never even get close to management. The typical entry-level worker passes through his or her job in short order, with an industry-average job tenure of less than six months. Since this is an average, it suggests that a large number of employees are there and gone in a matter of weeks. It is this pattern, a planned operation built around low skills and high turnover, that has given fast food jobs such a bad name. In order for the industry to keep functioning with such an unstable labor force, the jobs themselves must be broken down so that each step can be learned, at least at a rudimentary level, in a very short time. A vicious circle develops in which low wages are attached to low skills, encouraging high departure rates. Hence, although it is quite possible to rise above the fray and make a very respectable living as a general manager overseeing a restaurant, most crew members remain at the entry level and leave too soon to see much upward movement. Observing this pattern on such a large scale—in practically every town and city in the country—Americans naturally conclude that one can't get anywhere in a job like this, that there is no real future in it, and that anyone with more "on the ball" wouldn't be caught dead working behind the counter. . . . Mobility isn't necessarily that limited, but since that is not widely known, the negative impression sticks.

The stigma also stems from the low social status of the people who hold these jobs: minorities, teenagers, immigrants who often speak halting English, those with little education, and (increasingly in affluent communities afflicted with labor shortages) the elderly. To the extent that the prestige of a job refracts the social characteristics of its average incumbents, fast food jobs are hobbled by the perception that people with better choices would never purposely opt for a "McJob." . . . Entry-level jobs of this kind are undeserving of this scorn: more skill, discretion, and responsibility are locked up in a fast food job than is apparent to the public. But this truth hardly matters where public perception is concerned. There is no quicker way to indicate that a person is barely deserving of notice than to point out he or she holds a "chump change" job at Kentucky Fried Chicken or Burger King. We "know" this is the case just by looking at the age, skin color, or educational credentials of the people already on the job: the tautology has a staying power that even the smartest public relations campaign cannot shake.

Ghetto youth are particularly sensitive to the status degradation entailed in stigmatized employment. As Elijah Anderson (in *Streetwise*, University of Chicago Press, 1990)

and others have pointed out, a high premium is placed on independence, autonomy, and respect among minority youth in inner-city communities—particularly by young men. No small amount of mayhem is committed every year in the name of injured pride. Hence jobs that routinely demand displays of deference force those who hold them to violate "macho" behavior codes that are central to the definition of teen culture. There are, therefore, considerable social risks involved in seeking a fast food job in the first place, one that the employees and job-seekers are keenly aware of from the very beginning of their search for employment.

It is hard to know the extent to which this stigma discourages young people in places like central Harlem from knocking on the door of a fast food restaurant. It is clear that the other choices aren't much better and that necessity drives thousands, if not millions, of teens and older job-seekers to ignore the stigma or learn to live with it. But no one enters the central Harlem job market without having to face this gauntlet.

Tiffany started working in the underground economy bagging groceries when she was little more than ten years old because her mother was having trouble supporting the family, "checks weren't coming in," and there was "really a need for food." She graduated to summer youth by the time she was fourteen, but two years later she needed a "real" job that would last beyond the summer, so she set about looking—everywhere. As a young black teenager, she quickly discovered there wasn't a great deal open to her. Tiffany ended up at Burger Barn in the Bronx, a restaurant two blocks from her house and close enough to her high school to make after-school hours feasible.

The first Burger Barn I worked at was because nobody else would take me. It was a last resort. I didn't want to go to [Burger Barn]. You flip burgers. People would laugh at you. In high school, I didn't wanna be in that kind of environment. But lo and behold, after everything else failed, Martin Paints, other jobs, [Burger Barn] was welcoming me with open arms. So I started working there.

Tiffany moved to Harlem when she finished high school, and found she couldn't commute back to the Bronx. Still sensitive to the stigma attached to her old job, she tried her luck at moving up, out of the fast food business and into a service job with more of a "white-collar" flavor; she looked everywhere for a position in stores where the jobs are free of hamburger grease and hot oil for french fries, stores where clerks don't wear aprons or hairnets. Despite her best efforts, nothing panned out.

I'm looking at Lerners and Plymouth [clothing stores] and going to all these stores, but nothing is coming through. But [Burger Barn] was waitin' for me because I had two years of experience by then.

The new Burger Barn franchise was right in the middle of Harlem, not far from the room she rents over a storefront church, and it had the additional appeal of being "a black-owned business," something that mattered to Tiffany in terms of the "more cultural reasons why [she] decided to work there." She was glad to land a job, but worried that her high school diploma couldn't take her any farther than this entry-level position. It didn't augur well for the future.

William followed a similar pathway to Burger Barn, graduating from summer youth jobs in the middle of high school and looking for something that would help pay for his books and carfare. The Department of Labor gave him a referral to Burger Barn, but he was reluctant at first to pursue it.

To go there and work for [Burger Barn], that was one of those real cloak-and-dagger kinds of things. You'll be coming out [and your friends say], "Yo, where are you going?" You be, "I'm going, don't worry about where I'm going." And you see your friends coming [to the restaurant] and see you working there and now you be, "No, the whole [housing] project gonna know I work in [Burger Barn]." It's not something I personally proclaim with pride and stuff. . . . If you are a crew member, you really aren't shit there. . . . You got nothing there, no benefits, nothing. It was like that [when I was younger] and it's like that now.

William tried every subterfuge he could think of to conceal his job from the kids he knew. He kept his uniform in a bag and put it on in the back of the restaurant so that it would never be visible on the street. He made up fake jobs to explain to his friends where his spending money was coming from. He took circuitous routes to the Barn and hid back by the gigantic freezer when he spotted a friend coming in. The last thing William wanted was to be publicly identified as a shift worker at Burger Barn.

In this he was much like the other teen and young adult workers we encountered. They are very sensitive to stigma, to challenges to their status, and by taking low-wage jobs of this kind they have made themselves vulnerable to exactly the kind of insults they most fear. But the fact is that they do take these risks and, in time, latch on to other "narratives" that undergird their legitimacy.

Breaking the Stigma

One of the chief challenges facing an organization like Burger Barn involves taking people who have come to it on the defensive and turning them into workers who appear at least on the surface to enjoy their work. Customers have choices; they can vote with their feet. If ordering french fries at Burger Barn requires them to put up with rudeness or indifference from the person who takes their order, they can easily cross the street to a competitor the next time. It is clearly in the company's interest to find ways to turn the situation around. Ideally, from the industry's viewpoint, it would be best if the whole reputation of these jobs could be reversed. This is what McDonald's had in mind when it launched the Calvin series. But for all the reasons outlined earlier in this [reading], this probably won't come to pass, since the conditions that give rise to the stigma in the first place—low wages, high turnover, enforced deference—are not likely to change. Beyond publicizing the opportunities that are within reach, much of which falls on deaf ears, there is little the industry can do to rehabilitate its workers in the eyes of the public and thereby reduce the tension across the counter.

Yet behind the scenes, managers and workers and peers working together in restaurant crews do build a moral defense of their work. They call upon timeless American values to undergird their respectability. Pointing to the essential virtues of the gainfully employed, Burger Barn workers align themselves with the great mass of men and women who work for a living. "We are like them," they declare, and in so doing they separate themselves from the people in their midst who are not employed. And they have plenty of experience of individuals who don't work, often including members of their own families. They see beggars come around the restaurants looking for handouts every day; fast-talkers who walk into Burger Barn hoping for free food; agemates who prefer to deal drugs. In general, these low-wage workers are far less forgiving, far less tolerant, of these "losers" than are many liberal writers. Since they hold hard, poorly paid jobs, people like Kyesha or Jamal see little reason why anyone else ought to get a free ride. What the indigent should do is to follow their example: get a job, any job.

Ianna is an articulate case in point. She has had to confront the social degradation that comes from holding a "low job" and has developed a tough hide in response. Her dig-

nity is underwritten by the critique she has absorbed about the "welfare-dependent":

I'm not ashamed because I have a job. Most people don't, and I'm proud of myself that I decided to get up and do something at an early age. So as I look at it, I'm not on welfare. I'm doing something.

I'm not knocking welfare, but I know people that are on it that can get up and work. There's nothing wrong with them. And they just choose not to. . . . They don't really need to be on [welfare]. They just want it because they can get away with it. I don't think it's right, because that's my tax dollars going for somebody who is lazy, who don't wanna get up. I can see if a woman had three children, her husband left her, and she don't have no job 'cause she was a housewife. Okay. But after a while, you know, welfare will send you to school. Be a nurse assistant, a home attendant, something!

Even if you were on welfare, it should be like, you see all these dirty streets we have? Why can't they go out and sweep the streets, clean up the parks? I mean, there is so much stuff that needs to be done in this city. They can do that and give them their money. Not just sit home and not do anything.

Patricia, a mother of five children in her late thirties, has worked at Burger Barn for five years. She moved up to New York from Tennessee after her husband walked out on her, hoping to find more job opportunities than were available in the rural South. It took a long time for Patty to get on her feet; during the time she was really desperate, she turned to the welfare system to put food on the table. Eventually she broke free of her heavy-handed caseworker and landed her Burger Barn job. Given this background, one imagines Patty would be tolerant of AFDC recipients. After all, she has been there. Not so. Having finally taken the hard road to a real job, she sees no reason why anyone else should have an easier ride.

> There's so much in this city; it's always hiring. It may not be what you want. It may not be the pay you want. But you will always get a job. If I can work at Burger Barn all week and come home tired and then have to deal with the kids and all of that, and be happy with one twenty-five a week, so can you. Why would I give quarters [to bums on the street]? My quarter is tax-free money for you! No way.

Or, in a variation on the same theme, Larry reminds us that any job is better than no job. The kids who dare to hard-time Larry get nothing but a cold shoulder in return, because he knows deep down that he has something they don't have: work for which he gets paid.

> I don't care what other people think. You know, I just do not care. I have a job, you know. It's my job. You ain't puttin' *no* food on my table; you ain't puttin' *no* clothes on my back. I will walk tall with my Burger Barn uniform on. Be proud of it, you know.

Danielle is a little less confident, and allows that she doesn't advertise the nature of her job by wearing her uniform on the street. But she agrees with Larry that what is most important is that you work at all. What a person does for a living is less critical than willingness and ability to find and keep a job of any kind.

> Regardless of what kind of work you do, you still can be respected. Ain't saying I'm ashamed of my job, but I wouldn't walk down the street wearing the uniform. . . . Guys know you work there will say, "Hi, Burger Barn." I ain't gonna lie and say I'm not ashamed, period. But I'm proud that I'm working. You know,

my daughter's father . . . used to grab pigs and clean pigs all day. But he was respected for his job. I respected him because he worked, regardless of what kind of work it was. He got laid off a better job, and that was the only job he could find at the time. So he took it, and I respect him for that. Anybody who could work any kind of job should be respected. Because they was getting that money honestly. They don't have to go out there and get it illegal.

These conservative views trade on a sentiment shared by the working poor and the working class: work equals dignity and no one deserves a free ride. Of course, this means more coming from people who have stood on their feet for eight or nine hours at a stretch for the minimum wage. Virtually all they have to show for their trouble is the self-respect that comes from being on the right side of the chasm that separates the deserving (read "working") and the undeserving (read "nonworking") poor.

Other retorts to status insults are possible as well. Flaunting financial independence often provides a way of lashing back at acquaintances who deride young workers for taking jobs at Burger Barn. Brian, born in Jamaica but raised in some of Harlem's tougher neighborhoods, knows that his peers don't think much of his job. "They would just make fun," he says. "'Ah, you flipping burgers. You gettin' paid four twenty-five.' They'd go snickering down the street." But it wasn't long after Brian started working that he piled up some serious money, and everyone around him knew it.

> What I did was make Sam [the general manager] save my money for me. Then I got the best of clothes and the best sneakers with my own money. Then I added two chains. Then [my friends] were like, "Where you selling drugs at?" and I'm like, "The same place you said

making fun of me, flipping burgers. That's where I'm getting my money from. Now, where are you getting yours from?" They couldn't answer.

Media attention given to the glamour of the drug trade suggests that it is an attractive magnet for kids who need money. But the young adults we met in Harlem are frightened of the drug lords and want to stay as far away from their business as possible. They know too many people who are dead, in jail, or permanently disabled from the ravages of drugs. Kyesha explained:

> People like to down me, like this job wasn't anything, like it was a low job. Like selling drugs was better than working at fast foods. But I was like, "Nah." I never went that way, toward drugs, so I'm just gonna stick to what I do. Now they *locked up,* and I don't think I'm gonna get locked up for selling hamburgers and french fries!

If you aren't willing to join the underground economy, where are you going to get the money to dress yourself, go out on the town, and do the other things teens throughout the middle class do on Mom and Dad's sufferance? Harlem families cannot provide it. That leaves the youth themselves to earn the cash to support their lifestyle, a primary force pushing them to find jobs. A young man like Brian can remain a player in the local social scene by supporting his consumer needs with a job. He takes no small amount of pleasure outdoing his friends on style grounds they value as much as he does.

It might be comforting to believe that these hardworking, low-wage workers were, from the very beginning, different from their non-working counterparts, equipped somehow to withstand the gauntlet of criticism that comes their way when they start out on the bottom of the labor market. It would be comforting because we would then be able to sort the admirable poor (who recognize the

fundamental value of work and are willing to ignore stigma) from the rest (who collapse in the face of peer pressure and therefore prefer to go on the dole). This is simplistic. Burger Barn workers of all ages and colors have been the butt of jokes and the target of ridicule. Some, like Jamal, claim they don't care what other people think, but when you get to know them personally, they will admit that it took a long time, a lot of swallowed pride, to build up this confidence. The sting of public criticism did get to them.

How, then, did they manage to develop the backbone it takes to stay the course in a stigmatized job? How do ghetto residents develop the rejoinders that make it possible to recapture their dignity in the face of social disapproval? To some degree, they can call on widely accepted American values that honor working people, values that "float" in the culture at large. But this is not enough to construct a positive identity when the reminders of low status—coming from customers, friends, and the media—are relentless. Something stronger is required: a workplace culture that actively functions to overcome the negatives by reinforcing the value of the work ethic. Managers and veteran employees play a critical role in the reinforcement process. Together they create a cocoonlike atmosphere in the back of the restaurant where they counsel new workers distressed by bad-mouthing.

Kimberly, a twenty-year-old African-American woman, began working at Burger Barn when she was sixteen and discovered firsthand how her "friends" would turn on her for taking a low-wage job. Fortunately, she found a good friend at work who steadied her with a piece of advice:

> Say it's a job. You are making money. Right? Don't care what nobody say. You know? If they don't like it, too bad. They sitting on the corner doing what they are doing. You got to work making money. You know? Don't bother with what anybody has to say about it.

Kim's friend and adviser, a Burger Barn veteran who had long since come to terms with the insults of his peers, called upon a general status hierarchy that places the working above the nonworking as a bulwark against the slights. The advice Kim gleaned from her friend and her manager made a big difference in helping her to see that she deserves her dignity.

> Kids come in here . . . they don't have enough money. I'll be like, "You don't have enough money; you can't get [the food you ordered]." One night this little boy came in there and cursed me out. He [said], "That's why you are working at [Burger Barn]. You can't get a better job. . . ." I was upset and everything. I started crying. [My manager] was like, "Kim, don't bother with him. I'm saying, *you got a job.* You know. It is a *job.*"

Immigrants who have taken jobs in central Harlem are particularly in need of a defense against character assassination, because they are targets for the ire of African-Americans who resent their presence in a community with an insufficient number of jobs to go around. Ana, a native of Ecuador, had a very difficult time when she first began working as a hostess at Burger Barn. A pretty, petite nineteen-year-old, she was selected for the job because she has a sparkle and vivaciousness that any restaurant manager would want customers to see. But some of her more antagonistic black customers seemed to see her as an archetype: the immigrant who barely speaks a word of English and snaps up a job they may have tried to get themselves. Without the support of her bilingual Latino manager, she would not have been able to pull herself together and get on with the work.

> I wasn't sent to the grill or the fries [where you don't need to communicate with customers]. I was sent to the cash register, even though the managers

knew I couldn't speak English. That was only one week after my arrival in the U.S.! So I wasn't feeling very well at all. Black people were cursing me out, saying I shouldn't have that job. Thank God, three weeks later I met a manager who was Puerto Rican. He was my salvation. He told me, "Ana, it's not that bad." He'd speak to me in English, even though he knows Spanish. He'd tell me, "Don't cry. Dry off those tears. You'll be all right, you'll make it." So he encouraged me like no other person in that Burger Barn, especially when the customers would curse at me for not knowing English. He gave me courage, and after that it went much better.

Among the things this manager taught Ana was that she should never listen to people who give her a hard time about holding a job at Burger Barn. Having been a white-collar clerical worker in her native country, Ana was unhappy that she had slipped down the status hierarchy—and she still is. She was grateful to have a way to earn money, and her family was desperate for her contribution. But when customers insulted her, insinuating that someone who spoke limited English was barely worthy of notice, she turned to management for help. And she found it in the form of fellow Latino bosses who told her to hold her head up because she was, after all, working, while her critics, on the whole, were not.

With this moral armor in hand, Burger Barn workers often take the process of carving an honored identity one step further: they argue their jobs have hidden virtues that make them more valuable than most people credit. Tiffany decided in the end that there was more substance to her job than she initially believed:

> When I got in there, I realized it's not what people think. It's a lot more to it than flipping burgers. It's a real system of business. That's when I really got to

see a big corporation at play. I mean, one part of it, the foundation of it. Cashiers. The store, how it's run. Production of food, crew workers, service. Things of that nature. That's when I really got into it and understood a lot more.

Americans tend to think of values as embedded in individuals, transmitted through families, and occasionally reinforced by media images or role models. We tend not to focus on the powerful contribution that institutions and organizations make to the creation and sustenance of beliefs. Yet it is clear that the workplace itself is a major force in the creation of a "rebuttal culture" among these workers. Without this haven of the fellow-stigmatized, it would be very hard for Burger Barn employees to retain their dignity. With this support, however, they are able to hold their heads up, not by defining themselves as separate from society, but by calling upon their commonality with the rest of the working world.

This is but one of the reasons why exclusion from the society of the employed is such a devastating source of social isolation. We could hand people money, as various guaranteed-income plans of the past thirty years have suggested. But we can't hand out honor. Honor comes from participation in this central setting in our culture and from the positive identity it confers.

Roosevelt understood this during the Great Depression and responded with the creation of thousands of publicly funded jobs designed to put people to work building the national parks, the railway stations, the great highways that crisscross the country, and the murals that decorate public walls from San Francisco to New York. Social scientists studying the unemployed in the 1930s showed that people who held WPA jobs were far happier and healthier than those who were on the dole, even when their incomes did not differ significantly. WPA workers had their dignity in the midst of poverty; those on the dole were vilified and could not justify their existence or find an effective cultural rationale for the support they received.

This historical example has its powerful parallels in the present. Joining the workforce is a fundamental, transformative experience that moves people across barriers of subculture, race, gender, and class. It never completely eradicates these differences, and in some divisive settings it may even reinforce consciousness of them—through glass ceilings, discriminatory promotion policies, and the like. But even in places where pernicious distinctions are maintained, there is another, overarching identity competing with forms that stress difference: a common bond within the organization and across the nation of fellow workers. This is what makes getting a job so much more than a means to a financial end. . . .

37

American Untouchables
Homeless Scavengers in San Francisco's Underground Economy

Teresa Gowan

An early morning at Bryant Salvage, a Vietnamese recycling business, finds a variety of San Francisco's scavengers converging to sell their findings. Vehicle after vehicle enters the yard to be weighed on the huge floor scale before dumping its load in the back; ancient pickup trucks with wooden walls, carefully loaded laundry carts, canary Cadillacs stuffed to overflow with computer paper, the shopping carts of homeless men, a 1950s ambulance carrying newspaper, and even the occasional gleaming new truck. The homeless men unload their towers of bottles and cardboard while young Latino van recyclers shout jokes across them. Middle-aged Vietnamese women in jeans and padded jackets buzz around on forklifts or push around great tubs full of bottles and cans, stopping occasionally to help elderly people with their laundry carts. The van recyclers repeatedly honk their horns at the homeless guys to get out of the way. The homeless recyclers, silently methodical in their work, rarely respond.

Equivalent scenes can be found in Jakarta, San Salvador, or Calcutta. The collection and sale of other people's trash is a common means of survival for very poor people all over the world. At the moment full-time scavenging is most prevalent in poorer countries, where a huge variety of people collect, sort out and clean rags, paper,

cardboard, metals, and glass, often living on the dumps where they work. They either sell these materials for recycling, or directly recycle them into new products themselves. The United States and Western Europe have had their own share of trash pickers. The wharf rats and the tinkers, the rag and bone men, the mudlarks and the ragpickers, all lived off working the garbage of industrialization until the early twentieth century. However, in these countries welfare capitalism eventually absorbed most poor people into the waged working class, leaving only the formal municipal garbage workers and an insignificant scrap economy supplied by eccentric junk lovers, schoolchildren, and the occasional part-time cardboard or can recycler.

Trash is back. Over the last ten years the US recycling industry has mushroomed on both the formal and informal levels, taking the form of a double tiered system which relies heavily on informal labor for sorting and collection, while reprocessing is dominated by large capital enterprises. Informal labor in recycling falls into two distinct groups: the general population who sort their own household recycling for free (sometimes required by law), and those who collect and sort in order to sell. This paper is concerned with the second group. . . .

Informal Recycling in the Broader Political Economy

Homeless men are the most immediately visible group of San Francisco's recyclers, as they work in the daytime and collect from

Abridgment of "American Untouchables: Homeless Scavengers in San Francisco's Underground Economy," by Teresa Gowan, presented at the Regular Session on the Informal Economy, ASA 1995. Reprinted by permission of the author.

unsorted public and private trash. Making only a few dollars a load, many recyclers work more than 12 hours a day, sometimes taking in two or even three loads of 100–200 pounds each. However, the greatest volume of informal recycling is brought in by the van recyclers. Latinos and Asian Americans, many of them first generation and undocumented immigrants, use vans to collect large quantities of cardboard and bottles. Known by their competitors in the city's official recycling company as the "mosquito fleet," the van recyclers work at night and in the early morning, preempting the weekly runs of the curbside recycling program trucks or collecting the boxes and bottles put out by bars and restaurants every night. Small numbers of African American and white car-drivers specialize in computer paper and newsprint. Yet another significant group are elderly people who gather unobtrusively from public trash using plastic bags which they usually consolidate into laundry carts when they go to the recycling companies.

The increases in volume reported by the recycling business is repeated in the accounts of homeless recyclers. Clarence, who has recycled in the southern part of the So-Ma district since 1991, says that there are now 25–30 men working a patch that used to only support five of them. Sam reckoned that there were five times more recyclers in the 24th Street area than when he began five years ago.

The Loss of Formal Work

The increase of informal recycling has occurred in the context of the radical transformations of the country's political economy since the 1970s. These changes include a sharp decrease in industrial jobs, especially union ones, a scaling down of formalized relationships between the state and economic enterprises, and a general decentralization of economic activity.

California suffered the effects of restructuring later than the older manufacturing regions of the United States. The state was insulated from the manufacturing collapse of the early 1980s by its disproportionate share of defense contracts, its large share of booming computer and bio-tech companies, and a real-estate frenzy financed by the spectacular but ephemeral successes of the LA-based junk-bond market. The inability of these industries to really sustain the bulk of California's working class is now revealed. Working class Californians are suffering from a prolonged and severe recession, losing 1.5 million jobs in 1990–2, including 1/4 of all manufacturing jobs. Construction, always the best bet for unskilled male labor, has practically stopped—the rate of housing starts is the lowest since the Second World War. Within San Francisco the very disjunction between the collapse of heavy industry and the still booming informational industries has added to the problems of blue collar workers by bringing in large numbers of younger people with high disposable incomes who are willing and able to pay increasingly fantastic rents and house prices.

The experience of the recyclers I've interviewed suggests that the rise of recycling is at least in part a direct product of this job crisis. The new full-time scavengers started recycling as a last resort, after failing to find better paid work. Victoriano, a Mexican van recycler, described how he and several other van recyclers moved to California with the idea of getting construction work, but have had to settle for recycling instead. Anita, an elderly recycler, started the work when her daughter's data entry job was cut back to 20 hours a week.

For the homeless recyclers the process of moving into recycling was more drawn out and complex, given that they only noticed this line of work after they had already become homeless. The story tends to be that the multiple economic and emotional strains of long-term unemployment propelled these men on to the street. While they didn't even consider cart recycling before, once they were homeless recycling became "making the best of it," a partial solution to both extreme financial hardship and the indignities of their condition. The stories of Bill, Jordan, and Victor are typical in this regard. Bill previously worked for PG&E as a mechanic for 17 years, but was laid off in cutbacks in the fall of 1988. Jordan had a relatively well-paid union job as a forklift operator in Oakland before his company closed down. According to both of these men, unemployment transformed a controllable alcohol habit into a major problem, their families left them, and they became homeless. Victor, a skilled carpenter who moved here from New Mexico in 1994, spent six months unsuccessfully looking for construction work before ending up sleeping under the 101 freeway and recycling.

The Contraction of Welfare Benefits

The devastating effect of the job losses on the current Californian recession are intensified by their coincidence with severe welfare cuts on both the local and federal levels. While laid-off workers in Northern and Western Europe are still at least partially protected by social democratic safety nets, Americans left unemployed by the vast job losses of the last few years have had only minimal help from the welfare system, once their unemployment eligibility has run out.

Conditions have always been harsh for Americans living on benefits. However, the political and economic restructuring of the last 20 years has included a substantial reduction of the standard of living for the disabled, the unemployed, and their dependents. The US welfare system's historical principle of "less eligibility" requires that welfare benefits pay less than work,

with the argument that people will only work when they can make more by working than by claiming benefits. Union-busting, capital flight, and the subsequent mushrooming of temporary work and subcontracting combined to drive the going wage for the working poor below the existing level of welfare benefits.[1] . . .

Welfare contraction has not been coupled with looser work rules for those still receiving benefits. As a result, the benefit cuts force recipients into participation in the underground economy. Elderly people without family support or private pension schemes, single adults on disability, women with children on AFDC, and above all single able-bodied adults on welfare ("General Assistance" in California), simply cannot get by without supplementing their income through other means. Mary, a woman with bad arthritis who brings in about 70 lbs. of recycling every morning, started recycling after her SSI entitlement was reduced. . . . Most homeless recyclers are only eligible for GA, which comes to $345 a month, barely enough to cover a month's rent in a welfare hotel. The welfare system therefore simultaneously requires claimants to work and forces this work underground by surveilling and penalizing any work for money in the formal economy.

The "Capital Strategy" Analysis

For working class people caught between unemployment and welfare contraction, recycling has become an important subsistence strategy, attracting increasing numbers of homeless men, recent Filipino, Chinese and Latino immigrants, Southeast Asian refugees on welfare, and poor elderly people.

Through which wide-angle lens should we view this booming underground economy in trash? The dominant practice in the informal economy literature has been to see the growing underground economy as just one more element of the systemic offensive of capital against organized labor and government regulation. In this model, the formal and informal economies are not in competition but instead form interlocking systems which combine to maximize the profits of large capital. Castells and Portes clearly articulate this perspective when they describe the informal economy as "a new form of control characterized by the disenfranchisement of a large sector of the working class, often with the acquiescence of the state."[2]. . .

Castells and Portes' conception of informal economic activity as a capital strategy effectively explains the case of the recycling industry, where informal "production" is clearly dependent on a close relationship with large capital. The recycling collected in the informal sector eventually ends up in the hands of large corporations, as reprocessing technology is too expensive for small capital. Informal recyclers, therefore, function as essential intermediaries between consumers and capital, with thousands of informal recyclers in the Bay Area feeding perhaps a hundred small recycling companies, which in turn feed a smaller number of large buyers who export fiber, metal, and glass all over the world. In this globalized industry bottles, cans, and cardboard collected on neighborhood streets are more likely to end up in Asia or Australia than in local recycled products.[3]

Control by large capital is apparent on the local level. San Francisco's garbage giant, Norcal, dominates both the legal and the informal economies in trash. Norcal holds the city contract for both garbage collection and curbside recycling. The company also owns the two largest recycling companies in the city, both of which overwhelmingly buy from the professional scavengers of the informal economy.

It is unlikely that Norcal's official collection company would find it profitable to take over the frequent and comprehensive collection performed by informal recyclers across the city. Their weekly curbside program is too infrequent for small restaurants and bars with limited storage space, whereas the informal recyclers have a nightly circuit. In addition, the homeless and elderly recyclers get much of their material from unsorted trash which would end up as garbage. Through its recycling companies, Norcal still ends up with most of the recycling collected by the informals. "What do you say," laughs Samuel Stewart II of the city recycling department, "yes, we still make money from it!" In practice the informals provide a recycling labor force which is cheaper than the union workers of Norcal's curbside program, and greatly increases the company's volume of recycling.

The "capital strategy" implementation of San Francisco's recycling industry is therefore persuasive on the purely economic level. Rather than competing with formal industry, the informal recyclers serve as a cheap collection service for a few large companies, primarily Norcal's vertically integrated conglomerate. These companies would not have been able to rely on the efforts of the informal recyclers without so many other businesses shrinking their formal operations, creating a "fourth world" of workers permanently pushed off the bottom of the formal labor market and only partially supported by the state. Recycling is therefore both typical of capital restructuring and dependent on it at the same time.

There are, however, serious problems with the "capital strategy" model. The argument tends towards functionalism, jumping too quickly from what capital needs to what capital gets. I now turn to my participant observation with homeless recyclers, in hopes of showing that such an assumption strips away the living center of social life, thereby obscuring the processes by which informal economic arrangements are sustained and reproduced from day to day.[4]

Meanings of Recycling for Homeless Men

Even for men on the street, recycling is a choice, although it is a choice made within severe constraints. Homeless people are doing all sorts of things to get by: panhandling, washing car windows or shop windows, drug dealing, selling the Street Sheet paper, doing the service agency shuffle, performing music or poetry, stealing, selling clothes or books, and turning tricks.

All these occupations vary to some extent along the lines of race and gender. The typical recycler is a man in his 30s or 40s, most often African American, but with large minorities of whites and Latinos. The racial breakdown of recyclers is therefore not noticeably dissimilar from that of the general homeless population, although there are perhaps a few more white men. Gender, on the other hand, is extremely skewed. Out of hundreds of homeless recyclers on the San Francisco scene I have encountered only four women, all classically "butch," with a muscular and taciturn self-presentation. The two I know have long histories of doing male-dominated jobs. One of them used to be a traffic cop, the other a van driver. Recycling is almost exclusively a man's job. In general there are still many more men than women on the street.[5] However, the extreme scarcity of female recyclers is better explained by the gendered nature of the work. There are, after all, several homeless women who walk around with their husbands and boyfriends as they work; however, they studiously ignore the process of recycling, rarely even touching the cart, let alone actually doing any dumpster diving. While recycling can be made to fit certain masculinities, it repulses women with mainstream conceptions of femininity. One woman selling clothes on the street described recycling as a filthy job which "no woman should have to do. I'd rather stand in line all day."

If anything is clear from my field work it is that even for these most socially excluded and degraded informal workers, their work couldn't be further from the analytically empty space of hand to mouth "survival." Despite the low pay, many of the homeless recyclers really get into their work with enthusiasm. They do not express the sullen resentment of people acting only out of economic compulsion—a self-presentation which is overwhelmingly in evidence in social welfare establishments. The work is inherently hard. Clarence, a very strong but not particularly obsessive recycler, works 7 or 8 hours daily, dragging two carts tied together for about nine miles and collecting 250 pounds of recycling for his average $20 receipt. Bill the Mechanic has put in at least 16 hours on the days I've spent with him, barely ever stopping for a break. His daily income of under $30 works out at about $1.80 per hour of intense physical labor. Yet recyclers often push themselves beyond reasonable goals, working obsessively fast and energetically. Keeping their carts on the road for speed they steam along, leaning hard into their loads and darting searching glances from side to side. Several recyclers I know work for 12 or more hours a day, and it's not unusual to find lonely carts full of recycling whose owners have passed out from dehydration and exhaustion.

The recyclers are also eager to display their great efforts to other people. Sam, a middle-aged white man who died by the side of his recycling cart earlier this year, was always concerned with asserting the validity of his work to others. The first time I ever met him he pointedly told me a story of an argument with a "resident" the night before. "Hey, keep the noise down, I've got to *work* in the morning," the man had shouted out of a window. "What do you think I'm doing," Sam had shouted in return. "They just don't think, you know," he said in retrospect. "They think we do this for fun or something. I work hard,

I clear up the neighborhood. Don't beg, don't steal, don't deal drugs. You'd think people could be civil to me." Although Sam was unusual in his willingness to fight back at housed people, the same eagerness to impress the serious nature of their work on others is standard among the recyclers. Their physical movements themselves have elements of mime. Like the superhard stare of the gang-banger or cop, the obsessively workaholic self-presentation of many recyclers suggests how much they have to prove by *how* they do their work. We are already a long way from the simple economic self-preservation implied by the capital strategy model.

Why should the homeless recyclers be so emotionally involved in a job which is physically exhausting, low paid, and most of all, significantly stigmatized by much of the general population as not only disgusting but akin to stealing? To get at this question we need to take the experience of homelessness seriously, not only as an indication of extreme economic hardship, but as an extraordinary dehumanizing and frightening location on the American social map.

The Dominant Constructions of Homelessness

The recyclers are fighting a formidable and ancient set of discourses which set up homeless people as powerful symbols of deviance and decay. These can be simplified into two dominant strands which I call the exclusion discourse and the social welfare discourse.

The exclusion discourse sets up homelessness as a representation of fundamental and threatening outsiderness. Here homelessness is characterized by madness, the rejection of rules, and general failure or refusal to control the physical and emotional manifestations of the animal self. The disproportionately large number of African-Americans who are homeless adds in three centuries worth of white race-think which places people with dark skin somewhere on the border between culture and nature, human and animal. Through this lens people who are not homeless intuitively attribute disgusting and irrational impulses to homeless people. In the case of recyclers, the symbolic connection of homelessness and trash is often so powerful that others don't require any rational explanation for their dumpster diving activities at all. One of the bartenders I interviewed seemed surprised at the idea of homeless recyclers selling the bottles they collect every night from his bar. "Oh yes, I suppose they do sell them—I've never really thought about it," he said.

The exclusion discourse has recently taken on a new intensity. As long as homeless people were relatively rare, they could safely symbolize intemperance, dirt, and savagery without being considered a real threat. But with the huge growth in homelessness since the early 1980s, the meaning of homeless people in public space is in the process of reinterpretation. No longer isolated *representations* of disorder, the exclusion discourse represents the "new homelessness" as a full-scale *invasion* by disruption, madness, dirt, criminality, and free-roaming idleness. Exclusive practices against homeless people have become more hostile and the use of institutional force has intensified. Local politicians, police departments, and chambers of commerce have responded to the appearance of large numbers of extremely poor people who have nowhere to disappear to by redefining public space as private space with selective access for people who don't look poor. In the same commercial strips where "consumers" are encouraged to "browse" and "linger," homeless people are moved on, cited, and arrested. In the last year, San Francisco police have issued 15,000 tickets under the "Matrix" program for "encampment," "aggressive panhandling," "urinating in public" or "obstructing freedom of movement."

The exclusion discourse attacks homeless people as a threat to the shared values of the wider society. In contrast, the degrading practices of the welfare agencies set them up as incompetent victims. Welfare and health agencies move to analyze and tame the people outside by curing the poor of their problems and reincorporating them into housed society. In this kinder discourse, the problem of homelessness is now a pitiful state entered involuntarily, and the solution is a technical question of how to best help the vulnerable poor rehabilitate themselves. Homelessness represents not a free space but a pathetic and mundane condition. The dangerous, even visionary madness and hedonistic abandon portrayed in the exclusion discourse are contained and tamed by the social welfare discourse's mechanistic categories of involuntary mental illness, social disconnection, and substance abuse.

The American social welfare discourse is profoundly individualistic. Inability to prosper is an individual failure, stemming from personal deficiencies. For example, any analysis of a homeless person's economic activity focuses on how they consume resources, rather than how they produce value. Although agencies may recognize that a single person especially cannot live on GA alone, money-earning activity is uniformly classified as deviance rather than subsistence. By setting up "the problem of poverty" in this way the social welfare discourse draws a curtain over the self-sustaining (and self-defining) parts of poor people's lives.

Fighting Hostile Images of "The Homeless"

What both the exclusion discourse and the social welfare discourse have in common is their assertion that the state of homelessness is but an external representation of a profound internal difference from the rest of society. The response of the homeless recyclers is to argue through their work that they are neither strange nor evil nor incompetent, but just decent working men down on their luck. Rejecting both the criminality and insanity attributed to them by the exclusion discourse and the feminizing picture of pathetic incompetence and vulnerability created by the social welfare discourse, recyclers aggressively assert their normality, hard work, competence, and self-sufficiency.

Recyclers often complain of the indignities of social welfare institutions. Although few go so far as to quit the welfare system completely, recyclers turn their back on their status as welfare clients and embrace an identity based on their work. Differentiating themselves strongly from "stiffs" and "winos," recyclers are not heavy users of soup kitchens or shelters, only moving inside if they get sick or the weather hits freezing. Many would agree with Jordan: "I hate the shelters, don't like being around all the bums. It's depressing. You can't keep any self-respect."

For those who have spent long years in prison, dealing with the welfare system takes on an added significance. After doing eight years inside in the 1980s, James, a white man in his early forties, has turned his back on what he calls the "poverty system" completely. "When you've been in the joint, shit, you've done your time and you don't want to do any more. I'm a citizen . . . (sigh). Dealin' with the welfare and the hotels, it's like another sentence, it really is. I have to go through that any more? No. It's about time for life, real life." I asked him if recycling was real life. He laughed. "Well, that's a question. Mm. Yes, yes it is . . . it's *more* of a life anyway. You do your own thing, you know." After looking life in the eye from both locations James has decided that he prefers recycling and sleeping rough to living in the hotels and spending long hours in service agency lines. In defiance of the wider society's stigmatization of homelessness he insists that the recycling life allows him to be a man worthy of respect.

Rejecting the social welfare construction of the homeless man as a pathetic dependent, recyclers use their work to demonstrate that they are both self-sufficient and competent. Some emphasize physical strength and effort, others formal knowledge and resourcefulness. Those with technical education will often apply it to their work. Dobie is an African American recycler who works the prosperous Richmond neighborhood. He has customized a big cart, adding wheels with real tires and inner tubes. He demands respect for his work, striding along in the middle of the road, holding up traffic with imperious hand signals. Like Bill the Mechanic, Dobie applies technical concepts to the haulage aspects of recycling. Bill explains the best angle to hold your cart in relation to the road using math formulas. Dobie blinds with science in his discussions of the mechanics of weight distribution and cart design.

The recyclers are equally concerned with struggling against the exclusion discourse's representations of homelessness as criminality, madness, and disorder. Recyclers uniformly pride themselves on living as much within the law as is possible for a homeless person. Many people say explicitly that recycling is a way for them to do an honest day's work, without having to hustle or cheat. At the extreme is a person like Clarence, an African American man in his late thirties who had a desk job in the army for several years. Clarence sends in every receipt he gets to General Assistance, and will not touch the dumpsters rented out by the Norcal recycling company. Sam, who usually dropped by every couple of days, avoided me for weeks out of embarrassment over a small loan he was unable to repay.

A major priority for most recyclers is to build regular, exclusive relationships with suppliers in businesses and apartment buildings. Apart from the obvious benefits of stabilizing income, such connections are important points of pride, ways to convince themselves and others that people who are not homeless rely on their services and trust them to keep to a routine. These relationships are often referred to in formal business language: "I try not to default on my schedule," says Dobie. "I've got several long-standing accounts in the Castro area," says Jordan.

Relationships with suppliers make recyclers feel that they can claim to be part of "the community," rather than outside. To be seen to get on with one another is equally important. The exclusion discourse pictures homeless people as living outside rules and social restraint, acting on impulse. Two bartenders who refused to let homeless recyclers take their bottles both explained their decisions by their wish to avoid fights. "See, that would cause fights. We can't have them fighting outside the bar, it's bad for business," said one man. Neither of them had seen a fight between recyclers—but this is how they expected homeless people to behave.

Knowing that others are likely to see them in this way, recyclers strongly reject suggestions that they compete with each other for resources. Rather than fighting over scraps, recyclers treat each other as solidaristic blue collar workers. "There's no shortage, we don't need to be competing" is the accepted wisdom. It's not unusual to hear men who are only superficial acquaintances comparing their night's work after they have sold their load, telling each other where they found the best stuff. "Well, a man wouldn't just take that information and go and clean up ahead of me," Sam explained. "I mean, well, he would be embarrassed." Even Clarence, who has big plans for expanding into van recycling, and thinks of himself as an "entrepreneurial dude," puts group solidarity before financial gain. A couple of years ago he was working the area around where he lives too intensively and some of the older men asked him to cool off a bit. "Come on, Clarence, a man needs a smoke now and then." "And that was cool," says Clarence. "I don't want to be getting in anyone else's way. There's plenty out there for everyone."

Another way that the recyclers reject the antisocial characteristics attributed to them by the exclusion discourse is by forging a strict separation between work and leisure. They are acutely aware that the "unemployed" man becomes marked out from "decent" working class men when the crucial masculine work/leisure distinction blurs into the more ambiguous state of "hanging out." The recyclers' stigmatization as homeless people and their lack of privacy for leisure time combine to create a presumption of guilt—any moment of rest is liable to be interpreted by others as indication that they are a "bum." Many respond to this problem by hiding away alone in secluded space when they are not working. Others create clear spatial and temporal breaks between "work" and "leisure" by alternating vigorous work with a scheduled "breakfast break" or "lunch-hour" where they abandon their carts to socialize, eat, or drink in parks or street corners. One group of younger and more sociable African Americans in the So-Ma area regularly get together to barbecue and drink on a Friday or Saturday night. "We're single men, you know. We like to party."

Who Is Attracted to Recycling?

Men move towards recycling not just because it provides a way to demonstrate certain qualities, but also because it is the informal job they are best *able* to do. The majority of the homeless recyclers in my sample have a substantial history of stable blue-collar employment and only hit skid row life in their 30s or later. This kind of life-history tends to produce a man who is either uncomfortable or inexperienced with using his "personality" for direct economic gain. Socialized as a routinized blue collar worker, the typical recycler finds it difficult to change himself into a hustler, even an uncriminalized hustler such as a car washer or "street sheet" vendor. Victor describes himself as "an old-fashioned guy. I'm not real sociable. This (recycling) suits me because, in general I mean, no one bothers you much, you can get your pay without having to bullshit about it." Victor's self-contained, taciturn masculinity was sustainable, perhaps even essential in the lower-middle-class, Latino community where he spent most of his previous life. Now that he is homeless his refusal to take on a more communicative, more subordinate role has become a luxury he can afford by doing recycling.

Recycling therefore gives people an opportunity of making a living which is culturally and often spatially removed from the usual walkways of ghetto life. While this chance to make an honest buck outside of the ghetto economy is most clearly welcomed by men who feel profoundly "away from home" on skid row, recycling also appeals to cons and hustlers looking for a change. Spike spent two years stealing from cars with his best buddy Valentino, but now they are using recycling to keep straight:

> I've changed, don't want to get in trouble any more. I got one felony, I don't intend to get the other two. But I don't want to do that shit anyway. This is better. I like recycling. It's real interesting what you find out there when you put your mind to it. And you're not doin', anyone any harm.

Those recyclers who work the most strenuously tend to be men who previously held long-lasting and decently paid semi-skilled or skilled jobs in the formal economy. Many of them are white, but by no means exclusively. These mostly older men are more intense about their work, and rarely sociable with other recyclers. Clarence, who is a charitable sort of guy, says, "It's not that they're alienated or anything . . . they're just doin' their route, no time to chat." I disagree. My impression is that those men who have achieved some part of the American dream but then lost it find their homeless state a continual source of pain and shame. As a result they can't get much comfort from others in the same position. Only by totally immersing themselves in their recycling work can they feel that they are still men in the way they learned to think of manhood in their formative years.

The almost obsessive effort that these recyclers put into their work becomes understandable when you realize that every heave of the cart is a blow against the ever-present image of the welfare bum. This helps to explain why Bill the Mechanic, who has fallen from the prosperity of a suburban ranch house and two cars, works every waking hour; why his brother Sam worked himself to death on the job at 48.

Using Recycling to Redefine Homelessness

No matter how hard recyclers like Bill and Sam work, they cannot escape other people's perception of them as just another faceless private in the homeless army. In truth, far from proving difference from "the homeless" as constructed in mainstream discourses, doing recycling is a clear mark of the condition of homelessness, at least for work age men. These men have only got into recycling since they became homeless. In many years under the poverty line Valentino and Spike had never considered recycling, yet they instantly gravitated towards recyclers as a natural peer group within the homeless population, making their first rounds only one day after they had to move onto the street. I knew Valentino before he became homeless, and he called me a couple of days after he moved outside. "We've been

sleeping in this alley down by Folsom, doin' just fine," he said. "We met some nice guys down here. Showed us the tricks of recycling." Only one of the sample had done recycling before becoming homeless, and he was using a truck to collect valuable scrap metals like copper and brass.

Recyclers respond to the close connection between homelessness and recycling in two ways. Some still try to escape a homeless identity by trying to look as un-homeless as possible in their personal appearance, and by working all the time and not socializing with other homeless people. Neither Danny nor Jordan ever use the term "homeless" at all. Still in shock, Jordan looks only to the past or the future. "I'm just waiting for something to come up," he says. "I've got a (truck-driving) license, you know. . . . A man with a *license* shouldn't be in this position."

Others accept that they will be seen as homeless and consciously use their work to assert a "positive" homeless identity which contradicts the exclusion and social welfare discourses. In order to do this they often end up drawing new lines of exclusion: "Us recycling guys, well we're different from other homeless you know. We don't just bum around and do drugs."

Some of the recyclers have a more militant homeless identification. James is extremely angry about the collective abuse of the homeless by the SFPD, intensified under the current "Matrix program." Using a standard American individualist conception of citizenship he argues that recyclers provide for themselves economically and they harm no one. He therefore deserves the same presumption of innocence, the same common respect, and the same civil liberties as any other citizen.

While these approaches are radically different in their political implications, at the level of everyday self-presentation they work out much the same. All of these people work hard to present an image of competence and industry to the rest of the population, an image which contradicts the dominant meanings of homelessness.

In this way the recyclers make of their work a cultural project to transform the stigma of dumpster-diving into a public demonstration of normality and self-sufficiency. They thereby challenge the symbolic fault lines which separate homeless people from everyone else, making the implicit (and often explicit) argument that the problem of homelessness is not created by the differences and deficiencies of homeless people themselves, but is both part and product of the wider society.

> It makes me so mad when people are disrespectful. I mean, can't they see? It could have happened to them, to anybody almost, you know. I mean, you can't protect yourself against bad luck. I'm not a bad man. Can't they see?

Luther's question, "Can't they see?", is both metaphorical and literal. As he sees it, those who see *him* hard at work recycling should be able to figure out that he is an ordinary, decent man, rather than some shadowy representation of what they themselves are not.

Abstract versus Situated Labor

The capital strategy perspective emphasizes macro-structural limitations rather than the practices people develop within them. At its most extreme, it reduces the efforts of informal workers to pre-social survival by adaptation. But while objective constraints are indeed massive for the homeless recyclers, this desperately poor and socially degraded group refuse to compete aggressively or treat each other instrumentally, insisting instead on respect and solidarity as the basis of their relationships. Rather than scrabbling for survival as faceless victims of structural forces, the recyclers use their work to

enact the principles they believe in: self-sufficiency, community, work ethic, "dependable" behavior.

Although they are experiencing extreme poverty and often despair, homeless recyclers don't experience their work lives as new grooves "distributed" by capital to take advantage of their desperation. Within the harsh constraints imposed by homelessness, they have taken up this particular work because it suits their needs, skills, and sense of self better than the other ways they could make money. Other people on the street have very different orientations; Valentino described his friends among the street crack dealers as "*not* impressed" by his recycling. He thought it highly unlikely that any of them would try recycling, seeing as they had always been "different" from him. Most typically, recyclers welcome the opportunity to earn cash from "good honest labor" without either hustling or enacting dependency. Choosing the hard labor of recycling over the various forms of "hustling" performed by other homeless men, the recyclers tend to share a specific previous life experience—that of the male blue collar worker in a routinized workplace in the formal economy.

The move into recycling reflects not only a particular past but a particular reaction to being homeless. Without the status crisis of homelessness these proud native men would not even consider recycling, let alone invest it with such symbolic significance. However, once they become homeless, recycling becomes thinkable. And once they become recyclers, that experience becomes part of what they are and what they can and cannot do, shaping their future possibilities and limitations, likes and dislikes. Labor is part of a life, past, present, and future.

To say that recyclers make a social world out of picking up garbage, and that they have adopted this particular form of work available to homeless people because it "suits" them does not necessarily challenge the capital strategy analysis. It does, however, fill it out substantially. When we do ethnography, we are forced to replace the automatons of macro-social theory with real people. In this case, qualitative fieldwork shows us the concrete ways that a group of informal workers come to "consent" to their economic activity, even making of it a centerpiece of their lives. While the capital strategy analysis may outline the origins of informal recycling, only a closer look at the social world of the recyclers explains how it is sustained and reproduced by the people who do it. . . .

In the meantime, as the recyclers say, the recycling companies are a haven, the only environment where their homelessness does not become the basis for separate and unequal treatment. The recycling staff are generally curt but fair, the rationalized economic transaction is free from the usual compulsory humiliation rituals. "No hustle, no bullshit," as Carlos puts it. Given their stigmatized social position, recyclers are choosing to concentrate their efforts on using their work to redefine themselves as people with full humanity rather than victims. In this way they not only pull themselves back into the flows of capital, but also create self-respect in a hostile world.

NOTES

1. Blau, Joel. *The Visible Poor: Homelessness in the United States.* New York: Oxford University Press, 1992, p. 49.

2. Castells, Manual and Alejandro Portes. "World Underneath: The Origins, Dynamics, and Effects of the Informal Economy." In *The Informal Economy,* p. 27.

3. *San Francisco Business Times,* September 16, 1994.

4. Since September 1994 I have used a combination of participant observation and informal interviewing to study homeless recyclers working in San Francisco. I have got to know 21 of the recyclers well, by working with them and talking as we go. I have also had occasional conversations with about 30 other men.

I have also interviewed 14 bartenders about the relationship between bars and the recyclers that collect from them, four Latino van recyclers, a recycling consultant to Alameda County, an official in the San Francisco City Recycling Department, and a manager at one of the smaller recycling companies.

I made contact with the homeless recyclers by approaching them in the street or in the recycling company yards. I focused on two yards, the largest and best-known in the city, and a smaller Vietnamese-run business. Eight of the recyclers, five white and three Latinos, are based in the Mission, a large racially and ethnically mixed neighborhood of mostly low-income people. From the Mission they travel out to the more prosperous Noe Valley and Castro neighborhoods. Another eight, six of them African American, live in the main "skid row" areas of the city—the So-Ma and Tenderloin neighborhoods—from which they have access to the hundreds of bars and restaurants surrounding the downtown area. The other members of the group each recycle in different neighborhoods of the city; the wealthy Pacific Heights and Richmond areas; the heavily touristed North Beach; the mixture of high fashion and ghetto in Hayes Valley; and the predominantly African American neighborhoods of Hunters Point and Bayview.

5. Samples taken in eight American cities in the mid-eighties ranged from 78% to 97% male composition (see Snow, David A. and Leon Anderson, *Down on Their Luck: A Study of Homeless Street People* (1993), Berkeley: University of California Press). Many homeless women may be invisible to such tracking samples, as they are approached in male-dominated places like soup lines and public parks. Yet there are good structural reasons that there should be considerably more men than women on the street, not least the differences between AFDC and GA.

PART V

Work and Family

In her 1977 monograph on work and family in the United States, Kanter observed: "If any one statement can be said to define the most prevalent sociological position on work and family, it is the 'myth' of separate worlds" (p. 8). Kanter identifies the elements of this 'myth,' the most important being the idea that work and family "constitute two separate and non-overlapping worlds, with their own functions, territories, and behavioral rules" (Kanter 1977). Needless to say, sociologists have become increasingly critical of this conception of work-family relations and have profoundly rejected the "myth of separate worlds." In its place they have begun to explore the interconnections between work and family life, and the consequences of these relations for workers, families, employers, and society.

Balancing Work and Family Life

How do people balance work and family life? What factors make this balance attainable, and what barriers are likely to be encountered? One way to answer these questions is to examine the issues women and men face as they attempt to juggle their work and family responsibilities. The three readings in this section provide different views of this juggling act.

Although the Family and Medical Leave Act grants parental leave to both women and men, fathers are much less likely than mothers to take full advantage of this legislation. In Reading 8, Arlie Russell Hochschild draws on her research in one large company ("Amerco") to explore some

of the reasons for this. Many of the men she interviewed seemed to want to be more family focused, even constructing "hypothetical selves" who made family a priority. Nevertheless, Hochschild found that most men perceived the costs of a more balanced life to be too high; turning away from work toward family meant that they would have to sacrifice professional recognition and career success.

For reasons discussed by Hochschild, working men are much less likely than working women to have family caregiving responsibilities. The next two selections examine some of the ways that employed women manage the dual demands of work and family life. In Reading 39, Anita Ilta Garey examines mothers who work nights. Although the women she interviewed benefited financially from working the night shift, they also appreciated this schedule for its compatibility with their mothering ideals and responsibilities. In particular, mothers who worked the night shift could present themselves as "at-home" mothers who are available for their children. Being seen as an "at-home" mom while working a full-time job was not easy, however, and Garey examines some of the reasons women felt compelled to maintain this stance.

Working part-time is another strategy for balancing work and family life. In Reading 40, Cynthia Fuchs Epstein and her colleagues report results from their study of part-time lawyers. Understanding why women and men choose to work part-time, as well as some of the consequences of this choice for their personal and professional lives, are among the topics covered in this reading.

Family Work

Hochschild (1989) uses the term "second shift" to refer to the time women spend performing unpaid household work, in addition to their time working in the paid labor force. In her 1989 book on this topic, Hochschild (p. 7) quotes from a woman she interviewed: "You're on duty at work. You come home, you're on duty. Then you go back to work and you're on duty." The "second shift" is a pertinent issue for women in dual-earner households. Because women's entrance into the labor force has not been accompanied by any significant, corresponding change in their male partners' participation in family work, balancing the demands of work and family falls heavily on women.

In Reading 41, Hochschild introduces the concept of the "third shift" to capture the ways that families cope with limited time at home. Hochschild suggests that the family has become increasingly "Taylorized" (see Reading 6)—subject to "speed-ups" and efficiency concerns, while the workplace has become more relaxed. Families thus are taking on the least rewarding aspects of work and workplaces are incorporating the best aspects of family life. In Hochschild's view, children are particularly affected by this reversal of home and work, and she examines some of the social forces that have brought us to this point.

In the final selection, Arlene Kaplan Daniels returns us to issues raised at the beginning of the book and proposes new questions for analysis. Recall Rybczynski's discussion in Reading 1 of the social forces giving rise to our notions of work and leisure as distinct spheres. Kaplan Daniels returns to this theme, calling attention to the problems with viewing work as something separate from other spheres of life. She invokes the concept of "invisible work" to capture an array of activities that are typically overlooked by commonsense understandings of what counts as work. Kaplan Daniels challenges us to broaden our conception of work and consider the relations among the many important activities that make up people's daily lives.

REFERENCES

Hochschild, Arlie Russell with Anne Machung. 1989. *The Second Shift: Working Parents and the Revolution at Home.* New York: Viking.

Kanter, Rosabeth Moss. 1977. *Men and Women of the Corporation.* New York: Basic Books.

BALANCING WORK AND FAMILY LIFE

38

"Catching Up on the Soaps"
Male Pioneers in the Culture of Time

Arlie Russell Hochschild

"I've just talked to two men who took paternity leave."

—ARLIE HOCHSCHILD

"Oh? Who's the other one?"

—AMY TRUETT

Sam Hyatt was a gifted engineer, seven years with the company, and the father of a three-month-old baby boy. In 1990 he was one of two men in the company who requested and received formal parental leave. Amerco, like many companies nation-wide, offers six weeks of paid leave to the mother. Beyond that, it allows twenty weeks of unpaid leave that can be split in any fashion between husband and wife. Sam and Latesha Hyatt decided that Latesha should take eighteen weeks and Sam two.

After the birth of a child, many men at Amerco arranged informally with their bosses to take a few unpaid days off using accumulated sick leave because the forms for parental leave were said to be "a hassle." To his astonishment and dismay, Sam discovered that he was the first man in the company to apply formally for paternity leave. I asked Sam, a gentle thirty-three-year-old African American

man with an easy laugh, to tell me how he ended up being a trailblazer at Amerco.

"I come from a family of six children in Cleveland," he replied. "My mother was a single parent and worked several jobs to support us. I'm the third oldest and I had some responsibilities for my younger brother and sisters. We went through tough times, not just financially but emotionally." He described how he took college preparatory courses in a public school, was accepted by California Polytechnic Institute, and graduated in three years with a degree in mechanical engineering. While in college, he learned of an Amerco summer scholarship/intern program. The company offered him an internship and, pleased with his summer work, offered him a job upon his graduation. Along the way, he met and married Latesha, a chemical engineer who also worked for Amerco.

Amerco was a predominantly white company as was the town of Spotted Deer and its surrounding valley communities. But in pursuit of its mission to increase diversity, Amerco began in the late 1980s actively recruiting gifted minority students at technical colleges and universities, hiring them as summer interns, and, if all went well, offering them jobs when they graduated.

This pathway to Amerco placed Sam Hyatt in a curious mix of circumstances. The company was eager to draw the best from every racial and ethnic talent pool and was busy trying to make minority newcomers feel welcome. So, for example, Amerco made sure that one local radio station played music likely to appeal to many African Americans. The company also hired the only local barber skilled in black hairstyles. Yet it was also true that blacks, Chicanos, and Asians together still made up a very small percentage of Amerco's workforce. And the community lacked the sort of racial mix that might have reduced Sam's occasional sense that people expected him to represent the "black position" on whatever came up.

In fact, what the working-class whites who lived in the surrounding countryside knew about African Americans they seemed to have learned mainly from television shows about violent crime. When Sam first came to Spotted Deer, he got lost driving on a mountain road and stopped at a bar-restaurant to ask for change to make a call. The steely-eyed faces that greeted him made him think of some sheriff's posse in a small Mississippi town in the 1950s. He froze and backed out. That only had to happen once to impress him with a sense of his vulnerability as a black man in this white valley.

Still, at Amerco and at home, life was good. With a flourishing career, a loving wife, and a new house Sam happily prepared for the birth of their first child. Latesha planned to take four and a half months of maternity leave, and Sam's first official act as a father-to-be was to ask the company for time off.

Two months before Latesha was due, I approached my supervisor, somewhat unsure about how he would respond. Amerco had just published a paternity-leave policy in 1988. When I got my hands on it, I didn't realize that I was the first to use it. I'm not sure if I'm still the only one. I filled out the form and took it to my supervisor. We get along really well. I'm not uptight with him generally, but for some reason I was this time. He sensed my nervousness and said, "Don't

worry about it, this is great." In a matter of days or a week, it was signed by my manager. The form acted as an agreement that I could take leave without pay for two weeks.

Sam was doing well at work. His supervisor's professional development report noted that he "continuously met and usually exceeded his customers' requirements, and that he was doing a superior job as a department supervisor after a very short time in the position." When his wife was just about to have the baby, Sam noted,

I was working on a big project to design, fabricate, and test equipment, and it was time to install it—a difficult time to be away from work. But my father had missed my birth and then my boyhood, and maybe that's why I wanted to be there for my own child from the beginning.

After eight hours at the hospital, Sam greeted a squalling, eight-pound baby boy, wrapped him in a blue blanket, and laid him in his bassinet. As he nursed his wife back to health, he cared for the house and spent hours attuning himself to this new small being, whom they named Adam.

When, two weeks later, he returned to his nine-hour days, he encountered a wide variety of reactions:

To the women at the office, I was a great hero. Sam *cooks!* Sam does *laundry!* Sam takes *paternity leave!* But most of the guys I'm not close to ignored it. They all knew, but they acted as if they weren't supposed to know. They were thinking, "Where were you? On vacation?" My close friends teased me, "It must have been fun, what did you do? Did you change diapers? Come on, it must have been a *great* time. You sat around and watched TV." They thought I was using this time as an excuse to get away.

They saw Sam's paternity leave as time when he was not working, but relaxing, goofing off. They didn't link paternity leave to paternity.

Sam faced a choice. He could let the playful jabs about "catching up on the soaps" go and accept the obvious implications: that because women give birth to babies, babies are a women's thing; that men have no role at or around birth, so paternity leave is unnecessary or silly. Or he could respond. But he would have to be careful, he felt. He couldn't be too "politically correct" because, for many of his colleagues, the issue of paternity leave was fraught with unacknowledged tension. Many of them were feeling pressure from working wives who had sacrificed time from their own budding careers and yearned for appreciation as well as some parallel gesture of commitment, no matter how small.

Sam stood his ground but parried the jabs lightly:

I let them know what I really did. And I told them what it meant to me. They responded, "Well, it's not for me, but great, if that's what you want," that type of thing. I tried to convey the idea that this is a great opportunity for men. If I had it to do all over again, I told them, I'd take *more* time off.

A few younger men who perhaps dreamed of taking paternity leave themselves someday applauded Sam, as did a few older men who imagined that they might have taken one, had they been given the chance.

At home, Sam's leave, however brief, established a pattern:

I comb Adam's hair every morning and dress him. I hear guys say, "I'm going home to babysit." Or they say, "I have to play Mr. Mom," as if there's no such thing as Daddy or Father. I don't say anything, but I despise these statements.

I correct them when they say, "Do you have to babysit?" When they ask me, "What are you doing?" I say, "I'm going home to be a dad." Or, "I'm going home to be with my family." I don't honestly know if they sense the difference between "babysitter" and "dad."

After four and a half months, when Latesha returned to her regular schedule, they both began waking up at 5:30 A.M. to spend more time with Adam. At 7:30 A.M., they dropped Adam at his sitter's. "We rarely get a chance to see him at lunch," Sam continued. "We just can't manage the time. We pick him up at 5:30 P.M. and go home." After a year, Latesha decided to take part time, cutting her working day back to six hours. As Sam explained,

We've named Latesha as the primary caregiver. Still, my role is not to help, it's to act. All the time we're talking about who does what. We're still working it out. Latesha would like an equal partnership. But I wouldn't be comfortable being the one going part time. First, because of my work, and second, because she's more organized than I am.

As it was, Sam had begun to feel that he was pressing the limits of acceptability at Amerco. Because he rarely took work home and rarely worked weekends, he felt his superiors were watching him with an eagle eye. As he put it,

My use of time doesn't come close to that of my superiors. I don't know if I'm going to change or if, eventually, they are. I love the work. I just don't like the workaholism. Higher-level managers all tell you that family is "number one." Every moment they get, they talk about how their child just won the fifty-yard dash and show you pictures. It's number one to them, but you look at how they live and you have to wonder. To me, family life really is number one.

Still, Sam often found it hard to get out the office door anywhere near 5 P.M.:

> Often, I have a four to five o'clock meeting. Then I have to clean off my desk, return a few calls. If it's my turn to pick up Adam, I may call the babysitter and ask if she can hold out another twenty minutes or so. To leave at five o'clock, I need a good excuse. Adam's not a good excuse.

Sam and Latesha were still resisting the press of work, but without many allies. Their home life was not anchored to a circle of kin who called, visited, meddled, and supported. Both had moved far from their hometowns. Latesha missed her mother and sisters in particular. Even though she found most people at Amerco friendly and outgoing, a semiconscious vigilance against unwanted looks or remarks proved a strain for her, and so she found their time alone together a particular relief. She was as unwilling to give up their family time as Sam was to give up his idea of being a "real dad."

Upon learning that there were only two men in the company who had formally applied for paternity leave, a white manager asked me who the other one was. When I mentioned Sam Hyatt, he mused, "Maybe he got to take it because he's black." That made me wonder: Did the men who ribbed Sam for "catching up on the soaps" think that an exception had been made for him? Were they not asking for their paternity leaves because they were *white* and so had little chance of getting them? It was hard to know how Sam could win.

Certainly, if a boss wanted to resist setting a paternity-leave precedent in his division, he could always behave disagreeably when prospective fathers requested leaves. One worker found himself locked in a fierce struggle with his boss over his request for a single week of paternity leave.

"Call it vacation," his boss suggested.

"I'd like it in addition to vacation," the worker said. "Can you deduct it from my pay?"

"Take it for free, then," his boss replied, irritated.

"I'm not asking for something free," came the response.

"Well, I can't give you paternity leave. It's too much paperwork. Why don't you just take it unofficially?" The following summer, the worker discovered to his dismay that his boss had deducted his paternity leave from his vacation time. When that boss left for another job, the worker had to struggle with his new boss to restore his lost week of vacation time. Such were the isolated trials of male time-pioneers.

Had this worker and Sam Hyatt become fathers in Sweden, however, they would have been among the half of Swedish fathers who take six weeks *paid* paternity leave. In middle-class Swedish families, it would have been very much the thing to do, and even in working-class circles they would have encountered few objections. But at Amerco, the few pioneers of paternity leave were largely invisible and knew little of one another.

Sam Hyatt had, for instance, never heard of John West, who, like him, was consciously attempting to atone for an absent father (as well as an absent mother) by being there for his child. John was a shy, thin, thirty-two-year-old man with blond hair, who initially seemed more eager to tell the story of his wife's family than his own. "My wife's father was a workaholic veterinarian who put in ten- to sixteen-hour days. She didn't want me to be like her father." It was his wife's strong desire for him to take paternity leave that led him to request it.

As for his own story, he quickly filled in the details of his family's slow-motion collapse in Southern California—a childhood without Christmases, Thanksgivings, or any other symbols of family time or connection.

By age sixteen, he found himself in a "no-parent" family:

> My brother and I were left unsupervised for days at a time when we were in elementary school, really for ten years of our lives. It made us less trusting but more self-reliant. My brother cooked and I cleaned. Both of us still do that in our marriages today.

While John at first saw himself as merely his wife's proxy on the issue of paternity leave ("This was *really* important to her!"), his own eagerness for it soon showed through as well:

> As soon as Tamara was pregnant, I approached my supervisor. So I gave him six to seven months' notice. My supervisor is new at Amerco and he said, "Oh? Okay." I brought him the book, pointed to the page, and he said, "We'll see as time gets closer if it really fits into our work schedule." I hounded him and I got two weeks.

I asked John how it was being home on paternity leave.

> I cleaned and cooked and did all that good stuff while Tamara recuperated from her delivery. I tried to keep her in bed as much as possible, and I took care of the baby. It worked out really well.

His male coworkers were surprised to learn of the paternity-leave program and quick to evaluate it in financial terms:

> At first, they envied me a bit until I pointed out that it was unpaid. So then the envy went away, and they said, "Oh gosh, I'd never do that, I'd go broke." Well, *I* don't think they'd go broke.

For John, far more than money was at stake:

> In my family, there's nothing left. My mom lives in an apartment. My dad lives in a condo. I have no idea where all the toys and clothes and mementos I had when I was growing up are. I can't find the crib I was born in.
>
> When we go to visit my in-laws, I realize what a close family is. Tamara goes home to see her room with all her furniture and pictures just as it was. She can pass on to our daughter the toys she herself played with as a baby. Christy is wearing dresses Tamara used to wear. I can't tell you how much I enjoy that.

John also gave some tentative thought to trying to cut back his work hours:

> Tamara goes back to full time in January. I brought it up: "Hey, maybe I could go part time." We could split days so that I'm home when she's not, and she's home when I'm not.
>
> In the Research and Development Division where I work, there are some young couples who are breaking the ice with part time. So I think if I was ever to ask to work twenty to thirty hours a week, it might be possible.

But in the end John could not bring himself to ask for fewer hours, a decision he rationalized in this way:

> I'm a closet workaholic. There are times my wife has to jolt me back into family life. The last hour at work I get nervous that I've stayed at work too long. Going home in the car, I worry she'll be in a bad mood. My family comes first, but sometimes I ask myself, do I really *need* to be home? Or is this a passing thing? If I don't get home for an hour, is Tamara going to die? No, probably not. But if I don't meet this deadline at work, maybe the consequence will be severe.

When Tamara was home on maternity leave, John happily left it to her to be the watchdog of family time. She then declared that 6:30 P.M. would be their official dinner-time.

> Tamara keeps telling me that if I really work hard for eight hours, I can get everything done. I can come home and forget about work. So I try to gear myself to that. But sometimes I also want to linger and talk to colleagues and not dash right home.

John nevertheless wanted Tamara to keep him on what he called "the straight and narrow." He liked the idea of being called home by a waiting wife.

Interestingly enough, when Tamara returned to work after her maternity leave, John found himself taking on the same role, helping Tamara to limit her work time:

> My wife is very conscientious about work. She says, "I have to make this deadline," and, "Oh my God, I'm never going to make it, I'm so far behind." I ask her, "What happens if you postpone your deadline? Is there a problem with that?" She thinks it's dangerous not to meet her deadlines. But work isn't school. Nobody's grading you. Even project schedules aren't written in stone. You can talk to all the people who establish your deadline and see if you can get it moved.

Though both John and Tamara talked seriously of their need for more time at home—and each actually made moves to recapture small amounts of work time for their family life, for their child—their efforts to rein in each other's schedule told a somewhat different story. Whatever they believed their deepest time-desires to be, both of them were voting with their feet. For each of them, the pull of work was stronger than the pull of home, and only the constant application of self-control (or the control the other could apply) could right the balance. As for so

many other two-job couples like them, there was no one in the company, at home, or in the neighborhood capable of weighing in on the side of the family.

John's workplace response to his situation at home was a curious one. He began putting a certain amount of effort into helping colleagues get up the nerve to ask for flextime schedules. He recounted one such story:

> My coworker Betty told me her daughter was doing badly in school, but she couldn't get home from work early to help her. Betty told me, "I'm working so hard; there's no way I can go half time." So we talked about her coming in early, leaving at three o'clock, and taking a computer home. She said, "What if my boss says no?" I said, "So what?" "He's going to think badly of me," she said. I answered, "For two days. Then he's going to forget it." Eventually, Betty went to her supervisor and cut a deal. She leaves at three o'clock and works two hours at home on the computer.

John also went out of his way to encourage men to get on the paternity-leave bandwagon:

> I was talking to a guy on the company softball team I play on. His wife is expecting, and the guy was saying, "Oh, I could never ask for paternity leave. My boss wouldn't let me." I said, "How do you know? Did you ask him?" "No, no, but he just wouldn't let me." So I told him, "Asking is the hardest part. *Ask* him!"

John became an informal chronicler of people's efforts to get shorter hours. He told this story of a woman who wanted to come back part time after she'd had a child:

> Her boss hated the idea but didn't think he had the right to hate it. So he sabotaged it by killing her with kindness. He

eliminated all her responsibilities and arranged for her to still get paid. She was devastated. She was a very hard-driving person who wanted to do the work, not just get paid. In the end, her boss left the company, and now she's back full time.

By acting like a self-taught prison "lawyer" whom other inmates consult, John seemed almost to have convinced himself that he had actually altered his own schedule. But, in truth, he was an armchair revolutionary, part of an invisible army of working fathers who dream up hypothetical selves who share the second shift, play with their kids, and seldom postpone family time; while they themselves work like mad.

The Men Who Didn't Ask

Five years after the birth of his son, Jimmy Wayland felt he had completely missed the boat. A handsome, dark-haired consultant specializing in overseas sales, Jimmy had not even thought of paternity leave when his child was born. In fact, he had felt that his wife wanted the entire experience of a new infant for herself, and yet, to his puzzlement, she seemed to resent being left alone. "I had no idea what was stewing in her mind," Jimmy remarked. Both his mother and his mother-in-law pampered and fretted over the baby. Jimmy felt excluded and responded by immersing himself in his work.

As Jimmy described his domestic story,

My wife was in a hurry for us to reach what she felt was success. She's a good person, she just wanted to move more quickly than I did. She saw me as too "laid back." She was always dreaming about the next house, the next job, the next stage of life. My philosophy was to enjoy the one we had. She'd come home from work and start cleaning. If I had a sandwich in my hand, she'd be cleaning

up the mayonnaise before I'd finished. Maybe she was just nervous, but she expressed it by trying to make everything "perfect," the kitchen, the house, me.

With the pressure of a small baby and both of our jobs, my wife felt she was doing it all. And she felt it was too much to handle. I didn't have a clue she was as mad as she was. It was actually the day she was supposed to go part time that she left me and the baby.

She'd been so good all her life. At home, she was good. At community college, she had a 4.0 average. Then, when she got unhappy with me, she ran off with a rambling man and left me and Joshua when he was a year and a half. We had a big custody battle. Everyone sided with me and I won.

For a long time, Jimmy, who was thirty-two when I first met him, had felt his personal life was "in a shambles" while his work life flourished. But after the custody battle, he miraculously reestablished a friendship with his wife and in time gave her back half the custody he had legally won. Soon, they were "discussing everything" and splitting holiday care of their son. Each took care of Joshua when the other had to travel.

Jimmy's parents would pick up Joshua from the sitter if Jimmy had to work late or go back into work after dinner, and this helped. But even with the new, more collaborative arrangement, Jimmy felt there was a problem. "Joshua works an eight-to-five job just like I do," Jimmy remarked, "which is tough because he loves being home with me. Life has been hard enough for him, so I feel like he needs all the time I can give."

Jimmy elaborated,

Joshua is never going to know what a summer is like without having to get up and be shuffled off somewhere. He's never going to experience free time with me around. So I spoil him. I give him some leeway at home. If he doesn't want to eat supper right away, I don't force him, and sometimes he goes to bed later at night than he should. Maybe he's stalling for time, but he says the most hilarious things at nine-thirty at night. We have our best conversations then.

At work, Jimmy described himself as "not a sixty-hour man":

Here in the plant, we have a macho thing about hours. Guys say, "I'm an eighty-hour man!" as if describing their hairy chests. I personally work about forty-four to forty-eight hours. My boss is a nice guy. I can't tell you that my boss or my boss's boss refuses me permission to take time off. I almost wish they *would*. Then I'd *really* give them a piece of my mind.

Jimmy thought he spent too much time at Amerco not doing "real work," and this meant that he needed to add time at the end of the workday to get it all done:

Work begins at 7 A.M. since we start getting calls from overseas then. Between nine and nine-thirty, three people might grab me to talk about a sale. Then I have a meeting from ten-thirty to eleven, and probably between eleven-thirty and twelve noon someone will ask me to go out to lunch. I go around in a caffeine high from one meeting to another to another. Meetings are a whirlwind job within the job. It's like a tornado.

I really like my coworkers, but I now spend so much time saying, "No, I can't" take on more work or do more favors that those relations are getting strained. There are so many things to do on a given day. I'm gone for a couple of hours, and I have twenty electronic messages on my computer when I get back. People are working weekends; you can

see by the dates. They send things Friday at 10 P.M., Saturday mornings at 9 A.M., Sundays at 9 P.M. Of the twenty messages on my machine, I have to do something about twelve of them. My head spins. At the end of the day, finally, I'll think out a memo. That's my real work, and that edges out an early pickup for Joshua.

In his heart of hearts, Jimmy wanted to rise up the Amerco ladder. But he also wanted Amerco to understand, if not honor, men like himself who were caught between the demands of work and home. As he explained,

You have the high-risers grabbing all they can. Then you have the discontent of the lower-downs. Then you have confused people in the middle like me. A day doesn't go by where I don't talk about overload. It's an underground conversation here. You don't want to say it too loud. We're in this whirlwind; we work ourselves to death. Then when we die: What purpose did we serve? Is it worth it? But we're afraid to get off the roller coaster for fear we won't be able to get back on.

What made it hard on working parents like himself, Jimmy mused, was the absence of an "honorable middle rank." He continued,

Amerco isn't doing a good enough job matching people's opportunities for money or job titles to their family values. What if you don't want to go for the top, but you don't want to level out? We need to be assured that it's okay if we make that middle choice. We need to be told, "You may lose out on some money or a promotion down the road, but we still value you." A lot of us feel we can grow and should be rewarded—without becoming top managers. I don't worry about seeming like a loser, a goof-off, deadwood. I worry about not seeming like a serious player. We need to change the definition of serious player. A serious player now means someone who has aspirations to go as high as he can, someone who puts in an incredible amount of time, often at the expense of the family. Amerco needs to recognize serious players with serious families.

Three years later, when I visited Jimmy again, he seemed to be turning into the very man his ex-wife had wanted him to be—a rushed, rising executive who had left the "honorable middle" behind. Just as in 1990 he had thought managers in general "couldn't have a life," now he was a manager without much of a life. He had, he claimed, simply moved the "ambition bar" one notch upward. He had also found a steady girlfriend who had quit work to be a "wonderful stepmom" to Joshua. The result was that he and Joshua did fewer things together. "Joshua can play with his little sports figures on the floor for hours, then go outside and shoot baskets by himself," Jimmy commented wistfully. "Now, I have to invite myself to do things with him."

If, in 1990, Jimmy had agonized more openly about his situation than most of the other middle-level male professionals I interviewed, others found themselves, however silently, trapped in the same dilemma. These men ranged from middle managers to technicians, data entry workers to administrative support personnel. Those in the "middle," like Jimmy, often secretly dreamed of a more moderate work pace and way of life. Men in such jobs tended to be neither fully absorbed into a cult of professional workaholism nor pressed by desperate economic need. They worked hard. They wanted to be, as Jimmy put it, serious players. But half of Amerco's male middle managers had working wives; two-thirds had children under thirteen. In the absence of help from housekeepers or kin, they faced the need and often a fair amount of pressure to pitch in at home. So, many of them seemed inclined to resist very long hours.

Such men in the middle might seem poised to resist the process by which the worlds of home and work were being reversed; but they felt torn between the pressure to do more at home and a company-supported image of the serious player as a long-hours man. Even the smallest actual exchange of work time for home time became a monumental decision in their minds. Sam Hyatt took two weeks off for his child's birth, then tried to hold the line on extra hours, but when he was promoted and sent to another state, even that minimal level of resistance to the pull of work crumbled. John West and Jimmy Wayland both talked a good line about the need for more time at home, but neither of them could bring themselves to "walk the talk," and both ended up as long-hours men.

The sociologist William Goode has observed that upper-middle-class fathers advocated a greater role for men at home, though the pressures of career often prevented them from living out what they claimed to believe. Working-class men, on the other hand, often actually did more at home than they thought they should. Today, a confused group of men may be emerging between the other two, men who feel even more strongly than the upper-middle-class fathers that they *should* be doing more, and are even less able to live up to their ideals.

As Amerco's surveys showed, Amerco women were far more interested than Amerco men in expanding time at home, more informed about Amerco's family-friendly policies, and more likely to say they valued these policies. More surprising was the gap between men at the top and men in the middle. Larger percentages of men in the middle with children in childcare, for instance, supported paternity leave than did men above them in the corporate hierarchy.

In one 1990 Amerco survey, 13 percent of top male employees thought childcare leave for new fathers was a policy of "great value," while 26 percent of men one level down and 43 percent of administrative and technical men did. (Hourly workers were not surveyed.) Among women, 43 percent of top employees supported childcare leave for new fathers, while 38 percent of workers one level down and only 27 percent of administrative and technical workers agreed.

I can think of two possible explanations for these differences. Men in lower management were younger than men in upper management and perhaps more sympathetic to the idea of participating at home. In the administrative ranks, men were also more likely to work among women. In fact, over half of all administrative workers were women, which meant that these men talked with women every day. Maybe as a result they came to see the world a bit more from a woman's point of view. But no matter why they wanted more time for family life, the vast majority of them still weren't pressing for it. The reasons they gave for their inaction did not have to do mainly with money or job security, nor did they generally lack information about policies such as paternity leave or job sharing, nor were they avoiding the evil eye. Many of them simply could not imagine bucking Amerco and the kind of recognition it promised in return for a full-scale dedication of their time to the company. Both Amerco's official managed culture and the informal male culture of the workplace proved so overwhelmingly powerful that there seemed to be a silent pact to acquiesce to long hours. Did men submit to these hours because they "had" to, because the other guys were doing it, because they liked being at work, or because the pull of family life was too weak?

Jimmy Wayland spoke for many when he said, "I don't define my success as career success, but I'm living as if I do." In the end, for these men—and for increasing numbers of women as well—work was winning out. What had transpired both at Amerco and in society at large was a subtle but complete recasting of the notion of the "family man." Traditionally, "family man" meant a good provider, one who demonstrated his love of wife and children by toiling hard at the office or factory. In the modern workplace, however, "family man" has taken on negative overtones, designating a worker who isn't a serious player. The term now tacitly but powerfully calls into question a worker's masculinity. It was precisely to avoid being classified as a "family man" that the majority of men at Amerco, including Jimmy Wayland and John West, stayed clear of the policies that one might have expected a "family man" to embrace.

39

Motherhood on the Night Shift

Anita Ilta Garey

"My grandmother worked in a cannery for forty years, and I never knew it! She was just my grandmother. We'd go to her house and she'd bake cookies and—she was just *there*. I never knew she worked. I never knew she was a cannery worker." In the seminar in which my students interviewed their mothers and grandmothers about their work histories, they were now exchanging "discoveries." Many students were amazed to find that their mothers had been employed while their children were school-age. One student asked herself aloud: "How could I not know she worked?" How indeed?

In the aggregate, women's labor-force participation can be "invisible" in a number of ways. Feminist scholars, through their research and writing in the 1970s and 1980s, reclaimed what had been a hidden history of women's employment and economic production. Women's economic role had been omitted from most historical accounts, and feminist historians put women back in (Kessler-Harris 1982). The invisibility of mothers' labor-force participation has also resulted from the way in which survey and census data have been collected. Women engaged in agricultural labor, for example, are disproportionately undercounted in the censuses of most countries (Dixon 1982). Christine Bose found that, despite changes over time in the technical definitions of "employ-

ment," women's employment has been consistently undercounted in U.S. censuses. Bose argues that although changes in the way employment is counted have corrected a great deal of the undercount of women's employment that occurred in censuses before 1940, much of women's employment in the informal or irregular economy is still not counted (for example, in-home child care, piece work, domestic service, or giving piano lessons). Her larger point is that "census definitions, enumeration, and verification methods can be molded to conform to, and thus support, gender- or race-related ideologies" (Bose 1987:109). In other words, employment can be counted so that certain types of employment and employment of certain types of people remain invisible.

The students who were surprised to learn that their mothers and grandmothers had been employed were pointing to a different kind of invisibility. Rather than the aggregate invisibility of histories and censuses, they had touched upon the ways an individual woman's employment can be rendered invisible. Patricia Zavella's interviews with Chicana cannery workers revealed that although these women had worked in the cannery for many years, some of their husbands would deny the fact that their wives were employed by discounting seasonal work or by describing as temporary and short term a work history that had become ongoing and long term (Zavella 1987). The refusal to recognize their wives' employment status is connected to an ideology that sees women's labor-force participation as secondary, nonessential, and a potential threat to men's identification with being the family provider (Potuchek 1997). Mothers themselves often downplay their employment, and together wives' and husbands' presentations of self perpetuate the ideology of the male breadwinner (Hochschild and Machung 1989; Potuchek 1997; Zavella 1987). For example, many women emphasize maternal visibility in relation to their children by restricting their hours of employment to the hours their children are in school or to the hours their children are asleep. This strategy can render less visible the fact of a woman's employment. It is this kind of invisibility that my students discovered when they took the time to ask their mothers and grandmothers about their labor force participation.

Night-shift work takes place when no one is looking, when the house is quiet and everyone is asleep. Mothers who choose the night shift talk about their reasons for doing so in remarkably similar terms. None of them refers to herself as a night person; all of them talk about their fatigue and their need for more sleep; and all of them describe how working the night shift allows them to be the kind of mothers they want to be. The night shift enables these women to implement a strategy of being a mother that most closely resembles nonemployed "at-home mothers."*

Mothers who work the night shift (11:00 P.M. to 7:30 A.M.) link their strategies of being

---

*The common phrase "at-home mothers" infers that mothers who are employed are not in their homes, when clearly employed mothers are at home some of the time and nonemployed mothers are not at home all the time. It serves the same purpose as the phrase "full-time mothers," which is to signify that employed mothers are not "fully" fulfilling their roles as mothers. I use quotation marks to indicate that I am using these phrases to refer to the cultural conceptions embedded within them, conceptions with which both employed and nonemployed mothers must contend.

a mother to which hours they are at work— or, more accurately, *to which hours they are at home.* They leave for work after their children are in bed for the night and usually arrive back home after their children have left for school or day care. During the night, children have been with fathers or other relatives, and it is predominantly the fathers who get the children off to school in the morning. One thing that mothers who work the night shift thus avoid is the morning rush at home. Mothers who work day shifts at the hospital, which begin at 7:30 A.M., either have to leave before their children are awake, or they have to get both themselves and their children up and out the door at a very early hour. The morning is not only rushed and tense, but the mother's work schedule and her child's needs and wants are brought into head-on collisions on a daily basis. Some of the night-shift workers reported getting home before their children left for school, and these mothers emphasized the fact that they could then make sure that their children looked "cared for" before they left for school. But they were not the ones who actually got the children ready, and they did not need to hurry their children because of their own schedules, but only in terms of the children's school schedules. Night-shift nurses tiptoe out after the children are asleep and thus avoid the conflicts of a frantic morning exit.

Night-shift workers are home at the other end of their children's school day, when their school-age children return at around 2:00 or 3:00 in the afternoon. Day-shift hospital workers, on the other hand, leave work at around 4:00 or 4:30 in the afternoon and head into rush-hour traffic for the commute home. They rush to pick up children at child care, or they return to waiting children and dinner preparation as soon as they walk in the door. The importance of this after-school and evening time to mothers who choose the night shift becomes evident when we compare them to workers on the evening shift. If mothers work the evening shift (3:30 to 11:00 P.M.), they are home in the mornings to get their children up and off to school, and they are there during the day to be with their preschool-age children, but they are not there in the afternoons and evenings to help with homework, have dinner with the family, or put the children to bed.

In general, mothers with school-age children do not find the evening shift conducive to their strategies of being a mother, and the mothers I talked to who worked the evening shift fell into two categories: they worked part time and had children who were not yet in school, or they worked full time and had children who were grown and out of school. Thus being at home when children returned from school was not an issue for the women in these two groups.

Mothers who work the night shift use shift work to present themselves as mothers in ways that resemble the voluntary part-time workers' strategies of being employed mothers. Although most of the full-time night shift nurses said they would prefer to work part time, they did not have the economic resources that would enable them to take part-time employment. All of the night shift nurses I interviewed worked full time. Most of them were married, but their husbands were not employed in the professions and had less education and lower positions in the occupational hierarchy than the husbands of the voluntary part-time nurses. In addition to needed income, wives' full-time employment at the hospital often provided the medical insurance coverage and other benefits that the family needed.

There are direct economic reasons for nurses to choose the night shift. For example, the hospital gives a pay differential to nurses for working nights, and so nurses on the night shift earn more per hour than they would on the day shift. But my interviews

reveal that financial factors are only one part of a matrix of reasons for choosing the night shift and not the sole determining factor. Several nurses reported turning down opportunities for promotion and higher pay because the promotions would have entailed increasing their hours or being responsible as a supervisor even during their hours at home. Nurses explained their choice of shift in terms of their relationship to the profession, their children's needs, their definition of successful mothering, and their husbands' schedules, as well as their family's financial needs.

Another economic benefit of the night shift is that child-care costs are reduced because other family members are home at night to look after children. Night-shift nurses may not have the economic resources to work part time, but they are able to draw on family support resources for nighttime child care. The use of shift work by couples with young children is clearly a way of solving the child-care problems of availability, quality, and expense, and many dual-earner couples deal with the issue of child care by working different shifts and sharing the care of their children (Hertz and Ferguson 1996). Dual-earner couples with children under fourteen years are more likely to work nonday shifts than are dual-earner couples with children older than fourteen (Presser 1987:108). In one-third of dual-earner couples with children under six years of age, at least one parent works a non-day shift, and there is a strong correlation between non-day shifts and high rates of child care performed by family members, including fathers (Presser 1988, 1989).

But child care by family members was not primarily motivated by economic considerations. When it is the woman who works a night shift, the solution resolves more than the provision of child care. Concerns about leaving children with nonfamily child-care providers, coupled with concerns about their identities as primary caregiver mothers, were strong forces motivating these women's child-care arrangements.

When their wives are working, the husbands of the married night-shift nurses are the primary caretakers of their children. For the most part, it was fathers who got their children up and ready for school. Fathers' contributions to the care of their children remain important even when we remember that most of this care occurs between 10:00 P.M. and 8:00 in the morning. It does not occur during the hours when children are doing their homework, going to after-school or weekend activities, having their dinner, taking their baths, being read to, or getting tucked in for the night. The nighttime care of children does not occur when children have appointments with doctors and dentists, during parent-teacher conferences, during friends' birthday parties, or when the stores are open so that one can buy school supplies, clothes, Halloween costumes, sports equipment, dancing shoes, and the present for the friend who is having the birthday party. When fathers care for children while their wives are working night shifts, most of the care occurs while the children, and the fathers, are sleeping.

These men are not necessarily trying to escape parenting work. It is true that men are often resistant to sharing the second shift (Hochschild and Machung 1989), but some women are also reluctant to surrender symbolically key activities, especially those connected to their identities as mothers. In his study of dual-earner couples, Scott Coltrane notes that "the routine care of home and children are seen to provide opportunities for women to express and reaffirm their gendered relation to men and to the world" (Coltrane 1989:473). In addition, Coltrane found that fathers who perform activities normatively assigned to mothers often face negative reactions from male coworkers. Men may refuse to take on these responsibilities for the same reasons that many women

are reluctant to relinquish them: because the performance of these activities is symbolically linked to constructions of gender. The night shift enables mothers of school-age children to maximize "family time"—it does not take up after-school time or evening family time, and it gives mothers the most waking time with their children. Working the night shift is the way that some women attempt to reconcile the structural conflicts and the conflicting vocabularies of motive attached to motherhood and employment.

Night-Shift Nurses at Sierra Hospital

Most of the hospital workers who work nights are nurses. My interviews with night-shift workers included registered nurses and nurses' aides, in addition to involuntary part-time janitorial workers. At night, the physicians, physical therapists, social workers, secretaries, receptionists, administrators, and food service workers have all gone home. Several of the night-shift nurses remarked that this was one of the things they liked about working at night.

At Sierra Hospital, the night-shift nurses work eight-hour shifts, which begin at 11:00 P.M. and end at 7:30 in the morning. Many of these nurses live outside the city where the hospital is located and have commutes of up to an hour each way. Most of them reported getting home between 8:30 and 9:00 in the morning. Although they are entitled to a half-hour break during the night, heavy patient loads and exceptionally busy nights often mean that these breaks are not taken in an effort to keep up or catch up with the work that needs to be done. One night shift nurse put it this way:

> Doing a midnight shift on my area, *rarely* do we get half an hour break—*rarely*. You've got to move real fast. Why should I move real fast constantly? You

know, even if you take the half an hour break, I'd be so far behind.

Skipping their break also helps them to leave work on time or reduces the amount of time that they must stay after their shift ends. Before a nurse can leave her shift, she must update each patient's chart. Often nurses cannot finish their charting until the next shift arrives to take over the direct patient care. Nurses reported having to extend their workdays by thirty to forty-five minutes in order to finish their charting. Although nurses are technically entitled to overtime if they work after their shift, overtime is frowned upon by a budget-conscious administration, and the message conveyed to nurses is that "good nurses" finish their charting during their shift. Therefore, nurses who don't get their charting finished before their shift ends do so on their own time rather than risk being judged inefficient.

Being a worker is important to the night-shift nurses. However, while part-time nurses were sometimes frustrated by the extra effort it took to stay connected at the workplace when they came in only a few days a week, many of the night-shift nurses preferred the way that the night shift separated them from the daily activities of the ward. One nurse noted that working the night shift was "a family-like business" and different from the day shift, when "the bosses and everybody are there." Night-shift nurses were more removed from the professional aspects of their positions than were either part-time or full-time, day-shift nurses, and they interacted far less with other health professionals such as physicians, physical therapists, and social workers. This had its disadvantages, and several nurses remarked that they were not likely to be promoted or to have opportunities for specialization while they remained on the night shift.

Of the thirty-seven mothers I interviewed, seven were currently working full

time on the night shift. All but one of these women had children under the age of twelve years, and the person who didn't have young children had worked the night shift since her children, now grown, were young. In addition, many of the older nurses who were working full-time day shifts when I interviewed them had worked the night shift when their children, now teenagers or adults, were young. Mothers who no longer worked the night shift reported either that they couldn't handle the fatigue of working nights or that they had changed their shifts when their children were older or when there were changes in their circumstances, such as the availability of family child care.

While there are patterns and conclusions to be drawn, there is both overlap and diversity within the group of night shift workers. Short sketches of six of these women illustrate their commonalities and differences as well as the contexts in which each weaves a life.

Shirley Roberts

Shirley Roberts is a sixty-year-old, African-American practical nurse who has worked the night shift for twenty-six years. She is married, has five adult children and eight grandchildren, and lives in a older, working-class neighborhood with well-built and well-maintained Spanish-style homes and well-tended gardens. After her youngest child was born, Shirley went to night school for a year to get her practical nursing training, and her husband stayed with the children while she was in school. Shirley noted that after being home with five children for more than twelve years, evening classes had provided a break for her: "It was an outing for me also, to get away from the house." When her youngest child was six years old and in school, Shirley started to work at the hospital.

> So my husband would be home with them at night and I would be home in the daytime. They would be in school

until like 3:00, so that gave me a chance to sleep in the daytime, get up and cook dinner, then, you know, help them with their homework. And then that's what I been doing ever since.

Shirley does not live far from the hospital, and she does not have to do charting as the registered nurses do, so she is able to get home soon after her shift ends. When her children were growing up, she made sure that she got home before they left for school.

I always got home before they went to school, and I would see that they had their breakfast—their daddy would start it sometimes—and comb their hair, make sure they're okay when they're underage and all.

Shirley told me that her husband, who is a skilled laborer with a civil service position, worked the evening shift when the children were growing up. He would come home at night just as she was leaving for work. Between work schedules and sleeping, Shirley and her husband didn't see each other very much. Shirley explained:

But you have to be able to understand that. . . . You have to have a nice husband who understands that and helps you with the children. You can't do that alone, it's too hard. I mean mothers are doing it, but it's really hard. You need someone to help you. Fortunately, my husband was nice. . . . I didn't have no trouble with the children either.

Shirley never had to rely on nonfamily child care. She was home with the children while they were young, and when she went to work nights, her husband was with them. If the children were ill, Shirley would take vacation days or take the sick child to her mother's house. In the summer the boys would go to summer camp, and the girls would split the summers between both sets

of grandparents. At Christmas, Shirley would take vacation time, which she told me was "a big family time for them." Now that her children are grown and she is near retirement, Shirley continues to prefer the night shift because, she explains, the workload is lighter than on the day shift, when patients have to be fed, bathed, and moved. At sixty, Shirley finds that the night shift continues to work for her.

Janice Ramos

Janice Ramos is a thirty-year-old, Filipina registered nurse. She immigrated to the United States with her parents when she was a teenager. Janice is married and has two children, an eight-year-old child and a fourteen-month-old baby. Her husband, also a Filipino immigrant, works as a technician. The family lives in a large, custom-built, two-story house in a small town about a forty-five-minute drive from the city where Janice and her husband work.

Janice was very articulate, but there was a flatness in her voice, a lack of intonation and a strain that conveyed long-term fatigue. Janice is a planner: their children were planned, their house was planned, her continuing education and career goals were planned. "We plan our life situation," she told me. But Janice has had to face the unplanned and unexpected. Janice's ultimate goal is to become a nurse practitioner. That plan, however, was postponed when Janice's second child was born with health problems. The baby was in the hospital for five months and was still plagued by respiratory illnesses. This experience affected Janice's plans to continue her education and her and her husband's plans about future children (they decided not to have any more).

Doris Chavez

Doris Chavez is a thirty-four-year-old, Mexican-American registered nurse. Her parents both had eighth-grade educations, and she was the first in her family to attend college, where she earned her B.S.N. degree. She is proud of her parents, whom she described as having come from very poor families and as working hard and doing well. Doris and her husband, an electrician, have two children, ages seven years and four years.

I interviewed Doris at the hospital just after her shift ended at 7:30 in the morning. Doris's home is an hour's drive from the hospital and, although she makes this commute four days a week, she feels more sympathy for her husband, whose commute is almost twice as long. Doris and her husband could not afford to buy a house in either of the urban areas where they work, and commuting is the price they pay for buying a house in a more affordable outlying area. Doris added that where they live is "calmer" than the urban area where she works, and that she liked that for her family.

Doris had a lively manner and a quick sense of humor. While she did not hesitate to say that being a "working mother" is "hard" and that "it's not easy to do," Doris thinks of herself as fortunate. Often, after describing a problem or a difficult situation, she concluded, "But we do okay," or "But it works out."

Angela Cordova

Angela Cordova is a forty-three-year-old, Filipina registered nurse who immigrated to the United States when she was sixteen years old. Both of her parents and all four of her siblings have also immigrated. Her mother lives "mainly" with her, but "goes around" to the houses of her other children, being cared for by them and helping them to care for their own children. "In my family," Angela said, "we help one another." When she returned to work when her second child was six weeks old, it was her mother who cared for the baby: "She's the best—the mother of the mother."

Angela is married and has two school-age children, ages nine years and six years. Her husband, also a Filipino immigrant, has a college degree but has been unable to find a job commensurate with his education and now works for a package delivery company. The Cordova family lives in a large, six-bedroom house in a suburb that is a forty-five-minute drive from the city in which Angela and her husband work. When I arrived at her door, Angela opened it and told me that she had just woken up and that her house was not clean. I sat on the sofa while she darted around picking things up and cleaning off the dining room table, where we would sit to conduct the interview.

Angela was friendly and eager to help me with my research project. She was also very tired, and several times during the interview, when I thought she was too tired, I would start to wind it up, at which point she would launch off on another topic with renewed enthusiasm.

Julia Ginzburg

Julia Ginzburg is a forty-three-year-old, Jewish-American registered nurse. Julia's upper-middle-class parents had higher ambitions for her than nursing, but Julia worked in poorly paid social service jobs after college, became pregnant with her first child, and married a man with no education or skills. A nursing degree for Julia was seen as an answer to the problem of how to support her family while her husband obtained his GED and went to college. Julia, her husband, and her first child lived with Julia's parents, who paid for her nursing education, while she went to nursing school. After Julia began her career as a nurse, she and her husband moved into their own rented apartment and had another baby.

At the time I interviewed her, Julia had been working as a nurse for three years, and her children were nine years old and one year old. While still considering themselves a married couple, Julia and her husband have recently separated and live apart. Julia is the primary and often the only breadwinner in the family. Julia's husband takes care of the children during the nights she works at the hospital, and he is there many evenings on her days off, but the bulk of the child care and daily maintenance is left to Julia. Unlike Janice, Doris, or Angela, she is renting the house they live in, and she said of herself, "I'm old, I'm forty-three, and I've got—I've got—nothing—to fall back on."

My overriding impression of Julia was of weariness and disappointment; unlike Janice, Doris, and Angela, hers was not a story of upward mobility, future aspirations, and hope. Julia grew up in an upper-middle-class family; her mother stayed home to raise the children and support her husband's career, and a college education for Julia and her sisters was assumed. Julia's background and the idealism and optimism of the period in which she came of age promised expanding opportunities, but that sense of possibility and promise is no longer a part of Julia's perspective on life.

Patricia Anderson

Patricia Anderson is a fifty-three-year-old, African-American registered nurse. She has worked as a nurse for twenty years, is divorced, and has three adult children and a twelve-year-old daughter. Patricia and her daughter live in a two-bedroom rented apartment in a new apartment complex in a middle-class section of the city. Although most of the full-time nurses at Sierra Hospital work four shifts a week, Patricia works five shifts a week because, she told me, her daughter's dance lessons and other activities are expensive, and she needs the money.

Patricia likes being a nurse and she likes interacting with patients, but she does not like working in the hospital because of the administration, the paperwork, and the speed-up on the ward. If she got married again, which she would like to do, she said she would change her schedule from full time to part time. When I asked if she would quit working altogether if she could, she replied that she wouldn't take that risk and would stay working two days a week to keep her hand in "in case anything goes wrong."

Nationally, African-American nurses comprised only 4.2 percent of registered nurses in 1996 (Malone and Marullo 1997), and the number of African-American registered nurses at Sierra Hospital is larger than the national average but still a small minority. In an occupation in which 90 percent of the total population is white, Patricia had experienced a number of incidents that she characterized as "subtle racism." Patricia explained, for example, that whenever she was in a new situation, white people would assume she was not a nurse. Applying for her first nursing job twenty years earlier, she was told that applicants for the janitorial positions should apply at the office down the hall. After working as a nurse for a number of years, she interviewed for a different nursing position and discovered halfway through the interview that the personnel director assumed she was applying for a position as a nurses' aide. At Sierra Hospital, nurses and nurses' aides can be sent from their regular wards and loaned to another ward if needed; this is called floating. Patricia remarked that different assumptions were made when white women and black women "floated": "If a white person floats to another floor, they assume she's an R.N. If I float, they assume I'm a nurses' aide."

Most of the African-American nurses I interviewed mentioned both institutional and personal racism in the hospital. Different hospitals and different units within the same hospital had varying reputations regarding whether they were better or worse places for black nurses to work. "Each floor has a personality," Patricia told me, "like states—Louisiana is a man's state; Illinois is a white man's state; and California is strictly for kids." Sierra Hospital was considered a better place than many of the other hospitals in the immediate area, but some wards were considered definitely better than others.

A Mother's Place: "Being" at Home

The house as a symbol of family life is a recurring theme in the stories my interviewees told. Regardless of shift or occupational category, most of the women I talked to emphasized the importance of owning their own homes in the context of their feelings and plans about children. But there was another way in which the house as symbol was particularly salient for the night-shift workers. A house, to be a home, is where a mother is.

One of the most powerful images in modern theater is the door shutting as Nora Helmer leaves her husband and children in Ibsen's *A Doll's House* (1958 [1879]:68). This image juxtaposes the physical boundary of the house with its symbolic importance in the definition of family. Houses, the spaces within which homes are made, are important symbols in the construction of meanings about family. Ibsen represents Nora's desertion of her family with the sound of a closing door, by which the audience knows that she has crossed the threshold and is outside the physical space of the house. When the woman is removed from the house, definitions of home and family are called into question and must be reconstructed to account for or to conceal the fact of their missing central element.

The emotional content of home is mirrored in cliches such as "Home is where the heart is" and "Home is the place where they have to take you in." Another well-known saying is "A woman's place is in the home,"

the corollary of which may be "A home is where the woman is"—especially where a mother is. Night-shift "working mothers," in common with nonemployed mothers, are able to be home during the day.

Being at home during the day is related to cultural ideas of what a mother *does* and what a mother *is*, to both *doing* and *being*. To be at home during the day is to emulate nonemployed mothers, often referred to as full-time mothers. The term "full-time mothers" incorporates the idea that to be employed lessens the fullness or completeness of one's mothering. It is in response to this perspective that the night-shift workers are constructing a "working mother" who is a "full-time mother" because she does what "full-time" (nonemployed) mothers do. Even if her husband and children are not at home, the woman *of* the house is the woman *in* the house.

Janice Ramos, Doris Chavez, and Julia Ginzburg each have one child in elementary school and a child under five years old in some form of day care. Despite differences in ethnicity, age, and seniority at the hospital, their stated reasons for working the night shift are remarkably similar.

Janice had been at Sierra Hospital for less than a year but had worked in several hospitals before that, and I asked her if she had worked the night shift in her previous positions. Janice responded:

> I was always working nights. 'Cause it's easier to work nights with my young children. I like to be home with them, even [if] I'm sleeping, I like to be, you know, around.

Doris, who had worked at Sierra Hospital for ten years, immediately mentioned both owning a house and being home during the day when I said, "Tell me about working and having children." Doris replied:

> It's hard, real hard. I want my kids to go to college; we bought a house. I want

them to have a house. The things that I feel are important and so that's why I do it. And that's one of the reasons I work night shift. I feel more comfortable being at home in the daytime while they're— well, they go to day care. So my husband takes them to day care and then I get home in the morning and sleep. And I know that I'm home by the phone in case something happens to them. The school's right down the street so during school time it's nice—he walks home.

Julia, who had been at Sierra Hospital for almost three years, gave a similar response to my question about her reasons for working the night shift.

For me, it allows—I mean, if—I'm available. There's always a parent at home. If there's anything that comes up; if the kid is sick, it's no big deal, I'm here. Like now, when—during the summer— when my son is finished with his program at noon he comes home. I'm here. He can handle himself around the house. My small one I have in child care, but the big one comes home and can go and play with friends, he can go to the library himself, but—I'm here. . . . I'm asleep! But I'm here. If something comes up, I'm available.

"I'm here," "I'm home," "I'm around," "I'm available": these are striking refrains in two ways. First, they are coupled with the statement "I'm asleep." Second, for a large part of the time when these women are home, their children are not. Notice that both Doris and Julia use the word "comfortable" to describe their reasons for wanting to be home in the daytime. But being at home during the day, even if they are asleep and their children are at school or in child care, fits with their definition of motherhood. It not only enables them to respond instrumentally to daytime child-related needs and emergencies and to

be home when children return from school, but it places them in the symbolically appropriate place for mothers: in the home. A look at how each organizes her daily schedule illustrates this.

Janice gets home from the hospital at about 8:30 in the morning. Her husband, who has to be at work by 9:00 A.M., has already gotten their older child off to school, taken the baby to the neighbor who does child care for them, and left for work. Janice returns to an empty house and immediately goes to sleep. At 1:30 in the afternoon, she wakes up, gets the baby from the neighbor's house, and meets her son at the bus stop. She spends the next few hours feeding the children, playing with the baby, and helping her son with his homework. When her husband returns from work between 4:30 and 5:00 P.M., she goes back to bed and sleeps until about 9:00 P.M., at which time she gets up to leave the house at 10:00 P.M. for another night shift.

Shirley Roberts reported a similar method of getting enough sleep by going to bed as soon as she got home from work in the morning, sleeping until the children got home at 3:00 P.M., and then going back to bed after dinner and sleeping for another two or three hours. These routines are exceptions to the pattern reported by most of the other night-shift nurses, who don't go back to bed in the afternoon or evening for additional hours of sleep. Janice's intended routine gives her more sleep than the other nurses I interviewed. However, my interview with Janice indicated that things were often not routine in her household and that she averages far less sleep than claimed in her report of a typical day.

Except for her two days off each week, Janice spends about three of the thirteen-and-a-half hours she is home during the day with her children. The rest of the time the children are at school or child care, or they are home and Janice is sleeping. For Janice, working nights cannot be a way of spending more time with her children, since day-shift workers would have about as many child contact hours as Janice does. Nor does working nights give Janice more time with her husband, who takes over the care of the children as soon as he returns from work so that Janice can sleep. But, as Janice says, what working nights does do is to allow her to "be home with them"—to "be around."

Long commutes contribute to mothers' concerns about being at home during the day, near their children's schools and child-care locations. While the concern with being far from home does exist for commuters, many women cited the same reasons for working nights even when they had lived near the hospital in which they worked. Julia Ginzburg and Patricia Anderson, both of whom live within five miles of the hospital, talked about being home during the day in the same terms as did those with long commutes: they wanted to be around, to be available, to be home.

Doris Chavez lives over an hour from the hospital and usually does not get home until 9:00 in the morning. Her husband, who has a two-hour commute to work, gets the children up at 5:00 A.M., leaves the house by 5:30 to drop them at the child-care center, five minutes from their house, and then continues on his way to work. Their oldest child will be at the child-care center until 8:00 A.M., when he is bused to his elementary school, which is also near their home. Unlike Janice, Doris does not immediately go to sleep when she gets home; she does some housework, thinks about dinner preparations, unwinds a bit. She said she usually sleeps between 10:00 A.M. and 3:00 P.M., but when I asked her if that meant that she usually gets five hours of sleep, she told me that she averages about four hours of sleep on the days she works. She wakes at about 3:00 P.M. to welcome her son home from school and goes to pick up her youngest child from the child-

care center. Doris spends the rest of the afternoon preparing dinner, helping with homework, and caring for the children. When her husband comes home from work, they all have dinner together. Doris reported that evenings are spent playing games, reading with the children, or facilitating the oldest child's participation in sports or Cub Scouts. Doris tries to have the children in bed by 8:00 P.M., a challenge in the summer during daylight savings time, so that she can take a half-hour nap on the sofa in the living room before getting ready for work. She leaves the house at 9:30 at night to drive back to the hospital for another night shift.

Doris and Janice differ in the number of hours they are home and awake while their children are home and awake. Doris reported spending about twice as much contact time with her children as Janice, but for both of them what is salient is *which hours* they are home. As Doris said, "I know that I'm home by the phone in case something happens to them." Doris told me that the "overlap" period from 5:30 A.M. until 9:00 every morning, during which neither she nor her husband are at home, is a concern to her, and adds:

> But I'm usually home by nine, and I have been called before [by the school] and they know I'm sleeping. I get that straight with the teacher [laughs] right off the bat. You know, "I work nights, I'm home."

Doris lets her children's teachers know, and she emphasized the importance that they know, that she is a mother at home during the day. The work of making her presence at home visible to her children's teachers illuminates the symbolic nature of Doris's behavior. She is gesturing to herself, to her children, and to relevant others that she is an at-home mother.

Julia Ginzburg's separation from her husband and her position as the primary earner in her family make her life very different from both Janice's and Doris's, but her schedule is similar to the others. When I interviewed Julia, she was trying to implement and maintain a healthier sleep schedule than had been the case for the previous three years. She had been sleep deprived for so long that she reported that she was beginning to have physical and emotional problems. Before she took a break and got some rest, it would often take Julia two hours to leave the hospital after her shift, because she was so tired it would take her that long to finish her charting.* On her new schedule, Julia gets home between 8:30 and 9:00 A.M., after her husband has taken the children to school and child care. She sleeps until about 3:00 P.M., when her nine-year-old son comes home from school, at which time she leaves to pick the baby up from child care. In the summer, her older child gets home at noon from a summer program but takes care of himself while she sleeps.

Julia did not report as structured a family life as Doris did, but Julia is just as concerned about preserving certain symbols that represent a particular construction of motherhood, particularly one in which a mother is home during the day. Although Julia is asleep when her son returns from school, the fact that she is in the house is important to her, not only in terms of being physically present in case of an emergency, but also in symbolic terms. Julia explained:

> If I were working in the daytime, I wouldn't be comfortable with him coming home to an empty house. I don't want him to be—*I don't feel like he's a latchkey kid.* I'm here. I'm asleep! But I'm here.

---

*Other nurses I interviewed confirmed Julia's exhaustion and the time it took her to finish charting and leave the hospital in the morning.

Patricia Anderson expressed a similar sentiment when I asked her if it was her choice to work nights:

> I'd rather because—since I'm divorced and [my twelve-year-old daughter] is into a whole lot of different things [dance and sports activities]—to make sure that no one ever has an excuse for saying [in a singsong voice], "Well, my mommy wasn't home and I hit the streets"—just like that.

In Doris's, Julia's, and Patricia's narratives, there is an emphasis not only on the importance of being at home during the day, but also on the importance of being *seen* as mothers who are at home. Doris emphasizes that her children's teachers know that she is home during the day and available to be called; Julia stresses that her son is not a "latchkey kid"; and Patricia says that she works nights in part so that no one can say, retrospectively, that she neglected her daughter because she was away at work during the day. All three are emphasizing maternal visibility. There are two concerns being conveyed in their explanations: one is with the immediate safety of the child, and the second is with potential problems that might be said to be caused by the mother's behavior.

Being there in the afternoon to welcome children home from school and in the evening to supervise dinner, homework, baths, and bedtime is extremely important to these women. The night shift, unlike day or evening shifts, allows them to be present during both of these crucial times. Angela Cordova used a parable to explain her reasons for working the night shift:

> It's better for a mother to stay home in the evening. Because the children will be more calm. See, I grew up in the country, and I could see the chickens and the chicks, like when the sun is setting. The

chicks is "cheep cheep cheep" and then the mother hen will sit down and all goes underneath.

For Angela, being at home in the evening is part of a natural order that is pan-species but sex-specific.

A woman's presence at home in the evening has a symbolic, emotional, and instrumental importance. If mothers are at home during the afternoons and evenings, they can supervise older children during those hours when children are most likely to act independently or in association with their peers. The theme of supervision was particularly salient with Shirley, Angela, and Patricia, the night-shift workers with the oldest children. Angela told me with great amusement:

> I have only two [children] and I told my husband, "We have to watch them like a hawk" [laughs]—"a friendly hawk, though," I say. [Laughs.]

Shirley also mentioned the parental supervision of children as a reason for working the night shift:

> Working at night was good for my family. It kept them together. You keep your children out of trouble. . . . I don't think children should be left alone. I think that's where you find the problems. I think children should be supervised at all times.

When I asked Patricia if she ever considered changing shifts as her daughter got older, she replied:

> You know, see, every time I want to change [shifts] I see a [television] show or something about teenagers and so I think [about the] things they could do, and I know how I was. I was the goody goody two shoes *only* because my parents were exceptionally strict.

What these mothers are saying is not just that children need supervision, but that

mothers need to be the ones who are supervising at particular times or in particular circumstances. The supervision that only mothers can do is directly linked to concepts of being—being mothers and being at home. Men (fathers) are often seen by the women I interviewed as unable to provide this all-encompassing kind of supervision and are sometimes seen as either needing supervision themselves or being incapable of adequately supervising their children. Yolanda Lincoln, an African-American ward secretary who worked full time on the day shift, remembered the problems she had when she once tried working an evening shift.

> It was hard for the kids because I didn't get to spend as much time in the evening with them. And even my husband, you know, he said today he would never work evening again while the kids are little. It's family time, and especially as a mother and with children in school, just to oversee that they are doing their homework and things like that. My husband is capable, but sometimes he can be lax, you know? Because a lot of times of time [when] I worked evenings . . . a lot of times I would come home and homework wouldn't be done and he would say, "Oh, she didn't tell me she had homework." So I knew then I could never work evenings.

Like caring for younger children, being at home to supervise older children is gendered. It is considered a mother's responsibility not only to teach young children right from wrong, but also, by her presence, to keep older children from doing wrong. Angela told me that when her nephew got into trouble and was sent to Juvenile Hall, she looked to the structure of her brother and sister-in-law's home for an explanation of "what went wrong." Angela's sister-in-law works an evening shift, from 3:30 P.M. to 11:00 P.M., and Angela blames her sister-in-law for being absent during those crucial hours. She admits that when her sister-in-law goes to work, her brother goes out to see his friends and leaves the children with Angela's mother. Angela's sister-in-law feels that her husband should stay home and help with the children, and Angela agrees. But Angela added, "And then I said to myself, 'Maybe [my brother] feels the same way, he misses [his wife] in the evening.'" Although two other adults are responsible for the children, the children's father and grandmother, Angela thinks that the key to her nephew's delinquent behavior is the absence of the mother during the evening hours, an absence that leads the husband to go out at night, leaving his children with their elderly grandmother. Angela's judgmental comments about her sister-in-law are probably glossing other unspoken family strains, but Angela's disapproval of her sister-in-law is expressed in a story about the symbols of appropriate motherhood. Earlier in our conversation, Angela had described her sister-in-law as an "ideal mother [whose] house is clean, [and who] cooks so good," and had then launched into the story about how her nephew was sent to Juvenile Hall. Angela concluded:

> [My sister-in-law] likes [to work] in the evening because she can do more work in the daytime at home. Her house *very clean*. . . . And I told [my sister-in-law], I said, "Why you don't work nights?"—"I cannot function right at night," she said. But I don't know what's best. That's why the house don't get clean.

Angela was presenting a morality tale about priorities and motherhood, and she was also presenting her own strategy of being by positing what she presents as the failed strategy represented by her sister-in-law. Despite her disclaimer, Angela clearly feels that she does know what is best, and she invokes the theme of "being there" to present her own strategy of being a mother, a strategy in which she is at home during the day and early evening for her children. . . .

Both "Working Mothers" and "Stay-at-Home Moms"

Mothers who work the night shift use the cloak of night to render their employment less visible. They do not deny the fact that they are employed, but they do try to implement strategies of being that highlight their maternal visibility. The night shift allows "working mothers" to appear to be "stay-at-home moms." At issue is the preservation of a family form in which the mother is available to her children during the day, both as the person who performs symbolically invested activities, such as volunteering at her child's school or taking her children to dance lessons or sports activities, *and* as the person whose very being is symbolically invested—the woman in the house, the mother at home.

Night-shift nurses implement strategies of being employed mothers in three major ways: they limit the visibility of their labor force participation to their children and in the public spheres of their children's lives; they make themselves available to involve their children in symbolically invested activities outside the home, and they position themselves in the culturally appropriate place and time: at home, during the day. All three of these strategies work to highlight their visibility as mothers.

What explains this shared concern with being seen as "at-home moms"? It is not a commonality of cultural, ethnic, or class background. Doris is the daughter of Mexican-immigrant, working-class parents who were both employed while she was growing up. Julia came from an upper-middle-class, Jewish home with a father in the professions and a homemaker mother. Patricia's parents were middle-class African Americans who both held professional positions. Shirley grew up in a working-class, African-American home in which her father was the breadwinner and her mother stayed home and was not employed until Shirley was in elementary school. Janice immigrated to the United States from the Philippines with her college-educated parents, both of whom were employed. What they all face, however, are similar dominant cultural norms about motherhood. From their different backgrounds, they each interact with prevailing definitions of motherhood—they are not creating motherhood from scratch, and they are not immune to the culture around them.

Working the night shift enables these mothers to normalize family life so it looks and feels more like the dominant cultural ideal of a traditional family: a father who goes to work in the morning and a mother who is home during the day, welcomes her children home from school, has dinner on the table for her returning husband, and tucks the children into bed at night. Judith Stacey refers to this family form as the "modern family": "an intact nuclear household unit composed of a male breadwinner, his full-time homemaker wife, and their dependent children" (Stacey 1990:5). In historical terms, Stacey is correct; the prevalence of such families was historically recent and short-lived, as well as being culturally specific. But for the women I interviewed, this family form is conceptualized as traditional. If not a common family form in their modern world, it was still an ideal by which they measured themselves, and the word "traditional" best represents the concept that these "working mothers" were trying to convey.

As a group, they have similar constellations of resources that make night-shift employment a sensible strategy for negotiating norms about motherhood in their constructions of themselves as "working mothers." Except for Shirley, they all have qualifications as registered nurses. Except

for Patricia, each relies on her husband for nighttime child care. Unlike the voluntary part-time nurses, their husbands' jobs do not pay enough or provide the needed benefits that would enable them to work part time. Of course, similar resources are experienced differently by women in differing social locations and familial contexts. What it means, for example, to be the sole support of her family will be different for Julia, whose parents have economic resources she could call on in an emergency, than for Patricia, who is estranged from her parents and has grown children who still turn to her in times of need. They have traveled different paths (Cole 1986), but they talk in remarkably similar ways about how working the night shift enables them to be "working mothers" who are "stay-at-home moms."

REFERENCES

Bose, Christine E. 1987. "Devaluing Women's Work: The Undercount of Women's Employment in 1900 and 1980." Pp. 95–115 in *Hidden Aspects of Women's Work,* edited by Roslyn Feldberg, Christine Bose, and Natalie Sokoloff. New York: Praeger.

Cole, Johnetta B. 1986. "Commonalities and Differences." Pp. 1–30 in *All American Women: Lines That Divide, Ties That Bind,* edited by Johnetta B. Cole. New York: Free Press.

Coltrane, Scott. 1989. "Household Labor and the Routine Production of Gender." *Social Problems* 36:473–90.

Dixon, Ruth B. 1982. "Women in Agriculture: Counting the Labor Force in Developing Countries." *Population and Development Review* 8(3):539–66.

Hertz, Rosanna, and Faith I. T. Ferguson. 1996. "Childcare Choices and Constraints in the United States: Social Class, Race and the Influence of Family Views." *Journal of Comparative Family Studies* 27(2):249–80.

Hochschild, Arlie Russell, and Anne Machung. 1989. *The Second Shift: Working Parents and the Revolution at Home.* New York: Viking.

Ibsen, Henrik. 1958 [1879]. "A Doll's House." Pp. 1–68 in *Four Great Plays by Ibsen.* New York: Bantam.

Kessler-Harris, Alice. 1982. *Out to Work: A History of Wage-Earning Women in the United States.* Oxford: Oxford University Press.

Malone, Beverly L., and Geri Marullo. 1997. "Workforce Trends among U.S. Registered Nurses." A report for the International Council of Nurses ICN Workforce Forum. Stockholm, Sweden, September 21–October 1, 1997. ANA Policy Series. Washington, D.C.: American Nurses Association (www.ana.org/readroom/usworker.htm).

Potuchek, Jean L. 1997. *Who Supports the Family? Gender and Breadwinning in Dual-Earner Marriages.* Palo Alto: Stanford University Press.

———. 1988. "Shift Work and Child Care among Dual-Earner American Parents." *Journal of Marriage and the Family* 50(1):133–48.

———. 1989. "Can We Make Time for Children? The Economy, Work Schedules, and Child Care." *Demography* 26:523–43.

Zavella, Patricia. 1987. *Women's Work and Chicano Families: Cannery Workers of the Santa Clara Valley.* Ithaca: Cornell University Press.

40

The Part-Time Paradox
Time Norms, Professional Lives, Family, and Gender

Cynthia Fuchs Epstein, Carroll Seron, Bonnie Oglensky, and Robert Sauté

In the post–World War II era and for a time thereafter (Skolnick, 1991) the model of a stay-at-home, nonwage-earning mother caring for children represented an ideal in American society. Although women were actually moving into the workforce in ever-increasing numbers, the advent of the women's movement in the late 1960s imbued women's presence in the labor force with a legitimacy that went beyond the economic pressures driving them there. At the same time, restrictions on their participation in high-prestige professions were seriously curbed through Title VII of the Civil Rights Act of 1964 and a series of land-

mark court cases. In the years that followed, women flocked to the legal profession (Epstein, [1981] 1993) as they did to medicine and other spheres from which they had been excluded in the past. Indeed, mothers all over America have gone back to work after the birth of their children in numbers that have increased sharply in recent years. Fifty-five percent of new mothers returned to the workforce in 1995 within 12 months of giving birth, compared with 31 percent in 1976 when the Bureau of Labor Statistics started to track these figures (Fiore, 1997). Seventy-seven percent of college-educated women ages 30 to 44 juggle work and child rearing.

Of course, this trend conflicts with today's norms of motherhood, which specify standards for "intensive mothering" that have become ever more demanding (Coser and Coser, 1974; Hays, 1996). Standards for "quality time" with children have also escalated the

Excerpts from *The Part-Time Paradox* by Cynthia Fuchs Epstein, Carroll Seron, Bonnie Oglensky, and Robert Sauté. 1999. New York: Routledge. Reprinted by permission of Routledge, Inc., part of the Taylor & Francis Group, and the author.

numbers of hours each week parents are supposed to devote to involvement in their children's education, psychological development, and leisure-time activities (Hays, 1996).

At the same time, child care—private and public day-care centers, all-day nurseries, agencies that supply nannies and baby-sitters for those who can afford private solutions—all cater to the child-care needs of working parents. However, there is not enough high-quality child care generally available to meet demand, and there are also cultural perspectives that make the use of surrogates (except for family members) problematic.

The backlash against working mothers has been reflected in a stream of books (Hewlett, 1986; Mack, 1997; Whitehead, 1997), newspaper and magazine articles, and television news stories. From the mainstream press to the publications of right-wing organizations and "foundations," features are published constantly decrying the use of surrogate care. Working women are directly or indirectly chastised for selfishness in articles such as "Day Careless" (Gallagher, 1998) in *National Review*; "Day Care: The Thalidomide of the 1980s" and "Working Moms, Failing Children," in publications of the Rockford Institute; and cover stories in national newsmagazines such as "The Myth of Quality Time: How We're Cheating Our Children" in *Newsweek* and "The Lies Parents Tell About Work, Kids, Money, Day Care and Ambition" in *U.S. News and World Report*. News coverage focuses on stories about inadequate, inappropriate, and even lethal caregivers (Barnett and Rivers, 1997). Sociologist Arlie Hochschild's (1997) claim that Americans prefer working to dealing with the stresses of parenting received much media attention, including a cover story in the *New York Times Magazine*, and evoked a lively public response faulting American women for their selfishness in preferring the workplace to the home. And

the case of Louise Woodward, an English *au pair* worker acquitted in the death of an infant in her care in a Boston suburb, generated an avalanche of hate mail to the mother, a part-time physician, faulting her for not caring for her child herself.

The hostility and indifference expressed by the media to their child-care needs and the arrangements they make fuels guilt in working mothers and reinforces conventional negative attitudes about the advisability of full-time mothers' care for children (Faludi, 1991).

Women have written about the continuing conflict between their roles, seeing it as a war between their "selves." For example, in a book explaining her retreat from a high-powered publishing position to become a more attentive mother, Elizabeth Perle McKenna (1997:85) wrote:

> Every morning the bell would ring and out would come these two identities, sparring with one another, fighting for the minutes on the clock and for my attention.

Research that shows positive effects on the family well-being of dual-career couples (Barnett and Rivers, 1997; Parcel and Menanghan, 1994) does not evoke the same kind of media attention that bad experiences evoke, and virtually no media coverage focuses on the benefits to children of surrogate care or the successful management of roles by worker-mothers.

Thus, cultural contradictions of mothering have deepened rather than resolved concerns about the balancing of work and family obligations (Hays, 1996).

Though all the mothers among the lawyers interviewed for this study rely on at least part-time surrogate care, they are wary about delegating child care and seek to minimize it. Although even full-time working mothers express some ambivalence about assigning part of their mothering role to another person, part-timers have chosen reduced work schedules as a way to express their preferences and reduce their guilt, and, of course, to reduce role strain (Goode, 1957; Merton, 1957). A refrain common in many of the interviews with part-time lawyers was expressed by an associate at a large firm: "No one, no one, not a nanny, not a day-care center, will show my children as much love, and be able to care for my children the way that I can." Josh Levanthal, a supervising attorney in a government agency, worked part time to share in care for his children, as did his wife, Robin, another government attorney. Josh told us he agreed with his wife in thinking "a nonparent would not take the same sort of care that a parent would." Similarly, Sara Wright, an associate in a medium-size law firm whose office shelves were filled with photographs of her two toddlers, expressed concern that her children "have [my] moral values and not the babysitter's" and said this motivated her to take a part-time schedule.

Some of the lawyers interviewed expressed distrust of surrogates. Marina Goff, who cut back her work schedule after moving to a distant suburb so she could spend more time with her two-year-old son and five-year-old daughter, spoke of the "horror stories you hear, even from friends." Several other lawyers also spoke of the "absolute nightmare to find people who can watch your children." Fueled by newspaper accounts of horrible behavior by nannies, two of the attorneys interviewed admitted secretly videotaping their in-home child-care providers. Both were pleasantly relieved to discover that their children had exemplary care.

Of course, this cultural climate has had an effect on attitudes about how much commitment working mothers ought to have to their careers, and how much to the family. These cultural attitudes persuade many women to work less and a few to leave the workplace altogether for the sake of "moth-erhood," although discontent about the nature of their work may also contribute to retreat from career paths.

McKenna's (1997) study of women who decide to leave work found that when she scratched the surface, "women admitted that, yes, they wanted more flexibility and time for their children, but if they had been happier in their work, they would have figured it out somehow" (164). She pointed to the case of Alicia Daymans, who declared in an early part of an interview that she decided to leave the high-profile magazine she worked for because she wanted to spend more time with her daughter, but revealed later that the "real" reasons were the moral and philosophical differences she had with the publication's owners. Certainly, spending time with her preadolescent daughter was a big concern, but she admitted that this alone would not have prompted her to leave.

Certainly, many women feel it is appropriate to work full time and use child-care surrogates, and do. We interviewed scores of women attorneys in our study of lawyers in large corporate law firms (Epstein et al., 1995) who said they were comfortable with the balance of work and family in their lives and had worked with responsible and loving child-care surrogates who served their families well. This supported David Chambers's (1989) striking findings that women graduates of the Michigan Law School who were mothers showed the highest amount of contentment when compared with childless women (married and single) and with men. Although many of them worked part-time for some period after law school, many either consistently worked full-time or swiftly returned to full-time work after a brief leave. Consistent with our findings, women with children in Chambers's sample made more accommodations to career than men. Most for some period since law school ceased working outside the home or shifted to part-time work. A quarter of the mothers worked part-time or took leaves for periods totaling at least 18 months. But even women who do not feel guilty about sharing themselves with career and family must interact with others who question their behavior and punish them.

Several lawyer mothers complained that some "stay-at-home" mothers refused to make playdates with their children, if the nanny brought the child to their home. As a result many women are exposed to multiple and often contradictory messages. The women and the few men who choose part-time work, or the law jobs with "regular hours" considered less than the large-firm norm, are those who hope to reconcile the obligations and satisfactions of both spheres using an alternative equation. Part-timers particularly subscribe to the hands-on parenting norms popular today and are members of socioemotional communities that foster them. Pressures from spouses, children, coworkers, extended family members, and social acquaintances all affect what they say, believe, and do about balancing familial duties and professional calling.

It appears that the families of the lawyers who use part-time work in law firms to resolve the conflicts of work and child care are not so different structurally than the families of their full-time lawyer colleagues (Epstein et al., 1995). They are about the same size and are headed by spouses who work in similar occupations, for example.

More than 80 percent (62 out of 75) of the lawyers in this study who work or have worked part time chose to do so for child-care reasons. They are mothers (with two exceptions) whose children ranged in age from infancy to 13 years old. Several mothers chose to work reduced hours from the time that they returned to work from maternity leave; others chose it as their children moved beyond infancy, and still others after the birth of a second child. About 40 percent either

have returned or plan to return to full-time employment as their children mature (22 of 57), and 12 percent (7) are unsure of their plans. Almost half (28 lawyers) have no present intention of resuming full-time work. Additionally, most lawyers responding to a survey sent out by the Part-Time Network of the Association of the Bar of the City of New York (the LAWWS Network) (Schwab, 1994)—a group promoting part-time options in the legal profession—answered that they did not wish to return to full-time work in the future. A subset of our sample has migrated back and forth between full-time and part-time status as their families have increased in size, grown older, or been affected by other work or family pressures.

Decisions to Work Part-Time for the "Joys of Motherhood"

Just as these lawyers reported that their decisions to have children were worked out strategically in terms of their careers, more than half of the women part-timers in this study reported that when they were pregnant they were fairly certain that they would not return to work full-time after giving birth. Yet, of these, many told us that for strategic purposes, they behaved at work "as if" they were unsure about their postpartum plans. They did not want to reveal their intentions to work part-time prior to taking maternity leave because they did not want to lose quality work before they took leave, and they also believed they could negotiate a more favorable reduced-hours arrangement later. For most of the women in the study the decision to work part time was cushioned because they are wives of prosperous men. Thus, they were financially free to act on their feelings that it was necessary to spend more time at home.

Psychological reactions to motherhood compelled a number of lawyers interviewed to choose part-time work. Some reported their decisions to take extended periods of maternity leave or return on a part-time basis were spontaneous and emotionally unpredictable. As Patricia Clarke, a senior associate in a large Wall Street firm, described it:

> I fell madly in love with my son. . . . I just started to feel that I wouldn't be able to leave him every day and feel like someone else was raising my child. I didn't love my job enough to justify that. . . . It wasn't a trade-off worth making.

Cheryl Meany, a government attorney who left a position at a medium-size firm because she could not reduce her work schedule from four to three days a week, was agitated when she remarked, "I just felt desperate to be with my child." She admitted to being more traditional than other lawyers and wishing to stay home to take care of her two preschool-age daughters, but she was not alone in feeling "desperate."

Several mothers noted that the urge to work part time was fueled by jealous competition with their care providers. Gloria Mann, another government attorney, declared that she needed to spend "every waking hour" with her new son because:

> Being a mother to him . . . I felt like every minute, . . . every weekend I would be there for him to know that I was his mother, [not the] . . . baby-sitter.

Another mother admitted that she was heartbroken to find a local store clerk mistake her son's *au pair* for her.

Cultural lore stresses the value of witnessing a child's first steps or first words. The importance of these moments was internalized by many of the women (but was not reported by fathers in the same way). In her interview, Betty Forten, a full-time attorney, wept softly as she described her feelings at missing her son's first successful attempt at walking, a major regret of the women who worked full time. In her study of child-care providers, *Other People's Children* (1995), the sociologist Julia Wrigley found that nannies know the cultural importance of such infant milestones and that many refrain from telling parents when their children utter their first words or take their first steps, so that the mother or father will "discover" these achievements themselves.

The importance of witnessing and participating in the later development of a child was the rationale for their choice as Barbara Friedl, an eighth-year associate in a large, expanding firm, explained:

> I discovered that the more verbal they get, the more incredibly engaging they are. And the more my presence makes a difference to them. And right now, for a five-year-old . . . there is no one in the universe like me. . . . Her baby-sitter is wonderful and she adores her . . . but there is something absolutely extraordinary about having Mommy pick her up from school.

Negotiating Part-Time Status with a Spouse

Decisions about childbearing, time off, and part-time work were pondered and made by these lawyers within a broad context that incorporated economics, norms of professional commitment, and ideas about gender roles. The decision about which spouse will work part time is generally made against three criteria: a "rational" economic assessment, the couple's response to traditional sex roles, and their agreed-upon ideology. All of these criteria may be seen as ideological concepts that are intertwined and susceptible to challenge and negotiation.

There are economic repercussions on the family when a spouse cuts back work time and income, but because of the income differentials in the various sectors of the profession the impact on family lifestyle may vary. Usually, when a spouse cuts back on work time, family income falls precipitously. Virtually all families decide jointly whether to reduce paid labor from two full-time jobs, and most couples negotiate over how much their work schedules can be reduced and what child-care arrangements can be made. Many husbands initially were reluctant to accept their wives' working a reduced schedule, but others saw this as the wife's decision. Patricia Brooke said her husband, Tom, was skeptical about her working part time, for financial and professional reasons. "He was . . . thinking, 'Gee, we're now gonna be poor,'" she said. Tom is also a lawyer and has doubts about the seriousness and legitimacy of part-time lawyering.

> The fact that we're both lawyers in many ways makes the relationship difficult, because he has . . . standards, and he doesn't think of part-time lawyers as . . . serious. . . . He would never admit any of this, but I think his reluctance about part-time [makes him see] me as less legitimate as a lawyer because I'm only working three days.

The decision about which spouse will work full-time is rarely couched today in the language of traditional roles, but is usually justified in terms of maximizing income over a long time period. Yet studies show that it is common for men to regard themselves as the "breadwinner" no matter how much income a wife brings into the family (Potuchek, 1997). Indeed, we heard from a male government attorney that many of his colleagues had come to the agency because of idealistic motivations to "help people," but found their salaries could not support growing families, home mortgages, and wives who felt they should cut back in their own careers. Moving to legal work that was

more lucrative was, therefore, the "daddy track." Thus we see many decisions are interactive with people's views of appropriate roles and future needs. Couples weigh effort versus return; sacrifices are calculated against potential gains. Many husbands have incomes sufficient to forgo their wives' contributions. When the men are in independent professional practices or are small-business owners, couples usually decide it is more important to invest in his career than hers. Finally, families often use the language of economic rationalization when deciding which spouse should work part time. Karyn Post works four days a week as a senior associate in the corporate department of a prestigious midtown New York firm. She was hired on a part-time basis from a firm where she also had worked a reduced schedule. She has no plans to return to a full-time schedule and does not need to because her husband does very well working in the financial sector. She describes the process through which she and her husband agreed that she should work a reduced schedule:

> We decided that the financial rewards of partnership versus the hours that I would have to work to accomplish that were not worth it, and that it was better for me to go part-time and take on a bigger role at home. . . . I'm happy I was able to do that because I'd rather be at home and be with the kids. It was better to invest more in his career.

As we have seen, women report that they, together with their husbands, often make the decision to work part-time because they accept the idea that men will ultimately make more money than women. This is based on common knowledge that in general, women workers make less money for equal or similar work. Although this is not really the case for *professional* women who work in the same spheres as men and put in the same amount of time, couples still regard it as logical to invest in the husband's career.

Of course, powerful norms setting appropriate gender roles form a backdrop to all of these decisions even when the stated rationales are economic.

But sometimes, traditional sex-role assignments are a clearly stated factor in such decisions. Fiona Scott, a federal attorney, remarked that she was "more maternalistic than [her] husband was paternalistic." Others reported their husbands were uninterested in child rearing. Carrie Little, an associate at a large firm, explained that her husband did not consider reducing his work schedule because "he didn't really want to stay home and take charge. . . . He's more of a male." The traditional gender roles are not necessarily seen as "natural," but many regard them as inevitable. Jeannette Warren, a part-time partner at a prestigious firm, left her first job in the public interest sector in the early 1970s because it did not permit her to take a reduced schedule. She had the major responsibility for child care, a responsibility she desired. As she outlined her thinking:

> Women have . . . family responsibilities . . . that men just don't have. . . . My husband could do anything that I would do with my girls, but there were times when they just wanted me; and the other side of it is . . . maternal instinct, . . . I wanted to take them to the doctor; I didn't want him to take them to the doctor. . . . Women genetically or instinctively [are different].

Several mothers attributed their husbands' relative disinterest in child care to societal norms. "Of course, I wish my husband were more involved, but he's not. Society just doesn't value that for men, and he's just not that different from other men."

As the husband of a part-time lawyer described it, many attitudes come from the general society about the propriety of men

and women taking on certain work and family roles. Philip Smith, an associate in a large firm, talked to us about having considered going part-time himself. He and his wife discussed it "jokingly . . . with an edge of seriousness." Sex roles played a major part in his thinking:

> You're brought up and programmed to think you're supposed to be and do [certain things]. . . . And I guess you're brought up to think that well, if someone works part-time, it's going to be the wife. That's just how it is. And how shocking it would be if it was any other way.

Even if the subject is broached, the mechanisms that persuade people to conform to society's norms are sometimes right on the surface. Sharon Winick, a seventh-year associate in a large firm, recounted a discussion with her husband:

> Some of the issues [my husband and I discussed] were: Is it easy for a man to work part time? Is the stigma greater on a man? Can he ever redeem himself if he does that? Is it even possible to do that? He didn't experience the pull to want to be home. He experienced it as wanting to support me.

A part-time attorney whose husband is a lawyer who works at home confronted the cultural view of her husband's decision: "Real men do not work at home."

Ideological Renegades

When men chose to work part-time they explained it in ways that seemed a conscious attempt to subvert social norms and to offer themselves as alternative examples. They tended to have a political commitment to a gender-free ideology and a commitment to raising their children with maximum parental involvement. Robert Malcolm worked part-time for two years beginning four months after his first child was born. His father had played a very traditional role as a parent, which made him seek a different role. "I don't understand why men would want it to be any other way in . . . their relationships with their kids," he said. Equality of responsibility in child rearing is also a political issue, as he described it:

> In terms of household responsibilities . . . it's sort of a political issue. I come from the left side of the spectrum, and I'm a fairly strong feminist, and I think it's the proper way to live your life. . . .
>
> It was important to us that the kids viewed us equally. It was important to us that they didn't view the stereotyped roles for men and women in the household, . . . that the kids basically had parents home with them for most of the time.

His wife, Leila, has worked three days a week in a municipal agency for two years and will continue to do so for the foreseeable future; she supports his decision. She feels that the reward for this political commitment was the way in which their son was socialized. "My son was totally equally bonded to both partners. He didn't have one primary over the other," she said. Their larger political commitment to set themselves as an example was important in this decision:

> We did it [worked part time] for ourselves, but we were really happy [to] set an example. . . . When [only] a few men do it . . . you'll continue to have a situation where women rank behind men. Women will always be doing other things at home, and men will keep advancing their careers. So we both thought that the best thing would be if [we] share child-care responsibility.

In both cases where men worked reduced schedules to be with their children they became dissatisfied, feeling they were missing out on their careers and failing to enjoy their parenting roles. Both male lawyers returned to full-time work, leaving their wives to work part time. One of the men returned to a full-time schedule because he missed the supervisory role that is denied in his department to part-timers; the other, because of a trial that required his full-time participation. As we found in our study of large corporate firms (Epstein et al., 1995), most men find that attempts to adjust their work schedules to accommodate family needs meet extreme resistance from employers, and the costs they face are felt to be too high to pay (Rhode, 1997). It is simply easier for their wives to find accommodation in the workplace.

Furthermore, sometimes knowingly and sometimes quite unconsciously, many women place constraints on their husbands' interest in reducing their workloads and spending more time with their children. Some who have tried it find also that women in the community resist their attempts to participate in parenting that goes beyond the traditional father's role as a soccer or baseball coach. John Spiegel, a government attorney whose wife works for the same agency two days a week on site, two days at home, told us it was clear that his wife "had more of a need" to be with the children. He felt also that if he spent more time at home he would be more isolated because he didn't think he'd be included in the activities arranged by mothers. Several mothers were candid about not encouraging their husbands to reduce their work time, saying they wished to be in charge at home. With a husband whose commitment to child care might be the envy of many working mothers, Sara Atkins found herself feeling quite ambivalent. A woman with two post-graduate degrees from elite schools, she left a full-time, high-demand position in a firm because of health problems and a desire to mother her two children. She intimated that her husband's active involvement with the children threatened her role as "primary parent," and she felt somewhat competitive with him. Her work choice effectively undercut her husband's plan to share the parenting role in an equitable way.

Professional Ideology

Many factors influence an attorney's choice of part-time work. One of the issues for women in law is the conflict between motherhood and the ideology of professionalism. . . . Many of the profession's leaders regard law as a "calling." It is this sense of vocation that partly differentiates a profession from a craft and sets it above other occupations.

Mothers who choose part-time work must adjust to the perception that they are compromising their calling. Of course, many young lawyers, men and women alike, no longer accept this definition of a professional. (It was only among lawyers in government service that we found a sense of mission to accomplish socially useful objectives. Yet even there the attractions of law were its autonomy, variety of work, and potential for a high income, rather than a grandiose ideal.) Margaret Segrest, a recently laid-off counsel in a multinational corporation's legal department with two boys and an attorney husband, expressed a sentiment that was not uncommon:

> I enjoy practicing law. . . . I want to keep my foot in for economic reasons. . . . I like getting dressed and coming to work, and I like thinking, and I did invest a lot in going to law school.

What distinguishes a professional from a nonprofessional, in her view, is the professional's commitment to task without regard to other constraints. In contrast to a job in which one just does the required work within a given time period, a professional is supposed to be dedicated to producing the best she can and to provide service at its highest level.

In balancing physical, emotional, and time demands between lawyering and mothering, the allocation of energies required for mothering becomes less problematic for many part-time attorneys when the practice of law is reduced to "work, money, and prestige," as a lawyer sharing a job put it. The choice between children and career, as one woman expressed it, is a "no-brainer." Or as another joked, "There's a saying that on our deathbed nobody ever says, 'Gee, I wish I'd spent more time at work.'" . . .

Part-Time Work as a Solution for Role Strain and Role Inequities

Faced with cross-pressures to meet the norms of intensive mothering, the problems of surrogate child care, the curtailing of professional identity, and the continued strength of traditional gender roles in the family, what keeps women lawyers, who usually can afford to, from leaving the paid work force altogether?

Two issues predominate: the fatigue and isolation of parenting, and the attempt to maintain power in marital relationships.

Most of the women lawyers interviewed saw their work as a needed respite from domestic responsibilities. Elsie Marshak, the associate described earlier as working 35 hours a week in a large firm, considers work a condition for sanity: "I need to work. I would go crazy staying at home full time. But I was also going to go crazy doing everything at once." Using similar language, Laurie Potempkin, another part-time associate, asserted, "I think that I would go crazy staying at home. I need some structure to my life. I need the intellectual stimulation. And kids are great. But they're very demanding; it's very physically demanding and not as intellectually so in the early years." She went on to describe mothering as lonely and isolating:

> When I was on maternity leave, I found it lonely. There wasn't the camaraderie of working with people, the interaction with colleagues; you just sit with other mothers. But I guess maybe I didn't click with the other mothers. They were just always talking about kids and play days and stuff.

The gendered division of labor exists and persists because of differences in power between men and women. Some women respond to this imbalance by asserting their need for independence. Part-time work allows them to keep some control over their financial resources, social networks, and professional identities. In large part, they are defending a space with both real and symbolic territories. Their social networks and professional identities are reminders that they are more than mothers. Although, with a few notable exceptions, women attorneys do not earn enough in part-time positions to maintain their standard of living, their earnings are considerable compared to what they would earn in other occupations. Further, an independent income offers the possibility of autonomy; its absence means dependence. In negotiating conflicting norms, they often use their mothers' experience as a guide, stressing their continued employment as a safety net. Elsie Marshak reflected:

> My parents . . . had a rocky marriage for 30 years, and my mother always pushed me to be financially independent. . . . I'm not truly independent. Our lives are so intertwined with kids, but [it's important] knowing that, if I want independence, I can have it.

Though Deborah Seinfield, in her 40s, removed herself from the partnership track, staying in the labor force as a part-time associate gives her a sense of independence:

> I never thought I'd be able to depend on somebody else . . . for money. . . . One of the things that's always kept me from quitting, other than the fact that my husband says, "No," was I couldn't imagine asking him for money, for an allowance.

Neither of these attorneys believe their incomes make them self-sufficient, but they are grounds for claiming at least symbolic autonomy.

The integration of work roles and family roles is negotiated by husbands and wives on the basis of their philosophies, traditions, and practical concerns. Financial pressures, the number of children and their ages, and access to good child-care providers are all important factors, but all are weighed and interpreted within frameworks that mark the pair's private worlds and reflect the larger society.

REFERENCES

Barnett, Rosalind and Caryl Rivers. 1996. *She Works, He Works: How Two-Income Families Are Happier, Healthier and Better Off.* San Francisco: HarperCollins.
———. 1997. "Bashing Working Families." *Dissent* (Fall):13–15.
Chambers, David L. 1989. "Accommodation and Satisfaction: Women and Men Lawyers and the Balance of Work and Family." *Law and Social Inquiry* 14(2):251–287.
Coser, Lewis and Rose Laub Coser. 1974. "The Housewife and Her Greedy Family." In Lewis, Coser, *Greedy Institutions*, 89–100. New York: Free Press.
Epstein, Cynthia Fuchs. [1981] 1993. *Women in Law.* Chicago: University of Illinois Press.
Epstein, Cynthia Fuchs, Robert Sauté, Bonnie Oglensky, and Martha Gever. 1995. "Glass Ceilings and Open Doors: Women's Mobility in the Legal Profession." *Fordham Law Review* 64(2):291–449.

Faludi, Susan. 1991. *Backlash.* New York: Crown.

Fiore, Faye. 1997. "Full-Time Moms a Minority Now, Census Bureau Finds." *Los Angeles Times,* Nov. 26, 1.

Gallagher, Maggie. 1998. "Warning: May Be Harmful to Children: Day Careless." *National Review,* Vol. L, No. 1 (Jan. 26):37–43.

Goode, William J. 1957. "Community Within a Community: The Professions." *American Sociological Review* 22:194–200.

Hays, Sharon. 1996. *The Cultural Contradictions of Motherhood.* New Haven: Yale University Press.

Hewlett, Sylvia Ann. 1986. *A Lesser Life: The Myth of Women's Liberation in America.* New York: W. Morrow.

Hochschild, Arlie Russell. 1997. *The Time Bind: When Work Becomes Home and Home Becomes Work.* New York: Metropolitan Books.

Mack, Dana. 1997. *The Assault on Parenthood: How Our Culture Undermines the Family.* New York: Simon and Schuster.

McKenna, Elizabeth Perle. 1997. *When Work Doesn't Work Anymore: Women, Work and Identity.* New York: Delacorte Press.

Merton, Robert. 1957. *Social Theory and Social Structure.* Glencoe, IL: Free Press.

Parcel, Toby L. and E. G. Menanghan. 1994. *Parents' Jobs and Children's Lives.* New York: Aldine.

Potuchek, Jean L. 1997. *Who Supports the Family: Gender and Breadwinning in Dual-Career Marriages.* Stanford, CA: Stanford University Press.

Rhode, Deborah. 1997. *Speaking of Sex: The Denial of Gender Inequality.* Cambridge: Harvard University Press.

Schwab, Jolie. 1994. Report to the Committee on Women in the Profession. Unpublished paper.

Skolnick, Arlene. 1991. *Embattled Paradise: The American Family in an Age of Uncertainty.* New York: Basic Books.

Whitehead, Barbara Dafoe. 1997. *The Divorce Culture.* New York: Knopf.

Wrigley, Julia. 1995. *Other People's Children.* New York: Basic Books.

FAMILY WORK

41

The Third Shift

Arlie Russell Hochschild

Amerco, a highly profitable, innovative company, had the budget and the will to experiment with new ways to organize its employees' lives. Its Work-Life Balance program could have become a model,

Excerpts from *The Time Bind: When Work Becomes Home and Home Becomes Work* by Arlie Russell Hochschild. Copyright © 1997 by Arlie Russell Hochschild. Reprinted by permission of Henry Holt and Company, LLC.

demonstrating to other corporations that workforce talents can be used effectively without wearing down workers and their families. But that did not happen. The question I . . . asked is: Why not? The answer . . . is complex. Some working parents, especially on the factory floor, were disinclined to work shorter hours because they needed the money or feared losing their jobs. Though not yet an issue at Amerco, in some companies workers may also fear that "good" shorter-hour jobs could at any moment be converted into "bad" ones, stripped of benefits or job security. Even when such worries were absent, pressure from peers or supervisors to be a "serious player" could cancel out any desire to cut back on work hours. The small number of employees who resolved to actually reduce their hours risked coming up against a company Balashev. But all these sources of inhibition did not fully account for the lack of resistance Amerco's working parents showed to the encroachments of work time on family life.

Much of the solution to the puzzle of work-family balance appeared to be present at Amerco—the pieces were there, but they remained unassembled. Many of those pieces lay in the hands of the powerful men at the top of the company hierarchy, who had the authority and skill to engineer a new family-friendly work culture but lacked any deep interest in doing so. Other pieces were held by the advocates of family-friendly policies lower down the corporate ladder, who had a strong interest in such changes but little authority to implement them. And the departmental supervisors and managers, whose assent was crucial to solving the puzzle, were sometimes overtly hostile to anything that smacked of work-family balance. So even if the workers who could have benefited from such programs had demanded them, resistance from above would still have stymied their efforts.

But why *weren't* Amerco working parents putting up a bigger fight for family time, given the fact that most said they needed more? Many of them may have been responding to a powerful process that is devaluing what was once the essence of family life. The more women and men do what they do in exchange for money and the more their work in the public realm is valued or honored, the more, almost by definition, private life is devalued and its boundaries shrink. For women as well as men, work in the marketplace is less often a simple economic fact

than a complex cultural value. If, in the early part of the century it was considered unfortunate that a woman had to work, it is now thought surprising when she doesn't.

People generally have the urge to spend more time on what they value most and on what they are most valued for. This tendency may help explain the historic decline in time devoted to private social relations, a decline that has taken on a distinctive cultural form at Amerco. The valued realm of work is registering its gains in part by incorporating the best aspects of home. The devalued realm, the home, is meanwhile taking on what were once considered the most alienating attributes of work. However one explains the failure of Amerco to create a good program of work-family balance, though, the fact is that in a cultural contest between work and home, working parents are voting with their feet, and the workplace is winning.

In this respect, we may ask, are working parents at Amerco an anomaly or are they typical of working parents nationwide? In search of an answer, I contacted a company called Bright Horizons, which runs 125 company-based child-care centers associated with corporations, hospitals, real estate developers, and federal agencies in nineteen states. Bright Horizons allowed me to add a series of new questions to a questionnaire the company was sending out to seven thousand parents whose children were attending Bright Horizons Children's Centers. A third of the parents who received questionnaires filled them out. The resulting 1,446 responses came from mainly middle- or upper-middle-class parents in their early thirties. Since many of them worked for Fortune 500 companies—including IBM, American Express, Sears, Roebuck, Eastman Kodak, Xerox, Bausch and Lomb, and Dunkin' Donuts—this study offers us a highly suggestive picture of what is happening among managers and professional working parents at Amerco's counterparts nationwide.

These parents reported time pressures similar to those Amerco parents complained about. As at Amerco, the longest hours at work were logged by the most highly educated professionals and managers, among whom six out of ten regularly averaged over forty hours a week. A third of the parents in this sample had their children in child care forty hours a week or more. As at Amerco, the higher the income of their parents, the longer the children's shifts in child care.

When asked, "Do you ever consider yourself a workaholic?" a third of fathers and a fifth of mothers answered yes. One out of three said their *partner* was workaholic. In response to the question "Do you experience a problem of 'time famine'?" 89 percent responded yes. Half reported that they typically brought work home from the office. Of those who complained of a time famine, half agreed with the statement "I feel guilty that I don't spend enough time with my child." Forty-three percent agreed that they "very often" felt "too much of the time I'm tired when I'm with my child." When asked, "Overall, how well do you feel you can balance the demands of your work and family?" only 9 percent said "very well."

If many of these Bright Horizons working parents were experiencing a time bind of the sort I heard about from Amerco employees, were they living with it because they felt work was more rewarding than family life? To find out, I asked, "Does it sometimes feel to you like home is a 'workplace'?" Eighty-five percent said yes (57 percent "very often"; 28 percent "fairly often"). Women were far more likely to agree than men. I asked this question the other way around as well: "Is it sometimes true that work feels like home should feel?" Twenty-five percent answered "very often" or "quite often," and 33 percent answered "occasionally." Only 37 percent answered "very rarely."

One reason some workers may feel more "at home" at work is that they feel more ap-

preciated and more competent there. Certainly, this was true for many Amerco workers I interviewed, and little wonder, for Amerco put great effort into making its workers feel appreciated. In a large-scale nationwide study, sociologists Diane Burden and Bradley Googins found that 59 percent of employees rated their family performances "good or unusually good," while 86 percent gave that rating to their performances on the job—that is, workers appreciated *themselves* more at work than at home. In the Bright Horizons national survey, only 29 percent felt appreciated "mainly at home," and 52 percent "equally" at home and work. Surprisingly, women were not more likely than men to say they felt more appreciated at home.

Often, working parents feel more at home at work because they come to expect that emotional support will be more readily available there. As at Amerco, work can be where their closest friends are, a pattern the Bright Horizons survey reflected. When asked, "Where do you have the most friends?" 47 percent answered "at work"; 16 percent, "in the neighborhood"; and 6 percent, "at my church or temple." Women were far more likely than men to have the most friends at work.

Some workers at Amerco felt more at home at work because work was where they felt most relaxed. To the question "Where do you feel the most relaxed?" only a slight majority in the Bright Horizons survey, 51 percent, said "home." To the question "Do you feel as if your life circumstances or relationships are more secure at work or at home?" a similarly slim majority answered "home." I also asked, "How many times have you changed jobs since you started working?" The average was between one and two times. Though I didn't ask how many times a person had changed primary loved ones, the national picture suggests that by the early thirties, one or two such changes is not unusual. Work may not "always be there" for the employee, but then home may not either.

I should have asked what arena of life—work or family—was most engrossing. Amerco parents loved their children but nonetheless often found life at work more interesting than life at home. The workplace, after all, offered a natural theater in which one could follow the progress of jealousies, sexual attractions, simmering angers. Home, on the other hand, offered fewer actors on an increasingly cramped stage. Sometimes, the main, stress-free, "exciting" events at home came during the time Americans spend watching television. (According to one study, Americans spend about 30 percent of their free time in front of the television.)

For this sample, then, we find some evidence that a cultural reversal of workplace and home is present at least as a theme. Unsurprisingly, more people in the survey agreed that home felt like work than that work felt like home. Still, only to half of them was home a main source of relaxation or security. For many, work seemed to function as a backup system to a destabilizing family. For women, in particular, to take a job is often today to take out an emotional insurance policy on the uncertainties of home life. . . .

Behind Reversing Worlds

Although work can complement—and, indeed, improve—family life, in recent decades it has largely competed with the family, and won. While the mass media so often point to global competition as the major business story of the age, it is easy to miss the fact that corporate America's fiercest struggle has been with its local rival—the family. Amerco company officials worry about their battles for market share with companies in Asia and Europe. But they take for granted their company's expanding share of domestic time. For where the workplace invests in its em-

ployees, as at Amerco, it often wins the emotional allegiance of its workers—and so ever more of its workers' time.

The ascendancy of the corporation in its battle with the family has been aided in recent years by the rise of company cultural engineering and, in particular, the shift from Frederick Taylor's principles of scientific management to the Total Quality principles originally set out by Charles Deming. Under the influence of a Taylorist worldview, the manager's job was to coerce the worker's mind and body, not to appeal to his heart. The Taylorized worker was deskilled, replaceable, cheap, and as a consequence felt bored, demeaned, and unappreciated.

Using more modern participative management techniques, companies now invest in training workers to "make decisions" and then set before their newly "empowered" workers moral, as well as financial, incentives. Under Taylor's system, managers assumed that workers lacked the basic impulse to do a good job. Under Total Quality, managers assume workers possess such an impulse. Under Taylorism, the worker was given no autonomy. Under Total Quality, the worker has a certain amount of autonomy and is drawn further into the world of work by the promise of more.

As the Amerco work environment illustrates, the Total Quality worker is invited to feel recognized for job accomplishments. The company publishes a quarterly magazine, *Amerco World,* that features photos of smiling workers credited with solving problems, anticipating bottlenecks, inventing new products, reducing errors, and otherwise "delighting the customer." In describing its application of the Total Quality system before the House Subcommittee on Science, Research, and Technology, an Amerco vice president noted that the company preferred to reward quality work with personal recognition rather than money. Personal recognition, he pointed out, has proved an extremely effective motivational tool, one far less likely to create the jealousies that often result from giving financial rewards to some workers and not others. Company surveys confirm this.

At Amerco, employees are invited to feel relaxed while on the job. Frequent recognition events reward work but also provide the context for a kind of play. Amerco's management has, in fact, put thought and effort into blurring the distinction between work and play (just as that distinction is so often blurred at home). Fridays during the summer, for instance, are "dress down" days on which employees are urged to dress "as though" they are at home; and the regular rounds of company picnics, holiday parties, and ceremonies are clearly meant to invest work with celebratory good feeling. For white-collar workers at Amerco headquarters, there are even free Cokes, just as at home, stashed in refrigerators placed near coffee machines on every floor.

Amerco has also made a calculated attempt to take on the role of helpful relative in relation to employee problems at work and at home. The Education and Training Division offers employees free courses (on company time) in "Dealing with Anger," "How to Give and Accept Criticism," "How to Cope with Difficult People," "Stress Management," "Taking Control of Your Work Day," and "Using the Myers-Briggs Personality Test to Improve Team Effectiveness." There are workshops in "Work-Life Balance for Two-Career Couples" and "Work-Life Balance for Single Adults." At home, people seldom receive anything like this much help on issues so basic to family life. At home, there were no courses on "Coping with Your Child's Anger over the Time Famine" or "Dealing with Your Child's Disappointment in You or Yours in Him."

As a result, many Amerco managers and professionals earnestly confessed to me that the company had helped them grow as human beings in ways that improved their ability to cope with problems at home. Even in the plants, training in team building sometimes instills similar feelings in the workers. One Amerco handout for its managers lists a series of "qualities for excellence at work" that would be useful at home—an employee would be judged on whether he or she "seeks feedback on personal behaviors," "senses changes in attention level and mood," or "adapts personality to the situation and the people involved." Amerco is also one of about a hundred companies that enrolls its top executives in classes at the Corporate Learning Institute. There, managers learn how to motivate and influence others and manage conflict. The Institute offers an open-ended "personal focus program designed for people from all walks of life who have a genuine desire to explore and expand their unique possibilities." One can, at company expense, attend a course on "Self-Awareness and Being: The Importance of Self in the Influence Process."

The Total Quality worker is invited to feel committed to his company. When, in *Modern Times,* a speedup finally drives the Taylorized Charlie Chaplin crazy, he climbs into a giant complex of cogs and belts and is wound around a huge wheel. He has become part of the machine itself. How could he feel committed to a company that had turned him into a machine part?

Under Total Quality at Amerco, the worker is not a machine; he's a believer. This became clear to me when I witnessed a "Large Group Change Event," held in a high school cafeteria one summer morning in 1992. The event, Amerco's response to losing customers to a growing competitor, was staged somewhat like a revival meeting. Its purpose was to convince each worker to renew his commitment not to his spouse or church but to his workplace. . . .

At the end of the event, to signify their new "commitment," workers inscribed their names on one of the immense red banners that hung at the cafeteria entrance. They signed with fancy long *g*'s and tall *t*'s, with lines under their names, and curlicued *s*'s. Under some names they bracketed nicknames, others as in a high school yearbook were cleverly written inside one of the banner's larger letters that corresponded to the beginning letter of a name.

The event had climaxed with a promise of redemption. Workers had offered themselves up, name by name, to be "saved" from unemployment, and to save the company from falling profits. Amerco, too, wanted these workers to be saved, not laid off. It had already spent four million dollars to get the "mission" of Total Quality out to the plants—and now it was spending even more to save plants and jobs. That said something in itself, the workers felt: Amerco cared.

This sense of being cared for encouraged workers to adopt a more personal orientation toward work time. If, in *Modern Times,* Chaplin, like millions of real factory workers of his era, found himself the victim of a company-initiated speedup, Amerco's professionals, managers, and even factory workers were being asked to envision themselves as their own time strategists, their own efficiency experts. They were to improve their own production, to manage their own intensified work pace at their own plants, even in their own lives. Under the moral mantle of Total Quality, however, workers weren't being asked to consider the speed of their work— not directly anyway—only its "quality." Meanwhile at home, the same workers were finding that quality was exactly what they had to let go of in order to do a certain quantity of chores in the few hours left to them.

The Taylorized Family

If Total Quality called for "reskilling" the worker in an "enriched" job environment, capitalism and technological developments have long been gradually deskilling parents at home. Over time, store-bought goods have replaced homespun cloth, homemade soap and candles, home-cured meats and home-baked foods. Instant mixes, frozen dinners, and take-out meals have replaced Mother's recipes. Daycare for children, retirement homes for the elderly, wilderness camps for delinquent children, even psychotherapy are, in a way, commercial substitutes for jobs a mother once did at home. If, under Total Quality, "enriched" jobs call for more skill at work, household chores have over the years become fewer and easier to do.

Even family-generated entertainment has its own mechanical replacement—primarily the television, but also the video game, VCR, computer, and CD player. In the Amerco families I observed, TV cartoons often went on early in the morning as a way to ease children into dressing and eating breakfast. For some families in the evening, CNN or network news lent an aura of seriousness to the mundane task of preparing dinner. After dinner, some families would sit together, mute but cozy, watching sitcoms in which *television* mothers, fathers, and children talked energetically to one another. TV characters did the joking and bantering for them while the family itself engaged in "relational loafing." What the family used to produce— entertainment—it now consumes. Ironically, this entertainment may even show viewers a "family life" that, as in the sitcoms *Murphy Brown* and *Ink,* has moved to work.

The main "skill" still required of family members is the hardest one of all—the ability to forge, deepen, and repair family relationships. Under normal circumstances the work of tending to relationships calls for noticing, acknowledging, and emphathizing with the feelings of family members, patching up quarrels, and soothing hurt feelings. In the wake of the "divorce revolution," this sort of emotional work, always delicate, has become even more complicated and difficult. . . .

Family life can be baffling under the best of circumstances. But in a society based on the nuclear family, divorce creates extra strains. Blending and reblending people into remarriage "chains" can be much harder than the word "blend" implies. Stepsiblings in such families are rarely as close as biological siblings—and that's only one of many problems such new families face. One divorced Amerco employee complained that his stepchildren refused to obey him and instead confronted him with the challenge "You're not my *real* dad!" On the other hand, many divorced mothers also deeply resented the ways their remarried ex-husbands favored their new families. One divorced wife, for instance, observed bitterly that her ex-husband had managed to buy a new car and boat while remaining in arrears on his child support payments. Faced with such issues and in need of emotional "reskilling" few parents at home have the faintest idea where to look for "retraining."

At Amerco, successful completion of on-the-job training is rewarded with a recognition ceremony, a Total Quality pin, and possibly even a mention in the company magazine. At Amerco, large sums of money are spent to stage "commitment ceremonies" between the company and its workers whenever a "divorce" seems to threaten. But who rewards a difficult new kind of emotional work or watches for declining profit margins at home? Who calls for renewed vows of commitment there?

The Hydro-Compressed Sterilized Mouth Wiper

Working parents often face difficult problems at home without much outside support or help in resolving them. In itself time is, of course, no cure-all. But having time together is an important precondition for building

family relations. What, then, is happening to family time?

Working parents exhibit an understandable desire to build sanctuaries of family time, free from pressure, in which they can devote themselves to only one activity or one relationship. So, for instance, the time between 8 and 8:45 P.M. may be cordoned off as "quality time" for parents and child, and that between 9:15 and 10 P.M. as quality time for a couple (once the children are in bed). Such time boundaries must then be guarded against other time demands—calls from the office, from a neighbor to arrange tomorrow's car pool, from a child's friend about homework. Yet these brief respites of "relaxed time" themselves come to look more and more like little segments of job time, with parents punching in and out as if on a time clock. . . .

Paradoxically, what may seem to harried working parents like a solution to their time bind—efficiency and time segmentation—can later feel like a problem in itself. To be efficient with whatever time they do have at home, many working parents try to go faster if for no other reason than to clear off some space in which to go slowly. They do two or three things at once. They plan ahead. They delegate. They separate home events into categories and try to out source some of them. In their efficiency, they may inadvertently trample on the emotion-laden symbols associated with particular times of day or particular days of the week. They pack one activity closer to the next and disregard the "framing" around each of them, those moments of looking forward to or looking back on an experience, which heighten its emotional impact. They ignore the contribution that a leisurely pace can make to fulfillment, so that a rapid dinner, followed by a speedy bath and bedtime story for a child—if part of "quality time"—is counted as "worth the same" as a slower version of the same events. As time becomes something to "save" at home as much as or even more than at work, domestic life becomes quite literally a second shift; a cult of efficiency, once centered in the workplace, is allowed to set up shop and make itself comfortable at home. Efficiency has become both a means to an end—more home time—and a way of life, an end in itself.

A surprising amount of family life has become a matter of efficiently assembling people into prefabricated activity slots. Perhaps the best way to see this is to return to a classic scene in the film *Modern Times.* A team of salesmen is trying to persuade the president of Electro Steel, where Charlie Chaplin works on an assembly line, to install a J. Willicomb Billows Feeding Machine, which, as the mad inventor explains, "automatically feeds your men at work." The sales pitch, an automated recording, continues: "Don't stop for lunch. Be ahead of your competition. The Billows Feeding Machine will eliminate the lunch hour, increase your production, and decrease your overhead." In scientific-looking white lab coats, two sales demonstrators—with the muted smiles and slightly raised eyebrows of French waiters—point to the "automatic soup plate with the compressed air blower" ("no energy is required to cool the soup"); to the "revolving plate with automatic food pusher"; to the "double knee-action corn feeder with its syncro-mesh transition, which enables you to shift from high to low gear by the mere tip of the tongue"; and finally to the "hydro-compressed sterilized mouth wiper," which offers "control against spots on the shirt front."

The hapless Chaplin is chosen to test the machine, and a salesman straps him into it, his arms immobilized. The machine begins to pour soup into his mouth and, of course, finally down his shirt. Chaplin keeps a doubtful eye on the automatic mouth wiper, which periodically spins in to roll over his lips and, if he doesn't stretch up, his nose. Buttered corn on the cob appears, moving automatically back and forth across his

mouth. As a deskilled eater, his only job is to bite and chew. However, the corn, like the factory's conveyor belt, soon begins to speed up, moving back and forth so fast that he has no time to chew. The machine breaks. Impassive white-coated salesmen try to fix it, but it only malfunctions again, feeding Chaplin bolts with morsels of sandwich and splashing a cream pie in his face. The mouth wiper leaps out wildly to make a small, clean stripe across his smeared face, and Chaplin drops away from the machine in a faint.

The CEO of Amerco didn't have to introduce a Billows Automatic Feeding Machine. Many of his employees quite voluntarily ate lunch quickly at their desks to save time. This pattern is by no means unique to Amerco. A recent report commissioned by the National Restaurant Association found that these days business lunches are faster and fewer in number. Only 38 percent of adults polled in 1993 said they ate lunch out at least once a week, compared with 60 percent in the mid-1980s. According to Wendy Tanaka, an observer of San Francisco's business district, people take less and less time out for lunch, and many restaurants are being turned into take-out businesses to make ends meet. Customers who do sit down to lunch are more likely to bring work with them. As Tanaka observes, it is no longer unusual for someone to walk in with a laptop computer and have lunch opposite a project not a partner.

Perhaps more significant, though, a feeding-machine atmosphere has entered the home. *Working Mother* magazine, for example, carries ads that invite the working mother to cook "two-minute rice," a "five-minute chicken casserole," a "seven-minute Chinese feast." One ad features a portable phone to show that the working mother can make business calls while baking cookies with her daughter.

Another typical ad promotes cinnamon oatmeal cereal for breakfast by showing a smiling mother ready for the office in her square-shouldered suit, hugging her happy son. A caption reads, "In the morning, we are in such a rush, and my son eats so slowly. But with cinnamon oatmeal cereal, I don't even have to coax him to hurry up!" Here, the modern mother seems to have absorbed the lessons of Frederick Taylor as she presses for efficiency at home because she is in a hurry to get to work. In a sense, though, Taylor's role has been turned over to her son, who, eager for his delicious meal, speeds *himself* up. What induces the son to do this is the sugar in the cereal. For this child, the rewards of efficiency have jumped inside the cereal box and become a lump of sugar.

A Third Shift: Time Work

As the first shift (at the workplace) takes more time, the second shift (at home) becomes more hurried and rationalized. The longer the workday at the office or plant, the more we feel pressed at home to hurry, to delegate, to delay, to forgo, to segment, to hyperorganize the precious remains of family time. Both their time deficit and what seem like solutions to it (hurrying, segmenting, and organizing) force parents to engage in a third shift—noticing, understanding, and coping with the emotional consequences of the compressed second shift. . . .

42

Invisible Work

Arlene Kaplan Daniels

The notion of work as something set apart from the rest of life is a peculiarly modern and Western idea. Cross-cultural studies show us that other peoples are not inclined to make such distinctions. Production, religious practice, and family life are integrated. In our society work is a folk concept (Turner, 1957); we all have a commonsense notion of what work is. It is something that, whatever its status, is hard (it can be arduous, boring, taxing, challenging, stressful), yet we have to do it. Sometimes work is skilled, requiring training and experience. Other work can be monotonous or backbreaking. We usually associate the

Excerpts from "Invisible Work" by Arlene Kaplan Daniels. 1987. *Social Problems* 34:403–415. Reprinted with permission of the author.

former with high-status occupations and the latter with low-status jobs. We distinguish work from leisure activity (that we *want* to do because we enjoy it) and from other activities in the private realm of life—personal grooming, child care, homemaking. In modern, industrialized society perhaps the most common understanding of the essential characteristic of work is that it is something for which we get paid. This idea is associated with activity in the public world, which is dominated by men and separated from those private worlds of family and personal relationships where women predominate. There may be exchanges in households and friendships, but they are not monetary. Even activity in the public sphere, such as volunteering and community service, is not work if it isn't paid. However, any activity we do for pay, wherever it is found, even if we enjoy it, must, by definition, be work. But any effort we make, even if it is arduous, skilled, and recognized as useful—perhaps essential—is still not recognized as work if it is not paid.

I will show how our concept of work is affected by our understanding of three elements in the folk conception: (1) the differences between public and private activity; (2) the importance of financial recompense; and (3) the effects of gender on judgments about the legitimacy of calling an activity work—or if it is recognized as work, giving it a high value. In considering the restrictiveness of these commonsense understandings, I focus on the work that disappears from our observations and reckonings when we limit ourselves to the conception of work that develops from the relationship of these three ideas.

The Devaluation of Unpaid Work

It is admittedly difficult to shake free of our folk concept of work. Commonsense understandings about the place of work in social life are reflected and reinforced in our sociological researches. Our studies of stratification, for example, depend on occupation as a key variable in assessing socio-economic status of an individual and his (increasingly, also her) family as well (see Acker, 1973). But the significance of work lies deeper than its importance as an indicator of status. Work provides a clue to a person's worth in society—how others judge and regard him or her. To work—and earn money—is also to gain status as an adult. Thus, working is an important way to develop both a sense of identity and a sense of self-esteem. In this process, one not only comes to see oneself as an adult and a person of some worth; one comes to appreciate the larger normative order in which we participate. We earn our bread and work to keep society functioning at the same time. The value we place on this reproductive

process shows how we participate in the moral order. Study of the division of labor, as social scientists from Emile Durkheim to Everett Hughes have pointed out, is important for what it tells us about the moral order. Any recognition of an activity as work gives it a moral force and dignity—something of importance in a society. In a cash nexus economy like ours, this importance is recognized by payment for doing something. Work in what Illich (1981) calls the "shadow economy" can be included here, for payment can include trading services and goods where money is not—or not officially—exchanged. Payment signals the belief that somehow society needs that something done.

What about all that work outside the economy? The idealized separation of work from the home—the expected distinction between the public world where men went out to work and the private world where women remained at home to raise the family and prepare a place of respite for the working man—sharpened the distinction between productive workers (men doing "real" work for wages) and non-productive workers (women supporting, raising, and rehabilitating those real workers). Of course, lip service is paid to the importance of this work outside the market economy; but it is clear that the work in the private sphere is regarded as less important. It does not figure in the Gross National Product and in the records of divorce settlements. These records indicate that women are sometimes left virtually penniless while husbands keep much of their resources for themselves. Women who have always worked in the home and know no other livelihood become what has come to be called displaced homemakers. The problems of displaced homemakers show the generally low worth placed on the work of women in the home.

One consequence of the lesser esteem given to work in the private realm is that women themselves devalue work in the private world. An early feminist social scientist,

Charlotte Perkins Gilman ([1898] 1966), argued that this work should be rationalized and minimized by bringing more of it into the public sphere, e.g., community laundries, eating and child-care facilities. She thought stripped-down private houses—composed of little more personal space than bedrooms that individuals would tidy themselves—would solve the problem of completing the work that would otherwise be done in private life. Implicit in her argument is that the work is not significant—it is only mindless drudgery that women should not be asked to undertake individually. Instead, the work could be tackled as a societal problem. Then women, like men, could do the important work of society that is economically productive. This support of the commonsense or folk concept of what is important work forces a devaluation of everything that does not fit the definition. Further, since work is associated with adulthood, an implication of the folk concept is that those who do not work are not fully adults.

Today, of course, women who agree that work in the private sphere is not worth their effort have other alternatives. For example, they can hire other (lower-status and lower-paid) women to replace them in the home if they have sufficient means. Other modern, industrialized societies have gone further than our own in providing alternatives to child care at home, though none have made systematic efforts to create communal eating arrangements, with the exception of the Kibbutz experiments—and these experiments have not been widely adopted, even in Israel. Whatever the arrangements, the normative expectation in every industrialized society is that women will coordinate public and purchased services with the private requirements of their families. Even in households where women earn high wages, sometimes higher than their husbands, it is part of a woman's unpaid and uncounted work to tailor these arrangements to fit her circumstances (Hertz, 1986). This tailoring is thus part of the invisible work in social life. It shows us how gender expectations, and separation between the public and private worlds, are mixed together with paid work to create a special type of problem for which women are expected to take responsibility.

The lack of social validation implicit in disregard of all the tailoring required tells women this effort doesn't count as work; and they themselves often discount the effort it requires. Another area where the folk idea of work is too restrictive is in the distinction between paid and unpaid labor commonly associated with work—even in the public world. The work of community service volunteers is useful, but that it is not paid tells others—and the volunteers themselves—that it is not needed, not really important work despite all the lip service about the value of altruistic endeavor. Calling something altruistic is a way of saying it is not work. Since it is not remunerated, and though it may be recognized as a personal benefit—as well as one for society—it is not work. This view does not deny that women's efforts receive ceremonial attention: mothers have mother's days, and volunteers receive awards and other commemorations for faithful service. But these attentions are perfunctory. They are not part of the institutionalized aspects of life represented by salaried jobs and by occupational careers with their expectations of titles and promotions, security and fringe benefits—and by the larger normative framework within which these expectations are embedded. The framework includes the assumption that working activity is important, significant enough for someone to pay for it. A related assumption is that people who receive that pay are important. The pay is both an indicator that they are independent and autonomous, and a resource for making them so. For example, married women find, when they take paying jobs, that individuals making their own money are more independent and have more "say" in families than those who do not make financial contributions (Ferree, 1976). The position of the housewife before she takes a paid position reveals a problem in the definition of work. Many kinds of effort and skill are not recognized in the folk concept. This omission creates an ambiguous position for those in the grey area of working without pay. These people are mostly women—volunteers and housewives—whose efforts are, consequently, not seen as entirely serious, not the significant work of the world.

Recognition of Invisible Work and Resistance to Its Validation

The women's movement has called attention to the issue of just what is work by insisting on the importance of all the activities where women predominate. Feminists have argued that, when the housekeeping and child care activities of women have been ignored or glossed over with vague allusions to "women's work," the real work involved is not appreciated. This neglect arises even though these activities are the most easily observable parts of what I have termed invisible work. One way to draw attention to that work is to show how it is constructed, what effort it involves, and what it would cost if it were purchased in the market. Some of these costs are born by women themselves who go out to work and pay for their replacements out of salary or who work double time—on the job and in the home—to make up the difference. Other costs, like providing long-term care for the sick and elderly, are hard to assign when no women remain at home to provide that care. For example, Nona Glaser (forthcoming) points out that early hospital release for patients depends on whether someone will be at home to care for them. And, as Elizabeth El-

liott (1986) notes, home-care programs assume that costs of care can be lowered by replacing hospital-based personnel with someone who will learn how to deliver care to a chronically ill patient in the family for free. Still other costs involve the replacement of women's volunteer services to the community. Efforts to show the value of this work often involve estimating its dollar value or, if no social arrangements seem feasible for replacing volunteers with paid workers, speculating on how local communities would manage without it and asking what is lost when women no longer volunteer their full-time services.

Efforts to understand the nature of women's work through the analysis of tasks have a long history, stemming from the days of Victorian social reformers who undertook time and motion studies of the work women do in the home. These studies show both the arduousness of the work—especially for the lower classes—and also the pressures under which it is accomplished. The difficulties of work in the home before the advances of modern technology are well documented in such works as Stasser's *Never Done* (1982). But the pressures of the work continue irrespective of technology. For the middle class, they involve the boredom and resentment created by mindless routine and the consequent narrowing of vision, ambition, and sense of competence so well depicted in French's novel *The Women's Room* (1977). For the working class, they involve the pressure of making ends meet—often with spouses who are inadequate or sporadic earners and sometimes irresponsible or abusive as well. The studies by Luxton (1980), McKreindle and Rowbotham (1977), and Rubin (1976) highlight the difficulties and disappointments that working-class wives face as they try to manage family responsibilities under these conditions. These women work with inadequate supplies and resources to do the job according to their own performance expectations for such tasks as maintaining cleanliness or providing proper, nourishing meals. For both middle- and working-class wives, the pressures of household work often include isolation. The private work in the home is set off from the public affairs of the world, leaving many women with a sense of alienation and distance that can be oppressive—contributing to what Betty Friedan (1963) called the sickness without a name. The pressure of isolation is mitigated when women go out to work, but at its own costs. Studies (e.g., Berk, 1985) show that men do very little housework or child care at home and add very little further time when their wives go out to work. When men do work at home, it tends to be the more desirable jobs— reading to the children before bedtime or cleaning up the kitchen at a leisurely pace after the dinner hour. Women, on the other hand, usually undertake the high-pressure tasks with deadlines attached to them—getting children ready for school in the morning; rushing after work to pick up children at day care and then home to prepare dinner.

These problems are exacerbated by the lack of attention to and serious respect for the work in the private sphere. Studies of family life (e.g., Luxton, 1980) show that husbands do not rate the work of their wives as highly as their own. They see the valuable work as that of the breadwinner who can dole out the family allowance to his wife in the manner he chooses. The grim consequences for wives with improvident or unscrupulous husbands are well known. As the woman's movement has long argued, "most women [with young children to care for] are only one man away from welfare," (Steinem, 1983:8). The problems of displaced homemakers after divorce are also well known. As Weitzman (1986) points out, divorce settlements are often inequitable and unpredictable. Consequently, women can depend upon neither a fair nor a standardized recompense for years of homemaking. Even in states where commu-

nity property laws insure a 50-50 split of assets at the time of divorce, men have socially legitimated human capital—good jobs, training, and experience to further their earning power. These resources are not generally figured into the settlement. Even after equal division, women are not so likely to have these resources, particularly if they have been out of the labor market while raising their children. The recompense of homemaking is correspondingly chancy.

In short, a real pressure underlying the work of the homemaker is lack of validation. The work is private; there is no audience beyond the family and the work is personalized for the family members who rate it as they please. Under these circumstances it is not hard to see why women, family members themselves, do not understand some aspects of their activity as work. DeVault (1987) has pointed out that considerable effort and attention goes into a woman's provisioning the household and preparing meals. The work is "customized," as it were, to pick from the bewildering array of mass-produced products that suit the budget of the household and the tastes of individual family members. Furthermore, it requires continual checking and policing to note what stocks are running low. Even when tasks can be delegated to others, it is usually the wife and mother who notices what needs to be done and when. The others do not take this responsibility and so do not "see" the task until they are directed. Planning, restocking, improvising, and adapting to family quirks and demands require effort that the housewives themselves do not recognize as work; they say they cannot understand why they become so tired or use so much time in making the effort. The difficulty of recognizing it as work is compounded not only by the realization that no one else will see it as work, but also by a woman's own sense that much of it ought to be offered spontaneously—a gift or expression of love for her family. Yet, the expectation that she ought to provide these services provokes guilt if she slacks off on the extra touches or anxiety if she feels she is not doing enough. The stereotypic picture of the woman idly shopping, of shopping as a leisure-time activity of women, also obscures the work of the woman as consumer (Glaser, 1987). These ideas contradict the folk concept of work as something you *have* to do to receive payment. While, as noted earlier, some of the work women do *can* be translated into paid work equivalents, much of it cannot—the tailoring, planning, and specialized catering, for instance. Validation of an individual as a worker through this kind of activity is, then, very difficult.

The importance of public validation can be seen from studies of women who do venture from the home. Esther Benjamin (1979) found, in her research on reentry women at Northwestern University, that good grades meant a great deal to them. The grades were universalistic criteria for performance. Women competed for them and won them in an academic marketplace. The grades were a public standard for excellence that these women felt proud to meet. They recognized them as indicators of potential for salaried careers as well. They spoke of a rise in their self-esteem accordingly, a sense of self-esteem that success in raising a family, even maintaining an elaborate home establishment and attaining success in the public world of volunteering, did not create. The grades, as well as the common expectation that they might lead to good jobs, were generally understood and appreciated by a much wider circle of people than the family and volunteer circles where these women had already made their mark. My own research on volunteers who become civic leaders (forthcoming) supports these findings. Even the very successful and prominent

among them, if they had no or little experience working for pay, showed signs of self-doubt and anxiousness about their position vis-à-vis paid professionals.

However, the fact that these women have some doubts about their own legitimacy should not deflect us from seeing the skilled, systematic, and persistent effort involved. The women I studied were successful entrepreneurs in civic projects. They were experienced in fundraising, public relations, building organizations, and lobbying as advocates for a cause. Some became community service generalists or brokers sought after for their advice in all areas. Their work is valued in the cities and towns of this country—yet it is always seen as somehow anomalous or idiosyncratic, the work of some unusually talented women with free time on their hands. It is never seen as a widespread pattern of work involving local recruitment, training, and development of skills for women who become capable volunteer leaders in community and civic affairs.

Volunteer work in politics provides another example of hidden or obscured work for women. This example is important, for it overlaps with work in the folk concept in that successful volunteers can move into the prestigious and paid positions available to political appointees. However, men are more likely to be awarded such positions, while women remain in the background as volunteers. Margolis (1979) points out how women help create this obscurity in New England town democracies. The women who are important political leaders send prominent towns*men* (clergy, professionals) to lobby council members on key voting issues in the belief that men will be more persuasive than women. A social scientist who only polled decision makers about which people had lobbied them might never discover how many were directed by the women leaders in the town. This omission raises an important question, not only for political scientists, but also for sociologists of work. Students of work need to understand how the social fabric of life is constructed, how work goes on in areas we have not previously examined; but wherever work is necessary, people have to do it, and put forth skill and effort in its cause. The fabric of life requires this effort—or it is poorer if that work is absent. Most of the people expected to do it—or assumed to do it most easily—are women.

There is increasing recognition of such contributions, of course. Our society is changing, albeit slowly, under the impact of the women's movement. In response to the movement, we now have the examinations of women's lives—and women's work—that I have drawn upon here. But serious discussion of this work that would affect social policy is slow in coming. For instance, changes in inequitable insurance rates, revision of inheritance taxes (for widows who are not recognized as partners in a family business or farm), redress in patterns of divorce settlements that generally favor husbands, recognition for women in political advancement through their work in organizing and managing campaigns—all these are slow in coming. This slowness reflects a general reluctance to view women's work as a serious work equivalent to that of men, i.e., requiring the same or similar skills and competence to receive the same rewards (Feldberg, 1984). This reluctance is evident even in the area of women's paid work, where it is one of the reasons that comparable worth legislation to reassess the value of and reward for women's occupations to make them equivalent to male occupation standards is still so bitterly resisted (Steinberg, 1986). Where the assumption is prevalent that payment reflects skill, there is still widespread lack of recognition that the skills and education required for typical women's jobs have for so long been underrewarded.

The lack of validation attendant upon women's work in the family, in volunteer worlds, and in women's occupations affects the definitions women make of their own efforts. If women's work is so hard to conceptualize, and so hard to assess as equal to that of men even when it is recognized as public and paid, it is not surprising that many areas of women's activity receive a low judgment—as of little importance—from women as well as men. The closer the work to the activities of nurturing, comforting, encouraging, or facilitating interaction, the more closely associated it is with women's "natural" or "feminine" proclivities. Such activity is not seen as learned, skilled, required, but only the expression of the character or style of women in general. In the political arena, for example, Margolis (1979) reports that women take responsibility for organizing political meetings: making schedules, sending out flyers, phoning to urge people to come, arranging meeting halls, preparing refreshments. All these activities provide the background and support for (usually male) candidates who appear, speak, and then leave. The women's activities are absolutely essential to the success of campaigns but are not seen, even by the women themselves, as part of "important" political work. They speak of it as "drudge" work instead. The skills required in making decisions and judgments, sizing up prospects, and knowing how to influence and persuade—all these remain invisible. In the volunteer world, as I have noted elsewhere (Daniels, 1985), the women who produce community benefits and parties make the aura of sociability that not only encourages people to give generously to a cause but also develops the esprit to create and shape a sense of community. Yet the work involved in these efforts is colored by the assumption of triviality or frivolity attendant upon such endeavors. The skills needed to do the work and its importance for the community are ambivalently regarded, even, again, by the women themselves. They are, after all, members of the folk who share a concept of what real work is.

The aspect of these activities most difficult for everyone to conceptualize as work involves the warm and caring aspects of the construction and maintenance of interpersonal relations. In the commonsense view, these activities occur spontaneously. They are informal and unregulated—outside of bureaucratic rules and obligations. These activities are what Arlie Hochschild (1979) calls the positive aspects of "emotion work." They involve the following behaviors: (1) attending carefully to how a setting affects others in it—through taking the role of the other and feeling some of the same feelings; (2) focusing attention through ruminating about the past and planning for the future; (3) assessing the reasonableness of preliminary judgments by checking over the behavior of all respondents in an interaction—just as good hostesses do when they look for signs of how well people are enjoying a party, whether or not anyone appears ill at ease or left out; (4) creating a comfortable ambience through expressions of gaiety, warmth, sympathy, and cheerful, affectionate concern for, or interest in, another. Emotion work is an example of how gender expectations and the private sphere are interconnected in a job description, for it is women's job in our society to manage these tasks in the family. The behaviors detailed by Hochschild are essential to the support and encouragement of family members—both in their activities in the home and in support for these members as they enter and return from encounters in the public world.

Contradicting commonsense beliefs about these activities as part of the private world of family are other commonsense notions about the way pleasant or even close interpersonal relationships can make certain kinds of work in the public world go more

smoothly—team work, for example, or service work where the customer enjoys the pleasant, personalized ambience that workers can create. Hochschild (1983) focuses on this latter kind of work in her study of airline stewardesses to show that emotion work can be rationalized through recruitment and training of women who become adept at making nurturing and encouraging gestures even in the face of resistant or difficult clients. In these situations, emotive skills are developed and focused by the employers much as they might train their workers for any other occupational tasks. But as Hochschild notes, women are not likely to be highly rewarded for a "natural" talent that the airlines have helped them polish into a skill. Women are expected to dispense their interpersonal services in addition to their other services even under trying conditions—such as when greater numbers of customers are added to the workload. When the interpersonal services are an important part of the transaction from the employer's perspective, it is necessary to limit the number of clients each servitor must help—and offer resources and room for autonomy so that the servitors can do so. For example, people willing to pay for seats in the first-class cabins of airlines are served by less pressured attendants.

Under what conditions will we pay for such services? Many servitors in first-class establishments are men: maître d's in posh restaurants, porters and concierges in luxury hotels. These are relatively high-status jobs which we "naturally" expect men to fill. They combine authority with their efforts to please, and they are specially rewarded for their combination of interpersonal skills. When we talk about the other area where interpersonal relations make work go smoothly—team work—we think of the work usually assigned to men: leadership. The interpersonal skills involved in leadership are particularly rewarded when men perform them. After all, interpersonal and caring skills are *not* seen as natural for men. They receive more credit for showing these skills accordingly. Part of that credit includes offering men in these high-status jobs the resources (staff, time, independence) to perform at their best advantage. The symphony conductor, the military officer, and the politician or administrator are examples of individuals at work who are recognized as needing to add some important interpersonal skills—understanding and working well with others—to the performance of their tasks.

However, the same interpersonal skills that are rewarded when they are attached to recognized and prestigious occupations in the public sphere are harder to see in the private world of family where women become "specialists" in them. Pamela Fishman (1978) has shown that women engage in a disproportionate amount of the encouraging, facilitating behaviors of communications even in supposedly egalitarian households. When men initiate conversations, women supply the supportive remarks that help channel interactions as men direct. When women initiate, men do not offer the same encouragement; they show by unenthusiastic response, or by ignoring the topic, that they prefer their own topics. Women then drop their own pursuit—sometimes after several tries—to pursue the men's concerns. Sattel (1976) argues that women are expected to perform these interpersonal services for men and are reproached (or men show their disappointment) when women refuse. The expectation that women possess the natural skills for this type of service blends with the expectation that they *should* do them—helping men to express emotions, for example. Sattel confines his argument to the arena of personal relationships, but the expectations that women will facilitate and encourage in interaction spills over into the occupational

world. For example, in a study of student evaluations, Norma Wikler (1979) found students to be harder on women than men instructors when an instructor was not readily available, supportive or sympathetic to student problems. The expectations for women in this area were higher and they were sanctioned for not meeting them. A common complaint from women in the business world is that they are expected to show maternal or nurturant behaviors and are berated as hostile or even castrating if they, like male peers, do not.

The resistance to specifying and giving reward to the interpersonal skills of women as legitimate aspects of work is surely an aspect of the pervasive gender stratification noted earlier—i.e., activities, that when women do them, receive less reward than when men do them. The idea that emotional work should be natural for women contributes to the idea that their work is less skilled—or that this part of their work should get less reward. But there is additional resistance inherent in both the lay person's and the economist's perception of the significance of the wage: in general, the effort required to earn money is seen as distinctive and separate from other activity. Even when interchanges do not hinder but aid in the development of esprit, they are rarely seen as the significant skills of work. They are not significant even when what they accomplish is appreciated. As Wadel (1979:367) points out, focusing attention on pay for work and the specific product desired neglects the activities of work that produce such things as "social relations, technical and social skills, attitudes and values."

In addition to the narrow focus on the activities that produce the product for which the wage is granted, resistance to conceptualizing interpersonal activities as work comes from the expectation that emotional interpersonal gestures are natural expressions that come spontaneously. This view fails to recognize that such gestures are not merely expressive but must also be focused or directed so that they communicate the intended emotion. The idea of expressiveness also includes the view that spontaneous gestures that are loving or supportive are given freely and need not be equated with standard units in a monetized economy. The very idea is distasteful. When we speak of a woman "selling" herself in marriage it is a pejorative, repugnant image, although it is a vivid metaphor for a type of exchange that, as theorists since Engels ([1884] 1972) have pointed out, provides a useful insight into family relationships in a bourgeois economy. Of course, there is a general commonsense understanding that good interpersonal relationships are helpful in work. It meets the opposing understanding that personal relations should not be used for profitable advantage—as seen in the ridicule or disdain sometimes attached to the glad hander and the too obvious, smarmy or oily friendliness of the used car dealer or other high-pressure salesperson.

Importance of Reconceptualizing Work

In this discussion of what might be called work, we have moved from activities convertible into commonsense work categories—where a market value can be attached—to those where a wage value is difficult or even repugnant to consider. But the continuum is not a simple one to conceptualize. It is complicated by the mix of exploitive or trading aspects to be found in the most intimate interactions, on the one hand, and spontaneous or altruistic aspects of interaction to be found in work settings, on the other. Even housewives who say they love their husbands sometimes wheedle money or favors from them, trading an especially nice dinner or sex for the desired benefit (Luxton, 1980). The value of a nice ambience and a personal touch is also understood in

business. Buttering up the customers so that they will be loyal to a particular service goes better when feelings of warmth or sympathy can actually be summoned by the servitors. If workers summon up the feelings, this behavior is more likely to appear spontaneous. In consequence, supervisors teach airline stewardesses how to get themselves in the right frame of mind to behave this way (Hochschild, 1983). These mixtures raise questions about the idea that spontaneous and altruistic gestures are not part of work as well as the idea that spontaneous and altruistic behavior in the family may not be commingled with calculating and exploitive behaviors.

The mixtures also underline one aspect of the problem of definition: the nature of work changes over time and in various contexts. When, before industrialization, men and women worked together in a productive unit within the home, it was easy to see both as workers. The separation of home and workplace changed the meaning of the work men and women do. Thus, women today may have to bribe or entice their husbands for goods and services when the only way to get things is with money and the husband has sole or primary access to it. At the same time, mass production not only of goods but of services has isolated some of the nurturant activities characteristic of women and placed a market value upon them. Women are expected to produce these activities more readily or easily than men, and include them gratis in whatever labor power the women sell accordingly.

As Wadel (1979:369) notes, market prices can also affect definitions; they can determine what is work and what is not. Once goods and services can be produced both commercially and domestically, our commonsense definitions of work and non-work change to accommodate to the new situation. These changes explain why care of children or sick and elderly is not real work within a family setting but becomes easier to understand as work once these activities can be bought in the market.

The commonsense understanding of work, despite the importance it attaches to payment for labor, is distinct from an economic perspective; for it has, as Wadel (1979:371) also points out, a moral component. Having a job "is commonly held as a prerequisite for membership in the 'moral community.'" To "earn one's keep" is a commonsense phrase to express an expected common denominator of behavior on the part of any responsible person. Its importance can be seen in the emphasis parents place upon it and their exasperation when young adults don't fulfill it; for it is the *least* they can do. Working is thus an expression of moral values; but it is something more. It is also an arena for their development.

The work of developing and maintaining the moral force of social institutions can be seen in the family, the community, and the workplace. As Wadel (1979:371) instructs us, we need to look not only at "institutions as end results [but also at] the 'work' that has gone into their achievement." In this way we gain a new understanding and appreciation of many activities previously seen as extraneous or trivial—if noticed at all. The work of symbolically *creating family* occurs in the family events—e.g., the dinner hour and special celebrations held at that time—generally made possible by women who plan, provision, and then produce these occasions (DeVault, 1984). Such occasions symbolize the integrity of the family and provide concrete memories of sharing in an activity. The memories help create the sense of solidarity and commitment to the common aims of family that make it a special unit.

The work of *making community* arises through the efforts of many local volunteers who maintain the services and the sense of community required. They organize networks, plan events, get people together to formulate a way—through an organization, a campaign, a social service—to meet hitherto unmet needs in the locality. As people participate in these activities, they develop a sense of commitment to one another, to the purpose of their efforts, and to the community for which the organization or service is constructed. In short, they develop and strengthen moral convictions about what should and should not occur in their community.

The many informal interchanges that make the difference between a tolerable and an unbearable workplace depend upon the efforts of workers and managers to maintain an ambience that encourages commitment and esprit. Again, the work of creating the background for amiable and affiliative interactions can also create a sense of the reasonableness and rightness of work goals, reaffirming the moral necessity to perform at work in order to see oneself as a fully participant citizen in the work group.

In looking at these efforts, one comes to focus on how institutions are changed as well as maintained. For example, when women withhold their services as church workers, they may alter the nature of a religious community. As Susan Stall (1982) reports from her study of women in an agricultural area, fellowship is connected with sociable church activity like church suppers. When the women enter the labor market and have no time to prepare the suppers, the sense of fellowship dissipates, and a different religious institution appears. Similarly, changes in family structure—with more and more female-headed, single-parent households—also brings about changes in the nature and amount of work involved in building family, and a new kind of family appears. Robert Weiss (1979) reports that children take on some of the emotional as well as physical tasks formerly shared by parents. A new distribution of work in the family ensues. These changes call to our attention not only the new work but some of the invisible work—both emotional and physical—that, as Elise Boulding (forthcoming) tells us, children often do in families.

Changes in institutions bring to light not only the earlier work required for their maintenance but also the work implicated in creation of new institutional forms. If we examine changes closely, we can see what has been added or taken away in our society by the presence or absence of efforts that we have come to take for granted. We appreciate and want the efforts that make our institutions more workable though we wouldn't credit most of it as work.

Conclusion

I have argued that the concept of work should include all the work in the private world of the home, the volunteer work in the public sphere, and the emotion work in both public and private worlds. All these activities involve real work—only it is work that is sometimes difficult to fit into a commonsense perspective that focuses only on remuneration for effort. We need that other element inherent in both the commonsense and the sociological definition of work: work as a basic element in the moral order. Reconceptualizing work to include all the elements I have suggested does not imply that all aspects of work should be paid—or that all should have a dollar value assigned. Certainly, it is true that assigning monetary value too explicitly to acts which, after all, do contain spontaneous and altruistic elements, does dampen one's enthusiasm about them. For example, reckoning the exact cost of a dinner party, including the time and all labor involved, can put a blight on hospitable impulses. But recognition and validation of the work involved in all this invisible or unattended activity is still possible. What can we give that

is more than the perfunctory honors and sentimental accolades we now offer homemakers and volunteers, yet less than (or different from) a regular salary? Some forms of equivalences—e.g., insurance and pension programs for homemakers under various schemes for payment, cash equivalents for volunteer service—have already been suggested. My own suggestions at this stage are quite tentative. Once we appreciate the significance of all the pieces of emotional and physical work that now do not receive the dignity and moral force of definition as work, we can regard the workers in a new light, appreciating both their effort and their skills.

An analysis of invisible work tells us something about how the fabric of life is woven; it calls attention to what gives life its texture, to continue the metaphor. Should we call this work? Or should we distinguish it from work because it is not remunerated or because of the apparently spontaneous aspects, the appearance of intuitive responses in social settings? I have argued that it is work and that it is important to think of it as work. Even without remuneration, it at least shares one aspect of the commonsense definition in that some people are expected to do it and can be sanctioned for not doing it.

When there is a rift of some kind in the social fabric, public or private, at home or at work, it is often expected either that women *should* or that women *could* weave the fabric back into wholeness because they have the natural talents to do so. My argument is that, whatever their natural propensity, they are trained in these skills. In consequence, women are more likely to be able to do this job. Their practice comes from weaving the fabric together in their friendships, families, and work settings. The skill at this weaving comes from attending to the background comforts that make interaction pleasanter, from watching out for hesitances, likes, and dislikes of others in the social setting and trying to accommodate them. Once these behaviors become habitual, women are just "naturally" better at this work. Of course, social life would run more smoothly if every able-bodied person attended to those matters, rotating some tasks around or shifting them from one to another as a context permitted. Serious attention to the importance of this work in the social construction of reality may make that sharing seem more reasonable.

REFERENCES

Acker, Joan. 1972. "Women and Social Stratification: A Case of Intellectual Sexism." *American Journal of Sociology* 78:936–45.

Benjamin, Esther. 1979. "Changing Self Conceptions and Pressures for More Egalitarian Marriages: Women Return to School." Paper presented at the annual meetings of the Society for the Study of Social Problems, Boston.

Berk, Sarah Fenstermacher. 1985. *The Gender Factory.* New York: Plenum Press.

Boulding, Elise. Forthcoming. "Waiting as Invisible Work: An Exploration of Waiting in Families." In Kai Erikson (ed.), *Working.* New Haven: Yale University Press.

Daniels, Arlene Kaplan. 1985. "Good Times and Good Works: The Place of Sociability in the Work of Women Volunteers." *Social Problems* 32:363–74.

———. Forthcoming. *Invisible Careers: Women Civic Leaders from the Volunteer World.* Chicago: University of Chicago Press.

DeVault, Marjorie L. 1984. "Women and Food: Housework and the Production of Family Life." Unpublished Ph.D. dissertation, Northwestern University, Evanston, IL.

———. 1987. "Doing Housework: Feeding and Family Life." Pp. 178–91 in Naomi Gerstel and Harriet Gross (eds.), *Families and Work.* Philadelphia: Temple University Press.

Elliott, Elizabeth. 1986. "Who Cares and Where? The Relocation of Health Care Cost, Technology and Work in the Growing Business of Home Health Care." Unpublished paper, Northwestern University, Evanston, IL.

Engels, Friedrich. [1884] 1972. *The Origins of the Family, Private Property and the State.* New York: International Publishers.

Feldberg, Roslyn L. 1984. "Comparable Worth: Toward Theory and Practice in the United States." *Signs* 10:311–28.

Ferree, Myra Marx. 1976. "Working-Class Jobs: Housework and Paid Work as Sources of Satisfaction." *Social Problems* 23:431–41.

Fishman, Pamela M. 1978. "Interaction: The Work Women Do." *Social Problems* 25:397–406.

French, Marilyn. 1977. *The Women's Room.* New York: Summit Books.

Friedan, Betty. 1963. *The Feminine Mystique.* New York: Norton.

Gilman, Charlotte Perkins. [1898] 1966. *Women and Economics.* New York: Harper Torchbook.

Glaser, Nona Y. 1987. "Servants to Capital: Unpaid Domestic Labor and Paid Work." Pp. 236–55 in Naomi Gerstel and Harriet Gross (eds.), *Families and Work.* Philadelphia: Temple University Press.

———. Forthcoming. "Overlooked, Overworked: Women's Unpaid and Paid Work in the Health Services 'Cost Crisis.' " *International Journal of Health Services* 18.

Hertz, Rosanna. 1986. *More Equal Than Others: Women and Men in Dual-Career Marriages.* Berkeley: University of California Press.

Hochschild, Arlie. 1979. "Emotion Work, Feeling Rules and Social Structure." *American Journal of Sociology* 85:551–75.

———. 1983. *The Managed Heart.* Berkeley: University of California Press.

Illich, Ivan. 1981. *Shadow Work.* Boston: Boyars.

Luxton, Meg. 1980. *More Than a Labour of Love: Three Generations of Women's Work in the Home.* Toronto: Women's Educational Press.

Margolis, Diane Rothbard. 1979. "The Invisible Hands: Sex Roles and the Division of Labor in Two Local Political Parties." *Social Problems* 26:314–24.

McKreindle, Jean and Sheila Rowbotham. 1977. *Dutiful Daughters: Women Talk About Their Lives.* Austin: University of Texas Press.

Rubin, Lillian B. 1976. *Worlds of Pain: Life in the Working-Class Family.* New York: Basic Books.

Sattel, Jack W. 1976. "The Inexpressive Male: Tragedy or Sexual Politics?" *Social Problems* 23:469–77.

Stall, Susan. 1982. "The Work Women Do in a Small Rural Town." Paper presented at the annual meetings of the Midwest Sociological Society, Des Moines.

Stasser, Susan. 1982. *Never Done: A History of American Housework.* New York: Pantheon.

Steinberg, Ronnie. 1986. "The Debate on Comparable Worth." *New Politics* 1:108–26.

Steinem, Gloria. 1983. *Outrageous Acts and Everyday Rebellions.* New York: Holt, Rinehart and Winston.

Turner, Ralph. 1957. "The Normative Coherence of Folk Concepts." Proceedings of the Pacific Sociological Society. *Research Studies of the State College of Washington* 25:127–36.

Wadel, Cato. 1979. "The Hidden Work of Everyday Life." Pp. 365–84 in Sandra Wallman (ed.), *Social Anthropology of Work.* New York: Academic Press.

Weiss, Robert S. 1979. *Going It Alone.* New York: Basic Books.

Weitzman, Lenore. 1986. *The Divorce Revolution: The Unexpected Social and Economic Consequences for Women and Children in America.* New York: Free Press.

Wikler, Norma. 1979. "Sexism in the Classroom." Paper presented at the annual meetings of the American Sociological Association, Boston.